# Religion versus empire?

## British Protestant missionaries and overseas expansion, 1700–1914

### Andrew Porter

Manchester University Press
Manchester and New York

*distributed exclusively in the USA by Palgrave*

*Published by* Manchester University Press
Oxford Road, Manchester M13 9NR, UK
*and* Room 400, 175 Fifth Avenue, New York, NY 10010, USA
www.manchesteruniversitypress.co.uk

*Distributed exclusively in the USA by*
Palgrave, 175 Fifth Avenue, New York,
NY 10010, USA

*Distributed exclusively in Canada by*
UBC Press, University of British Columbia, 2029 West Mall,
Vancouver, BC, Canada V6T 1Z2

*British Library Cataloguing-in-Publication Data*
A catalogue record for this book is available from the British Library

*Library of Congress Cataloging-in-Publication Data applied for*

ISBN  0 7190 2822 1  *hardback*
      0 7190 2823 X  *paperback*

First published 2004

13  12  11  10  09  08  07  06  05  04      10  9  8  7  6  5  4  3  2  1

Typeset by
D R Bungay Associates, Burghfield, Berks

Printed in Great Britain
by CPI, Bath

# Religion versus empire?

Published in our
centenary year
2004
MANCHESTER
UNIVERSITY
PRESS

# Contents

# Acknowledgements

In writing a book of this kind, assistance and encouragement have inevitably come from many quarters over a long period and have been of many different kinds. For resources to travel, to meet other scholars, and to carry out research, I am most grateful to the British Academy; to King's College London for its provision of sabbatical leave; to the University of London's Central Research Fund; and to the Pew Charitable Trusts of Philadelphia through its support of the North Atlantic Missiology and Currents in World Christianity Projects. For access to collections, for the help of their staff, and for permissions to cite materials and published work, I am grateful to the Bodleian Library; Cambridge University Library; the Church Mission Society; the Council for World Mission; material references to the American Board of Commissioners for Foreign Missions are by permission of the Houghton Library, Harvard University, and Wider Church Ministries of the United Church of Christ; the editors of the *Historical Journal* and the *Journal of Imperial and Commonwealth History*; Lambeth Palace Library; the Trustees for Methodist Church Purposes; the National Library of Scotland; Oxford University Press; Ridley Hall, Cambridge; the Keeper of Archives and Special Collections, School of Oriental and African Studies; Trinity College, Cambridge; University College London; the Yale Divinity School Archives and Library; Hilary Carey; Ronald Davies; Richard Elphick; Alan Guenther; Nils Kristian Hoimyr of the Norwegian Mission Society; Wilbert Shenk; John Vickers. I have gained greatly from the members of the North Atlantic Missiology Project; the Currents in World Christianity Project; and the Imperial History Research Seminar at the Institute of Historical Research, London. Among other friends and colleagues I must mention Clyde Binfield; Arthur Burns; Penny Carson; Greg Cuthbertson; Kevin Grant; Hans Hillebrand; Roger Louis; Ged Martin; Colin Matthew; Jenny Murray; Richard Pierard; Lamin Sanneh; Rhonda Semple; Rosemary Seton; Martha Smalley; Brian Stanley; Sarah Stockwell; John Stuart; Luke Trainor; Grant Wacker; Andrew Walls; and Jon Wilson. David Killingray and Peter Marshall were far more than generous in reading and commenting on a late draft of the manuscript, as too was a reader for Manchester University Press. To my wife Mary no acknowledgement can suffice.

# Abbreviations

| | |
|---|---|
| ABC | ABCFM Archives |
| ABCFM | American Board of Commissioners for Foreign Missions |
| BDCM | Gerald Anderson (ed.), *Biographical Dictionary of Christian Missions* (Grand Rapids, MI, 1999) |
| BFBS | British and Foreign Bible Society |
| BMS | Baptist Missionary Society |
| BSIMS | *Bulletin of the Scottish Institute of Missionary Studies* |
| CIM | China Inland Mission |
| CMI | *Church Missionary Intelligencer* |
| CMS | Church Missionary Society [now Church Mission Society] |
| CMS Register | *Church Missionary Society. Register of Missionaries (Clerical, Lay, & Female), and Native Clergy, From 1804 to 1904* (Privately Printed: London, n.d.) |
| CSSH | *Comparative Studies in Society and History* |
| CVES | Christian Vernacular Education Society |
| CWC | Currents in World Christianity Project |
| CWM | Council for World Mission |
| DEB | Donald M. Lewis (ed.), *The Blackwell Dictionary of Evangelical Biography, 1730–1860*, 2 vols (Oxford, 1995) |
| DSCHT | Nigel M. de S. Cameron (ed.), *Dictionary of Scottish Church History and Theology* (Edinburgh, 1993) |
| FCMMR | *Free Church Monthly Missionary Review* |
| FCS | Free Church of Scotland |
| FCSMR | *Free Church of Scotland Missionary Review* |
| FMC | Foreign Missions Committee |
| HJ | *Historical Journal* |
| IBMR | *International Bulletin of Missionary Research* |
| ICHR | *Indian Church History Review* |
| IJAHS | *International Journal of African Historical Studies* |
| JAH | *Journal of African History* |
| JEccH | *Journal of Ecclesiastical History* |
| JICH | *Journal of Imperial and Commonwealth History* |
| JRA | *Journal of Religion in Africa* |
| LMS | London Missionary Society |
| MCA | Methodist Church Archives |
| MS.Afr.S.216–219 | W.M. Macmillan Collection, Rhodes House Library, Oxford |
| NAMP | North Atlantic Missiology Project |
| NLS | National Library of Scotland |

| | |
|---|---|
| *ODNB* | *Oxford Dictionary of National Biography* (Oxford, 2004) |
| *OHBE* | *Oxford History of the British Empire*, 5 vols (Oxford, 1998–99) |
| PP | Parliamentary Papers, House of Commons |
| *SAHJ* | *South African Historical Journal* |
| SCM | Student Christian Movement |
| SPCK | Society for the Promotion of Christian Knowledge |
| SPG | Society for the Propagation of the Gospel |
| SUM | Sudan United Mission |
| SVM | Student Volunteer Movement |
| SVMU | Student Volunteer Missionary Union |
| UMCA | Universities' Mission to Central Africa |
| WMMS | Wesleyan Methodist Missionary Society |
| YMCA | Young Men's Christian Association |
| YWCA | Young Women's Christian Association |

# Maps

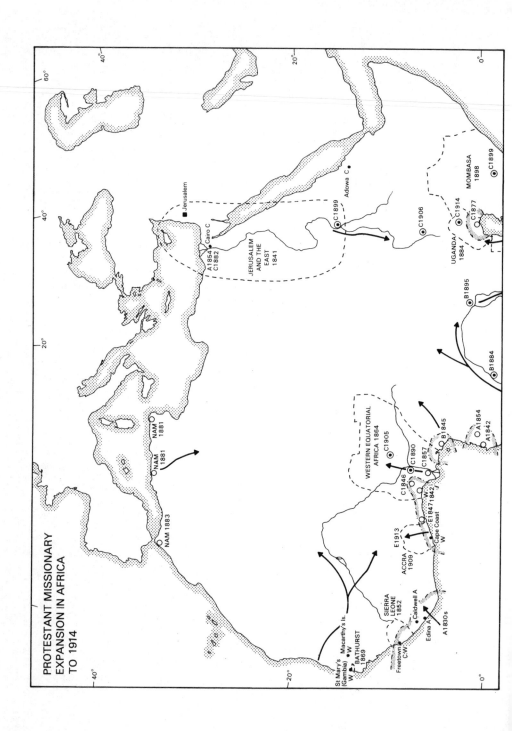

PROTESTANT MISSIONARY
EXPANSION IN AFRICA
TO 1914

NAM 1883

NAM
1881
NAM
1881

NAM
1881

St Mary's
(Gambia). W
BATHURST
1869
Macarthy's Is.

SIERRA
LEONE
1852

Freetown
C·W
Edina A
A1830s

Caldwell A

ACCRA
1909

E1913

E1847 1842
Cape Coast
W

C1846
W
C1857
C1890

C1905

WESTERN EQUATORIAL
AFRICA 1864

B1845
A1842
A1854

B1884

B1895

Jerusalem

A1854 Cairo C
C1882

JERUSALEM
AND THE
EAST
1841

Adowa C

C1899

C1906

C1914
C1877
UGANDA
1884

MOMBASA
1898

C1899

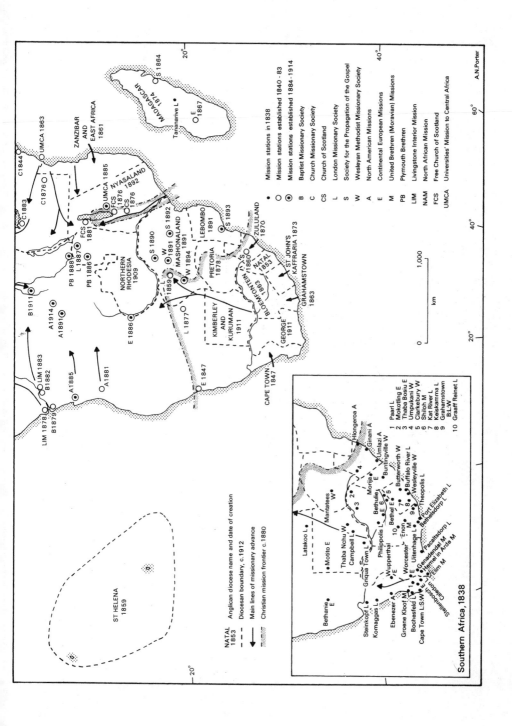

Southern Africa, 1838

Mission stations in 1838 •
Mission stations established 1840 - 83 ○
Mission stations established 1884 - 1914 ⊙
Baptist Missionary Society B
Church Missionary Society C
Church of Scotland CS
London Missionary Society L
Society for the Propagation of the Gospel S
Wesleyan Methodist Missionary Society W
North American Missions A
Continental European Missions M
United Brethren (Moravian) Missions M
Plymouth Brethren PB
Livingstone Interior Mission LIM
North African Mission NAM
Free Church of Scotland FCS
Universities' Mission to Central Africa UMCA

NATAL 1853    Anglican diocese name and date of creation
- - -    Diocesan boundary, c.1912
→    Main lines of missionary advance
▨    Christian mission frontier c.1880

ST HELENA 1859

MADAGASCAR
Tananarive L
S 1864
E 1867
E 1874

ZANZIBAR AND EAST AFRICA 1861
UMCA 1863
C1844
C1876
C1883
UMCA 1885
NYASALAND 1892
UMCA 1892
FCS 1881
CS 1876
S 1876
PB 1888
PB 1886
L 1887
NORTHERN RHODESIA 1909
E 1886
L 1877
KIMBERLEY AND KURUMAN 1911
GEORGE 1911
CAPE TOWN 1847
E 1847
BLOEMFONTEIN 1863
NATAL 1853
ST JOHN'S KAFFRARIA 1873
GRAHAMSTOWN 1863
ZULULAND 1870
LEBOMBO 1891
S 1893
W 1894 1891
PRETORIA 1878
MASHONALAND 1891
W 1891
S 1890
S 1892
L 1859
LIM 1878
B1879
LIM 1883
B1882
A1885
A1881
B1911
A1914
A1891

A.N.Porter

km
0          1,000

20°          40°          60°

Bethanie E
Steinkopf L
Komaggas L
Ebenezer A
Groene Kloof M
Bochesfeld L·S·W
Cape Town L·S·W·E
Steinendal M
Caledon
Genadendal M
Elim M
Riemen in Arde M
Pacaltsdorp L
Port Elizabeth L
Bethelsdorp L
Grahamstown
B·L·W
Uitenhage L
Enon M
Theopolis L
Worcester E
Wupperthal E
Philippolis L
Campbell L
Thaba Nchu W
Griqua Town L
Motito E
Latakoo L
Mantatees W
Bethulie E
Bethel E
Morija
Buntingville W
Butterworth W
Buffalo River L
Clarkebury W
Wesleyville W
Shiloh M
Kat River L
Keiskamma L
Umlazi A
Ginani A
Hlongeroa A

1 Paarl L
2 Mokotling E
3 Thaba Bosiu E
4 Umpukani W
5 Clarkebury W
6 Shiloh M
7 Kat River L
8 Keiskamma L
9 Grahamstown B·L·W
10 Graaff Reinet L

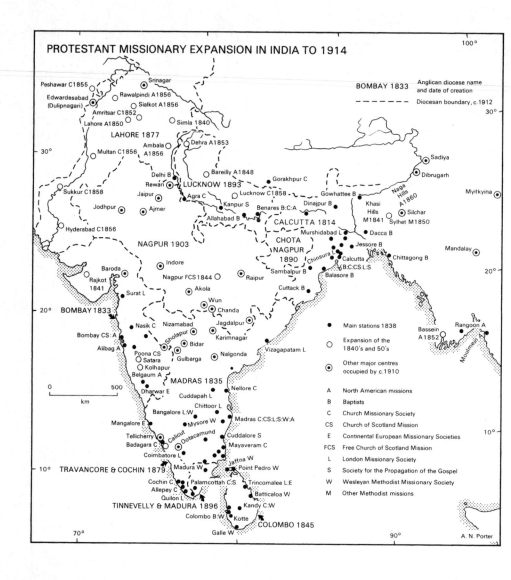

PROTESTANT MISSIONARY EXPANSION IN INDIA TO 1914

BOMBAY 1833 — Anglican diocese name and date of creation

– – – – – — Diocesan boundary, c.1912

Peshawar C1855
Edwardesabad (Dulipnagari)
Rawalpindi A1856
Srinagar
Sialkot C1856
Amritsar C1852
Lahore A1850
Simla 1840
LAHORE 1877
Multan C1856
Ambala A1856
Dehra A1853
Sukkur C1858
Delhi B
Rewari
Bareilly A1848
Gorakhpur C
LUCKNOW 1893
Jaipur
Agra C
Lucknow C1858
Gowhattee B
Jodhpur
Ajmer
Kanpur S
Benares B:C:A
Dinajpur B
Naga Hills A1860
Myitkyina
Allahabad B
CALCUTTA 1814
Khasi Hills M1841
Silchar
Hyderabad C1856
NAGPUR 1903
Murshidabad L
Sylhet M1850
Indore
CHOTA NAGPUR 1890
Dacca B
Mandalay
Baroda
Nagpur FCS1844
Raipur
Chinsura
Calcutta B:C:CS:L:S
Chittagong B
Rajkot 1841
Akola
Sambalpur B
Balasore B
Surat L
Wun
Cuttack B
BOMBAY 1833
Chanda
Nasik C
Nizamabad
Jagdalpur
Bassein A1852
Rangoon A
Bombay CS:A
Sholapur
Bidar
Karimnagar
Alibag A
Poona CS
Gulbarga
Nalgonda
Vizagapatam L
Satara
Kolhapur
Belgaum A
MADRAS 1835
Dharwar E
Cuddapah L
Nellore C
Bangalore L:W
Chittoor L
Mangalore E
Mysore W
Madras C:CS:L:S:W:A
Tellicherry
Calicut
Ootacamund
Cuddalore S
Badagara C
Coimbatore L
Mayaveram C
TRAVANCORE & COCHIN 1879
Madura W
Jaffna W
Point Pedro W
Cochin C
Palamcottah C:S
Trincomalee L:E
Allepey C
Batticaloa W
Quilon L
TINNEVELLY & MADURA 1896
Kandy C:W
Colombo B:W
Kotte
COLOMBO 1845
Galle W

● Main stations 1838
○ Expansion of the 1840's and 50's
◉ Other major centres occupied by c.1910

A North American missions
B Baptists
C Church Missionary Society
CS Church of Scotland Mission
E Continental European Missionary Societies
FCS Free Church of Scotland Mission
L London Missionary Society
S Society for the Propagation of the Gospel
W Wesleyan Methodist Missionary Society
M Other Methodist missions

0        500
km

A. N. Porter

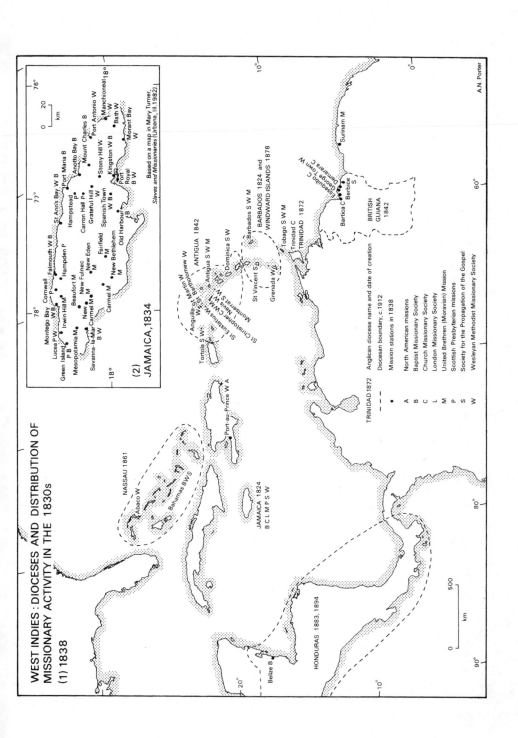

WEST INDIES : DIOCESES AND DISTRIBUTION OF
MISSIONARY ACTIVITY IN THE 1830s

(1) 1838

NASSAU 1861

Abaco W

Bahamas B W S

Port-au-Prince W A

JAMAICA 1824
B C L M P S W

HONDURAS 1883, 1894

Belize B

(2)
JAMAICA, 1834

Montego Bay   Cornwall
Lucea P W .    . W B   Falmouth W B
Green Island   .      . Hampden P
        P B
Mesopotamia M .         Beaufort M
    New .    . New Fulnec
Savanna-la-Mar Carmel M    . New Eden
        B W          M
        Carmel M   . Fairfield
                M
            . New Bethlehem
                W

St Ann's Bay W B
        . Port Maria B
Hampstead P .   . Anotto Bay B
Carron Hall P .   Mount Charles B
Grateful Hill    . Port Antonio W
    W      . Manchioneal 18°
Spanish Town  . Stony Hill W  . Bath W
    W B    . Kingston W B
        Port .    . Morant Bay
Old Harbour   Royal      W
        B    B W

Based on a map in Mary Turner,
Slaves and Missionaries (Urbana, III.1982).

Anguilla S W
Tortola S W   . St Martin W
        . St Bartholomew W
St Eustatius C W M .   . Antigua S W M
St Christopher's W M .   ANTIGUA 1842
        Nevis W .   . Montserrat S

        . Dominica S W

            . Barbados S W M
St Vincent S .
        . BARBADOS 1824 and
Grenada W S .   WINDWARD ISLANDS 1878
        Tobago C
        . Trinidad W
        TRINIDAD 1872

Essequibo C   . Demerara C
        George Town W
        . Berbice
Bartica C      S
    . BRITISH
    GUIANA   . Surinam M
    1842

TRINIDAD 1872   Anglican diocese name and date of creation
------   Diocesan boundary, c.1912
.   Mission stations in 1838

A   North American missions
B   Baptist Missionary Society
C   Church Missionary Society
L   London Missionary Society
M   United Brethren (Moravian) Mission
P   Scottish Presbyterian missions
S   Society for the Propagation of the Gospel
W   Wesleyan Methodist Missionary Society

A.N. Porter

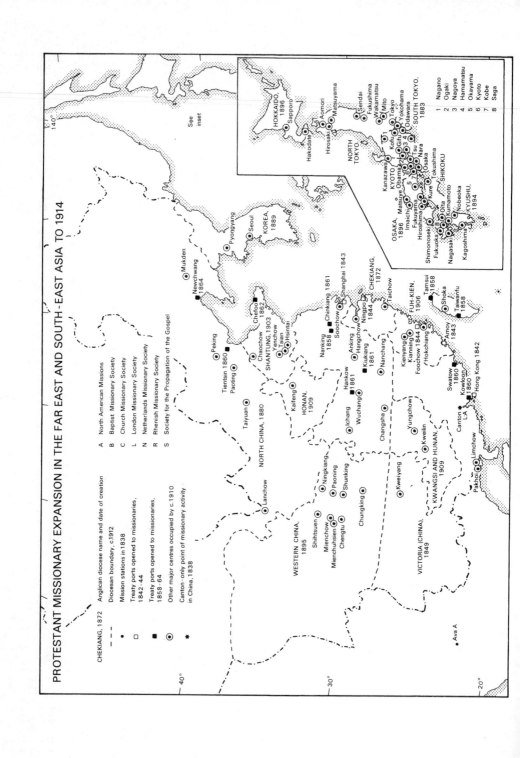

PROTESTANT MISSIONARY EXPANSION IN THE FAR EAST AND SOUTH-EAST ASIA TO 1914

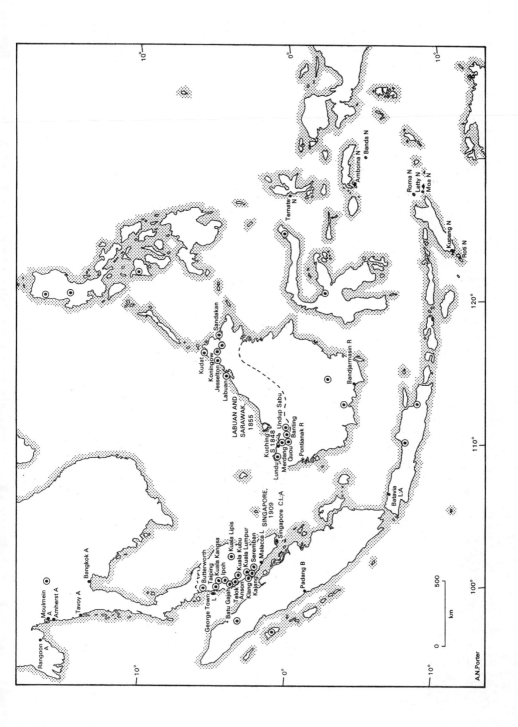

Rangoon A
Moulmein A
Amherst A
Tavoy A
Bangkok A

George Town L
Butterworth
Taiping
Batu Gajah
Ipoh
Telok Anson
Kuala Kangsa
Kuala Lipis
Kuala Kubu
Klang
Kuala Lumpur
Kajang
Seremban
Malacca L
SINGAPORE, 1909
Singapore C L A

Padang B

LABUAN AND SARAWAK, 1855
Kudat
Koningow
Jesselton
Labuan
Sandakan

Kuching S 1848
Lundu
Merdang
Quou
Banting
Undup Sabu
Pontianak R

Batavia L A

Bandjarmasin R

Ternate N

Amboina N
Banda N

Roma N
Letty N
Moa N

Kupang N
Roti N

0    500
km

10°

0°

10°

100°

110°

120°

10°

0°

10°

A.N.Porter

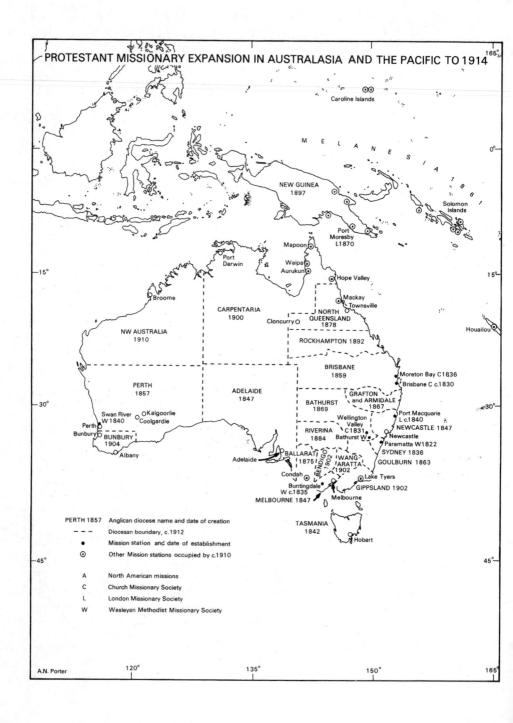

PROTESTANT MISSIONARY EXPANSION IN AUSTRALASIA AND THE PACIFIC TO 1914

165°

Caroline Islands

M E L A N E S I A

NEW GUINEA
1897

Solomon
Islands

Port
Moresby
L1870

Mapoon

Port
Darwin

Weipa
Aurukun

Hope Valley

Broome

Mackay
Townsville

CARPENTARIA
1900

NORTH
QUEENSLAND
1878

Cloncurry

Houailou

NW AUSTRALIA
1910

ROCKHAMPTON 1892

BRISBANE
1859

Moreton Bay C1836
Brisbane C c.1830

PERTH
1857

ADELAIDE
1847

GRAFTON
and ARMIDALE
1867

BATHURST
1869

Swan River
W 1840

Kalgoorlie
Coolgardie

Wellington
Valley

Port Macquarie
L c.1840
NEWCASTLE 1847

Perth
Bunbury

BUNBURY
1904

RIVERINA
1884

C 1831

Bathurst W

Newcastle
Paramatta W1822

Albany

BALLARAT
1875

SYDNEY 1836

GOULBURN 1863

Adelaide

WANG-
ARATTA
1902

Lake Tyers

Condah

GIPPSLAND 1902

Buntingdale
W c.1835

Melbourne

MELBOURNE 1847

TASMANIA
1842

Hobart

PERTH 1857     Anglican diocese name and date of creation

- - -           Diocesan boundary, c.1912

●               Mission station and date of establishment

⊙               Other Mission stations occupied by c.1910

A               North American missions

C               Church Missionary Society

L               London Missionary Society

W               Wesleyan Methodist Missionary Society

A.N. Porter

120°          135°          150°          165°

15°

30°

45°

BENDIGO 1902

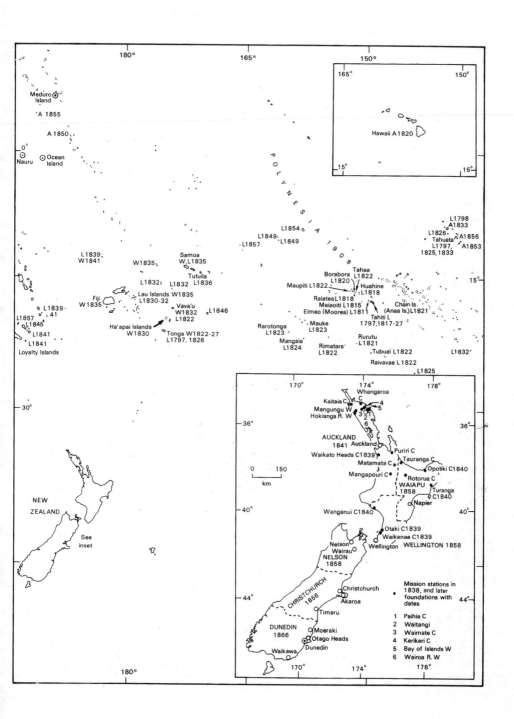

180°   165°   150°

165°                150°

Meduro Island

A 1855

A 1850

Nauru   Ocean Island

0°

Hawaii A1820

15°                15°

P O L Y N E S I A 1908

L1798
A1833

L1854   L1826-   A1856
L1849.   Tahuata   A1853
L1857   L1849   L1797,
1825, 1833

L1839   Samoa
W1841   W,L1835

W1835   Tahaa
Tutuila   Borabora   L1822
L1832   L1832   L1836   L1820   Huahine
Maupiti L1822   :L1818
Lau Islands W1835   Raiatea L1818   Chain Is.
Fiji   L1830-32   Maiaoiti L1815   (Anaa Is.)L1821
W1835   Vava'u   Eimeo (Moorea) L181   Tahiti L
L1857   W1832   L1846   1797,1817-27
L1845   L1822   Rarotonga   Mauke   Tahiti L
Ha'apai Islands   L1823   L1823   1797,1817-27
L1841   W1830   Tonga W1822-27   Mangaia'   Rurutu
L1841   L1797, 1826   L1824   Rimatara'   L1821
Loyalty Islands   L1822   ,Tubuai L1822   L1832'
Raivavae L 1822

15°

30°

L1825

170°   174°   178°
Whangaroa
Kaitaia C   C   4
Mangungu W   5
Hokianga R. W   3 2 1
6

36°               36°

AUCKLAND
1841   Auckland
Puriri C
Waikato Heads C1839   Tauranga C
Matamata C   Opotiki C1840
Mangapouri C   Rotorua C
WAIAPU
1858   Turanga
C1840
Wanganui C1840   Napier

NEW
ZEALAND

See
inset

40°               40°

Otaki C1839
Waikanae C1839
Nelson   Wellington   WELLINGTON 1858
Wairau
NELSON
1858

CHRISTCHURCH
1856   Christchurch   Mission stations in
Akaroa   1838, and later
foundations with
Timaru   dates

44°               44°

1   Paihia C
2   Waitangi
DUNEDIN   3   Waimate C
1866   Moeraki   4   Kerikeri C
Otago Heads   5   Bay of Islands W
Waikawa   Dunedin   6   Wairoa R. W

180°   170°   174°   178°

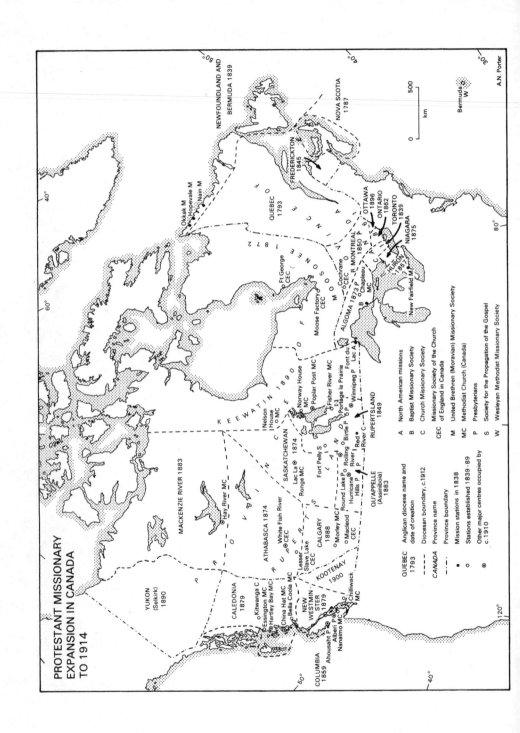

PROTESTANT MISSIONARY
EXPANSION IN CANADA
TO 1914

YUKON
(Selkirk)
1890

CALEDONIA
1879

COLUMBIA
1859

NEW
WESTMIN
STER
1879

Ahousaht P
Alberni P
Nanaimo MC
Chilliwack
MC

Kitwanga C
Essington MC
Hartley Bay MC
China Hat MC
Bella Coola MC

KOOTENAY
1900

MACKENZIE RIVER 1883

ATHABASCA 1874

Hay River MC

White Fish River
CEC

Lesser
Slave Lake
CEC

CALGARY
1888

Morley MC
Macleod
CEC
Hurricane
Hills P
Round Lake P
Rolling
River P
Birtle P

SASKATCHEWAN

Fort Pelly S

Lac La
Ronge MC

Lac La
1874

Nelson
House
O MC

QU'APPELLE
(Assiniboia)
1883

RUPERTSLAND
1849

Winnipeg P
Portage la Prairie
Red
River P

Fisher River MC

Poplar Post MC

Norway House
MC

KEEWATIN 1890

Font du Lac P

Lac A

MONTREAL
1850

ALGOMA
1873

New Fairfield M

HURON
1857

B
Chapleau
MC

Cochrane
CEC

Moose Factory
CEC

Ft George
CEC

QUEBEC
1793

FREDERICKTON
1845

OTTAWA
1896

ONTARIO
1862

TORONTO

NIAGARA
1875

NEWFOUNDLAND AND
BERMUDA 1839

NOVA SCOTIA
1787

Okkak M
Hopedale M
Nain M

A    North American missions
B    Baptist Missionary Society
C    Church Missionary Society
CEC  Missionary Society of the Church
     of England in Canada
M    United Brethren (Moravian) Missionary Society
MC   Methodist Church (Canada)
P    Presbyterians
S    Society for the Propagation of the Gospel
W    Wesleyan Methodist Missionary Society

QUEBEC   Anglican diocese name and
1793     date of creation

——— Diocesan boundary, c.1912

CANADA   Province name

————  Province boundary

·——·  Mission stations in 1838

o     Stations established 1839–89

⊙     Other major centres occupied by
      c.1910

Bermuda
W

0        500
km

A.N. Porter

# Introduction

The subject of this book is at once the entanglement of British missions with Britain's empire and the extent of their separate development, in a context of global perceptions and worldwide processes of change. Conversely it is a general history neither of missions nor of empire, taken separately. It is not a study of the myriad local impacts made by evangelists around the world. Moreover it is a history that cannot begin at the beginning. The geographical and chronological range of its subject is too great for any one scholar or single volume. Since at least the twelfth century, British, still more English, empire building has been if not a persistent then at least a recurrent process.[1] Conquest, settlement and other kinds of economic, social and political penetration have intermittently, at times persistently, displaced existing communities, pressed ahead with their cultural adaptation and imposed on them a 'colonial' status. The Christian urge towards missionary activity aimed at the religious conversion of peoples near and far is not only older still, but geographically has far outreached any of the world's formal territorial empires.[2] Such populations have sometimes been viewed benevolently, Pope Gregory's reputed observation before despatching Augustine to Britain itself, 'non angli sed angeli', being but an early if perhaps purely symbolic instance. More often, if with equal ignorance, they have been variously classified or demonised by terms such as 'barbaric', 'savage', 'pagan' or 'uncivilised'. At all times Britain's religious evangelism, like its empire-building, has been held to combine in varying proportion elements of benevolence, obligation, sympathy, utility, inevitability or historic necessity. Equally, both have found not only their supporters but also their bitter critics, who have emphasised the corruption, destruction, racial conflict, authoritarianism and exploitation associated at home and abroad with all forms of British overseas expansion.

The growth and adaptation of Christian missions and the processes of empire-building or dissolution have often coincided in both period and place. Periodically intertwined as they have been, the relevance of the one to the other in particular settings overseas has been much discussed. Nevertheless, even for the period 1790–1914, when the modern missionary movement got into its stride and

*[Handwritten margin notes: "Britain has been and still is colonising"; "Religion spreading / similar to colony taking"; "Both have fans and critics"; "Growth of the two usually coincides"]*

1 A.F. Madden, *Select Documents on the Constitutional History of the British Empire and Commonwealth, Vol. 1 'The Empire of the Bretaignes', 1175–1688* (Westport, New York and London, 1985); David Armitage, *The Ideological Origins of the British Empire* (Cambridge, 2000); Stephen Howe, *Ireland and Empire: Colonial Legacies in Irish History and Culture* (Oxford, 2000); David Landes, *The Wealth and Poverty of Nations* (New York and London, 1998).
2 P.R.L. Brown, *The Rise of Western Christendom*, 2nd ed. (Oxford, 1997); R.A. Fletcher, *The Conversion of Europe: From Paganism to Christianity, 371–1386 AD* (London, 1997); Ian Wood, *The Missionary Life: Saints and the Evangelisation of Europe 400–1050* (Harlow, 2001).

enthusiasm for imperial expansion reached its peak not only in Britain but throughout western Europe and the Atlantic world, there has been no general recognition
or study of the problem as a whole.

General histories published in the 1970s and 1980s indicated at best a passing
awareness of the question. *The New Cambridge Modern History*, for example,
simply referred to overseas missions as one more among the myriad forms of
'humanitarian, educational, philanthropic and social' reforming causes increasingly
taken up by believers in the late nineteenth century. Occasionally it was acknowledged that missionary activity contributed to imperial expansion, but the manner
in which it did so remained undefined. There was a tendency for religious questions to be treated in the context simply of the growing secularisation of European
society, and for histories of Europe to ignore the significance of overseas agents
such as missionaries for the continent's own domestic transformation.[3]

These limitations are not to be explained simply by an appeal to the nature of
general histories, for at the same time the subject received no more attention even in
standard accounts of religion and the churches. The example set by Owen
Chadwick in his masterpiece on *The Victorian Church*, where overseas missions
received no mention at all, may have been unfortunately powerful. However, the
lack in other significant studies of any reference to the expression of religious
enthusiasm, revivalism and material Christian commitment, either Protestant or
Catholic, in foreign missionary expansion, suggests that it may also have been
symptomatic of a wider oversight, parochialism or general lack of interest among
ecclesiastical and religious historians.[4] The interests of historians of empire also lay
elsewhere, in the constitutional, political and economic aspects of Britain's overseas
expansion. For reasons recently summarised by Norman Etherington, 'the study of
Christian missions has not developed as a recognized and coherent branch of
British Imperial and Commonwealth history'.[5]

It is of course true that research by historians of Africa, Asia and the Pacific,
by historians of missions *per se* as well as sociologists and anthropologists, has
partly compensated for this neglect of the relations between missions and empire
by historians of metropolitan Britain, empire and continental Europe. Since the
early encyclopaedic studies of missions by scholars such as Richter, Latourette and
Neill, there have been many lines of academic descent.[6] For example, Groves's

---

3  F.H. Hinsley ed. *Material Progress and World-Wide Problems, 1870–1898: New Cambridge Modern History* Vol. II (Cambridge, 1976 edn), pp. 118, 180, 402, 404, 406, 624; James Joll, *Europe Since 1870* (Harmondsworth 1976 edn), p. 80; Norman Stone, *Europe Transformed 1878–1919* (London, 1983).

4  Owen Chadwick, *The Victorian Church*, Vol. 1 (3rd edn, 1971) and Vol. 2 (2nd edn, 1972); Hugh McLeod, *Religion and the People of Western Europe, 1789–1970* (Oxford, 1981).

5  Norman Etherington, 'Missions and Empire', in Robin W. Winks (ed.), *OHBE Vol. 5 Historiography* (Oxford, 1999), pp. 303–14. Quotation at p. 303.

6  K.S. Latourette, *A History of the Expansion of Christianity*, 7 vols (London, 1937–45); *Christianity in a Revolutionary Age*, 5 vols (New York, 1957–61); Stephen Neill, *A History of Christian Missions* (2nd edn, Harmondsworth, 1986), with comments on Julius Richter's work at p. 480.

survey of the African continent was followed by important regional studies, now classics in their own right, such as Oliver on East Africa, Slade on the Congo and Ajayi and Ayandele on Nigeria.[7] Southern Africa's history has also been greatly enriched by historians of the missions and Christian churches.[8] Missionary work in India, notably in Bengal, Madras and the Punjab, has received serious attention from British and American scholars and that in China has benefited especially from American studies.[9] Apart from these detailed examinations of missions at work in the field, there have also appeared biographical studies of individual missionaries and official or sometimes unofficial histories of major missionary societies.[10] Alongside studies of the growth in Asia and Africa of the western churches, of the transmission overseas of western theologies, rituals and ecclesiastical forms, of missionary work in education or medicine, much interest has been shown in local perceptions of and contributions to Christian practice and traditions. There are now many studies of the multifarious 'independent', native-led churches and of the developing relationships between traditional religious systems and Christian beliefs. The variety of subject and perspective is enormous, but

7  Charles P. Groves, *The Planting of Christianity in Africa*, 4 vols (London, 1948–58); Roland Oliver, *The Missionary Factor in East Africa* (1952; 2nd edn, London, 1965); Ruth Slade, *English-Speaking Missions in the Congo Independent State, 1878–1908* (Académie Royale des Sciences Coloniales, Tome 16, Brussels, 1959); J.F.A. Ajayi, *Christian Missions in Nigeria 1841–1891* (London, 1965); E.A. Ayandele, *The Missionary Impact on Modern Nigeria 1842–1914* (London, 1966). Most recently but rooted in an older tradition, Bengt Sundkler, *Christianity in Africa* (Cambridge, 2001).

8  Richard Elphick, 'Africans and the Christian Campaign in South Africa', in H. Lamar and L.M. Thompson (eds), *The Frontier in History: North America and Southern Africa Compared* (New Haven, 1981); Jeff Guy, *The Heretic: A Study of the Life of John William Colenso 1814–1883* (Johannesburg and Pietermaritzburg, 1983); Jean and John Comaroff, *Of Revelation and Revolution*, 2 vols (Chicago, 1991 and 1997); Richard Elphick and Rodney Davenport (comp. and eds), *Christianity in South Africa: A Political, Social and Cultural History* (Oxford and Cape Town, 1997); Elizabeth Elbourne, *Blood Ground: Colonialism, Missions and the Contest for Christianity in the Cape Colony and Britain, 1799–1853* (Montreal and London, 2002).

9  For Asian examples, Jeffrey Cox, *Imperial Faultlines: Christianity and Colonial Power in India, 1818–1940* (Stanford, 2002); Penelope S.E. Carson, 'Soldiers of Christ: Evangelicals and India, 1784–1833', (unpub. Ph. D. thesis, London, 1988); Susan Bayly, *Saints, Goddesses and Kings: Muslims and Christians in South Indian Society 1700–1900* (Cambridge, 1989); Avril A. Powell, *Muslims and Missionaries in pre-Mutiny India* (London, 1993); Henriette Bugge, 'Mission and Tamil Society: Sixty Years of Interaction, 1840–1900 (unpub. Ph. D. thesis, Copenhagen, 1991); Paul A. Cohen, 'Christian Missions and Their Impact to 1900', in J.K. Fairbank (ed.), *The Cambridge History of China*, Vol. 10 (Cambridge, 1978); Jerome Chen, *China and the West: Society and Culture 1815–1937* (London, 1979); Jacques Gernet, *China and the Christian Impact* (Paris, 1982; English trans., Cambridge, 1985); Helen Ballhatchet, 'Between Idolatry and Infidelity: the Christian Missionary in Japan, 1874–1912', (unpub. Ph.D. thesis, London, 1985).

10  Recent examples include Andrew Ross, *John Philip (1775–1851): Missions, Race and Politics in South Africa* (Aberdeen, 1986); Brian Stanley, *The History of the Baptist Missionary Society 1792–1992* (Edinburgh, 1992); Daniel O'Connor and others, *Three Centuries of Mission: The United Society for the Propagation of the Gospel 1701–2000* (London, 2000); Kevin Ward and Brian Stanley (eds), *The Church Mission Society and World Christianity, 1799–1999* (Grand Rapids and Richmond, 2000).

recent work by scholars such as Adrian Hastings and Richard Gray has none the less gone some way to demonstrate the possibilities of making this overwhelming volume of material more manageable and less daunting.[11]

It is not from any desire to play down the importance of such studies to say that they have nevertheless often militated against an integrated understanding of missions and empire. One consequence of recent scholarly advances is that missionary sources have come to be seen chiefly as routes to a fuller appreciation of local non-European societies. That is one of their great virtues. However, although that historiographical function and important intellectual goal has been fulfilled, the missions themselves have as a result been pushed to the margin. Authors' perspectives have echoed that of the reviewer who saw in Gordon Hewitt's history of the Church Missionary Society (CMS) evidence that 'missionary history is no longer very interesting, except to those in some way specially concerned with it. What we want to know about today is the slow emergence of genuinely Asian and African churches ... a theme that cannot be adequately handled in terms of one society only, however eminent.'[12] Historians of Africa have argued strongly for the fundamental irrelevance of metropolitan thinking and missionary theory or theology to what took place in Africa itself. Terence Ranger observed as long ago as 1979 that the significance of missions rightly 'seems to belong more and more to European than to African history' and Richard Gray noted that however much missions differed in theory about what they were doing and how it might best be done, 'during these early decades [1900–40], African realities forced most missionaries to adopt remarkably similar practices'.[13] The inescapable triumph or dominance of local conditions over imported traits provides the ultimate justification for localised, essentially internal studies, quite properly diverting attention away from any preoccupation with the interplay of missions and empire. 'There is no need', wrote one historian of missions and church growth in Uganda, 'to bring in explanatory factors drawn from the European arena. The attitudes of the European actors can best be explained by the influence of developments within the African arena.' Others clearly agreed.[14] Many area specialists thus came to favour an exclusive concentration on their locality, dismissed metropolitan influences as of no

11 Richard Gray, 'Christianity', in A.D. Roberts (ed.), *The Cambridge History of Africa Vol. 7 1905–1940* (Cambridge, 1986); *Black Christians, White Missionaries* (New Haven and London, 1990); Adrian Hastings, *A History of African Christianity, 1950–1975* (Cambridge, 1979); *The Church in Africa 1450–1950* (Oxford, 1994); Elizabeth Isichei, *A History of Christianity in Africa* (Grand Rapids, 1995).

12 Gordon Hewitt, *The Problems of Success: A History of the Church Missionary Society 1910–1942.* Vol. 2 (London, 1977), reviewed by John Iliffe, 31, 1 *JEccH* (1980), 126–7.

13 Terence Ranger, 'White Presence and Power in Africa', *JAH* 20 (1979), 463–9; Gray, 'Christianity', p. 143.

14 Holger B. Hansen, 'European Ideas, Colonial Attitudes and African Realities: The Introduction of a Church Constitution in Uganda, 1898–1909', *IJAHS* 13, 2 (1980), 240–80. See also T.O. Beidelman, 'Social Theory and the Study of Christian Missions in Africa', *Africa* 44 (1974), 235–49;

more than minimal significance and appeared to see little future in comparative generalisations.

Such conclusions are reminiscent of the way in which the debate surrounding the supposed distinction between British colonial policies of 'indirect rule' and the French preference for 'assimilation' was laid to rest. Once it was realised how far in practice local African conditions prevailed, the lack of significant differences between the two seemed plain. Similar tendencies could be seen in the contemporaneous work of Caribbean historians.[15] As the fragility or instability of white communities and the restricted or temporary nature of the white presence and impact in the ex-colonial world has been brought to the fore, so the significance of any interplay between metropole and periphery, mission and empire, has been steadily eroded. The logic of such developments suggested that the study of missions and empire might founder on either the autonomy of non-Europeans' own history or the insularity of the British.

Supporters of missions continued to study their own history, but their handling of it has often failed to win the confidence of 'secular' historians. Their own evident confessional commitment, the tendency to hagiography or institutional piety, the study of the missionary past with the commitment of the determined reformer intent on future success, both seem almost as strong as ever. Even so scholarly a work as Shenk's study of the influential mid-nineteenth-century CMS Secretary Henry Venn appeared in a series devoted to 'new and creative approaches to the understanding of mission'. Its foreword stressed the need to 're-appropriate' Venn's views for their anticipation of late twentieth-century missionary strategies and highlighted the author's particular qualifications as those of 'a creative thinker in the realm of world mission theory and strategy and an experienced administrator'.[16] Such approaches may also have helped to perpetuate a preoccupation with over-arching missionary theory or ideology at the expense of the historical workings and development of the missionaries' own world.[17]

In the 1980s the main currents of historical specialisation and the overwhelmingly secular preoccupations of the academy were thus not such as to encourage a dispassionate or nuanced examination of the relationship between missions and empire. The paradox posed by the simultaneous downplaying of missions' impact

'Contradictions between the Sacred and the Secular Life: The Church Missionary Society in Ukaguru, Tanzania, East Africa, 1876–1914', *CSSH* 23 (1981), 73–95; *Colonial Evangelism: A Socio-Historical Study of an East African Mission at the Grassroots* (Bloomington, 1982); Robert Strayer, *The Making of Mission Communities in East Africa: Anglicans and Africans in Colonial Kenya, 1875–1935* (London, 1978).

15  W.A. Green, 'The Creolization of Caribbean History', *JICH* 14, 3 (1986), 149–69.

16  Wilbert R. Shenk, *Henry Venn – Missionary Statesman* (Maryknoll, NY, 1983), pp. v, xi–xii. See also Margaret Blunden, 'The Anglican Church and the Politics of Southern Africa, 1888–1909', (unpub. D.Phil. thesis, Oxford, 1980); Jocelyn Murray, *Proclaim the Good News: A Short History of the Church Missionary Society* (London, 1985).

17  For instance, L. Vander Werff, *The Strategy of Christian Missions to Muslims: Anglican and Reformed Contributions in India and the Near East 1800–1938* (South Pasadena, 1977).

and the elevation of the role played by local Christians, while continuing to depict western missions as forceful and effective agents of empire and colonial control, was not even addressed.

With hindsight, it is possible to see that Brian Stanley's book *The Bible and the Flag*, published in 1990, both reflected the limitations of the existing literature and demonstrated that serious attempts were being made to transcend them.[18] In his words, 'the belief that "the Bible and the flag" went hand in hand in the history of Western imperial expansion is fast becoming established as one of the unquestioned orthodoxies of general historical knowledge'. His intention was therefore to reach those readers untouched by monographs or scholarly articles, not 'to exonerate Christian missionaries from all the charges which have been levelled against them' but 'to convey an informed historical understanding of the issues involved'.[19] This was in every respect a book for the times. It was in part confessional, readily admitting the high-handed arrogance and easy dismissiveness with which many missionaries had approached religions and cultures other than their own. While acknowledging the 'imperial' implications of Christian religion, it also offered in response to critics a thesis defending the possibility of Christian missionary activity without empire. Finally it had much to say about the ambiguities of the missionary enterprise in an imperial setting and the world from which the missionaries came.

Since then, area specialists have begun to retreat from the more extremely dismissive of these positions and there has been a renewal of interest in the subject of missions and empire, not least in response to the growth of work in cultural history and a growing attention to the impact of imperial possessions on Britain itself.[20] Nevertheless, it remains the case that existing histories of British imperialism still pay only limited, if any, attention to the religious and missionary dimensions of overseas activity.[21] Historians of Britain's own domestic ecclesiastical and religious past, while appreciative of the work on the missions, have so far paid little attention themselves to the popular outpouring of evangelical enthusiasm, funds and volunteers for work overseas, which occurred irrespective of denomination and was often channelled into specific colonial possessions.[22] Among students at least of

---

18  Brian Stanley, *The Bible and the Flag: Protestant Missions and British Imperialism in the Nineteenth and Twentieth Centuries* (Leicester, 1990).

19  *Ibid.*, p. 12.

20  Additional evidence of this concern may be found in the activities of the North Atlantic Missiology and Currents in World Christianity Projects run by Dr Stanley from the University of Cambridge.

21  See for instance Bernard Porter, *The Lion's Share* (3rd edn, London, 1996); T.O. Lloyd, *The British Empire, 1558–1995* (Oxford, 1996). By contrast, Ronald Hyam, *Britain's Imperial Century, 1815–1914: A Study of Empire and Expansion*, 3rd edn (Basingstoke and New York, 2002), gives them due weight.

22  David Bebbington, *Evangelicalism in Modern Britain* (London, 1988); David Hempton, *Religion and Political Culture in Britain and Ireland* (Cambridge, 1996); *Religion of the People: Methodism and Popular Religion, c.1750–1900* (London, 1996). A notable exception is Steven Maughan,

Africa it is clearly still possible to present Protestant missions as the most unequiv-ocal and effective cultural imperialists and empire-builders, even as fellow histori-ans and anthropologists have begun to reveal the possibility of understanding Africa far more fully through sources that link the Christian impact both to reli-gious motive on each side and to 'the religious project which brought the mission-aries in the first place'.[23]

There thus exist at present three relatively distinct and enormous literatures, the first on Britain's imperial history, another on Britain's domestic religious and ecclesi-astical past and that concerned with the local histories of distinct regions or colonial societies around the globe. All have a potential interest in the phenomenon of Christian missionary expansion, whether as agents of British expansion overseas, as expressions of popular and provincial British religious commitment or as a critical influence in shaping local politics and identities. Nevertheless, time and the pressures of specialisation have militated against cross-fertilisation in this field as in so many others. This book has therefore also been written in the belief that its central theme, drawing as it does on all these scholarly traditions, may be of some value in con-structing a bridge, however rickety, across the historiographical gulfs that persist.

The following chapters explore the specific theme of the interplay of missions and empire and suggest that this may reveal fresh connections between British and overseas regional or global history. The book thus inevitably touches the perenni-ally vexed question of the consequences for Britain itself of its colonial ventures overseas. In what ways have the acquisition of colonies and imperial rule, or even of informal influence overseas, shaped the development of metropolitan Britain? This question perturbed figures as disparate as Edmund Burke and Richard Cobden and now preoccupies numerous historians of British or English culture and 'identity'. They too are currently engaged in exploring relationships between metropolitan Britain and the outside world in the development of which evangelicals and missionaries appear to have played a part.

In her recent writings, Kathleen Wilson, for example, has made a case for an influential missionary contribution to existing English perceptions of themselves in the late eighteenth century as members of a superior Protestant nation. As a result in particular of the London Missionary Society (LMS)'s expedition to Tahiti in 1796, 'cultural relativism was eschewed in favor of a more uncompro-mising view of antipodean savagery that sought to establish simultaneously the redemption, superiority and proprietary rights of the English settlers'.[24] Susan

'Regions Beyond and the National Church: Domestic Support for the Foreign Missions of the Church of England in the High Imperial Age, 1870–1914' (unpub. Ph. D. thesis, Harvard, 1995).

23 Comaroff, *Of Revelation and Revolution*; reviews of Comaroff, Vol. 1, in 'Book Feature', *SAHJ* 31 (1994), 273–309; Leon De Kock, *Civilising Barbarians: Missionary Narrative and African Textual Response in Nineteenth-Century South Africa* (Johannesburg, 1996); J.D.Y. Peel, *Religious Encounter and the Making of the Yoruba* (Bloomington, 2000), pp. 4–5.

24 Kathleen Wilson, *The Island Race: Englishness, Empire and Gender in the Eighteenth Century* (London and New York, 2003), p. 82.

Thorne's work has vigorously propounded the view that 'Missionaries were considerably more successful in securing imperialism's hegemony in Britain than in their foreign fields of operation' and focuses her attention on 'their influence on social relations and political identifications in Britain'.[25] Foreign missions were 'one among the myriad sites at which ordinary Britons encountered the colonies' and the 'imaginative relationship to the empire encouraged by missions contributed ... to some of the central developments of British social history in this period', including class formation, gender relations and their relationship to the concept of race.[26]

Catherine Hall has also devoted much attention to the place of race in the empire and its association with gender differentiation in British social and political culture. In the words of her most recent book, 'If gender hierarchy was inscribed at the heart of the missionary enterprise, so was that of race.'[27] In ways not dissimilar to Thorne, she has suggested that missions have played a vital role in popularising empire with large sections of the British public. As they mobilised public opinion behind missions – especially perhaps in the case of Jamaica – so missionaries entrenched racial stereotypes and notions of racial hierarchy, 'constitut[ing] themselves as colonisers' and non-whites as the colonised.[28] At the same time, it is said, they encouraged ordinary British individuals to see themselves as members of a chosen people whose future would involve them as an imperial power lording it over much of the world.

There is much in this book relevant to the concerns of these authors, but their preoccupations are not often addressed directly in what follows. There are several reasons for this. There are good intellectual grounds for thinking that the important questions they have raised deserve further consideration at length and in their own right, not as subordinate issues overshadowed in a work of a different kind. Some readers may nevertheless regret, for instance, the decision not to discuss at any length here the issue of gender. This of course offers a very valuable bridge between the histories of Britons, male as well as female, at home and overseas. Missions in particular were a most important means of mobilising women for employment both in Britain and abroad, especially and increasingly for positions in teaching, medical care and work with indigenous women and children. So much was this so that by the 1890s the majority of British mission workers in the field were female. Especially if single, their responsibilities were often markedly heavier and their status more elevated (if still imperfectly recognised) than they would have been at home. Their presence significantly reinforced the trend in

25 Susan Thorne, *Congregational Missions and the Making of an Imperial Culture in Nineteenth-Century England* (Stanford, 1999), p. 10.
26 *Ibid.*, pp. 5, 7, 15–17.
27 Catherine Hall, *Civilising Subjects: Metropole and Colony in the English Imagination, 1830–1867* (Cambridge, 2002), p. 97.
28 *Ibid.*, p. 12; for earlier instances of this view, Ajayi, *Christian Missions*, pp. 261–2.

missionary activities towards the practical concern with welfare.[29] In dealing with the specific theme of this book, however, their presence and its importance may be taken as understood, even while there remain many dimensions to be more fully explored.[30]

There are, however, also certain differences between the approach and working assumptions adopted by these authors and those shaping the analysis of missionary enterprise attempted here, that are less easily reconciled. Wilson, for instance, argues not only that 'the ultimate goal of evangelicalism was to create universal Christian subjects in the eyes of God', but that the LMS demonstrated the powerful 'imperatives to convert, subdue and possess the world through the cultural power and superiority of English Protestantism'.[31] No more than her bald assertion that the 'new missionary societies were well-connected to the abolitionist cause' will these bear much analytical weight. It will become clearer below that human beings were already 'equal in the eyes of God' and that the making of Christian 'subjects' was scarcely evangelicals' 'ultimate goal'. No more were conversion, subjugation and possession necessarily linked in missionary minds and to suggest so is surely to confuse much evangelical thought and motive with entirely different and distinct forms of imperial activity. In assigning an influence to the role of missions in the making of eighteenth-century English nationalism, the activities of Methodists, Moravians and the Society for the Propagation of the Gospel (SPG) are likely to have a better claim to consideration than the LMS.[32]

The same tendency, to remodel the inherently flexible and variegated character of so much in the activity of missions and agencies of imperial expansion into a series of rigid functional connections between empire, national identity and missions, is also detectable in Thorne's work. In writing of the 'birth of modern missions' she argues that 'missions ... were ... a product of the transformation in

29  Steven Maughan, 'Regions Beyond and the National Church', chap. 3; Rhonda Semple, '"Ladies of Much Ability and Intelligence": Gendered Relations in British Protestant Missions, 1865–1910', (Ph.D., London, 2000), now published as *Missionary Women: Gender, Professionalism and the Victorian Idea of Christian Mission* (Woodbridge, 2003); Jane Haggis, 'Professional Ladies and Working Wives: Female Missionaries in the London Missionary Society and its South Travancore District, South India in the Nineteenth Century' (unpub. Ph.D. thesis, Manchester, 1991).

30  See Chapter. 12, below. pp. 319–20, 322. Also Sean Gill, *Women and the Church of England from the Eighteenth Century to the Present* (London, 1994), chap. 8 'Women in the Mission Field'; Fiona Bowie, Deborah Kirkwood and Shirley Ardener, *Women and Missions: Past and Present* (Providence and Oxford, 1993); Jocelyn Murray, 'The Role of Women in the Church Missionary Society, 1799–1917' and Guli Francis-Dehqani, 'CMS Women Missionaries in Persia: Perceptions of Muslim Women and Islam, 1884–1934', in Kevin Ward and Brian Stanley (eds), *The Church Mission Society and World Christianity, 1799–1999*, (Grand Rapids and Richmond, 2000) pp. 66–90, 91–119; Norman Etherington, 'Gender Issues in South-East African Missions, 1835–85', in Henry Bredekamp and Robert Ross (eds), *Missions and Christianity in South African History* (Johannesburg, 1995), pp. 135–52; and works by Gaitskell, Grimshaw and Robert, in bibliography.

31  Wilson, *Island Race*, p. 81.

32  See Chapter 1 below.

the British colonial project, a means of governing colonies whose indigenous inhabitants could no longer be eliminated, enslaved or removed'.[33] If this is eccentric in the case of the LMS, dominated as it was from the start by concern with the Pacific where British colonies did not yet exist outside New South Wales, it is no less so given the difficulty missions had even in securing entry into areas under British control, let alone in becoming a 'means of governing'. It is also claimed that 'colonial officials invariably referred to [missionaries] in public in highly favourable terms': for many years this was scarcely contemporary experience in India, the British West Indies or Cape Colony. Neither by the imperial government nor by the missions themselves were missions 'conceived of ... as an alternative to the increasingly authoritarian forms of rule by which the British state hoped to avoid a repetition of the American Revolution'.[34]

As a divinely favoured nation, possessing in its empire as in its wealth, its political stability and its victory at Trafalgar, marks of that favour, Britain was widely held to have a reciprocal obligation to promote the spread of Christianity. To that end, the Methodists, for example, spent £34 on their missions to St Kitts and almost £200 on Antigua in 1805–6; £1064 went to their Irish mission, £516 to the Welsh. The Liskeard circuit ceased to contribute after 1804–5 when it found almost £8; and the worshippers of Colne scrupulously counted up subscriptions of £15 5s 6½d in 1805.[35] Such gifts were not intended to underwrite empire, any more than fluctuations in money raised were signs of discontent with imperial progress. They were expressions of personal faith, signs of recognition of a widespread need for preachers and true religion, evidence of concern that the country's obligations and Christ's last command might not be met. Methodist anger at Thomas Coke's mishandling of the accounts reflected neither an expression of outraged patriotism nor a sense that consequently empire might be endangered. In a world where missions and empire occupied separate if sometimes overlapping spheres, it was evidence of discontent at the thought that through carelessness the Lord's coming might be delayed.[36]

There are issues enough here to suggest the value of a fresh attempt to understand the world of the eighteenth-and nineteenth-century missionary movement and its encounter with empire. There is the same evident need for understanding in the case of the missionaries themselves. Catherine Hall's recent book, *Civilising Subjects*, for example, comes with a gentle, unobtrusive, but none the less surprising disclaimer. 'My focus is on the social, cultural and political world of nonconformists; I do not pretend to be a theologian.'[37] It is hard to reconcile this position with the historian's need to recognise that Nonconformists, evangelicals and others

---

33  Thorne, *Congregational Missions*, p. 41.
34  *Ibid.*, pp. 38, 41. For discussion of these issues, see Chapter 3, below.
35  Figures taken from *Methodist Annual Reports*.
36  For Coke see below, pp. 29, 31–2, 34.
37  Hall, *Civilizing Subjects*, p. 444, footnote 29.

took their theology and religion seriously and applied them to considerable practical effect. The chapters that follow this Introduction provide, amongst other things, a commentary on various missionary beliefs and their implications for the approaches of missions both to empire and the world beyond British control. They suggest that historians should perhaps be prepared to take not only theology but a good many other things as seriously as did most missionaries of the day. It ought to go without saying that this involves a major methodological point. It is not a suggestion that historians writing about religious expansion have to be theologians and committed supporters of missions; that would be as absurd as an insistence that today's historians of empire or any other subject should approach it from a particular intellectual standpoint. It is simply to ask that the relevant historiography should be generously defined and that sources of missionary inspiration should receive a full consideration, rather than be arbitrarily confined to their supposedly rational and secular components, generally found more comprehensible if not congenial by most of today's scholars.

It is to be hoped that this book lives up to its own injunction. In some respects it is a conventional construction. It explores and presents arguments and themes within a chronological framework, selectively referring to particular examples of missionary work and individual geographical areas as seems appropriate.

The opening chapter is concerned with developments that took place from the beginning of the eighteenth century. Instead of adopting the conventional starting point marked by the formation of the principal voluntary societies in the 1790s, it begins with the operations of the Anglican SPG and to a lesser extent those of the Society for the Promotion of Christian Knowledge (SPCK). The evangelical revival was brought rapidly into connection with overseas missions as a result of the work of continental European protestants, the Moravians and Wesleyan Methodists, notably in North America and the West Indies. Together these provided a theological legacy and a territorial context important in shaping the initiatives of the 1790s and 1800s. In the course of those two decades, dealt with in Chapter 2, continuing revival led to the foundation, reorganisation and further development of several major societies, notably the Baptist Missionary Society (BMS), the London Missionary Society, the Church Missionary Society and the Wesleyan Methodist Missionary Society (WMMS).

Chapters 3 and 4 are concerned with the ways in which, once established, the new missionary societies began to define their approaches to the contemporary world, both in terms of their own general strategy for expansion overseas and at the local level of their encounter with particular interest groups and political authorities. Missions were increasingly involved in agitating for unfettered access to all British colonial possessions, in the continuing campaign against slavery, with the debate about Christianity's links with the expansion of British commerce and the adoption of policies of 'westernisation' towards non-European societies. Particular attention is devoted to missions and white planter or settler societies in the West Indies and South Africa and to relations between the imperial authorities and missions in India and Sierra Leone. Chapter 5 explores some of the ways in which, in the early nineteenth century, the international connections of the movement also continued to provide a reminder of the distance that existed between British missions and the building of a British empire.

The decades 1830–50 witnessed a further major wave of missionary expansion. The ways in which this process was organised and the crucial significance for that expansion of the mission societies' relationship with the humanitarian movement are at the heart of Chapter 6. New-found prominence and respectability prompted missionary organisers to plan the future of their enterprise and the building up of 'native churches'. Chapter 7 not only examines the nature of these plans but, with special reference to India, southern Africa and the West Indies, considers the reasons why so many in the missionary movement thought that they had substantially failed in the 1850s and 1860s. The mid-century's mounting sense of failure or at least stagnation went hand in hand with several new departures. Chapter 8 therefore considers the implications for the ties between missions and empire of the emergence of the new 'faith missions', the extension of Protestant evangelism into China and a newly developed concern with Islam.

New or radical departures were less common than the reshaping of existing missionary frameworks, intellectual and administrative, in ways designed to revive the movement's enthusiasm and sense of direction. Chapters 9 and 10 run in parallel and overlap in various ways. They analyse the manner in which from c.1870 missionary traditions underwent extensive adaptation and analyse the implications for empire as well as some consequences of those adjustments. They embrace the development of high church responses in the form of the Universities' Mission to Central Africa (UMCA) and the Oxford and Cambridge missions to north India; the Niger crisis of the 1880s and 1890s; the impact of the late-century revivalism associated with the Keswick movement; the experience of Scottish and Wesleyan missions in India; and the involvement of missions in the process of African partition. Chapter 11 explores from several angles the ways in which, when the empire was at its peak between 1890 and 1914, both the development of the missionary movement and individual missionaries were increasingly led to distance themselves from the identification of imperial and British missionary interests. The growth of the international students' movement and the ecumenism associated with the World Missionary Conference of 1910 contributed to this process. Also of particular interest is the realignment once more of the missionary with the humanitarian movement, in response both to domestic attitudes and to conditions in areas such as China, India and the Congo. The year 1914 marks the start of the destruction and reconstruction of missionary enterprise associated with the First World War, a hiatus in many of the developments examined here and thus an appropriate terminal date. Chapter 12 offers concluding reflections on both the argument of the book and some of its omissions.

Although the organisation may seem conventional, the arguments are perhaps less so. Much importance is attached to the concern of missionaries with their own independence and their rooted aversion to 'politics'. Their engagement with empire more often than not took the form of bitter experience. This taught them the lessons that independence was a chimera and, more positively, that selective engagement was nevertheless both possible and at times advantageous to the pursuit of their own distinct goals. Missions thus saw themselves much of the time as 'anti-imperialist' and their relationship with empire as deeply ambiguous at best. Viewing the scene from standpoints other than their own, they may have been wrong in this perception. The extent to which missionaries were identified by local peoples with conquerors and colonisers, damned by proximity to settlers and their own ministrations to administrators, was often seriously underestimated at the time. It has subsequently been a focus for those keen to demonstrate the impossibility of missionaries being other than essential agents of colonialism. Nevertheless, modern scholars are also faced with missions aware of the problem and working to rid themselves of guilt by association.[38] It continues to be important for historians to appreciate the roots of that missionary misunderstanding and to examine any consequences of missionary attempts to remedy the situation.

A further assumption is that issues of theology, belief and ideas about the nature of the church are to be taken seriously. However much missionaries may have been constrained by local circumstances, historians are not entitled to dismiss their motives as insignificant and of no consequence or interest. Missionaries viewed their world first of all with the eye of faith and then through theological lenses. The book attempts to demonstrate that the fluctuating dynamism of the missionary movement, as well as the timing, direction and form of missionary initiatives, owes much to theological persuasion. Not only 'religious revival' but also the content of those revivals and the denominational twist given to the implementation of missionary policy, could have a marked impact in the mission field. Thus views about the millennium, biblical interpretation, the course of Roman Catholic and Islamic expansion, the criteria for or evidences of conversion, could affect missionary relations not only with their home constituency but with both government and local people overseas, whether Christians or not.

Another purpose of the book is thus to suggest that there is still value for all historians in paying attention to the metropolitan roots of missionary enterprise. The pattern and nature of missionary activity on the ground were also affected by metropolitan developments other than those narrowly concerned with matters of faith. Particular attention is given here to the shifting relationship between missions and humanitarianism and to the international dimensions of the missionary movement. Both frequently placed missions at odds with the practical consequences of imperial expansion and rule. In doing so they raise a further question mark over the easy identification of what are often and inaccurately labelled 'British' missions with the limited realities of 'British' empire-building.

---

38  For example, John Barton (Agra) to Henry Venn (CMS Secretary.), 4 April 1863, CMS Archives, CI 1/037, no. 30; for Barton see below, pp. 178–81

# Missionary practice and precedents,
## 1701–89

William Carey's famous essay *An Enquiry into the Obligations of Christians, to use Means for the Conversion of the Heathens* (Leicester, 1792) and his part in the formation at Kettering in October that year of what became known as the Baptist Missionary Society, were for the Society's most recent historian a 'turning-point in the history of Christian missionary endeavour'.[1] Brian Stanley's careful choice of words reflects how the star of the Baptist missionary has waned in recent years. Realisation of the extent of Carey's dependence on numerous friends and collaborators 'for insight and a wide range of initiatives' has necessarily modified the traditional emphasis on his central role in 'beginning the modern era of Protestant missionary work'. Like many other missionary 'heroes', he is no longer so likely to be seen as that 'great, solitary figure who towered above his contemporaries'.[2]

Carey's pamphlet, his departure for India in 1793 and his residence with colleagues from 1799 at the Danish settlement of Serampore, just outside Calcutta, are thus losing their significance as conventional markers for the beginning of the modern missionary movement. British departures in the 1790s, it is being argued, should be seen instead as adding further dimensions to a movement at once trans-Atlantic and Europe-wide that was already under way.[3] In a similar fashion, the place of the later 1780s and 1790s in the history of imperial expansion has also been reconsidered. Associated with the loss of the American colonies and the mounting impact of the Industrial Revolution, these decades were often seen as pinpointing the threshold of Britain's nineteenth-century empire. In recent years the roots of that empire, nurtured by new forms of 'gentlemanly capitalism', a sense of national identity linked to Protestantism and constitutional liberty and

---

1 Brian Stanley, *The History of the Baptist Missionary Society, 1792–1992* (Edinburgh, 1992), p. 2.

2 A. Christopher Smith, 'William Carey 1761–1834. Protestant Pioneer of the Modern Mission Era', in Gerald H. Anderson et al. (eds), *Mission Legacies. Biographical Studies of Leaders of the Modern Missionary Movement* (Maryknoll, NY, 1994), p. 246; E. Daniel Potts, 'William Carey', in Donald M. Lewis (ed.), *The Blackwell Dictionary of Evangelical Biography 1730–1860* (Oxford, 1995), pp. 197–8.

3 Andrew F. Walls, 'The Eighteenth-Century Protestant Missionary Awakening in its European Context', in Brian Stanley (ed.), *Christian Missions and the Enlightenment* (Grand Rapids and Richmond, 2001), pp. 22–44; W.R. Ward, *The Protestant Evangelical Awakening* (Cambridge, 1992); J.C.S. Mason, *The Moravian Church and the Missionary Awakening in England 1760–1800* (Woodbridge, 2001).

bureaucratic reconstruction in response to the needs of war, have been steadily pushed back before 1750. To adapt the phraseology of one distinguished recent account, 'elements of a new Empire already co-existed with those of the old early in the eighteenth century'.[4] Certainly for the questions addressed in this book earlier eighteenth-century precedents have considerable significance. By the time Carey set sail, developments in Britain's Atlantic and Caribbean colonies had long and amply illustrated the chief missionary problems and possibilities which were constantly to recur and shape the connections of missions and empire.

## I

The first entanglements of Protestant missionary work and British colonial enterprise are to be traced in the North American colonies. Until c.1700, these missionary activities were slow to get going and few and far between, and were for the most part both sporadic and geographically restricted. With few exceptions they were largely unproductive either of conversions or of more than temporarily improved relations between Indians and settlers. Even some of the best-known attempts – the 'New England Company' and the Presbyterian John Eliot's work with the Naragansett and closely related groups, or Harvard's Indian College, both of which continued over a period of about forty years – demonstrated unequivocally the place of missions as perhaps adjuncts of empire but in no real sense its effective agents.[5] Surviving correspondence of the New England Company and the reports of the Bishop of London's commissaries, the Reverend James Blair appointed to Virginia in 1690 and the Reverend Dr Thomas Bray to Maryland in 1696, who were entrusted to investigate and take steps to improve the state of the colonial churches, confirmed this very bleak picture.[6] Eliot's story was taken up by later generations of missionaries as a shining example of selfless devotion to the missionary cause. However, it is no less possible to set hagiography aside and to see in its history a combination of persistent yet ultimately fruitless evangelism with a vigorous but

4  Cf. P.J. Marshall, 'Britain without America – A Second Empire?', in *OHBE* (ed.), *Vol. 2 The Eighteenth Century* (Oxford, 1998), p. 577.

5  Sidney H. Rooy, *The Theology of Missions in the Puritan Tradition* (Delft, 1965); William Kellaway, *The New England Company, 1649–1776: Missionary Society to the American Indians* (London, 1961), and for Eliot see chaps 5–6; James Axtell, *The Invasion Within: The Contest of Cultures in Colonial North America* (New York and Oxford, 1985); Louise A. Breen, 'Praying with the Enemy: Daniel Gookin, King Philip's War and the Dangers of Intercultural Mediatorship', in Martin Daunton and Rick Halpern (eds), *Empire and Others: British Encounters with Indigenous Peoples, 1600–1850* (London, 1999), pp. 101–22.

6  [New England Company], *Some Correspondence between the Governors and Treasurers of the New England Company in London and the Commissioners of the United Colonies in America, The Missionaries of the Company and Others between the Years 1657 and 1712* (London, 1896); Thomas Bray, *A Memorial representing the present State of Religion on the Continent of North America* (London, 1700); W.S. Perry (ed.), *Historical Collections relating to the American Colonial Church*, 5 vols (New York, 1870–78), Vol. 1, Virginia, Vol. 4 Maryland, passim.

largely unavailing defence of Indian rights and lands in the face of white encroach-
ment. The fate of Eliot's fourteen Indian villages or 'praying towns' provided
evidence of the persistent problems. Designed to prompt conversion and encourage Indian adaptation to white ways, they were instead destroyed in 'King Philip's
War' (1675), when many of their inhabitants joined the hostile Indian forces against
the colonists. Their destruction anticipated very similar events in the settler wars of
the Cape Colony 175 years later.[7]

Of much greater direct importance to both the immediate and long-term development of missionary enterprise was the establishment of the Society for the
Propagation of the Gospel in Foreign Parts in June 1701. This was the second of
three societies organised by the same small group of high church Anglican reformers led by Dr Thomas Bray. Two years before, in response to fears for the quality of
Christian instruction and daily living, the Society for Promoting Christian
Knowledge had been formed to provide religious literature and even complete
libraries of approved books for needy parishes, both at home and overseas.[8] Two
decades later, in 1723, the Associates of Dr Bray were established as a foundation to
manage funds which Bray had accumulated by a bequest from Holland for the
education of African Americans.

The SPG, constituted by royal charter, directed its attention exclusively to the
colonies. It was the first body to promote the systematic recruitment of episcopal
clergy for new or vacant parishes, to foster religious teaching through the provision
of missionaries and schoolmasters and to lobby the imperial governments for episcopal oversight and provision in Britain's overseas possessions.[9] Under the presidency of the Archbishop of Canterbury and the general direction of those bishops
who chose to become members and therefore vice-presidents, the Society was
incorporated with powers to acquire property and to raise and disburse funds in
order to tackle the religious shortcomings of the overseas empire. For all its establishment and clerical flavour, it was none the less a voluntary society, essentially
dependent on subscriptions, collections and the commitment of unpaid time. In
due course, the Society's efforts made an essential contribution to the spread of
Anglicanism throughout British North America and, it has been claimed, by 1776
had become 'central to the religious development of Britain's American colonies'.[10]

As the preamble to the charter explained, 'in many of our Plantations, Colonies
and Factories beyond the Seas ... the Provision for Ministers is very mean. And

---

7  *BDCM*, p. 197.
8  The SPCK may have existed in embryonic form since 1696.
9  For the history of the SPG, C.F. Pascoe, *Two Hundred Years of the S.P.G.: An Historical Account of the
   Society for the Propagation of the Gospel in Foreign Parts, 1701–1900*, 2 vols (London, 1901); H.P.
   Thompson, *Into All Lands: The History of the Society for the Propagation of the Gospel in Foreign Parts
   1701–1950* (London, 1951); Daniel O'Connor and others, *Three Centuries of Mission: The United
   Society for the Propagation of the Gospel 1701–2000* (London and New York, 2000).
10 Jon Butler, *Awash in a Sea of Faith: Christianizing the American People* (Cambridge, MA, and
   London, 1990), p. 34.

many others ... are wholly destitute and unprovided of a Maintenance for Ministers and the Public Worship of God; and for Lack of ... such, many ... do want the Administration of God's Word and Sacraments and seem to be abandoned to Atheism and Infidelity and also for Want of Learned and Orthodox Ministers to instruct Our ... Subjects in the Principles of true Religion, diverse Romish Priests and Jesuits are the more encouraged to pervert and draw over Our said Loving Subjects to Popish Superstition and Idolatry'.[11]

Although neither indigenous peoples – North America's Indians – nor black slaves were explicitly mentioned in the charter, the term 'subjects' meant for many in the Society more than simply white emigrants and settlers. The Dean of Lincoln glossed the charter's formality in his anniversary sermon in 1702. 'The design is, in the first place, to settle the State of Religion as well as may be among our *own People* there ... and then to proceed ... towards the *Conversion* of the *Natives* ... this is ... the greatest Charity we can show ... especially ... to the souls of many of those *poor Natives* who may by this be converted from that state of *Barbarism* and *Idolatry* in which they now live'.[12]

The early Instructions for the missionaries set out the desired approach via 'natural religion' to instructing '*Heathens* and *Infidels*'. 'Native' was increasingly and explicitly taken to include both the Indian peoples of North America and the imported African slave population and its descendants, not only in the eventual thirteen colonies but throughout the Caribbean and the Atlantic world. In 1710, responding warmly to the visit of the 'Four Indian Kings' – an Iroquois diplomatic delegation – to London, the Society made plain its resolve: 'the design of propagating the Gospel in foreign parts does chiefly and principally relate to the conversion of heathens and infidels: and therefore that branch of it ought to be prosecuted preferably to all others.'[13] This commitment by the SPG was no less genuine for reflecting the optimism and hopes among both English and Indians generated by the pressures of a new phase in the war with France (the War of the Spanish Succession, 1702–13). It sprang from the general sense that the interests of church and state were fundamentally one and that opportunities provided by *raison d'état* were there for the Society to turn to its advantage. In practice, however, the Society's immediate promise of missionaries to the Iroquois eventually came to little. The appointment of the first missionary, William Andrews, was delayed until 1712 and the mission was abandoned in 1719.

If the general object of missionary evangelism was not consistently given the widespread prominence attached to it on this occasion, it was nevertheless a matter to which the Society frequently returned. On the eve of the Seven Years War (1756–63) fresh instructions were sent from London to the Society's missionaries,

---

11  Pascoe, *Two Hundred Years*, Vol. 2, p. 932.
12  *Ibid.*, Vol. 1, pp. 7–8, original emphases.
13  'Instructions for the Clergy employed by the Society' (1706), Pascoe, *Two Hundred Years*, Vol. 2 pp. 838–9, original emphases; Vol. 1, p. 69; Thompson, *Into All Lands*, pp. 27, 78–9.

urging them to seize every opening for converting Indians. This 'good work is not only pious and Charitable in the more important Views of Religion, but highly beneficial likewise in a Civil View, as promoting the security and Interest of the American Colonies'.[14] Archbishop Secker, looking ahead a little later, felt that 'we ought to have more [missionaries] upon the frontiers; at least when it shall please God to bless us with a peace. For Missionaries there might counteract the artifices of the French Papists; and do considerable services, religious and political at once, amongst the neighbouring Indians; both which points the Society hath been heavily charged, on occasion of the present war, with having neglected.'[15]

An equally direct concern was expressed for the colonial slave population, which began to increase rapidly after the Treaty of Utrecht (1713). Christopher Codrington, for example, attached considerable importance to the Society's intentions and in his will of 1710 left his Barbados estates together with several hundred slaves specifically for its support. He expected the Society to provide a model of the manner in which, through the education and conversion of the slaves, Christianity and slavery might be reconciled and plantation society in the Caribbean transformed. Ill-informed and desultory oversight from England combined with local management and a continuing preoccupation with profits to produce total failure. On the American mainland, professed intentions similarly outran practical results despite more evidence of conscientious missionary activity. A limited number of schools existed and a handful of devoted missionaries persevered with the religious instruction and education of slaves in the face of persistent obstacles raised by slave-owners. Relying on such evidence, historians of the SPG have often been at pains to defend the Society against charges of failing to evangelise the black and Native American populations. In the case of the African Americans, however, such criticisms have often arisen from the unwillingness of the Society to antagonise white slave-owners and its refusal to come out in support of emancipation, rather than from consideration of such evangelisation as was attempted. It might be argued that the Society's policy was the only one that stood a chance of success in a society where acceptance of slavery and determination to maintain the institution were all but universal. It is nevertheless impossible to disagree with the conclusion that 'By 1770 it was evident that, in the British colonies at least, hopes for the Christianization of slavery had been ill-founded.'[16]

There is no doubt that the SPG's missionary work was directed chiefly at the white colonial population, when, from the 1690s onwards, increasingly systematic attention was given to establishing the Anglican church more securely in colonial America. As a direct result, colonial politics and the fight for material endowment

---

14  Frank J. Klingberg, *Anglican Humanitarianism in Colonial New York* (Philadelphia, 1940), p. 81.
15  In 1758, *ibid.*, p. 93.
16  David Brion Davis, *The Problem of Slavery in Western Culture* (1966. Penguin edition, Harmondsworth, 1970), p. 247. For Codrington, *ibid.*, pp. 243–6; and J. Harry Bennett, *Bondsmen and Bishops: Slavery and Apprenticeship on the Codrington Plantation of Barbados, 1710–1838* (Berkeley, 1958).

and episcopacy in the face of expanding Dissent and denominational diversity received far more attention than the teaching and conversion of Indians and African Americans.[17]

A conventional but none the less central assumption on all sides in the Society and among its supporters was that the SPG's missionary activity contributed to the good order of colonial government and society, a matter of importance not only to local inhabitants or colonial citizens but to the imperial government and its subjects at home. The work of the SPG was officially supported to a limited extent in order to establish in British North America religious activity possessing an established status and institutions which paralleled those of the Anglican church at home. Good government, social order and established religion were regarded as inseparable in an ideal world and the desirability of their connection was demonstrated in many different ways. The SPG, for instance, itself ordained in 1702 that all bibles which it distributed should be bound together with the Book of Common Prayer, thus symbolically linking the preaching of the word with the maintenance of proper standards of church order and liturgy. In the provision and continued support of clergymen, the Society neither intended nor expected to rely only on its own financial resources. Its original anticipations of sufficient clerical support from local sources within three years of an appointment were totally unrealistic and by 1710 the possibility of an open-ended liability had been accepted. However, even while meeting mixed success, it never ceased to press both in London and on the ground for the implementation of those Acts and imperial instructions to colonial governors which might assist their cause.[18] By 1715, the Church of England was established in four colonies; although it remained very weak in North Carolina, by 1720 South Carolina had thirteen parishes, Maryland twenty and Virginia fifty. Their colonial assemblies and vestries were required to fund the active propagation of the Gospel. This necessitated in practice at least the provision of glebe land or a crop tax – 16,000 lb of tobacco to each minister per annum in Virginia – regarded as sufficient to produce an income to support the necessary numbers of parish priests and schoolmasters. Additional support was also forthcoming at intervals in the shape of grants from Queen Anne's Bounty and from such proceeds as were generated by occasional Royal Letters requiring parishes at home to raise funds for the Society's work.

Even where they were not legally established and often faced particular hostility from colonial assemblies – in the middle colonies and in New England – Anglican ministers regarded themselves as members of a state church, obliged to minister to everyone and consequently committed to evangelism as a primary task. To some historians, most notably perhaps Carl Bridenbaugh, the character of

---

17  Robert T. Handy, *A History of the Churches in the United States and Canada* (Oxford, 1976), chaps 2–3, and 5, for a survey of the conditions for missionary expansion and church growth from 1650 to 1800.

18  W.W. Manross, *The Fulham Papers in the Lambeth Palace Library: American Colonial Section Calendar and Indexes* (Oxford, 1965).

the Society was therefore such as to leave no doubt that it represented 'British imperialism in ecclesiastical guise'.[19] Its missionaries were an arm of the English state and it has been argued that the Society rapidly became the 'central agency' for the promotion of the Anglican church rather than simply the transmission of the Gospel. Such was the speed with which its missionaries 'invaded the colonies by force and employed tactics worked out by the prelates in London' and so keen its commitment to the extension of royal control that by 1718 only Connecticut had no episcopal church. Setting out 'to overcome the colonial conditions which had reduced the Church of England to the status of a sect in the colonies north of Maryland', the winning of political influence and proselytisation at the expense of rival denominations became the main preoccupation of Anglicans. At once symbolic of its intentions and an important practical route to attainment of its goal were the SPG's periodic public campaigns for the appointment of an Anglican bishop for the American colonies. Always a subject of interest especially on the part of colonial Anglicans, according to Bridenbaugh, it was promoted with particular vigour until the death of Queen Anne, then again in the 1740s and above all in the 1760s as part of the more general reconstruction of a centralised empire after the Seven Years War.[20]

This is an exaggerated depiction of the integration of empire and Anglican missions, one that reflects the wishful thinking of a limited number of contemporaries rather than the reality of circumstances on the ground either in London or in North America. Appeals from local SPG clergy for the establishment of effective episcopal authority and integrated ecclesiastical structures were constantly despatched to London. Many of the writers saw the satisfaction of these requests in the first instance as essential to sustain Anglican Christianity and teaching for those colonists who wanted it, rather than as a necessary basis for any concerted campaign against colonial Dissent. The local co-ordination and strengthening of Anglican religious life and the consequent necessity for a local source of religious and ecclesiastical authority *within* the church, were their first priorities.

Throughout the century to 1790 congregations and clergy suffered in different ways from the lack of organisation quite as much as limited resources. The Bishop of London's Commissary in Pennsylvania was obliged to point out that 'The members of our Church are not the Richest in the Place, the Riches generally centring in the Quakers & High Dutch who are very numerous & carry all before them and our Church labours under very great discouragement as we have no legal Establishment (as they have at New York) not so much as a Charter of Incorporation to enable us to manage our Business to the best advantage.'[21] These were none the less by no means the problems of Pennsylvania alone.

---

19  Carl Bridenbaugh, *Mitre and Sceptre: Transatlantic Faiths, Ideas, Personalities and Politics, 1689–1775* (New York, 1962), p. 57.
20  *Ibid.*, pp. 25–7, 119, and chap.10 'The Great Fear', 1766–1770.
21  Rev. Dr Robert Jenney to SPG Secretary, 26 Oct. 1749, Perry, *Historical Collections*, Vol. 2, p. 260.

Frustration, inefficiency and loss of morale were closely connected to the absence everywhere of periodic or regular visitations, local and prompt scrutiny of parish reports and even of rapid responses to death and illness. Only a bishop could administer the sacraments of confirmation and ordination, with the consequence that local candidates for the priesthood had no alternative but to bear the difficulty and cost of travelling to London. In William Sturgeon's words, 'The Church of England without a Bishop is left to the care only of a few private Clergymen who have no person to oversee or call them to an account upon their misbehaviour, nor to encourage and support them in the best cause. This leaves them and their respective Congregations to do the best they can and indeed sometimes it is bad enough.'[22] From time to time ministers or missionaries themselves could go completely off the rails, but still remain in place to do incalculable damage for want of local authority to suspend or replace them. Such a one was the incumbent at Duck Creek in Pennsylvania, whose behaviour prompted a despairing general observation. 'For as in this Province we have no establishment by Law and obtain a preference only by the purity of our doctrine and the testimony of our own good lives and examples, so one irregular Clergyman … will pull down more in six months than a diligent Missionary can build up in almost as many years.'[23]

It is not surprising that episcopal clergy often felt isolated and vulnerable if not resentful and frustrated as a result of their comparative powerlessness. Although it was always possible to find examples of Dissenters and Anglicans living as neighbours in amicable toleration, hostility was widespread and indignities, often petty, common at all levels of society. Feelings ran particularly high in parts of Massachusetts where the Congregationalists were firmly entrenched. At Hopkinston near Boston, for instance, the incumbent reported meeting 'with some opposition and spite there from the Dissenters, particularly in regard to the Building our Church, who are the Owners of the Saw mills in that Town and have disappointed us of our Boards and other materials for Building'.[24] Pamphlet warfare and battles with the Assembly included a specific legislative challenge to the SPG and its *raison d'être* which was finally resolved only by the intervention of the Archbishop of Canterbury and royal disallowance of the offending Act.[25] Even in Virginia, where the Church of England's position was supposedly secure, the political weight and organisation of Dissent and the strongly erastian tradition of the Anglican gentry, were such that by mid-century the Governor and Bishop of London had lost control over the appointment and induction of most parish clergy.

---

22  Rev. Wm. Sturgeon to Archbishop of Canterbury, 29 Nov. 1758, Perry, *Historical Collections*, Vol. 2. p. 268.
23  Rev. Philip Reading to SPG Secretary, 26 March 1747, Perry, *Historical Collections*, Vol. 2, pp. 244–5.
24  Rev. Roger Price to SPG Secretary, 23 April 1749, Perry, *Historical Collections*, Vol. 3, p. 431.
25  For the Act of 1762, promoting a new society 'for Propagating Christian Knowledge among the Indians of North America', Perry, *Historical Collections*, Vol. 3, pp. 471–97.

Disputes over interpretation of the Act of Toleration, the licensing of meeting houses and itinerant preachers, were incessant. However, Anglican complaints about Dissenters' sharp practice as often as not fell on stony ground. Persistent provocation from the Reverend Samuel Davies elicited from the Lords of Trade an exhortation to mutual respect and caution: 'as Toleration and a free Exercise of Religion is so valuable a branch of true liberty and so essential to the enriching and improving of a Trading Nation, it should ever be held sacred in His Majesty's Colonies'.[26] Disingenuous this might be, but it clearly indicated the extent to which the church was left on its own in normal times.

Wariness mingled with indifference to the SPG and its concerns was the predominant attitude among officials in London. In their eyes the overwhelmingly Protestant character of British North America was a sufficient guarantee that colonial ambitions would not result in the encouragement of French territorial expansion. To provoke colonial religious dissent or domestic political conflict by favouring Anglicanism, even an Anglicanism stripped of its temporal or civil powers, was therefore generally regarded as unnecessarily provocative and politically unwise. Capturing the often easy-going expediency of the day, one Governor observed of Pennsylvania's Germans, 'They fled from oppression and after having tasted the sweets of a British Constitution, it does not seem probable to me that they will ever look back to their old masters.'[27] Even Anglican bishops favourable to a new Anglican diocese were disinclined to force the issue in the face of successive ministerial objections on political grounds.[28]

This official imperial detachment from Anglican missionary ambition was modified only temporarily and in very particular circumstances, with reference not to white colonists' fractiousness but to Indians and colonial security. The SPG's sporadic efforts among the Mohawk were ignored until the threat of war made their alliance strategically valuable. Then Sir William Johnson (British Commissioner for Indian Affairs, 1744–74) and the SPG missionary John Ogilvie (1749–62) worked closely together on the New England frontier to secure their loyalty to the British side in the Seven Years War. Both men believed that conversion and support for the British went together, as indeed on this occasion they did.[29]

These were none the less alliances of convenience and often brief at that. Johnson and William Shirley, Governor of Massachusetts, equally supported other missionaries at the time and no provision was made for Ogilvie and his work once Montreal was captured in 1760. After the Seven Years War, there was a noticeable burst of enthusiasm for missions to Indians, as thanksgiving for British victory, as a way of earning additional favours and in anticipation of forthcoming stages in

---

26  Rev. Wm. Dawson to Bishop of London, 16 Aug. 1751, Perry, *Historical Collections*, Vol. 1, pp. 380–1.

27  Governor Thomas to Bishop of Exeter, 23 April 1748, Perry, *Historical Collections*, Vol. 2, p. 256

28  S.J. Taylor, 'Whigs, Bishops and America: The Politics of Church Reform in Mid-Eighteenth Century England', *HJ* 36, 2 (1993), 331–56.

29  Thompson, *Into All Lands*, pp. 82, 139.

God's plan.[30] Nevertheless, plentiful enthusiasm had its distinct limits, notwithstanding a measure of official approval. Although Johnson went on to become a
member of the SPG in 1766 and a valued adviser, his views in support of the
Society failed to count for much in official circles and his offer of 20,000 acres of his
own land for the support of an Anglican bishop was ignored.[31] High churchmen for
their own part were at times no more mindful of state interests. Welcoming the
British victories and the extension of British territory into the heart of the continent late in 1760, Thomas Barton's first thoughts were not for wealth or empire but
for the many heathen newly made into British subjects and his hopes were that they
would be at once well provided with missionaries.[32] However, as Pontiac's War of
1763–4 demonstrated, professed Protestantism and missionary contacts were ineffective in preventing treaties being broken by both sides. For some time after 1763
no more official imperial enthusiasm was shown for Indian missions than for episcopacy. Not until the 1780s, when the imperial government found itself strategically caught between Roman Catholic dissent in Nova Scotia, Quebec's staunchly
Catholic French Canadians and the newly-independent United States, did it turn
once more to the possibilities of additional support from an established church's
missionary expansion. Again with the white colonists and the need to counter-
balance Roman Catholicism uppermost in mind, it created bishoprics in Nova
Scotia (1787) and Quebec (1793).[33]

In other respects, many of the issues encountered by the eighteenth-century
Society were more nearly those common to other mission societies and individual
missionaries at all times. As in all colonies of white settlement, continued emigration, natural population increase, commercial disputes, land-hunger and speculation, greed, mutual fear and misunderstanding culminated in broken treaties,
unmitigated cruelty and warfare between indigenous groups and newcomers. The
SPG not only found itself unable to moderate these conflicts to any significant
degree, but from time to time, starting with the 1715 Carolina war, suffered losses
because of them. Its members also divided over questions of responsibility for the
violence and the appropriate legal or political responses to it. White abuses
commonly prompted the conclusion that the reformation of the colonists themselves was of the utmost urgency. As he left Albany after a year of fruitless waiting
on Mohawk goodwill, Thoroughgood Moor lamented, 'to begin with the Indians is
preposterous; for it is from the behaviour of the Christians here, that they have had
and still have, their notions of Christianity, which God knows, hath been generally

---

30  P.J. Marshall, 'Presidential Address: Britain and the World in the Eighteenth Century: Part 2,
    Britons and Americans', *Transactions of the Royal Historical Society* 6th Series, 9 (1999), 7–8.
31  Klingberg, *Anglican Humanitarianism*, chap. 3 'Sir William Johnson and the S.P.G.'.
32  Rev. Thomas Barton to SPG Secretary, 6 Dec. 1760, Perry, *Historical Collections*, Vol. 2,
    pp. 294–5.
33  Peter M. Doll, *Revolution, Reaction, and National Identity. Imperial Anglicanism in British North
    America, 1745–1795* (Madison and London, 2000), pp. 195–7; Judith Fingard, *The Anglican Design
    in Loyalist Nova Scotia, 1783–1816* (London, 1972), chap. 2.

such that it hath made the Indians to hate our religion'.[34] Equally these abuses intensified the commitment which many individual SPG clergy and missionaries felt to the non-white populations.[35]

The themes of white colonists' own need for evangelisation, of their resistance to the evangelisation of Indians and slaves and of their turning non-Europeans against Christianity thus became perennial causes of complaint. Sixty years on in Georgia, the Reverend Samuel Frink re-echoed Moor's complaints: efforts to convert Indians were 'all to no purpose while many of the white people' were 'as destitute of a sense of religion as the Indians themselves'. From New York Elias Neau reported that most of its white inhabitants opposed evangelisation of slaves with the argument that 'Christian knowledge ... [would] make their Slaves more cunning and apter to wickedness'.[36] At the opening of the Seven Years War, Thomas Barton lamented that unlike the French the English had merely sent to the Indians 'abandon'd profligate men ... who defrauded and cheated them and prac- tised every vice among them that can be named, which set the English and the Protestant Religion in such a disadvantageous light, that we have reason to fear they detest the name of both'.[37]

Comments such as Moor's and Frink's also point to the territorial limits of SPG missionary work. The Indians encountered by ministers and missionaries were for the most part 'settlement' Indians, those who were close neighbours of the colonists rather than those who were distant and remote. Whether out of fear, pref- erence for a degree of comfort or conviction that time could be more productively spent elsewhere, missionaries 'rarely visited Indian Country to spread the word'.[38] Encounters with Indians at any distance beyond the colonial frontiers were still less likely, for the SPG Charter confined the Society's activities to the colonies them- selves. Converts were thus only those who had experienced a measure of English civil authority, those who had not done so being generally cause for despair, as the SPG missionary William Andrews made plain in 1719. 'They are a sordid, merce- nary, beggerly people having but little sense of Religion, honesty or goodness among them, living generally filthy, brutish lives ... through their own sottishness, sloth and laziness ... They are [moreover] of an inhumane savage Nature [who] Kill and Eat one another. ... Heathens they are and Heathens they will still be'.[39]

Where it survived, commitment to the local people in turn opened the missions up to debate on their own methods, especially in connection with the organisation

---

34  Pascoe, *Two Hundred Years*, Vol. 1, p. 68.

35  For instance Rev. W. Andrews with the Mohawk, *ibid.*, Vol. 1, pp. 70–1; Klingberg, *Anglican Humanitarianism*, passim.

36  Pascoe, *Two Hundred Years*, Vol. 1, pp. 28, 64.

37  Rev. Thomas Barton to SPG Secretary, 8 Nov. 1756, Perry, *Historical Collections*, Vol. 2, pp. 279–80.

38  James H. Merrell, '"The Customes of Our Countrey": Indians and Colonists in Early America', in Bernard Bailyn and Philip D. Morgan (eds), *Strangers within the Realm: Cultural Margins of the First British Empire* (Chapel Hill, 1991), p. 147; Axtell, *Invasion Within*, p. 242.

39  Axtell, *Invasion Within*, p. 263.

of schools. To what extent were the vernacular languages either an appropriate or the best medium for instruction? What part should local people play as catechists or missionaries to their own communities? Should education and conversion be pursued while preserving traditional Indian ways of life, as William Johnson argued? Or should Charles Inglis's vision of their transformation as a Christian agricultural peasantry be the missionaries' goal? To what degree was successful evangelism compatible with the status of slavery, or were SPG members in pursuit of converts bound to favour policies of amelioration or even emancipation in pursuit of this goal, irrespective of the damage this would cause to their relations with plantation and slave owners? For the SPG as for all other evangelists Christianity was increasingly likely to raise questions as to the social, political and economic structure of the colonial societies within which they worked.

Of these issues and their consequences for different missionary bodies and for the governments with whom they had to deal we shall see more below. For the moment we must stay with the implications of the established Anglicanism for which the SPG was the main vehicle. A glance at the territories where the Society operated in the eighteenth century reveals at once the greatest of the limitations on its missionary work: it could work only in the wake of the imposition of an established colonial government. This was a missionary enterprise dependent on state initiative quite as much as on its anticipation of state support. It was one that embodied a narrowly territorial vision of the church and its authority, as distinct from the broader vision of the church as community, conscious of its individual members irrespective of their origins. The organisation provided by the SPG in the eighteenth century was one in which missionary activity was intended increasingly to draw church and state together. It represented the missionary activity of an ancien regime, in which such activity was felt to require the approval and support of political authorities. Not only was missionary enterprise unthinkable in circumstances where the state might fail to follow; it could not be contemplated where state authority did not already exist. This was a model which was to be ever more vigorously questioned from the 1790s on.

From its beginnings, however, there were features of the SPG which modified any narrowly national identification of church, state and missionary enterprise. The view that 'a transatlantic focus is a sine qua non' for the study of American religion is becoming generally accepted and the same insistence on its multiple origins is a feature of recent work on the overseas Protestant missionary movement.[40] Despite its evidently Anglican and episcopal character, the SPG was also to some degree a cosmopolitan body sharing these expanding contacts and horizons. Perhaps one-third of its missionaries were English, but among the rest there were significant numbers of 'strangers within the realm', from Wales, Ireland and Scotland as well as others from continental Protestant communities in Germany, Holland, France, Piedmont and Switzerland. From its earliest years the SPG was in

---

40 Butler, *Awash in a Sea of Faith*, p. 5; Mason, *The Moravian Church and the Missionary Awakening*.

correspondence with Protestants in mainland Europe. In North America – in the Carolinas and New York, for example – the Society assisted French Protestant communities wishing to join the Church of England and supported German immigrants too poor to provide their own ministers' salaries. Even if 'most Germans', for instance, appear to have 'remained within the Lutheran and Reformed denominations', Anglican co-operation with them was readily forthcoming. Not only ministers but also books in translation were supplied to emigrant congregations such as the German-speaking Palatines and the Swiss in South Carolina.[41] Elsewhere English missionaries conducted services in Italian and French. Continental Protestants – such as the Frenchman Elias Neau – were employed in various stations throughout the century.[42] Outside the Atlantic world, the SPCK supported the Danish Halle mission in India from 1709 and adopted their own Lutheran missionaries there from 1725.[43]

It is unclear how far this contributed to reconcile to British rule many of the eighteenth-century European Protestant emigrants, who were to be found everywhere from Virginia to Newfoundland. Moreover, it is difficult to define precisely the contribution made to the Society's own work by these blended traditions. Frequently the SPG's assistance was regarded as a useful bridging device, integrating the Protestant cultures of the Atlantic world. Governor John Lawrence of Nova Scotia felt that by providing pastors and schoolmasters, 'in a little time, the German language may fall into disuse and with it, their manners and Customs, so apt to create differences and to prevent a thorough union and harmony with the rest of His Majesty's subjects'.[44] In due course, on the death in 1799 of one such missionary to the 'German congregation in Halifax', Bishop Inglis reported that 'a German preacher is no longer needed, as they all speak English'.[45] A little deference not only to language but to continental customs was also reckoned to go a long way. The Germans of Lancaster (Pennsylvania) were regarded as sympathetic to the Anglican message, 'But the want of an organ of which these people are extremely fond, & in which they place almost half their devotion, has hitherto kept them back. Many Lutherans who gladly embrace every opportunity to teach their children the Religion, Manners and Customs of England, would come to our Church if we had but an Instrument to celebrate the praises of God in the manner that they have been used to.'[46] One must be careful not to exaggerate the significance of such wide-ranging co-operation and

---

41  Patricia U. Bonomi, *Under the Cope of Heaven: Religion, Society and Politics in Colonial America* (Oxford and New York, 1986), pp. 81–2; O'Connor, *Three Centuries of Mission*, p. 28.

42  Elias Neau (1703–32); Daniel Bondet (1709–22); John Frederick Hager (1710–17); Francis Le Jau (1700–1, 1706–17); John Jacob Oel (1722–77). Charles Boschi (1745–49), Bartholomew Zouberbuhler (c.1745–66); Michael Houdin (1760–66); Paul Bryzelius (1767–73): Pascoe, *Two Hundred Years*, Vol. 1, 63–5, Vol. 2, 849, 851, 855, 856, 861; and William W. Manross, *S.P.G. Papers in the Lambeth Palace Library: Calendar and Indexes* (Oxford, 1974), pp. 118–22.

43  O'Connor, *Three Centuries of Mission*, p. 28.

44  Doll, *Revolution, Religion and National Identity*, p. 63.

45  Manross, *S.P.G. Papers*, Vol. 10, 46–7.

46  Rev. Thomas Barton to SPG Secretary, 6 Dec. 1760, Perry, *Historical Collections*, Vol. 2, p. 294.

evident sympathy, but they remain pointers to what was to become the increasingly international character of the British missionary movement.

## II

In comparison with the SPG's work in colonial North America, the dissenting bodies – Baptists, Congregationalists, Presbyterians – were if anything still less inclined to push their missionary work beyond the boundaries of the white communities. Missionary initiatives were no more forthcoming from the metropole than they were from the colonial congregations. At root this sprang from a rationalistic form of hyper-Calvinism with its belief in the predestination of the elect which for long inhibited missionary enterprise of any kind, especially overseas. The absence of missionary dynamism also reflected the dissenting focus on the congregation and the tight-knit community of the religiously like-minded requiring a minister's constant attention. It was further encouraged by the absence before the 1790s of nonconformist missionary societies committed theologically and institutionally to evangelism as a prime concern. In a world where so many colonists not only feared and despised Indians but anticipated their eventual extinction, sustained missionary work on that broader front was likely only if provided with financial support largely independent of congregational giving or approval. Regardless of the measure of Anglican establishment achieved in the different colonies and despite the supply of funds from Britain itself, even the SPG was unable to surmount this difficulty.

Among dissenting ministers the early eighteenth century saw the intensification of attempts to establish influence and control over their white members; the development of regular clerical and congregational meetings; and a good deal of church building. Baptists (as one consequence of their own serious internal divisions), Quakers, Congregationalists (or Independents) and Presbyterians in particular focused on the potential for growth in the white settlements. Then and later, these continued to be the primary concerns of all the denominations. They were aimed at protecting existing positions, keeping up with the expansion of immigration and the frontiers of trade or settlement and also at drawing ahead in the heightened competition for members with other rivals, which was a feature of the years from about 1740 up to the Revolution.

It should not surprise us that even the impact of the linked revival movements, the Evangelical Revival in Britain itself and the 'Great Awakening' which commenced early in the 1740s in the colonies, did little to alter this emphasis. The experience of religious revival and the evangelical promotion of missions are by no means necessarily connected. Above all in the eighteenth century it is worth noting the gulf to be bridged between the revival of what were regarded as moribund ecclesiastical establishments or existing Protestant communities in need of renewal and the incorporation of non-Christian, pagan peoples into the Christian world. Although Europe's erstwhile emigrants settled abroad might readily appear to have lapsed in their faith (even if for no fault of their own), they were just as easily seen as subjects ready for reclamation. Indians and black Africans more commonly prompted mixed feelings as to whether they could ever be Christianised to start with. John Wesley might memorably assert that 'the world is my parish' and his lieutenant Thomas Coke reject the distinction between 'home' and 'foreign' missions. But neither could deny that shortage of resources and estimates of likely results compelled organisers to be selective of sites for their missions, home or overseas. The haphazard dispersal of overseas missionary activity was an inescapable consequence of these uncertainties, as can be seen in the case of both Moravian and Methodist missionary enterprise.

The Moravian Brethren took much of their inspiration from the pietist revival movement within the Lutheran church, associated with Halle and the leadership of P.J. Spener and A.H. Francke. Reconstituted by Count Nicholas von Zinzendorf at Herrnhut in 1722, the community quickly turned to missionary work. In search of tolerant governments, they followed the example of Bartholomew Ziegenbalg and Heinrich Plutschau, who had settled in the Danish trading centre of Tranquebar, south India. They established themselves first in the Danish colonies of St Thomas, St John and St Croix in the Caribbean (1732–41) and Greenland (1733) and briefly in the Dutch Cape Colony (1737–44). They subsequently put down roots in the British colonies of Jamaica (1754), Antigua and Tortola (1756), Tranquebar (1760), Barbados (1765), Labrador (1771), in Danish Serampore (1776) and in Tobago (1789). This expansion was assisted by the connections the Brethren built up in Britain. There their popularity during the 1730s and 1740s rested on their being an episcopal church and culminated in the parliamentary Act of 1749 encouraging their settlement in British North America.

Although they experienced serious disorganisation, financial difficulties and loss of support in the 1750s, after Zinzendorf's death in 1760, his successor, August Spangenberg, took the church in hand and restored both its fortunes and its reputation for orthodoxy. At the Synod of 1764 a new constitution was approved and its Protestant episcopal character re-emphasised; David Crantz's history of its Greenland mission, published in 1766, was circulated widely and attracted considerable attention; the missionary society was revived in 1768, with a strong input from London and drawing in friends not actually members of the church.[47] By 1771 there were twenty-two congregations in Britain and a campaign to restore its credibility and respectability involved both the politicking needed to secure approval for the Labrador mission and increased attention to publicising its work. From 1789 the society regularly published its Periodical Accounts.[48]

The reputation of the Moravians as desirable settlers in British North America was dependent on the character of their mission stations. They were small nuclear settlements, designed to be politically unobtrusive and economically self-sufficient.

47 A.G. Spangenberg, *A Candid Declaration of the Church known by the name of Unitas Fratrum, relative to their labour among the heathen* (London, 1768).

48 For the importance of the Moravians, the starting point must now be Mason, *The Moravian Church*.

The Moravians set out in each one to develop artisanal skills, agriculture and trade, while stressing their essential quietism. As Spangenberg defined their approach, 'We are very attentive that the bond between the government and the heathen may not in the least suffer by means of evangelical tenets; for should this appear unavoidable in any place ... we should in that case rather choose to retire from thence.' 'We never attempt, by means of our missions, to obtain the least influence in civil or commercial affairs but are contented with what we can earn by our industry in useful employments for our support, to the satisfaction of the government.'[49] Mindful of their European background, they aimed to impress by example and to avoid giving offence by any aggressive evangelisation. However, this was not necessarily a recipe for success. The difficulties of the Greenland mission made a substantial contribution to their near ruin in the 1750s; the barrenness of Labrador later posed a similar problem; and the Dutch Reformed Church persuaded the Dutch East India Company to close the mission at Baviaans Kloof (Genadendal) in 1743. It was not reopened until 1792.

Notwithstanding the essentially missionary nature of Methodism itself, within the ranks of the Wesleyan Methodists, overseas missions were much slower to get off the ground.[50] This may be attributed in part to John Wesley's own instructive experience as an SPG missionary and parish minister at Savannah, Georgia, from 1736–38. It impressed him with the magnitude of the effort needed to establish vital religion even among the white colonists and, despite his admiration for the Moravians' work, left him with no illusions as to the ease of reaching either slaves or Indians. Notwithstanding the revivalist impact of George Whitefield's itinerant preaching on his numerous visits to British North America between 1738 and 1770, this task of reaching the Europeans became hardly less demanding. Francis Asbury, who volunteered at the English Methodist Conference of 1771 and was sent by Wesley as a missionary to the American colonies, emerged by 1784 as leader of America's Methodists. His journals indicate clearly the priority given not only to itinerancy and mission but almost inevitably to the white colonists.[51] Asbury had to contend with the scattered nature of white settlement; the gruelling demands of itinerancy, even more testing for those who could not match his own restless journeying; and the constant attention to securing the cohesion of the Methodist connection and individual congregations, for instance by cultivating friendly Moravians or Quakers. These restricted his encounters with other sections of the

---

49  Spangenberg, *Candid Declaration*, paras. 4–5.
50  The standard history is G.G. Findlay and W.W. Holdsworth, *The History of the Wesleyan Methodist Missionary Society*, 5 vols (London, 1921). More recently, John A. Vickers, 'The Genesis of Methodist Missions', *NAMP Position Paper 10* (Cambridge, 1996) and David Bundy, 'The Development of Models of Missions in Methodism during the early American Republic with attention to the antecedents of the Holiness Movement', *NAMP Position Paper 48* (Cambridge, 1997).
51  Elmer T. Clark (ed.), *The Journal and Letters of Francis Asbury*, 3 vols (London and Nashville, 1958).

population. Native Americans hardly feature at all either in his or in other Methodist writings.[52]

Even African – 'Negro' – families were reached chiefly as a consequence of ministering to those whites who permitted their slaves to attend meetings. Sometimes the Africans were separately provided for, for example at Georgetown, when 'in the evening the Negroes were collected and I spoke to them in exhortation'.[53] From time to time Asbury recorded his pleasure at African participation with the rest of those present at meetings; but this was never the prelude – as was frequently so with whites – to closer acquaintance or his recording of individual names. Rather it confirmed him both in his universalist theology, by revealing God as 'no respecter of persons' and in his hectic itinerancy, which he felt provided him with effective protection against 'partiality'.[54] Many people felt that by their rules against slavery Methodists had already demonstrated excessive partiality towards Africans and the resentment these bred only contributed to increase hostility and resentment on the part of the colonists against Wesleyans themselves.[55] Asbury's political sense was sufficiently acute to appreciate that greater efforts to evangelise enslaved Africans were only likely to endanger the Methodist enterprise as a whole.

Methodist missionary activities therefore relied heavily on the haphazard initiatives of individual members. The earliest of these were Nathaniel Gilbert (1760), John Baxter (1778) and, although he died before arrival, Jeremiah Lambert, in the British island of Antigua. Early and isolated personal ventures began to acquire a little more substance in the late 1770s when the Reverend Dr Thomas Coke started to collect funds for overseas missions from several English circuits and called in 1778 for volunteers to go to West Africa.[56] Rank and file support, however, did not generate official sanction. Wesley himself discouraged Coke from pursuing this course and the Annual Conference in 1778 rejected a West African request for missionaries. In the early 1780s, Wesley's concern to take a renewed grip on Methodism and to organise its recovery after the serious disruption inflicted by the American War of Independence also deflected Coke's missionary ambitions. Coke and Asbury were appointed Superintendents of the American Methodists, a position involving Coke in prolonged journeys across the Atlantic in 1784–5, 1786–7, 1789 and 1791. Inevitably he was diverted from sustained attention to missionary schemes. His 'Plan of the Society for the Establishment of Missions among the Heathens' (1783), his contacts with Benjamin La Trobe and the Moravians whose West Indian work he admired and thoughts exchanged in 1784 with Charles Grant, the East India Company director, about a mission to the East Indies, all for the time being fell by the wayside.[57]

---

52  Findlay and Holdsworth, *History of the WMMS*, Vol. 1, part 2, chap. 9 'The Gospel among the Red Men'.

53  8 Dec. 1772, Clark, *Asbury, Journal and Letters*, Vol. 1, p. 57.

54  17, 21 Nov. 1771, and 7 July 1776, *ibid.*, Vol. 1, pp. 9–10, 222.

55  30 April and 15 Nov. 1785, *ibid.*, Vol. 1, pp. 488, 498.

56  For details of Coke's career, John A. Vickers, *Thomas Coke Apostle of Methodism* (London, 1969).

57  Vickers, *Thomas Coke*, chaps 8–9.

In 1786 John Wesley and the Conference were at last prepared to offer a little support to Coke's latest appeal for West Indian missions, although they still focused principally on the American mainland and on Nova Scotia where the Anglican church seemed intent on reviving its ecclesiastical control.[58] Nevertheless, this was enough for Coke to link his American tours of duty with visits to the Caribbean to oversee missionary activity and assess the prospects there for Methodist expansion. He also began to reconsider the outlook in West Africa, in the form of a mission to Sierra Leone. For the moment, however, Methodist missions remained fundamentally dependent on Coke alone, for funds, encouragement, oversight and supervision. It was a fragile one-man band, a construction constantly at risk from Coke's own impulsiveness, his chaotic personal control, swelling debts and a complete lack of any financial or administrative system.

## III

To understand the implications for the future relations of missions and empire of those eighteenth-century developments considered so far requires, finally, an examination of major facets of the theological and intellectual fashions of the time. Of critical importance were the waning popularity of notions of election and predestination. They were displaced in part by ideas developed from the writings of the late sixteenth-century Dutch theologian Jacobus Arminius (1560–1609) and by an evangelical, activist Calvinism associated with the outstanding American theologian, Jonathan Edwards (1703–58) and his British followers. Eighteenth-century Christians increasingly rejected the view that the future state of all believers was already settled irrespective of how they led their lives. They turned instead to the doctrine of justification by faith, the belief that an unqualified acceptance of the Christian faith was sufficient to put the believer right with God. Many Christians as a result developed a new confidence from the understanding that atonement for the wickedness of mankind achieved by Christ's death was available to all individuals without exception through divine grace, rather than to an elect but unknown few. The conscious acceptance of these ideas and the assurance of ultimate delivery from death and everlasting hell were not only central components in the evangelical understanding of individual conversion. They were experienced with an enormous sense of relief, joyful excitement and an impulsive wish to share one's faith, all of which contributed hugely to the emotional fervour of the century's religious revivals.[59] Where certain Calvinist tenets could be held to make missionary activity superfluous if not essentially pointless, these 'arminian' and evangelical notions only encouraged missionary enterprise. They gave fresh

---

58  Thomas Coke, *Address to the Pious and Benevolent, proposing an annual subscription for the support of the missionaries in the Highlands and islands of Scotland, the Isles of Jersey, Guernsey and Newfoundland, the West Indies, and the Provinces of Nova Scotia and Quebec* (London, 1786).
59  M.R. Watts, *The Dissenters*, 2 vols (Oxford, 1978, 1995), Vol. 1, esp. pp. 428–34.

point to the Gospel's missionary command, 'Go ye therefore and teach all nations'.[60]

This Protestant rediscovery of theological justification for Christian missions and the benefits or rewards of faith readily complemented both the optimism and the emphasis on the obligation to benevolence found in much contemporary secular thought. It also had practical consequences in the form of encouraging Christians to think about the means through which they might advance evangelism. Here novelty lay in the emerging realisation that believers themselves were intended to be the chief means of Christianity's expansion. The context and direct experience of domestic revivals, both in Britain and in the American colonies, brought out not only the possibility but also the ease with which Christians themselves could become evangelists. In the increasingly integrated world of the North Atlantic it could seem no great imaginative or even practical step to move from participation in evangelisation at home to involvement in overseas missions. Struck by the proliferation of knowledge, communication, shipping and trade – a process symbolised for many by Captain James Cook's Pacific voyages – evangelicals saw the responsibility for taking advantage of such opportunities as devolving directly upon their ministers and increasingly on themselves. 'Glory to God!', wrote Francis Asbury, 'I can leave all the little affairs of this confused world to those men to whose province they pertain; and can comfortably go on in my proper business of instrumentally saving my own soul and those that hear me.'[61]

In addition to the fruitful interplay of personal conversion and communal revival, there existed further doctrinal elements of great general importance. These were a mounting general preoccupation with the providential working out of God's plan and promises for the world and a focused belief in the coming of the millennium and the apocalypse. 'All enthusiastic movements, in their effort to detach people from worldliness, are apt to talk the language of chiliasm.'[62] At every social level, the period of the Evangelical Revival and the Great Awakening offers much evidence to support Knox's dictum. In particular the 1740s and 1750s produced an explosion of speculation about Christ's Second Coming and the Last Days. What were the indications of the approaching millennium and how if at all might it be advanced? The religious excitement and revivals on both sides of the Atlantic were themselves seen as heralds of the coming great event. So too the French and Indian wars, the growth of American prosperity, the Lisbon earthquake and a host of other contemporary events were interpreted as 'signs of the times'. Together they were regarded as evidence of an impending biblically predicted age of peace, plenty and international harmony, associated with the fall

---

60  Matthew, 28. vv.18–20; Mark, 16. v.15.
61  26 March 1776, Clark, *Asbury, Journal and Letters*, Vol. 1, p. 182.
62  R.A. Knox, *Enthusiasm: A Chapter in the History of Religion with Special Reference to the XVII and XVIII Centuries* (Oxford, 1950; repr. 1959), pp. 545–6.

of the Antichrist, variously identified with Islam, infidelity (France) and
the Papacy. Differences of opinion revolved around the question whether the onset
of the millennium would be gradual or cataclysmic and there was disagreement
as to whether it would be preceded or followed by the Second Coming.[63]
Differences of interpretation notwithstanding, however, Christians of all denominations held that its occurrence was both certain and likely to take place soon.
Thomas Coke, admitting himself 'fully convinced that these are no common days',
dismissed what he regarded as minor differences: 'of this we may rest ourselves
assured, that the great period of the consummation is at hand, – that it is even at
the door'.[64]

Theological books, printed sermons and other pamphlets passed both ways
across the Atlantic, fostering vigorous debate, denominational variety and a flourishing international Protestant culture. A response to popular demand stimulated by
the major revivals, this traffic was also enthusiastically fostered by publishers, adver-
tisers and merchants. Religious literature formed a most important ingredient of the
trans-Atlantic consumer society of the eighteenth century.[65] In what were comparatively literate societies, these issues were thus widely considered and were not treated
merely as remote or abstract theological inquiry. Knowledge of the Bible inevitably
prompted speculations about prophecies of the future, notably those contained in the
books of Daniel and Revelation. If at a popular level they seem now to represent no
more than enthusiastic fantasies, they could be none the less real to those who entertained them. Educated and scholarly writers took them very seriously as matters for
elucidation and textual commentary. Jonathan Edwards paid special attention to the
unfulfilled prophecies and the coming of the apocalypse, attempting constantly to
match current events with prophetic chronology and the occurrence of revivals with
the divine plan for the world.[66] In the 1770s Asbury recorded how he spent time not
only in reading and rereading Revelation but in studying prophetic literature and

---

63  Ruth H. Bloch, *Visionary Republic: Millennial Themes in American Thought, 1756–1800*
    (Cambridge, 1985), esp. chap. 2.
64  Thomas Coke, *The Recent Occurrences of Europe Considered in relation to such prophecies as are either
    fulfilling or unfulfilled. First published in 1807, in an appendix to his Commentary on the Bible* (London,
    1809), pp. v, ix, 314.
65  Susan O'Brien, 'A Transatlantic Community of Saints: The Great Awakening and the First
    Evangelical Network, 1735–1755', *American Historical Review* 91, 4 (1986), 811–32; 'Eighteenth-
    Century Pubishing Networks in the First Years of Transatlantic Evangelicalism', in Mark A. Noll,
    David W. Bebbington and George A. Rawlyk (eds), *Evangelicalism: Comparative Studies of Popular
    Protestantism in North America, the British Isles, and Beyond, 1700–1990* (New York and Oxford,
    1994), pp. 38–57.
66  Iain H. Murray, *Jonathan Edwards: A New Biography* (Edinburgh, 1987, repr. 1996), pp. 49–50.
    See *The Works of Jonathan Edwards Vol. 5: Apocalyptic Writings*, ed. Stephen J. Stein (New Haven
    and London, 1977), which includes his *Notes on the Apocalypse*; his highly influential *An Humble
    Attempt to promote Explicit Agreement and Visible Union of God's People in extraordinary Prayer for
    the Revival of Religion and the Advancement of Christ's Kingdom on Earth* (1747); and the sermons
    appearing posthumously as *History of the Work of Redemption* (1774).

noting where it could be tied to the actual course of historical events.[67] In Britain too, separate and no less popular strands of eschatological reasoning have been traced in both Scotland and England.[68] In Dundee, for example, John Willison wrote *The Balm of Gilead, for Healing a Diseased Land … And a Scripture Prophecy of the Increase of Christ's Kingdom and the Destruction of Antichrist*; published in 1742, it went into eight editions by 1786 and was very widely read. South of the border, a succession of Anglican bishops – Robert Lowth, Richard Hurd, William Warburton – developed their eschatological views not least in their published anniversary sermons delivered to the SPG and Bishop Thomas Newton's volumes on prophecy were especially well thumbed.

These preoccupations are relevant here for their association with discussion at the time of the role Christian missions might have in preparing the way for the millennium by increasing the extent of Christ's kingdom. There were those who, while perhaps acknowledging the desirability, for instance, of American Indian conversion, nevertheless attached much greater importance to 'the internal renewal' of white colonial society and so stressed the significance of domestic missions for this process. For the more liberal of Congregationalists and those few Anglicans in British North America who took a gradualist view of the unfolding prophetic chronology, the progress of Indian conversions was a certain indicator of the millennium's approach and a precondition of its onset.[69]

These views were associated in turn with a more persistent division of opinion over the two basic approaches to missionary work. The first tendency maintained that missions were best promoted by preaching, translation of the Bible and reliance on the working of the Holy Spirit to bring about individual conversions. The other, held most strongly by Scottish mission theorists, inclined to the view that conversion was to be looked for as the outcome of a gradual, developmental or 'civilising' process, fostered by missions and involving the cumulative workings of Divine Providence together with the operation of human reason and will.

Jonathan Edwards, himself a missionary to Native Americans for much of the 1750s after being ejected from his own pulpit, was an influential spokesman for the first of these positions. In 1749 he published his *Account of the Life of the Late Reverend Mr David Brainerd*, a close friend and missionary who died of tuberculosis in Edwards's home at the age of twenty-nine after four years' work, most notably with the Delaware Indians. No ordinary missionary biography, it was the first full such life to be published and became an inspirational classic of missionary endeavour. Its success owed much to the evidence it claimed to provide as to the promise of Indian conversion, but more still to its compelling portrayal of Brainerd's own power as a

67  Clark, *Asbury, Journal and Letters*, Vol. 1, pp. 92, 113, 115, 127, 268–70, 292, 314; Vol. 3, p. 365.
68  J.A. De Jong, *As the Waters Cover the Sea. Millennial Expectations in the Rise of Anglo-American Missions 1640–1810* (Kampen, 1970), chaps. 4–5.
69  Bloch, *Visionary Republic*, pp. 48–9.

preacher and his unremitting self-sacrifice, typifying the requirements of Christians in the Last Days.[70] Edwards's writings became extremely influential towards the end of the century in stimulating the interest of British Baptists, Congregationalists, Church of Scotland and Church of England figures in the theologically timely as well as practically important role which missions could play.[71]

Missionary activity as an essential component of eschatological concern was presented in the second of these ways by the work of the Scottish SPCK (1709) both in the Scottish Highlands and, after 1730, in North America. The Indians were regarded by the missionaries in much the same light as the uncivilised Highlanders. The SSPCK's dominant approach was based on the establishment of schools in which religious teaching was closely linked to rigorous supervision of a highly prescriptive syllabus. Conversion was anticipated as part of a broader cultural transformation and involved the Society's members in debates about language and instruction that clearly herald many of the debates later heard in the nineteenth century. Nevertheless, for all the anticipations of modernity which have been read into the Society's work, it has been well demonstrated that 'the chief "driving power" behind Scottish missionary activity at this time' was the prominent eschatological concern of the Scottish evangelicals.[72]

## IV

By the end of the 1780s, it was widely felt that the consequences for both missions and empire of nearly a century of British Protestant missionary activity had been disappointingly slight. Pessimism as to the outcome of evangelistic work with the heathen was everywhere the most common result of practical experience. This was only echoed two hundred years on by the historian of the New England Company. 'Eliot's plan of bringing the wandering Indian tribes into settled habitations had remained for more than one hundred and twenty years the most likely way of converting them. But it also remained supremely difficult to change a deeply rooted pattern of living ... The Indian population of New England was constantly dwindling, disease and rum continuing to take their toll. But if converts were few, so were those who attempted to make them: a few missionaries practising what so many propagandists had preached.'[73]

Nevertheless, from the confused patchwork of ecclesiastical structures and personnel and the varied stock of theologies and missionary strategies, there were

70  Murray, *Jonathan Edwards*, pp. 300–10. The *Life* went into many editions. For the latest scholarly edition, *The Works of Jonathan Edwards Vol. 7*, ed. Norman Petit (New Haven and London, 1985).

71  Ronald E. Davies, 'Jonathan Edwards and His Influence on the Development of the Missionary Movement from Britain', *NAMP Position Paper 6* (Cambridge, 1996).

72  Donald E. Meek, 'Scottish Highlanders, North American Indians and the SSPCK: Some Cultural Perspectives', *Records of the Scottish Church History Society* 23, 3 (1989), 378–96; De Jong, *As the Waters Cover the Sea*, pp. 141–51, quotation p. 149.

73  Kellaway, *The New England Company*, p. 276.

lessons to be learnt. Most obviously, in their competition with other agents of empire – settlers, merchants, local assemblies, colonial agents, imperial politicians – to shape the processes of empire-building and manage colonial society, missionary interests had carried little weight, irrespective of denomination. The SPG struggled to realise its pretentions to be the missionary wing of the established church in a local colonial context involving both substantial popular resistance and forms of episcopal direction which were distant and frequently ineffectual. Its experience demonstrated that attempts to tie missionary enterprise to the interests of the imperial government were likely to fail or be at best only very temporarily successful. The imperial government's commitment was too fickle and unreliable, too vulnerable to shifting political assessments of domestic or colonial demands and too reluctant to increase ecclesiastical power and resources, even for a national church such as the Church of England to rely on its links to the secular power to sustain its missionary activities. Dissenters had long known this and even found their influence over government policies declining from the mid-century on.[74] Anglicans increasingly feared as much, but were reluctant to accept it. The lesson was finally learnt only in the 1830s and 1840s, but by 1790 the writing was on the wall. Those who could read therefore began to look for alternative models of Anglican missionary enterprise.

Dissenters and nonconformists often felt themselves less constrained than the SPG clergy, having less expectation of winning advantages by wooing local colonial or imperial authorities, either in satisfaction of their own needs or in relief of external pressures placed on them. However, their missionary efforts suffered at least equally with the SPG's from a lack of effective 'denominational' or overall control. Methodists, anxious to steer clear of independency while avoiding the danger of an ossified establishment, hoped to balance religious freedom and ecclesiastical order in a system of itinerant preachers, circuit organisation and annual conferences. However, where the source of missionary initiative and authoritative regulation of missionary activity should lie in such a system remained obscure. As Coke's career shows, individual initiative was easily scuppered by denominational prejudice or inertia, but was no less capable of becoming a thorn in the denominational flesh. Moravians did not scruple over the firm, even dictatorial, central control of their missionaries, but were vulnerable to their uncompromising insistence on the self-sufficiency required of each mission station.

In all cases, the extent and character of missionary endeavour during the eighteenth century was overwhelmingly influenced by the vagaries of individual inclination subject only to the limited power of such central organisation and authority as existed. At the same time all evangelical communities found it difficult in any systematic fashion to recruit missionary volunteers and prepare them for the field (even if that preparation was thought necessary, which commonly it was not).

---

74 Alison Olson, 'The Eighteenth Century Empire: The London Dissenters' Lobbies and the American Colonies', *Journal of American Studies* 26, 1 (1992), 41–58.

These characteristics were not only connected with each other but were reinforced by the absence of a coherent theology or practical strategy for promoting Christian missions. For much of the century this meant that an important spur to the development of denominational organisation specifically devoted to the promotion and administration of overseas missionary activity, as well as a powerful inspiration to missionary volunteers, was missing. By the 1780s, however, it was clear that millennial concerns provided committed Christians with a powerful incentive to personal involvement with missions and that the framework offered by millennial speculation and conviction of the working-out of a divine plan had become broadly supportive of missionary endeavour. This connection was to become still closer in the following decades as missionary enthusiasts turned to the solution of the practical problems they faced.

## ~ 2 ~

# The reorganisation of
# missionary enterprise, 1790–1812

The story of Britain's expanding interests in many different parts of the world during the second half of the eighteenth century scarcely needs retelling. In the fifty years since the appearance of Vincent Harlow's first volume on the reshaping of Britain's empire after the Seven Years War, historians' understanding of the complexity of that process has been constantly developed and redefined. So too at the time, contemporaries at all levels of society came to see clearly that they inhabited a world far more varied and extensive than that of the North Atlantic. As a consequence of the Anglo-French conflicts that lay at the heart of the intermittent global war, British imperial rule was greatly extended – in Bengal and South India, Canada and the Caribbean. International rivalries, military ambition and commercial interest both national and individual attracted British attention to territories such as China and South America well outside Britain's colonial empire. They were linked to the extension of maritime and land-based exploration, especially in the Pacific and West Africa. Expanding geographical awareness was combined with a burgeoning scientific and travel literature, the growth of societies and scientific institutions, administrative requirements, ethnographic observation and reform movements such as that against slavery. Together they provided new knowledge and heightened curiosity, bringing home to Britons the now enormous range of their encounter with non-European peoples and Britain's own global reach.[1]

One major consequence of these developments was a many-sided reassessment of Britain's overseas responsibilities, not least to indigenous populations. Acknowledgement that such responsibilities existed and the idea that Britain's own overseas interests might in some degree depend on their recognition, were always contentious issues. Nevertheless, in the 1780s, these principles became widely and explicitly accepted as a result of the public debate about the British presence in India and the gathering momentum of the anti-slavery movement, with its prime

---

1 Vincent T. Harlow, *The Founding of the Second British Empire, 1763–1793*, 2 vols (London, 1952, 1964); P.J. Marshall and Glyndwr Williams, *The Great Map of Mankind: British Perceptions of the World in the Age of Enlightenment* (London, 1982); C.A. Bayly, *Imperial Meridian: The British Empire and the World, 1780–1830* (London, 1989); P.J. Marshall (ed.), *OHBE Vol. 2 The Eighteenth Century* (Oxford, 1998); 'Britain and the World in the Eighteenth Century', 4 parts, *Transactions of the Royal Historical Society* 6th Series, 8–11 (1998–2001); John Gascoigne, *Science in the Service of Empire: Joseph Banks, the British State and the Uses of Science in the Age of Revolution* (Cambridge, 1988); Richard Drayton, *Nature's Government: Science, Imperial Britain and the 'Improvement' of the World* (New Haven and London, 2000).

focus on West Africa and the transatlantic trade.[2] Chief among these responsibilities for many British people at home and abroad who were serious Christians was
the spreading of their faith to those without it. This course of action, virtuous in
itself, was also felt likely to produce many reciprocal benefits for those who adopted
it. The evangelical Anglican Charles Grant (proprietor and director of the East
India Company) developed the case for Christian missions in India not only from a
sense of Christian duty but firmly convinced that they held the key to the moral,
political and commercial transformation of India.[3] In a similar vein in 1789,
William Wilberforce addressed the hard-headed among his House of Commons
listeners, begging them to 'make reparation to Africa ... by establishing a trade
upon true commercial principles'; right in itself, an end to the slave trade would
also mean that 'we shall soon find the rectitude of our conduct rewarded by a regular and growing commerce'.[4]

# I

In provoking evangelical responses, worldwide changes also provided the context
for the striking wave of new missionary societies formed in the 1790s: the Baptist
Missionary Society (1792), the (London) Missionary Society (1795), the
Edinburgh (Scottish) and Glasgow Missionary Societies (1796) and in 1799 the
Society for Missions to Africa and the East (known as the Church Missionary
Society from 1812). Their appearance so close together was no mere coincidence,
but rather the result of networks of influence and contacts built up over nearly half
a century.

It has been shown, for example, that 'The connections between the three
English societies was extremely close.'[5] Of central importance to the emergence of
the BMS was activity within the Baptist associations in the English Midlands – in
particular Northampton, Leicester, Olney, Kettering, Bristol and Birmingham.
Leading Baptists in this region, such as John Ryland, John Sutcliffe, Andrew
Fuller and William Carey himself, had close connections with figures playing a
central role in the organisation of the CMS. Family ties, personal friendships and
correspondence and geographical proximity, connected the Baptists with
Anglicans such as John Venn, Thomas Scott and John Newton. Fuller, the first
secretary of the BMS, attracted subscriptions from the Anglican evangelicals of

---

2  Roger Anstey, *The Atlantic Slave Trade and British Abolition, 1760–1810* (London, 1975); David
   Brion Davis, *Slavery and Human Progress* (New York, 1984); Robin Blackburn, *The Overthrow of
   Colonial Slavery, 1776–1848* (London and New York, 1988).
3  Charles Grant, *A Proposal for establishing a Protestant Mission in Bengal and Behar* (unpublished;
   London, 1787); *Observations on the State of Society among the Asiatic Subjects of Great Britain,
   particularly with respect to morals; and the means of improving it ... written chiefly in the year 1792, PP*
   (1812–13), Vol. 10.
4  Quoted in Reginald Coupland, *Wilberforce* (Oxford, 1923), pp. 128 ff.
5  Michael M. Hennell, *John Venn and the Clapham Sect* (London, 1958), p. 227.

the Clapham Sect – Wilberforce, Grant and Henry Thornton.[6] Ideas were readily shared and principles debated, for instance when Thomas Haweis, moving spirit in the LMS, was invited to share in the discussions of the Anglican Eclectic Society where the crucial steps to the formation of the CMS were taken. Thomas Coke and Grant, Grant and Wilberforce, were writing to each other about missions in the 1780s. Books were also recommended and passed on. John Erskine, leading moderate in the Church of Scotland, known for his millennial ideas and strongly supportive of the Edinburgh Missionary Society in 1796, sent among other volumes Jonathan Edwards's *An Humble Attempt* to John Ryland. Edwards's *Life of David Brainerd* as well as Moravian and Baptist *Periodical Accounts*, Crantz's *Greenland* and Sierra Leone Company reports, were among those works acquired to inform the early deliberations of the CMS committee in November 1799 and to start up the Society's library.[7]

Personal connections, a widely shared stock of ideas and a much-debated theological literature went together with a developing common sense of the practical issues to be addressed in promoting missions. For the increasing number of missionary enthusiasts, the territorial expansion of Britain's colonial empire allied to the growth of geographical and ethnographic information had two principal results. It rapidly increased their sense of opportunity, their awareness of the openings available to them for conveying to the heathen the Gospels' good news of saving grace. Simultaneously it enhanced the general sense of dissatisfaction with their inheritance of earlier eighteenth-century missionary efforts.

William Carey's career exemplifies the process experienced by members of all denominations. Even while he lacked the formal education and wider experience of many dissenters and nonconformists, Carey's origins in an 'obscure little village ... in the dullest period of the dullest of all centuries' were not as remote from the century's broader changes as this later biographer implied.[8] His intellectual curiosity, an early interest in reading and study and his time spent as a village schoolmaster, prompted him to draw in however magpie-like a manner on the widening contacts and geographical knowledge of the period. Section 3 of his *Enquiry into the Obligations of Christians* was given over to 'a Survey of the present State of the World', categorising populations as to numbers and religion and territory by geographical extent. 'It must undoubtedly strike every considerate mind, what a vast proportion of the sons of Adam there are, who yet remain in the most deplorable state of heathen darkness, without any means of knowing the true God, except what are afforded them by the works of nature; and utterly destitute of the

---

6 Stanley, *History of the BMS*, pp. 1–20; Elizabeth Elbourne, 'The Foundation of the Church Missionary Society: The Anglican Missionary Impulse', in John Walsh, Colin Haydon and Stephen Taylor (eds), *The Church of England c.1689–c.1833* (Cambridge, 1993), pp. 247–64.

7 Stanley, *History of the BMS*, p. 4; Elbourne, 'Foundation of the CMS'; Charles Hole, *The Early History of the Church Missionary Society for Africa and the East to the end of A.D. 1814* (London, 1896), pp. 48, 51.

8 George Smith, *The Life of William Carey, D.D., Shoemaker and Missionary* (London, 1885), p. 9.

knowledge of the gospel of Christ, or of any means of obtaining it.'[9] These openings were the more challenging given the limited attempts hitherto to take them up. Carey's Section 2 surveyed the history of 'former Undertakings for the Conversion of the Heathen'. Although acknowledging some eighteenth-century successes, he none the less dispensed in three brief paragraphs with everything from John Eliot onwards.[10]

Others were drawn along the same critical line of reasoning. Thomas Coke returned from his first visit to America in 1784 with first-hand observation and 'strongly biased against the Anglicans' for their neglect of need and opportunity. In Virginia 'The clergy in general ... never stir out to church, even on a Sunday, if it rains', preferring their role as 'the parasites and bottle companions of the rich and great'.[11] Notwithstanding such strictures, there were Anglicans, clerics as well as laymen, who shared Coke's passion. As befitted a bishop of London, while Coke fumed at Anglican shortcomings, Beilby Porteus made the SPG his point of departure. Whatever its previous record, Porteus appreciated its irrelevance to America after the crisis resulting from the total disruption of its work by war and independence. In his SPG Anniversary Sermon of 1783 he therefore developed two lines of argument. He maintained the traditional insistence on English settlers' rights to worship in the established manner, but also pointed to the existence of new openings involving both whites and blacks in existing spheres of SPG activity in the British West Indies and Canada.[12] David Brown, appointed to India in 1785, became the first of a series of 'pious chaplains' working with the East India Company at Calcutta. He was of like mind with Porteus, as was his mentor, the Reverend Charles Simeon of King's College, Cambridge. Still more interest was evident among the members of the Clapham Sect, which included Charles Grant after his return to England in 1790.

Thomas Haweis, on the eve of the formation of the LMS, commented in more eirenic fashion on the opportunity afforded by the 'South Sea islanders' and British neglect of them so far. 'We have discovered them and in a sort have brought them into existence; but I read with *pity*, that we have hitherto only exercised their curiosity to admire our ships and the colour of our skin; with *grief*, that we have contaminated them with our vices, and with *indignation* behold them perishing with diseases communicated by those who bear the Christian name, without an effort to inform them of the paths which lead to salvation, or to impress them with a sense of moral obligation.'[13]

---

  9 Carey, *An Enquiry*, pp. 62–3.
 10 *Ibid.*, pp. 36–7.
 11 Vickers, *Thomas Coke*, pp. 85, 100.
 12 G.D. McKelvie, 'The Development of Official Anglican Interest in World Mission, 1783–1809: With Special Reference to Bishop Beilby Porteus', 2 vols (unpub. Ph.D. thesis, Aberdeen, 1984), pp. 32–3, 67–8.
 13 T[homas]. H[aweis]., 'The Very Probable Success of a proper Mission to the South Sea Islands', *Evangelical Magazine*, 3 (July 1795), 261–70.

This last passage highlights several other features of evangelicals' reactions to late eighteenth-century conditions which persuaded them of the need for their involvement in greatly enhanced missionary endeavours. Openings for missionaries were understood not only as a consequence of deepening awareness on the part of Christians but as providential opportunities brought into existence and made plain by God himself. It followed that failure to respond was cause not for a mild New Year's resolution but for remorse and guilt, as much at the blindness to divine leading as to neglect of the duty of benevolence owed to the heathen themselves. Reparation or atonement for wrongs past was required particularly of a nation such as Britain, seen almost universally as especially favoured by Providence – in religion, political stability, material wealth and technical advancement. This argument, drawing on the obligations derived from good fortune and prosperity, was widely used not only by evangelicals to win support for the missionary cause but by humanitarians to secure backing for reforms as diverse as abolition of the slave trade and the protection of climbing boys (chimney sweeps).[14]

Dissatisfaction with past achievements and a focus on new opportunity were to remain inseparable from missionary enthusiasm throughout the nineteenth century. This depended in part on the impatience generated by the constant recruitment, throughout the nineteenth century, of young turks insensitive to the problems of their predecessors and elders.[15] At all times, however, in a community either innocent of or firmly resistant to biblical criticism and convinced of the efficacy of prayer, it was nourished by an underlying prophetical awareness in evangelical minds of the drift of world events. Rationalising – for that is how it was then conceived, using the indisputable foundations of biblical evidence – his proposal for a South Seas mission, Haweis was quietly confident. '[W]e know that the fullness of the Gentiles is determined; that the signs of the times give every reasonable hope that it is near, even at the door; and providential openings point the way for the execution of what every true Christian is praying and hoping God in his tender mercy will hasten.'[16]

In the light of lessons to be learnt from past failures, how did the supporters of missions think they should move forward? If existing models of missionary organisation were unsatisfactory, what should replace them? Part of the evangelical response to these questions lay, first, in defining and in playing down apparent obstacles to missionary activity and then in emphasising how propitious circumstances now were for

---

14  For the manner in which these spurs to action were incorporated into missionary goals, see Chapter 4.

15  For example, of LMS male recruits from 1835–1869, 52 per cent were aged 20–24, 90 per cent 29 or under and for 1870–1914, 42 per cent and 88 per cent: Alan F. Perry, 'The American Board of Commissioners for Foreign Missions and the London Missionary Society in the Nineteenth Century: A Study of Ideas' (unpub. Ph.D. thesis, Washington, 1974), p. 571.

16  *Ibid.*, pp. 263–4 and below at notes 34–5; 'Report of the Third Annual General Meeting of the Missionary Society', *Evangelical Magazine* 5 (June 1797), 243; J.H. Pratt (ed.), *Eclectic Notes: or, Notes of Discussions on Religious Topics at the Meeting of the Eclectic Society, London, during the years 1798–1814*, 2nd edn (London, 1865), pp. 259–61, 367, 452.

its success. Carey's analysis was succinct. The problems lay in the heathens' 'distance from us, their barbarous and savage manner of living, the danger of being killed by them, the difficulty of procuring the necessaries of life, or the unintelligibleness of their languages'.[17] In the conditions of his own day Carey felt some of these 'obstacles' insignificant. Of 'distance' in particular, 'nothing can be alleged for it, with any ... plausibility in the present age', given progress in shipping and maritime communications. Other forms of enterprise managed to survive in unpromising circumstances: 'trading companies' and 'commerce lies in many of the places where these barbarians dwell'. Indeed, '*navigation*, especially that which is *commercial*, shall be one great mean of carrying on the work of God', in effect confirming the implication of Isaiah 60: 9 that 'commerce shall subserve the spread of the gospel'.[18] As for a 'barbarous way of living', this was no problem for the apostles and '*is* no objection to commercial men'. Other supposed difficulties only reflected pusillanimity. The threat of death was unreal: 'I greatly question whether most of the barbarities practised by the savages upon those who have visited them, have not originated in some real or supposed affront and were therefore, more properly, acts of self-defence, than proofs of ferocious dispositions ... .*Elliot* [*sic*], *Brainerd* and the *Moravian missionaries*, have been very seldom molested.' Similarly, the physical needs for survival could be met by locally grown foods; and with languages, 'the missionaries must have patience and mingle with the people, till they have learned so much of their language as to be able to communicate their ideas to them in it'.[19]

The impediments to missions perceived by Carey were of an essentially practical character, surmountable by practical measures. Others, less confident of human ingenuity given past experience, trusted that the '*Lord will remove the* OBSTACLES *which lie in the way of the conversion of the heathen nations*'.[20] This less optimistic conclusion arose not surprisingly from consideration of certain more intractable conditions likely to shape missionary activity. There was '*the unhappy contentions and divisions which subsist among Christians*', encouraging in any non-Christian audience a low opinion of its believers. The '*impurity of those who are styled Christians*' and the '*horrible cruelties committed by those who profess the Christian religion*', while echoing Carey and much earlier experience in colonial North America, were not for some commentators to be overcome by good missionary practice. 'The SLAVE TRADE, therefore, that infamous commerce in human blood ... must be relinquished before the inhabitants of Africa will receive the Gospel.' Other '*internal* difficulties' were identified as lying in the character of heathen societies, '*the ignorance of the mind*, the *rebellion of the will* and the *sensuality of the affections*'. Although neither 'so numerous and of such a nature' as those classified as 'external', these hindrances were presented

17  Carey, *An Enquiry*, p. 67.
18  *Ibid*., pp. 67–8.
19  *Ibid*., pp. 68–9, 71, 74.
20  'Remarks on the Prophecies and Promises relating to the Glory of the Latter Day', *Evangelical Magazine*, 1 (Oct. 1793), 163.

with the implication that considerable time at least would be required for Gospel teaching to take effect.[21]

Such utterances can easily be seen as betraying their authors' insularity and naive optimism. However they did not blind Carey to the central problem which, as argued above, vitiated much missionary enterprise – that of providing financial support, a framework of authority and discipline for missionaries and their converts on the ground and continuity of operation. In considering 'what Means ought to be used', Carey turned again to commercial models. Drawing the analogy with a trading company, he pressed the case for a voluntary society with lay and clerical members; governed by a set of rules, in which subscribers would emulate shareholders; and which would have an executive committee to attend to its administration.

With the youthful impetuousness which was to be characteristic of so many who became caught up in the missionary movement, Carey did not remain content with elaborating schemes on paper. He was a supporter of direct action and made no secret of the fact. Even prayer by itself was insufficient. 'We must not be contented, however, with praying, without *exerting ourselves in the use of means* for the obtaining of those things we pray for', he wrote, doubtless conscious of the barb it carried. Thus it is no surprise to find Carey energetically pressing his case until, in May 1792, he secured from his colleagues in the Northamptonshire Baptist Association the crucial resolution to draw up a plan for a society. This was done. 'The Particular Baptist Society for Propagating the Gospel among the Heathen' was formed in October 1792, with Carey one of its five managing Committee members.[22]

## II

Although Carey had directed its sights away from commerce to missions, there was of course much in his suggestion that was familiar from the existing trading or colonising companies. Moreover, as Carey noted,[23] the continuing appeal of such a pattern had only shortly before been confirmed by attempts to establish a settlement for poor blacks and freed slaves in West Africa. This private initiative was first developed by Henry Smeathman (botanist and West African explorer) and the abolitionist Granville Sharp. It originated in the wish to provide for the growing numbers of poor blacks in Britain's towns, especially the larger ports, and in the work of the Committee for the Black Poor formed in London in January 1786. At the same time, momentum was added by the wider mobilisation of anti-slavery opinion, evident in the London Committee for the Abolition of the Slave Trade, formed in May 1787 and of which Sharp was member. In April that year, with the

---

21 *Ibid.*, pp. 164, 165.
22 Carey, *An Enquiry*, p. 81; Stanley, *History of the BMS*, pp. 9–15; Smith, *Life of Carey*, pp. 50–3.
23 Carey, *An Enquiry*, p. 80.

aid of Treasury grants and naval transports, Sharp sailed with 411 black and white settlers for his so-called 'Province of Freedom'. The chaotic administrative arrangements for the settlement, deaths and disputes among the settlers and the destruction of Granville Town by local Africans in December 1789, put a rapid end to Sharp's project and the Government refused further backing.[24]

Supporters in London, however, led by Henry Thornton, banker and member of the Clapham Sect and urged on by petitions from abolitionists all over England, obtained a parliamentary act of incorporation for a new Sierra Leone Company. Sharing the same fundamental humanitarian concerns for freed slaves' well-being, the new company was intended to address the problems of finance, economic support and defence far more systematically than had been possible under Sharp's quaintly anachronistic and idealistic plans. With government assistance a large number of fresh black colonists were recruited from freed slaves and black loyalists in Nova Scotia and settled in Freetown, site of the original Granville Town, in March 1792. Shortly afterwards a new system of government was introduced, based on the recently evolved 'crown colony' pattern of governor and advisory council.

Neither venture was designed as a missionary enterprise, but the support of religion and the extension of Christianity were taken for granted. To a certain extent this was anticipated as a natural development, arising from the fact that many of the settlers belonged to one Protestant denomination or another. Expectation that the settlement would develop ties with the surrounding communities, and provide an example of black achievement consequent on abandonment of the slave trade, carried with it diffusionist assumptions. To add impetus to this process, chaplains were appointed with parochial and missionary responsibilities – in 1787 Peter Frazer (Fraser), recently ordained as an Anglican, formerly a Presbyterian and in 1792 Nathaniel Gilbert and his cousin Melvill Horne, again Anglicans but sympathetic to the Methodism of many of the new settlers. Horne indeed had long worked closely with the Wesleyans. Schoolmasters were also provided.[25]

These hopes were nevertheless soon dashed. Frazer, ill and refused a church by his intended flock, abandoned the settlement after only ten months and Gilbert left in July 1793. Similarly, after little more than a year, during which he had preached a single missionary sermon through an interpreter, Horne returned to Britain, convinced that 'I could not effect my purpose'.[26] As enterprises whose funds and preoccupations necessarily embraced all aspects of the settlement's organisation,

24 Christopher Fyfe, *A History of Sierra Leone* (Oxford, 1962), pp. 13–25; Philip D. Curtin, *The Image of Africa: British Ideas and Action, 1780–1850* (London, 1965); J.R. Oldfield, *Popular Politics and British Anti-Slavery: The Mobilisation of Public Opinion against the Slave Trade, 1787–1807* (London, 1998), chaps 2–3.
25 Fyfe, *Sierra Leone*, pp. 25–58; *DEB*, Vol. 1, pp. 439–40, 572–3.
26 Melvill Horne, *Letters on Missions; addressed to the Protestant Ministers of the British Churches* (Bristol, 1794), p. iii.

there was neither sufficient money nor time for the London Committee or their local governor to pay special attention to these problems. The history of the Company's appointments was endlessly problematical and their positive impact correspondingly restricted even in vital matters such as the removal of slavery.[27]

Gilbert and Horne were at least well regarded. According to Zachary Macaulay in his first stint as governor, Horne in particular was a fine preacher. With 'fire, perspicuity and simplicity', he was able to move a congregation appropriately to the occasion.[28] However, the lack of a local language, and the burden of the chaplain's work in Freetown, in Horne's view limited any wider influence. Subsequently missionaries sent out by Thomas Coke were regarded as a serious disappointment. A later party from the General Missionary Society (as the LMS was sometimes called) was so disputatious that, as Thornton unflatteringly put it, Macaulay had had to send them to separate places lest they should destroy each other like game cocks travelling in the same bag![29]

As missionary enthusiasm in Britain intensified, Sierra Leone's 'experiment in freedom' thus seemed at first to provide a final demonstration of the failings of older models. The settlement's and company's early experience pointed to the need for far more concerted and extensive *missionary* efforts, rather than limited evangel-istic work undertaken in the manner of the Sierra Leone ventures as but one aspect of broader concerns. This was precisely the lesson urged by Horne on his arrival home. Having reflected on his Freetown experience, he immediately published his general analysis of the missionary problem. The trifling number of converts made since the Reformation was for him proof that Christians had gone about evangelisa-tion in the wrong spirit and the wrong way. Missionary societies and ministerial action to launch them were the answer, not the despatch of single individuals, isolated as Horne himself was in West Africa or David Brainerd in North America. Even if good and practical men, 'their success will always be inadequate to the object of Missions, which is an extensive spread of Christ's religion'.[30] Thus Horne felt able to praise the Moravians and unable to assess the success or otherwise of the Dutch, Swedes and Danes. Working together in ardent, pious, voluntary groups, agreed on doctrine, modes of teaching and discipline, Moravians led regular lives. They were not only backed up from home; 'mutually supporting and inspiriting one another' on the spot, so they ensured 'the zeal and abilities of an individual' could be truly effective. Methodists too he felt had their strengths and advantages; although 'no one plan can be formed, which will equally apply to [different]

27 Michael J. Turner, 'The Limits of Abolition: Government, Saints and the "African Question", c. 1780–1820', *English Historical Review* 112 (1997), 319–57.

28 7 and 18 July 1793. *Zachary Macaulay and the Development of the Sierra Leone Company, 1793–4. Part I: Journal, June–October 1793*, ed. Suzanne Schwarz (2nd edn, Leipzig, 2000), pp. 26, 32.

29 Thornton to Macaulay, 13 June 1796 and to Hannah More, 18 March 1798, Thornton Family Papers, Add.7674/1/L1, ff. 85–6, 128, transcripts; Fyfe, *Sierra Leone*, pp. 67–8, 75–6.

30 Horne, *Letters*, p. 33.

Nations', numbers were crucial and Coke could have done far more in the West Indies with united support.[31]

Missionary associations Horne thought should be quite separate and distinct bodies. While avoiding any direct criticism of the Sierra Leone venture, he insisted that they should not be linked to commercial interest, for the danger then was that 'gain became a pedestal for godliness to stand upon'. Equally they should keep their distance from governments and the state. Piety, benevolence and an 'unassuming modesty' were the essential requirements of missionaries. These qualities were their own advertisement and source of protection, whereas close relations between religion and government or commerce corrupted both parties. 'By affecting the favour of the great, we degrade our ministry, endanger our own salvation and render the men we flatter and fawn upon worse than they were before.' This, after all, had brought down the Jesuits. No less than favour from or dependence on governments, missions should also avoid acquiring authority, especially secular authority, over their own converts. 'We say that religion flourished most when she had to contend with the State, and had no other support than what she derived from her own native strength.'[32]

The publication of Horne's *Letters* was very timely. On the evangelical circuits of England and among moderate churchmen in Scotland, discussion of overseas missionary possibilities was gathering momentum.[33] The *Evangelical Magazine*, launched in 1793, was fired with the conviction that 'Thousands read a Magazine, who have neither money to purchase, nor leisure to peruse, large volumes. It is therefore a powerful engine in the moral world.'[34] Bringing together virtually all shades of evangelical opinion, the *Magazine* devoted increasing space to missionary issues. It reviewed missionary publications such as Christian La Trobe's *History of the Missions of the United Brethren among the Indians in North America* and the first Baptist *Periodical Accounts* and recorded in its 'Religious Intelligence' section the births of new societies and the spread of the prayer movement for missions. The Worcester Evangelical Society, for example, founded on 1 January 1795, reportedly had as its object 'the support and spread of the Gospel in this and other countries ... [and] to co-operate occasionally with other societies in the *encouragement of missionaries abroad*'.[35] With its pungent style, wide range of reference and practical wisdom from personal experience, Horne's book was at once taken up, read widely and enthusiastically reviewed in the *Evangelical Magazine* by Thomas Haweis.[36]

---

31  *Ibid.*, pp. 33–7, 41.
32  *Ibid.*, pp. 51, 53–4, 133.
33  Roger H. Martin, *Evangelicals United: Ecumenical Stirrings in Pre-Victorian Britain, 1795–1830* (Metuchen, NJ and London, 1983); Allan K. Davidson, *Evangelicals & Attitudes to India, 1786–1813: Missionary Publicity and Claudius Buchanan* (Sutton Courtenay, 1990), chap. 5.
34  *Evangelical Magazine*, 1 (July 1793), 3.
35  *Ibid.*, 3 (Feb.–March 1795), 77–81, 114, 122–3.
36  *Ibid.*, 2 (Nov. 1794), 476–8.

Not unlike Carey two years before, Horne was offering further telling criticisms of what were established features of an essentially 'Anglican' approach to missionary work, still characteristic of the Sierra Leone Company as much as they were of the SPG. It was an approach that placed missionaries under the authority of the governor, linked them to 'the state', attempted to combine missionary with parish responsibilities and in practice left missionaries largely isolated whether or not that was thought appropriate. However, although Horne urged the reading of Carey, he did not go on like Carey to accept the necessity of a denomination-based missionary society.[37] His appeal was directed to Christians of many kinds and his recommendation was for a missionary society that would be non-denominational. This was a suggestion attractive for many reasons. It was thought likely to reduce the divisions among Christians, to avoid confusion over Christian essentials and help to stimulate active evangelical faith at home. It would maximise support and detach missions from politics, religious establishments and government and was not, the evangelical Anglican in Horne hastened to add, simply the covert promotion of dissenting principles or independency. 'It is not Calvinism, it [is] not Arminianism … It is not the hierarchy of the Church of England; it is not the principles of Protestant Dissenters, that [the missionary] has in view to propagate. His object is to serve the Church Universal.'[38]

Among those to whom Horne's arguments most strongly appealed was that denominationally mixed body of men who, having debated his ideas at length, came together in late September 1795 to establish the (London) Missionary Society and approve its first venture, a mission to 'the South Seas'. At their meeting in May 1796, held, like so many of the early missionary planning meetings, at the Castle and Falcon inn in Aldersgate Street in the City of London, the Society's directors approved what became known as their 'fundamental principle'. 'As the union of God's People of various Denominations, in carrying on this great Work, is a most desirable Object, so, to prevent, if possible, any cause of future dissension, it is declared to be a fundamental principle of the Missionary Society, that our design is not to send Presbyterianism, Independency, Episcopacy, or any other form of Church Order and Government (about which there may be differences of opinion among serious Persons), but the Glorious Gospel of the blessed God to the Heathen: and that it shall be left (as it ever ought to be left) to the minds of the Persons whom God may call into the fellowship of His Son from among them to assume for themselves such form of Church Government, as to them shall appear most agreeable to the Word of God.'[39]

---

37  Carey, *An Enquiry*, p. 84; Minutes of the Meeting, 2 Oct. 1792, Resolution 2, Smith, *Life of Carey*, p. 52. A General Baptist Missionary Society was formed in 1816.

38  Horne, *Letters*, p. 60.

39  *Evangelical Magazine*, Aug.–Nov. 1795; Richard Lovett, *The History of the London Missionary Society 1795–1895*, 2 vols (London, 1895), Vol. 1, pp. 49–50. Every *Annual Report* contained a statement of the Fundamental Principle. It was incorporated as Article III into the Plan and Constitution of the LMS, which replaced the earlier Regulations in 1870.

Throwing off denominational attachments or revising past practices was never-theless rarely easy. In time the LMS found it impossible to sustain this ecumenical principle unalloyed and became identified ever more as a Congregationalist society. Nevertheless, the significance of the principle as a statement intended to define the practice and context of mission bodies in the 1790s remains unchanged. Nowhere were the difficulties of striking out in new directions demonstrated more clearly than among those evangelical Anglicans wishing to reinvigorate the missionary efforts of the Church of England. Men of such views were found in various quar-ters. Beilby Porteus, still in the mid-1790s a lone figure on the bench of bishops, and Charles Grant have already been mentioned, as have David Brown and Charles Simeon. To these prominent individuals can be added assorted members of the growing number of English clerical societies, such as those at Elland, Rauceby and Hotham; and members of one particular such society, the Eclectic Society, formed in January 1783 as a regular discussion group by evangelical clergy living in or close to London.

Once agreed in their wish to promote Christianity on a global scale and accept-ing that missionary societies were essential to the tasks of raising funds, adequate numbers of recruits and effective administration, mission enthusiasts were faced, broadly speaking, with four possible courses. A society might organise itself on a basis at once voluntary and non-denominational, as did the LMS, which was left entirely to its own devices notwithstanding the later growth of a distinct denomina-tional identity and the slow development of Congregational unions. Alternatively a society might be identified with a single strand or denomination of Christianity, but, while existing within the church, remain as a separate voluntary body in no way controlled by any church authorities. This was essentially the position of the BMS, which developed as a national society in no way subordinate to the Baptist Union that came into being in 1813. Likewise the CMS prided itself on being both independent and a 'church' society. Then again, a missionary society might be constituted as a formal arm of the church or denomination, subject to church lead-ers and those to whom they delegated their authority. This arrangement was essen-tially that of the SPG within the Church of England. It provided a far less flexible structure because, notwithstanding the limited involvement of church or political leaders in day-to-day business, it brought to bear on the formulation of missionary policy the opinions of many who could not be relied upon for their interest, sympa-thy or knowledge. Finally and often equally constraining, there was the Wesleyan Methodists' arrangement in which their missionary society was in a very real sense one with the denomination. The mission society secretaries, such as Jabez Bunting, were also the national officials who ran the Methodist connection and the mission house was also for many years the only national headquarters the Methodist church possessed.

It was not only logic and economy that at first pointed Anglican reformers towards the revival of the SPG as the necessary way forward. Even while they wished the BMS and LMS well, their genuine attachment to the Church of England and its episcopal character made it hard for them to contemplate working towards a non-denominational society. However, in the late 1780s and 1790s, redirection of the SPG's activities had become a very unpromising proposition. After withdrawing from 'colonial' America in 1785, the Society under Archbishop Moore (1783–1805) was intent on putting together the pieces of its work in what remained of British North America, catering for the displaced loyalists and responding to the needs of a growing settler and immigrant population.[40] This renewed emphasis on traditional priorities was in keeping with the inclinations of the SPG's long-serving secretary, Dr. William Morice. His period of office (1778–1819) was officially damned as one of 'stagnation' and Morice as 'not the man to introduce fresh ideas or infuse fresh life'.[41] Stimulus from the Society's wider membership was also lacking. Most were deeply suspicious of the religious 'enthusiasm' associated with voluntary societies, interdenominational fraternising and the pressures for reform; they also treasured their established status. As a result, those with evangelical or humanitarian leanings increasingly found themselves out of sympathy with the atmosphere at SPG.

Even Porteus, the one bishop both well informed and seriously concerned since as early as 1773 with missions to 'the heathen', was not only alone among church leaders but in evangelical eyes was cautious to a fault. He showed not the slightest interest in the BMS or LMS. Although implicitly critical of SPG work in the West Indies, when his suggestions of 1783–84 for changes were rejected in March 1784, he did not contest the issue despite his great personal disappointment. Sympathetic to missions in India, again he seems to have made no direct and open attempts to persuade political or church leaders to modify their opposition. In the parliamentary debate of 1793 on renewal of the East India Company charter and the insertion therein of the so-called 'pious clauses' obliging the Company to promote religious instruction, he spoke reluctantly and indecisively on the main issue. Porteus in his reticence may have been politically realistic. However, he was also governed throughout by the conviction that for the established church to engage in missions required the supportive involvement of the imperial government. Without that, the church could not move and if no church, then no mission.[42] This placed him at a great distance from a cleric such as Thomas Scott, member of the Eclectic Society and Anglican biblical commentator. For Scott such entanglements only confirmed his view that 'the connexion of religion with politics is one grand antichristian abuse ... universally adopted at the reformation, by which modern Christianity is most strikingly discriminated from ancient'.[43] Although behind the scenes Porteus tried gentle persuasion and influence in many quarters, he remained too tied to older ideas to sympathise with the radical movements of his day towards new voluntary societies.

---

40  Fingard, *The Anglican Design*; Thompson, *Into All Lands*, pp. 104–73.
41  *Ibid.*, p. 110.
42  McKelvie, 'Development of Official Anglican Interest', pp. 146, 149–50, chap. 5, 793–815, 855–70.
43  Letter of 28 Aug. 1799, John Scott, *Letters and Papers of the Late Rev. Thomas Scott* (London, 1824), p. 229. For Scott, *DEB*, Vol. 2, pp. 989–91.

The failure to move the SPG left reformers with no alternative to a society of their own. The difficulties they faced have been well and most recently scrutinised by Elizabeth Elbourne.[44] In the context of a limited 'Anglican missionary culture', they wished to appropriate the means of the dissenters and nonconformists while at the same time not simply avoiding accusations of disloyalty and subversion but securing the actual approval of the Anglican bishops. This was necessary both to satisfy their own commitment to Anglican church order and, opposed as they were to the use of laymen, to obtain episcopal ordination for their missionaries.

The hesitant progress towards their goal and the central roles played by the Eclectic Society, John Venn and Charles Simeon, are well known. Early Eclectic discussions about missions – for example to the 'East Indies' and Botany Bay – were somewhat desultory, almost as if assuming that 'the best way of propagating the Gospel in the East Indies' was likely to be peculiar to the territory rather than a missionary society with a general remit. However, the launching of the LMS and the sudden possibility of a bequest to finance an Anglican initiative spurred the Eclectic Society on 6 February 1796 to discuss 'With what propriety and in what mode, can a Mission be attempted to the Heathen, from the Established Church?' Interestingly at this stage, in answer to the question Anglican enthusiasts produced no book standing in relation to the formation of the CMS as Carey's *Enquiry* and Horne's *Letters* had done for the two earlier societies. None the less, discussions continued, and a further three formal meetings early in 1799 were the final stages in the launch of the CMS on 12 April. Although its rules and plans for a countrywide representation were agreed by the end of May, further action was delayed until July 1800, the time it took Wilberforce to elicit in response to the Society's letter a private but not unfriendly undertaking from the Archbishop to view its activities sympathetically.[45]

The decision to focus its title and efforts on 'Africa and the East' was also carefully considered. For the moment at least it avoided giving offence to friends in other societies, allowing the Baptists their more explicit preoccupation with India and steering clear of the LMS in the Pacific and the Cape Colony. More important, it clearly side-stepped any appearance of wishing to rival either the SPG or (although never publicly stated) the Methodists, with their primary focus on British North America and the British West Indies. In the words of the second resolution of the foundation meeting, 'as it appears from the printed reports of the Societies for Propagating the Gospel and for Promoting Christian Knowledge that those respectable Societies confine their labours to the British Plantations in America and to the West Indies, there seems to be still wanting in the Established Church a society for sending missionaries to the Continent of Africa, or the other

---

44  Elbourne, 'Foundation of the CMS'; but also Hennell, *John Venn*, chap. 5.
45  Elbourne, 'Foundation of the CMS'; Hennell, *John Venn*, chap. 5; Hole, *Early History*, pp. 4–64; Eugene Stock, *The History of the Church Missionary Society: Its Environment, Its Men and Its Work*, 4 vols (London, 1899, 1916), Vol. 1, pp. 68–74.

parts of the heathen world'.[46] Many of those involved in the infant society already had close interests in Sierra Leone, dating from 1786–87 and, from earlier still through Grant, in India. Other missions had moved with less deliberation. Carey had come to settle on Bengal largely by chance encounter with John Thomas, another example of Grant's ubiquitous encouragement who had also previously evangelized there. Thomas Coke's emerging interest in India rather later on seems to have reflected the twists and turns of his own personal inclinations.[47] In the Anglican selection, however, there seems to have been a degree of careful consideration not immediately apparent in their competitors.

During the 1790s, the interest and efforts of small nuclei of committed evangelicals within the major Christian groupings had brought about considerable institutional advance and had won wider sympathy for the cause of overseas missions. At the start of the new century it remained to be seen whether momentum could be sustained, or increased, by turning sympathy into financial support and acceptable missionary volunteers.

### III

Divisions within these Christian communities were a continuing feature of the religious scene, threatening both their involvement in missions and co-operation between them as denominational distinctions hardened through to the 1860s. Conservative dissenters looked askance at the LMS, General Baptists kept their distance from the Particular Baptists and Christians in every camp argued over the wisdom of diverting finance abroad. Anglican leaders were very lukewarm towards the CMS: no bishop would join its General Committee or preach an Anniversary Sermon until Bishop Ryder in 1814. Even those welcoming the spread of Christianity might deny the utility of missions. Richard Watson, Bishop of Llandaff, felt 'It will not be easy for missionaries of any nation to make much impression on the Pagans of any country, because missionaries in general, instead of teaching a simple system of Christianity, have perplexed their hearers with unintelligible doctrines not expressly delivered in Scripture ... Christianity is a rational religion; the Romans, the Athenians, the Corinthians ... all, at length, exchanged their Paganism for Christianity; the same change will take place in other countries, as they become enlightened by the progress of European literature and become capable of justly estimating the weight of historical evidence, on which the truth of Christianity must, as to them, depend'.[48]Amongst the wider population indifference and vehement criticism were both common and mockery not only entertaining but usefully subversive of activities often seen as destructive and malign.

---

46 Hole, *Early History*, p. 37.
47 Stanley, *History of the BMS*, pp. 16–17; Vickers, *Thomas Coke*, pp. 335–50.
48 *Anecdotes of the Life of Richard Watson, Bishop of Llandaff; Written by Himself at Different Intervals and Revised in 1814* (London, 1817), p. 198.

In 1802, speaking to the proposal for an increase in the parliamentary grant to the settlement of Sierra Leone, General Isaac Gascoyne disapproved of the colony as a failure and waste of money, but had a still greater dislike of missions. 'All the advantage that could be drawn from the settlement was, the importation of Methodist piety and British spirits.' He had decided not to oppose the grant 'as it might be the means of ridding this Country of a great number of field preachers who would otherwise be troublesome ... and who would be induced to take a voyage to the Colony in the capacity of Missionaries'.[49]

The Reverend Sydney Smith was perhaps more fluent and stingingly dismissive than most. He wrote for many when he acknowledged the obligation to promote religion, but disputed the circumstances in which it was practicable and dismissed missions as an inappropriate means. 'We admit it to be the general duty of Christian people to disseminate their religion among the Pagan nations who are subjected to their empire .... We believe that we are in possession of a revealed religion; that we are exclusively in possession of a revealed religion; and that the possession of that religion can alone confer immortality and best confer present happiness. This religion, too, teaches us the duties of general benevolence: and how, under such a system, the conversion of Heathens can be a matter of indifference, we profess not to be able to understand.' However, 'there is scarcely a parish in England or Ireland, in which the zeal and activity of any one of these Indian apostles would not have done more good ... than can be expected from their joint efforts in the populous regions of Asia'. Moreover, the 'duties of conversion appear to be of less importance, when it is impossible to procure proper persons to undertake them and when such religious embassies, in consequence, devolve on the lowest of the people ... The wise and rational part of the christian ministry find they have enough to do at home ... But if a tinker is a devout man, he infallibly sets off for the East. Let any man read the Anabaptist missions; – can he do so ... without feeling that they are benefiting us much more by their absence, than the Hindoos by their advice?'[50]

On paper at least, missionary supporters gave as good as they got, the periodical reviews losing few opportunities to set right the sceptical or ill-willed. One *Eclectic* reviewer, for example, pulled no punches in assessing William Tennant's *Indian Recreations*. 'With the labours of Christian Missionaries in Hindoostan, Dr. T[ennant]. is not at all acquainted; and to what he says on the subject, not the smallest regard is to be paid ... we are compelled to say, that the Dr. never appears to less advantage, than when the christian religion is his theme. A very improper use is made of the phraseology of the sacred Scriptures; and it is sometimes introduced with a levity (to give it the gentlest name) which fills us with disgust'.[51] In

---

49  11 June 1802, *Parliamentary Register*, 18 (1802), p. 685. Gascoyne was MP for the slave-trading centre of Liverpool, 1802–30.

50  'Indian Missions', *Edinburgh Review*, 12 ( April 1808), 169–70, 171, 179–80.

51  *Eclectic Review* 1, 12 (Dec. 1805), quotation at p. 898.

the same issue, Captain Philip Beaver's *African Memoranda* became the occasion for a sustained defence of Sierra Leone in particular and missionaries in general against Beaver's 'presumption' and 'want of acquaintance with his subject'. 'Gentlemen who dictate on topics of this kind, should reflect, that the doctrines alluded to are no more comprehensible to their own minds, than to that of a savage; and they should inform themselves of facts which have usually attended the promulgation of the gospel, before they venture to arraign the conduct and to depreciate the characters, of Christian missionaries.'[52] Works regarded as themselves of little importance were given space so that reviewers might dilate on a subject they considered important. Such was John Savage's *Some Account of New Zealand* (London, 1807), which prompted an assessment of the European impact on Tahiti and other islands. This led to the predictable conclusion that 'There is but one gift that it is in the power of Europeans to make, which may, in any degree, compensate for the miseries to which they have subjected these islanders – the introduction of the Gospel of Christ.'[53]

Polemical vigour, however, could not disguise the fact that in most respects the life of the missionary societies was more visionary than substantial. The SPG's subscriptions rarely topped £500 per annum between 1783 and 1819 and in only two of the thirty years before 1814 does its income seem to have exceeded £5000. Normally it fell notably short of that figure, buoyed up by unpredictable donations and dividends from investments. In most years the Society remained in credit only because its level of activity and hence outgoings were kept low. Average total income a year from 1786 to 1812 was £3922.[54]

Baptist Missionary Society income was liable to serious fluctuations, but in its first twenty years to 1812 a total of nearly £50,000 averaged out at £2411 per annum.[55] Unsurprisingly, early Methodist accounts are not to be found. However, as the annual Conference's Committee began to take charge away from Coke, details began to emerge and between 1803 and 1809 they seem to have received some £3419 per annum. Greater oversight, however, still left them not only unable to compile figures for 1806–7 but liable to receive gifts in kind. 'Also from a Gentleman at Huddersfield, twenty yards of fine black kerseymere, for Missionaries cloaths.'[56]

At the two extremes of missionary giving were the LMS and the CMS. The LMS drew on an open-ended base of subscribers and resorted to the tactic of

---

52  *Ibid.*, pp. 881–91, quotation at p. 884. For Beaver, disillusioned after involvement in the Sierra Leone project at an early stage and formerly colleague of Thomas Clarkson, see Curtin, *Image of Africa*, pp. 110–12, 127, 265, 268.

53  *Eclectic Review* 3, 2 (Oct. 1807), quotation at p. 868.

54  Pascoe, *Two Hundred Years*, Vol. 2, pp. 822–32; McKelvie, 'Development of Official Anglican Interest', appendices D–G, pp. 1043–9.

55  *The Centenary Volume of the Baptist Missionary Society, 1792–1892* (London, 1892), pp. 332–3.

56  *Methodist Reports*, passim; *A Statement of the Receipts and Disbursements of the Methodist Missions, in the years 1803 and 1804* (London, 1804), p. 5.

collecting in Baptist and Methodist chapels. Although it was criticised for the latter, the overall advantage was plain in an income averaging £6795 per annum from 1796 to 1812. Even taken together the SPG and CMS were unable to match this record. The CMS alone offered a sorry contrast. Its receipts continued to illustrate the force of Henry Thornton's observation in 1795 as to the relative stinginess of Anglican giving compared with that greeting the new LMS. Not until 1805 did the CMS receive more than £1000 and the average from 1799 to 1812 was a mere £1436.[57]

Such figures are of course subject to various caveats, as, for example, assessments of the potential of different denominational organisations for raising funds. Other bodies, old and new, were there to attract such evangelical resources as were available. The SPCK still contributed to the upkeep of the Lutheran missionaries in India. The Religious Tract Society (1799) and the British and Foreign Bible Society (1804) offered new and important support to missionary efforts at home and abroad. The evidence is nevertheless also illuminating. They seem to reflect for instance the relative poverty and internal divisions that existed within the Baptist and Methodist communities, as they do the high level of commitment of the evangelicals behind the LMS. Equally striking is the lack of concern with the Church of England. Not surprisingly, with the societies anxious to place as many missionaries overseas as quickly as possible, the pattern of funding fits closely that of recruitment and deployment.

Volunteers were no easier to come by than were funds and, inevitably, the more exacting the requirements the fewer there were to be found. Again the LMS and the CMS represented the two poles of the picture. The CMS story was particularly telling. Not until 1804 did it recruit its first missionary and of the fifteen accepted to the end of 1813 only three were English, the rest being German-speaking.[58] Anxious for men in holy orders, it proved at first impossible either to attract ordained clergy or to obtain ordinations for CMS candidates. Only through the German Carl Steinkopf, Lutheran chaplain of the Savoy Chapel in London (1801–59) and connections made with Johann Jänicke's recently established Missionary College in Berlin, could volunteers be found. With some reluctance, therefore, the CMS in 1804 took on the first two of many subsequent missionaries in Lutheran orders. Not until 1817 did missionaries from home begin to outweigh those from the continent. Men were taken from Alsace and Württemberg as well as Berlin and later also from Hanover and Jena. In 1819 the first two missionaries were commissioned from the Basel Institution, where Steinkopf's links were especially strong. With its Württemberg catchment area Basel became from then on the main, as well as a steady, source of continental recruits for the CMS until about 1860.[59]

---

57  Lovett, *History of the LMS*, Vol. 2, app. 3; Hennell, *John Venn*, p. 228; *Chronological Chart of the Progress of the Church Missionary Society.*

58  *Church Missionary Society Register of Missionaries and Native Clergy, From 1804 to 1904* (CMS, privately printed, London 1895).

In the early years the scale or sphere of CMS operations was no less restricted than its sources of men. Twelve of the first fifteen missionaries went to Sierra Leone or very nearby, only six of whom survived on three stations by 1813. At Samuel Marsden's urging, the remaining three – in fact 'lay settlers', neither missionaries nor catechists – went as an advance party for a New Zealand mission, two of them leaving London in 1809 although the mission did not get under way until December 1814.[60] An official survey by the Society of its current state in 1812 was strong on the grandeur of the missionary design, with the benefits of Christianity outlined for the hundreds of millions of Africa's and Asia's population. Other particularly enticing prospects for missionary expansion were specified in Abyssinia, Ceylon, the Persian Gulf and the Malayan archipelago. However, it is impossible to miss the mingled faint hopes and disappointment, the making of bricks without straw, that lay beneath this scheme. In Sierra Leone, it was noted, attention was being switched from adults to children, in the hope of more rapid progress. Additionally 'The Society has attempted to lay the foundation of a Settlement on the large and populous Island of New Zealand – with the view of introducing civilization among that interesting race, preparatory to the introduction of the Gospel.' Putting as favourable a gloss as possible on the continuing shortage of missionaries, reference was made to future plans for the use of Christian Africans from the United States and – earlier failures notwithstanding – to the education of African youths in Britain.[61]

Better funding and more candidates to choose from did not necessarily guarantee greater success. The LMS launched itself with a great flourish. In 1796 it despatched for Tahiti four ordained missionaries and twenty-six others with various skills – shoemakers and bricklayers, for example – on board the Society's own ship *Duff* bought for the purpose. Within three years, however, two-thirds of the members had abandoned the enterprise; the mission had withdrawn from the outer islands of Tongatapu and the Marquesas to Tahiti; and the *Duff* with a second party had been lost as a prize of war to the French. These losses and the complete failure of the LMS project in Sierra Leone only confirmed for Thomas Scott, a CMS founder, his doubts as to the LMS and its management. To his eye, they selected the wrong sort and were altogether too zealous, insufficiently wise and too uncritical of 'favourable providential appearances and second causes'.[62] Even the centenary historian of the LMS was unusually frank in presenting these early

---

59  *Ibid.*, List I, entries 25, 26, 33, 34, 54, 55, for recruits from Hanover, Jena and Württemberg; Paul Jenkins, 'The Church Missionary Society and the Basel Mission: An Early Experiment in Inter-European Cooperation', in Kevin Ward and Brian Stanley (eds), *The Church Mission Society and World Christianity, 1799–1999* (Grand Rapids and Richmond, 2000), pp. 43–65. For Steinkopf, *DEB*, Vol. 2, p. 1047.

60  *CMS Register*, List I, entries 8, 9 and 15; Hennell, *John Venn*, pp. 243–4. Marsden was Anglican chaplain and agent for the LMS at Sydney, NSW.

61  *Summary View of the Designs and Proceedings of the Society for Missions to Africa and the East* (London, 1812), pp. 16–21, quotation at pp. 18–19.

62  Scott, *Letters and Papers*, p. 185.

ventures as disasters. On the part of the Directors they were 'a conspicuous example of zeal outrunning discretion' and 'the enormous waste of resources' was a
major object lesson for the future.[63]

In Bengal, Carey's experiences were such that only 'an extraordinarily high
degree of personal motivation on the part of its leaders' ensured even its survival.
At times the mission certainly represented little more than that. For six years
family disasters and his own personal survival were Carey's main concern; earning
enough to live on took priority over evangelisation. Conditions eased with the
arrival in 1799 of four more missionaries and their families and the decision to
settle at the Danish possession of Serampore on the south bank of the Hugli
river.[64] This made possible much more translation work and the development of
schools, but Carey and his colleagues were always too hurried and seriously over-
stretched. The community was increasingly divided in itself, especially by the
presence of younger missionaries who were often it seemed little more than 'religious adventurers' and in 1811–12 it suffered drastically from deaths and the
destruction of the mission in a fire. For the BMS leaders at home there were few
triumphs to report for the delectation of subscribers and volunteers and only
skilful management by the Secretary, Andrew Fuller, held things together until his
death in 1815.[65]

These essentially metropolitan British perspectives on the need for new forms
of missionary enterprise, their nature and their consequences, reveal some of the
limitations of the movement in the two decades either side of 1800. In one sense
there is nothing new in that. Contemporary evangelicals used this evidence to illustrate the enormity of the Christian task and to drum up support for God's cause.
Later generations of missionary supporters with longer runs of statistics to hand
used them to demonstrate how great the cumulative achievement had been over
fifty or one hundred years. Such contrasting perspectives have provided the back-
bone of much missionary history.

## IV

The same material, however, is helpful in illuminating the changing relationship
between religious expansion and empire. In this period it is difficult not to be struck
by the comparatively insignificant place occupied by empire in the minds of many
evangelicals. To a degree that at times could leave onlookers quite bemused and

---

63  Lovett, *History of the LMS*, Vol. 1, pp. 46–7, 57–64, quotation at p. 59; for subsequent develop-
    ments, *The History of the Tahitian Mission 1799–1830 written by John Davies Missionary to the
    South Sea Islands*, ed. C.W. Newbury (Hakluyt Society 2nd series, 116, Cambridge, 1961).
64  For a map, Smith, *Life of William Carey*, p. 125.
65  Stanley, *History of the BMS*, pp. 36–43 and for Fuller, pp. 15–34; Stephen Neill, *A History of
    Christianity in India, 1707–1858* (Cambridge, 1985), p. 189 ff.; E.D. Potts, *British Baptist
    Missionaries in India, 1793–1837: The History of Serampore and Its Missions* (Cambridge, 1967),
    p. 23.

evangelicals themselves open to ridicule, their thinking was dominated by the concept of an all-embracing, superintending Providence.[66] It was the workings of Providence which governed the unfolding of the divine plan for the world and revealed at intervals to believers the direction and nature of its course. As was to be expected, there was nevertheless a certain mystery as to the operations of Providence. The books of Roger Anstey and Boyd Hilton have demonstrated the significance for contemporary evangelicals of two different modes of providential action. 'General' or 'natural law' Providence operated in a regular, mechanical, non-interventionist way, working through 'natural and immutable laws of cause and effect'. 'Special' or 'particular' Providence was manifested in sudden or catastrophic interventions that provided direct indications of divine intention or judgement. These were, in Hilton's words, '*ad hoc* and *ad hominem* interventions in terrestrial affairs'; and for Anstey they involved 'the particular direction of the individual godly man's life by God'.[67]

It was not always easy to distinguish between the two modes of operation; nor was attention to Providence necessarily to be associated with a particular interest in apocalyptic and eschatological matters. However, in an age dominated by the upheavals in America, social and economic disruption and the earth-shaking events of the French Revolution and Europe's wars to 1815, signs of providential activity were to be detected everywhere and many people were only too ready to point out their relevance to assorted millenarian speculations or congruence with those eschatological signs indicated in the prophetic books of the Bible. At various social levels these uncertainties and the search for explanatory frameworks of belief were widely manifested in the commotion associated with figures such as Richard Brothers and Joanna Southcott, and with other popular strands of millenarianism at the time. Very different in the main, although not always as easily distinguishable as they thought themselves, were the serious evangelicals. Many of them engaged in 'speculation about the nearness of the millennium' and contributed to the 'spate of sermons and pamphlets on Daniel and Revelation ... in the 1790s'. They shared 'the general religious ethos of bible-centred, Protestant evangelicalism ... favourable to an apocalyptic interpretation of events in Europe' in ways 'entirely orthodox and respectable'.[68]

Fulfilment of the Great Commission to preach and convert the heathen was not only assured but also, evangelicals believed, just how and when it might happen would become plain through progressive revelation. That had always been so and there was as a result widespread insistence on the foolishness of anticipating

---

66  For ridicule, Sydney Smith, 'Ingram on Methodism', *Edinburgh Review*, 11 (January 1808), 341–62.

67  Anstey, *The Atlantic Slave Trade*, pp. 126, 129–40 and quotation at pp. 173–4; Boyd Hilton, *The Age of Atonement: The Influence of Evangelicalism on Social and Economic Thought, 1785–1865* (Oxford, 1988), pp. 10–17, quotations at p. 13.

68  See in particular J.F.C. Harrison, *The Second Coming: Popular Millenarianism 1780–1850* (London, 1979); for the quotation, p. 207; Perry, 'The ABCFM and the LMS', esp. chaps 2–4.

Providence. Thus William Carey was sternly reprimanded by J.C. Ryland in 1785 or 1786, on the grounds that the times were clearly not right, as being 'a miserable enthusiast' for asking whether all ministers were not obliged to 'teach all nations' at every opportunity.[69] Thomas Scott, an obvious supporter of new missionary activity, advised a similar caution. In his view, 'the patience of waiting' for the Lord to bless the work was 'the most essential requisite for a modern missionary'.[70] However, one man's premature anticipation could be another's correct interpretation of the signs of the times.

Early in 1793, shortly after it began publication, the *Evangelical Review* was in bullish mood. 'That there is a time of peace, prosperity and purity awaiting all the nations of the earth, appears evident from the prophecies and promises in the sacred Scriptures, ... from a serious attention to the *signs of the times*, we may indulge the hope that this grand jubilee is at hand. The present period is a crisis replete with great events.' Armed with a battery of biblical references, the author approvingly quoted Jonathan Edwards's comments on Isaiah 11 and 47. 'It seems evident that the time will come, when there will not be one nation remaining in the world, which shall not embrace the Christian religion.'[71] A little later, Melvill Horne was explaining why, plainly, 'The latter ends of the world are fallen upon us and we have many considerations to excite us ... to more than apostolick labours.' 'In the West, the Roman Antichrist, accursed of God and man, is sinking under the reiterated strokes of divine vengeance. The God of the Christians is baring his arm and exposing the nakedness of the Scarlet Whore ... Yet a little while and we shall hear the cry, *Babylon the Great is fallen.*'[72]

Horne's exposition is characteristic of many in evangelical circles, especially those drawn to the LMS, and more than a few in Anglican society. W.H. Oliver has usefully identified the general hallmarks: 'a resolute if somewhat perfunctory identification of papacy and Antichrist, a system of biblical interpretation based upon allegory, a belief that most supernatural events would come at the end of the millennium, a constant concern with the prophecies on the future of the Jews, a tendency to diminish the difference between the millennium and the present world, a belief that God worked among men through men and institutions and often a lively interest in the role of Great Britain as an agent of providence'. Members and supporters of the new missionary societies set out to engage with Catholics in Ireland and continental Europe. The LMS and the CMS played crucial parts from 1801 in channelling the early work that resulted in formation of the London Society for Promoting Christianity amongst the Jews (1809). 'All three conversions, of heathens, Jews and Catholics were held together in a web of prophetic

---

69  Stanley, *History of the BMS*, pp. 6–7; Smith, *Life of Carey*, pp. 31–2.
70  Scott, *Letters and Papers*, p. 133.
71  'Remarks on the Prophecies and Promise relating to the Glory of the Latter Day', *Evangelical Magazine*, 1 (Oct. 1793), 157–8, 162.
72  Horne, *Letters*, p. 20.

interpretation. All three, in some manner, would accompany the Second Coming and the millennium.'[73]

Although Baptists and Methodists were often more lukewarm towards specifically prophetical enthusiasm and interpretative debates than were members of other denominations, all shared the view that in this providentially guided, divinely driven world it was for 'the modern missionary', through prayer and watchfulness, to discern the means available for the spreading of true religion. In such a world national developments might have their place, empire might provide an arena for providential fireworks, but no necessary priority was to be attached to either. Empire in the form of British rule could never be more than one among many such means, each of varying importance, to be employed or ignored as Providence thought fit. Thus evangelicals also identified exploration, commerce, science, individual Christians, as well as the new missionary societies, among the necessary and efficacious means now available.

Empire, however, was not only one means among many. It was constantly cut down to size and could appear to be of limited potential when set within the far wider global perspective associated with evangelical Christianity. Christ's death was for all people, as were the promises of grace and salvation. The interpretation of prophecy, the dynamic consequences of the millennium and Second Coming, the demonstration of the historical case for and against particular mission strategies, all hinged on the use of examples or evidence gathered worldwide and on a universal outcome.

Such assumptions and characteristics are present not only in the influential founding texts such as those by Horne and Carey but in many others. Thomas Haweis, for example, penned a worldwide review in 1812 in which he began with the prophetical setting, insisting that his readers should consider the signs of the times.[74] 'The events we have lately seen and the appearances in providence and grace, encourage the hope, that the time of the fulfilment of prophecy speedily approaches.' Global evidences were produced in support of this claim. Nevertheless, while it was optimistic in outlook, Haweis's essay was not a triumphalist tract. It expressed something of the newly emergent confidence not so much in empire as in British expansion as a force for good, while also retaining an older awareness of empire's evils. Britain was evidently not alone in the providential scheme even if it 'seems peculiarly destined to be the instrument ... to carry his salvation into the end of the earth'. Reservations too were in order because 'the greatest obstacle to the conversion of the Heathen will be found in the unseemly

73  W.H. Oliver, *Prophets and Millennialists: The Uses of Biblical Prophecy in England from the 1790s to the 1840s* (Auckland, 1978), pp. 84, 90. For the LSPCJ, Martin, *Evangelicals United*, esp. chap. 9; and W.T. Gidney, *The History of the London Society for Promoting Christianity among the Jews, from 1809 to 1908* (London, 1908).

74  Thomas Haweis, *A View of the Present State of Evangelical Religion throughout the World; with a view to promote missionary exertions* (London, 1812).

conduct of those who profess the Christian name'. Moreover, the 'spirit of conquest and the thirst for gain, however inimical in themselves to a kingdom not of this world, have, with extended empire, opened a vast field for Missionary labours; and good hath thus, as is often seen, arisen out of human evil'.[75] Providential means had created the sphere in which missionary efforts could now get under way.

Perhaps these reminders came appropriately from Haweis, whose personal history had included missionary failures and a sense of earlier eighteenth-century limitations. But in looking ahead, he also emphasised for his readers that missionary enterprise was no crudely national or British – to use an anachronistic term – 'imperial project'. As seen above in the CMS's ties with Berlin and Basel, it was an international undertaking and increasingly so. Along with most members of the missionary fraternity, Haweis was well aware that at one of its earliest meetings the Directors of the LMS had sent circular letters not only to ministers and friends in Scotland but also to foreign Protestant churches. These had produced enthusiastic responses. Not only had most of the newly formed missionary associations in Scotland become auxiliaries of the LMS, but 'on the Continent, from places as far apart as Rotterdam and Basle, Frankfurt and Norkopping, letters of sympathy and liberal contributions came promptly to this appeal'. New contacts were made in Holland and Switzerland; an agent for the Society was established in Paris to push on the continental work; and students trained in Berlin and Rotterdam for the Netherlands Missionary Society were taken on by the LMS for work in Java.[76]

In his review, however, Haweis not only anticipated greater European co-operation but went on to link British missionary fortunes with America. The American Board of Commissioners for Foreign Missions, set up in Boston in 1810 as the engine for east coast congregationalism, was already in contact with British societies. Although the British and the Americans 'may never again coalesce into one people', their co-operation was the order of the day. Corruption in America as in Europe notwithstanding, 'America is still a land of real Protestants … the American colonies appear, not only rising into a vast consolidated empire, but reviving in efforts to promote the kingdom of the Lord … and are, I hope, destined with us to spread the everlasting gospel to the ends of the earth, whither their commerce next to our own extends'.[77] The 'international' of activist Protestants, the existence of which is now recognised by growing numbers of historians, was steadily widening its embrace.

Evangelical responses to Britain's changing presence overseas had involved in the 1690s the limited establishment of new agencies to entrench the Christian faith as part of that process. A century later, the evident weaknesses of those early institutions and a broader approach to similar demands stimulated a marked proliferation of

---

75  *Ibid.*, pp. 5, 29–30.
76  Lovett, *History of the LMS*, Vol. 1, pp. 44, 75–7, 94–5, 105.
77  Haweis, *View of the Present State*, pp. 53–4.

missionary societies. The connections between, and the goals of, mission supporters were also extended, this time well beyond the confines of Britain and its existing colonies, even if evangelical rhetoric often outstripped recruits, funds and actual evangelism. The further recasting of missionary endeavours was to take place in the 1860s and 1870s and again at the turn of the nineteenth century. In each period, the reshaping of evangelical enterprise had inescapable consequences for Britain's presence overseas and for extra-European populations. To some of these consequences in the years to 1830 it is now necessary to turn.

## ~ 3 ~

# Missions, governments and empire:
# the terms of engagement, 1800–30

On 18 March 1799, the Eclectic Society turned its attention to a proposal for discussion from John Venn. 'What methods can most effectually be used to promote the Gospel among the heathen?' At the head of Josiah Pratt's notes of the ensuing debate was the basic principle that in all things 'God's providence must be *followed*, not *anticipated*'.[1] The consequence of such a starting point for missions was that it inclined them to follow in the wake of imperial expansion, rather than to strike out on their own. In this shared theological outlook may perhaps lie one justification for attributing to the Clapham Sect and many of its supporters an implicit 'Christian imperialist agenda'.[2] However, concentration on the colonial theatre at once both was a sign of the societies' continuing weakness and, in the missions' early retreat from independence, provided plentiful evidence of the difficulties they faced in implementing plans of their own. Colonialism was by no means necessarily conducive to missionary activity.

Evangelicals had no ultimate intention of confining activity to colonial territory, for, as Venn acknowledged, 'the world is an extensive field'. In most parts of 'Africa and the East' Britain's possessions were no more than toeholds; for all the furore which had accompanied expansion in India there was little reason to regard anything other than Bengal as a 'British bridgehead'. Yet Venn's colleague Thomas Scott early in the century looked forward to seeing CMS missionaries enter China and Japan. William Carey himself had thought originally of going to China.[3] For those calculating with Carey the numbers of unredeemed heathen, to others thinking in millennial or apocalyptic terms, or who preached the universal availability of grace and salvation to a single humankind, the perspective was inescapably global and only in very small part imperial. Nevertheless, although the LMS and the Baptists began their work in India outside the reach of British authority, their preference was otherwise and was soon implemented. The CMS commenced in Sierra Leone and then, after more than a decade, Madras. In the Caribbean Methodists opened up their first stations in Antigua and Jamaica; the BMS not only followed the connection into Jamaica, but were responding to appeals from the black Baptist, loyalist emigrants who settled there after the American War of Independence.[4]

---

1 Pratt (ed.), *Eclectic Notes*, p. 97.
2 Elbourne, 'Foundations of the CMS', p. 250.
3 Hennell, *John Venn*, pp. 245, 248.
4 For the BMS and the Caribbean, Stanley, *History of the BMS*, pp. 68–70.

Such strategic choices are unsurprising. Interpreters of providential design were inclined to view empire as a source of obligation. Possession entailed the duty to Christianise; failure to do so risked incurring divine displeasure and loss of the opportunity for atonement or national redemption. However, they also reflected less a specific preference for those parts of the world due to be coloured red on the map, than the continuing state of comparative ignorance about the world as a whole. They illustrate the relative ease of communication and the frequency of trade with some places rather than others. Decisions were based on the accidents of attention captured or imagination stimulated by chance intrusions on popular awareness, for example, by Pacific or West African explorers. If the LMS parties to Tahiti were somewhat off the beaten tracks, they found their justification not only in the Cook connection but also in the extension of existing commercial links. 'My idea is', Thomas Haweis explained, 'that our society should have a transport ship, chartered to carry convicts to Norfolk Island or Botany Bay and to have a home freight from China on account of the India Company: This on the usual terms. From Norfolk Island to Otaheite [Tahiti], the voyage to China would be very inconsiderably lengthened.'[5]

As even Haweis's passing reference to convict transportation suggests, there was to be no escape for the missions from encounter and engagement with, even dependence on, governments, whether imperial or colonial. At first, however, neither side sensed where events were leading and neither state nor mission societies wanted dealings with each other. The Anglican chaplain in Calcutta, Claudius Buchanan, saw government's initial endowment of a few Indian bishoprics being rapidly displaced by the interest and support for Christian expansion of the local evangelical community. As the responsibility and function of the evangelical community as a whole was reinterpreted in the 1790s, so many of its members thought that the state could be edged aside. Indeed, the new Protestant missionaries thought they were better off without state aid. This had been characteristic of Spanish and Portuguese Catholic missions and the Jesuits, for example, were often seen as having destroyed themselves by such connections. By contrast, in the absence of government ties, Moravian missions seemed to have flourished. Melvill Horne argued forcefully that 'By affecting the favour of the great we degrade our ministry, endanger our own salvation … religion flourished most when she had to contend with the State, and had no other support than what she derived from her own native strength.' By 1830 the impossibility of avoiding entanglement was plain and a competition was in progress to settle the terms of engagement. How the pattern of that engagement was worked out, and its inevitability accepted for the time being, is the subject of this chapter.[6]

---

5  *Evangelical Magazine*, 3 (July 1795), 269.
6  Claudius Buchanan, *Colonial Ecclesiastical Establishment* (London, 1813), pp. 33–9; Horne, *Letters*, quotation at pp. 53, 133 but also pp. 30–1, 34, 51–3.

# I

In the early 1800s, the colony of Sierra Leone consisted of little more than Freetown itself and a few square miles of peninsular land between the sea and the Sierra Leone river. Its population seemed to the Company and its officials impoverished and frequently cantankerous. It was undoubtedly of very mixed origins – poor blacks from Britain, free blacks from Nova Scotia and several hundred Maroon settlers from Jamaica who arrived in 1799. Religiously they belonged to several denominations – Methodists, the Countess of Huntingdon's Connection, Baptists – or to none. Their relations with local African communities were often violent and several missionary initiatives in and around the colony had collapsed ignominiously – the BMS (1795), Methodist (1796) and the LMS and Scottish missions (1797).[7]

The situation was radically changed in 1807 by the abolition of the British slave trade. Freetown was selected as the base where the Royal Naval squadron's captains would liberate those slaves (Liberated Africans or 'recaptives') freed from the slavers along the West Africa coast. Sierra Leone's population began to rise steadily and the social and ethnic diversity of the town greatly increased, well beyond the capacity of the government to provide for its new inhabitants as envisaged by apprenticeship or enlistment. A policy therefore began to take shape of settling the recaptives in a series of villages around the peninsula.

The effective establishment of missionary activity was achieved at the same time. From 1806–12 the CMS missionary, Gustav Nylander, built up a very popular school in Freetown in part as a support to the mission inland and won considerable material support from the government. The Welsh Methodist William Davies arrived in 1815, crossed swords with the Nova Scotian Methodists and, with the freedom of initiative still available in a denomination whose mission society had not yet been formalised, he moved on to work in the Liberated Africans' villages. Initiatives of this kind provided the basis for the direct partnership between colonial government and missions that emerged under governors Maxwell (1811–14) and MacCarthy (1814–24). By 1813 Wesleyan hopes and CMS attempts to advance beyond Freetown, across the river and to the north among the Susu, had proved ineffectual and new outlets were therefore needed. As Pratt, the CMS Secretary, observed, 'The natives appear most unjust and ungrateful. What shall we say of men, who, after they have seen you residing in their country for no end but to confer blessings on them, will allow you to stay only on condition of selling by a larger measure than you used to do and buying by a smaller!' Wesleyan officers felt much the same, reassuring subscribers that, contrary to the position in

---

7  John Peterson, *Province of Freedom: A History of Sierra Leone, 1787–1870* (London, 1969), chap.1; Fyfe, *Sierra Leone*, chaps 4–5; Stiv Jakobsson, *Am I Not a Man and a Brother? British Missions and the Abolition of the Slave Trade and Slavery in West Africa and the West Indies, 1786–1838* (Uppsala, 1972), pp. 82–118.

other colonies, their difficulties in Sierra Leone 'have not arisen from the state of the laws, the persecuting spirit of the inhabitants, or the influence of other denominations'.[8]

Local missionaries were divided over strategy but also well aware of the potentially better openings not just for teaching but for primary evangelisation in Freetown and its immediate neighbourhood. Although there was some fear that schoolmasters paid by government might be lost to the mission,[9] its members were on surprisingly good terms with officials. Governor Maxwell cultivated both the missionaries and the CMS in London by providing land and a schoolmaster's salary, a policy continued by MacCarthy and resulting in the building of the CMS Institution for higher education. MacCarthy had in mind the establishment of a full CMS mission in Freetown, which would play an indispensable role not only in education but in solving the central problem of an orderly administration for the Liberated Africans.[10]

In 1816, Edward Bickersteth visited Freetown on behalf of the CMS Parent Committee and was completely won over to MacCarthy's vision. It is, he wrote, 'very important to mark the indications of a providential leading. Among these I consider the protection of an established government, the facility and safety of intercourse with the people, the economy attending the mission and the number that may be easily gathered together'.[11] The promise of religious influence, funds for a house and chapel in each village, clergy salaries, overall organisation sufficient to embrace the growing numbers and a culturally coherent settlement resting on Christian education won over both Whitehall and the CMS to the new system of parish administration and local government. In 1817 the CMS finally withdrew from its inland mission and the new arrangements were introduced. While the CMS took charge of most of the villages, the Wesleyan Methodists concentrated on the liberated Africans in Freetown itself and a few settlements nearby, such as Congo Town and Soldiers' Town.[12]

A system that seemed to satisfy so many different interests could hardly last for long. Once the lubricant of generous Treasury grants was challenged after MacCarthy's death in 1824 and a parliamentary enquiry instituted, change became inescapable. However, for a time at least Sierra Leone continued to provide a model of mission–government relations that had been unexpected and remained unmatched elsewhere. After such a slow start, the CMS could not allow its first mission to fail and the Methodists had no wish to advertise their internal divisions by withdrawal. No more than in 1801 or 1807 could either the imperial

---

8   J. and J.H. Pratt (eds), *Memoir of the Reverend Josiah Pratt* (London, 1849), pp. 106–10; Pratt to Rev. L. Butscher, 16 May 1815, *ibid.*, pp. 110–11; *Annual Report of the State of the [Wesleyan] Missions, Foreign and Domestic* [for 1813] (London, 1814), p. 14.

9   *Annual Report of the State of the [Wesleyan] Missions* [for 1814] (London, 1815), p. 17.

10   Fyfe, *Sierra Leone*, pp. 127–46; Pratt to Rev. L. Butscher, 21 Nov. 1814, Pratt (eds), *Memoir*, p. 119.

11   Quoted in Peterson, *Province of Freedom*, pp. 74–5.

12   Jakobsson, *Am I Not a Man and a Brother?*, pp. 143–65.

government or the anti-slavery lobby afford to see Sierra Leone founder. Here was a rare opportunity to restore credibility on all sides that an ambitious governor could not miss.

## II

In the three decades after 1770, the attitude of the East India Company, towards missionary work in its territories seems generally to have cooled.[13] Support for those missions the Company had already approved, such as the SPCK Lutherans in Madras, was continued as long as they avoided provoking local inhabitants and provided religious services needed by the British. New ventures, however, were not encouraged and their promoters sensed that permits would not be forthcoming. This divergence between the focus of evangelical enthusiasm on new missionary fields and the drift of East India Company opinion was already evident in the politely negative response to Charles Grant's plans in the 1780s. It was more starkly demonstrated in the 1790s. Parliamentary debate in the summer of 1793 on the renewal of the East India Company's charter revealed some support in both Commons and Lords for Wilberforce's and Grant's proposals to promote Christianity in India. However, once the Company mobilised its backers, hopes of securing approval for a religious establishment and for ministers, schoolmasters and others to be regularly sent out at Company expense 'to promote ... the Interest and Happiness of the inhabitants of the British Dominions in India ... and ... their religious and moral improvement', were overwhelmingly rejected.[14]

Following such a setback and in the setting of further British territorial gains after 1798, there was no escaping the need to engage regularly with the imperial government and its officials if India was to become a serious field for British missionaries. Missions had no alternative but to enter imperial politics, developing the arguments of British self-interest as well as Indians' well-being and cultivating secular political alliances that would add weight to their cause.

In India itself, missionaries who had despaired of permission from East India Company headquarters in Leadenhall Street but trusted to Providence and arrived illegally without licences, often found themselves more welcome than they had expected. This was especially so in the south, where missionaries had long been in evidence.[15] Even dissenters and nonconformists, despite their position outside the establishment, were not ineffective in outflanking the law. William Carey, for example, became the model individual exception to the rules. Good behaviour, mild and deferential manners, his demonstrable utility as a linguist and his worth as a teacher

---

13  This section relies heavily on Carson, 'Soldiers of Christ.

14  Quotation from the first of the two 'pious clauses', resolutions passed by the House of Commons, 14 May 1793, *Journals of the House of Commons* 48, 778; Carson, 'Soldiers of Christ', 33.

15  Carson, 'Soldiers of Christ', chap. 3; 'An Imperial Dilemma: The Propagation of Christianity in Early Colonial India', *JICH* 18, 2 (1990), 169–90.

after 1800 at the government's Fort William College all won him friends. Blind eyes were turned to his missionary operations, even when they were moved into the British sphere. Fort William College was an essentially Anglican institution: headed by the two Anglican chaplains, David Brown and Claudius Buchanan, its statutes required religious tests of its professors. 'Lecturers' and other 'teachers', however, were exempt, thus allowing for Carey's appointment. Carey had no qualms in professing his loyalty to the governor-general: even if he doubted his own linguistic ability, 'I certainly am not disaffected to the state'.[16] However, the tolerance of men such as Sir John Shore and Lord Wellesley[17] avoided the issue of principle; it left anyone so placed open to rationalist critics and pedantic legalism, the prejudices of individual officials, or changes in the climate of opinion. Both LMS and Baptist missionaries at times felt officials discriminated against them at will and there can be little doubt that such arbitrary actions exacerbated the jealousy and envy which often marked the attitudes of missionaries towards each other in Calcutta.[18] Security for themselves, not to mention protection for any converts, could be assured only if the law were changed.

The mutiny among sepoy troops at Vellore, not far from Madras, in July 1806 was precisely the kind of event to make life difficult for missions dependent on no more than goodwill. Some two hundred European troops were killed or wounded and the supposed cause – rumours of a policy of proselytisation, stimulated by new dress regulations introduced by the Commander-in-Chief, Sir John Cradock – produced a powerful, even if ill-founded, backlash against missions, especially in London.[19] There were demands for the recall of all missionaries and an end to the circulation of missionary translations, as the only way of protecting Britain's position in India. In Bengal Sir George Barlow, the acting governor-general, served an expulsion order on two Baptists freshly landed at Calcutta and introduced stiff curbs on religious teaching, preaching and literature distribution. These actions were in many respects eased once the main crisis was over, but, when news reached London, Grant, together with LMS and BMS leaders, had to work hard to ward off the criticism and divert blame for the mutiny from evangelicals.

It has recently been demonstrated clearly how in the years following the Vellore rising British missionaries in India felt themselves seriously beleaguered.[20] Barlow's replacement, the new Governor-General Lord Minto, reimposed tight restrictions on the missions, despite pleas by his chaplains. Although these too were

---

16  Smith, *Life of Carey*, p. 218.
17  Governors-General, 1793–8 and 1798–1805 respectively.
18  See Henry Martyn's journal, Calcutta, 3 Sept. 1806: S. Wilberforce (ed.), *Journals and Letters of the Reverend Henry Martyn*, 2 vols (London, 1837), Vol. 1, p. 491.
19  For Vellore, Carson, 'Soldiers of Christ', pp. 73–90; Davidson, *Evangelicals & Attitudes to India*, pp. 164–81; Burton Stein, *Thomas Munro: The Origins of the Colonial State and His Vision of Empire* (Delhi, 1989), pp. 144–6; Neill, *History of Christianity in India*, pp. 149–51; S.K. Mitra, 'The Vellore Mutiny of 1806 and the Question of Christian Missions to India', *ICHR* 7 (1973), 75–82.
20  Carson, 'Soldiers of Christ', chap. 5.

subsequently relaxed, the British takeover of Serampore in February 1808 finally placed its missionaries unequivocally under East India Company control. Missionary leaders looked for signs of support in the exchanges between London and Calcutta, but there was no mistaking the general determination to prevent any missionary activity thought likely to alarm Indians or which suggested that official policy supported Christianisation. Subject to these general considerations, new missionaries were permitted into India, especially the south, but their places of settlement were firmly controlled. LMS employees were allowed into Vizagapatam and Bellary, but not Seringapatam; BMS personnel were directed to Agra and away from the Punjab frontier. John Chamberlain of the BMS, a perpetual nuisance in official eyes, was ordered by the government back to Calcutta; Pritchett and May of the LMS barely escaped deportation back to Britain; and two other Baptists were actually expelled.[21]

The imperial and Company governments preferred, if possible, control and containment of the missionaries to the more extreme policy of expulsion. In part this reflected the fact that officials, while concerned at the dangers of unregulated missionary activity, were themselves quite frequently committed Christians and were not necessarily averse to compromises over evangelisation. While deportation might smack of intolerance and therefore carry with it the danger of political reper-cussions at home, stricter regulation and enforcement of the licence system held out the possibility of frightening missionaries into careful compliance. On the other hand, many missionaries were not inclined to be overawed by secular authority and there were those who even relished confrontation. Moreover, although there is no evidence of a concerted policy among the home societies, dissenting missionaries were arriving in India with greater frequency and in larger numbers. While some might be challenged or be subsequently penalised for ill conduct, most were likely to become settled. A policy on the part of the societies of careful instructions to departing missionaries and frequently reiterated respect for East India Company controls, was likely to win through.

Anglican policy for promoting missions and Christianity in India, unlike that of the BMS and LMS, was essentially two-pronged. The expansion of activity by the CMS was associated with the further strategy of promoting an Anglican establish-ment there. This was strongly supported not only by Grant, Wilberforce and their friends but by the growing number of evangelical chaplains finding preferment with the East India Company. Of particular importance as an establishment propa-gandist was Claudius Buchanan. Along with Henry Martyn, David Brown, Daniel Corrie and Thomas Thomason, Buchanan was one of Charles Simeon's early protégés and through the Grant connection was appointed first to Barrackpore (1797) and then Calcutta (1799). Playing a key role in the planning of Wellesley's Fort William College, he became vice-provost and professor of Greek and Latin (1800–6). Using his official position, Buchanan played a particularly important part

---

21  *Ibid.*, pp. 106–10.

in publicising the problems of missions in India and in linking their needs and the propagation of Christianity with the role of government.[22]

At this stage, the Anglicans more than any among supporters of missions tended to follow in the footsteps of territorial empire. In one of his most famous sermons, Buchanan, recapitulating evidences for the timeliness of disseminating Christianity, included 'the subjugation of so large a portion of Asia to the British dominion'.[23] Only by means of the imperial tie, it was believed, could the link be preserved between church and state and missionaries avoid the dangers associated with unbridled 'enthusiasm' and itinerancy by being subject to ecclesiastical authority and direction. Not until the 1820s did the practical problems inherent in such episcopal control begin to surface; for the moment, the CMS was anxious to win the bishops' approval rather than argue over the division of official responsibility in the mission field.

Buchanan raised the issue of a religious establishment in the specific setting of Wellesley's recent victories over Mysore and the Maratha states. These events more than ever called for an expression of those 'national sentiments of humanity and Christian duty' towards both Europeans and native Indians, which would have been naturally excited had they occurred nearer home. 'The perpetuity of the Christian faith amongst Europeans in India and the civilization of the natives, must rest equally on a foundation which, as yet, we have not; and that is, an Ecclesiastical Establishment.'[24] It was a forceful appeal, sharing elements of Bishop Porteus's older thinking while at the same time looking resolutely ahead. Whereas Porteus confronted with Cornwallis in the 1780s met little interest, Buchanan believed that civil government under Wellesley was opening up the possibility of helpful reforms. Buchanan's contacts with the Baptists and his hopes for the CMS raised the prospect of further missionary expansion. To the younger man, lacking Porteus's inhibiting experience and seeing state and missions on the move, their alliance with the church looked perfectly possible. The point had often been made in the past that empire by itself carried with it the danger of evil and corruption for its rulers, but for Buchanan, unlike many, the answer to this problem did not lie in the rejection of empire. Instead, tying together church, state and missions he argued would embody a sufficient 'religious precaution' to prevent the possibility of decay.[25]

Buchanan's sense of the importance of history was strong. Central to the knowledge indispensable to missionaries, he told the CMS at its tenth anniversary, was 'an accurate knowledge of the BIBLE and a general knowledge of the

---

22 Davidson, *Evangelicals & Attitudes to India*, provides by far the fullest treatment of Buchanan's career.

23 'The Star in the East', delivered at Bristol, 26 Feb. 1809, reprinted in Claudius Buchanan, *Eight Sermons* (new ed, London, 1812), pp. 46–7.

24 Buchanan, *Memoir of the Expediency of an Ecclesiastical Establishment for British India* (London, 1805), pp. xii–xiii.

25 *Ibid.*, p. 15.

HISTORY of the world'. 'The History of the World illustrates the Word of God; and the Book of Providence, when devoutly studied, becomes a commentary on the Book of Revelation. But if the preacher be ignorant of the great events of the world, "the word of prophecy" is in a manner lost in his ministry; particularly in relation to the revolutions in Eastern nations.'[26] His own historical sense, however, was selective if not defective. At this stage it did not include, for example, the cautionary lessons that might have come from the SPG's experience.[27] Consequently, for a time he was optimistically expectant. 'Let us first establish our own religion amongst ourselves and our Asiatic subjects will soon benefit by it. When once our national church shall have been confirmed in India, the members of that church will be the best qualified to advise the state as to the means by which, from time to time, the civilization of the natives may be promoted.'[28] Buchanan had no great fear of engaging with government; from his standpoint, the involvement of church, episcopacy and established missions in politics was only natural.

Confidence, however, could easily be shaken. When the mutiny broke out at Vellore, Buchanan was on tour not far away and ridiculed throughout the idea that missions bore any responsibility for the crisis.[29] He was especially infuriated when, as part of the restraints immediately imposed on missionaries, the advertisement and printing of his own sermons on Christian prophecy were subjected to a ban.[30] In November 1807, in one of the early salvoes in the pamphlet war waged over missions in India until 1810, he launched a vigorous attack on the Company's government. From then on he returned constantly to his theme of establishment as offering a vital support to the propagation of Christianity, but he also continued as an outspoken defender of missions against what he saw as government interference. Returning home to Britain in 1808 just as the polemical exchanges there were reaching their height, he was most concerned to prevent what he saw as the main issues from being lost to sight. Made newly aware of the missions' lack of staunch friends, Buchanan's emphasis shifted away from the possibility that ecclesiastical interests might call the tune to make more of the argument that religion needed the protection that establishment could provide. He continued to develop the case for establishment in his sermons and, in his efforts to persuade the East India Company, the Board of Control and the Anglican hierarchy, continued to draw out fresh temporal advantages. He claimed that a 'Protestant Establishment is wanted in our Empire in the East, not only to do honour to Christianity ... but to counteract the influence of the ecclesiastical power of ROME: for in some provinces of Asia, that power is too strong for the religion of Protestants and for the unprotected and defenceless missionaries'. Mindful perhaps of Jesuit experiences in China, he also claimed that a Protestant establishment on the spot would afford

---

26  'A Sermon', 12 June 1810, Buchanan, *Eight Sermons*, pp. 199–200.
27  See Chapter 1 above.
28  Buchanan, *Memoir of the Expediency*, p. 20.
29  Davidson, *Evangelicals & Attitudes to India*, pp. 165–6.
30  *Ibid.*, pp. 168–9.

guarantees against the corruption of Christianity by its being blended with local rites.[31]

Buchanan's experience in the aftermath of Vellore did not dim his optimism, for the reason that it rested – as he frequently explained – on the twin foundations of Providence and Prophecy. History – the direction of its main currents and the guide to his own sense of historical significance – was sacred history. Preaching for the benefit of the CMS in Bristol in February 1809, shortly after his return, he argued that there was proof aplenty to show that the time had arrived for diffusing Britain's religion in the East. It was not simply that the needs of Indians were obvious. Also in its favour there were 'the general contemplation of the prophecies … the commotion in the bands of infidelity against it … the revolution of nations and "the signs of the times"'. Among the latter were 'the state of the Jews in the East, confirming the truth of ancient prophecy' and the contemporary moves to convert them.[32]

Although some evangelical Anglicans, such as Lord Teignmouth (formerly Sir John Shore),[33] found Buchanan needlessly strident, he contributed hugely to keeping the issue of missionary freedoms in the public eye. Methodists and dissenters also welcomed this impetus given to the missionary cause, even while seeing in Buchanan and his fellow chaplains untrustworthy allies – at one moment supporters, at another rivals, determined to cut back dissenters' influence through checks on their mobility or controls over translations of the scriptures.[34] The common objective for evangelicals in general, however, was toleration of their activities and the freedom to promote the expansion of Christianity where, as and when they saw fit. Everywhere this overrode evangelical objections to involvement in politics and the lobbying of governments. For non-Anglicans recent experience pointed to the need to institutionalise their religious freedoms and rights in a manner that would leave them as untrammelled as possible, not only by Anglicans but also secular interests strongly represented on such bodies as the East India Company. For Anglicans, the goal of establishment itself was looked to for the defence of their liberties, perhaps also as a practical aid to their ascendancy in the face of expansion by denominational rivals and a guard against obstruction from secular quarters. The nature and status of missionary enterprise thus inevitably became linked to debates over the renewal of the Company's charter in 1813.

William Wilberforce, his allies and the missionary societies began in 1812 to prepare the ground for the forthcoming parliamentary battle by organising pamphlets, articles, discussions in the East India Committee of the SPCK and deputations to the

31  'The Three Eras of Light', preached before the University of Cambridge, 1 July 1810, Buchanan, *Eight Sermons*, pp. 275–7.
32  'The Star in the East', *ibid.*, pp. 28, 40, 42; and 'The Three Eras of Light', *ibid.*, p. 278.
33  First Baron, formerly Sir John Shore, East India Company servant 1768–89, Governor-General 1793–98, member Board of Control 1807–28, President of BFBS 1804–34, Vice-President of CMS, *DEB*, *Vol. 2*, pp. 1010–11.
34  Davidson, *Evangelicals & Attitudes to India*, pp. 155–6.

Prime Minister, Lord Liverpool. This process and the ensuing debates have been the subject of detailed recent examination.[35] The parliamentary battle began on 22 March 1813, with the introduction of the government's proposals by the Foreign Secretary, Viscount Castlereagh. It ended in July with the relaxation of the Company's monopoly on British trade with India, the acceptance of a 'pious clause' and the commitment of the Company to support from its own local revenues a bishopric and three archdeaconries to superintend the British settlements.

The 'pious' clause in the final Act began as follows: 'And whereas it is the Duty of the Country to promote the Interests and the Happiness of the Native Inhabitants on the British Dominions in India and such Measures ought to be adopted as may tend to the introduction among them of useful knowledge and of religious and moral improvement, and in furtherance of the above objects, sufficient facilities ought to be afforded by Law to persons desirous of going to and remaining in India, for the purpose of accomplishing those benevolent designs so long as the authority of the Local Governments respecting the Intercourse of Europeans with the interior of the Country be preserved, and the Principles of the British Government, on which the Natives of India have hitherto relied for the free exercise of their religion be inviolably maintained.'[36] It then proceeded to details. Its inclusion marked an advance not only over the House of Commons resolutions and the evangelicals' parliamentary defeat of twenty years earlier but also over Castlereagh's original proposals in March. These had included no such clause. That the change occurred was the consequence of astute parliamentary manoeuvring by Wilberforce and his friends and an extensive petitioning campaign pushed ahead in the country especially by the BMS and LMS. There was also a measure of restraint on all sides: by the ministry, aware that it could compromise with opinion at home while retaining the controls thought essential to political stability in India; by the Church of England, content with the extension of its influence and potential controls over missionaries through the concession of a bishopric; and by dissenters' leaders who, while they accepted that wholly unrestricted missionary access was unobtainable, were pleased with the clear statement of principle in the Act and were at least relieved that appeals against Company decisions were now allowed.[37]

The outcome was, nevertheless, a limited victory for missionary interests. Missionaries had no greater freedom than before to go to India, and the Company retained fundamentally unchanged the power to determine whether missionaries had behaved in such a way as to forfeit its protection. The 'pious' clause simply gave formal definition to current practice, modified only by the necessity of responding with a plausible case to any appeal against restriction and deportation by the Company. In this way missionaries, who were still not specifically mentioned in the revised charter, were placed on an equal footing with all other Europeans. As

---

35  Carson, 'Soldiers of Christ', chaps 6–7; Davidson, *Evangelicals & Attitudes to India*, chaps 13–14.
36  53 Geo.3.c.155, Section 33.
37  Carson,'Soldiers of Christ', pp. 140–5.

William Carey concluded, writing home in 1814, 'our going into the interior depends as much upon the rule of Government as before'.[38] The future of missionaries in India was to remain as much as ever a matter contested between missions and governments, with the outcomes hardly less variable or less subject to individual views and prejudices than they had been before 1813. In 1828, the LMS Directors still felt it necessary to reassure the imperial authorities of their value. They impressed on their missionaries 'the duty and the policy … of manifesting in their own conduct and promoting also in others a sincere and affectionate respect to the Government and to the authorities which it appoints'. Contrary to the views of those on the spot, Directors considered 'this admonition … so essential and indispensable', so important to their own credibility, that violation of it would provide grounds for instant dismissal.[39]

For Anglicans the outlook was perhaps brighter. In his 'Prospectus of an Ecclesiastical Establishment for India', written at the reformers' request early in 1812, Buchanan had called for an extensive system including numerous chaplains, schoolmasters, plans for an Indian ministry and a church building programme, the whole to provide for both Indians and Europeans and to be overseen by four bishops. His proposals, ambitious but soberly presented, were taken up by the Clapham Sect. They became the basis of discussions both within the East India Committee of the SPCK and between the SPCK, the Archbishop of Canterbury and other high churchmen. With Archbishop Sutton's backing and his promise of political support, they were widely distributed. The new establishment approved by the Act did not match this grand design. However, the consecration of T.F. Middleton as Bishop of Calcutta and his arrival with his three archdeacons in November 1814, identified the state with the missionary enterprise much more directly than before and promised both to strengthen and control the work of the CMS whose first missionaries had arrived in Madras shortly before.[40]

## III

In the eyes of missionary organisers and volunteers the Cape of Good Hope had a compelling, even romantic, significance.[41] In the general view it had long been

---

38 Carey to Andrew Fuller (BMS Secretary), 4 Aug. 1814, in Carson, 'Soldiers of Christ', p. 188.

39 Laurence Kitzan, 'The London Missionary Society and the Problem of Authority in India, 1798–1833', *Church History* 40 (1971), 457–73, esp. 468–9.

40 Neill, *History of Christianity in India*, pp. 261–6; *CMS Register*, List I, entries 16, 17, for J.C. Schnarre and C.T.E. Rhenius.

41 It has also been subject to much attention from historians, including Richard Elphick and Hermann Giliomee (eds. and comps), *The Shaping of South African Society 1652–c.1840* (Cape Town and Middletown, CT, 1989); Timothy Keegan, *Colonial South Africa and the Origins of the Racial Order* (London, 1996); Elphick and Davenport (eds), *Christianity in South Africa*; Henry Bredekamp and Robert Ross (eds), *Missions and Christianity in South African History* (Johannesburg, 1995); Elbourne, *Blood Ground*.

recognised as the most important of the stations on Europeans' great commercial route to the East. Carey's depiction of missionary enterprise on the model of trading companies was readily linked to the examples of the half-dozen East India companies, especially the English, French and Dutch.[42] The East Indiamen, echoing the prophet Isaiah's 'ships of Tarshish' which had so impressed Carey with the assistance commerce might lend to missionary enterprise,[43] were an obvious first link in the process of Christian expansion. For missionaries in the 1790s the Cape was an obvious base for extending their work into Africa; it was already the starting point on the 'road to the north', so significant in the later history of the Cape's own territorial and economic expansion. Captured by Britain in 1795, but returned to the Batavian Republic in 1802, it again came under British control, permanently as it turned out, in 1806. Nevertheless, it was not necessarily the displacement of Dutch authority with British potential that appealed to evangelical onlookers, so much as the Cape's symbolic importance. Henry Martyn, visiting the Baptists at Serampore in 1803, noted that an 'idea thrown out by [Carey] pleased me very much, not on account of its practicability but its grandeur, i.e. that there should be an annual meeting at the Cape of Good Hope, of all the missionaries in the world'.[44]

There was, however, little grandeur surrounding the first arrival of British missionaries at the Cape, a small party of four from the LMS in March 1799 led by Dr Johannes Theodorus Van der Kemp. Van der Kemp had been attracted to the Society in 1797 through Moravian connections in Zeist (Holland) and had helped the LMS establish a sister society in the shape of the Netherlands Missionary Society, based in Rotterdam.[45] He and his colleagues had taken advantage of free passages on the convict transport, the *Hillsborough*, heading for Botany Bay and disembarked with some relief after four months of near mutiny, disease and death in the wretched conditions of the ship's holds.

In its small way the voyage demonstrated the impossibility for missionaries of escaping the embrace of government, whatever illusions they might entertain as to the likelihood or desirability of independence. Enthusiastic haste to be up and doing, the perceived need for economy with their funds, the expectation that they could take advantage of a government offer or facilities (however apparently 'providential') without risk of compromise or obligation, were to be perennially recurrent features of missionary thinking and much travelled pathways to 'political' involvement with empire.

This lesson was reinforced as the new arrivals considered where best to settle themselves. Exhortations to support the new missionaries, brought to Christians at

---

42  Carey, *An Enquiry*, p. 83.

43  *Ibid.*, p. 68.

44  Wilberforce (ed.), *Journals and Letters of Henry Martyn*, p. 466.

45  Ido H. Enklaar, *Life and Work of Dr. J.Th. Van Der Kemp, 1747–1811: Missionary Pioneer and Protagonist of Racial Equality in South Africa* (Cape Town and Rotterdam, 1988), pp. 44–58. Enklaar also provides the fullest treatment of Van der Kemp's varied and colourful earlier life.

the Cape by Van der Kemp from the LMS Directors, were rapidly taken up. In April 1799 the South African Society for Promoting the Extension of Christ's Kingdom was founded. In its constitution, however, far from urging avoidance of politics in the manner of the dissenting traditions of the LMS, the Society aligned itself with the conservatism of the Dutch Reformed Church and its many well-to-do members. It insisted on 'the general duty of every Christian, to render all submission and reverence to the temporal Power, for the Lord's sake and carefully to refrain from anything which may be repugnant to the rules that have been promulgated in things civil and ecclesiastical'.[46] This was to repeat the stance taken up by the Moravian missions, for whom it was already clear that Genadendal, since its resettlement a few years before and notwithstanding its political quietism, was continuing its existence only on sufferance of the local white population. As a later historian of Christian missions in South Africa was to note, in consequence of this commitment, 'the Society was considerably hampered in its work'.[47]

To be hampered or constrained in this way was far from the LMS party's intention, but it was soon evident that freedom from controls was likely only while the mission's activities fell into line or at least avoided conflict with official preferences. Promises of aid and protection from the Governor, Francis Dundas, could not but come with strings attached. In the north, however, for the moment few problems seemed to present themselves. Reinforced in September 1800 with more recruits both locally and from London and Rotterdam and after a brief, abortive mission by these horrified novices to the San people, some half-a-dozen missionaries were subsequently scattered in three stations well beyond the administrative reach of Cape Town and local *landdrosts* (magistrates).[48] Poor, isolated and vulnerable, they were of little concern to either colonial or indigenous authorities. More serious in their own way were problems internal to the mission, personal conflicts and the tendency to be diverted into trading – notable particularly in the Tswana mission on the Kuruman river – about which the LMS Directors and its local sympathisers could do little.

Van der Kemp, determined on a mission to the Xhosa, was altogether another matter. He slowly made his way from Cape Town in May 1799 via Graaff Reinet, the Great Fish and the Kat rivers, to Ngqika's kraal at Tyumie. He was reluctantly permitted to select a site some distance away across the Keiskamma and throughout 1800 he moved between there and Ngqika's. As a result of the third Frontier War (1799–1803), however, local conditions were very violent and disturbed and official hopes on both sides that he might prove a useful diplomatic intermediary came to little. Finally, in December 1800, Van der Kemp therefore agreed to Dundas's and his successor's (Sir George Yonge's) repeated requests to return to Graaff Reinet.[49]

46  J. Du Plessis, *A History of Christian Missions in South Africa* (London, 1911), p. 93.
47  *Ibid.*, 93 and 94–8 for its early years.
48  These were at the Kuruman River, the Zak River and Rietfontein.
49  Enklaar, *Life and Work*, pp. 86–109.

Van der Kemp's unsupervised activities in the frontier war zone, his dealings with colonial outlaws such as Coenraad de Buys and his personal security were of sufficient concern for the British Governors to wish to place him where he might be more conveniently controlled. This became more urgent still, as Van der Kemp's evangelising among the Khoi refugees at Graaff Reinet and their use with the local magistrates' agreement of the church buildings, provoked serious upheavals in the form of Afrikaner rebellion and violence against both the missionary and his congregation.[50] His relations with the South African Missionary Society also began to deteriorate as the Society unilaterally took the placement of missionaries into its own hands.

To restore public order in Graaff Reinet and ease the immediate tensions over the position of the Khoi, the Cape government offered Van der Kemp land and assistance in removing himself and his people to a new settlement at Algoa Bay. With some support from the *landdrosts*, Bresler and Maynier, at Graaff Reinet, Van der Kemp was uncompromising in his criticisms of the local farmers and other white settlers. The 'unchristian and inhuman dislike which the boers bear to the poor oppressed heathen being taught the Gospel and the cruelties inflicted upon these unfortunate beings, are evidently amongst the causes of God's chastisement on this country ... there is no other way of saving this country, than by the government doing justice to the natives. In no other way can the boers escape the hand of Providence than by acknowledging their guilt'.[51] Nevertheless he saw the value of the offer and its significance as a base for expansion in the eastern Cape. In March 1802 he therefore took possession first of one then finally a second, more secure farm that was to become the LMS's main station at Bethelsdorp. The object of Van der Kemp and his closest colleague James Read was that 'the Hottentots [Khoi] should be perfectly free, upon an equal footing in every respect with the Colonists and by no sort of compulsion brought under a necessity to enter into their service'.[52]

Notwithstanding Van der Kemp's brave plans, Bethelsdorp was seen to languish by both British and Batavian governments. Early visitors were appalled by the condition of the settlement. Van der Kemp's persistent affronts to local conventions by his personal lifestyle, the apparent ignorance and indolence of the Khoi, the dearth of religion and their unwillingness to labour even on their own behalf became staples in a critical litany of failings. Relationships with the Batavian authorities deteriorated to the extent that Van der Kemp and Read were summoned to Cape Town and detained by the Governor. The establishment of further mission stations within the colony was prohibited and frontiers redefined in order to force missionaries still further away into the interior.[53]

---

50  Elphick and Davenport, *Christianity in South Africa*, pp. 35–6; Elphick and Giliomee, *Shaping of South African Society*, pp. 344–7.
51  12 Nov. 1801, Enklaar, *Life and Work*, p. 122.
52  Elphick and Giliomee, *Shaping of South African Society*, p. 380.
53  Keegan, *Colonial South Africa*, p. 85; Du Plessis, *Christian Missions*, p. 113.

The restoration of British imperial control in 1806 saw little change. To those, like Henry Martyn, who relied on the LMS's written accounts, Bethelsdorp was a striking achievement. However, even after Bethelsdorp was well established, potentially sympathetic visitors still expressed serious reservations as to the conduct of missions on these lines. 'We had been willing to believe', wrote the Moravian Christian La Trobe, 'that the very unfavourable accounts, given by travellers of Bethelsdorp, were greatly exaggerated, if not altogether false and that it was not to be credited, that a Society, possessed of such ample means, would suffer any of their settlements to remain in so disgraceful a state, as to be always brought forward against them, as a proof of the unprofitableness of their missionary exertions in this country. But I am sorry to say, that as to its external situation, nothing can be more miserable and discouraging.' Inevitably, he felt, despite a warm welcome from the missionaries, this was reflected in the character of the inhabitants.[54]

Bethelsdorp conformed to neither the Moravian model of a politically well ordered and paternalistic mission station nor to the local ideal of pliant centres of reliable labour. Van der Kemp's evangelism was linked closely with his determination to establish bulwarks for the Khoi against loss of land and property, compulsory labour on public works, the abuse of labour contracts creating conditions akin to slavery, and discrimination in the courts. James Read, nominally superintendent of the LMS stations after Van der Kemp's death in 1811, continued this approach. Like Van der Kemp he too reinforced his ties by marrying into the local community and, accentuating the Khoi's independence, again posed a challenge to the local racial order.

Other LMS missionaries, perhaps less independently minded than Van der Kemp, were more inclined to work within the system, either for politic reasons or out of deference to their instructions from the Society. William Anderson, at Klaarwater (Griquatown) on the northern frontier, found his influence with the local Bastaard (Griqua) leaders growing as a result of missionary marriages, colonial contacts and the development of a church. However, while attempting to nurture their independence, he also found himself under tightening controls and growing pressure from Cape Town to act, against both his Instructions and personal inclination, as an agent for the colonial government.[55] In the manner of British officials in India, governors from Janssens (1803–5) on had insisted on their authority to license missionaries and to dictate their teaching, breaches of their instructions being threatened with the withdrawal of licences or other sanctions. However, even if government recognition conferred a certain status that could be turned to evangelistic advantage, there were limits to this possibility. From 1814 onwards, Anderson faced demands for him to take on responsibilities related to the defence and stabilisation of the frontier and meet colonial requirements for military

---

54  Wilberforce (ed.), *Journals and Letters of Henry Martyn*, p. 59; C.I. Latrobe, *Journal of a Visit to South Africa in 1815 and 1816* (London, 1818), pp. 206–9.
55  Elphick and Giliomee, *Shaping of South African Society*, pp. 264–5, 268–9, 270–4.

recruits. The result in this case was a loss of favour with both Griquatown and Cape Town. Griquas resented attempts to limit their independence from the colony, which agreements approved by the missionaries in 1809 and 1813 had seemed to confirm, and Cape Town was critical of Anderson's failure either to deliver what the government wanted or to prevent violent Griqua protest.

There followed the dispersal of part of the Griqua people. Anderson remarked on a fall-off in support for the church and the government turned on the mission. Some mission centres run by Khoi evangelists were closed. Governor Somerset then refused to allow a new party of missionaries to settle outside the colony, thus raising the whole issue of the freedom to appoint and dismiss them. Subsequently, after extending the new magistracy of Beaufort West to include the Griquatown mission, Somerset pressed for its break-up and resettlement elsewhere within the colony. In 1820, facing official threats of closure, Anderson gave up and left in despair, convinced that there was no way forward other than colonial expansion and a British takeover of the territory.[56]

The examples of Van der Kemp, Read and Anderson illustrate the rapidity with which missions were drawn inexorably into colonial politics, whether they willed it or not. They also demonstrate more generally the various conflicts of interest arising from the missionary presence in settler societies. These occurred between missionaries and white colonists; between missions and local governments, the latter often but not necessarily in sympathy with colonial citizens; and between missions and indigenous peoples, suspicious of missions' partiality or disappointed by their limited capacity to influence colonial authorities. In the early nineteenth century, the mission directors at home naturally expected their employees to resolve such problems locally. Not only did missionaries frequently not have the time, resources and contacts or influence enough to win through. They were often driven to conclude that they were confronted not merely by individual wickedness but by the evil workings of a system that required means far more powerful than they possessed to bring it down. In such circumstances, with local solutions unobtainable, they turned to the imperial government itself and to political forces in the metropole.

The career of Dr John Philip, appointed director of the LMS's South African operations in 1817, demonstrates more than any other the process by which the arena for missions' engagement in politics ultimately came to be enlarged.[57] The example is the more telling for Philip, arriving at the Cape in February 1819 with his fellow commissioner John Campbell to inspect and reorder the LMS settlements, was both under instruction and predisposed to restore good relations

56  *Ibid.*, pp. 272–3.
57  Andrew Ross, *John Philip (1775–1851)*; Elbourne, *Blood Ground*; Keegan, *Colonial South Africa*; W.M. Macmillan, *The Cape Colour Question: A Historical Survey* (London, 1927); *Bantu, Boer and Briton: The Making of the South African Native Problem*, 2nd rev. and enlarged edn., (Oxford, 1963).

between the missionaries and Somerset's government. Indeed Philip's appointment illustrates how the non-episcopal mission societies were also drawn towards government because they shared a common interest in controlling individual missionaries, many of whom thought they should have a free rein. Debate as to how this control might be secured was often vigorous. Before Philip reached Cape Town South Africa's missionaries were sorely divided between those who welcomed the idea of a superintendent and those who did not. Charles Pacalt observed vehemently that 'To put all the missionaries under one is to remove the Pope from Rome to Bethelsdorp.'[58] The Directors at home thought otherwise. So too did the imperial government, on behalf of whom Lord Bathurst told a LMS deputation to the Colonial Department that he highly approved of a 'Resident Director with whom Governors could correspond as [a] proper representative of the Society'.[59]

John Philip was at first impressed by Somerset and his officials and, based in Cape Town, accepted many of the conventional criticisms made of men such as Read and Van der Kemp. Philip not only supplied the government with a copy of his report but also obtained the restoration of missionaries' freedom of movement. Robert Moffat of the 1817 party was at last permitted to travel to Kuruman (Lattakoo). But good relations did not last. Somerset himself, temperamental and self-important, swung completely against Philip after differences over the government's treatment of complaints by the '1820 settlers' in the eastern Cape. At the same time, Philip came to understand far more clearly the embattled position of the Khoi, as well as to share Read's sympathy for their plight and his view of the role of Bethelsdorp in their defence.[60] When, in response to the serious problems besetting the settlers in the Eastern Cape, the imperial government set up the Commission of Eastern Enquiry into the colony's affairs, Philip intervened through friends in London to have the Khoi covered in its terms of reference and on its arrival in Cape Town carefully cultivated some of its members. He was convinced that progress would be achieved only by calling external political forces into play and influencing imperial policy.

This was not the first time LMS missionaries, blocked at the level of colonial government, had played the imperial card. Van der Kemp's appeal to London for assistance in securing justice for the Khoi in the Cape courts had contributed to the establishment of the circuit courts in 1811 and the – to local farmers – notorious 'Black Circuit' of 1812. This compelled many employers for the first time to answer cases brought against them by the Khoi with missionary assistance.

Philip, however, went further. Long delays in the Commission's report prompted him to go to London in 1826 to press the issue, somewhat to the disquiet of the other LMS Directors who were still anxious for the Society's reputation at home. Too many demands for action risked appearing importunate and threatened

---

58 Report of Cape Town Meeting, 12 Aug. 1817, MSS Afr.s.216/1/26–7.

59 2 Dec. 1818, MSS.Afr.s.216/1/46.

60 Ross, *John Philip*, chap. 4.

political complications, so Philip was at first left alone to promote the Khoi cause and the need for reform of the colonial government with the help of T.F. Buxton, members of the Clapham Sect and the Anti-Slavery Society. The wealth of information he was able to provide and the elaboration of his arguments in his book, *Researches in South Africa*, as the LMS Directors steeled themselves to intervene, helped to win sufficient public and parliamentary backing for the Tory government to accept a Commons resolution in July 1828 requiring colonial legislation. Given the deep-rooted imperial reservations about compulsion in matters of colonial legislation, this was no slight achievement.[61]

Legislation, already in progress at the Cape and designed to meet the growing agitation, almost immediately arrived in London in the shape of Ordinance 50 (1828), which asserted the principle of equality before the law for the Khoi and ended both the offence of 'vagrancy' and compulsory labour. It is interesting that even at such a moment, when the LMS's encounter with the state and dependence on the imperial government was fully exposed, Philip emphasised how he was not asking for direct imperial support. Rather, 'in asking protection for the people, from colonial rapacity and cruelty, we ask all the efficient aid which government can afford us in the prosecution of our labours. Government may support an ecclesiastical establishment ... but a missionary society ... is an apparatus, which human government can neither fabricate nor conduct with success.'[62]

Philip's campaign had enough momentum and his advocacy requisite persuasiveness to secure the permanence of Ordinance 50 by its adoption as an imperial Order-in-Council in January 1829. This further step was of far more than merely formal significance. Cape landowners were worried by their growing inability to control local African labour as firmly as they had once done. After the imperial Act of 1833 they also faced the full emancipation of their slaves no later than 1838. The colonists therefore persuaded the colonial government to attempt to recoup the position by passing a new Vagrancy Ordinance in 1834, with the purpose of compelling liberated slaves, apprentices and others to take work with white employers, regardless of the conditions and wages offered. Philip's precaution of 1829 not only obliged Governor D'Urban to refer the new Ordinance to London for approval in the knowledge that it conflicted with the imperial legislation but eased the process of its unqualified disallowance by the imperial government.

Shortly before this episode, reflecting on recent events, John Philip summed up the reasons for his necessary involvement with the imperial government in pursuit of missionary goals. 'It is a curious fact that the perspicacity of Dr Van der Kemp's mind never penetrated the veil which connected the system of oppression, under which the colonial population suffered and which ultimately broke his heart and killed him. He conceived that the evil was partial, that it belonged to the character

---

61  The erosion of the imperial government's reluctance to intervene is charted in D.J. Murray, *The West Indies and the Development of Colonial Government 1801–34* (Oxford, 1965).

62  Dr John Philip, *Researches in South Africa Illustrating the Civil, Moral and Religious Condition of Native Tribes*, 2 vols (London, 1828), Vol. 1, p. xxvii.

of certain men with whom he came in contact and never discovered that the men he had to contend against were acting under a system, on which the whole principle of the colonial government was conducted. His mistake is to be traced to his remoteness from the seat of government.'[63] Even as early as 1821–22 Philip had little doubt that 'If you are to give extension and permanency to your missions, Cape Town must be pressed into the service of Missions.'[64] This powerful sense of the need to be in Cape Town or in direct touch with London was never to leave him, much though it disquieted other missionaries who felt that it inevitably and seriously diverted him from their primary task of evangelisation. Taking up the protective thread of Van der Kemp's and Read's work inevitably gave him further grounds to favour the anti-slavery cause. Philip saw here the answer to those who criticised him as overly 'political'. He had become convinced that ending all forms of slavery for the inhabitants of the Cape would achieve more for Christianity than anything else, simply because missionary activities in present circumstances were confined to their institutions and these were the only places where the Khoi had 'a shadow of protection'.[65] Before long the same conviction was to bring him again to London to give evidence before the Aborigines' Committee of 1835–7 and it engaged his energies on behalf of Khoi and Xhosa until his death in 1851.[66] It established a tradition of active and critical missionary engagement with South African governments and imperial policy-makers which was still alive in the 1880s and 1890s in the work of John Mackenzie of the LMS and the Methodists working with the Tswana.

For all missions, effective evangelisation was compatible with certain types of society and incompatible with others. White settler societies, more often than not, were among those seen as inimical to evangelisation and so stimulated a libertarian if not humanitarian response on the part of some missionaries, requiring the interposition of imperial political controls. The politics of white settler societies with their dynamic demand for political liberty and devolution awoke in sections of the missionary fraternity a quite contrary movement in favour of centralised imperial intervention and control. Appeals to the power of the imperial state for missionaries such as Philip was the necessary last resort of men anxious to win the competition with white settlers for control of the future of indigenous peoples such as the Khoi.

## IV

The controversies over missions' relationship to the imperial and colonial governments in India and in South Africa had implications for other colonies. In October 1812, Josiah Pratt, the CMS Secretary, persuaded Claudius Buchanan as his final

63 Philip to Rufus Anderson, 13 Dec. 1833, ABC 14/1/69.
64 Philip to W.A. Hankey (LMS Secretary), n.d., MSS.Afr.s.216/1/143.
65 Philip, *Researches in South Africa*, Vol. 1, p. xxx.
66 *DEB*, Vol. 2, pp. 880–1; see below, Chapter 6, pp. 139–40, 148–9.

contribution to the forthcoming charter campaign to sketch out in full his thoughts about ecclesiastical establishment. Buchanan agreed, notwithstanding his recent stroke, and by mid–March 1813 his book of more than two hundred pages was circulating rapidly.[67] Although there was plenty of familiar material, on this occasion, as the full title makes clear, Buchanan did not confine his attention to India but instead widened his outlook. Discussing in general terms how, as it now seemed, 'The Responsibility of extending Christianity has devolved on Great Britain', Buchanan defined the 'rational and legitimate' means of evangelisation as sending out missionaries, translating and publishing the Scriptures and 'To extend the Native Church'.[68] Britain's performance in the last, he suggested, was a notable failure, amounting to no more than bishoprics in Nova Scotia and Quebec and two bishops consecrated for the American states. This amounted to a serious dereliction of duty. Buchanan then proceeded to echo arguments developed many times before in pre-revolutionary representations to the SPG. 'Episcopal superintendence is required in remote regions, in order to ordain natives on the spot; to dispense the ordinance of Confirmation; to direct the labours of the Missionaries; to form and regulate the growing church; and to preserve the unity of religion, as much as may be, within our own dominions.' Finding such neglect both inexplicable and indefensible, he floated the idea of a 'General Colonial Ecclesiastical Establishment', to be supported for a brief initial period by the three Anglican societies, the SPG, SPCK and CMS, before it became self-supporting. 'The greatest blessing, certainly, which the nation could impart to her children throughout the world, would be, to give them a simple Ecclesiastical Establishment, with full toleration to all who dissent from it. While such a constitution would be replete with advantage to ourselves, it would give to the religion of the denominations differing from us, a degree of order and stability, which at present they do not possess.'[69]

In few places was this more necessary, Buchanan felt, than in the West Indies where, like the East, missionaries 'are at this moment in a state which may be called one of persecution'.[70] Doubtless Buchanan's own brush with the authorities led him to exaggerate the predicament of missions in British India, but he might justifiably have referred instead to the parallels between British possessions in the West Indies and the settler colony at the Cape. His strictures on conditions in the Caribbean colonies would have sounded sadly familiar to Van der Kemp, James Read and some of their colleagues. Buchanan noted the great hostility to missionary Christianity among the whites, especially in Jamaica where recent legislation against missions ignored the imperial government's disallowances. Everywhere, he

---

67  *Colonial Ecclesiastical Establishment: Being a Brief View of the State of the Colonies of Great Britain and of her Asiatic Empire, in respect to Religious Instruction: Prefaced by some considerations on the National Duty of affording it. To which is added, A Sketch of an Ecclesiastical Establishment for British India. Humbly Submitted to the Consideration of the Imperial Parliament* (London, 1813).

68  *Ibid.*, pp. 10, 16–28.

69  *Ibid.*, pp. 28, 51–2.

70  *Ibid.*

concluded, the church was 'entirely subject to the secular authority', to a degree, indeed, unparalleled anywhere in Britain or India; 'the neglect of Christian ordinances and the relaxation of morals are the most serious evils'. In the manner of John Philip later, Buchanan saw intervention by an external authority as a vital element in any solution. 'Both the Planter and the Slave need the paternal interference of the Imperial Parliament.'[71] One particular form of that interference which, significant as it was to Buchanan, would not have commended itself to Philip, was episcopal oversight and defence of Anglican missionaries. Bishops were to come in due course, as we shall see below, but most of the early nineteenth-century missionaries – overwhelmingly Baptists, LMS and Methodists – were anxious above all for imperial intervention on their behalf in other ways.

The slave societies of the British Caribbean colonies at the turn of the eighteenth century presented missions with some of their most difficult challenges. For none perhaps was this more the case than for those free blacks who, frequently touched by the religious revivals in North America, either came or were invited to the islands. Often working as preachers or missionaries, many were Baptists and arrived especially in the wake of the War of Independence. Their successors were to play notable parts both in the nineteenth-century movement of black missionaries to Africa and as pastors or church leaders alongside the white missionaries throughout the Caribbean.[72] However, as the anti-slavery movement crystallised in Britain, so too evangelicals of all denominations associated themselves with the abolitionist cause and the future of the British territories. Missionaries, especially Methodists, were identified almost as a matter of course by white colonial society as enemies of the plantation system. No less readily, they were seen by many slaves and free coloured inhabitants as humanitarian sympathisers and Christian reformers.

Mission society organisers were alive to the divided loyalties that this situation created for their missionaries. However, they were also determined that their conversionist enterprise should not be diverted or jeopardised by missionary entanglement in the politics of anti-slavery. As a result, instructions to missionaries departing for the West Indies were unusually plain-spoken in their prohibition on involvement with politics or anything else that might risk an encounter with colonial or imperial authority.

Wesleyan instructions included a special section on the West Indies. These were 'stations of considerable delicacy ... which require, from the state of society there, a peculiar circumspection and prudence on the one hand and of zeal, diligence and patient perseverance, on the other'. Missionaries were warned that 'your only business is to promote the moral and religious improvement of the slaves to whom you may have access, without in the least degree, in public or private, interfering with their

---

71  *Ibid.*, pp. 59–60.
72  For figures such as George Liele and Moses Baker see Stanley, *History of the BMS*, pp. 68–70 and David Killingray, 'The Black Atlantic Missionary Movement and Africa, 1780–1920s', *Journal of Religion in Africa* 33,1 (2003), 3–31.

civil condition'. 'The Committee caution you against engaging in any of the civil disputes or local politics of the Colony to which you may be appointed, either verbally, or by correspondence with any person at home, or in the Colonies.'[73] Presbyterians were told 'Never converse with the natives on political subjects. Such conversation, you may be almost certain, will be misrepresented and turned as an engine against you.' Baptist letters were no less blunt. 'Do not intermeddle with politics ... Remember that the object is not to teach the principles and laws of an earthly Kingdom, however important a right understanding of these may be, but the principles and laws of the Kingdom of Christ. Maintain toward all in authority a respectful demeanour. Treat them with the honour to which their office entitles them. Political and party discussion avoid as beneath your office.'[74] However, explicit though these prohibitions might be, they were in practice unworkable for conscientious missionaries. They found their neutrality and non-involvement being eroded from two directions.

From many planters and other members of white society there came a steady barrage of harassment and persecution. Not all whites hated the missionaries, but most feared their influence and few supported them warmly. Men such as Hermanus Post at the plantation Le Resouvenir in Demerara, who welcomed LMS missionaries to live on his estate, were few and far between.[75] If others were generally civil, they were also easily alienated by aspects of slave evangelisation, especially if a missionary seemed successful and slave congregations grew. On a daily level there was what the Methodists' official historians played down as the 'private hostility', 'the ruffianism of West Indian colonial life'. Broken windows, disrupted services, spies in the congregation, intimidation and insulting behaviour were all commonplace.[76]

They were of course not uncommon at home in Britain and many missionaries, despite their youth, were doubtless well practised in fending off the unruly. However, if such things discomfited the inexperienced or sensitive, even the thick-skinned were vulnerable to manipulation of the law and legal process against them. In a society where planters, magistrates, Council or Assembly members, town council, jury or parish vestry members and their electors so often overlapped, illegitimate pressure and injustice were easily brought to bear. Conditions were such that this was not merely a Caribbean problem. At the Cape of Good Hope, for example, mission stations had been threatened with perverse interpretations of

---

73  'Instructions to Missionaries', Clause VII paras 1, 6, 9, from *The Report of the Wesleyan-Methodist Missionary Society for the year 1822* (London, 1823).

74  Quoted in Mary Turner, *Slaves and Missionaries. The Disintegration of Jamaican Slave Society 1787–1834* (Urbana and London, 1982), pp. 9–10.

75  Emilia Viotti da Costa, *Crowns of Glory, Tears of Blood: The Demerara Slave Rebellion of 1823* (New York and Oxford, 1994), pp. 88–9.

76  Findlay and Holdsworth, *History*, Vol. 2, pp. 64, 83; for an LMS example, Donald Wood, 'A Slave Missionary and the Worldly Powers: John Wray in Guiana', in Holger Bernt Hansen and Michael Twaddle (eds), *Christian Missionaries and the State in the Third World* (Oxford and Athens, GA, 2001), p. 32.

local tax laws.[77] In Jamaica's rather different conditions, the Assembly expressed its concern in the preamble to an Act in 1802 that 'there now exists in this island an evil, which is daily increasing and threatens much danger to the peace and safety thereof, by reason of the preaching of ill-disposed, illiterate, or ignorant enthusiasts, to meetings of Negroes and persons of colour, chiefly slaves, unlawfully assembled; whereby ... the minds of the hearers are perverted with fanatical notions'.[78] This Act was modelled on an earlier measure from St Vincent designed to break up the circuit network of Methodist preachers and for the time being permitted the harassment and imprisoning of missionaries in dispute over their licences and accusations of unlawful assembly. Disallowed in London after two years, its substance was redrafted in the form of revised policing regulations for the town of Kingston.

William Gilgrass, who was in consequence imprisoned and his chapel closed for conducting a singing class, was driven to write home to Thomas Coke. 'If we can have no redress from home, we must leave the island ... We dare meet no more Classes, the corporate body [the Corporation] having given orders to the police-officer ... that all the punishment in their power shall be inflicted. Nothing appears to satisfy them but our banishment.'[79] Re-enactment of the slave code in 1807 brought another onslaught on Methodist teaching and preaching and again it was disallowed in 1809. The following year further legislation made licences more difficult and expensive to obtain, and missionaries more vulnerable to frivolous or vexatious complaints. Thomas Coke's report to Methodist subscribers in 1808 was understandably gloomy. 'All our chapels in this island are now shut up, the Missionaries silenced and the work of God, to all appearance at a stand.'[80]

Missionaries were divided in their responses to obstruction. While the anti-slavery movement made only slow headway, the process of protest and disallowance of legislation in London was cumbersome and sometimes fruitless. Missionaries meanwhile wanted effective protection and toleration in order to establish themselves on a permanent basis. On occasion, disruption caused by blacks could be dealt with by missionaries' own recourse to the local courts. In Barbados, William Shrewsbury told a Manchester friend how 'We have recently been prosecuting one of our drunken hearers for disturbing the Congregation during public worship; he suffered nearly 3 months imprisonment for his offence. This measure we hope will prove salutary; I am sure it was one of urgent necessity.'[81] Where whites were responsible, however, protection and redress required far more positive intervention from an imperial government that was only slowly

---

77  Basil le Cordeur and Christopher Saunders (eds), *The Kitchingman Papers: Missionary Letters and Journals, 1817 to 1848* (Johannesburg, 1976), pp. 72–5.

78  Jakobsson, *Am I Not a Man and a Brother?*, p. 283.

79  Findlay and Holdsworth, *History of the WMMS*, Vol. 2, pp. 76–7.

80  *The Annual Report of the State of the Missions which are carried on both at home and abroad by the Society late in Connexion with the Rev. John Wesley* (London, 1808), p. 20.

81  W.J. Shrewsbury (Barbados) to Rev. John Smedley, 6 July 1821, MCA, PLP 97-9-26.

losing its reluctance to override the powers of elected assemblies and the non-cooperation of planters even in Crown Colonies.

In May 1823 the humanitarians won a significant advance when Liverpool's ministry committed itself to the amelioration of slave conditions. As part of this shift of emphasis, bishoprics were set up in Jamaica and Barbados to inject some vigour into the Anglican parish system and extend its responsibility to the slaves. That Christian teaching was a central feature of this policy was, however, a mixed blessing for the missions; they rightly anticipated increased resistance to them on the ground. Finding themselves drawn willy-nilly into play as agents of imperial policy, they still found themselves lacking the means to give full practical effect to their role. This was confirmed when white responses to the Demerara slave rebellion in August included the widespread destruction of mission property and victimisation of Christian slaves and led to the death of the LMS missionary, John Smith.[82] Fearful of repercussions, some of the Jamaica missionaries circulated a series of resolutions, intended to defend their own neutrality and to head off planter anger, only to find themselves at the centre of a violent storm over accusations of supporting slavery. The response of the WMMS secretaries, warning the missionaries to avoid cheapening church membership by the over-hasty or too easy admission of converts and repeating admonitions against engaging in social and political controversy, was hardly helpful in its balancing of principle with inaction.[83]

Intervention in politics and appeals for external assistance were not only driven by the missionary commitment to religious freedom and desire for an end to white harassment. This was after all only to wage on a more extreme front a battle still being fought at home, one which was to continue over lesser forms of discrimination long after the emancipation of Catholics and repeal of the Test and Corporation Acts in 1828–29. The conflict in the Caribbean was fuelled no less powerfully by the inexorable drift of many missionaries into an unqualified abolitionist position, as result of their day-to-day encounter with slave society. The restrictions on meetings and worship; punishment of slaves for attending churches and chapels; prohibitions on religious education and literacy; the extreme difficulty of any orderly family life; the ethical and sexual corruption on all sides in a society so given to violence and compulsion; all made a properly Christian existence impossible and mocked missionary efforts. John Smith was only twenty-four on arrival in Demerara in 1816. Wakened in the mornings to the sounds of slaves being flogged, realising gradually that with few exceptions his only sources of friendship, warmth and happiness were the slaves, like his predecessor John Wray he found his abolitionist inclinations confirmed. 'Time and again, in spite of his conscious efforts to comply with established norms', he found he could do nothing other than

---

82  For Smith and the Demerara rebellion, da Costa, *Crowns of Glory*.
83  Findlay and Holdsworth, *History*, Vol. 2, pp. 87–9; for colonial reactions to 1823, Jakobsson, *Am I Not a Man and a Brother?*, chap. 7.

encourage beliefs and practice that 'undermined the system of sanctions and assertions that maintained slavery'.[84] It was all but impossible to do otherwise. 'Barbados
is Barbados still', wrote Shrewsbury. 'Wickedness prevails, I think more than ever,
in this Sodom of the West and I am afraid will never be extirpated, until some
signal judgment is manifested against this land.' For the moment, however, it was
Shrewsbury who suffered the 'signal judgment': his chapel in Barbados was
destroyed in the aftermath of Demerara's rebellion and he was transferred for his
own sake to the Cape Colony.[85]

   These were the experiences that progressively sapped the reservations of
missionaries and their societies about their involvement in public affairs. Planters
seemed never to learn and incapable of change. The aftermath of the Demerara
events saw anti-missionary campaigns in other parts of the West Indies.[86] In 1826
the Jamaican Assembly again revised the slave code and took the opportunity to
attack the missions. This legislation – again wending its way to disallowance and
revision – was followed by the formation of the Secretaries Committee to investigate missionary misdemeanours and by a flood of contested arrests, imprison-
ments, preaching and licensing cases. The cycle witnessed in 1816 and 1823 of
rebellion, severe repression, persecution of missions and uproar among their evangelical supporters in Britain was then repeated most dramatically in the 'Baptists'
War' in Jamaica in 1831.[87]

   The significance of these events in the Caribbean colonies has been considered
by historians chiefly for the final impetus they gave to the humanitarians' anti-slavery campaign of the early 1830s, the legislative emancipation of slaves within the
empire in 1833 and in the contribution made by missionary conflicts to the 'disintegration of slave society'. However, they also have their place in the wider evolution
of missionary attitudes towards religion, church and state. The Caribbean colonies,
more even than the Cape and India, not only impressed on missionaries the impossibility of detachment from politics and government. They also brought home the
necessity of cultivating both secular authority as a vital aid to their undertakings
and the popular opinion needed at times to compel authorities to act in their
defence. The fundamental conditions of protection and toleration were not easily
established, either inside or outside the colonial empire. This lesson was potentially
worrying for encouraging doubts about the workings of Providence that had
seemed so promising in the 1790s. It was nevertheless also compatible with an optimism derived from faith and millennial thinking. It was slowly and reluctantly
learned by 1830 and was confirmed by the implicit bargain struck at emancipation,
that in return for support the missions would instruct the freed slaves through their

---

84  Da Costa, *Crowns of Glory*, pp. 291–2 and chap. 4.

85  Shrewsbury to Smedley, 6 July 1821, MCA, PLP 97-9-26.

86  For the Barbados story, Findlay and Holdsworth, *History of the WMMS*, Vol. 2, pp. 198–208.

87  Turner, *Slaves and Missionaries*, chap. 6; for the Baptist experience, Stanley, *History of the BMS*,
    pp. 70–82; K.R.M. Short,'Jamaican Christian Missions and the Great Slave Rebellion of 1831–2',
    *JEccH* 27, 1 (1976), 57–72.

apprenticeship and beyond. Not for another three decades was it again to be seriously challenged.

It was also a lesson repeatedly reinforced during the century. When the centenary history of the LMS was written, its author had no hesitation in accepting that the 'no politics' rule could not be binding. Slavery, the treatment of 'Hottentots' and 'Kafirs', idol-worship in India and the opium trade were for Richard Lovett instances where the government of a country allied itself with 'cruelty, social wrongs and oppression'. Missions had no alternative but actively to oppose such things and to work against government support for them.[88] As will be seen below, this was to bring missions equally into conflict with indigenous authorities.

---

88  Lovett, *History of the LMS*, Vol. 1, p. 544.

# ~ 4 ~

# Missionary religion and secular influences: Christianity, commerce and civilisation, 1800–35

The sense of embattlement felt by missionaries in the early decades of the nineteenth century was particularly marked in India, South Africa and the British West Indies. In each case missions were drawn into engagement with local governments or rival interest groups and turned to the imperial government for assistance and protection. In Sierra Leone, the Methodists and the CMS fell back on the colonial government for want of success outside the colony. No less noticeable, however, is the growing vigour and weight that the societies at home were able to throw into their struggles especially after 1823. On the eve of the debates over India in 1813, they were struggling on all fronts and, as was seen above, the outcome of the 1813 campaign was no resounding success. Countered by the widespread fear of an infectious 'radicalism' and measured in terms of income and recruits, much of the buoyancy and enthusiasm for the cause of 'vital religion', so evident in the founding decade of the 1790s, had evaporated.[1] Nevertheless, by 1830 and seen from the metropolitan end the missionary movement was beginning to look quite different. For all the societies, recruitment had become far more promising and in most cases subscriptions had risen year on year since 1815.

After its feeble start, for example, the CMS began to make great strides. The numbers of workers sent out by the Society jumped to seven in 1815 and remained at a yearly average of ten from 1820–1830. Its annual income tripled overnight from £3046 (1813) to £10,793 (1814) and then barely faltered before reaching a temporary peak of £54,010 in 1829. This expansion owed a great deal to the energetic promotion from 1813 of local CMS associations to canvass on the Society's behalf. The LMS, with an income five times that of the CMS in 1813, also increased its funds steadily but more slowly than its rival, with the result that it was overtaken by the Anglicans in 1819–20. Although Baptist income rose sharply to a new level c.1820 it then remained fairly steady before rising again in the 1830s. After their missionary society was hammered into shape by Jabez Bunting and Beecham in 1818, the Wesleyans went from strength to strength, doubling their income in the 1820s to roughly £40,000 per annum and then doubling it again in the 1830s.

What did these new and increasingly generous subscribers think they were supporting? At one level, of course, the answer is simple: the conversion of the

---

1 Above, pp. 40–53, 58–62.

heathen everywhere to Christianity. However, the simple answer as so often does not get us very far. We have already seen in Chapter 3 how missions and their organisers, many of them starting out as political innocents, were steadily forced to adjust their perceptions and practices in order to create circumstances in which they could carry on their work. In the same way that they had to create a legal and political framework for evangelism, so missionaries found that they had to wrestle with the content of their religion and its relation to British metropolitan cultures in order to find forms in which it could satisfactorily be transmitted to culturally alien societies.

## I

The missionary movement was gathering renewed strength not only by drawing on its reserves of evangelical enthusiasm but from the continuing debate about the meaning of 'civilisation' and especially the possibility of civilising, or improving the conditions of, non-European peoples. Even by the end of the century there had been little disagreement as to the characteristics of 'civilisation'; Britain's own capitalist culture and institutions provided the principal yardstick. Already in the 1760s Adam Smith had established the progressive stages through which human societies advanced to their culmination in 'the commercial age'. Under the influence of Scottish writers, it had become ever more conventional to assume that with commercial progress there went political sophistication. Development of the political arts meant good government, order and the liberty of individuals. Britain's commercial and industrial pre-eminence also produced moral benefits, for these pursuits provided 'bulwarks against passions, vice and weakness'.[2] In matters of faith and ethics, Protestant Christianity embodied the peak of religious perfection, a point on which for once even Sydney Smith could speak for almost everyone. 'We believe that we are in possession of a revealed religion; and that the possession of that religion can alone confer immortality and best confer present happiness.'[3] Such pre-eminence and good fortune were very widely felt to create obligations to less fortunate societies.

There were felt to be many such societies, for, by 1815 there were increasingly few who took a broadly tolerant – let alone uncritical – view of non-European peoples and their cultures and fewer still who admired their achievements. The duty of benevolence was enjoined on both secular and religious grounds; its fulfilment necessitated the civilisation of the peoples of Africa, the Pacific and Asia. There were, not unnaturally, still sceptics and others who ridiculed such arguments. The general result, however, in the words of the *Eclectic Review*, was that 'The melioration of the condition of the human race, in every form, never employed so great a number of active and benevolent minds, as at the present time

---

2  Marshall and Williams, *The Great Map of Mankind*, pp. 147, 149.
3  *Edinburgh Review* 12 (April 1808), 170.

... one directs his views to one object and another to another ... but all unite in endeavours to augment the sum of human felicity.'[4] British religion, law, commerce, good government, literature and education were all it seemed for export and even those inclined to ridicule the missionary himself were likely to approve his purpose. Sydney Smith, again, was one of the many who roundly asserted the obligation to disseminate Christianity abroad as well as at home. 'This religion ... teaches us the duties of general benevolence: and how, under such a system, the conversion of Heathens can be a matter of indifference, we profess not to be able to understand.'[5]

Consideration of how an overall state of 'civilisation' might be achieved naturally encouraged attention to processes, to priorities and to the ways in which aspects of civilised society might be connected with each other, if not mutually supportive. The precise relations between Christianity and commerce, evangelism and trade thus became important to the discussion. In debates about the policy to be adopted towards India or Africa, or discussion of the best missionary methods, further distinctions were frequently drawn between Christianity itself on the one hand and civilisation on the other. Not only was the place of commerce in the overall picture to be considered, but there were questions to be addressed as to which – Christianity, commerce or civilisation – either could, or should, be introduced first, in what forms and with what degree of overlap. Contemporaries in debate were often confused.[6]

For some, concerned often with law or administration, there was no doubt that 'civilisation' should be introduced first and so prepare the way for the Christian religion. Churchmen often felt obliged to reproach such apparently secular-minded critics for making the 'common, but absurd mistake, that the sublime doctrines of the gospel are not to be addressed to heathens, because their untutored minds are not prepared to comprehend them'.[7] However, members of the churches were themselves divided over how the different agencies of improvement ought to be introduced. Richard Watson, Bishop of Llandaff, expected little from missionary work *per se*; rather it was through the 'extension of science and commerce ... [that] India will be christianized by the government of Great Britain'.[8] Civilisation under government auspices he felt would bring Christianity in its train. Not surprisingly many Evangelicals despaired at such opinions, as for example when the Reverend William Tennant wrote hopefully of agriculture and the level of manufactures in India but appeared 'to consider attempts to convert the Hindoos, in their present state, as a fruitless effort'. 'Exceedingly sorry we are, to perceive such sentiments

4  *Eclectic Review* 1, 2 (Oct. 1805), 762.

5  See note 3 above.

6  For recent contributions to this historiographical debate, Brian Stanley (ed.), *Christian Missions and the Enlightenment* (Richmond, Grand Rapids and Cambridge, 2001).

7  *Eclectic Review* 1, 2 (Dec. 1805), 884.

8  Watson, *Anecdotes of the Life of Richard Watson*, p. 198.

drop from the pen of a clergyman and a chaplain of his Majesty's army', complained one outraged reviewer.[9]

Even supporters of missions fell out over the priority of civilisation or Christianity, the experience of the Moravian Brethren, for example, being used as ammunition on both sides of the argument.[10] Within the Presbyterian Church of Scotland a long-running dispute was carried on between moderate or rational Calvinists and their evangelical counterparts. Among the former were men such as George Hill and John Inglis, who believed that a degree of 'civilisation' in the form of acquired knowledge and rationality was an inescapable prerequisite for the comprehension of Christian truth and experience of conversion. Evangelicals, such as the outstanding scholar and minister Thomas Chalmers, denied this, trusting that the true and universal religion could be grasped without such preparation by human beings who were everywhere the same.[11] From his experience of contrasting Scottish parishes, Chalmers had no qualms about broader generalisation. He was convinced that 'There is no controverting the existence of a moral sense in the rudest of barbarians ... in all countries you have ground upon which you can enter.'[12] Nevertheless, even while many evangelicals argued that Christianity *could* perfectly well precede civilisation, there was certainly no clear feeling that it should *necessarily* do so. Samuel Marsden, Anglican chaplain at Port Jackson (New South Wales) and agent for the LMS and CMS, often understood as an exponent of the Scottish moderate 'civilisation first' position, in fact saw civilisation and Gospel teaching proceeding together in the hands of intelligent and industrious missionaries. 'To preach the Gospel without the aid of the Arts will never succeed amongst the heathen for any time.'[13]

Christians carried on these discussions within the framework of a providentialist theology. As indicated in Chapter 2, this was the world of Bishop Butler's *Analogy*, Archdeacon Paley's *Evidences of Christianity* and William Wilberforce's *Practical View of Religion*. Nevertheless, just as Christianity and civilisation were not always seen as organically linked, so commerce and Christianity were often regarded as essentially separate issues. They had not yet been integrally linked in the way that was to become common fifty years later. Commerce, particularly

9  *Eclectic Review* 1, 2 (Dec. 1805), 896, 898.
10  *Edinburgh Review* 21 (Feb. 1813), 64–6, reviewing Henry Lichtenstein, *Travels into Southern Africa*; Rev. W. Hanna, *Memoirs of the Life and Writings of Thomas Chalmers*, 4 vols (Edinburgh, 1849–52), Vol. 1, pp. 390–2.
11  Ian Douglas Maxwell, 'Civilisation or Christianity? The Scottish Debate on Mission Methods, 1750–1835', in Stanley (ed.), *Christian Missions and the Enlightenment*, pp. 123–40; Gavin White, '"Highly Preposterous": Origins of Scottish Missions', *Records of the Scottish Church History Society* 19, 2 (1976), 111–24.
12  W.J. Roxborogh, 'Thomas Chalmers and the Mission of the Church With Special Reference to the Rise of the Missionary Movement in Scotland' (unpub. Ph.D. thesis, Aberdeen, 1978), pp. 307, 359. For Hill, Inglis and Chalmers, *DSCHT* (Edinburgh, 1993), pp. 158–61, 407–8, 429–30.
13  Marsden, quoted in Brian Stanley, 'Christianity and Civilisation in English Evangelical Mission Thought, 1792–1857', in Stanley (ed.), *Christian Missions and the Enlightenment*, p. 185.

foreign trade, was a fundamental characteristic of a civilised society, but 'civilisation' which lay at the centre of the general concern was felt both to comprise far
more than commercial activity and to be clearly distinguishable from Christianity.
The understanding of commerce above all as the exchange of primary produce or
raw materials for manufactures and the identification of such a system of exchange
as a prime factor in the dissemination and support of Christianity among non-
Europeans were not features of late eighteenth- and early nineteenth-century
debates about evangelisation.

We have already seen how William Carey touched on what were essentially
superficial connections or parallels between evangelisation and commercial activity.
He saw in the adventurousness of the trader evidence that heathen territories were
closer than one might think and a reproof to Christians who nevertheless preferred
to turn their backs on the wider world, rather than an inescapable auxiliary for the
contemporary evangelist.[14] So too, the newly founded missionary societies of the
1790s, as well as the later Wesleyan Methodist Missionary Society (WMMS), were
at pains to dissociate themselves from commercial activity. 'It is a positive rule',
declared the Wesleyan 'Instructions to Missionaries', 'that no Travelling Preacher
shall "follow a trade". You are to consider this rule as binding upon you and all
Foreign Missionaries in our Connexion. We wish you to be at the remotest distance
from all temptations to a secular or mercenary temper.'[15] However, just as the societies had been keen but were ultimately unable to avoid direct engagement in 'political' matters, so the same was to be true of commerce.

As a measure of the distance missionaries found themselves travelling, one can
take the speech delivered by Bishop Samuel Wilberforce at Leeds in May 1860 on
behalf of the newly established Universities' Mission to Central Africa (UMCA).
'"What," some simple-minded man might say, "is the connection between the
Gospel and commerce?"' The bishop's answer to his rhetorical question was char-
acteristically robust. 'There is a great connection between them. In the first place,
there is little hope of promoting commerce in Africa, unless Christianity is planted
in it; and, in the next place, there is very little ground for hoping that Christianity
will be able to make its proper way unless we can establish a lawful commerce in the
country.' Britain's part in forging the connection was abundantly clear. It was 'the
intention of God to make the interest of this, the most active, the most ingenious
and the freest people on the face of the earth, to be up and doing and to be in
earnest in the far more important work of spreading His Gospel throughout the
world. Was it written in vain by the prophet, "and the ships of Tarshish first"? Was
it not meant that God had given us our commerce and our naval supremacy – that

---

14  Carey, *An Enquiry*, pp. 67, 81–2; also pp. 44–5 above.
15  David Bogue, 'Objections against a mission to the heathen, stated and considered', *Sermons preached
in London at the Formation of the Missionary Society* (London, 1795), pp. 132–3; 'Instructions', clause
ix, *The Report of the Wesleyan Methodist Missionary Society for the Year ending December, 1822*
(London, 1823), p. xi.

industry, that patience which enabled us to subdue the earth wherever we had settled ... our wealth, with our mutual trust in each other, that we might as the crowning work of all these blessings, be the instruments of spreading the truths of the Gospel from one end of the earth to the other?' Of course the answer was 'yes', for, as Wilberforce argued, drawing examples from the early history of the Christian church, the connection rested on a dual principle. 'The providence of God ... has ordained that when Christianity is placed in any great centre, it should be borne everywhere by the natural power of commerce itself ... commerce ... is intended to carry, even to all the world, the blessed message of salvation.' Just as commerce furthered Christianity, so the reverse was also true. Christianity, according to Wilberforce, has 'the effect of training the human race to a degree of excellence which it could never attain in non-Christian countries', giving 'value to life', 'dignity to labour' and 'security to possession', with the result that a Christian people would tend to be 'a wealth-producing people, an exporting people and so a commercial people'.[16] Missionaries could not but approve and encourage such commercial development.

These sentiments are revealing in several respects. They reflect, first, the growth of Britain's own nineteenth-century commerce and may be seen as a measure of the rapid economic transformation the country and its consumer society had undergone. They also indicate the persistence into the mid-century of that earlier providentialist theology in which world events were readily interpreted as auguries for the success of Britain's missionary enterprise.[17] However, they also demonstrate the extent to which the missionary movement consciously and unconsciously had come to terms with the economic character of the age, adapting its message to the characteristics of capitalist society in its various guises. To appreciate the process by which the Christian message was elaborated and the content of evangelical missionary Christianity given greater definition, it is useful first to turn again to India and Sierra Leone as continuing subjects of evangelical concern.

## II

In the case of Sierra Leone, despite the direct commercial interest and missionary concern of its evangelical promoters, a pattern of attitudes can be discerned in which there emerged no instrumental connection between commerce and Christianity. After the failure of Granville Sharp's project for a self-sufficient, self-governing settlement, the Sierra Leone Company took over Sharpe's concession in 1790 with a view to 'the Introduction of Civilization into Africa'.[18] This the

16  Speech at Leeds, 25 May 1860, Samuel Wilberforce, *Speeches on Missions*, ed. Henry Rowley (London, 1874), pp. 212–13.
17  Brian Stanley, '"Commerce and Christianity": Providence Theory, the Missionary Movement and the Imperialism of Free Trade, 1842–1860', *HJ* 26 (1983), 72, 93.
18  *Report from the Committee on the Petition of the Court of Directors of the Sierra Leone Company, PP* (1801–2) 2 (339), p. 7.

Company expected to achieve by the establishment of a trading settlement handling tropical produce; this would build up links with neighbouring tribes and serve as an example to them by its own industry, peace and prosperity. Persuasion by rational example would contribute to the abolition of the slave trade, the root cause of Africa's barbarity.

Civilisation by means of 'legitimate trade', however, did not involve the intimate linking of commerce and Christianity which the Company's association with the Clapham Sect might lead one to expect. Others have noted how 'the Sierra Leone Company began with hardly any thought about the possible uses of either education or missionary work'.[19] In the early days of the venture there were perhaps good reasons for this. As we have seen, the Company was mounted hastily in order to rescue the earlier immigration scheme and the main body of early settlers – the Nova Scotians – were in many cases regarded already as educated Christians. The missionary movement was itself only just beginning. The accent on legitimate trade may have owed more than anything to domestic political necessity: Henry Thornton, the Company's chairman and his friends found in that idea something beneficial with which to counter the pro-slavery lobby's arguments that slavery was ineradicably rooted in African conditions and that abolition would seriously damage Britain's interests.[20] However, this predominant concern with the secular aspects of civilisation persisted throughout the Company's life.

The emphasis certainly owed a lot to bitter experience, not least of recalcitrant colonists and intractable physical conditions. Parliamentary defenders of the Company in 1802 made much of claims to some educational progress. Castlereagh mentioned details and Thornton, in a desperate if unwitting extension of historical stage theory, appealed to the 'wisest legislators and the most celebrated writers [who] agreed in this position, that the introduction of knowledge must ever precede civilization'. In submissions to the parliamentary Select Committee examining their affairs, the Directors observed that it 'need scarcely be remarked how much Civilization is forwarded by promoting regular Industry and good Order, by affording complete Protection, by facilitating the fair Acquisition of Property and by securing the quiet enjoyment of legitimate Influence and Power'.[21] However, these were only piecemeal gains. By 1807, Thornton could claim no more than to have proved what he had professed to believe when setting up the Company nearly twenty years before, 'the practicability of civilizing Africa'.[22]

Thornton's explanation of his conviction is worth noting. 'What were the great impediments to the improvements of a country?', he asked his House of Commons audience. 'Either something, first, in the climate; or, secondly, in the soil; or, thirdly,

---

19  Curtin, *The Image of Africa*, p. 262.
20  *Ibid.* and pp. 105–7; Ralph A. Austen and Woodruff D. Smith, 'Images of Africa and British Slave Trade Abolition: The Transition to an Imperialist Ideology, 1787–1807', *African Historical Studies* 2 (1969), 69–83.
21  11 June 1802, *Parliamentary Register* 18, (1802) pp. 683–7; *PP* (1801–2), 2 (339), p. 22.
22  29 July 1807, *Cobbett's Parliamentary Debates*, 9, 1004.

in the character of the inhabitants.' He then commented on each to show that in 'no one of these respects was there any insuperable obstacle to civilization'. Not only was the creation of an expanding trade possible; thanks to the Company, there now also existed 'a body of colonists on the coasts of Africa, speaking the English language, attached to the English people, advancing in civilization and morals and increasing in numbers'. From both the trade and the colonists, Britain might expect 'substantial advantages'.[23]

Here, any mention of Christianity and the role of conversion was notable by its absence. Despite the wish of the Company's supporters to introduce 'among the natives … the blessings of religion',[24] there was no suggestion that hopes for commerce rested on the establishment of Christianity or that commerce would in any way be the vehicle for religious progress. In India many evangelicals either ignored or were frankly sceptical about commercial prospects. In Sierra Leone, where it was impossible to ignore the future of legitimate trade, they were convinced of its potential. Yet in the talk of civilisation there was still no marriage of trade with religion, in either theory or practice. Most graphically illustrative of the separation was the complete removal from Sierra Leone of the sons of local notables; for their education and religious instruction they were brought to board beside Clapham Common.[25]

Once Sierra Leone became a Crown Colony, however, a different equation was gradually developed.[26] Such missionary activities as grew up there went with the adoption of patterns of schooling which were already established in England and were later to become familiar in India. Wherever possible, the village school, plus a range of English learning, religious literature and preaching, made up the preferred mode. This pattern of development owed very little to missionary reflection or choice of strategy and virtually everything to the practical necessities of government. At first the missions in Sierra Leone had little incentive either to consider or to reconsider the implications of their work. The Maxwell–MacCarthy programme was the only practicable one and the missions had a keen interest in making it a success. In this they were assisted by Freetown's developing position as the seat of government for the West African settlements, site of the Mixed Commission Court adjudicating captures of slaving vessels, naval base and military centre. Government spending, for example on rations for the liberated Africans and after 1815 a steady recovery of local trade and shipping, contributed to stifle questions about the status quo. The English language necessarily took precedence over any vernacular.

---

23  *Ibid.*, 1003–5.
24  Thornton, 11 June 1802, *Parliamentary Register*, 18, 686–7.
25  Evidence of William Greaves, *PP* (1801–2), 2 (339), 30–1; Henry Thornton to Hannah More, 26 Oct. 1798 and n.d. [Nov. 1800?], Add. 7674/1/L2, ff. 11, 117–19.
26  The following has drawn heavily on material in Fyfe, *Sierra Leone*, pp. 139–81; Peterson, *Province of Freedom*, pp. 123–74; and Jakobsson, *Am I Not a Man?*, pp. 192–230.

However, MacCarthy's system bred its discontents. Evangelicals increasingly chafed at the administrative demands imposed on them; MacCarthy criticised the CMS for failing to supply sufficient numbers of missionaries and schoolmasters; denominational rivalries offended all but the self-righteous; and the high death rate among Europeans made for work left undone and tasks badly performed. The result was the CMS withdrawal in 1824 from both the parish administration and the recruitment of teachers and the installation of a new regime under MacCarthy's successors which made substantial reductions in expenditure. The new dispensation left the missions with far less control over or easy access to the liberated Africans and their education. With the constant shortage of helpers, this threatened to undermine their work.

The missions' solution to this problem was to pay much more attention to educating the liberated Africans, looking to them to fill the gaps caused by death as soon as possible and to take over far more responsibility in the village churches. The CMS had closed its Christian Institution on Leicester Mountain after it had been deserted by Principal Bull and only two pupils remained. The Society now reopened it on a new site at Fourah Bay in 1827. Its English syllabus was intended chiefly to serve missionary requirements, but it proved equally valuable to the liberated Africans in equipping them for trade as well as other positions in Freetown. No longer so closely regulated by the colonial government, the liberated Africans organised their own affairs to an ever greater extent, beginning to accumulate property and acquire social status, something often related to position in the local Christian congregations.

The evangelistic consequences of early missionising in Sierra Leone thus owed far less to missionary adaptation than to uncommon constraints. Despite a well-disposed colonial government and a place at the centre of the colony's affairs, the chaotic social make-up of the population left missionaries with few choices. Numerous vernaculars and limited European command of them made the use of English inescapable; English and its adaptation as Krio were well-attuned to the West African commercial setting; and liberated Africans' interest in legitimate trade could hardly be discouraged. By the mid-1830s Christianity and commerce were therefore important identifying features of Sierra Leone's distinctive 'creole' or Krio culture. In this colony the links between Christianity and civilisation were thus defined by the ambitions of a newly formed legitimate commercial society, in what probably came as close as anywhere could to a straight missionary transfer of British beliefs and values. Pursuit of the missionary goal was unavoidably associated with and underpinned by the fortunes of legitimate trade.

## III

On Indian questions, the views of Charles Grant carried particular weight with supporters of missions. Grant seems always to have accepted the maxim that benevolence, whether in the promotion of good government or in fair trading, brought reflex benefits. Following his conversion in 1776, his faith in the potential of the East India Company as an agent of improvement and civilisation was strong, but the conviction grew on him that good laws and decent customs were of no use without the integrity and moral discipline that Christianity alone could produce in those who directed or lived under the company's administration. As a result he became increasingly critical of the company's past policies on the grounds that the value of its work had been totally undermined by its lack of concern with Christian teaching even for its own employees and its effective prohibition of missionary activity among Muslims and Hindus. By 1792 Grant was clear in his own mind that the civilisation and reformation of Indian society was not only necessary, but entailed nothing less than the steady introduction of the whole of Western learning.[27] He pressed increasingly for the dissemination of Christianity, not just as a body of doctrine or collection of sublime truths but as the essential ingredient required to bind Western ways and culture together.

Grant's strategy was education, his medium the English language and missionaries his agents. Missionaries he also defended not for any contribution which they might make to economic advance but for their cultivation of the sense of community and common values between rulers and ruled: nothing could do more to secure Britain's government in India. Grant wholeheartedly opposed the expansion of commerce which many proposed to achieve by opening India to all traders. Preservation of the East India Company's monopoly, the restriction of trade, was essential, for it supported the company's administrative structure, the only agent capable of encouraging religion and so of changing India for the better. He was prepared to admit that 'moral improvement would lead to economic improvement and help our commerce', but trade in any direct sense was irrelevant to the propagation of his faith.[28] In Grant's mind conversion had almost, one might say, driven out trade.

Given the great importance of commerce in the Divine dispensation to Britain itself, why did evangelicals feel commerce of so little importance to their work in India? If Grant had been alone in his views, he might be dismissed as someone concerned simply to reconcile his religious opinions with a vested interest in the company's own chances of profit. His suggestion that missionaries contributed to security might be written off as one more instance of the facility with which evangelicals and humanitarians attempted to win wider support by claiming that their policies served fundamental national interests.[29] In fact his arguments were widely representative and carried conviction because they rested on both historical fact and present experience. This was demonstrated in the debates on renewal of the Company's charter and the admission of missionaries to India in 1813.

---

27  Charles Grant, *Observations on the State of Society among the Asiatic Subjects of Great Britain, written in 1792*, printed in *PP* (1812–13), Vol. 10, *Report from the Select Committee on the Affairs of the East India Company*, General Appendix I.

28  A.T. Embree, *Charles Grant and British Rule in India* (London, 1963), pp. 47, 118, 142–4 and passim; Grant, *Observations*, p. 88.

29  See their arguments as set out in Anstey, *The Atlantic Slave Trade*, chap. 14; and cf. Thomas Chalmers, *The Utility of Missions ascertained by Experience*, 2nd edn, (Edinburgh, 1816), p. 19.

Evangelicals pressing for changes in the charter were convinced that commerce as such had done nothing to improve India, even if it appeared that the Company had been reformed since the supposedly rapacious days of the mid-eighteenth century. The past record of trading activity hardly suggested a latent capacity for supporting effective evangelism. It is, after all, very noticeable that, while supporters of missions were happy to see pressure from all sides put on the Company to change its ways, they avoided aligning themselves directly with free traders anxious to open India to all and sundry.[30] Many evangelicals seem to have been ready to accept the company's own argument that, while there might be honourable traders, nevertheless 'far the greater number would be adventurers of desperate or needy circumstances'.[31] Supporters of the admission of missionaries and the appointment of more clerics were consequently at pains to impress on Parliament by contrast their own sobriety and orderly intentions. For example, 'all the ministers and licentiates [of the Church of Scotland] have received a regular university education, which qualifies them both for teaching schools and for performing the services of religion and which at the same time affords a presumption in favour of their discretion and the propriety of their conduct'.[32] Programmes of action were to be similarly restrained. The LMS stated its intention 'to rely for their success upon the divine blessing attending a candid statement of the evidences which sustain the Christian religion, of the sacred doctrines, promises and precepts of which it principally consists and on their exemplary and blameless lives, attended by deeds of kindness and good-will to the natives'.[33] William Wilberforce emphasised the great importance of the general education and diffusion of knowledge which missionaries would also provide. These he saw as the essential counterpart of the religious instruction, in that they broadened the native mind and placed local superstitions in a different light. The combination of reason and truth, enlightenment and Christian mission, would be irresistible: 'the natives of Hindostan ... would, in short, become Christians, if I may so express myself, without knowing it'.[34]

It might be objected that these were just arguments for the occasion, since missionaries at the time certainly needed to defend their own character and the reasonableness of their brand of religion. Moreover, prolonged uncertainty as to the likely outcome of the Charter's revision compelled evangelicals to avoid arguments that might antagonise trading interests on either side. Representations in favour of a preaching and educational strategy were arguably calculated to do both.

However, there was more to this initial distancing of Christianity and the missionary cause from commerce than either an historical assessment of India's progress or calculations of immediate political expediency. Although practical caution may have prompted supporters of missions to India to present their case in

---

30 See the Petitions from supporters of missions in 1813, *Parliamentary Debates*, 25 and 26.
31 Speech by Grant, 31 May 1813, *Parliamentary Debates*, 26, 453.
32 Petition of Elders and Ministers of the Provincial Synod of Glasgow, 28 April 1813, *ibid.*, 25, 1092–3.
33 Petition, 14 April 1813, *ibid.*, 817–18.
34 22 June 1813, *ibid.*, 26, 832–3.

ways which played down links between the expansion of commerce and that of Christianity, even on occasions when connections were made it was with a view to assisting or justifying the missionary presence rather than drawing out any direct instrumental link between conversion and economic pursuits. Grant in his *Observations* wrote of the diffusion of 'our religion and knowledge' as 'the noblest species of conquest' adding 'and wherever, we may venture to say, our principles and language are introduced, our commerce will follow'. Claudius Buchanan spoke at the CMS's tenth Anniversary Meeting in 1810, emphasising both the inadequacy of commercial means and the importance of missionary societies linked to individual initiatives. In the run-up to the 1813 debates Wilberforce himself called only reluctantly for an alliance with commercial interests, not because he expected the diffusion of Christianity to be assisted by freer trade but in order to increase his political chances of abolishing the restrictive powers of the Company.[35]

In fact the case had gone against making any such link for two chief reasons. On the one hand, circumstances were such that prospects for the expansion of British trade with India were widely regarded as poor or non-existent. On the other, few who believed in a rosy commercial future saw in the introduction of Christianity a sufficient condition for growth: India's stunted development was the product of the East India Company's monopoly and only its abolition could open the way for expansion. It was thus possible for both commercial pessimists and optimists to believe that Christianity and civilisation might flourish apart from commerce and that the best means of promoting Christianity were independent of trade. Lord Teignmouth, for example, had no doubt that entry for missionaries into the Company's territory was desirable, that conversion was possible and that the introduction of Christianity 'would tend to the improvement of [the Hindu's] civil condition'. But when asked if an improved civil and moral condition 'would tend to increase their consumption of the various manufactures of their own or of any other country', he was certain it would not.[36] Teignmouth and many others who gave evidence to the parliamentary inquiry into the Company's affairs argued that the reason for the limited trade of India and the Company's own losses lay chiefly in the poverty of most Indians, their lack of purchasing power and the absence of any actual need for European goods.[37] Economic facts of life rather than the religious and moral state of India's inhabitants governed the levels of trade.

Not only did the promotion of Christianity not further trade; expanding trade neither promised nor depended on religious conversion. Thomas Grenville put the

---

35  Grant, *Observations*, PP (1831–32), 7 (734), General Appendix I, p. 88; Buchanan, 'A Sermon preached at the Parish Church of St. Andrew by the Wardrobe ... June 12, 1810', *Proceedings of the Church Missionary Society for Africa and the East* 3 (London, 1810–12), 9–50; R.I. Wilberforce and S. Wilberforce, *The Life of William Wilberforce*, 5 vols (London, 1838), Vol. 4, p. 14, diary entry, 14 Feb. 1812.

36  *PP* (1812–13) 7, 18.

37  Evidence of Thomas Graham and Major-Gen. Alexander Kyd, April 1813, *Parliamentary Debates* 25, 493–500, 527–32, 648–56; evidence of Mr Bruce, May 1813, *ibid.*, 26, 436.

anti-monopolist view that trade once opened would perpetuate itself unaided. 'By commerce, commerce will increase and industry by industry. So it has ever happened and the great Creator of the world has not exempted India from this common law of our nature. The supply, first following the demand, will soon extend it. By new facilities new wants and new desires will be produced. And neither climate nor religion, nor long established habits, no, nor even poverty itself, the greatest of all present obstacles, will ultimately refuse the benefits of such an intercourse to the native population of that empire. They will derive from the extension of commerce, as every other people has uniformly derived from it, new comforts and new conveniences of life, new incitements to industry and new enjoy-ments in just reward of increased activity and enterprize.'[38] In his view neither Hinduism nor Islam was a barrier to commerce and such obstacles as existed required not a religious transformation but the divorce of secular sovereignty from commercial monopoly.

That freer trade had little to offer the evangelicals seemed to be further confirmed by their first-hand experience. Even the most enthusiastic Baptists had found themselves drawn rapidly into teaching and the scholarly work of translation and publishing. Moreover, such economic activities as they became involved in seem to have had little to do with trade. Their concern was overwhelmingly with poor relief and the encouragement of subsistence through limited agricultural improvements.[39] It is therefore not surprising to find evangelicals, well before the public debates of 1813, firmly convinced as to the only worthwhile methods of propagating the Gospel. Discussing two of a series of dissertations 'on the best Means of Civilising the Subjects of the British Empire in India and of diffusing the Light of the Christian Religion throughout the Eastern World', the *Eclectic Review* was gratified 'that both the present writers, though of different national establish-ments, concur ... in the opinion we formerly intimated, that it is from the united measures of circulating the scriptures and of employing suitable missionaries, [i.e. well-trained, educated men] that we most reasonably may hope for the advance-ment of Christianity in the Eastern World'.[40] Preaching and teaching were the essential means; their effectiveness was to be increased by improving their quality and volume, not by linking them up with economic agencies. Allied to the mission-ary societies, the British and Foreign Bible Society, strongly supported by Grant, Teignmouth and Wilberforce and the Religious Tract Society, were the purest expressions of contemporary missionary strategies.[41]

---

38  April 1813, *ibid.*, 25, 739–40. Grenville was President of the Board of Control, 1806–7.

39  Potts, *British Baptist Missionaries in India*, pp. 70–4; Kenneth Ingham, *Reformers in India, 1793–1833: An Account of the Work of Christian Missionaries on Behalf of Social Reform* (Cambridge, 1956), chaps 2–5, 7.

40  *Eclectic Review* 2, 2 (July 1806), 536.

41  As examples of this commonly held view, William Wilberforce to Lord Wellesley, 6 April 1813, Wilberforce, *Life*, Vol. 4, p. 111; and Henry Martyn, *Sermons* (Calcutta, 1822), No. 20, on the BFBS.

## IV

In the early years of the century, the missions thus tended to hold to the traditional forms of religious instruction as the best means of transmitting their message. The absence of any obvious readiness on their part to link Christianity to a particular political economy, or to identify it with the commerce which it was generally agreed heralded a major advance in civilisation, was the result of several influences. No less important to the supporters of missions than the concept of civilisation and the idea of progress toward it by historical stages, were their traditional individualistic understanding of conversion and religious commitment and belief in the universality of human reason and conscience. Convinced as they were that Christianity was universally acceptable and beneficial to any society that embraced it, they were inclined to reject the idea that Christianity and a particular culture – whether or not it was 'commercial' – necessarily went hand in hand. In their emphasis on the overriding importance of teaching, literacy and the diffusion of the Scriptures, they were also drawing on the rationalist features of eighteenth-century thought in matters other than theology to support their continuing belief that Christianity could be introduced by universally applicable means. Missionaries did not understand preaching, schooling and the circulation of the Gospels in translation to be tied inevitably to particular forms of social and economic change. Thus when the LMS opened its Missionary Academy for training volunteers at Hoxton in 1825, it did so in the conviction that 'Education and the [printing] press are the two great means, which in connection with preaching, will bring about the moral revolution of the world.'[42]

Their belief in the efficacy of these methods reflected not only the slow growth of contemporary knowledge concerning non-European societies but also observations of their own world. Britain was still a society where rank and hierarchy were important, where many thought that while a man might rise, most were still born to their station. Where no one class was yet regarded as the national repository of universal virtues, it was natural to reflect that 'here and every where, the success of the Gospel is and always has been, greater among the lower and the middling classes of society, than among the rich, noble and wise'. For the evangelical, concerned as often as not with the reformation of manners and extirpation of vice at all levels of society at home as well as with missions overseas, the conclusion was unavoidable: although 'a high state of civilisation presents *advantages* for the introduction of Christianity, it may ... be attended with *disadvantages* which overbalance them'.[43] In such a world, commercial advance and religious conversion were not easily linked. However, changes began to take place in the mission field;

---

42  J.A. James, *Missionary Prospects: A sermon the substance of which was delivered ... at the opening of Hoxton College as a missionary academy* (Birmingham, 1826), p. 24. Hoxton, part of Shoreditch and Hackney, in east London, was already well known for its older dissenting academy.

43  *Eclectic Review* 2, 1 (May 1806), 364.

socio-economic circumstances altered at home; and as a result the evangelical formulation of the links between civilisation, Christianity and commerce also changed.

V

Missionary attitudes to their task in India in some respects remained the same, but in others changed quite sharply. Notwithstanding the expansion of British commerce after 1813 and the further expectations of growth once the East India Company's monopoly of the China trade was ended in 1833, an educational strategy remained central to missionaries' thinking. Although the Serampore Trio had noted, as the Scottish missionary Alexander Duff was later to do, the stimulus given by commercial growth to the local interest in learning English, commercial activity seemed to bear no relation to successful evangelism or conversion and the total numbers of converts remained very small. Rather than rely on trade to pave the way for a religious transformation, it therefore seemed to mission strategists more sensible to alter the form and content of the education that missionaries were providing.[44] With Scottish missions taking a leading role, the curriculum was progressively broadened in order to relate Christianity far more closely to Western learning as a whole.

There was nothing remarkable in the Church of Scotland's genuflection towards educational activity as the essential adjunct of missions when its Assembly decided to establish its work in India in 1824. When it came to foreign missions, the pattern of church expansion in Scotland and the intimate connections between parish school and parish church had shaped the thinking of the two major parties within the church.[45] For the evangelicals, Thomas Chalmers continued to reason from the universality of human nature to identity of methods at home and abroad. 'If schools and bibles have been found to be the engines of civilisation to the people of Britain it is altogether a fair and direct exercise of induction when these schools and bibles are counted upon … as equally powerful engines of civilization to the people of other countries.' Leading moderates such as Inglis felt 'it cannot be doubted that a man of an understanding mind, habituated to thought and reflection, has an advantage over others, for estimating both the evidence of Christian doctrine and its accommodation to human wants … We should, therefore, do injustice to the hope which we entertain of the universal prevalence of the gospel, if we did not make a fair allowance for the corresponding disadvantage under which others labour. It is obvious that whatever shall tend to remove such an obstruction to the success of the gospel, must have the effect to facilitate its progress in the

---

44  Smith, *Life of Carey*, p. 378; James, *Missionary Prospects*, pp. 24–5, 36–7.
45  Andrew F. Walls, 'Missions', *DSCHT*, pp. 567–94, esp. 567–72; D. Chambers, 'The Church of Scotland's Nineteenth Century Foreign Missions Scheme: Evangelical or Moderate Revival?', *Journal of Religious History* 9, 2 (1976), 115–38.

world.'[46] The difference between the two parties still lay in the balance struck between the direct transmission of religious truth to individuals and the place to be given alongside it to other educational subjects.

Metropolitan preferences for vernacular instruction in local schools were fed into Scottish plans by the small group of ministers entrusted with working out the practical details of the General Assembly's commitment. Of particular importance were Inglis, now chairman of the church's Committee for the Propagation of the Gospel in Foreign Parts and the evangelicals Alexander Thomson and Alexander Brunton, all three of whom had been closely involved with education and mission-ary schemes in Edinburgh and the Highlands.[47] Such sentiments were perfectly compatible with developing practice elsewhere in the mission field, both where Scots worked alongside others, as in the ranks of the LMS, or alone, for example, in the Glasgow and Edinburgh Societies. Indeed, this congruence of Scottish theoris-ing and local needs helps to explain the persistence in the 1820s of 'metropolitan' traits in a man like John Philip, at odds with colonial administration and settler practice in South Africa.

The language of instruction was nevertheless of great significance and a matter for some dispute. In 1805 Carey and his colleagues had drawn up a state-ment of their missionary principles, in which they placed great emphasis on the education and training of native Indian preachers. 'It is only by means of native preachers we can hope for the universal spread of the Gospel through this immense continent. Europeans are too few and their subsistence costs too much.'[48] A commitment to the use of the vernacular languages by local Christian agents was thus essential. This priority underlay the immense programme of translations car-ried on by Carey at Serampore. It shaped the organisation of the Serampore system of local schools, founded in response to the new encouragement to educa-tion shown by the Company Government of India from 1815. Finally, in building on the principles set out in Joshua Marshman's *Hints relative to Native Schools*, vernacular education was entrenched alongside the study of both Sanskrit and English in the Baptists' Serampore College launched in 1818.[49] In Carey's view this was to be no 'Christian College' but a college of both arts and sciences, with the addition of a divinity faculty for those who wanted it and catering to both converts and non-converts.[50]

To implement its plans for educational missionary work, the Scottish Assembly in 1829 appointed Alexander Duff, who had come under Chalmers's influence at

46 Roxborogh, 'Thomas Chalmers', pp. 298, 314.
47 M.A. Laird, *Missionaries and Education in Bengal, 1793–1837* (Oxford, 1972), chap. 7, esp. pp. 198–200; Chambers, 'The Church of Scotland's Nineteenth Century Foreign Missions Scheme'.
48 John Clark Marshman, *The Life and Times of Carey, Marshman and Ward*, 2 vols (London, 1859), Vol. 1, pp. 228–9.
49 *Ibid.*, Vol. 2, pp.116–27, 157–9, 168–75; J.C. Marshman, *Hints relative to Native Schools, together with the outline of an institution for their extension and management* (Calcutta, 1816).
50 Smith, *Life of Carey*, pp. 381–410.

the University of St Andrews from 1823 to 1827. On arrival in Calcutta in May 1830, with instructions to establish a higher educational institution outside the city for the training of native vernacular teachers, Duff instead allowed his own assessment of local conditions to override the Assembly's wishes. He rapidly became convinced that 'in regard to education, elementary English schools are best adapted to the present circumstances'.[51] Aware that the expansion of Calcutta's trade and its European population had created a considerable demand for English, Duff both noted Indians' willingness to pay fees and felt that they would be unlikely to attend a new vernacular training college. He therefore planned to multiply the numbers of English-speaking Indians in the expectation that, especially if commercial demand had peaked as he suspected, there would soon be candidates enough anxious to train as English-medium teachers for 'an Institution of a Higher order' to thrive. To assist the efficient and economical use of money, time and energy, Duff also preferred a central site in Calcutta, particularly in a climate where travelling was difficult. The novelty of his methods he regarded as justification enough for his intrusion where many other missionaries were already at work.[52]

Within six months Duff was reporting that 'hitherto … [the school] has proved successful, if not triumphant' in attracting and holding pupils, especially those of the higher castes. Soon his perception of the value of English schools was, he claimed, attracting 'unanimous consent' and not only sympathy but growing practical interest at the highest levels of government. He also began to win over students from the nearby Hindu College, set up in 1817 to introduce Indians to the new secular learning but seen increasingly by conservative Hindus and missionaries as the purveyor of an undesirably Western culture. In the course of 1832 Duff began to press on the home Committee the need for the most advanced classes to be removed to a new central building, open to all and designated a College. Despite some dissenting missionary voices, his plans gathered momentum and while home on leave in 1835 Duff was able to win over the church to his vision, at least for the time being. Speaking before the General Assembly in May, he developed his theme that 'The English language … is the lever which, as an instrument, is destined to move all Hindustan.'[53] The General Assembly subsequently approved similar higher educational institutions set up in Bombay (1832), Madras (1837) and Nagpur (1844).[54]

To see the process in motion one can take the example of Dr John Wilson, the Scottish church missionary who had arrived at Bombay in February 1829. Wilson was not only an excellent linguist but strongly committed to vernacular schooling.

---

51  Duff to Inglis, 23 Aug. 1830, NLS MS7530, f. 35; for Duff's impact, Laird, *Missionaries and Education*, esp. pp. 200–41, 249–60; for commentary on his ideas about syllabus and curriculum, Gauri Viswanathan, *Masks of Conquest: Literary Study and British Rule in India* (New York, 1989; repr. Delhi, 1998), chap. 2 'Praeparatio Evangelica'.

52  Duff to Inglis, 23 Aug. 1830, 9 Nov. 1831, NLS MS7530, ff. 26–38, 84.

53  Alexander Duff, *The Church of Scotland's India Missions* (Edinburgh, 1835), p. 20.

54  Far less successful was the Anglican Bishop's College, Calcutta, founded 1820, Neill, *History of Christianity in India*, pp. 264–6.

Following the Baptist pattern, his 'instrument was the vernaculars of a varied population' – Marathi, Gujarati, Hindi, Hebrew and Portuguese – 'with Persian, Arabic and Sanskrit in reserve for the learned classes'.[55] However, following Duff's lead, Wilson launched an 'English School, connected with the Scottish Mission' in March 1832. In doing so, he was responding not only to indigenous interest but also to the 'English laymen, chiefly officials' who subsequently went on to make up the new corresponding committee which the General Assembly decided in 1835 to install with each of its missions, to provide local oversight and direction.[56] In the same way that English displaced Sanskrit at Serampore College by 1834, so Wilson's new model soon established itself. For the annual examinations in March 1842, 'The subjects and text-books were those of the Scottish Universities, not excluding Greek and Hebrew. Prize essays were read by natives on domestic reform and the practice of idolatry. Geology was the science studied that session. Dr. Wilson lectured on the evidences of Christianity and Biblical Criticism and used Hill's *Lectures* as the text-book of systematic divinity.'[57]

These were important departures and mirrored developments within the Company's government. As administrators felt under growing pressure from the perennial demand for financial economy, the perceived need for an efficient administrative class and a mixture of utilitarian or evangelical considerations, the same view became dominant during Lord William Bentinck's governor-generalship (1828–35). In response to growing contacts with the West, the expansion of private Indian-controlled schools offering similar opportunities also began to occur. As a result, where they had previously made only limited, tentative moves in this direction, the other Protestant denominations also now followed suit, modelling their 'English' schools on the Scottish General Assembly's Institution in Calcutta and cementing their relationships with the official, professional and merchant classes as they did so.[58] It gradually became clear that there were considerable limitations to such a missionary strategy, in the number of Indians educated, in the quality and distribution of schools and colleges across India and still more in the number of conversions thereby achieved by the missionaries. Nevertheless, the commitment to English continued to shape government educational policy and remained central to missionary enterprise. Notwithstanding the limited encouragement given to elementary vernacular education under new legislation in 1854 for grants-in-aid, the provision of high-level English-language education remained a prime aim in the process of evangelism for many years to come. In following Duff's example, missions reduced the significance hitherto attached to instruction in the classical and vernacular languages of India. They shifted significantly towards the provision of syllabuses designed to introduce

55  George Smith, *The Life of John Wilson, D.D., F.R.S.* (London, 1878), pp. 79 and 68–77.
56  *Ibid.*, pp. 78, 245, with lay names at p. 76.
57  Marshman to Wilson, 23 Sept. 1834, *ibid.*, pp. 246–7, 249; George Hill, *Lectures in Divinity*, 3 vols (Edinburgh, 1821).
58  Laird, *Missions and Education*, chap. 8 'Scottish and English Missionaries, 1830–1837'.

into India modern, secular, Western knowledge combined with a moral and Christian education. In so doing, they furthered the ambitions of both a significant body of opinion within the government of India and those Indians who saw advantages in collaborating with agents of imperial rule and Western contact.

## VI

When Dr John Philip settled in Cape Town in 1819, mission stations were of two kinds. There were those within the administrative frontiers of the Colony, established on land either bought by the missionary societies themselves or granted to them by the colonial government, of which Genadendal and Bethelsdorp were the most important. Other stations were set up beyond the colony's notional border, such as the LMS's Griqua Town (originally Klaarwater) and Kuruman (originally Lattakoo) or, a little later, the chain of Wesleyan stations, beginning with Wesleyville, in what was known to contemporaries as Kaffirland (later the Ciskei and Transkei). Most of these were the result of missionary responses to what they understood to be expressions of interest or direct requests by local African leaders for a missionary presence in their territories. Such pleas in the discourse of the day to 'come over and help us' were encouraged and enthusiastically reported back to societies' headquarters. They were readily interpreted as evidence of Africans' awareness of the significance of the Gospel and the numerous openings for evangelism and were a major feature of missions' fund-raising efforts.

Privately, however, missionaries were often more sceptical, sometimes cynical, in their comments on the local motivation behind such approaches. As Thomas Hodgson noted in his journal, 'it is to be feared that most of the calls for missionaries in the "come over and help us" which ring through the religious world [?], arise from an idea that the residence of missionaries will be an advantage in a temporal sense'.[59] This view was echoed from the colonial side, for instance when Governor Somerset wanted to strengthen his system of agents beyond the frontier. The following letter from the Colonial Secretary provides a clear illustration of the way in which missionaries were used by the civil authorities and of the resultant need for the missionaries to fight their own corner. 'His Excellency is convinced that he shall better consult the immediate interests of this settlement and put an end more easily to those inhuman massacres and ruinous plunderings which take place on our borders, by complying with the wish of the Caffer chief to have a zealous and enlightened instructor sent to replace Mr. Williams than by any acts of hostility towards the offending Caffers.'[60] Writing to the Wesleyan Mission Secretaries,

59  12 Jan. 1823, R.L. Cope (ed.), *The Journal of the Rev. T.L. Hodgson Missionary to the Seleka-Rolong and the Griquas, 1821–31* (Johannesburg, 1977), p. 106.

60  Lt-Col. Christopher Bird to Rev. John Brownlee, 30 Dec. 1818, John Philip Papers, Mss.Afr.s. 216/1/51. Brownlee resigned from the LMS and was officially appointed 'government' missionary to the Xhosa at Ngqika's kraal, the successor to Rev. Joseph Williams (LMS) who had resisted taking on this role.

William Shrewsbury regretfully agreed with Hodgson: 'those Chiefs & their people who have desired Missionaries, have been mainly influenced by *worldly principles*; they supposing – & indeed truly – that it would tend in various respects to their outward advantage, & especially be a means of preserving them from the various marauders of this continent, by the friendship they would be able, through our medium, to maintain with the Colony'. Shrewsbury nevertheless acknowledged that, whatever the motive, the foot in the door that it provided was both beneficial and providentially designed for the achievement of greater things. 'From this consideration arises much of the respect shown to the Missionary, & much of the importance which attaches itself to his character. And for this reason, a Missionary is sure to have the shield of protection thrown over him by whatever Chief he lives with against all direct Persecution, Oppression & Wrong. All this is ordered by Divine Providence for the accomplishment of much higher & more glorious purposes than the people themselves have contemplated by desiring us to sojourn with them, as acknowledged Teachers of the Word of God.' The problem for the missionaries lay of course in that 'those principles which have induced them to desire our residence in the Country, will not lead them to renounce ungodliness & Sin'.[61]

To persuade Africans to take that further step, missionaries were initially inclined to agree that the first requirement lay in establishing stable, settled communities. While this might be seen as an attempt to hasten their progression from the stage of nomadism and hunting to that of settled agriculture and commerce, it had another far more immediate importance for missionaries who needed at least a constant, attentive and preferably concentrated audience to receive their preaching. Failure to secure this was for a mission to fall at the first fence. No wonder therefore that Van der Kemp's colleagues Johannes Kicherer and William Edwards, having made no discernible impression on the San, picked themselves up, shook off the dust of Namaqualand and headed for greener pastures. Still more was stable concentration necessary if that further necessity, the school, was to be established: 'it is only by its means that we can indulge a hope of raising up *Native Interpreters, Schoolmasters & Preachers*'.[62]

However, the early experience of the LMS seemed to suggest that missionary stations given over essentially to preaching and teaching were also less than effective in fostering wider change. The poverty of Bethelsdorp under Van der Kemp was a case in point, too often providing no more than a sanctuary for those who had nowhere else to go. Philip quickly realised that there would be little to write home about if missionary activities were confined to LMS 'institutions' simply because they were the only places where the Khoi might find 'a shadow of protection'.[63]

61  W.J. Shrewsbury to Mission Committee, 31 March 1831, WMMS South Africa Albany Correspondence, 1831/7.
62  William Shaw to Mission Committee, 26 April 1826, *ibid.*, 1826/21.
63  Philip, *Researches in South Africa*, Vol. 1, p. xxx.

Mission stations needed to be far more than self-contained centres for basic evangelism, reliant on a bare, or even a successful, subsistence economy. Sometimes, however, it seemed as if this development might be impossible under policies devised in London. Questioning whether it was right for them to continue funding some of the South African stations, the Directors wrote to Philip suggesting that 'settlements somewhat approaching towards the state of those established by Moravians and rendered capable by exercise of trades of supporting themselves appear to Directors very desirable'.[64] For reasons of economy and efficiency, Philip at first had some sympathy with this line of thought. Shortly after his arrival in South Africa, for example, he proudly referred to the Caledon Institution, founded by the LMS near Swellendam in 1811, as quite likely to become 'the Genadendal of our Institutions in this country'.[65] However, his support subsequently cooled for a course of action which could be seen as revealing the weaknesses of the Moravian model. 'The Moravian method of forming a colony under the direction of several missionaries is very pretty. But it will require thousands of years before the heathen will be converted by their mode of proceeding. A missionary fixed among a few hundred Hottentots should not consider this as a fixed abode but as a place of residence for a few years from which after preaching the Gospel he is to remove to some other tribe ... [otherwise] his usefulness must be circumscribed and there is danger of his sinking into a mere farmer.' Privately Philip regarded the Moravians as conservative in their outlook and practice and 'the great men in this colony who were constantly praising the Moravians' as at best uncritical or having as their object to run down the LMS.[66]

Philip's alternative crystallised rapidly as he travelled round the colony, gradually drawing together a vision of uninhibited evangelism and the political as well as economic conditions essential to its success. The vision he set out at length in his *Researches*, as part of his efforts to inform British domestic opinion of the true conditions in South Africa. It has been much written about and needs little more than to be summarised here.[67] Starting from belief in the fundamental and universal equality of humans everywhere, Philip argued that Christianity, commerce and civilisation inevitably developed together. The relationship of man and society was so constituted 'that no improvement can take place in any part of the one or the other without diffusing its influence over the whole man and over the whole frame of society. The thorough knowledge of one science requires a general acquaintance with many others. With the improvements of science, the arts and manufactures of

64  W.A. Hankey and George Burder (LMS Secretaries) to Philip, 9 April 1819, John Philip Papers Mss.Afr.s.216/1/70.

65  Philip to the Directors, c.Aug. 1819, *ibid.*, 74; and *ibid.*, 73, for plans to cultivate cotton, flax and hemp.

66  Philip to David Bogue, 18 May 1821, *ibid.*, 151; to Directors, 19 Jan. 1824, *ibid.*, 216/2/330.

67  Most recently by Andrew Ross, *John Philip*, pp. 84–102 and Elbourne, *Blood Ground*, pp. 240–52; for the best presentation of the general circumstances within which Philip was working and to which his *Researches in South Africa* was a response, Keegan, *Colonial South Africa*.

a country may be expected to keep place ... It is the same as it respects the progress of genuine religion.' The unfettered efforts of missionaries towards their main goal of conversion, therefore, inevitably brought with them 'innumerable advantages, connected with the improvement of the world, in their train'. Missions made possible 'the triumphs of reason over ignorance, of civilisation over barbarism and of benevolence over cruelty and oppression'.[68] 'Civilisation bears to religion a relation similar to what the foliage bears to the tree.'[69]

Philip's vision of society was essentially libertarian and the role of government he saw as that of guarantor of rights and freedoms, notably rights to the security of property both in land and labour and freedom from arbitrary compulsion and unjust laws. Missionaries and Africans, he argued, were at one here and missionaries required no special privileges beyond the 'protection ... from colonial rapacity and cruelty' which was not only all that government could provide but the common right of everyone.[70] True religion would triumph just as genuine ability would secure its right reward, albeit within a society increasingly differentiated by class distinctions rather than colour.

In practice, Philip thus wanted the LMS stations or institutions to emerge as outward-looking centres, integrated socially and economically on equal terms into the broader community. As producers of, for example, cotton, flax, hemp and other marketable commodities and as consumers, the Khoi would accumulate wealth and education; they would set an example through the improvement of their stations and become steadily more involved in the life of the colony. Tribes beyond the colony, secure in the assurance of protection by the imperial government, would be able to hold their own and develop in a similar way. Rather than increase the size of individual institutions and the numbers of Africans they accommodated, Philip wanted the numbers of missionary stations throughout the colony and elsewhere to be increased. Ultimately the position of the Khoi throughout the Colony and the Xhosa beyond would be equally secure and respected.[71]

Influential as Philip's views became and well known as they are, there were other missions working their way towards what in important respects were similar conclusions. The Wesleyan missions at the Cape got properly under way with the arrival of Methodist preachers such as William Shaw and John Ayliff, who emigrated from Britain with the '1820 settlers'. These settlers, some four thousand in all, were brought in by the imperial government in part to reconstruct the eastern defences of the Cape Colony after the War of 1819. Centred on Graham's Town, the Wesleyans developed a much greater sympathy with the ambitions of white colonists than did other denominations, especially at the time of the eastern

---

68  Philip, *Researches*, 1, pp. vii–viii, x, with further discussion at Vol. 1, pp. 355–70.
69  *Ibid.*, p. 204.
70  *Ibid.*, p. xxvii.
71  Not only Ross but Macmillan, *The Cape Colour Question* and *Bantu, Boer and Briton*, quote extensively from Philip's writings and correspondence on these issues.

frontier war of 1834. They saw the invasion of the Colony in that year as further evidence of the 'predatory warfare' characteristic of the Khoi and Xhosa with their 'semi-barbarous state of society'; and they rejected out of hand the idea that it had been provoked by the colonists. Methodists had early on criticised Van der Kemp and Read for such faults as 'antinomianism', 'laxity' and 'disrespect for the Sabbath' and William Shaw in particular emerged as a persistent critic of Philip and the humanitarians.[72]

Missionaries such as Philip saw themselves as protectors of African interests against white oppression and violence, requiring to be backed up by the power of the imperial government in the absence of sufficient support from the colonial authorities. Shaw and his colleagues by contrast saw their missionary role as that of mediator between 'the Muskets of the white people and the Assagays [*sic*] of the Caffres'.[73] They accepted the legitimacy of colonial ambitions, for, as one missionary in Graham's Town observed, 'I have never known a community of Europeans *so free* from illiberal prejudices.' And they were convinced of the need to retain the 'present salutary impression of the superior power of the Colonial Government, by the *prompt* and *severe* punishment of wrongs inflicted on the Colony or on Colonists in Kafirland'.[74] This lack of sympathy with the humanitarian perspective did not simply reflect conventional thought among settlers in the eastern Cape, nor did it depend entirely on the issues at stake. Methodist leaders completely removed from the scene were equally inclined to dismiss 'the sickly sentimentalism of certain philanthropists, who would make the Natives angels' and to criticise Philip personally with an animus which owed much to his own criticisms of their missionaries.[75]

Nevertheless, the Methodists and the more conservative spirits among the LMS members developed with Philip's party a common view of the political economy appropriate to building up Christian communities. On the missionary stations, not only the encouragement of commercial agriculture but the establishment of stores was essential: 'by this means', Shaw wrote from Wesleyville, 'our people would be enabled, by a little industry, to rise to the enjoyment of many of the comforts & conveniences of civilized life'. As Shaw later reported, iron cooking pots, hatchets, handkerchiefs and calicoes were all exceedingly

72  Cope (ed.), *Journals of the Rev. T.L. Hodgson*, p.90; Shaw to Mission Committee, 2 Feb. 1826, warned the London officers against Philip; Shaw to Philip, 6 April 1838, WMMS South Africa Albany Correspondence, 1826/6, 1838/2; William Shaw, *A Defence of the Wesleyan Missionaries in South Africa: Comprising Copies of a Correspondence with the Rev. Dr John Philip DD* (London, 1839). See also Dr John Beecham to Rev. Jabez Bunting, letters 1836–38, MCA, PLP 7-2-30 to 34 and correspondence in W.J. Shrewsbury File, *ibid.*, PLP 97–9.

73  Shaw to Mission Committee, 1 April 1830, WMMS South Africa Albany Correspondence, 1830/12.

74  W.J. Shrewsbury to Mission Committee 30 March 1833, *ibid.*, 1833/10; Wm B. Boyce to Gov. Sir B. D'Urban, 31 March 1834 (copy), *ibid.*, 1834/13.

75  Dr John Beecham to Rev. Jabez Bunting (n.d., 1834?), MCA, PLP 7-2-25.

popular.[76] The plough too was vital, increasing the cultivable area and, he hoped, revolutionising the position of women who had hitherto dug the fields with wooden spades.[77] William Shrewsbury felt the consequences to be a quiet revolution. 'Commercial enterprize, which is not without its moral disadvantages, & its tendencies, in the hands of some men, to corrupt even the heathen, ... is, *upon the whole*, productive of good in various respects. It is evidently a mean in the hands of Providence, both of promoting that Civilization for which the gospel has prepared the people, & of opening a more frequent intercourse with interior tribes, which will facilitate the establishment of Christian Missions amongst them also.'[78]

Underpinning the whole system, however, was the need for security of African rights to possess the land, both within and without the Colony. This was confirmed for the Methodists by the War of 1834. Shaw, for instance, argued vigorously for the importance of land rights in evidence to the Parliamentary Select Committee on Aborigines in 1835.[79] 'The local government should support and protect them in the enjoyment of their rights, and especially of their rights in the soil, without which the Caffres must ultimately prove a great scourge to the colony. If we deprive them of the soil, we deprive them of the means of sustenance and we compel them to become robbers and thus war must be perpetuated till we have extirpated them.'[80] He was also closely involved in the writing and publication by his colleague William Boyce of a vigorous defence of Wesleyan views on the question.[81] As Shaw explained to John Beecham, the Mission Secretary, Boyce was 'a decided convert to all the most important of *our principles*, especially the essential one, that the only way to secure the interests of the Aborigines, *is to secure their lands* ... The correct principle as to Colonization maintained in your admirable pamphlet on that subject, are maintained in Boyce's book and sustained by weighty facts ... To prevent their predatory habits on the one hand and to secure their right in the soil on the other, is the only method that can be devised to save the Aborigines from ultimate annihilation'.[82]

---

76  Shaw to Mission Committee, 17 Aug. 1825; also 20 Aug. 1827, 13 July 1828, WMMS South Africa Albany Correspondence, 1825/29, 1827/?, 1828/22. For Shaw's Wesleyville store, Roger B. Beck, 'Cape Colonial Officials and Christian Missionaries in the Early Nineteenth Century', in Holger Bernt Hansen and Michael Twaddle (eds), *Christian Missionaries and the State in the Third World* (Oxford and Athens, GA, 2001), pp. 76–86.

77  Shaw to Mission Committee, 9 Dec. 1831, WMMS South Africa Albany Correspondence, 1831/34.

78  Shrewsbury to Mission Committee, 29 March 1832, *ibid.*, 1832/8.

79  *Aborigines (British Settlements): Report from the Select Committee*, PP (1836) 7 (538), QQ. 596–762, 1062–71, 1099–1129.

80  *Ibid.*, 7 Aug. 1835, Q. 663.

81  William B.Boyce, *Notes on South African Affairs, from 1834 to 1838* (Graham's Town, 1838).

82  Shaw to Beecham (private), 10 Nov. 1838 and also 1 Feb. 1839, WMMS South Africa Correspondence, 1838/? and 8; D. Coates, John Beecham and William Ellis, *Christianity the Means of Civilization* (London, 1837) brought together the missionary evidence to the Select Committee for a wider audience.

## VII

There were still many issues in dispute between the different missionary groups at the Cape. Were African rights, for example, however 'secure', none the less to be qualified by the recognition of their tenures as 'colonial fiefs'; or were occupancy and possession to be defined in some more absolute manner? These were questions that remained to be answered. Nevertheless it is clear that by the mid-1830s, in the Cape Colony as well as the very different settings of British India and colonial Sierra Leone, missions had begun to develop and offer prescriptions for political and economic change. Such alternatives as already existed – like the hunting or peripatetic pastoralism still found in parts of Cape Colony – seemed to them scarcely more conducive to conversion than was compulsory labour for white masters. T.L. Hodgson prayed for the San and the Griqua to 'cease their indolent wandering habits' and, sharing his conviction that 'idleness is irreconcilable with experimental religion',[83] many missionaries began to support openly not only the cause of slave emancipation but that of legal protection for free labour and the recognition of rights to land-ownership. They thus came to favour the acquisition of property, the accumulation and the security of a settled existence for non-Europeans as essential supports to an independent Christian way of life, to the future of local churches and the freedom of missionaries themselves to move on to new fields.

It was the progress of their settlements, first of all Bethelsdorp, that brought home to LMS missionaries the links between encouraging the Khoi as both producers and consumers, deeply involved in the commercial life of the colony and the advance of Christianity.[84] At the same time there was here a general principle, made explicit in the LMS Resolution of October 1818. 'It is a duty which the Directors owe to the great cause of propagating the Gospel ... to press on the attention of all their missionaries the obligation of finding their support from the people among whom they labour. This principle is of the greatest importance and the acting upon it in any station will be in itself a security for the progress of the Gospel in that place.'[85] The development of mission stations from 1820 onwards – Griqua Town, Philipolis, the Kat River settlement and Wesleyan settlements beyond the Fish River – seemed only to confirm the possibilities inherent in an alliance of commerce and Christianity. By the 1830s the missions had learned that their obligation to seek means for the conversion of the heathen required of them that they should become not only political animals but also political economists. There was little room it seemed for a man like Shrewsbury who begged to be excused the responsibilities of mission administration on account of his ineptitude in money matters. The Philips and the Shaws were inheriting the earth.

---

83  Cope (ed.), *Journals of the Rev. T.L. Hodgson*, pp. 66, 76.
84  James Read to Sir John Cradock, 23 Jan. 1812, copy, LMS 5/1/B/12.
85  Lovett, *History of the LMS*, Vol. 1, pp. 540–1.

# 5

# International connections and domestic networks in the missionary movement, 1815–50

In order to give effect to their religious imperatives, British missions and those who organised them had been forced to come to terms with the real worlds of political authority and economic activity. However, the unanticipated extent of this accommodation was seen neither as inescapable surrender nor as a source of perpetual dependence. Early nineteenth-century evangelical views of the relationship between missionary religion and imperial or indigenous authority were distinguished by their sense of self-sufficiency under a divine superintendence, rather than by any conscious or actual dependence by them on secular agencies or dynamism. Recognition by evangelicals of limiting conditions, whether imposed by governments or material circumstances, must always be clearly distinguished from both reliance on or subservience to them. To understand this requires historians to recognise the reality of missionaries' faith, their belief and trust in Providence, their conviction of the reality and reliability of divine promises and revelation offered in the Bible. Only if this is done can one explain the incurable optimism and missions' persistence in the face of death, hardship, deprivation and the tiny numbers of converts.

For the missionary, faith placed the empire in perspective. 'Empire', like 'civilisation', was at best something to be turned to missionary advantage, a means to an end but equally something to be ignored or rejected out of hand if it failed to serve the missionary's main purpose. 'It is very well in its place', wrote Philip, 'to urge the civilizing influence of a missionary society. But this is not the main object of such an institution. It is not the end; it is only the accompaniment. It is a never-failing collateral and may be used as a lawful instrument in fighting the battles of the missionary cause.'[1] In Philip's view, if people would but realise it, far from missions depending on empire, the reverse was the case. 'While our missionaries, beyond the borders of the colony of the Cape of Good Hope, are everywhere scattering the seeds of civilization, social order and happiness, they are, by the most unexceptionable means, extending British interests, British influence and the British empire. Wherever the missionary places his standard among a savage tribe, their prejudices against the colonial government give way; their dependence upon the colony is increased by the creation of artificial wants; confidence is restored; intercourse with the colony is established; industry, trade and agriculture spring up; and every

---

1 Philip, *Researches in South Africa*, Vol. 2, p. 360, quoting with approval Thomas Chalmers.

genuine convert among them made to the Christian religion becomes the ally and friend of the colonial government.'[2]

To a modern reader it may seem perverse for contemporary commentators – not least one as insecurely placed as Philip – to invert the balance of power between missions and government. They did so because, like Philip in his *Researches*, they were at pains to develop arguments that might appeal to a general public, not because they themselves necessarily took them seriously and certainly not because to uphold empire was itself a primary missionary goal. It was the task of imperial rulers to look after empire; if they were wise, they would facilitate missionary enterprise. Missions could be generally confident of catching the approving eye of Providence; the survival and success of empire were essentially uncertain. However, there were also other developments that enabled the eye of faith to behold signs of success and grounds for perseverance, to which missionaries attached much more significance. Of particular importance was the growth of global missionary networks, fostered by the active pursuit of common goals and the inter-marriage of members of missionary families

# I

International missionary networks and the generation of public support both at home and abroad continued to be an important source of practical assistance and encouragement. For British missions, North American contacts were of particular significance and took many, often overlapping, forms in the course of the century; personal friendships, professional contacts, exchanges of information and litera-ture, political co-operation and the transfer of revivalist impulses were all involved. In the first half of the century, the history not least of the LMS offers very instruc-tive examples of the way in which these connections and influences operated. They arise especially from areas such as the Pacific or southern Africa where LMS missionaries came into close contact with those of the American Board of Commissioners for Foreign Missions (ABCFM).

By 1815 LMS contacts with American supporters were plain enough. In its report for that year were listed seventeen Foreign Directors. Alongside those from Basel, Berlin, three from Rotterdam, East Friesland, Denmark, Sweden, Altona and Malta, a further six were from the United States; three of them represented missionary societies, in New York, Connecticut and Massachusetts.[3] George Burder, LMS Secretary from 1803 to 1827, had established a correspondence with his opposite number at the ABCFM in Boston, Jeremiah Evarts, which continued to grow under their successors. A significant part was played in this development by William Ellis, LMS Foreign Secretary from 1831 to 1841.

---

2  *Ibid.*, Vol. 1, pp. ix–x.
3  *Report of the [London] Missionary Society, 1815*, List of Directors. Samuel Marsden in New South Wales was listed as the seventeenth.

Ellis was originally sent in 1816 to join the LMS's Tahitian mission and first made acquaintance with the Americans when he accompanied an LMS deputation in 1822 to visit the recently established ABCFM Sandwich Islands mission in Hawaii. Ellis was so well liked and his linguistic skills so valuable, that he was invited to stay by the American missionaries and the local rulers and the two mission boards agreed to his transfer to Hawaii. Ellis returned to Britain from the Sandwich Islands in 1824 on account of his wife's serious illness and found it necessary to travel eastwards, first taking ship via Cape Horn to New Bedford, Massachusetts. He spent four months in Boston and New York, preaching and lecturing at the request of the American Board and forming important friendships, especially with Rufus Anderson, about to become the Board's Foreign Secretary. Ellis's wife meanwhile recovered sufficiently in the homes of American Board committee members to face the rest of their homeward voyage.[4]

Ellis was excited by the stirring of religious revival in the eastern United States and was enthused by the warmth of his reception. Everywhere, 'it has been highly gratifying to me to observe, in various classes and particularly in religious society, such a friendly feeling towards England and such a desire to co-operate with all associations of good men there, in … promoting righteousness, peace and happiness among all the families of mankind'.[5] More than forty years later Anderson paid generous tribute to the importance of Ellis's contribution to the work of the Board 'in many parts of the Northern and Middle states'.[6]

Once back in Britain, Ellis gained a reputation not only as an expert on Polynesia but as the chronicler of the local 'progress' in Christianity and civilisation brought about by the missionary societies.[7] In the preface to his *Polynesian Researches*, he explained how his volumes showed the transformation of 'the barbarous, cruel, indolent and idolatrous inhabitants of Tahiti and the neighbouring Islands, into a comparatively civilized, humane, industrious and Christian people. They also comprise a record of the measures pursued by the native governments, in changing the social economy of the people and regulating their commercial intercourse with foreigners, in the promulgation of a new civil code … the establishment of courts of justice and the introduction of trial by jury.'[8] There was,

---

4 John Eimeo Ellis, *Life of William Ellis Missionary to the South Seas and to Madagascar* (London, 1873), chap. 6: William Ellis, *Memoir of Mary M. Ellis* (London, 1835), pp. 151–3; Ellis's correspondence with Anderson, in the ABCFM Archive. Unless otherwise stated, all Ellis letters cited are from this archive. The series ABC 14, 'Miscellaneous Foreign Letters', consists of seven volumes covering principally the years 1831–99 and 1910–19; it contains the extensive correspondence addressed to the Board and its officers in Boston by members of foreign missionary societies and other individuals overseas.
5 Ellis to Burder, 8 July 1825, from Dorchester (USA), CWM South Seas 5/4.
6 Rufus Anderson, *History of the Sandwich Islands Mission* (Boston, 1870), pp. 59–60.
7 This was based on William Ellis's *Narrative of a Tour through Hawaii* (London, 1826); and *Polynesian Researches, during a residence of nearly six years in the South Sea Islands*, 2 vols (London, 1829).
8 *Polynesian Researches*, p. ix.

of course, more to this than an historical account of indigenous social and cultural change. Polynesian experience provided indisputable justification for the missionary movement: 'such facts as those presented to the world, in the recent history of the Society and Sandwich Islands, prove, that CHRISTIANITY ALONE supplies the most powerful motives and the most effective machinery, for originating and accomplishing the processes of civilization'.[9]

However, Ellis was also acutely aware that this Anglo–American achievement was seriously threatened by the continuing incursion of other Europeans into the Pacific, many of whom were far less willing than most missionaries to admit the existence of indigenous 'interests'. The visit of the King and Queen of Hawaii to Britain in 1824 not only provided a very timely reminder of those interests but, as a result of their tragic deaths from measles in London, stimulated a great deal of benevolent concern. Widespread curiosity about the Pacific and Britain's presence there was revived and the region re-emerged after India and the Cape Colony as yet another focal point in that wider struggle between the missionary societies and critics of their role in British expansion. It was the interest of the LMS in Melanesia and Polynesia and of Ellis more particularly in Hawaii, which ensured that the argument was co-ordinated and taken up on both sides of the Atlantic.

Ellis had both prepared and checked his own Hawaiian journal with his American colleagues before leaving the South Seas and en route he left a copy in Boston with a view to its publication in the United States. The interest it aroused during 1826 on its appearance in Britain undoubtedly owed much to recent events, as did other publications at this time, especially the *Voyage of H.M.S. Blonde to the Sandwich Islands in the Years 1824–1825*.[10] The two volumes were the subject of a *Quarterly Review* article early in 1827 which forcefully criticised the missionaries, especially the Americans, as mischief-makers. Pursuing a common line of attack, the reviewer praised the achievements of the Protestant Moravian Brethren's missionaries in linking civilisation and Christianity as against the 'amazing absurdity' of their counterparts in Polynesia, who 'have so little judgment and are so little acquainted with the human heart, as to let their zeal out-run discretion on many occasions and in many shapes'.[11] The review attracted plenty of attention. Ellis and the Directors thought it had been written by Richard Charlton, the British consul for the Sandwich, Society and Friendly Islands (Tonga), who was regarded as no friend to missions. They immediately set about correcting the errors and misrepresentations they found in it, through the *Edinburgh Review*, the *Eclectic Review* and in a letter to the *Quarterly* itself that the Society then published. Ellis even visited

9 Ellis, *Narrative*, Preface.

10 This account of the journey home of the dead Hawaian monarchs in a royal naval vessel, based on material supplied above all by the ship's chaplain and officers, was published in London (1826), by Maria Graham, cousin of its commanding officer, Captain Lord Byron.

11 *Quarterly Review* 35 (March 1827), pp. 419–45, quotation from p. 438; see also the Note with a letter from Na-Boki, p. 609 and *ibid.*, 36 (June 1827), Note, p. 298.

Charlton's friends and relatives in Falmouth.[12] From Baltimore, one of the American Board missionaries, outraged by 'so many palpable falsehoods contained in so small a space of print', told Ellis of his own attempts to counteract the *Quarterly*'s message in the local religious press.[13]

Thus the Pacific was caught up along with the Caribbean colonies and Sierra Leone in the processes of justifying the missionary task by appeal to its civilising impact, exposing the brutality and selfish interests of so many of its white expatriate critics and winning support at home for evangelical enterprise, not least among Britain's social and political elites. To this end, Ellis spoke, wrote and travelled a great deal. He spent the summer of 1827, for example, cultivating Viscountess Lifford, Viscountess Powerscourt, Lady Lowton, Lady Westmeath, Lord Gosford and others during a prolonged Irish tour. Kept up-to-date by his own letters to and from the islands as well as those of the Society, he corresponded and dined with Lord Byron in his campaign to get Charlton removed from his official position. Byron's high opinion of Ellis was matched by his willingness to enter the dispute in public support of the missionaries.[14] Discovering for himself as he itinerated the extensive public attention, not least in Scotland, he emphasised that the LMS 'should not deprive itself of the high and continued interest on behalf of the Sand[wic]h Islands which prevails in this country'.[15]

His own *Polynesian Researches*, partly written in the midst of this hectic journeying, also contributed to the blending of persistent propaganda with enlightenment and edification. He was not alone in his satisfaction at its sympathetic reception in the *Quarterly Review*, where the poet Robert Southey felt 'A more interesting book than this, in all its parts, we have never perused'. That Southey had his own conservative ecclesiastical agenda in mind was evident from his closing suggestion, that as 'the missionaries desire that the great good which they have done should be rendered permanent, it behoves them … to procure for their church the best human security that can be obtained, by connecting it with the state'.[16] But the nonconformist Ellis was not to be put off. Accepting an invitation from Southey, he found him most hospitable and stayed long. That pleasure mingled with calculation is clear from his account afterwards to the Secretary in London. 'Not that I anticipate much from him individually but the circle in which

---

12  William Orme, *A Defence of the Missions in the South Seas and Sandwich Islands against the misrepresentations contained in a late number of the Quarterly Review in a letter to the editor of the Journal* (London, 1827); Ellis (Leicester) to W.A. Hankey, 12 April 1827, CWM South Seas 6/4; Niel Gunson, *Messengers of Grace: Evangelical Missionaries in the South Seas, 1797–1860* (Melbourne, 1978), pp. 143, 170.

13  Elisha Loomis (Baltimore) to Ellis, 21 July 1827, CWM South Seas 6/4.

14  Ellis to Rev. J. Arundel, 21 June (from Dungannon) and 10 December 1827, CWM Home 5/1; George A. Byron, *An Examination of Charges against the American Missionaries at the Sandwich Islands, as alleged in the Voyage of the Ship Blonde and in the Quarterly Review* (Cambridge, 1828); J. Dyer (Admiralty) to Arundel, 13 April 1826, CWM Home 4/8.

15  Ellis to [Arundel?], 9 July 1829, from Edinburgh, CWM Home 5/4.

16  *Quarterly Review* 43, 1 (1830), pp. 1–54; quotations at 1, 54.

he moves and the extent of his writings render it exceedingly desirable that he should be favourable. I have heard of several gentlemen to whom he had spoken favourably of the results of the Mission to Tahiti.'[17]

Contacts with the American Board in Boston were an essential part of this activity. Rufus Anderson not only welcomed copies of Ellis's notes and manuscripts, but in return supplied him with private information about the British consul from his own correspondents. He also sent details of the Board's own publishing plans as well as copies of publications and reports on legal action being taken against ship owners for the actions of their captains and crews.[18] A prime object of these exchanges was not only to share information but also to maintain a common front. The two societies' common objectives would be greatly assisted by the fact that, as Anderson happily noted, 'In all the multiplied facts, which are mentioned directly and incidentally on both sides of the water, I do not find any discrepancy worth mentioning. In all the great points of fact and reasoning we agree perfectly, though writing 3000 miles apart and with distinct sources of information.'[19]

After Ellis's own *Narrative*, among the most obvious early fruits of this co-operation was a London edition of the journal of the former American missionary, the Reverend Charles Stewart. Covering events in the Sandwich Islands from 1823 to 1825 and, according to Anderson, 'exceedingly and deservedly popular' in America, it was edited and extensively annotated by Ellis. Ellis used it to put paid to the *Quarterly Review*'s errors of the previous year and also as a further move in the concerted effort to have Charlton replaced with a more amenable appointment.[20] Behind the scenes Ellis, Anderson and their colleagues continued to pool their information, about atrocities carried out by British or American merchant seamen and naval personnel, as well as the details of ships involved and their owners, their intention being where possible to have employees disciplined. They recorded for each other details of their dealings with government and politicians. Anderson, for example, kept Ellis abreast of the Court of Inquiry into the abuses alleged against crew-members of the American *Dolphin*, while Ellis recounted his contacts with Wilberforce, Sir Thomas Baring and government departments as to the consulship and legislation against atrocities.[21]

17 Ellis to Arundel, 21 June 1830, from Penrith, CWM Home 5/5. Also Ellis to Arundel 8 June 1830, in *ibid.*; and R. Southey to Rev. Neville White, 27 Aug. 1830, in Charles Cuthbert Southey (ed.), *The Life and Correspondence of the late Robert Southey*, 6 vols (London, 1849–50), Vol. 6, p. 114.

18 Rufus Anderson to Ellis, 21 Nov. 1827, 15 and 28 Jan. 1828, ABC/2.01/1, ff. 32–3, 40, 41 and following. The series ABC/2.01 and 2.1 contain the Foreign Secretaries' 'Out' Letters. Unless otherwise stated Anderson wrote from Boston, Massachusetts.

19 Anderson to Ellis, 15 Ja. 1828, ABC/2.01/1, f. 41.

20 Charles Samuel Stewart, *Journal of a Residence in the Sandwich Islands, during the years 1823, 1824 and 1825 ... With an Introduction and occasional notes by William Ellis* (London, 1828).

21 Anderson to Ellis, 23 May 1828, ABC/2.01/1, ff. 54–6; Ellis to Jeremiah Evarts, 29 Nov. 1828, ABC/14/1/24.

The pattern of contacts Ellis had established in the 1820s, on the basis of first his own and increasingly the two societies' common interest in the evangelisation of the Pacific islands, was naturally extended in the 1830s when on the death of Reverend William Orme, the LMS Foreign Secretary, Ellis was himself persuaded to take the appointment.[22] In his new position, as he explained to Rufus Anderson when exchanging with him portrait drawings of the mission secretaries, Ellis regarded their correspondence as vital to their effective work in the field and to further increasing or maintaining support at home. 'The better we understand each other,' he wrote, 'the more effectually shall we be enabled to cooperate.'[23] The two secretaries shared a common positive perception of Pacific islanders' capacities and a common diagnosis of the threats to their realisation. Their correspondence offered one means of co-ordinating a successful defence.

This was not just conventional politeness or a routine performance. Information exchanged was often inspiration shared. In Ellis's words, 'The accounts we continue to receive from your side of the Atlantic are very encouraging and give increased energy to our exertions here. Your *Herald* I look for with great anxiety and receive with much satisfaction.'[24] Exchanges of letters easily spilled over into mutual assistance with publication. Anderson and Ellis discussed the exchange of their own and others' manuscripts; the inclusion of material of particular interest to different audiences for separate British or American editions; how to outwit pirate publishers; obtaining books on particular subjects from the other's country; and the steps each was taking to refute the calumnies of missionaries' critics.[25]

A striking example was the publication of Ellis's vigorous *Vindication of the South Sea Missions*, brought out in response to the recent English translation of the Estonian Otto von Kotzebue's account of his world voyage which included serious criticisms of British and American missions and had been published a few years earlier in German. With a limited circulation in the original, Kotzebue's opinions and book had hardly seemed worth countering. Translated and favourably noticed in one or two journals, the position looked more serious.[26] As Ellis now explained, 'the account is made the vehicle of one of the most virulent and malicious, as well

22  17 Dec. 1830, Minutes of the London Secretaries Association, Vol. 1, British and Foreign Bible Society Archives, University Library, Cambridge; Ellis to Arundel, 23 Feb. 1831 and Rev. Dr Paterson to Rev. John Clayton, 4 Nov. 1831, CWM Home 5/6; Ellis to Anderson, 31 March 1831, ABC/14/1.

23  Ellis to Anderson, 19 July 1832, ABC/14/1.

24  Ellis to Anderson, 27 March 1830, ABC/14/1. *The Missionary Herald* was the American Board's periodical.

25  Ellis to Anderson, 20 April 1830; 14 Nov. 1830; 31 March 1831; 28 Feb. 1833, ABC/14/1; 24 Nov. 1838 (Private), ABC/14/2; Jeremiah Evarts to Ellis, 30 April 1828, Anderson to Ellis, 28 Feb, 21 Oct. 1828, 12 Nov. 1830, 21 March 1834, ABC/2.01/1, ff. 47–9, 109, 268 and ABC/2.01/2, f. 530.

26  O.E. von Kotzebue, *A New Voyage round the World in the years 1823, 24, 25 and 26*, 2 vols (London, 1830), Vol. 1, pp. 119–223 'O Tahaiti', passim; for Bingham (referred to as 'Bengham'), Vol. 2, pp. 151–265 'The Sandwich Islands'. For the irritation it caused, Gunson, *Messengers of Grace*, pp. 171–2.

as unfounded, attacks upon the introduction and influence of Christianity in those islands, which it has yet had to endure'. [27] Not only did Ellis devote eight chapters to a point-by-point demolition of Kotzebue's veracity and reliability; he also played a nationalist card, pointing out 'palpable indications of prejudice against the English government and nation'. For good measure he used the Appendix to hammer again other critics and to correct 'misapprehensions' in Captain F.W. Beechey's otherwise well regarded *Narrative of a Voyage to the Pacific and Beering's Strait*, which echoed Kotzebue and had been given recent currency in the *Edinburgh Review*. A copy went to Anderson hot off the press and the Bostonian was still reporting to his friend two years later the 'good use made of your *Vindication*' in countering critics in the United States. [28] When next evidence of misrepresentations appeared, Ellis was quick to respond fully and was ultimately able to tell Anderson of his success in getting corrections published in Prussia. [29] These were continuous refrains, spanning the years between the *Vindication* and his equally forthright defence of the Americans' Hawaii mission in 1866. [30]

Information and inspiration also went hand in hand with extended perspectives. As illustrated above, the 1820s and 1830s witnessed a growing appreciation among the missions of the need for pressure behind the scenes to secure official protection in the face of the most serious threats. Shortly after his return to England, Ellis was telling his Boston friends of the efforts being made to persuade the British government to appoint a consul to the islands. [31] But it was not long before his outlook rapidly widened. His own early experience had included spending the latter months of 1816 involved with Samuel Marsden's work with the Aborigines at Paramatta near Sydney. He and Anderson discussed prospects and plans for extending their operations in Siam, Singapore, Malacca and other Asian centres. [32] No one in his position could ignore the cumulative evidence – from South Africa, the West Indies, New South Wales and New Zealand, as well as other Pacific islands – of the combined threat to both indigenous societies and missionary activity posed by uncontrolled white expansion. It is scarcely surprising to find Ellis in 1830 voicing a general concern that aboriginal tribes should 'be preserved and protected in the occupation of the land of their fathers'. [33]

27  William Ellis, *Vindication of the South Sea Missions from the Misrepresentations of Otto Von Kotzebue, Captain in the Russian Navy, with an Appendix* (London, 1831), p. 11.

28  Beechey's work was published in London, 1831; it was the subject of an article in the *Edinburgh Review* 53 (March 1831), pp. 210–31; Anderson to Ellis, 2 Jan. 1833, ABC/2.01/2, f.29.

29  Ellis to Frederick Krohn (Berlin), 3 Jan. 1833 and to Anderson, 28 Feb. (enclosing Krohn's letters) and 2 June 1833, ABC/14/1/24.

30  *Vindication of the South Sea Missions*; *The American Mission in the Sandwich Islands: A Vindication and an Appeal in relation to the proceedings of the Reformed Catholic Mission at Honolulu* (London, 1866).

31  Ellis to Jeremiah Evarts, 29 Nov. 1828, ABC/14/1.

32  Their correspondence during the 1830s contains many such examples.

33  Ellis (Halifax) to Anderson, 20 April 1830, ABC/14/1. For a recent consideration of the contemporary South African debate, Elizabeth Elbourne, 'Freedom at Issue: Vagrancy Legislation and the Meaning of Freedom in Britain and the Cape Colony, 1799 to 1842', *Slavery and Abolition* 15, 2 (1994), 114–50.

These were, of course, issues with enormous resonance for anyone aware of North America's past, as Ellis himself realised. Together with the other mission secretaries, Dandeson Coates of the CMS and John Beecham of the Wesleyans, Ellis became steadily more involved with the political movements orchestrated by Thomas Fowell Buxton, which culminated in the appointment of the parliamentary Select Committee on Aborigines in 1836–7. In preparing himself and his colleagues to give evidence to the committee, Ellis again called on Anderson, asking him for advice on the history of North American Indian relations with the white settlers: 'I am desirous of obtaining all the information I can on the subject.' In response the Bostonian jotted down a long list of possibilities since (as he later told Ellis) there was no one work which would suffice and proceeded to secure his Committee's consent to the purchase and despatch of a dozen volumes 'with a request that they may be placed in the Library of your Society'. The ABCFM's generosity not only gave Ellis much pleasure and greatly benefited the LMS's library.[34] It was also an example, albeit a particularly munificent one, of a constant process which was helping to build up missionary libraries on both sides of the Atlantic.[35]

As a further result of Ellis's concern, the missionaries' case to the Select Committee, perhaps even its final recommendations, were also significantly strengthened. North America's own record, north and south of the 49th parallel, was interpreted as providing more than sufficient proof that indigenous peoples and invading white communities could not be brought to adapt to one another unless the missions and Christianity were guaranteed a central place in the process of adjustment. North America's failure to date should not be repeated. Ellis took the opportunity in his own evidence to use material drawn directly from American sources and experience in the Pacific, including his own recent correspondence with Hiram Bingham, leader of the Hawaii mission.[36]

As the first mission for each of the societies, Pacific affairs remained a perennial preoccupation. At intervals, Ellis and Anderson exchanged ideas about renewed expansion into the Marquesas and Washington Islands, each anxious to avoid acting without the full knowledge and co-operation of the other. Their efforts to have Consul Charlton removed continued.[37] This same detailed attention was still evident in their correspondence and publications in the 1860s.[38] Ellis also had no doubt as to the value of discussing general missionary problems or dilemmas with Anderson. Some of the most serious had to do with their common,

---

34  Anderson to Ellis, 4 Oct. 1837, ABC/2.1/1, ff. 469–70; Ellis to Anderson, 12 April 1837, ABC/14/1, 7 Feb. 1838, ABC/14/2/67.

35  See also above, Chapter 2, pp. 40–41.

36  *Report from the Select Committee on Aborigines (British Settlements)*, *PP* (1837) 7 (538), QQ. 4294–5, 4304–6, 4320, 4328, 4365, 4375, 4389, 4396–4402, 4416. See also Chapter 6, pp. 139–49.

37  Anderson to Ellis, 30 Jan. 1832, ABC/2.01/1, f. 400; and 2 Jan. 1833, ABC/2.01/2, ff. 24–7; Anderson to Ellis, 4 Oct. 1837, ABC/2.1/1 ff. 470–1.

38  Letters of Ellis to Anderson in ABC/14/4 (1860–71).

if sometimes touchingly naive, aversion to 'political' involvement. Both men regarded Roman Catholic missionaries as a dire threat to their societies' efforts and were deeply resentful of their contribution to the eventual French seizure of Tahiti in 1842. For all Protestant evangelicals, the Tahiti episode – 'one of the most painful that has occurred in the annals of modern missions' – was especially shocking. It was their first direct experience of 'Catholic aggression' and the revival under Pope Gregory XVI (1831–46) of the missionary enterprise of the Roman Catholic Church and an episode in which their vociferous co-ordinated protests made no impact.[39] Just like the earlier onslaught of unscrupulous traders and whalers, so now the Roman invasion gave point and added vigour to the societies' common front. However, for both secretaries the wish to call in their governments' aid to exclude Catholics conflicted with their equally fervent wish to avoid supporting any infringement by the state of the principles of political and religious liberty. They agonised too over the implications for their principled avoidance of politics, of local rulers' wishes to take the missionaries' advice on matters of state.[40] Despite this setback, there were nevertheless many other occasions when joint action was the order of the day. Ellis pressed for ABCFM help in the LMS's attempts to curb the trade in spirits; he discussed the division of territorial spheres, the practical problems of recruiting unmarried females and the desirability of medical missionaries.[41] Knowing of Ellis's close relationship with Anderson, LMS missionaries in their turn felt free to confide in Anderson and to use him as a safe post box for despatches they feared might otherwise be interfered with en route.[42]

## II

The construction and operation of international networks in the interests of the global missionary cause also played an important role in John Philip's work. The principle they embodied Philip announced in the preface to his *Researches in South Africa*. 'I view the different missionary societies … as so many divisions of the same army; … The Christian missionary … labours for the conversion of the heathen to a common christianity … without caring to which division of it they may belong.'[43] Philip was of a slightly older generation than Ellis and from a different background, but during his visit to Britain from 1826 to 1829 he too began to

---

39  The description is from Ellis to Anderson, 25 April 1843, ABC/14/2. Gunson, *Messengers of Grace*, pp. 174–9; John Garrett, *To Live Among the Stars: Christian Origins in Oceania* (Geneva and Suva, 1982), pp. 253–7; Aarne A. Koskinen, *Missionary Influence as a Political Factor in the Pacific Islands* (Helsinki, 1953), pp. 160–81.

40  Ellis to Anderson, 22 June 1831, ABC/14/1 and 25 April 1843, ABC/14/2/72.

41  Ellis to Anderson, 2 June 1833, 16 Dec. 1833, 18 April 1835 (Private), ABC/14/1 and 7 Feb. 1838, ABC/14/2/67.

42  See, for example, George Pritchard's letters to Anderson, 1835–43, in ABC/14/1–2.

43  Philip, *Researches in South Africa*, Vol. 1, pp. xii–xiii.

develop close contacts with both continental European Protestants and colleagues in America. These have been hitherto virtually ignored.[44]

Philip's initiatives in both cases arose from his wish to encourage the establishment of strong centres of evangelism beyond the colony's borders. 'I am a strong advocate for the concentration of a strong missionary force in the commencement of a missionary undertaking among nations previously without any knowledge of the Gospel.'[45] These would provide both the most effective aids to conversion and secure defences against colonial wrongdoing. In giving effect to this Philip began in 1828–29 to draw on the LMS's well-established continental links. The LMS, like the CMS a few years later, had taken some of its early missionaries from Jänicke's centre in Berlin, together with others from the Netherlands Missionary Society. Now Philip travelled in France and Germany recruiting for South Africa; he was successful in Paris, where the Evangelical Missionary Society provided three men and at Elberfeld, where, after a last-minute visit to the headquarters of the Rhenish Missionary Society, four volunteers were selected. All sailed with Philip to Cape Town in July 1829.[46] After their settlement at Motito near Kuruman, a second Paris Evangeletical Society party was seen off from Gravesend by the LMS in November 1832 and with Philip's help took up a station at Moriah under the control of the Sotho ruler, Moshoeshoe.[47] Not only did Philip (greatly assisted by his wife) continue as the Cape Town agent for the Paris Society, but an early meeting with the Moffat family and the relative proximity of their stations to that of the LMS's Robert Moffat at Kuruman led to a great deal of contact on the ground between the two societies.[48]

At the same time, Philip came to American attention as a result of his agitation on behalf of the Khoi, his publications and the persecution he experienced in the Cape Colony, details of which were readily available in the missionary publications crossing the Atlantic. As Superintendent of the LMS's stations, he was approached in 1832 by a group of students at the Princeton Theological Seminary intent on becoming missionaries. In asking him for information about opportunities for missionary work in Africa, their motive was twofold: a wish to take advantage of the revivals then sweeping the eastern United States and to atone for the guilt of American involvement with slavery and the slave trade.[49] Philip's very full reply

---

**44** For passing reference to his role in establishing the American Board Mission in Natal, Ross, *John Philip*, pp. 95, 224; Macmillan, *Bantu, Boer and Briton*, pp. 13, 95 n.2; *The Cape Colour Question*, pp. 105–6.

**45** Philip to Rufus Anderson, 18 March 1835, ABC 14/1.

**46** Du Plessis, *Christian Missions*, pp. 200–2, 211–18; Lovett, *History of the LMS*, Vol. 1, pp. 76, 526–7. It is not known what if any contacts Philip may have had with the Berlin Missionary Society; formed in 1824, its first party of missionaries to South Africa was sent out in 1834.

**47** Du Plessis, *Christian Missions*, pp. 190–4; Eugene Casalis, *My Life in Basutoland: A Story of Missionary Enterprise in South Africa* (London, 1889), chap. 4, pp. 59–60, 67–8.

**48** Lovett, *History of the LMS*, Vol. 1, pp. 588–9. See also Ross, *John Philip*, pp. 1, 111, 162.

**49** J.B. Purney to Philip, 16 March 1832, in D.J. Kotze (ed.), *Letters of the American Missionaries, 1835–1838* (Van Riebeeck Society: Cape Town, 1950), pp. 21–7, with Philip's reply, pp. 28–45. For

eventually reached the American Board in Boston and was published by them in the November 1833 issue of *The Missionary Herald*. It had a powerful impact.[50] Together with a further lengthy analysis of the state of South Africa and the case for a mission prepared for Rufus Anderson, Philip helped to shape the Board's eventual decision in July 1834 to send two missionary parties, one inland to Mzilikazi's Ndebele, the other to the Zulu in Natal.[51] As with the continental European Protestants, Philip received the new arrivals at Cape Town, introduced them to the country and made many of the arrangements for their onward journeys. Similarly he continued to act as their adviser and an important link with their home society.

Philip's own reputation and perhaps the interdenominational as well as Congregationalist sympathies characteristic of both the ABCFM and the LMS, help to explain these early moves. However, they should not be given undue weight. The American Board's contacts with the CMS were just as extensive.[52] Philip's ready responses and his interest thereafter in maintaining a regular correspondence with the Bostonians, reflected more than an obliging nature; that the same might be said of the ABCFM's principal Secretary can be traced in their surviving letters.[53] The tone of the correspondence is at once respectful, friendly and – especially on Philip's side – authoritative, betraying the characteristics which so impressed the French Protestant missionary, Eugene Casalis. A large and impressive figure, his 'expression of ineffable goodness and Christian simplicity gained for him immediately both confidence and affection. He belonged to that fine type of British piety full of sap and originality to which attach the names of ... David Bogue, Clarkson, Wilberforce and Angell James. His was a large and liberal spirit, which looked on all questions from a high point of view.'[54]

At root, Philip undoubtedly felt that he and the Americans were partners in the same enterprise. Embattled as he so often was and sensing that his *Researches* had gained him less support even at home than he felt he deserved, the interest and enthusiasm of the Americans provided welcome encouragement. Sensing their seriousness, appreciating both their willingness to plan carefully and their awareness of a need for patience, he was, he wrote, 'particularly pleased with the views entertained in America, as to the means by which missions to savages and barbarians should be conducted'.[55] Subsequent events during the 1830s only confirmed

the best known of the American missionaries to the Cape see Edwin W. Smith, *The Life and Times of Daniel Lindley (1801–80)* (London, 1949).

50  For one captivated by it, *The Journal of an American Missionary in the Cape Colony 1835 by George Champion*, ed. Alan R. Booth (Cape Town, 1968).

51  Rufus Anderson to Rev. Dr John Philip, 10 Aug. 1833, ABC/2.01/2 ff. 363–6 and 16 July 1834, ABC/2.01/3 ff. 89–93; Philip to Anderson, 13 Dec. 1833, ABC/14/1/69.

52  Anderson to Philip, 16 July 1834, ABC.2.01/3, f. 93.

53  Unless otherwise stated, all Philip's letters cited here are to be found in the ABCFM Papers, Houghton Library, Harvard University.

54  Casalis, *My Life*, pp. 67–8.

55  Philip to Anderson, 13 Dec. 1833, ABC/14/1/69.

his conviction: 'We are engaged in a common cause', he wrote, echoing Anderson's earlier sentiment and 'We feel that your Society and ours were made to cooperate.'[56]

In part this conviction rested on the sense of shared principles and a common background, in which an equal accessibility for all to divine grace was commonly recognised as the foundation for evangelicals' anticipation of worldwide conversion. For Philip and many of his contemporaries it was this uniformity which also made possible co-operation between missionaries of different nationalities. Differences between Americans and Englishmen, such as the formers' partiality to revivalist meetings, might often occasion comment, but were essentially superficial. After all, Philip wrote, 'Human nature is the same in its grand leading principles in all the countries of the world.'[57] Not only common principles but a shared history united British and American endeavours. Philip felt able to draw on a common stock of analogies with the past. He not only referred to the shared experience of work in the Pacific as providing lessons in missionary strategy; when obliged to warn that the 'same spirit which contributed to the years of Elliott [*sic*] and Brainerd's labours threatens' to isolate the missions and their work, he was clearly confident that his references would be understood and his fears taken seriously.[58] Events he encountered on the frontiers of contact and settlement beyond the Cape Colony only too frequently had parallels elsewhere, as he knew Anderson and his colleagues would appreciate. On an earlier occasion, Philip had seen fit to celebrate 'the savage American', who, 'forgetting the sound of the war-whoop', had 'joined the sweet singers of Israel'. Together with his own subsequent study, however, twenty years at the Cape had sobered his judgement. 'From what you have seen in America, you can judge of the results in Africa and other countries colonised from Europe.'[59] The ABCFM was not only well versed in the gloomy history of white contact with North American Indians, but was extensively engaged in its own programme of Indian evangelisation. Along with other societies in the 1830s, it was beginning to extend its operations beyond the Mississippi. Indeed, when the retreat of its mission to Mzilikazi in 1837 brought about the concentration of the Americans in Natal and removed the immediate need for reinforcements, the Board was clear as to the consequences. Anderson wrote to Natal telling his agents that 'Since the amalgamation of your two missions, the designation of the two missionaries, appointed to S. Africa, has been changed to the Rocky Mountain Indians.'[60]

---

56  *Ibid.*, n.d., from London; received in Boston 26 June 1837, ABC/14/1; Anderson to Philip, 16 July 1834, ABC/2.01/3, f. 93.

57  *Ibid.*, 18 March 1835, ABC/14/1.

58  *Ibid.*, Dec. 1839, ABC/14/2/134 and 7 Jan. 1845, ABC/14/3/356. In 1837, Ellis had made similar references in his evidence to the Aborigines Committee, *PP* (1836) 7 (538), Q. 4416.

59  John Philip, *Necessity of Divine Influence. A Sermon preached before the Missionary Society ... May 12, 1813* (London, 1813); Philip to Anderson, n.d., from London; received in Boston 26 June 1837, ABC/14/1.

With such foundations, Philip saw no difficulties and much to be gained in cultivating close relations with the ABCFM and its workers. Throughout the 1830s and 1840s his missionary efforts were inseparable from his prolonged battle to check the unregulated expansion of white settlement. At an early stage he emphasised the problems to Anderson. 'Since the Hottentot question was settled and since my return to the Colony, there is another evil of great magnitude which I have had to contend against. In the second sentence of my *Researches* you will perceive in what manner the colonial boundary has been extending for the last thirty years. This system is as much opposed to sound policy as it is to the interest of justice and humanity; but the colonists will think of nothing but an extension of territory and more land, so long as they can hope that they will be indulged in their wishes ... The indulgence of those feelings by the extension of the colonial frontier is attended with ... the destruction of the natives who have been killed in defending their territories, or have perished by the evils which have followed their expulsion.'[61]

Philip's aim was to stabilise the frontiers of white settlement by means of imperial government intervention and beyond them to establish mission communities, under either imperial protection or that of local rulers. This missionary presence he believed would secure time for the conversion and civilisation of African peoples, who would in the process establish peaceful relations with the Cape Colony. Philip felt that European and American ventures had their places in this grand design, a position in the American case reinforced by their explicit concern to avoid areas already populated by whites.[62] The ABCFM's involvement could not but contribute to his own plans. Not only was there safety in missionary numbers when facing up to both whites and Africans, but the concentration of missionary effort in particular centres rather than the diffusion of isolated individuals had other advantages. Conversion was more likely to result and working together would help Philip, as he put it, 'to introduce between the Colony and the natives and Zulus beyond our colonial limits a system of international law'.[63] After his visit to London to give evidence about the Cape Colony's War of 1834 to the Aborigines Committee, Philip wrote 'We have got a breathing time and that should be sedulously improved [?] by setting among them [the Zulus] the seeds of divine truth which will in a short time raise them to a condition that will command the tempest of white power and set bounds to their encroachments.' It was a time for optimism. 'If you can but evangelize the Zoolahs you will be able to raise native agencies among that people that will be felt across a great portion of Africa.'[64]

---

60  Anderson to the Brethren of the South African Mission, 24 Jan. 1838, in Kotze (ed.), *Letters*, p. 221. For the beginnings of the American advance see John D. Unruh, *The Plains Across: Emigrants, Wagon Trains and the American West* (1992 edn; first pub. 1979).

61  Philip to Anderson, 13 Dec. 1833, ABC/14/1/69.

62  *Ibid.*; and Anderson to Philip, 5 July 1836, ABC/2.1/1, ff. 130–3.

63  Philip to Anderson, 18 March 1835 and 11 March 1836 (from St Helena), ABC/14/1. For local white hostility to the connections of Philip with the American missionaries, Kotze (ed.), *Letters*, pp. 116–17.

64  Philip to Anderson, n.d., received 26 June 1837, ABC/14/1.

Pleased with what he felt was the high quality of the American missionaries,[65] Philip hoped to benefit from the trans-Atlantic connection in other ways. Sensitive to the cool reception of his own Society to his *Researches* and its lack of interest in promoting it, he was hopeful that an abridged edition might be published through the Board's good offices in the United States. 'You understand things of that kind better in America than they are understood in England', wrote the expatriate Scot.[66] More important still to Philip was Anderson's frequent provision of American missionary literature and the latest 'approved books and journals'. 'You cannot do us a greater service than to send us your publications and in that way to [press?] upon us that portion of the American mind and American policy which they contain.' Too many British societies failed to see the importance of this kind of communication, with the result that missionaries 'have returned to a state of child-hood in which nothing interests, beyond the barren localities of their immediate neighbourhood'. Few people he felt appreciated 'how much of our active benevo-lence we owe to our sympathy with the great affairs of the great world and these great affairs cannot affect us if they are not made known to us'. In other words and *mutatis mutandis*, it was necessary for locals to know 'that the Cape of Good Hope did not include all that was worth knowing in the world'.[67] If not travel then at least missionary networks should broaden the mind, for the benefit of all concerned.

Of course, this was a two-way process. Philip reciprocated with information, accounts and papers which 'will, I doubt not, surprise and interest Americans' and even sent exhibits for the American Board's museum.[68] He arranged the earliest possible despatch to Boston of materials relating to the Aborigines Committee, seeing their importance at a time when 'great questions such as this ... are agitating England and America'.[69] The Americans' knowledge of their own country, as well as their local practical experience, confirmed for them the wisdom of much in Philip's diagnosis of South African conditions. In particular, the Boer migration out of the Cape Colony on their Great Trek northwards had serious repercussions. Not only was the American mission to Mzilikazi destroyed in 1837, but even the regrouping of the missionaries with their colleagues in Natal seemed for a time to be threatened by white expansion.

Indeed, the leader of the American party, Daniel Lindley, saw little remaining promise in their situation. 'The emigration of the Boers was a thing, we believe,

65  *Ibid.*, 27 May and 29 Oct. 1835, ABC/14/1; Robert Moffat agreed, Kotze, *Letters*, p. 85. Also Robert Moffat to J.S. Moffat, 14 Jan. 1836 (copy), ABC New Series 5, Special Collections, Livingstone and Moffat Correspondence 1807–58.

66  Philip to Anderson, 26 Jan. 1834 (continued 14 March 1834), ABC/14/1.

67  *Ibid.*, 29 Oct. 1835, ABC/14/1 and 7 July 1848, ABC/14/3/361. Anderson had started to send material to Philip with his very first letter in 1833 (note 51 above) and shared Philip's view, see letter to Philip, 3 June 1835, ABC/2.01/3, ff. 335–7.

68  *Ibid.*, 18 March 1835, ABC/14/1; Dec. 1839, 26 Oct. 1842, ABC/14/2/134, 139; 30 July 1846, 7 July 1848, ABC/14/3/360, 361.

69  *Ibid.*, n.d., received 26 June 1837, ABC/14/1.

unthought of, when we first came into the country; and a thing by which we would have been in no way affected, had Moselikatsi [*sic*] not attempted their entire destruction ... The Emigrant Boers at present think they will settle not far from Natal, in order that they may trade at that port; and ... It is now quite evident that no very long period will elapse before a considerable white population will be settled at and around that port; and when this shall take place, we may expect that the natives ... will be compelled to give way to the wishes and interests of white men. We cannot think of the American Indians and of the natives in this country, without fearing that years of missionary labor among [them] may yet be sacrificed to what is called the enterprise of civilized man.' Without British intervention to protect the Zulus, their state and the mission would be destroyed.[70]

Lindley and his colleagues increasingly came to believe that nothing could control the movement of Boers and other settlers in southern Africa. Analogy buttressed experience. After all, wrote Lindley, 'what can prevent the emigration of Americans to the west? ... The boundaries of the Cape Colony ... are not impassable and it is not in the power of government to make them so ... The natives of this region are sinking for the last time.' This was a still more pessimistic prognosis than Philip's, assuming as it did a repetition of the consequences of American conflicts, rather than reflecting on the numerical preponderance and resilience of local South African peoples. Nevertheless, it pointed in the same direction, towards the immediate need for many more missionaries if conversion were to be achieved. 'There is no other hope for them.'[71]

As war engulfed Natal in 1837–38, the American mission was for a time compelled to retreat once more, on this occasion to the Cape. Against this threatening background, Philip's voice was that of reassurance and optimism, interpreting events in ways designed to prevent 'the attention of the American churches [turning] away from Africa. That is what I most of all dread.'[72] Members of the ABCFM came to accept, as Philip himself had previously done, that imperial intervention beyond the Cape colonial frontiers offered an essential guarantee of missionary security and hence of the preconditions for conversion. The mission eventually adapted itself both to the British annexation of Natal in 1842–43 and to working in an imperial rather than an independent African setting.[73] The advantage of so doing was gradually accepted by Rufus Anderson himself. In 1836 he was already concerned that South African peoples might experience the same fate as that of North America's Indians in confrontation with settlers expanding westward. After the troubles of 1837–38, he even told Ellis, 'The prospect now is, that

---

70 American missionaries (Daniel Lindley) to Anderson, 2 May 1837, in Kotze (ed.), *Letters*, pp. 173–4.

71 Lindley to Anderson, 1 Dec. 1837, Kotze, *Letters*, p. 213.

72 Philip to Anderson, 18 May 1838, also 26 Oct. 1842, ABC/14/2/132, 139.

73 This was achieved only with difficulty and on several occasions Philip anticipated their withdrawal from South Africa: Philip to Anderson, 18 May 1838, 9 Dec. 1842, ABC/14/2/132, 140; 26 Jan. 1844, 7 Jan. 1845, ABC/14/3/355, 356.

we shall be driven out of South Africa; and what is far more important, that the whole aboriginal population will vanish before the emigrant white man!' However, writing to the members of the Zulu mission in 1852, the year after Philip's death, he had attained a new calm. 'Perhaps each one of you will do more for the world to come, by having an Anglo-Saxon empire growing up around you, than if you had the natives all to yourselves. I really suppose that it will be so … It is a great thing to plant the gospel and its institutions in a great, fertile and healthy country in advance of colonization and so to shape the infancy of empires.'[74]

## III

There is more, of course, to the forward momentum imparted to the missionary movement than can be illustrated by examining the individual careers of Ellis, Philip and Anderson. The critical role of Berlin and Basel in the first half-century of the CMS has already been mentioned.[75] Elsewhere the BMS, for example, had established links through William Ward and W.H. Angas with sympathisers in the Netherlands. The consequence was the formation of the Netherlands Auxiliary Society which for twenty-five years, until the formation of their own society in 1847, gave sums of up to £200 annually to aid Baptist efforts. Angas also raised similar sums in Switzerland, the German states and East Prussia in the same period.[76] Evangelical contacts through bible, school and temperance societies sustained Swedish connections that led to the formation of the national Swedish Missionary Society in 1835. The spread of its local auxiliaries in the next decade produced a steady flow of funds to the LMS and to the Wesleyans.[77]

As the movement broadened, so the undergrowth of trans-Atlantic and globally peripheral cross-connections became more tangled. More missionaries came and went. Just as the number of long and distinguished missionary careers rose, so after a few years of evangelising many turned their energies to other occupations. By no means every missionary who returned home for good did so incapacitated by illness, as a gesture of rejection towards the societies or tarnished with the venom of the lapsed evangelist. Many continued in one way or another to act within their churches; all naturally took their missionary experience with them. A sense of the missionary role, an acquaintance with the realities facing the missionary, thoughtfulness as to the prospects or limitations of the movement, even an engagement with the debates integral to the missionary community, generally increased and

---

74  Anderson to Philip, 5 July 1836, ABC/2.1/1 ff. 130–3; to Ellis, 9 June 1838 (Private), ABC/2.1/2 ff. 116–17; letter of 1852 quoted by Norman Etherington, 'An American Errand into the South African Wilderness', *Church History* 39 (1970), 69.

75  See above, Chapter 2, p. 56.

76  James R. Hertzler, 'English Baptists Interpret Continental Mennonites in the Early Nineteenth Century', *Mennonite Quarterly Review* 54, 1 (1980), 42–52.

77  Hanna Hodacs, *Converging World Views: The European Expansion and Early-Nineteenth-Century Anglo-Swedish Contacts* (Uppsala, 2003), pp. 118–19, 146–7.

deepened. Characteristics formerly regarded as eccentricities of the movement came to seem less odd; its isolation was gradually eroded, by respectability, greater familiarity and communal involvement. By the late 1830s every denomination sported alongside its mission society both its publications and its auxiliary missionary associations enmeshed in local fundraising. Publications from the societies themselves were beginning to diversify well beyond the originally severe format of annual reports, with their limited listing of subscribers and comforting outlines of developments in individual fields. Religious periodicals of a more general kind as a matter of course often gave room to missionary news.[78]

The growth of the missionary movement itself spawned all manner of attachments at home and abroad. Within societies, organisers multiplied: between 1815 and 1832 the LMS increased the number of its Directors from 168 to 252 and the CMS its episcopal vice-presidents from two to four by 1824 and thereafter steadily to the point where by 1845 bishops normally accepted the Society's invitation. Societies forged links with each other. The BMS, for example, began to exchange publications with Boston on a grandiloquent note: 'the object in which you are engaged is fact enough to constitute a bond of union, even though, most probably, we shall never personally meet on this side [of] eternity'.[79] From Edinburgh Thomas Chalmers expressed to Anderson his gratitude on election as a Corresponding Member, and Richard Knill his sense of obligation unfulfilled as an Honorary Member, of the ABCFM. John Dunmore Lang, ambitious as ever, reproduced Philip's style in his own expansive plans for Australasia to be served by German missionaries and, with the help of the American Board, American Presbyterians.[80]

Missionary correspondence also had a complex place in constructing the worldwide web of connections. Most commonly the surviving records of the missionary societies encourage researchers to think above all in bilateral terms, working with the exchanges of letters between missionaries on their stations and either mission headquarters or family relations in Britain. It should not be forgotten, however, that missionary correspondence – much of it doubtless now lost – was carried on within and across geographical fields and denominations. In 1820, for example, the Wesleyan Barnabas Shaw, James Kitchingman of the LMS and their wives journeyed to visit the Lutheran Johann Schmelen on his station at Bethany (Namaqualand). Schmelen and Kitchingman had worked together in Besondermeid (Steinkopf) for a year and later Schmelen's children stayed with the Kitchingman family at Paarl for about two years. Evidently the two were frequent correspondents, but only fragments seem to have survived.[81] Except in rare cases,

78  See below, Chapter 6, pp. 156–9.

79  Thomas [surely John] Dyer (BMS Secretary) to Anderson, 24 April 1839, ABC14/1/2/56.

80  Chalmers (from Edinburgh), 29 Dec. 1841; Knill, 28 Dec. 1839; Lang (from Sydney, New South Wales), 11 Aug 1838, all to Rufus Anderson, ABC/14/2/49, 112, 113. For Knill's career in India and Russia, *DEB*, Vol. 2, pp. 656–7; for Lang, see *DEB*, Vol. 2, pp. 667–8.

81  Le Cordeur and Saunders, *Kitchingman Papers*, pp. 13, 94, 96.

official archives and collections, such as the classic editions of David Livingstone's correspondence prepared by Schapera, can be unintentionally but nevertheless seriously misleading in the impressions they create of who wrote to whom. It is hard to imagine from the surviving record that missionary wives could ever have written to one another, but in fact it is harder still to believe that they did not.

Missionary marriages provided an unceasing source of anxiety to society secretaries and treasurers, in much the way that single female volunteers were to do later in the century.[82] Fundamental questions were raised at once by their appropriateness. Few – certainly not Anderson and his colleagues – would have disagreed with John Philip in thinking it axiomatic that 'in a great majority of instances the usefulness of the missionary will be greatly retarded, or promoted, according as the spirit and temper of his wife are favourable or unfavourable to the great object of the mission'.[83] Mission committees were anxious not to lose good men, but worried at their lack of control over marriage partners. However, beyond this there lay recurrent issues of salaries and their increase, child allowances, pension rights and payments, house building and travelling costs. As societies got firmly into their stride, their secretaries were anxious not to squander resources to stimulate unhelpful competition for volunteers by allowing different denominational rates to get markedly out of line.[84] This problem was perhaps greatest for those missions such as the Methodists, organised within the church, where returning missionaries expected automatic redeployment in a domestic circuit and where financial demarcation lines between church and mission could be serious matters of public debate. John Beecham (Mission Secretary, 1831–56) tried to explain the practicalities for the Wesleyan leader, Jabez Bunting: 'Is not this the whole of the grievance in respect of the Contingent Fund – Missionaries come home with families and want houses and are obliged to be sent to circuits where young married preachers would otherwise be employed and this being on the Contingent Fund a burden which it would not have had to bear and to meet which burden they [missionaries] have previously contributed nothing by begging for the fund on their stations as the home preachers in their Circuits?'[85] Beecham proposed a solution that was agreeable, not only because it stilled objections by leaving no one feeling contributions were inequitable, but it also tended 'to promote the oneness of the home and mission work'.[86]

---

82  See 'Peter Williams, "The Missing Link": The Recruitment of Women Missionaries in some English Evangelical Missionary Societies in the Nineteenth Century', in Fiona Bowie, Deborah Kirkwood and Shirley Ardener (eds), *Women and Missions: Past and Present. Anthropological and Historical Perspectives* (Providence and Oxford, 1993), pp. 43–69; also Rhonda Semple, *Missionary Women: Gender, Professionalism and the Victorian Idea of Christian Mission* (Woodbridge, 2003).

83  Philip to Anderson, 13 Dec. 1833, ABC/14/1/69; also Anderson to Philip, 25 Nov. 1834, 2 Jan. 1835, ABC/2.01/3, ff. 183, 252.

84  London Secretaries Association, Minutes, Vol. 1, 13 Feb. 1834, 12 Feb. 1835, 12 March 1835, 10 Jan. 1839, 14 Feb. 1839, BFBS Archives.

85  Beecham to Bunting, 22 March 1832, Methodist Church Archives, PLP 7-2-1.

86  *Ibid.*

Still less remarked upon but not unremarkable was the part which marriage played in integrating missions with each other as well as into society at large. There is more of significance for the themes of this chapter, for instance, in the marital record of the Paris Evangelical Missionary Society in South Africa than Gallic romance. Shortly after arriving at the Cape in 1829, Samuel Rolland married the English Miss Lyndall; she in turn arranged a match for his colleague, Eugene Casalis, with Miss Sarah Dyke, the sister of an LMS missionary. Robert Moffat's daughter Anne leavened a Scottish LMS family by her subsequent marriage to Jean Frédoux. David Livingstone, another of Moffat's sons-in-law by virtue of marriage to Mary in 1845, in turn exploited Moffat's French and Parisian links for the education of his own daughter Anne in 1865. These links were still vigorous in 1877 when Robert Moffat himself spent several weeks in Paris, speaking and meeting prominent French Protestants such as Theodore Monod. In 1861, François Coillard, then based with the PEMS at Leribe, married the daughter of a Scottish minister met in Paris. In Calcutta, Joseph Mullens's wife from 1845 was Hannah, daughter of the first Netherlands Missionary Society then LMS missionary, Alphonse Lacroix.[87] It is undoubtedly the case that there were more such marriages between English women – some of them, such as Anna Hinderer, later well known in their own right – and members of the Basel Mission working through the CMS.[88]

These international connections did not produce so readily the dynastic missionary families that can be found at home in Britain itself during the later nineteenth century. The Moules within the CMS, the Broomhalls of the China Inland Mission (CIM) and the Guinness family, show the missionary movement at its most self-contained and self-perpetuating and stand out clearly in the missionary registers. However, there is another dimension to the picture. Although the ramifications and ripples caused by extra-British links are less easily recaptured, genuinely international, cross-denominational ties between societies, among individuals and within families were plentiful. They demonstrate how the Protestant missionary world drew its energy from sources and continued to organise itself in ways that transcended narrowly national, domestic and imperial categories. British, American and continental European societies drew each other together. As they did so, they paid less heed to the presence or absence of empire than they did to the proximity and possible duplication of each other's efforts and the expanding scope for evangelical co-operation.

---

87 Casalis, *My Life in Basutoland*, chap. 14; Lovett, *History of the LMS*, Vol. 1, p. 174; Peter Sanders, *Moshoeshoe Chief of the Sotho* (London, 1975), p. 143; Timothy Holmes, *David Livingstone Letters and Documents 1841–1872* (Livingstone, Lusaka, Bloomington and London, 1990), pp. 144, 150; for Coillard, Lacroix and Mullens, *BDCM*, pp. 142, 379, 480. Also François Coillard, *On the Threshold of Central Africa* (London, 1902); C.W. Mackintosh, *Coillard of the Zambezi* (London, 1907).
88 Jenkins, 'The CMS and the Basel Mission', gives many examples.

# The new wave: missionary expansion
# and plans for the future, 1834–50

Historians of the WMMS's centenary wished readers to remember the Reverend William James Shrewsbury for his career in the West Indies and stalwart resistance to white planter persecution in Barbados in 1823.[1] His later South African years were collectively glossed along with those of colleagues with the observation that 'no further reference need be made to Missionaries who in South Africa, as elsewhere, proved themselves to be men of gifts which would have made them remarkable in any sphere of work'.[2] One further reference only was made, to Shrewsbury's 'powerful and self-obliterating ministry', an unfortunate (and, one assumes, unthinking rather than uncharitable) choice of words, given that he was severely censured and dismissed from his position as a missionary in Cape Colony in 1835–36.[3] The reticence of the centenary authors about this episode is understandable. However, the events responsible for Shrewsbury's disgrace are well worth recalling for the light they throw on the broader development of the missionary movement.

When the Sixth Frontier War erupted in December 1834, the Cape government and its military forces, caught unawares, were anxious to sound out local opinion and keep the white community on their side. As Shrewsbury recorded at the time, 'I have been much importuned by Col: Smith, now commanding the Forces, to put on paper a few thoughts, concerning the mode of conducting the Kafir War. Though I refused to bear arms, I did not think I should be justified in declining this service to my King & Country in such an extraordinarily critical period.'[4] The advice Shrewsbury offered was forthright. In a brief and trenchant paper he suggested, for example, that 'The Chiefs who have invaded the Colony to forfeit their chieftainship, & their people to forfeit their Country, their Arms and their Property. This accomplished, the righteousness of British Law, & the equity of British Judges may decide the rest.' In Article 3, he went on, 'The actual murderers of British subjects, to be everywhere demanded; & when obtained, executed on the spot, that the Kafirs may see that *murder* with Britain is an unpardonable crime.

---

1  See above, Chapter 3, pp. 87–9.

2  Findlay and Holdsworth, *History of the WMMS*, Vol. 4, pp. 251–2.

3  *Ibid.*, p. 258.

4  Shrewsbury to Mission Committee, 16 Jan. 1835, WMMS South Africa Albany Correspondence, 1835/4; Henry (later Sir Harry) Smith, administrator of Queen Adelaide Province, Governor of the Cape and High Commissioner (1847–52), *Dictionary of South African Biography* Vol. 2, pp. 673–7.

Every chieftain to be informed that if he substitute *innocent persons* for the really guilty, the chieftain himself will forfeit his own life, as being himself the friend of murderers and the cause of the shedding of innocent blood, under the cover [colour?] of Law and Justice.'[5]

When Shrewsbury's paper came to light, with its further comments on 'Kafir enemies' and 'deserters' and the postwar settlement, it caused an outcry. His own lengthy justification to the Society – that he wrote from first-hand experience, expecting at any moment to be overwhelmed by the Xhosa; and that his necessary brevity had led to misunderstanding – was found wholly inadequate. In his despatch of 26 December 1835 repudiating Governor D'Urban's postwar arrangements, including the annexation of Queen Adelaide Province that Shrewsbury had recommended, Lord Glenelg took the opportunity to dismiss the missionary's views out of hand. His devastating response made the decision of the Wesleyan Missionary Committee inevitable, when it met four days later. Chaired by the President of the Methodist Conference, the Committee, after making all possible allowance, recorded its 'most entire and unqualified disapprobation' of Shrewsbury's action. 'They judge that the advice given by him to the Commander of the Forces ... if understood in its obvious and literal meaning was in various particulars most unwarrantable and revolting to the principles and feelings of humanity and religion' and censured him accordingly. Glenelg was immediately informed of the Committee's disavowal of everything Shrewsbury had written.[6]

Shrewsbury was mortified, claiming not least that, although he alone had signed his original letter to Smith, it represented the views of his colleagues on the ground, whose opinions he had sought on it. For long after, there also remained those who thought him entirely wronged by the outcome.[7] However, the failure of Shrewsbury's plea in self-defence and the Committee's unreserved condemnation owed little to political miscalculation and presentational failings by the missionary and his friends. It testified far more strongly to the fact that by the mid-1830s the missionary societies were riding high on the back of the humanitarian tide. The anti-slavery movement, led in very different ways by Wilberforce, Buxton, William Knibb and Joseph Sturge, had forged ahead since 1823. It had done so powered above all by the sense of moral outrage felt among a domestic religious public ever more aware of the dismissiveness, damage and insults directed at the missions its

---

5 Shrewsbury to Mission Committee, 24 Dec. 1835, giving details of his paper and his defence, *ibid.*, 1835/40. Original emphases.

6 *Ibid.*; Glenelg to D'Urban, 26 Dec. 1835, *PP* (1836), 39, 279, pp. 59–73; Minutes of a meeting of the Committee of the Wesleyan Missionary Society, 30 Dec. 1835, and Mission Committee to Glenelg, 9 Jan. 1836, WMMS South Africa Albany Correspondence, 1835/42.

7 Shrewsbury had some grounds for feeling hard done by: see, for instance, the similar views in Rev. William Boyce to Sir Benjamin D'Urban, 31 March 1834, 'Best Means of preserving the peace of the Colonial frontier written at His Excellency's request' (copy), in *ibid.*, 1834/13; J.V.B. Shrewsbury, *Memorials of the Rev. William J. Shrewsbury* (London, 1867, 2nd edn 1868), esp. Chapter 10; and review in *The Methodist Recorder*, 27 Dec. 1867, cutting in MCA, PLP 97-9-25.

members supported and the deprivation this inflicted on the slaves. Regard at home for the missionary movement had continued to grow, as a consequence of the victimisation of its activists overseas and its alignment with the humanitarians and their influential leaders. Missionary organisers in Britain were well aware of this, however much they still stressed the priority of their religious concerns. Anything, therefore, that threatened this identification of the missionary with the broadly humanitarian temper of the day could not be countenanced. In such circumstances and because he was carrying responsibility for the mission during William Shaw's absence in England, such uninhibited utterances meant Shrewsbury had to go.

Shrewsbury was also dismissed, in effect, because he had only limited sympathy with this prevailing outlook. From his viewpoint, if humanitarian prescriptions also threatened the success of evangelisation, then so much the worse for them. Reflecting on his past and present circumstances, Shrewsbury believed that freedom had its drawbacks and even slavery its spiritual benefits. In the British Caribbean, 'the circumstances of their [the slaves'] temporal thraldom have in many ways contributed to their spiritual liberty and everlasting happiness. It has brought them under the British Government, which in itself is a vast blessing; & when compared with the tyranny of many African chiefs, the Slavery of Africans under British Laws may, in some respects be denominated Liberty. It has caused them to become acquainted with the knowledge of Letters, & of the written word of God. It has led to an embracing of the Gospel as the *only* source of consolation; and to their union in Christian Societies to an extent which could never have been realized in their own country, where they indulged in wandering habits, & lived in a predatory manner, plundering & destroying one another.' In South Africa, however, whether 'as a Nation or as Tribes, we have to do with a haughty, fierce, proudly independent people; and they are too apt to consider themselves alike independent of God and Man'.[8] For the most part Shrewsbury hoped that the perfection and universal suitability of Wesleyan organisation would suffice through its expansion to overcome these obstacles. But at times – for instance, from mid-1832 on which at the time he felt the least fruitful portion of his career and when his regard for the settlers warmed – he hoped for greater success all round 'without making much noise about political rights & political oppressions'.[9] Such an outlook in a world where missions were to lead by persuasion and example, not coercion, made Shrewsbury a liability. The fact that he would not have hesitated to label himself a 'humanitarian' also points to the need for historians to recognise the varied guise in which humanitarianism could be said to display itself.

---

8  Shrewsbury to Mission Committee, 30 June 1830, WMMS South Africa Albany Correspondence, 1830/26.
9  *Ibid.*, 31 Dec. 1826, 30 June 1832, 31 Dec. 1832 and quotation from 30 March 1833, WMMS South Africa Albany Correspondence, 1826/40, 1832/18, 40, 1833/10.

This is not to suggest that the situation of the missionaries was dictated entirely by consideration of humanitarians as political allies. The extent to which the latter depended for information and political influence on missionaries overseas and on the church, or chapel-goers at home, inevitably pushed the missionary societies to the fore and strengthened their hands. Humanitarian leaders had learned to depend on men such as Philip for local knowledge and comment on government failings; they could not rely on the Shrewsburys of this world, watchdogs disinclined to bark. As missionaries were gradually drawn into and adapted themselves to the processes of policy formation and as governments listened more carefully to the missions, this mutual dependence became ever more marked. In 1835, moreover, it was still the case that, in return for greater official consideration, a diplomatic measure of deference was called for. No missionary society would have dared ignore Glenelg's rejection of Shrewsbury's suggestions and involvement. After thirty years in which they had come to terms with governments and had accumulated the political capital that flowed from the Demerara rebellion and Jamaica's Baptist War, a refusal on this occasion, however oblique, would have risked too much. The wisdom of that decision became abundantly clear in the outcome of the parliamentary Select Committee of Enquiry into the aboriginal populations of the colonial empire in 1836–37. That enquiry not only markedly strengthened the self-confidence of the missions but greatly illuminated the nature of the relation between missions, humanitarians and government.

## I

After parliamentary legislation was passed in 1833 legally emancipating the empire's slaves, humanitarian attention was directed once more but with new vigour towards those peoples who, while notionally free, were seen as suffering seriously from the impact of European expansion – Canada's Indian peoples, Pacific islanders, New Zealand's Maoris, the Aborigines of Australia and the indigenous peoples of South Africa. While slavery had remained their first priority, humanitarians' interest and intervention on behalf of aboriginal populations had been fitful, something seen in their temporarily taking up narrowly focused issues such as that of the Khoi under pressure from John Philip in 1826–29. Occurring against the background of a wider unease, the Cape Colony's Frontier War of 1834–35 changed this. Suspicions of white provocation, appalling reports of atrocities, astonishment at the drastic overriding of African sovereignty involved in the colonial government's imposed peace, together bred an urge to investigate. In the House of Commons, T.F. Buxton and his friends secured the establishment of a Select Committee to consider not only the Cape's own circumstances, given the disputes surrounding the recent war, but the wider global question: 'what Measures ought to be adopted with regard to the NATIVE INHABITANTS of Countries where BRITISH SETTLEMENTS are made and to the neighbouring Tribes, in order to secure to them the due observance of Justice and the protection of their Rights; to promote the spread of Civilization among them, and to lead them to the peaceful and voluntary reception of the Christian Religion'?[10]

These terms of reference were widely defined, in part as a result of pressure on Buxton from his female relatives.[11] They were no less widely interpreted geographically, as is clear from the extension of the Committee's search for evidence far beyond southern Africa. Witnesses testified on developments in Newfoundland, New South Wales, Van Diemen's Land, New Zealand and the Pacific islands, in addition as mentioned above to the United States.[12] Committee members thus addressed what they understood to be a global issue, the growing 'evil' of 'the oppression of the natives of barbarous countries'. This they agreed would simply increase if decisions were not taken in Britain 'as to the policy we should adopt towards ruder nations'.[13] There were nevertheless important distinctions to be drawn between different aspects of both the general problem under investigation and the policy designed to tackle it. British North America and the Cape provided examples of the problems confronting settled British colonial governments; the United States offered comparisons with the policies adopted by other independent states. New Zealand by contrast provided a demonstration of the alarming rapidity with which conflict and dispossession could escalate in the absence of effective authority. Moreover, there were several separate goals to be attained. Lawlessness and aggression had to be checked, whether rooted in greed, ignorance, fear, or self-defence; the right of the strongest, revenge and retaliation had to be replaced by a just and equitable system of law and political authority. The 'rights of those who have not the means of advocating their interests or exciting sympathy for their sufferings' had to be identified and protected. Finally 'the national necessity of finding some outlet for the superabundant population of Great Britain and Ireland', an equally 'benevolent and laudable object', had to be served if the basic causes of conflict were to be removed.[14]

As the inclusion of Christianity and conversion in the Committee's remit suggests, Britain's Protestant missions were always likely to play an influential role in its proceedings. This proved to be the case, notwithstanding the diversity in churchmanship among members of the Committee, which ranged from that of the high Anglican churchman W.E. Gladstone to the Quakerism of Thomas Fowell Buxton. Dr Philip, urged by Buxton to come to London specially,[15] remained in

---

10  The reports and proceedings are in *PP* (1836) 7 (538) and *PP* (1837) 7 (425); quotation, *Report*, p. 3, *PP* (1837) 7 (425).
11  For the establishment of the Select Committee, Elbourne, *Blood Ground*, pp. 283–7; Zoe Laidlaw, 'Networks, Patronage and Information in Colonial Government: Britain, New South Wales and the Cape Colony, 1826–43' (unpub. D.Phil. thesis, Oxford, 2001).
12  On the United States, Elisha Bates (Society of Friends) QQ. 4419–67; Richard King, QQ. 5369–5412; Thomas Hodgkin, QQ. 3865–3922, 5330–68, all in *PP* (1836) 7 (538).
13  *Report*, p. 75, *PP* (1837) 7 (425).
14  *Ibid*.
15  Philip to Rufus Anderson, 11 March 1836 (from St Helena), ABC 14/1.

close contact with him and was a constant fount of information behind the scenes. Individual missionaries such as William Shaw, the Reverend William Yate (CMS, New Zealand) and John Williams (LMS, 'South Seas') were questioned at length. The Secretaries of the three principal societies (Dandeson Coates, CMS; Reverend John Beecham, WMMS; Reverend William Ellis, LMS) appeared as a triumvirate, exploiting their public platform to the full and afterwards publishing their evidence in popular pamphlet form.[16] Of the forty-six witnesses examined, fourteen – almost one third – were missionaries. Not only did their experience range more widely than that of the thirteen military men and administrators called, who were drawn with only one exception from the Cape Colony, but all bar one of the missionary spokesmen were still in post after long periods of service.

There were of course many missionaries possessing a wealth of relevant experience but none the less absent from the Committee. Among them was the Reverend Samuel Marsden, effective promoter and overseer of the CMS mission to New Zealand. Marsden, who died in May 1838, was well known to and highly regarded by Buxton and others of his circle. He was probably debarred as much by distance, age and infirmity, as by any decision not to call on him. Had he travelled to London, however, there can be no doubt that his evidence would only have reinforced that of his colleagues. The tenor of Marsden's New Zealand letters for more than thirty years, from his first meeting with Josiah Pratt at the CMS late in 1807, is only too plain, the evolutionary shifts in his arguments by now only too familiar in the light of those witnessed in other settler societies.[17] That he did not travel to the Committee only reinforces one's sense of the evident extent of the missionary consensus. Notwithstanding the 'barbarous' customs and character of the Maoris, the young Marsden had argued, experience suggested them to be 'a noble and intelligent race and prepared to receive the blessings of civilization and the knowledge of the Christian religion'.[18] Their suspicion and violence towards outsiders had resulted from 'the wanton acts of oppression, robberies and murders committed upon … the natives of New Zealand [which] have completely destroyed all confidence in the Europeans'.[19] Marsden's own confidence that this would be remedied by regular contact with missionaries, new skills and practical and religious instruction, never faltered. When the transformation proved slower than anticipated, he and the other missionaries had a ready diagnosis: a lack of recognised and competent authority, unregulated commerce and settlement, disputes associated with the trade in arms, drink and women and European embroilment in local conflicts, were the causes. Visiting ships' captains and crews needed to behave themselves well,

16  For their evidence: Beecham, Coates and Ellis, QQ. 4269–418; Philip, 4468–521, 5321–9, 5413–52, 5460–517, 5711–51; Shaw, 596–762, 1062–71, 1099–129; Yate, 1586–871; Williams, 5563–710, in *PP* (1836) 7 (538). D. Coates, John Beecham and William Ellis, *Christianity the Means of Civilization* (London, 1837).
17  J.R. Elder, *The Letters and Journals of Samuel Marsden, 1765–1838* (Dunedin, 1932) pp. 50–1, 61.
18  Marsden and others to Secretary CMS, 25 Oct 1815, *ibid.*, p. 39.
19  Marsden to Secretary CMS, 22 Sept. 1814, *ibid.*, p. 132.

since 'New Zealanders will not be insulted with impunity and treated as men without understanding, but resent to the utmost of their power any injury heaped
against them'.[20]

Marsden's solution lay in the control especially of European behaviour. His
small beginnings involved his own strict regulation of the CMS missionaries themselves – trying to curb their involvement with trade and dismissing those like
William Yate whose personal morals he found corrupt, while increasing the
numbers of reliable men.[21] To foster progress he approved the gradual and piecemeal extension of governmental authority from New South Wales – the offer of
protection for Maoris (1813), the appointment of a magistrate (1814), the official
recognition of greater chiefly powers, prohibition of trades such as that in tattooed
heads and eventually the establishment of a British Resident (1832). By 1830, all
else having failed, Marsden was recommending to Governor Darling in Sydney 'a
small armed King's vessel, with proper authority' as 'most likely to prevent much
mischief, as she might visit all the harbours into which the European vessels
enter'.[22] On his seventh and last tour of inspection from February to May 1837, as
the Aborigines Committee set about its inquisition at Westminster, Marsden was
pleased at the apparent progress and prospects of Christianity and missionary
education. But advances he felt had been made against all the odds and British
authority was still virtually powerless. At Waimate, he reported, 'Several
Europeans keep public houses and encourage every kind of crime. Here drunken-
ness, adultery, murder, etc., are committed. There are no laws, judges, or magistrates, ... Some civilized government must take New Zealand under its protection
or the most dreadful evils will be committed from runaway convicts, sailors and
publicans. There are no laws here to punish crimes.'[23] Thus Marsden, himself no
unduly sensitive soul, finally concluded like many other observers that direct
British control was necessary and inescapable. Without an overarching authority
and effective power, neither Maoris nor whites could manage for themselves the
conflicts arising from uncontrolled contact.[24]

Missionary influence was manifest not only as a visible presence during the
proceedings but in the Select Committee's final *Report*. This arrived at much the
same conclusions as Marsden and the missionary witnesses. It was convinced that
'the effect of European intercourse ... has been, upon the whole, hitherto a
calamity upon the native and savage nations', that Europeans were generally at fault

20 Marsden, First Journal, June 1815, *ibid.*, p. 130. Note the status implicit in Marsden's use of 'New
   Zealanders' rather than 'Maori'.
21 *Ibid.*, pp. 139–40, 410–12, 421–2; and on the subject of Yate, disciplined after his return from the
   Select Committee in London, see pp. 515, 518–19; Judith Binney, 'Whatever Happened to Poor Mr
   Yate? An Exercise in Voyeurism', *New Zealand Journal of History* 9, 2 (1975), 111–25.
22 Elder, *Letters and Journals*, pp. 497–8; see also p. 499.
23 Marsden to Secretary CMS, 27 March 1837, *ibid.*, p. 523.
24 Peter Adams, *Fatal Necessity: British Intervention in New Zealand, 1830–1847* (Auckland and
   Oxford, 1977).

where conflicts occurred and that immediate government intervention was essential. Non-intervention and the absence of regulation served no national interest. 'On the contrary, in point of economy, of security, of commerce, of reputation, it is a short-sighted and disastrous policy. As far as it has prevailed, it has been a burthen on the empire.' Moreover, in reviewing the past and considering the way forward, not only self-interest but obligations and responsibilities should be borne in mind. 'The British empire has been signally blessed by Providence and her ... advantages, are so many reasons for peculiar obedience to the laws of Him who guides the destinies of nations. These were given for some higher purpose than commercial prosperity and military renown ... He who has made Great Britain what she is, will inquire at our hands how we have employed the influence He has lent to us in our dealings with the untutored and defenceless savage; whether it has been engaged in seizing their lands, warring upon their people, and transplanting unknown disease and deeper degradation ... or whether we have, as far as we have been able, informed their ignorance, and ... afforded them the opportunity of becoming partakers of that civilization, that innocent commerce, that knowledge and that faith with which it has pleased a gracious Providence to bless our own country.'[25]

Paternalistic in tone, unquestioning of Britain's self-evident superiority, the *Report* was at the same time perceptive, in its deeply critical assessment of British neglect and expatriate activities. It was alive to the practical difficulties of legislation and enforcement and worried about the principle of equity as between different cultural groups. Appalled by the prospect that, without intervention, conditions would deteriorate as emigration continued to mount, and conscious that Britain's power rendered indigenous peoples ultimately unable 'to resist any encroachments, however unjust, however mischievous, which we may be disposed to make', the Committee tried to define the principles of a system which might 'enforce the observance of their [indigenous] rights'.[26]

The purposes of its recommendations were clear. 'Whatever may be the legislative system of any Colony, we ... advise that, as far as possible, the Aborigines be withdrawn from its control' and placed in the 'more impartial hands' of imperial executive officials. All labour legislation and contracts should be regulated to preserve the freedom, if people wished, to sell 'their labour at the best price and at the market most convenient for themselves'. The acquisition and sale of land should be closely controlled to guarantee just returns, not least in the form of 'religious instruction and education' should native inhabitants want them. The *Report* aimed less at imposing imperial arrangements or insisting on wholesale adaptation to a British culture than at adjusting as peacefully as possible 'the disparity of the parties'.[27]

---

25  *Report from the Select Committee on Aborigines (British Settlements)*, *PP* (1837) 7 (425), pp. 74–6.
26  *Ibid.*, p. 3.
27  *Ibid.*, pp. 3, 77–8.

These recommendations were not merely rhetorical and cosmetic. The Committee had clearly identified the main areas and issues that continued to preoccupy British administrators and humanitarians for the rest of the century and beyond. In the light of suggestions canvassed at the time, its failure to take more seriously the possibility of restricting or even prohibiting land transfers may seem short-sighted. However, such a course was precluded by belief that it was incompatible with a prior respect for indigenous rights, as well as by confidence (to which missionary spokesmen contributed a great deal) in the possibilities of assimilation. Other ideal alternatives also seemed impractical. Although 'the safety and welfare of an uncivilized race require that their relations with their more cultivated neighbours should be diminished rather than multiplied', British subjects simply could not be tightly hemmed in behind precisely defined colonial frontiers. Even officially negotiated treaties were 'rather the preparatives ... for disputes than securities for peace', given 'the superior sagacity which the European will exercise in framing, in interpreting, and in evading them'.[28] As the missionaries and now the Select Committee members knew only too well, Britain's apparent strength and Imperial authority were often incapable of expression in an effective exercise of power. At the time, the *Report*'s carefully considered suggestions were regarded as imperfect but the best available.

For the missionary movement of the day the *Report* was a triumph. Reflecting the persuasiveness of missionary evidence to the Committee, it placed considerable emphasis on the increasing role of missions as mediators between the British and local peoples. Indeed, missions were explicitly made the sole exception to the wish to restrict contact between an 'uncivilized race' and 'their more cultivated neighbours'. As the heading to Section XI expressed it in the language of the billboard, 'Missions to be Encouraged'. 'To protect, assist and countenance these gratuitous and invaluable agents is amongst the most urgent duties of the Governors of our Colonies.' This placed a grave responsibility both on those charged with selecting and training missionaries and also on the missionaries themselves to take a broad yet balanced view of their obligations: 'piety and zeal, though the most essential qualifications of a missionary to the Aborigines, are not the only endowments indispensable to the faithful discharge of his office: ... it is necessary that with plans of moral and religious improvement should be combined well-matured schemes for advancing the social and political improvement of the tribes and for the prevention of any sudden changes which might be injurious to the health and physical constitution of the new converts'.[29]

Notwithstanding their own differences of opinion over implementation, missionaries such as Philip, Shaw and Williams and the Society secretaries were able to read into the *Report* a wholehearted endorsement of their principles and prior interests over those of other whites. Coates, Beecham and Ellis had no doubt

---

28  *Ibid.*, p. 80.
29  *Ibid.*, pp. 80–1.

that, whatever reservations had existed about European activity overseas in the eighteenth century, they had been steadily multiplied and confirmed. In words taken from their evidence and recapitulated in the *Report*'s Conclusion, they were unanimous as to the calamitous impact of the European encounter and its tendency 'to prevent the spread of civilization, education, commerce and Christianity'. They were at one with the writers of the *Report* in thinking that only priority given to Christianity would enable these other conditions to flourish.

Strongly influenced by South African and New Zealand evidence that the appropriation of native lands and attempts to control their labour were generally the greatest of indigenous grievances, the *Report* called for the strengthening of colonial governors' powers, for more carefully chosen colonial officials, for the extension of colonial jurisdiction beyond the formal frontiers and official backing for missionaries. This was essentially the programme which figures such as John Philip, for example, had pressed for since the 1820s. Like Philip before them, both witnesses and Committee members were now prepared to consider that measures essential to native security and independence might reduce contact with white colonisers while at the same time enabling commerce to increase. The recommendation of official support for missionaries was based on the belief that their presence not only reduced conflict but positively promoted trade. If, as these proposals were designed to ensure, 'commerce were conducted on truly Christian principles [it] might be made the means of communicating the most substantial benefits to the different aboriginal nations of the world'.[30] Commerce between whites and blacks, then seen as capable of producing a relationship of equal exchange, held out more promise for all than did white agriculture based on black labour.[31]

Discussion of the results expected from the prior introduction of Christianity pointed in one clear direction. Although in practice Christianity should be first on the scene, its effects were such that 'the moment Christian principle begins to bear upon the mind of man, from that moment his condition as a civilized being advances and hence Christianity and civilization advance *pari passu*'.[32] Asked whether he knew 'any class of missionaries who, in their attempts to instruct the natives in Christianity, combine the principles of Christianity and civilization', Shaw responded with a mixture of eagerness and resignation. This 'was precisely the plan on which the missionaries of the Wesleyan society endeavoured to act'. When called to the witness stand a year later, the LMS South Seas missionary John Williams agreed. He reiterated the proposition put to him by his questioner Edward Baines: 'undoubtedly ... I would advise' that 'civilization and the acquisition of the useful arts should be going on at the same time with Christianity, by

---

30  *PP* (1837) 7 (425), *Report*; *PP* (1836) 7 (538), QQ. 4345–7 (Coates, Ellis) and quotation at 4367 (Beecham).
31  Saunders, *Kitchingman Papers*, p. 272; Philip to Miss Buxton, 15 March 1832, MSS Afr.s.219B, f. 328.
32  *PP* (1836) 7 (538), Q. 4383 (Coates).

which means they may assist each other'.[33] Christianity in effect paved the way, since without it any attempts to adjust the encounter to foster good relations and material progress would fail.

It was the testimony of the Mission secretaries that most directly confirmed the shift in outlook that was taking place. They at last followed their subordinates from stations in the field in making explicit their acceptance that the establishment of Christianity required an appropriate cultural underpinning. After guaranteeing peace and 'an inalienable right to their own soil', 'It is also necessary ... to their moral and religious improvement, to encourage industry [i.e. individual effort and application] and commerce.'[34] Here again was an opening for the British govern-ment to act as an essential complement to the missionary societies: it should send out 'individuals to promote agriculture and manufactures among uncivilized tribes on the borders of our colonies'. That done, it 'would not be perhaps too much for a government standing in the position which the British Government does, to afford to people in such circumstances every facility and encouragement in commerce which the remission of ... duties would afford'.[35] Freer trade would thus also assist 'moral and religious' transformation. The introduction of Christianity and 'social improvement' was itself referred to not only in an older language which still spoke of compassion, benevolence and atonement for wrong but also now as 'a fair remu-neration for the loss of their lands', in other words in the developing language of contract and exchange.[36]

## II

The proceedings of the Aborigines Committee were a milestone in revealing the adaptation of the missionary movement to the world of expanding British commerce. They also confirmed the acceptability of missions to a wider domestic public and demonstrated a general recognition on the part of the societies and government that both parties could and should do business with each other.

Missions had begun in the 1820s to realise the value of linking Christianity and commerce. Progress at Bethelsdorp, then later at Griqua Town, Philipolis and the Kat River settlement demonstrated the relationship between African production, consumption and the advance of Christianity.[37] Experience in the Pacific, where inadequate missionary salaries, extreme isolation, infrequent and irregular contact with the outside world and the shortages or expense of supplies were common, showed that subsistence itself was dependent on trade. There were always a few

---

33  *PP* (1836) 7 (538), QQ. 1116–17 (Shaw, 21 Aug. 1835), Q. 5635 (Williams, 29 July 1836). For Baines, Select Committee member and MP for Leeds 1834–41, *DEB* Vol. 1, pp. 47–8.

34  *PP* (1836) 7 (538), QQ. 4371, 4375 (Coates, Beecham and Ellis).

35  *Ibid.*, Q. 4375.

36  *Ibid.*, Q. 4367 (Beecham).

37  Andrew Porter, '"Commerce and Christianity": The Rise and Fall of a Nineteenth Century Missionary Slogan', *HJ* 28, 3 (1985), pp. 597–621.

missionaries, such as George Pritchard, for whom trading 'acquired a virtue of its own' and risked diverting them from missionary work.[38] However, most followed William Ellis and his colleagues at Huahine. They attempted to develop local involvement in trades in oil and arrowroot and took commodities themselves in exchange for medicines and copies of the Gospels, with a view to offsetting their expenses.[39] The complications of such exchange reinforced John Williams's and Samuel Marsden's insistence on the need for missionary vessels and regular contact. Keen to reduce missionary costs in pursuit of further expansion, mission secretaries at home began to emphasise the need for local Christians to support their own activities.[40]

The Aborigines Committee illustrated how changes, although slow at first, had begun to have a marked effect. During his 1826–29 visit home, Philip had made heartfelt pleas: 'permanent societies of Christians can never be maintained among an uncivilized people without imparting to them the arts and habits of a civilized life'. At the same time he argued that 'Agriculture and commerce can never flourish, unless private property is respected and the laws which guard the possessions of individuals are the first principles of industry.'[41] More flexible and widely held attitudes developed under the pressure of collective experience and were justified by an extension of Providential reasoning. In Jamaica, James Philippo and William Knibb pressed ahead from 1835 with schemes for free villages and freehold land as providing the key to emancipated slaves' genuine independence of the planters.[42] By 1836 what had once been Philip's frustrated insistence on the need for secure, independent settlements had, ten years on, become Shaw's calmly stated common sense, even conventional wisdom. The Wesleyan told Buxton's Committee that 'government should support and protect them [local peoples] in the enjoyment of their rights and especially of their rights in the soil, without which the Caffres must ultimately prove a great scourge to the colony. If we deprive them of the soil, we deprive them of the means of sustenance and we compel them to become robbers and thus war must be perpetuated till we have extirpated them.' John Williams, also appearing in 1836, not only recognised but was also sanguine about the developments that had taken place. In the Pacific, 'there is a great advantage accruing to our country, by means of missionary labours, in a commercial point of view' as a consequence of changing patterns of consumption.[43] Neither Williams nor Shaw showed any signs of the older and far more stringent argument which appealed to white

38  Gunson, *Messengers of Grace*, pp. 115–21, 136. For Pritchard see Jane Samson, *Imperial Benevolence: Making British Authority in the Pacific Islands* (Honolulu, 1998).

39  Ellis, Davies and Barff to Burder, Mission Secretary, 15 July 1820, 17 June 1821, CWM South Seas 3/2; Barff to Hankey, Mission Secretary, 26 June 1822, *ibid.*, 3/7.

40  Above, Chapter 3, pp. 65, 67, 78–83.

41  Philip, *Researches in South Africa*, Vol. I, pp. 219, 382.

42  Stanley, '"Commerce and Christianity"', pp. 72, 93; Catherine Hall, 'White Visions, Black Lives: The Free Villages of Jamaica', *History Workshop* 36 (1993), 100–32.

43  *PP* (1836) 7 (538), QQ. 5677, 5687–91.

settlers and especially in the next decade to Wakefieldian colonisers, that labour and effective occupation alone created rights.[44]

Naturally missionaries from the field were delighted at the turn of events. At St Helena on his way to give his evidence, Philip had written optimistically to Rufus Anderson at the American Board. 'We have I believe the policy of the British Government upon our side and I doubt not ... that we shall be able, by the blessing of God, to enlist on the same side the religious feelings and principle of the nation.'[45] A year later he was jubilant. He described to Buxton's wife events reminiscent of the earlier anti-slavery campaigns, how public meetings of four to eight hundred people held in the large towns were declaring themselves keen on government action. He and his travelling companions from South Africa – the Reads father and son and their exemplary African converts Andries Stoffel and Dyani Tshatshu – did much to encourage throughout the country conviction as to the value of missionary activity. As he tried to get an early copy of the Committee's proceedings for Anderson, he told the Bostonian how 'Glenelg's views have fallen in with ours', 'the evidence on our side is triumphant'. Despite their deceits, 'The abettors of the old system here are biting the dust ... their teeth are broken and there is not a dentist in London that can replace them.'[46]

In the longer run, as historians know well, Philip's hopes were to be dashed.[47] However, for the moment he saw in the imperial government's refusal to approve Benjamin D'Urban's annexation of Queen Adelaide Province and the appointment of a senior official to oversee a treaty system negotiated with the Cape's eastern frontier peoples, something that gave them security and the missions an important opening. The new Lieutenant-Governor Andries Stockenstrom's official instructions seemed to serve Philip's aim to make 'every tribe to know its own limits, to be content with its own and respect its neighbours – & to drink with eagerness from the fountains of our religion civil policy and science'.[48] The settlement would assist not just British missions but the Americans, who were to work with the Zulu and exploit the latter's regional influence and connections.

As the Wesleyan mission's superintendent and suffering the financial consequences of the recent war in the destruction of Methodist settlements, Shaw took a different line. He seized on the *Report*'s advocacy of government financial support for missions and pressed the Cape government for annual subsidies of £100 to every mission station. Impressed by rumours about the future of Natal, he also left his home committee in no doubt either that 'We must have a Mission

---

44  For contemporary elaboration of the term 'humanitarian' in association with debate about 'rights', Mark Hickford, 'Making "territorial rights of the natives": Britain and New Zealand, 1830–1847', (unpub. D.Phil. thesis, Oxford, 1999).

45  Philip to Anderson, 11 March 1836, ABC 14/1.

46  Elbourne, *Blood Ground*, pp. 288–92; Philip to Mrs Buxton, 13 Dec. 1836, Mss.Afr.S.217/5/999; to Anderson, n.d. but 26 June 1837, ABC 14/1.

47  See esp. Ross, *Dr. John Philip* and Elbourne, *Blood Ground* and below.

48  Draft of Philip's evidence to Select Committee, Mss.Afr.S.217, Vol. 5, f. 1007.

there, if a colony is established', or of the strong case for government provision in aid of missionaries who might in any case go there.[49] Shaw's concerns may seem more prosaic than Philip's and his plans certainly envisaged closer ties between missions and imperial advance than did any of Philip's arrangements. However, they were in their way no less shaped by the concern to exploit evangelistic opportunities which the combination of domestic politics and local South African events had provided.

In making these claims the Cape Methodists were belatedly beginning to move towards taking up parliamentary grants especially for schools, a path already trodden by missionaries of most denominations, first in Sierra Leone and then the West Indies.[50] However, there was an additional buoyancy and optimism at this time that, no less than the sense of weakness and embattlement prevalent in the 1820s, was drawing missions into ever closer involvement with government and commerce. Consequently, missions were in danger of becoming captives of empire, as a result either of their growing dependence on direct government subvention and support or from reliance on general conditions created by government action and maintained by official intervention. However, the heady sense of imminent breakthroughs was sustained by a series of developments around the world sufficient to brush to one side most reservations about such relationships.

There was, for a few years at least, little diminution in the combined popular enthusiasm of the religious and humanitarian publics. Whatever the reservations held by leading figures such as Buxton or John Dyer (BMS Secretary, 1817–41) about particular objects of enthusiasm, they recognised its practical value to the missionary cause as well as its political potential. Hardly had Buxton's *Report* on the Aborigines appeared when the new campaign for the full and final emancipation of the ex-slaves through the ending of apprenticeship took wing, led by Joseph Sturge.[51] Sturge was assisted in the West Indian colonies by Baptist missionaries and the threat of black revolt, in the country by his first-hand information and eloquent histrionics and in Parliament by enthusiasts for both missionary and humanitarian causes such as Sir Eardley Wilmot.[52] Buttressed with the weight of more than four thousand petitions received in the early months of 1838, Sturge's campaign was finally successful in April in putting an end to apprenticeship for all the ex-slaves as from 1 August 1838.

Differences among humanitarians, between Buxton's supporters and those of the more radical Sturge, led at this point to the collapse of the Anti-Slavery Society

---

49 Shaw to Mission Committee, 4 March 1837, quotation from 10 Nov. 1838 (Private), 1 Feb. 1839, WMMS South Africa Albany Correspondence, 1837/12, 1838/7 and 1839/8.

50 Jakobsson, *Am I Not a Man*, pp. 526–49; see also above, Chapter 3, pp. 66–8.

51 Jakobsson, *Am I Not a Man*, pp. 561–73; Alex Tyrrell, *Joseph Sturge and the Moral Radical Party in Early Victorian Britain* (London, 1987), esp. Chapter 7 'The Battering Ram of Public Opinion (1836–38)'; 'The "Moral Radical Party" and the Anglo-Jamaican Campaign for the Abolition of the Negro Apprenticeship System', *English Historical Review* 99 (1984), pp. 481–502.

52 Sir John Eardley Wilmot, anti-slavery campaigner, MP for North Warwickshire.

and eventually to Sturge's formation in April 1839 of the British and Foreign Anti-Slavery Society. However, this does not seem materially to have affected the strength of the humanitarian–missionary alignment. Anxious to keep the movement alive and under his own control, Buxton responded in July 1838 by founding the African Civilization Society and by providing it with a programme which redefined humanitarian goals in a more distinctly evangelical form. The success of this manoeuvre was demonstrated by his carrying Baptists, Quakers, Wesleyans and Scottish Presbyterians with him into the new body.

Buxton shared the evangelical view that mobilizing the popular conscience and government power behind humanitarian causes should not only eradicate sin but also atone for past wrongdoing. This atonement involved not only penitential acts but the performance of good works from which the doer might also benefit. Buxton proceeded to demonstrate in new plans for Africa set out in two books, *The African Slave Trade* and *The Remedy*, the possibility of marrying Christian duty with secular self-interest under the umbrella of his new society.[53] In a prolonged echo of Wilberforce's earlier ideas linking abolition with Sierra Leone, Buxton demonstrated the continuing extent of the slave trade after more than thirty years of British abolition and laid out a programme for the rejuvenation of Africa. 'Legitimate commerce would put down the Slave Trade, by demonstrating the superior value of man as a labourer on the soil, to man as an object of merchandise; and if conducted on wise and equitable principles might be the precursor, or rather the attendant, of civilization, peace and Christianity, to the unenlightened, warlike and heathen tribes who now so fearfully prey on each other, to supply the slave markets of the New World. In this view of the subject, the merchant, the philanthropist, the patriot, and the Christian, may unite'.[54]

In developing his ideas for West Africa, Buxton relied heavily on the 1837 Aborigines *Report*, attaching great importance to it as a statement of policy.[55] In the emphasis he now placed on government protection and support in financial, administrative and naval terms and especially in the importance he attached to the role of Christian missions in Africa's transformation, he took his cue time and again from the discussions of three and four years before. In seeking to reapply the formula devised for the settler colonies to the different conditions of tropical Africa, Buxton was also attempting to sustain the same coalition of interests intended to give his plans practical effect. Slave traders black and white, like settler commandos, murderous seamen or native peoples set on revenge, he argued, were amongst the many contributors to the fact that Christianity 'had made but feeble inroads'. However, 'were this obstacle removed' by establishing the conditions for

53 Published sequentially in 1839, they were then combined in a single volume, *The African Slave Trade and Its Remedy* (London, 1840).

54 *Ibid.*, p. 306.

55 Charles Buxton (ed.), *Memoirs of Sir Thomas Fowell Buxton, Bart.*, new edn (London, 1882), pp. 184–5.

legitimate trade and civilisation, 'Africa would present the finest field for the labours of Christian missionaries which the world has yet seen'.[56]

It was of the greatest importance, Buxton said, that missionaries should be placed in all these centres of legitimate trade as agents of Christian instruction and civilisation and in justifying this argument he quoted extensively from the Aborigines Committee evidence.[57] The missionary interests, as they had been in 1837, were naturally delighted. The CMS associated itself closely with the humanitarian vision; John Beecham of the WMMS, won over by the reception of his ideas at Buxton's 1837 Committee, now supported him fully as did other missionary societies.[58] In this manner missionary supporters rallied again to the flag of legitimate peaceful trade; humanitarians, impressed by missionary evidence in 1837 and continuing missionary sympathy, now believed there were few if any more reliable supporters of their cause to be found.

Publicity for Buxton's plans generated considerable interest and excitement. Despite the fears of some ministers as to the costs and consequences of intertwining Britain with tropical Africa in a web of treaties, land purchases, trading and peacekeeping expeditions, the Whig government also fell in behind Buxton. A shared anti-slavery sentiment and political weakness outweighed practical reservations to the extent that the ministry agreed to support the first phase of Buxton's initiative in the form of a major diplomatic, scientific and commercial expedition up the Niger River. With expert crews, equipped with the latest technology and costing more than £100,000, three ships left Britain for the Niger in May 1841.[59] The CMS interest was represented by the Basel-trained Reverend Friedrich Schön (linguist and missionary at Sierra Leone since 1832) and Samuel Crowther, a liberated Yoruba, native catechist and later Bishop of the Niger. They both joined the party when it arrived at Freetown late in June, while other missionaries unable to secure berths on the official vessels tagged along as camp-followers.[60]

This is not the place to re-examine the misfortunes of the expedition. Almost one-third of the white members died of fever and by mid-October it had withdrawn from the Niger in disarray. The settlement upstream at Lokoja was abandoned and the African Civilization Society dissolved; Buxton died deeply disappointed in 1845. With the loss of his leadership the humanitarian movement in Britain rapidly lost much of its direction. The Aborigines Protection Society, legatee of the 1837 Select Committee's ideals, never made much impact under its

---

56  T.F. Buxton, *The African Slave Trade* (2nd edn, London, 1839), pp. xi–xii.

57  T.F. Buxton, *The African Slave Trade and Its Remedy* (2nd edn, London, 1840), chap. 6 'The Elevation of Native Minds', pp. 502 ff.

58  J. Gallagher, 'Fowell Buxton and the New African Policy, 1838–42', *Cambridge Historical Journal* 10 (1950), 49.

59  Howard Temperley, *White Dreams, Black Africa: The Antislavery Expedition to the Niger* (New Haven and London, 1991); Curtin, *Image of Africa*, chaps 12–13.

60  For Schön and Crowther, *DEB* Vol. 1, 277–8 and Vol. 2, pp. 981–2; also *BDCM*, pp. 160–1, 602–3. Two Baptists travelled on a supporting collier to Fernando Po: Stanley, *History of the BMS*, p. 107.

Quaker founder, Dr Thomas Hodgkin. Far more prominent was the British and Foreign Anti-Slavery Society (BFASS), but Sturge himself remained a contentious figure and the movement was constantly riven by disputes over where and how best to promote the anti-slavery cause.[61]

The decline of humanitarian activism, however, did not drag the missionary movement down at the same time. Notwithstanding the extent to which it had depended on and benefited from humanitarian organisation and support, the enthusiasm for missions generated between 1834 and 1841 was sufficient to surmount the Niger fiasco. The momentum enabled the movement to take up new openings which more than compensated for the Niger setback. One might reasonably suggest that Buxton's last great public act contributed significantly to the missionary cause rather than directly to that of anti-slavery. There is a melancholy but fitting symbolism in that while Commander Bird Allen, with his Buxton family connections and Dr Theodor Vogel, the official botanist, were among those who died on the Niger, Schön and Crowther comfortably survived to report on the expedition and support missionary expansion.[62] Much as Buxton's friends invoked the religious imagery of martyrdom in offering condolences for those who failed to return,[63] on this occasion it was not the missionaries who were the victims of the 'white man's grave'. Far more potent in associating the aura of martyrdom with the missionary movement was the murder of John Williams at Eromanga in the southwest Pacific in 1839. Occurring only two years after his evidence to the Aborigines Committee and his resoundingly successful tour of England to launch his memoir, Williams's death was a source of inspiration for years to come.[64] Missionary survival on the Niger and death in the Pacific neatly emphasise the distinctiveness of their interests and fortunes in the continuing counterpoint with their humanitarian allies.

## III

An important indicator of the newly enhanced popularity of missions at this time was the level of missionary income. These were, moreover, essential to the societies' ability to pick up where the humanitarians left off. Brian Stanley has demonstrated how, despite the general economic hardship experienced throughout Britain between 1837 and 1842, the societies' income showed 'an impressive and in some

---

61  Howard Temperley, *British Anti-Slavery 1833–1870* (London, 1972); A.M. Kass and E.H. Kass, *Perfecting the World: The Life and Times of Dr Thomas Hodgkin, 1798–1866* (Boston and New York, 1988).

62  Temperley, *White Dreams*, pp. 42, 73, 77, 138–9; J.F. Schön and S.A. Crowther, *Journals of the Rev. James Frederick Schön and Mr Samuel Crowther* (London, 1842).

63  Temperley, *White Dreams*, p. 138, quoting for example Buxton's business partner, Robert Hanbury.

64  John Williams, *A Narrative of Missionary Enterprises in the South Sea Islands* (London, 1837); Garrett, *To Live Among the Stars*, pp. 164–7; Dorothy Shineberg, *They Came for Sandalwood* (Cambridge, 1967), pp. 58–9, 205–7.

cases spectacular, increase in both money and real terms', representing 'a rapidly increasing share of national resources'.[65] At the same time 'a flood of missionary candidates' made it possible to send large numbers to the field, amongst them David Livingstone, C.G. Pfander and Octavius Hadfield.[66] Despite some fallback in 1841–42, unexpectedly high levels of giving were sustained through the 1840s, subsequently defying any attempt by historians to establish a predictable relationship between missionary income and economic fluctuations. This is precisely the point made in more general terms by the Wesleyan Society's chroniclers reviewing their much longer time-span in 1921. Although 'National impoverishment and ... commercial depression ... reduce the means of willing givers', it was surprising how little this had affected the Society. 'The curve of national income and that of missionary revenue, during the century, exhibit no general correspondence'.[67] Missions were clearly in the ascendant round about 1840 while, no less strikingly, other recent crowd-pulling causes were ceasing to be so. The picture provided, for example, by the Aborigines Protection Society and still more the British and Foreign Anti-Slavery Society, was far less rosy. The latter averaged £2000 per annum in the 1840s and only half that sum in the 1850s and 1860s.[68]

Explanation for the availability of plentiful resources in straitened times has been sought in the fact that missionary revenues 'are governed by wholly different forces'.[69] To expand on this coy, even cryptic, observation, the historian is not compelled to fall back on the miraculous or supernatural. Rather it is possible to look to the emergence in many minds of powerful combinations of perceived opportunities for missionary work and a heightened sense of religious obligation. As has already been seen, these were perfectly capable of creating a momentum and sense of direction at odds with the accountant's calculation of profit and loss.[70]

If the Niger seemed at least temporarily a lost cause and with it government support for joint action there with humanitarians and missionaries, elsewhere – even in West Africa – missions found considerable encouragement. Optimism regarding West Africa originated in the conjunction of two circumstances. First, there was a renewed interest from recently liberated slaves, both in the Caribbean and especially at Sierra Leone, in returning to their West African homes. At the same time, local disturbances arising particularly from the Yoruba wars (c.1825–40) prompted attempts by local leaders to secure missionaries and teachers as sources of support and protection for their people. White mortality itself stimulated a growing demand for the greater use of black agents.

---

65  Brian Stanley, 'Home Support for British Overseas Missions in Early Victorian England, c.1838–1873' (unpub. Ph.D., Cambridge, 1979), chap. 1, quotations at pp. 25–7.
66  For Pfander (Agra, 1840) and Hadfield (Waimate, New Zealand, 1838), *CMS Register*, List I, entries 264, 295.
67  Findlay and Holdsworth, *History of the WMMS*, Vol. 1, p. 186.
68  Stanley, 'Home Support', pp. 156–8.
69  Findlay and Holdsworth, *History of the WMMS*, Vol. 1, p. 186.
70  Chapters 2 and 3 above, pp. 55–6, 91.

The components of this picture have been well studied.[71] In Sierra Leone, the growth of Freetown and the multiplication of new villages since the mid-1820s had left its inhabitants neither prosperous nor contented. Settlers and liberated slaves both felt an acute lack of opportunity and serious tensions existed between the different communities, rooted in economic and social rivalries and expressed in growing segregation. Border conflicts with the Temne and epidemic yellow fever in the late 1830s only heightened discontents. Seeking a future in trade, especially along the coast, liberated Africans, many of them partly at least mission-educated, began to re-establish contacts with their own peoples. Significant numbers of Yoruba among them, displaced by the wars, opened up contacts with Abeokuta via Badagry from 1838–39 if not earlier.

For the Methodists, who had sustained no more than a very fitful presence on the Gold Coast since 1835, this exodus was not to be ignored. Thomas Birch Freeman, based at Cape Coast Castle since January 1838, was sent to Badagry in autumn 1842. Not to be outdone, the CMS despatched Henry Townsend to Abeokuta in January 1843, with Crowther following him in 1845. Both missions were settled in Badagry by 1845 and Abeokuta the following year, negotiating their continued presence amidst the complex local politics of the region.

Parallel developments took place as a direct offshoot from the post-emancipation excitement in the West Indies. From Jamaica the initiative of local Baptists, egged on by William Knibb and his colleagues, produced a mission to Fernando Po by 1843–44. Again their competitors were anxious to show themselves no less forward. Scottish Presbyterians took up the idea of a mission in 1841, encouraged by Hope Waddell of the Scottish Missionary Society in Jamaica, and in response to African requests established their first mission at Calabar in 1846.[72]

These advances coincided, of course, with Britain's annexation of New Zealand, that notable early-nineteenth-century expression of general humanitarian sentiment and specific missionary concern, clinched by the Treaty of Waitangi in 1840. In the sentimental climate created by the Select Committee of 1837, powerful pressures not least from the missionary lobby with its well-established presence in North Island were reinforced by appeals for defence against the very real threat from French expansion. Within six years of their arrival in 1838, Roman Catholic leaders had settled forty-one missionaries and twelve stations among a Maori population that was widely recognised as susceptible to conversion; their presence was strongly supported by French naval and diplomatic pressure. The question of

71 Fyfe, *Sierra Leone*, pp. 168–240; J.F. Ade Ajayi, *Christian Missions in Nigeria 1841–1891: The Making of a New Elite* (London, 1965), chap. 2 'The Return of the Exiles'.

72 Ajayi, *Christian Missions*, pp. 43–6, 53; Martin Lynn, 'John Beecroft and West Africa, 1829–54' thesis (unpub. Ph.D, London, 1978), chaps 4–5; Stanley, *History of the BMS*, pp. 106–10; for Waddell see his *Twenty-nine Years in the West Indies and Central Africa, 1829–58* (London, 1963 edn).

British control thus became ever more a Protestant as well as a Palmerstonian preoccupation.[73]

Missionary confidence was also greatly enhanced by events in the Far East. Ever since the 1790s China had loomed up on the Protestant horizon as one of the greatest challenges to missionary dedication. Its remoteness, physical extent and enormous population – by Carey's reckoning, sixty million undifferentiated 'pagans' – placed it perhaps second only to India in the global calculus of spiritual need. For Robert Haldane, Scottish evangelical philanthropist and theologian, it was China's existence – that 'world of souls in itself' – that invested missionary efforts in Bengal with strategic purpose.[74] The subsequent development of the missionary presence in India accentuated China's exceptionalism. Its impenetrability further heightened that challenge and provoked the sustained attention of a handful of missionaries – Robert Morrison, William Milne and Samuel Dyer of the LMS, Elijah Bridgman of the American Board and the essentially freelance Karl Gützlaff. From bases in Canton or Macau and commercial centres further afield such as Penang, Malacca or Singapore, they worked away at translation, the technical problems of printing in Chinese characters, the distribution of tracts and surreptitious evangelism, both along China's coast and sometimes well inland.[75] Gützlaff and Bridgeman were among those who set up the Society for the Diffusion of Useful Knowledge in 1834.

Missionary progress amongst the Chinese was nevertheless regarded as limited. As late as 1839 John Philip noted that while 'China is hermetically sealed ... Africa is open', an awareness of which he argued owed much to Buxton's recent efforts.[76] This perception was widely shared. The first tentative exploration by the CMS who sent out Edward Squire in 1836 reported in 1840 that there was 'no opening' and the sense of Africa's continuing comparative advantage influenced David Livingstone's early career. Impatient with waiting for the chance to enter China, Livingstone allowed his growing preference for 'Africa' to be confirmed by Robert Moffat, whom he met at the LMS boarding house in London shortly after his acceptance by the Society in the summer of 1839. However, unrest in China and the Opium War of 1839–42, which gave rise to Livingstone's frustration, was soon seen as providing a providential opening for missionary

73 James Belich, *Making Peoples: A History of the New Zealanders from Polynesian Settlement to the end of the Nineteenth Century* (Auckland, 1996) pp. 135–6, 180–7; Adams, *Fatal Necessity*; Garrett, *To Live Among the Stars*, pp. 48–55, 67–70. Palmerston was Foreign Secretary in Melbourne's government, 1836–41.

74 Carey, *An Enquiry*, p. 46; Haldane in *The Missionary Magazine* (Jan. 1797), quoted in Smith, *Life of Carey*, p. 336.

75 Brian Harrison, *Waiting for China: The Anglo-Chinese College at Malacca, 1818–1843 and Early Nineteenth-Century Missions* (Hong Kong, 1979); Elijah C. Bridgman. *Glimpses of Canton: The Diary of Elijah C. Bridgman 1834–1838*, with a Foreword by Martha Lund-Smalley (New Haven, C, 1998).

76 Philip to Rufus Anderson, Dec. 1839 [no day], ABC/14/2/134.

expansion. The Treaty of Nanking (1842) brought British possession of Hong Kong and opened the so-called 'treaty ports' of Ningpo, Foochow, Shanghai and Nanking not only for Western trade but for the free operation of Christian missionaries.

Commercial euphoria was more than matched by no less speculative displays of religious excitement. As a result, James Legge, Livingstone's contemporary, having contented himself with a place at Malacca in 1840, was rapidly resettled at Shanghai during August 1843. Not only did enthusiastic new recruits turn to China. An older missionary such as Walter Medhurst, with patience born of the knowledge that European governments could be as restrictive as the Chinese, also moved from Batavia to a new life in Shanghai.[77] The CMS's caution evaporated. Another exploratory party was sent out in June 1844 and by the end of the year it was being reported in its *Quarterly Papers* that 'China does not present so many difficulties to Missionary enterprise as most other Heathen countries'. A mission was started in 1847. After the initial heady enthusiasm, however, the colonial status of Hong Kong itself was no necessary recommendation for a missionary base. After the CMS's investigations, only one of its first four missionaries was based there, the others going to Ningpo and Shanghai.[78]

## IV

Not all the missionary advances of the early 1840s caused such a stir as China and New Zealand. Some were wholly unexpected. Thus the CMS arrived at Rabai, Mombasa, in 1844 'more by accident than design' according to Oliver.[79] Johann Ludwig Krapf simply saw it as a suitable base from which to rescue his hitherto unsuccessful mission to Abyssinia and the peoples of the north-east. It was a venture quite unconnected with either the commercial treaty of 1839 between Britain and the Sultan of Muscat and Oman or the appointment of J.A. Hamerton as consul in 1841. There were also instances of reluctant retreat. The CMS, contrary to the lessons of experience and Samuel Marsden's advice, had maintained throughout the 1830s a mission to the Aborigines at Wellington Valley, New South Wales. Despite the Society's continuing humanitarian as well as missionary

---

77  Medhurst was critical of the Dutch authorities' 'selfish system of excluding foreigners from their colonies', Medhurst to Rufus Anderson, 16 Feb. 1838, ABC/14/2/124. For his career, Harrison, *Waiting for China*; *BDCM*, pp. 451–2; and *Oxford Dictionary of National Biography* (forthcoming, 2004).

78  *Quarterly Papers of the Church Missionary Society*, 95 (Michaelmas 1844); George Smith, *A Narrative of an Exploratory Visit to each of the Consular Cities of China and to the Islands of Hong Kong and Chusan, on behalf of the Church Missionary Society* ... (London, 1847); Kate Lowe, 'The Beliefs, Aspirations and Methods of the First Missionaries in British Hong Kong, 1841–5', in Pieter N. Holtrop and Hugh McLeod (eds), *Missions and Missionaries. Studies in Church History Subsidia 13* (Woodbridge, 2000), pp. 50–64.

79  Oliver, *Missionary Factor*, pp. 5–6.

commitment, however, low expectations of benefits to the Aborigines, inadequate funds and the Colonial Office's refusal of further land grants prompted abandonment of the station in 1840–41.[80]

No setbacks however were yet sufficiently weighty to dim the general evangelistic enthusiasm. The reflex influence inside Britain of expanding missionary opportunities is plain to see, not only in the spheres of successful recruitment and philanthropic giving. By 1838, for example, the CMS had decided that it was time to give supporters a clearer picture of missionary activities around the globe. Secretary Coates wrote to colleagues in other societies for up-to-date details and incorporated them in the *Missionary Map of the World distinguishing the Stations of all Protestant Missionary Societies*.[81] If the pre-eminence of the CMS was becoming plain, nevertheless the international nature of missionary enterprise was no less evident. This map seems to have been the first of its kind, but such publications soon caught on. The SPG produced its own *Colonial and Missionary Church Map of the World* in 1842; the SPCK followed suit with an identical title in 1853.[82] The appearance of missionary atlases was only a matter of time, with the CMS again to the fore. Its *Church Missionary Atlas* (London, 1857) soon needed regularly updating; a fifth edition appeared in 1873, the eighth in 1896.[83]

Other publications also began to appear at this time, directed towards a wider general and sometimes younger, audience. The Church of Scotland began in 1838 to publish far more information about its work in its *Home and Foreign Missionary Record*, as did the WMMS in the *Wesleyan Missionary Notices* commenced in 1839. The CMS and the Baptists aimed more consciously not least at juvenile readers: the CMS brought out the *Church Missionary Juvenile Instructor* from 1841 and the BMS its *Juvenile Missionary Herald* for the first time in 1845.

It is impossible to overlook the intensified missionary confidence and optimism evidenced here in the societies' attempts to engage a new and enlarged audience and their energetic pursuit of subscriptions and donations. Significant advances into new geographical areas went hand in hand with a boldness of attitude towards governments of all kinds that disguised for the time being continuing dependence on secular authorities. This mood was powerful enough to reinvigorate not only the lay voluntary societies but to influence the development of even that most erastian and conservative body, the SPG.

---

80  Hilary M. Carey, '"The debt of justice": Aborigines, Missions and the Humanitarians 1830–1845', *NAMP Symposium Paper* (Boston, 1998).

81  Published by the CMS, London, 1838.

82  See also J. Wyld, *An Atlas of Maps of different parts of the World designed to show the Stations of the Protestant Missionaries* (London, 1839); *The Protestant and Missionary Map of the World* (London, 1846).

83  Roman Catholics were slower off the mark, with important publications from Germany, home of much professional late nineteenth-century cartography, in the 1880s: see *Atlas des Missions Catholiques. Par le R.P. O. Werner* [trans. from the German, orig. published, Freiburg, 1884] (Bureau des Missions Catholiques, Lyons, 1886).

As seen above, the SPG was essentially untouched by the eighteenth-century revival; moreover, its organisers lacked initiative and its financial support remained very limited.[84] From 1814, onwards through the 1820s, its funds and activity were very largely dependent on the continuing receipt and administration of parliamentary grants to the church in Nova Scotia and the Canadas. However, this position was rapidly becoming unsustainable. As British overseas emigration rapidly grew, so too did both the claims made on behalf of the church in new areas of settlement and the social and political importance of religious dissent among colonial populations. Both in Britain's colonies and at home, material endowment and other forms of government support for the Anglican church at the expense of rival denominations steadily became more unpopular, an ever more serious political liability. The inevitable consequences were a decade of adjustment in the relation of church and state during the 1830s, marked by a series of legislative and administrative measures. These included the establishment of the Ecclesiastical Commission (1835–36), the Registration Act of 1836 and other reforms touching tithes and church rates. In the white settlement colonies reforming pressures were also at work. In New South Wales, for example, after only eight years the Church and Schools' Corporation – Anglicanism's vehicle for the administration of its official funds – was brought to an end. For the SPG a redefinition of its missionary role was inescapable.[85]

Reform for the SPG was precipitated by the Whig government's decision in 1832 that the parliamentary grants for the colonial church establishments should cease. Although the outcry was such that transitional arrangements had to be negotiated to ease clerical hardship and sustain ecclesiastical provision, the logic held fast. Since all denominations could not be funded, equality of treatment required that they should finance themselves; the ending of state aid thus necessitated either a massive increase in colonial Anglicans' self-support or the SPG's discovery of new funds, or possibly both. The first seemed unlikely in any short term and occasional parish collections under Royal Letters (such as those of 1819 for Bishop's College, Calcutta and 1835 for schools and chapels in Mauritius and the West Indies) were sporadic and unreliable. The SPG therefore had no alternative but to follow the well-tried example of other missionary societies. It turned to a far more systematic organisation and regular use of Parochial Associations and district committees, both started in 1819, for fund raising through the circulation of missionary literature, appeals and public meetings.[86]

This strategy was successful and owed much to the appointment first in 1833 of Archibald Campbell as Secretary and then of Ernest Hawkins as Assistant Secretary in 1838 and Campbell's successor in 1843. Despite the continued refusal of the SPG to attend the monthly London Secretaries Meeting, both men were

---

84  Above, Chapter 2, pp. 50–1, 55–6.

85  For these processes see E.D. Daw, *Church and State in the Empire: The Evolution of Imperial Policy 1846–1856* (Canberra, 1977); Stanley, 'Home Support', pp. 76–91.

86  Pascoe, *Two Hundred Years*, Vol. 2, pp. 825–8b, 830–2.

energetic and well informed, not least in their awareness of the growing public prominence of their rivals. In the daily affairs of the Society the vital importance of missionary information in stimulating donations was not lost on them, with the result that to the Society's *Occasional and Quarterly Papers*, commenced in 1833, were added in 1843–34 *The Church in the Colonies* and *Missions to the Heathen*. Extending the evidence of voluntary self-help within the Church of England it was hoped might impress governments with a sense of duty or political necessity and enhance the SPG's influence in ways akin to that of the other missionary societies.

On issues of religious principle, the reformers were critical of government pretensions in matters of ecclesiastical reform and were sympathetic to Tractarian views of the Church with the importance they attached to the role of bishops as the prime source of doctrinal authority and discipline. This inclined reformers such as Charles Blomfield (Bishop of London) and Samuel Wilberforce (later Bishop of Oxford) to take the colonial church and the SPG's missionary activity out of the hands of an increasingly unsympathetic or interfering state. They found themselves facing problems very similar to those of their eighteenth-century counterparts, especially in the reluctance of imperial authorities to create dioceses, appoint bishops and attend to the anomalies of ecclesiastical law and jurisdiction.[87] Faced with government inaction or inappropriate changes and with mounting challenges from denominational rivals and colonial politicians, they wished to reduce the encumbrances of establishment and give the church itself more control over its own affairs. As one important step to this end, in 1841 they set up the Colonial Bishoprics Fund, with Hawkins as Secretary.[88]

The creation of the Fund had both an immediate and sustained impact on SPG work. Beginning in October 1841 with the consecration of G.A. Selwyn as bishop to the newly established colony of New Zealand, the 1840s closed with the creation in 1849 of the diocese of Victoria (Hong Kong), making a total of fifteen bishops appointed during the decade. The SPG was also instrumental in setting up St Augustine's College, Canterbury, in 1848, for the training of colonial clergy.

Although the SPG still envisaged its principal task as the provision of parish clergy and bishops to the burgeoning white colonial populations, one major consequence of the reforms was the greater practical importance it now attached to the evangelisation of indigenous populations. This shift might be said to have been restarted with the transfer to the Society in 1825 of the SPCK's missionary operations in India, as a result of which German Lutherans were gradually replaced with missionaries in Anglican orders.[89] It was fostered more generally, however, in response to two circumstances.

---

87  See Chapter 1 above, pp. 20–4.
88  W.F. France, *The Oversea Episcopate: Centenary History of the Colonial Bishoprics Fund, 1841–1941* (London, 1941).
89  Neill, *History of Christianity in India*, pp. 214–15; John E. Pinnington, 'Common Principles in the early years of the Church Missionary Society: The Problem of the "German" Missionaries', *Journal of Theological Studies* 20, 2 (1969), pp. 527–32.

First, there was the perennial need for funds. Despatching and supporting cler-gymen to colonists, or, as they were later christened, 'missions of recovery', were widely felt among churchgoers to be less interesting, even less important, than those of 'discovery' to foreign peoples often well beyond Britain's formal colonial territo-ries. To be successful, appeals for funds to support SPG activities needed to reflect this. Figures such as Hawkins realised this only too well, conscious as they were that competitors might move in where for lack of resources the SPG was unable to tread.[90]

The interests of SPG clergy themselves also contributed to the change. One particularly influential example was Bishop Selwyn. While not all SPG members shared his high view of the church and its authority, they were more than ever before agreed on the need for church and mission to expand together.[91] Committed to his position as a religious leader for the colonial populations, Selwyn made no play with notional distinctions between an imperial or colonial and a missionary role. He was a 'missionary bishop', consecrated to the task of building up the church from its very beginning, consulting the opinions of his fellow clergy in doing so but acting essentially on his own authority. Even if part of his work led him to operate inside colonial territory, it was immaterial that much of it did not. Highlighting the universal, global outlook of the missionary movement, the geographical limits of his diocese stretched far beyond any area of formal British control. Church and mission transcended empire, with colonial possessions provid-ing not only an evangelical arena but also a missionary launching pad.

Selwyn recognised the need for the church to keep irreligious colonists in check and to promote the interests of local peoples. He not only aimed to bring New Zealand's Maoris to Christianity but used the colony itself, his own diocese and his cathedral as a base for missions into the Western Pacific. Church and mission he claimed would be jointly best served by 'building up the colonial churches as missionary churches' rather than by separating the different aspects of their central missionary concern. In a published letter to Gladstone, part of the domestic debate about church–state relations, Selwyn argued that 'every plan, intended for the improvement of our own Church Establishment, should also have in view the more effectual propagation of the Gospel throughout our Colonies and among the heathen generally … The Church of England cannot be worthy of the English nation if it be not a missionary as well as a domestic Church.'[92] Just as other missions focused on missionary stations and schools, so for Selwyn the nerve centre of missionary activity and basis for all episcopal initiative was everywhere the cathedral and the community built around it. Selwyn and his supporters also shared with missionaries of other denominations a common sense of providential

90  O'Connor, *Three Centuries of Mission*, pp. 54, 67–9.

91  Anthony Grant, *The Past and Prospective Extension of the Gospel by Missions to the Heathen. The Bampton Lectures for 1843*, 2nd edn (London, 1845), pp. xi, xvi.

92  G.A. Selwyn, *Are Cathedral Institutions Useless? A Practical Answer to this Question addressed to W.E. Gladstone, Esq. M.P.* (London, 1838), pp. 46–7, 55–6.

guidance and inspiration. In language which might equally have come from an earlier figure such as Buchanan, the new bishop on arrival in New Zealand in May 1842 spoke in apocalyptic terms: 'if we know that the fulfilment of prophecy and the completion of promises and the growth of Christ's kingdom, all portend the coming of the end ... what need we any further argument, [or] stronger motive ... to devote ourselves ... to this great and hopeful work?'[93]

For those keen to reassert the power of the church and its leaders, to exploit the advantages of establishment while distancing the church from the state, the timing of Selwyn's appointment was critical. As was to be the case with other colonial appointments, New Zealand was witnessing the setting up of a church while a colonial government was still either weak or non-existent. Just as the early arrival of the CMS missionaries was thought to have given men such as Henry Williams enormous influence, so Selwyn saw great advantages in the initial simplicity 'and entire freedom from all political connection' of his own church.[94] Not only was he pleased when 'After much discussion with Government, I have gained the full power of organizing my own diocese, without interference on the part of the State.' He evidently felt that separation from the state placed him above local colonial conflicts, making possible a wider range of friendships – for example, with successive governors – and enhancing his influence as mediator or peacemaker.[95] However, this could not be expected to last. 'The Missionary must always expect that colonization will follow in his train, that he will not be allowed to retain his own authority unimpaired, nor to draw a line around his native converts, within which no contamination shall be allowed to enter. The world will find its way to them, or they will break forth into the world.'[96] However, although Selwyn was overtaken by the complications of local encounters far sooner than he had expected,[97] an early start could do much to establish not only the equal partnership of church and state but also the genuine independence of the missionary enterprise. An important aspect of this process, one which was to take up a great deal of his time, was the Melanesian Mission which he established under his own direct control in 1847.[98]

---

93  G.A. Selwyn, *How shall we sing the Lord's Song in a Strange Land? A Sermon preached in the Cathedral Church of St. Peter, Exeter ... previous to his departure from England* (1842); *Thanksgiving Sermon: Preached ... on His Arrival in His Diocese* (Paihia, 1842), p. 12.

94  Rev. H.W. Tucker, *Memoir of the Life and Episcopate of George Augustus Selwyn, D.D.*, 2 vols (London, 1879), pp. 55, 163–4; G.A. Selwyn, *A Charge delivered to the Clergy of the Diocese of New Zealand at the Diocesan Synod ... September 23, 1847* (repr. London, 1849), p. 9.

95  Selwyn to C.J. Abraham, 20 Oct. 1841, in Tucker, *Memoir of the Life*, Vol. 1, pp. 77, 225–6.

96  Selwyn, *A Charge*, p. 17.

97  For example, his intervention critical of Governor Grey's land policy, which was a focus of vigorous debate in the House of Commons, 13 Dec. 1847, *Hansard Parliamentary Debates* 3rd series, 95 (1847), cols 1003–30. Subsequently, see W.D. McIntyre (ed.), *The Journal of Henry Sewell, 1853–7*, 2 vols (Christchurch, 1980).

98  H. Laracy, 'Selwyn in Pacific Perspective', in Warren E. Limbrick (ed.), *Bishop Selwyn in New Zealand 1841–68* (Palmerston North, 1983), pp. 121–35; David Hilliard, *God's Gentlemen: A History of the Melanesian Mission* (St Lucia, 1978).

## V

Evangelical responses to events in China and New Zealand emphasise not only the heightened enthusiasm of these few years but also the insistent, inescapable variety of British expansion. No more than those of any other period do they reveal clear-cut relationships between the extension of the missionary presence and the establishment of Britain's secular political authority. They provide no evidence to suggest that 'the bible' naturally either followed or preceded 'the flag'. As the West African examples show, the sources of initiative were variously local converts, missionaries branching out from work in an existing colony, or the headquarters in Britain often interested in uncharted areas. New mission ventures might be responses to local requests for a missionary or school, to perceived problems arising from the intrusion of outsiders (traders, settlers and others), to personal ambition or the challenge of rival denominations. They can provide examples of withdrawal at a time of pronounced missionary enthusiasm for expansion and they offer no consistency in either the timing or the type of imperial authority established in areas where missions were at work or planned to advance.

Far more certain were the domestic status, respectability and degree of independence the missionary movement had acquired by the early 1840s. Together with new openings and more ample resources than it had previously known, these circumstances were responsible for the optimism and self-confidence marking the missionary endeavour. In competing with the other agencies of British expansion either to secure their influence or position by being early on the scene, or by shaping the pattern of imperial rule and expansion through pressure on governments, missions could point to at least some successes. Whether they could now exploit their openings and deploy finance, manpower and the missionary family in order to build on those early achievements had now to be demonstrated.

# 7

# Missionary goals, colonial experience and the waning of enthusiasm, 1850–70

Missionary progress towards a converted world and the movement's ability to take advantage of British expansion, or at least to contain the worst of its excesses, required not just territorial openings and material resources but the winning of converts and their effective deployment. However energetic the propagation of Christianity by figures such as Duff, Moffat and Selwyn, it did not modify the fundamental reality for missionaries everywhere that their task was ultimately one for indigenous Christians. Europeans could do little more than kick-start the process of global conversion. This fact, often at first accepted as an abstract proposition, was impressed on successive generations of missionaries by their own experience.

David Livingstone disembarked at Simon's Town in March 1841 and after ten weeks of winter trekking inland from Algoa Bay reached his destination, Robert Moffat's station at Kuruman, on 31 July. One year later and after a further lengthy journey to the north and north-east of Kuruman, he knew where he stood on the question of 'native agents'. Although his opinions in many respects later changed, he still shared – was doubtless in some respects reinforced in – many of the period's dismissive ethnocentric views of African cultures. The Tswana he felt were 'sunk into the very lowest state of both mental and moral degradation, so much so indeed it must be difficult or rather impossible for Christians at home to realise anything like an accurate notion of the grossness of the darkness which shrouds their minds'.[1] Attributing this condition to 'the lamentable deterioration of my species', Livingstone concluded that the nature, the extent and the urgency of the problem facing the missionary rendered the role of the convert central to its solution. Expressing his sadness 'when I contemplate the prospects of these large masses of immortal souls', 'I see no hopes for them except in native agents. The more I see of the country, its large extent of surface, with its population scattered and each tribe separated by a formidable distance from almost every other, I feel the more convinced that it will be impossible if not impolitic for the church to supply them all with Europeans. Native Christians *can* make known the way of life.' He offered examples from his own experience and suggested the value not only to the church but to the converts themselves of their being encouraged in this way as soon as

---

1 Livingstone to J.J. Freeman (LMS Secretary), 3 July 1842, in I. Schapera (ed.), *Livingstone's Missionary Correspondence 1841–1856* (London, 1961), p. 18.

possible.[2] It integrated them into the mission, tapped their own benevolence towards neighbouring Africans and exploited their ability to put across something of Christianity to children and others not easily reached by Europeans. This was the case both with those Africans hostile to Europeans and others who 'have not yet learned to despise the Gospel' as a result of such contacts.[3] Although not all missionaries – including Robert Moffat, Livingstone's mentor – agreed with him on the rapidity with which native agents could readily be put to evangelistic use, the principle itself was generally endorsed.

The search for converts as well as its success or failure always reflected local social and political conditions. Early LMS experience in the Pacific continued to fuel the expectations held by missionaries in different fields that their conversion of local rulers or social elites would perhaps in time percolate the lower classes. That same focus on elites, however, could also be encouraged by missions' frequent vulnerability and their reliance on local authority for permission to operate and for continued protection. However, as we have seen, missionaries were often uncomfortably aware of what seemed to them the mercenary calculations involved in attention to the Christian message. High-caste Indians profiting from a missionary education, rulers such as Moshoeshoe benefiting politically from the missionary presence in their kingdoms, were rarely among those most ready to encourage the education and conversion of others, even if eventually becoming Christians themselves. Inevitably therefore other approaches had to be adopted if missionaries were to draw in a wider cross-section of each society. Those possessing only a limited stake in local societies – which might include the ill or destitute, orphaned, enslaved, insane, vagrant and the criminal, figures often seen as marginal or in some other way deviant – were therefore frequently either attracted to mission stations or became the object of missionary attention. At one time or another, Robert Moffat's evangelistic career illustrates all these evangelical calculations at work.[4] In north India, the same considerations came into play. There it was estimated in 1862 that 'with the exception of Meeruth, nearly three fourths of the whole number of Christians in the North West Province and Punjab ... are orphans or the children of orphans'.[5]

## I

Beyond the initial quests for converts, however, lay the question of their future roles, the shape of indigenous churches and the development of the missions themselves. Although the desirability of comparative reflection on the experience of the

---

2  *Ibid.*, p. 19.
3  Livingstone to T.J. Prentice, 2 Dec. 1841, in Holmes (ed.), *David Livingstone Letters and Documents 1841–1872*, pp. 16–21.
4  Moffat, *Missionary Labours and Scenes*, esp. pp. 133–6, 354–72, 389–90, 401, 465.
5  John Barton to Henry Venn, 21 Feb. 1862, CMS Archives CI 1/037, no. 19; also 2 Oct. 1861, no. 16.

various missions in order to address such issues had been noted even in the 1820s, little systematic consideration seems to have been given to them until the 1840s.[6] Reasons for this were several. Mission organisers had for years given their chief attention to building up the networks of support at home, while the handling of events in the field was left largely in trust to the missionaries on the spot. Many of the latter were first generation missionaries, conscious of their pioneering status, possessing a sense of their own authority and high purpose with an ego to match, which could inhibit acceptance of others' ideas. Other circumstances such as the patchy and piecemeal development of any one missionary society's operations could also make comparisons difficult. Distance and the gathering of accurate information were major problems being only slowly overcome. At its most extreme this process included Daniel Tyerman's and George Bennett's tour of the LMS stations which took seven years, between 1821 and 1829 and at one point involved them in waiting for six months at Port Louis, Mauritius, for a cattle boat to visit the newly established station in Madagascar.[7] However, as the missionary movement grew, answers were wanted to these questions about future policy which went far beyond continued adherence to basic patterns of evangelism carried on within the framework of the original rules and regulations of individual societies. Given the ups and downs of the missionary record, a reliance on Providence and its interpretation, the assumption that there was a self-evident design in the evolution of the missionary enterprise, or reliance on the value of Pauline models and attempts to emulate recent individual success stories, no longer seemed quite sufficient. Although a belief in Providence inclined missionaries to accept the existence of empire, their sense of what either could or should be made of the opportunity it offered was not static. In the context of increasingly plentiful resources generated at home and converts beginning to emerge in numbers sufficient to facilitate a systematic use of native agents, the mood round about 1840 of confident missionary expansionism prompted the steady development of comparative and constructive practical thinking.

Mobilising native converts as the next step for the missionary movement was also pushed to the fore after 1840 by its potential contribution to solving a host of practical problems. That in turn explains much of its heightened attractiveness and popularity, even though the preoccupation itself was not new. The LMS's early strategy of trying to win over kings or other influential local leaders automatically allotted an important role to the leadership and example of highly placed converts. The sheer scale of the missionary task in Bengal and now China, set against the limited Western input, impressed on the Serampore trio, together with Duff and Gützlaff, the need for a rapid and extensive delegation of responsibilities to

---

6  Wilbert R. Shenk, 'The Role of Theory in Anglo-American Mission Thought and Practice', in *Changing Frontiers of Mission* (New York, 1999), pp. 34–47.

7  James Montgomery (ed.), *Journal of Voyages and Travels by the Rev. Daniel Tyerman and George Bennett*, 2 vols (London, 1831).

indigenous but modestly placed evangelists. Finances and European volunteers, it emerged, were inadequate to the global missionary task even at the best of times. Inevitably, therefore, questions arose about the possibilities for deploying in greater numbers local agents, who were also far cheaper to employ than Europeans. Mortality among white missionaries, experienced notably in tropical West Africa, caused disruption and prompted speculation that acclimatised indigenous agents might be the only dependable missionaries for the future. Robert Moffat's fondness for the station he had founded and developed at Kuruman, together with his reluctance to promote converts unless they met his high expectations, illustrated how the European missionary might become stranded and expansion itself curbed if ways were not found to bring on local helpers or expand the mission in other directions.[8]

Mobilising converts was clearly about more than populating mission stations and filling gaps on the new missionary maps. It was above all a response to the urgency that missionaries and still more their supporters at home, attached to their enterprise. This has to be understood in theological terms. The divine command, as we have seen, obliged missionaries to be up and doing. It was also imperative that 'the heathen' should be reached as quickly as possible, for otherwise there was no saving them from hell. Although the conviction that hell lay ahead even for those who had never heard the Gospel was beginning to weaken,[9] many missionaries continued to feel the force of saving the heathen from everlasting punishment as a most powerful spur to action. The need to act speedily was also strengthened by eschatological considerations. A quickened millennial interest in the 'signs of the times' was commonly a consequence of religious revivals. These were not lacking in the early 1840s, for many people years of intense religious activity. Fed by currents of revivalist enthusiasm from America, which for the first time introduced to Britain Charles Finney and his influential *Lectures on Revivals in Religion*, notable revivals occurred in Wales and Scotland from 1839 to 1843.[10] Evangelicals every-where took note even if taking no direct part. Occurring in the context of interna-tional events – not only the Opium War but Roman Catholic overseas missionary revival and conflicts in the Middle East between the Ottomans and Egypt's khedive, Mehemet Ali – they coincided with a flurry of millennial writing and speculation.[11]

---

8  Livingstone to Arthur Tidman (LMS Secretary), 17 Oct. 1851, in Schapera, *Missionary Correspondence*, p. 185. Cf. Andrew C. Ross, *David Livingstone: Mission and Empire* (London, 2002), p. 56.

9  Geoffrey Rowell, *Hell and the Victorians: A Study of the Nineteenth-Century Theological Controversies Concerning Eternal Punishment and the Future Life* (Oxford, 1974), esp. pp. 16, 105, 107, 118, 122, 190–2.

10  Bebbington, *Evangelicalism in Modern Britain*, pp. 114–17. Finney's *Lectures* were published in 1835; for his continuing influence see below, pp. 199, 244, 301.

11  For example, a trawl of the British Library catalogue using the keyword 'millennium' points to a cluster of 13 titles in 1841–5, with others occurring in 1829–33 (18 titles) and 1858–60 (15 titles), with two or fewer titles per annum at other times.

## II

Indications of the newly focused concern can be seen, for instance, in two well-attended meetings of the London Secretaries Association. A dozen gathered together at CMS House to consider 'the best way of training Natives for employment as catechists and missionaries in their several missions'; at the Wesleyans new premises in Bishopsgate Street their topic was 'The importance of a Native Agency and the best means of Training it.' The allied question of how to ensure that 'Native Christian Churches may ultimately provide for themselves' was debated in March 1841.[12] Of critical importance to this process of discussion was Henry Venn, appointed honorary part-time secretary at the CMS in 1841 and full-time from 1846. As son of the Reverend John Venn, founder member of the Clapham Sect and the CMS, Henry's evangelical credentials were of the highest. He came to the CMS while incumbent of a parish in Holloway, north London and shortly after his wife's death. Living only a stone's throw from the CMS's Training Institution in Islington and within walking distance of its offices in Salisbury Square, just off Fleet Street, Venn retired only in 1872.

Venn's career as the most influential mission administrator and strategic thinker of his age is well known.[13] During the 1840s and 1850s he was instrumental in focusing much of the movement's attention on how indigenous native churches might be developed. This goal, 'the chief work of his official life', was evident in his Letter Addressed to Converts throughout the World, approved by the CMS Jubilee Meeting in 1848 and one of the earliest CMS public documents to accept 'the number and position of Native Converts, as sufficient to warrant their recognition in a corporate capacity'.[14] He also contributed decisively to the debate within the Church of England and other episcopal churches as to how these native churches might be brought under episcopal leadership, about which more below.[15] The end point of his thinking on native Christians he set out in an overview of the CMS's work in 1865. He began by highlighting 'the danger of regarding all heathendom as a field to be evangelised by European and American Missionaries'. The impossibility of this task made it the duty of the Christian church 'to establish in each district and especially where there are separate languages, a self-supporting, self-governing, self-extending native Church'. With the growth of these churches, Venn believed, the mission itself would move on to new unevangelised fields and the parent church would then concern itself only with fixing 'the spiritual standard in such schemes', not in a disciplinary sense but 'by securing for them a supply of the

---

12  London Secretaries Association Minutes, 9 Jan. 1840, 10 Feb. 1842 and 19 March 1841.

13  C. Peter Williams, *The Ideal of the Self-Governing Church: A Study in Victorian Missionary Strategy* (Leiden, 1990); T.E. Yates, *Venn and Victorian Bishops Abroad: The Missionary Policies of Henry Venn and thl Repercussions upon the Anglican Episcopate of the Colonial Period, 1841–1872* (Uppsala and L do , 1978); Shenk, *Henry Venn.*

14  illi K ght, *Memo of e R H. Venn* (London, 1880), p. 277.

15  lo . 1 , 225 37.

vernacular Scriptures and a sound theological literature, which, in this country and in the English language, so happily abounds'.[16]

Here historians have the 'three-selves formula', so familiar to students of missions and applicable to the development of Christian communities and churches irrespective of denomination or field. Local 'native' churches should strive to become self-financing; this would both justify and make possible their self-government; once in control of their own affairs, the implementation of their own mission would enable them to be self-extending or self-propagating. Venn cannot claim sole authorship or inspiration. His wide-reaching contacts with missionaries and church leaders in Britain and abroad brought him into touch not least with Rufus Anderson, his exact contemporary at the ABCFM, whose thoughts were moving on very similar lines.[17] It is no surprise that Venn's office was Anderson's first port of call when he stopped off in London for a month en route to India in the summer of 1854.[18] However, in the British setting it was Venn who in a series of important papers and in his extensive correspondence explored and constantly refined the process by which converts, local teachers, catechists and ordained indigenous pastors could be brought together in mature and independent Christian communities and churches.[19] Venn never lost sight of the fact that missions were to be a temporary or transitional phase in the life of any society and that the route to the indigenous church lay in building it up from below, not through imposition from above or from outside either by society or by bishop.

In looking to the future, Venn's thinking was not simply ecclesiological; it drew on important aspects in the developing relationship of missions and British expansion.[20] While placing indigenous Christians at the centre of his plans and recognising the watershed now reached on account of their growing numbers, Venn was also aware of their vulnerability. He had a keen practical awareness of both the need to exploit other available means to sustain infant churches and the conditions under which they had to

---

16  Henry Venn, *Retrospect and Prospect of the Operations of the Church Missionary Society 1865* (London, 1865), pp. 4–5.

17  Dana L. Robert, 'Rufus Anderson', *DEB*, Vol. 1, pp. 19–21; Paul W. Harris, *Nothing but Christ: Rufus Anderson and the Ideology of Protestant Foreign Missions* (Oxford and New York, 1999); William R. Hutchison, *Errand to the World: American Protestant Thought and Foreign Missions* (Chicago, 1987).

18  Wilbert R. Shenk, 'Rufus Anderson and Henry Venn: a special relationship?', *IBMR* 5 (1981), pp.168–72; Andrew Porter, 'Language, "Native Agency" and Missionary Control: Rufus Anderson's Journey to India, 1854–5', in Pieter N. Holtrop and Hugh McLeod (eds), *Missions and Missionaries. Studies in Church History Subsidia 13* (Woodbridge, 2000), pp. 81–97.

19  For Venn's three most influential papers, of 1851, 1861 and 1866, Shenk, *Henry Venn*, app. I. These were eventually published together as *The Native Pastorate and Organization of Native Churches* (London, n.d.). See also Knight, *Memoir of Venn*, pp. 305–6, 318–21; and for a full guide to CMS papers on the theme, Williams, *Ideal of the Self-Governing Church*, pp. 269–74.

20  This paragraph is based on J.F.A. Ajayi, 'Henry Venn and the Policy of Development', *Journal of the Historical Society of Nigeria* 1 (1959), 331–42; J.B. Webster, 'The Bible and the Plough', *Journal of the Historical Society of Nigeria* 4 (1963), 418–34.

survive. This can be seen most clearly in his plans for (especially West) Africa. The anti-slavery, Buxtonian legacy was of particular importance, embodied as it was in the growth of British diplomatic negotiation and anti-slave-trade treaties, backed up by a naval presence and active consular intervention on behalf of legitimate trade. The growth of that trade was not simply a British interest, but – as the Sierra Leoneans' history demonstrated – reflected Africans' own expansive ambitions. Long recognised as an enthusiast for the development of African societies, Venn's support for this cause went well beyond warm rhetorical endorsement of 'civilisation' or a search for staples on the lines of the early Sierra Leone Company. It embraced a much more interventionist approach, in which schooling not only in literacy and English language but in practical industrial skills and direct investment in projects to grow cotton, cocoa and other crops, were all important. Here in the links of commerce with Christianity were the keys to the economic and social foundations of the new churches. Still more than the 'modernised' commercial societies of which they were to be a part, these churches were to be led by a burgeoning business and professional class. In a formula, which has close parallels with Duff's hopes in Calcutta, it was not European but African entrepreneurs who were to provide the motor of reform and the dynamics of church growth.

Venn's vision was that of a providentially ordained world, in which conversions were everywhere widespread and Christian churches firmly established at the centre of transformed local societies. It neither identified any one empire with that world nor envisaged British missions acting naturally as Britain's imperial agents. However, it took as axiomatic that in the interests of Christian influence and expansion missionaries and converts would harness such means to that end as British government, overseas agencies and imperial control might appear to offer. It was not least a bid on a grand scale to determine the nature of Britain's empire as a contributor to the missionary movement's own wider universalist ambition.

### III

If one asks what became of Venn's vision, it is clear with hindsight that at the highest level of expectation harnessing the energies of indigenous Christians and European missionary efforts met limited success. This was the case with both the CMS and other societies. Notwithstanding continuing sporadic bursts of evangelical expectation, conversion of the world and the Second Coming did not take place and to most contemporaries the millennial period of peace and plenty heralding the Last Judgement seemed somewhat distant. At the other extreme, within the CMS, Venn's ideas continued to influence the society's policy until the early years of the twentieth century. However, they did so in truncated forms and in the face of mounting opposition, both from missionaries in the field and in the committee rooms at Salisbury Square.[21] Venn, one could say, identified the mid-century

---

21  Williams, *Ideal of the Self-Governing Church*, chaps 4–6.

moment for strategic thinking, but in the end was unable to seize it with sufficient force or immediacy to put a permanent mark on the pattern of British expansion. It is necessary here to explore the reasons for this failure and to chart the evaporation of missionary enthusiasm. Subsequent chapters examine the consequences of these developments for the evolving encounter of religion and empire.

Notwithstanding the professional distaste for hagiography, there is something still to be said for the heroic tradition of missionary historiography. Individuals – sometimes entire communities – do have heroes and are capable of being power-fully inspired by those they regard as heroic. John Williams, later David Livingstone and James Chalmers undoubtedly fall into that category. John Philip's and Mary Slessor's careers demonstrated that heroic standing was not simply conditional on a dramatic death. To explain why they caught the nation's imagina-tion, to account for their success as speakers when on furlough, to dissect the appeal of their books and the impact of their example, can tell the historian much about the place of overseas missions in Victorian society. So too there is a class of anti-heroes, to which Henry Venn and perhaps others among his unsung secretarial colleagues such as E.B. Underhill, Eugene Stock, Ralph Wardlaw Thompson and Professor Thomas Lindsay might be said to belong. However influential behind the scenes, however important their contribution to sustaining the missionary universe within which individual comets made their appearance, no more than civil servants were mission administrators likely to catch the public's attention.

Venn was not a forceful propagandist, least of all on his own behalf. A prodi-gious worker and skilled committee-man, he was also modest and self-effacing, preferring to win his arguments by reasoned persuasion and likely to pull his punches in the process. The breadth of his strategic thinking has endeared him to modern scholars, for his memoranda have all the persuasive clarity of the best state papers. They often seem to cut through the tangle of awkward information from missionaries on the spot, exposing the immediate way forward and providing a clear view of the Society's goals. At the same time, however, his planning by the very virtue of its generous scope was vulnerable to contrary developments in indi-vidual mission fields. If, for instance, converts were not forthcoming in sufficient numbers, if pastors were not to be found, or if English and even vernacular educa-tion were put to the service not of the missions but only secular ambition, then hopes for the native churches were in danger of shipwreck.

One notable exchange with Rufus Anderson illuminates only too well the prob-lems that faced Venn and his programme even at a relatively early stage. The deputa-tion which took Anderson to India in 1854 found him worried by the apparently meagre results of the American Board's missions, full of disquiets about the methods they employed and determined to set them right. At the heart of his concerns were the numbers of converts won, the emphasis on schooling and the importance attached ever since the Scottish initiatives of the 1830s to the use of English. The American Secretary's nine pointed questions to Venn betrayed no disagreement with the goals of mobilising converts and organising new churches: the 'three selves' were inviolate. It was the means to these ends that provoked Anderson's doubts.

The American was particularly keen to know Venn's mind on three matters. 'How far', he asked Venn, 'would you be in favour of excluding the English language, as a medium of instruction from schools sustained by Missionary Societies [?]'; was 'training from boyhood in missionary schools ... found to be the most effective way of obtaining Native Preachers and Pastors'?; and ought there to be a rule 'that no school should be sustained in which the vernacular language is not made the grand medium of instruction'?[22]

Venn's answers were carefully considered. 'I conceive that English must be retained in two classes of schools. (1) In every extensive system of vernacular schools there should be a few English schools to give a *complete* education to the few who are destined to take the lead in Native society. For as in this country a classical education gives a man many advantages, – much more abroad an English education enlarges the mind and furnishes it with elements of thought far beyond what a mere vernacular education can supply. In many districts if Missionary Societies do not give this superior education no other parties will. In some places it is provided by other parties but in an objectionable form. (2) Another class of English schools which appear to me a legitimate department of Missions are those established in the Presidencies of India and other large towns where the acquisition of English is an object of desire with the wealthy classes. These classes will send their children to Mission Schools for the sake of the English education and it is the only way in which those classes are reached by the Missionary. Such schools are preaching places for the benefit of young men of the upper classes, as much as the Bazaars are preaching places for the lower orders.'[23]

As to missionary schools' success as nurseries of native preachers and pastors, Venn confirmed that they were the best although not the only or even a very productive source of such men. He urged Anderson not to worry about the small numbers, which in any case were proportionately far greater than was the case in England; to expect more would be unrealistic and patience was necessary. In his conclusion Venn not only warned his visitor again against over-hasty judgements, but then appeared to qualify even his own advice. 'In conclusion I will only remark that while the present era is one for the development of Missionary Principles of action, it is also one of incompetent theorising and with a tinge of Missionary romance. It is most important to remember that principles which may apply to one Mission will often be inapplicable to a different field, as well as different stages of advancement in the same field. And beyond any principles, as we call them, we must never forget that some of the most signal successes of modern Missions have been granted not to measures devised by wisdom and skill, but to individual zeal following out the leadings of divine Providence, without regard to fixed principles of action. Whatever rules or principles we may lay down we must never lose sight of "the glorious footsteps of divine Providence" ... For my own

22  Venn to Anderson, 6 Sept. 1854, ABC 14/3/506.
23  *Ibid.*

part I am more and more disposed to follow this providance [*sic*] than to trust to my Rules.'

Intellectually honest, politely sensitive to the inclinations and rather different views of his interlocutor, Venn's conclusion was a guarded one which seemed to lack the courage needed to carry his convictions. Certainly it allowed Anderson to leave for Bombay confident that he had heard little to still his misgivings and pleased that other informants had strongly agreed with him.

## IV

Venn's exchanges with Anderson are one of many indications in the 1850s of mounting reservations about the efficacy for missionary purposes of attempting to combine Christianity with commerce and Western English-language education. Signs of a general uneasiness together with specific misgivings were noticeable not least among those involved with India and where India led other fields often followed. Perhaps this was to be expected. The likelihood that any model of missionary enterprise would long remain generally acceptable was of course unlikely. No more than the older recipes of Brainerd, Eliot and the Moravians were the approaches of Duff and Venn likely to remain unchallenged, especially in a widening and ever more diverse world.

Doubts about Duff's prescriptions were never stilled, notwithstanding the tendency towards consolidation represented by the Scottish church's absorption of the Scottish Missionary Society in 1834, the moderates' pro-Duff victory which had overtaken the General Assembly by 1838 and the decision of the Scots missionaries to stay with the Free Church after the Disruption in 1843. From western India, from Bombay and still more Poona, letters reached the secretaries in Edinburgh insisting on the priority of the vernaculars, 'the grand medium for the instruction of the millions of the people' as John Wilson put it. He felt no less able to accept the need of 'the higher classes of the native' in Bombay itself for an English education.[24] His colleagues were ready to elaborate on this need. 'We can never expect to find, at such a station as Poona, that desire for a knowledge of English which is to be found in large trading cities. It is here worthy of remark that in Poona and through the whole of the Dakhan [Deccan], a knowledge of English is not particularly an object of desire even with the great and wealthy … Marathi is and must for a long period continue to be, the medium of intercourse. The case is very different at the great *Emporia* of the country'.[25]

The Duff strategy, moreover, continued to worry the faithful at home. Too much evidence of class teaching suggested a regrettable neglect of preaching; attention to the vernaculars risked appearing to ignore General Assembly policy;

---

24  Rev. Dr. John Wilson (Bombay) to Alexander Brunton, 14 Nov. 1836, NLS MS 7531, f. 51. See also above, pp. 106–9, 169–72.

25  Rev. Dr. J. Stevenson (Poona, writing from Bombay) to Brunton, 28 Nov. 1836, *ibid.*, ff. 60–1.

and the use of English textbooks spawned fears of secularism. These difficulties of mutual comprehension, between missionaries in western India and the Foreign Mission Committee (not to mention the wider public) at home, are plain in the tiniest details. One 'List of Books required for the General Assembly's Institution Bombay' included one hundred copies of Reid's *Geography*, 'not the Sacred Geography formerly sent by mistake'.[26] Whether this represented an unintended mistake or calculated correction, to the mission house clerk something was clearly wrong. How, one might wonder, could the Great Lakes come before the Sea of Galilee? Secretaries worked hard at editing the missionary correspondence, seizing on references to the growth of Indian interest, progress made in female education and the subversion of caste, while suppressing references to the advancing study of chemistry. For their part, missionaries resented misrepresentation to the home audience and the disguising of significant realities such as the need for flexibility and discretion in subject and method.[27] They all had an uphill task in making the case for the 'scientific consideration of the works of God' as 'most salutary and corrective to the idolatrous and superstitious mind of India'. Sensitive to his diverse audience, Wilson first emphasised for mercantile supporters and other 'civilisers' that it might be 'attended with the most important results in the development of the resources of the country'. To reassure the evangelicals, however, 'Human science, I trust, will ever be communicated in our mission in subordination to Divine Knowledge, in natural and friendly alliance with the doctrines of the Bible.'[28] More difficult even than the general argument for a Western education was the crafting of justifications for specific needs, for instance Mitchell's request for a galvanic battery. This would, he suggested, prevent his pupils being 'plunged necessarily into the gloomy caverns of their own metaphysics'.[29] That this was not a peculiarly Scottish problem and that Venn too felt the need to police the boundaries of appropriate English learning, is evident in his conveying the CMS Committee's alarm at the use of Pope and Milton as class texts.[30]

By the mid-1850s there were voices everywhere not only noting a lack of converts and limited indigenous involvement in the church but also attributing this shortfall to the preoccupation with English schooling. Too often, it was said, the latter was associated with overmuch concentration of effort and finance on a large central site, with a simultaneous neglect of the vernacular, preaching and the villages. As an example of best missionary practice, it was regarded as having little more value than the common placement of missionaries in garrison towns and commercial centres where they tended to minister to European congregations and neglect the local people.

26  30 Sept. 1840, NLS MS 7532/1, f. 69.
27  John Aitken (Poona) to Brunton, 16 June 1841, *ibid.*, f. 156; Rev. John Anderson (Madras) to Brunton, 14 Nov. 1839, NLS MS 7532/2, ff. 345–50. See 'Letters from Bombay 1840–42' for many examples of editing.
28  Wilson to Brunton, 1 March 1841, NLS MS 7532/1, f. 112.
29  John Murray Mitchell (Poona) to Brunton, 30 Sept. 1840, *ibid.*, f. 73c.
30  Henry Venn to James Long (Bengal), 11 July 1843, CMS Archives CI1/L3, f. 40.

In Scotland the defence of Duff's ideas was often privately half-hearted, as Rufus Anderson discovered. The Convenor of the Established Church's Foreign Missions Committee, while supporting their school system admitted nevertheless that 'it has resulted in but few conversions and that most of their beneficiaries go into worldly pursuits ... they have as yet no experience how it will work when they station their pupils in the country'.[31] The missionary administrator and historian Dr William Brown expressed to Anderson his whole-hearted disbelief in 'the Duff scheme' as 'contrary to Scripture and reason'; 'he believes it will fail; but says the Scotch people must have another five-and-twenty years to try it. He would have gone against it in his history but for his personal friendship towards Dr. Duff. In the long run, he believes that far greater results will follow from a main reliance in India upon preaching. – When Dr. Duff started his plan, it was objected to by many, but the Doctor's eloquence finally carried all before him.'[32] Concluding from what he heard north of the border that 'The Duff School rests as yet upon theory', Anderson encountered similar views in London. Beecham, still at the WMMS and 'a common sense man', was sceptical 'as to the use of schools and the English language', as too was the Reverend George Candy, temporarily home from his post as Corresponding Secretary of the CMS Committee in Bombay.[33]

That others thought on similar lines is shown in a deputation sent out to India at this time by the BMS. Coincidentally E.B. Underhill, BMS Foreign Secretary, found himself a fellow passenger with Anderson on the ship to Bombay. They got on well and continued to share ideas and papers from then on. Determined to revive BMS activities, Underhill's starting point was Calcutta. He was concerned to achieve a sizeable reduction in the extensive commercial activities of the Serampore press and to encourage the local election and support of Indian pastors. BMS concern that business was driving out mission was duplicated in Anderson's worries about his own mission press at Bombay and in those misgivings that had recently led the CMS to close its press at Madras.[34] If Underhill emerged from his visit with a restored confidence in the value of the press and Bombay's need to engage in English teaching, he remained dissatisfied with the work of the schools; it was essential 'to employ some of the best native preachers as missionaries'.[35] 'I have begun to act upon it ... as opening the way for the independent action of the native church. I am more and more convinced that many evils follow the state of dependence in which they have hitherto been kept. Very many of the complaints of the character of converts originate in this. We have all the faults and results of pauperism, without getting one step towards independency; indeed only rendering it impossible.'[36]

---

31  Entry, 30 Aug. 1854, Rufus Anderson Journal I, ABC 30/12.
32  *Ibid.*
33  Entry, 12 Sept. 1854, *ibid.*
34  Stanley, *History of the BMS*, pp. 149–54; entries, 6 Sept. 1854, 14–18 May 1855, Rufus Anderson, Journal I and III, ABC 30/12.
35  Underhill (Serampore) to Anderson, 7 Aug. 1856, ABC 14/3/497.
36  Underhill ('on the Ganges') to Anderson, 26 Oct. 1855, *ibid.*, 496.

Also in contact with Underhill and by chance meeting Anderson in Madras, was one of Venn's secretarial colleagues, the Reverend William Knight, who had been deputed to resolve problems afflicting the CMS Ceylon Mission. His rapport with both Underhill and Anderson was considerable and he was responsible for introducing the Bostonian to CMS missionaries in Bengal, including James Long, also 'all for the vernacular'.[37] Joseph Mullens, by 1855 ten years at the LMS station of Bhowanipore, near Calcutta, was another of those who impressed Anderson as he did others. He too counted himself with 'the great *majority* [holding] vernacular preaching to be *the* most important branch of missionary labour' and argued for the priority of vernacular rural missions with only a limited place for English education in the cities.[38]

Regardless of denomination and from widely separated parts of India, missionaries and supporters thus retailed similar dissatisfactions – the widespread failure of schools to act as feeders to congregations and churches, the use of English education by Indians as a way out of the local district and a route to self-advancement.[39] Discontent was by no means universal, but it was very widespread.

It was also the offspring of record keeping. With the occasional exception such as Thomas Coke, missionary societies were often ahead of government in their passion for measurement – populations, missionary volunteers, conversions, baptisms, cases of discipline (these not for public consumption), income and so on. Statistical series offered first a yardstick for individual missions' progress and subsequently a basis for comparative judgements. As these general indicators of 'progress' in Indian missions began to be regularly published from c.1850, they sapped the optimism that had launched the previous decade and the strategic planning which had been its outcome. Joseph Mullens made a decisive contribution to this process.

In the *Calcutta Review* of October 1851, he considered that year's Reports of the Calcutta and the Madras Auxiliary Bible Societies. His review was published separately the following year in London.[40] His message was plain. Although a case for progress could be made and India's unique scale and difficulty provided extenuating circumstances, none the less the missions' achievement was poor both relative to other fields and as befitted a 'great continent, with its vast resources and countless population … placed under the rule of a small island in the western world'.[41]

---

37  Knight (Madras) to Anderson, 5 July 1855, *ibid.*, 271. For Long and his world, *CMS Register*, List I, entry 301; Geoffrey A. Oddie, *Missionaries, Rebellion and Proto-Nationalism: James Long of Bengal 1814–87* (Richmond, 1999); David W. Savage, 'Evangelical Education Policy in Britain and India, 1857–1860', *JICH* 22 (1994), 432–61.

38  Mullens to Anderson, 22 Sept. 1855, 8 Dec. 1856, ABC 14/3, nos 323, 325; Lovett, *History of the LMS*, Vol. 1, p. 174. Original emphases.

39  For further instances, entries, 6 and 15 Nov. 1854, 11 and 23 April 1855, Anderson Journal, ABC 30/12.

40  Joseph Mullens, *Results of Missionary Labour in India* (London, 1852).

41  *Ibid.*, pp. 3–4.

The genie of dissatisfaction was loosed. Mullens rapidly left his desk in Calcutta to tour the Madras Presidency from January to March 1853. Turned into lectures, his investigations were again also published in London a year later.[42] The impact of his work and the questions it raised for assessment of missionary achievements and prospects were considerable. It can be seen the next year both in David Livingstone's ironic reference from Linyanti to his own problems and the indirect impact of missions for Mullens's consideration and in the proceedings of the first all-India missionary Conference at Calcutta, which Mullens himself was instrumental in organising.[43] Far from providing easy answers, statistics were soon regarded as muddying the waters more than ever. Complaints reached Venn that 'The statistical returns, as usually given, only deceive one as to the real results of mission work.'[44]

The missions were increasingly aligned in their discontent with critical members of the East India Company's government. Led by Lord Dalhousie (Governor-General, 1846–56), growing numbers of officials were also conscious of the limited achievements of the Bentinck era. This, recent historians would argue, far from stimulating a significant Westernisation, had continued to foster a 'traditionalisation' of Indian society.[45] Under the severe cumulative pressures of government debt after the wars of 1838–42 (Afghanistan), 1843 (Sind) and 1845–49 (Punjab), local imperial authorities were determined to reverse this process and push on with developing and modernising British India. That they were inclined to consider closer partnership with missionaries as one means to this end indicated not just a surviving concern to control a potentially unruly minority. It was both a reflection of the position as educators that the missions had come to play and a sign of their widely established social respectability. No longer were the subterfuges necessary that had secured Carey for Fort William College. Dr John Wilson's close contact with John Elphinstone (Governor of Bombay, 1853–59) intermeshed easily with his roles as government censor and intelligence officer reading intercepted Indian correspondence during the Mutiny and as a founder – later vice-chancellor – of the university of Bombay.[46] Since the 1830s missions and government had worked out a *modus vivendi* over the propagation of Christianity. The Company's insistence on official 'religious neutrality' remained in principle but had been modified in practice. A series of legislative measures had struck out some of the religious customs most objectionable to missions and there was considerable tolerance for those officials who wished in their private capacity to support missionary activity.

42  Joseph Mullens, *Missions in South India Visited and Described* (London, 1854).

43  Livingstone to Arthur Tidman, 12 Oct. 1855, Schapera (ed.), *Livingstone's Missionary Correspondence*, p. 300.

44  John Barton (Agra) to Venn, 19 Nov. 1862, CMS Archives, CI 1/037, no. 25.

45  D.A. Washbrook, 'India 1818–1860: The Two Faces of Colonialism', in Andrew Porter (ed.), *OHBE Vol. 3 The Nineteenth Century* (Oxford, 1999), pp. 395–421.

46  Above, Chapters 3 and 4, pp. 68–70 and 107–8; Smith, *Life of John Wilson*, pp. 506–8, 534–8.

Most missionaries had devised a system which incorporated Christian instruction while avoiding the appearance of directly imposing Christian beliefs on their pupils and they had learned to live with the occasional exodus of pupils to the 'secular' private or government schools in reaction against religious offence. Both missions and government found they could accommodate the sporadic public protests sparked off by occasional cases of conversion.

The multiplicity of local compromises that evolved under this system was not universally popular. A balance between preaching, proselytisation, different modes of religious instruction and formal English-language education, acceptable to missionary supporters at home, missions on the spot, British officials and Indians themselves was difficult to achieve. In the hope of injecting more purpose and direction into India's schools, the government in 1854 introduced grants-in-aid for secular schooling. Subject to inspection, funds became available to schools that met government requirements for instruction of a more practical and developmental character at every level, from the most elementary with fresh emphasis on 'useful knowledge' to the new universities proposed for the three Presidencies.[47] India's missionaries were placed in a difficult position. While there remained those who were highly critical of governments for not doing more to support them, there were also those who wished to take advantage of the new government patronage and funding.[48] The government in India, anxious to prevent schools ever being exclusively dependent on official resources, nevertheless wanted to benefit from missionaries' assistance as far as was politically possible. Debates about the new education policy therefore persisted, particularly with the nonconformist LMS and BMS who were far less happy than many in the CMS with abridging the voluntary principle by linking themselves to government through receipts of grants-in-aid. Experience shortly afterwards of the Mutiny (1857–58) also intensified missionary criticism of governments' insufficient promotion of Christianity. It simultaneously confirmed official insistence on a policy of promoting religious neutrality through even-handedness towards Christianity as well as its major rivals.

The reshaping of education policy and the reorganisation of India's government in response to the Mutiny insured that missions addressed the evident discontents of the early 1850s with piecemeal attempts at gradual reform, not by radical rethinking of the Duff and Venn approaches. The sheer scale and complexity of the Indian enterprise did not simply offer what Mullens had seen, namely a partial explanation for limited success; it also made overall change almost impossible to contemplate, even within the limits of a single missionary society. India's variety offered newcomers and old hands opportunities for hopeful fresh initiatives within the existing framework. When combined with the approachability and positive appreciation of missionary interests which, as Wood demonstrated, could

---

47  R.J. Moore, *Sir Charles Wood's Indian Policy 1853–66* (Manchester, 1966), chap. 6.

48  See the favourable review of the 1854 Despatch and its requirements by the Free Church of Scotland missionaries John Wilson and Robert Nesbit, in Smith, *Life of John Wilson*, pp. 531–3.

characterise a Secretary of State, then pragmatism seemed preferable to attempts at root and branch transformation.

Henry Venn's exchanges with the Reverend John Barton, sent out to India as Joint Secretary to the Calcutta Corresponding Committee in October 1860, are revealing of the situation facing all the societies. By the 1860s their administrative organisation was such that it was all but impossible to imagine a repeat of the process whereby thirty years before Duff had readjusted to his own way of thinking the policies not only of his own society but others as well. To one impetuous suggestion said to require only that CMS headquarters be put more directly in touch with Indian reality, Venn again revealed his gentle scepticism as he had to Rufus Anderson. 'My very dear Friend', he wrote, 'I smile at this misconception surrounded as I am by so experienced old Indians – & having for twenty years conversed with hundreds who have been engaged in India, in these very educational questions.'[49] His letter is weighed down with understatement, on the problems inherent in the missionaries' situation, and the reasoned conservatism as well as the expertise born of long experience. Assembled around mission committee tables, these constrained the mission secretary no less than the neophyte. On the precise educational issues, of the value of schools and English versus the vernacular, the society he wrote would hold to its traditional position, favouring 'education as one branch of Missionary operations' and 'intermediate ... between those societies which relinquish all heathen schools and those which devote their main resources to schools'. Meanwhile, faced with a shortage of those willing to teach, the sub-committee charged to look into it had 'advised the procuring of new "Returns" from all our Missions'.[50] No less than the latest new enthusiast, Venn, while demonstrating the caution appropriate to introducing change, was evidently also coming to terms with the language of the fashionable statistics.

Both Venn and Barton at this point concluded that there was little reason to do other than work within the system. Venn, the elder by forty years, was of a generation still mindful of how missions had adjusted their own preconceptions about politics and had fought to deal with governments on equal terms. Reluctant to forgo anything of those contacts and practical gains, Venn's thinking on acceptable levels of missionary engagement with politics and government over the years became increasingly sophisticated, some might even say sophistical.[51] Aware how easily governments could become backsliders, he finally supported the compromise issuing from review of the 1854 legislation whereby bible teaching became available in government-aided schools outside school hours to those wishing for it.[52] This outcome he thought

---

49  Venn to Barton, 26 Sept. 1861 (Private), CMS CI1/L5, f. 441.

50  *Ibid*.

51  For the fullness of his thinking see Venn's Instructions to Missionaries, 28 Sept. 1860, reprinted in Shenk, *Henry Venn*, pp. 130–7; also William Knight, *Memoir of Henry Venn B.D.* (London, 1882) pp. 468–79; and Venn and William Knight to G.G. Cuthbert (Secretary, Calcutta Corresponding Committee), 25 May 1860, CMS CI1/L5, f. 262.

52  Moore, *Sir Charles Wood's Indian Policy*, pp. 118–19.

offered a better balance of the society's responsibilities and committed government to provide from its own resources for the direct support of religion; it reduced the perceived secularism of government, something Indian missions had long fought for and offered an undertaking which they could easily police. Barton, by contrast inheritor of a more experienced and self-confident movement and highly critical of the often poor quality of biblical instruction where not under missionary control, looked ahead to distancing the CMS from government. The Society would call the tune by improving its own schools, exploiting grants-in-aid to its own advantage simply through the competitive quality of missionary provision and secure the quality of bible teaching at the same time. Barton was encouraged in this by belief that the government of India would favour giving up its own schools if their quality could be assured by those taking them over. [53]

Barton's position is peculiarly revealing, because he went to India fully sharing the home-based suspicion of schools and feeling that poor results in numbers of converts and pastors necessitated much more direct preaching in villages and bazaars. India's variety pushed him inexorably to a less exclusive position. 'My own views have been most marvellously changed in this respect, ... It was only natural that I should be prejudiced against Mission Schools on a large scale, when I found such men as French, Shackell, Stuart, Vaughan and many more, all agreeing in thinking such work to be out of the province of a true missionary, when our object is to win souls. I am quite sure that they are wrong.'[54] It was his own experience in charge of the CMS College at Agra and its potential as a central College for the North West Province, which caused him to favour a continual adaptation of the 'Duff model'. Aware how the grants-in-aid could also work against mission schools, Venn doubted Barton's optimistic outlook. 'Many of us entertained this hope once ... [and] we trust that you will make it [Agra College] an exception to the general depression of a Missionary Institution in juxtaposition with a Government Institution. But I write in reference to all India.' Barton, however, could play the variety card as well as anyone. In rebutting Venn's uncertainty as to Agra's potential, he stressed how 'it is not fair to compare the NWP. [North Western Provinces] with Bombay and South India. You might almost as well compare France and Germany.'[55]

These debates rapidly descended from the level of missionary strategy to issues of practice and implementation in different settings. Venn was uncomfortably aware of renewed pressure on funds and manpower, where Barton was only beginning to learn the financial art of the possible. Barton's interest in Agra did not

53 Barton to Venn, 20 June, 4 July, 17 Aug., 14 Sept. 1861, 19 June 1862, CMS CI1/037, nos 11, 12, 14, 15, 23. For gossip about government thoughts on withdrawal from schools, Barton (Agra) to Venn, 14 May 1861, *ibid.*, no. 9.

54 Barton (Agra) to Venn, 19 April 1861, *ibid.*, no. 8; *CMS Register*, List I, entries 416, 538, 417, 494.

55 Venn to Barton, 8 July 1861 (Private), CMS CI1/L5, ff. 396–8; Barton to Venn, 14 Sept. 1861, CMS CI1/037, no. 15.

prevent him supporting the work of the Christian Vernacular Education Society (CVES), designed to foster vernacular education in the wake of the Mutiny and established in 1858 as result of Venn's leading and CMS initiatives.[56] Other missionary secretaries in London were also happy to support the CVES, both for the assistance that it gave to selected schools and for its promise in promoting 'a cheap, efficient Native Agency'.[57] Barton was increasingly responsive to variable conditions. Captivated by the promise of the CVES even if irritated by some of its early shortcomings, he was before long also supporting the CMS's withdrawal from schools altogether in certain parts of Bengal.[58]

The missionary use of grants-in-aid and the CVES were nevertheless but small steps towards tackling the disquiets of the mid-century, addressing the scale of India's challenge to the missionary movement, or shifting opinion towards an agreed balance in any British educational programme for India. The decade following the 1854 Education Despatch brought home again to the missions their very real weakness. Once the imperial or even a colonial government put its financial muscle behind the wheel of policy, missionaries who disagreed with its direction were at a severe disadvantage. 'It is madness to think of running a race against Government schools', Venn wrote to Barton.[59] In thus restricting his reference to education, Venn's vision may for once have been narrower than the seriousness of the situation warranted.[60]

In most areas, however, the continuing absence of converts and indigenous agents, whether teachers, catechists or ordained pastors, remained the fundamental problem, whatever the preferred educational recipe. Pressed by Venn to acknowledge that missionaries in north India should be giving their time to organising native churches and systematic itineration, Barton demurred: 'where are our agents? where are our native churches?', he asked. North India he felt sure was still at the point where 'it was allowable to spend the strength of able missionaries in nursing up from infancy a future generation of native Christians ... for the whole of N.W.P. and Punjab we have but 22 men who are considered worthy of the office of a catechist and 13 of that of Reader. And ... more than half of them ... [consist] mainly of converts who are set to do Readers' or Catechists' work merely because the missionaries can find no other employment for them and in the faint hope that some day they may improve.'[61] After thirty years' labour, with only four hundred

56  Oddie, *Missionaries, Rebellion and Proto-nationalism*, pp. 61–7; Savage, 'Evangelical Educational Policy', pp. 444–5; William Knight to Rufus Anderson, two letters both 31 May 1858, ABC 14/3/269–70.

57  H.Carre-Tucker (Secretary, CVES and member, CMS Parent Committee) to Rufus Anderson, 18 Sept. 1858, quotation from 22 Jan. 1859, *ibid.*, 485–6.

58  Barton to Venn, 21 Feb. and 19 April 1862, CI1/037, nos 19, 22.

59  27 May 1861, CMS CI1/L5, f. 374.

60  Viswanathan, *Masks of Conquests*, pp. 146–54, elaborates further the argument that 1854 marked a defeat for the missions.

61  Barton to Venn, 21 Feb. 1862, CI1/037, no. 19.

native Christians and ten native agents who had not begun as orphan children dependent on the CMS, Barton saw it would be necessary to persist in using all possible means to conversion for a long time to come. Only then could the example of south India be followed. It is therefore not surprising to find Barton subsequently laying out at length the arguments for rejecting the crude distinctions so often drawn between direct and indirect evangelism, between preaching and education in schools, between the use of English and the vernacular.[62] At the same time Mullens was compiling his account of changes since his first survey. On education his conclusion was a gloomy one. 'Missionary education in India at the present time can hardly be regarded as in a satisfactory position. Unsettled in itself, its relation to mission work undefined, inadequate to the wants of the Christian converts, still more inadequate to the overwhelming need of the heathen people of the country, it is a branch of labour which requires the most anxious care of wise and experienced men and demands thorough consideration at their hands.'[63]No wonder the patterns of Indian mission practice changed little in most places and that missionaries for want of clear answers continued to plough what had often already been deemed infertile furrows.

## V

The mid-century experience of India was in many ways a sobering one. As one of the oldest and certainly the largest fields of the modern missionary movement, India frequently provided the rock on which youthful illusions about evangelisation were dangerously exposed if not altogether wrecked. It was not, however, the only source of experience which deflated the optimism of the early 1840s. Similar lessons undermining the assumptions of those days were to be learned or relearned elsewhere in the mid-century. New generations of missionaries came to see that independence for evangelists was an illusion. They could only make headway in so much as others decided they were useful, useful in ways the missions themselves also found acceptable.

The British colonies in the Caribbean were a mounting cause for concern. Supporters of missions, along with humanitarians, in 1840 found every reason to view the future with hope and excitement. Emancipation had unleashed a torrent of religious enthusiasm and large numbers of emancipated slaves joined the Christian churches, especially the Baptists and Methodists. In Jamaica between 1833 and 1840 the number of Wesleyan church members apparently doubled to 22,884 and the regular ministerial circuits increased from thirteen to eighteen. As a result, the character of Wesleyan activity took on far more that of a settled church than a mission field.[64]

---

62  *Ibid.*, 1 April 1862, no. 20.
63  Joseph Mullens, *A Brief Review of Ten Years Missionary Labour in India 1852–61* (London, 1863), chap. 8 'Missionary Education', quotation at p. 118.
64  Findlay and Holdsworth, *History of the WMMS*, Vol. 2, pp. 328, 354.

The CMS in 1842 decided to cease its work in Jamaica, Trinidad and also Malta. Too much significance can be attached to the coincidence of this step with worries in Salisbury Square at the sudden serious slump in society funds.[65] Set against the upsurge of local involvement, the Society's action is more readily understood as seizing the opportunity to redirect its resources where they were more needed and in the direction its founders had always intended, 'Africa and the East'. For the CMS ventures in the West Indies had always seemed anomalous. Although there lingered on one remaining mission, to the Amerindians at Bartica Grove, British Guiana, this too was overwhelmed by the influx of coloured settlers and was relinquished to the Bishop of Guiana as a parish in 1853.[66] Confidence in a prosperous future and a steep reduction in any reliance on home funds were also the message of a Wesleyan deputation sent to Jamaica in 1843. For the BMS in 1842, Jamaica's rocketing numbers and ample church receipts made the decision of the Jamaica Baptists to form their own independent Union with charge of its own affairs and finance equally welcome and natural.[67]

With hindsight, theological urgency, economic advantages and the missions' humanitarian enthusiasm made an unfortunate combination. Looking back twenty-five years later, Henry Venn admitted that this reaction to West Indian events had proved premature, with everyone's hopes 'unduly raised by a state of religious excitement consequent upon emancipation'.[68] All three societies soon found themselves unexpectedly the recipients of fresh and persistent requests for support. Each felt mounting resentment at any suggestion of restoring the missionary tie when disengagement and local independence was their goal. The BMS deputation to Jamaica in 1846 rejected the case for financial aid. Despite falling numbers and increasing difficulty in making ends meet, images of the recent revivalist wave were too recent and too intellectually comfortable for supporters in Britain to see in the situation more than local churches whose members were unwilling to pull their weight. In similar fashion the imperial government before long was refusing to act on appeals to reverse its damaging commercial policy.[69]

Only when Edward Underhill undertook a deputation in 1859–60, reporting back on achievements and problems, did the accumulated damage of Britain's free trade policies and the continuing obstructiveness of planter-dominated government find an effective missionary spokesman.[70] In addition to Jamaica to which he

65  For example, by Williams, *Ideal of the Self-Governing Church*, p. 3.
66  For J.H. Bernau, missionary at Bartica 1835–53, *CMS Register*, List I, entry 207; M.N. Menezes, *British Policy towards the Amerindians in British Guiana 1803–1873* (Oxford, 1977), pp. 220–2.
67  Findlay and Holdsworth, *History of the WMMS*, Vol. 2, pp. 351–3; Stanley, *History of the BMS*, pp. 83–4.
68  Knight, *Memoir of Henry Venn*, pp. 211–22.
69  Stanley, *History of the BMS*, pp. 87–8; Thomas C. Holt, *The Problem of Freedom: Race, Labor and Politics in Jamaica and Britain, 1832–1938* (Baltimore, 1992), pp. 264–70.
70  Holt, *Problem of Freedom*, pp. 270–3; Hall, *Civilising Subjects*, pp. 223–43. Missionaries locally, while critical, had no impact either there or in London.

gave most attention, Underhill visited Trinidad, Haiti, Cuba and the Bahamas. He still found much to criticise in the conduct of the local churches, but the generally sympathetic tone of his report and his book, as well as the perceptiveness of his comments on peasant agriculture and the future of the plantations demonstrated a willingness to think further ahead.[71] His approach to the Colonial Office early in 1865 was of crucial importance in forcing into the open debate about the islands' condition and the need for government remedial action. The timing of Underhill's initiative and Governor Eyre's dismissive handling of the local responses to it contributed to the pool of local miseries and discontent that spilled over in the Morant Bay Rebellion of October that year.

The story of Morant Bay has often been recounted.[72] The missions were caught up in the public protest that greeted Governor Eyre's brutal suppression of the violence. Their historic ties made this inevitable, just as the current extent of their connection limited their involvement.[73] The Caribbean colonies were no longer a significant missionary field. Unlike 1823 and 1831, missionaries there were declining in numbers and authority. In and after 1865 local Christians and the churches were expected to fend largely for themselves, exercising the responsibilities they had claimed for their own affairs. Missionary interests, because increasingly focused elsewhere than the West Indies, had little to gain from a renewed identification with the humanitarian movement by way of Jamaica. Hence the absence of any references to it in the standard missionary histories of the period.[74] For the time being the significant work of the missions in the Caribbean was complete. The image remaining from the 1850s and 1860s for the societies was essentially one that they had helped to create for and shared with many people in Britain, that of an 'experiment in freedom' which had so far met with limited success. The disaster that was Morant Bay demonstrated how in their own eyes imperial authorities, the local black and coloured population and the missions had each been failed by the others.

## VI

Measured against the expectations of the early 1840s, the outcome of the missions in southern Africa was hardly more cheering, either within the colonies of the Cape and Natal or beyond the colonial frontiers. In the case of the latter, David Livingstone's experience is revealing. Despite his own enthusiasm for 'native

71 Edward Bean Underhill, *The West Indies: Their Social and Religious Condition* (London, 1862), pp. 179–459 for Jamaica; Stanley, *History of the BMS*, pp. 87–95.
72 Most recently, Gad Heuman, *'The Killing Time': The Morant Rebellion in Jamaica* (London, 1994); Holt, *Problem of Freedom*, chap. 8 'A War of the Races'.
73 Bernard Semmel, *The Governor Eyre Controversy* (London, 1962).
74 Interestingly Morant Bay is not referred to in Stanley, *Bible and the Flag*, but see his *History of the BMS*, pp. 98–9; Findlay and Holdsworth, *History of the WMMS*, has a fleeting reference at Vol. 2, pp. 368–9, 372–3.

agency' and his pleasure at Robert Moffat's conversion to this new (especially metropolitan) priority during his spell in Britain (1839–43),[75] by 1848 his own preferences had shifted. At first his inherent restlessness was contained by the novelty of Kuruman, the freedom during Moffat's absence to explore the territory and in building a new station nearby at Mabotsa. Marriage to Moffat's daughter and the birth of two children similarly impressed on him the need for a settled berth. However, not wishing to stay at Kuruman, he followed the mission's African patron, Sechele, first to Chonuane and on again in 1847 to Kolobeng. The slowness and drudgery involved in creating new stations Livingstone found insupportable. These were activities happily to be neglected in favour of further travels – to Lake Ngami in 1849 and to Sebitwane, chief of the Kololo on the Zambezi in 1851 – and the peripatetic evangelising of fresh audiences which he regarded as 'real' missionary work.[76]

Livingstone's attitude was common enough. John Barton in India, himself at first instinct with what was also the Cambridge volunteers' sentiment of the 1860s favouring itinerant preaching over settled schooling, recognised the type and quickly came to reject it. He regarded that perpetual restlessness, which led many missionaries to crave for unfettered evangelism in 'the regions beyond',[77] as the search for an easy option, doubtless often unconscious but none the less enabling advocates to avoid the hard painstaking effort inseparable from conversion and church building. In the words of a later CMS Secretary, such ambitions were part of a failure to recognise in 'the attempt to be independent ... an escape from reality'.[78]

These passions eventually got the better of Livingstone. He negotiated paid leave from the LMS. He made his case in terms of the search for suitable stations well away from marauders including the Boers, the cultivation of native agents and the encouragement of Christianity linked to trade in the interior. He sent his family to Scotland and embarked from Cape Town in June 1852 on the transcontinental journey which made his name, taking him first to Loanda on the west coast and then back across to Quelimane on the east. Arriving there in May 1856, he left for London where in December he was given a triumphant reception led not by the LMS so much as the Royal Geographical Society and its President, Sir Roderick Murchison. Publication of his *Missionary Travels and Researches in South Africa* the next summer, followed by a lecture tour culminating in a rousing challenge delivered in Cambridge to the universities to take up the missionary cause, established him as an heroic figurehead periodically of value to the missionary movement well into the next century.

---

75  Livingstone to T.L. Prentice, 2 Dec. 1841, cited by Holmes, *David Livingstone*, pp. 17–18.

76  For the most recent account, Ross, *David Livingstone*.

77  A common phrase, denoting as yet unevangelized territory, casually used by Livingstone e.g. to T.L. Prentice, 3 Aug. 1841, in Holmes, *David Livingstone*, p. 14.

78  Barton to Venn, 17 Aug. 1861, CMS Archives CI 1/037, no. 14; M.A.C. Warren, *Crowded Canvas: Some Experiences of a Life-Time* (London, 1974), p. 113.

Although Livingstone continued to regard himself as a missionary, it was nevertheless as one with whom the LMS, preferring more biddable, settled employees, was no longer comfortable. The 1853–56 journey quietly brought formal connections to an end when Livingstone resigned in October 1857, although there was value to both parties in allowing a popular imaginative link to continue. Far more to the fore after 1857 was Livingstone's employment and support by the British government and the scientific community associated with the Royal Geographical Society. As Robert Stafford has shown, Murchison as its President was of particular importance. The man who 'transformed the obscure missionary into one of Victorian Britain's archetypal heroes', he found Livingstone's reports congenial and so published them; he secured both the publication of his book and a government consular appointment.[79] Government and the scientific community, like the LMS, were eventually to find Livingstone unmanageable, but in the same way were content to offer him continuing informal approval for the public interest and popular political support he could attract.

In such a context, Livingstone's hopes for a time turned to the possibility of founding an English colony and he worried about potential rivals in 'discovery', such as Richard Burton and Samuel Baker. His next project – an expedition to open up central Africa via the Zambezi – bore striking resemblances to the Niger expedition two decades before. Sufficient support, much of it self-interested, especially in the Admiralty and the Foreign Office as well as scientific and commercial circles, was cultivated to secure for him both a consular appointment ultimately for five years and funds enough for a grander expedition than Livingstone himself wanted.[80] Its object was to open the way for Christianity and commerce. Seeing a notable opportunity, missionary interests tried to keep in touch by shaping their own plans in the shadow of those devised by Livingstone and his sponsors. The LMS, not entirely happy, despatched two missions in June 1858, to the Kololo and to the Ndebele; and in February 1861 a new high church mission, the Universities' Mission to Central Africa (UMCA), sent out its first party under Bishop Charles Frederick Mackenzie, to be guided by Livingstone's advice in its choice of station.[81]

This expedition – again not unlike the Niger – was a disaster. From his earlier journey Livingstone had seriously miscalculated the navigability of the Zambezi and his attempts now to redirect both his own and the UMCA's venture towards Lake Nyasa via the Shire and Rovuma rivers created new and unexpected problems. In 1860 the LMS Kololo mission was almost wiped out when Livingstone failed to make his rendezvous and the mission tolerated by Mzilikazi at Inyati

---

79 Robert A. Stafford, *Scientist of Empire: Sir Roderick Murchison, Scientific Exploration and Victorian Imperialism* (Cambridge, 1989), pp. 172 ff.

80 Ross, *David Livingstone*, pp. 202, 243; Livingstone to A. Sedgwick, 6 Feb. 1858 and to W.C. Oswell, 2 April 1859, Holmes, *David Livingstone*, pp. 49–50, 60. There were public subscriptions, for instance £2000 from Glasgow and on 11 Dec. 1857 Parliament approved a grant of £5000.

81 Owen Chadwick, *Mackenzie's Grave* (London, 1959).

remained a forlorn prospect throughout the 1860s. In January 1862, Bishop Mackenzie died; his settlement at Magomero, caught up in the local wars, like Lokoja came to nothing; and under his successor Bishop Tozer the party retreated to Zanzibar in December 1863.[82]

Others have noticed how this record, with its underlay of bitter personal disputes, did little for Livingstone's reputation. His dismissal of the UMCA party as 'fit only for well-behaved ladies' boarding schools' and Tozer's move to Zanzibar – 'The first Protestant mission which in modern times has turned tail without being driven away' – were more notable for asperity than either charity or accuracy.[83] Although Livingstone retained a regard for Mackenzie, when he returned home in 1864, his own missionary credentials glowed less brightly and his popularity was significantly reduced. The extent to which Livingstone's reports and findings had fallen in with Murchison's own geographical, geological and economic theories gave the latter personal reasons for vigorously promoting Livingstone's written account of the journey.[84] None the less his patrons had to work hard to extract real gold from the low-yielding ore of the expedition's prospecting.[85] Livingstone's value was not entirely exhausted, as the offer of another jointly funded consular appointment by the government and Royal Geographical Society demonstrated. However, other explorers such as Samuel Baker were attracting attention and Livingstone's virtual disappearance from the public eye for five years from 1866 offers a striking contrast with his prominence ten years before.

The shift that had occurred in the live Livingstone's reputation is indicative of developments which, like those in India and the West Indies, pointed to the flagging energies and revealed the limitations of the mid-century missionary movement. In south central Africa new stations were not emerging; native agents were non-existent; and such government interest or support as was forthcoming was proving of no more than incidental value to the missions' cause. Perhaps still more important were the subtle changes in understanding of the equation between Christianity and commerce. Livingstone's own sense of who fulfilled the missionary role at times broadened to the point where the missionary task and British expansion fused together. 'I view the end of the geographical feat as the beginning of the missionary enterprise. I take the latter term in its most extended signification and include every effort made for the amelioration of our race; the promotion of all those means by

---

82  Doug Stuart, 'The Making of a Missionary Disaster: The Makololo and the London Missionary Society', *NAMP Position Paper 29* (Cambridge, 1997); Landeg White, *Magomero: Portrait of an African Village* (Cambridge, 1989 edn), pp. 3–70.

83  Livingstone to James Young, July / Aug. 1863 [?], to George Frere, 22 Dec. 1863 and to A. Sedgwick, 24 Aug. 1866, Holmes, *David Livingstone*, pp. 86–8, 157–8. Cf. to A. Sedgwick, 26 March 1865, *ibid.*, p. 117.

84  David Livingstone and Charles Livingstone, *A Narrative of an Expedition to the Zambesi and its Tributaries and of the Discovery of the Lakes Shirwa and Nyassa, 1858–1864* (London, 1865).

85  Stafford, *Scientist of Empire*, p. 181 refers to its 'disappointing results' and, p. 184, 'scanty scientific findings'.

which God in His providence is working and bringing all His dealings with man to a glorious consummation.'[86] This went well beyond conventional talk of the obligation of a favoured nation to promote Christianity. It is therefore of little wonder that his use of the term 'colony' at times seemed to mean more than the flourishing Christian centre which he had hoped would emerge at Magomero or among the Kololo. Such experiences of failure helped bring Livingstone to the conclusion that the presence of the Portuguese and slave traders called for a full-scale onslaught involving well-intentioned traders and government resources. It is therefore no surprise that, after careful thought, he and Murchison took the 'unusual' step of dedicating the *Narrative* as well as *Missionary Travels* to Palmerston.[87]

Missionary and African initiatives by themselves were unlikely to work in central Africa. Livingstone appeared at times as if wishing merely to apply West African thinking to the rest of the continent. 'Wishing to get our material system as on the West engrafted on the East with the world system', he scribbled to Oswell as he sent him the last pages of manuscript for perusal.[88] However, there is in his writing a sense that times had changed. He had not only learned for himself the hard lesson that missionaries rarely had either the authority or the power to work alone. Old remedies were insufficient in a world of new obstacles, where the presence of the Portuguese and Arabs introduced an international competition. For all his admiration of African capabilities and his dependence on their assistance in his own travels,[89] Livingstone, once beyond the Cape frontiers, was irresistibly drawn into anticipation of the scramble for Africa and its ultimate partition. If native agency, the Bible and the plough were to further the expansion of Christianity, they required both a more secure setting than Livingstone ever encountered on his journeys and greater authority behind them than the missions could normally provide.

Circumstances within the South African colonies went a long way to reinforce these views. At the beginning of the 1840s, not least among those missions who had to reconstruct their work after the War of 1834–35, conditions were such as to justify the optimism associated with native agency and Venn's model of development. Throughout the Ciskei and Transkei there was developing on the mission stations a significant class of skilled and educated African Christians, with widely varied ethnic and geographical backgrounds.[90] Symptomatic of this growth was the foundation and opening in July 1841 of the Glasgow Missionary Society's new

---

86  David Livingstone, *Missionary Travels and Researches in South Africa* (London, 1857), pp. 673–4.

87  Livingstone to W.C. Oswell, 22 May 1865, Holmes, *David Livingstone*, p. 135.

88  15 May 1865 [?], Holmes, *David Livingstone*, p. 134.

89  Donald Simpson, *Dark Companions: The African Contribution to the European Exploration of East Africa* (London, 1975).

90  Donovan Williams, 'Social and Economic Aspects of Christian Mission Stations in Caffraria 1816–1854', 2 parts, *Historia* 31, 2 (1985), 33–48 and 32, 1 (1986), 25–56; Janet Hodgson, 'A Battle for Sacred Power: Christian Beginnings among the Xhosa', in Richard Elphick and Rodney Davenport (eds), *Christianity in South Africa. A Political, Social and Cultural History* (Oxford and Cape Town, 1997), chap. 4.

Lovedale Institution, to provide not only elementary education but a training for both European and African schoolmasters, catechists and mission agents.[91] The growth of such a body – self-conscious, independent, familiar with new artisanal and agricultural techniques as well as the developing market economy and including teachers, interpreters, church elders and property owners – was widely viewed with misgiving. Local rulers, white colonists, even some missionaries, resented those aspects of the missions' work that more than ever seemed to pose a subversive challenge to indigenous traditions and to the emerging settler capitalism.

These developments, however, were soon seriously disrupted. From the War of the Axe (1847), through intermittent conflict on the Sotho frontiers (c.1848–54), the Frontier War of 1850–52, to the great Cattle Killing of 1857, many mission stations were destroyed and numbers fell drastically. The Wesleyans experienced serious losses on both the north and east frontiers before the Orange Free State was established in 1854. Their centenary history estimated that recovery had barely been achieved by 1865 and even then 'the feeling of depression remained'.[92] Such reconstruction and new expansion as the Wesleyans undertook into the 1870s was seen as drawing missionaries, government and settlers closer together. In its stations, 'there was manifested a kindly, paternal care for the people and wise counsel was always ready to guide and direct the chiefs at critical moments, so that outlying Mission stations became in a very real sense bulwarks of empire, protecting in the best possible way the British Colonists and the more peaceful tribes within the Colony. Not infrequently missionaries received the thanks of the Government for their intervention when it seemed likely that the tribes might once again begin the wars that had proved so disastrous.'[93] After the experiences of 1834–35 and 1850–52, the Wesleyans were more anxious than most for their future security.

Others were better placed. Lovedale, for example, was closed in the War of 1847 and requisitioned for the military, but survived the war of 1850–52 physically unscathed, owing to the new military post of Fort Hare nearby.[94] The LMS was forced to abandon Theopolis in 1849. It also experienced the final destruction of the Kat River settlement in the early 1850s and saw its people join the rebels in the war against the colonial forces. Other LMS stations were little affected. Two tours of inspection, by the Reverend William Thompson (Dr Philip's successor as LMS agent at Cape Town) from October 1852 to January 1853 and by William Ellis in 1855, both suggested that recovery and resources were enough to justify the Directors proceeding with their policy of local self-financing.[95] This had been under fresh consideration for a few years, the intention being to consolidate the

---

91  Robert H.W. Shepherd, *Lovedale South Africa: The Story of a Century 1841–1941* (Lovedale, 1941), chap. 3.
92  Findlay and Holdsworth, *History of the WMMS*, Vol. 4, pp. 288–9.
93  *Ibid.*, p. 307.
94  Shepherd, *Lovedale*, pp. 108–18, 126–8.
95  Thompson, CWM Archives, South Africa/Journals/4/113; William Ellis, *Three Visits to Madagascar* (London, 1858), pp. 193–251.

work in Bechuanaland and explore new possibilities in central Africa. The recent deaths of both John Philip and James Read Sr drew the teeth of such opposition as there was to this move. The Directors were not only influenced by the West Indian example of withdrawal from a colonial setting deemed fit to attend to its own affairs, but had to face a similar outcome to that sketched above. Initial success in raising funds and levels of congregational activity, especially in education, were not kept up. Missionaries suffered serious privation and tenants on the Society's land were unwilling to change their status. Only very slowly and not before Cape legislation under which the government resumed control of the lands originally granted to the Society, was the LMS withdrawal completed.[96] It was a messy and undignified exit, with local compliance only grudgingly given, while the Society's new plans for the north were, as seen above, either abortive or long delayed.

## VII

The 1850s and 1860s were marked by hiatus if not stagnation in important areas of missionary activity overseas. They were decades when the movement as a whole, frustrated in the attainment of long-standing goals, lost much of its momentum. The movement's own historians, despite their expertise in the manufacture of silver linings, agreed that 'languor' had set in, a widespread 'reaction from the impulse to world-expansion which possessed Christendom in the earlier decades of the nineteenth century'. [97] Eugene Stock presented a wealth of melancholy detail to illustrate the general decline in the fortunes of the missionary societies paralleling more general changes in the evangelical world. He pointed to the passionate and bitter controversies – over disestablishment, education and the theological issues raised by the publication in the early 1860s of *Essays and Reviews* and Bishop Colenso's writings on the Pentateuch.[98] Biblical authority and scholarship, faith with its transmission and its liturgical expression, were widely seen as threatened, especially by the Anglican parties forming the English Church Union (1859) and the Church Association (1865) as defences against rationalism, ritualism and Rome. 'Such a time', Stock wrote, 'is never a time of missionary advance.'[99]

Patchy results overseas and domestic diversions gradually reinforced each other. Stock felt that such revivalist fervour as was sparked off in the late 1850s was channelled entirely into home missions and domestic controversy. In the 1860s, the CMS had far fewer candidates than in the previous decade and by 1870 the state of the funds

---

96  I am grateful to James Lumley for being able to read his unpublished essay 'Progress or Decline? The Funding of the LMS Missions in Cape Colony, 1848–1872'; Lovett, *History of the LMS*, Vol. 1, chap. 21.

97  Findlay and Holdsworth, *History of the WMMS*, Vol. 1, pp. 128–9.

98  *Essays and Reviews* (London, 1860); J.W. Colenso, *The Pentateuch and Book of Joshua critically examined*, 4 vols (London, 1862–63). For the controversies and their important missionary dimensions, Guy, *The Heretic*; Stock, *History of the CMS*, Vol. 2, e.g., pp. 46, 336–8, 358, 378.

99  *Ibid.*, p. 338.

was such that vacancies had to remain unfilled and an embargo was placed on any further appointments of native agents. In 1872 the CMS Committee was lamenting that
'for the first time for many years ... not one single University man had offered for missionary service'.[100] For the CMS, according to Stock, the period 1849–61 provided
246 candidates including sixty-two university graduates; 1862–72 only 159, of whom
no more than twenty-three were graduates. It was scant consolation to note that other
societies had fared no better and that the combined number of missionaries maintained in India by the CMS, SPG, LMS, BMS and WMMS had fallen between 1862
and 1872 from 262 to 234.[101] For the LMS more than any other the first half of the
1850s 'were years of unbroken gloom'. Although the troubles afflicting the Wesleyans
at that time had only a limited impact on their missionary income, Methodism's
internal divisions hardly helped to stimulate home support of a non-financial kind.
Although financial shortages were temporarily reversed by generous popular
responses to appeals arising from the Indian Mutiny and the China crisis of 1856–60,
all the societies found themselves in difficulties again by 1862. Not for another decade
did things improve again.[102]

Despite the continued use of slogans and well-worn rhetoric, working within the
framework of 'civilisation, commerce and Christianity' was producing diminishing
returns both in the mission fields and at home. The societies had not yet seen either
the opportunity or the need to resurrect the humanitarian dimensions of their work
which had proved so valuable as a support until the 1840s. Confidence in missions'
ability to exploit to their own advantage the political dimensions of their expansion
with indigenous, colonial and imperial authorities was often misplaced. For example,
the eventual return of the LMS to Madagascar in 1861 after twenty-six years of
expulsion was dictated entirely by internal political crises and indigenous manoeu-
vrings.[103] India not least had hammered home some hard lessons. The Government of
India had proved only marginally useful to missions. Its failure to fulfil the providential obligations of empire not only laid it open to renewed evangelical criticism but
raised the unattractive prospect of British expansion multiplying the points of friction between missions and empire. Cultural and economic developments in India,
rather than working in favour of the missions, had illustrated their limited ability to
influence colonial civilisation. Instead, they had been brought face to face with their
own lack of independence in tackling what seemed an ever more herculean task. It is
therefore necessary now to turn to those who looked to new ways forward. Often their
plans entailed recasting the relations of missions with empire.

---

100  *Ibid.*, p. 336.
101  *Ibid.*
102  Stanley, 'Home Support for Overseas Missions', quotation from p. 40 and pp. 36–40, 56–9.
103  Bonar A. Gow, *Madagascar and the Protestant Impact: The Work of the British Missions, 1818–95*
     (London, 1979); Françoise Raison-Jourde, *Bible et Pouvoir à Madagascar au XIXe siècle* (Paris,
     1991), Part I.

# 8

# New directions:
# the challenge of the 'faith missions',
# China and Islam

Vulnerable to profiteers and open to charges of extravagance as well as temptation, missionaries were regularly called on to justify their expenditure. William Ellis, like so many an innocent abroad and already fleeced by Sydney's colonists with a quick eye for a greenhorn, nevertheless had to admit that the LMS Directors might have a case for criticising his order for a secretaire rather than 'a plain chest of drawers'. That apart, 'I do not know of any things that can appear extravagant except the porter, which was the only beverage we had, save some tea and it was taken for the sake of health and not for self gratification.'[1] As the enterprise grew and property was acquired, so finance committees multiplied in order to watch the mission accounts.

However, the questioning of costs and the criticism of wasteful or immoderate use of funds which arose in the 1860s and were still more a feature of the 1880s and 1890s, were of a different order to a mission's routine housekeeping. Directed at churches and chapel building, missionary housing, schools, the employment of teachers or medical missionaries and printing presses, they called into question an entire system of evangelisation. More and more people identified the pursuit of 'Christianity, commerce and civilisation' with the creation of expensive, large-scale establishments. Geographical expansion entailed proliferating administration, which in turn spawned committees and fund-raising machinery, both regarded as far from the real work in the field, and demands for more – and more prestigious – accommodation at home and overseas. The missionaries' central task and universal message were felt to be in danger of suffocation in the cultural wrapping of Western practice and civilisation. The BMS's special jubilee fund in 1842, for instance, was given over to paying off its debts and building new central offices in the City of London, both necessary but none the less prosaic.[2] Dean Stanley, preaching on 'the ends and the means of Christian Missions', reminded his audience that 'In these days – when there is so much temptation to dwell on the scaffolding, the apparatus, the organization of religion, as though it were religion itself – it is doubly necessary to bear in mind what true Religion is'.[3] When regular

---

1 Ellis (Huahine) to George Burder, 4 Aug. 1819, CWM South Seas, 3/1.
2 Stanley, *A History of the BMS*, pp. 213–14; the centenary was likewise marked by debt relief, pp. 226–7.
3 F. Max Müller, *On Missions. A Lecture delivered in Westminster Abbey on December 3, 1873. With an Introductory Sermon by Arthur Penrhyn Stanley Dean of Westminster* (London, 1873), pp. 7–8.

income also faltered and church growth stalled, it was only natural that calls – in today's vocabulary – for self-appraisal and the formulation of new strategies would be heard.

The programme that gradually emerged was for a range of reforms simplifying mission work. The very term 'missionary society' was to be abandoned in favour of 'mission' and much of the societies' home organisation should be dismantled. Highly orchestrated fund-raising programmes were unnecessary and indeed undesirable, for subscribers should not be encouraged to expect dramatic visible results in return for their giving. Missions required no more than a small committee of referees to vet those missionaries sent out, to receive donations as they were freely given and to dispatch all such money to a designated head at work in the field. He alone could be sufficiently in touch with its needs to take decisions on policy. Simplicity was the keyword. The links uniting Christianity and commerce ought to be severed in favour of an emphasis on direct evangelisation by lay preachers and teachers, native and European. Methods of working should minimise any association of Western culture with the Christian religion. Freed from the trammels of direction by Home Committees, wholly non-denominational in approach, they should assimilate themselves as far as possible to native ways of living, in food, attire and lodgings. Only in these ways would a serious impact be made on the heathen world.

## I

Even before the 1860s such demands were not unknown. They were implicit in the debate about the just balance to be struck between preaching and teaching which had rumbled on since Carey's early days and so divided Scottish opinion. They influenced the conflict between the Serampore founders and the new generation of BMS organisers in the 1820s and 1830s. More occasionally they were explicit, perhaps most dramatically so in Edward Irving's anniversary sermon for the LMS in 1824.[4] Minister at the Scottish Church in Hatton Garden, London, Irving was rapidly growing in reputation as a fashionable preacher able to attract large and socially distinguished congregations. However, far from commending the LMS, Irving threw convention overboard and vigorously attacked the prevailing organisation and record of all the missionary societies, including those in Scotland of which he had some direct experience. The 'lame and partial success which has attended modern Missions by the way of conversion, compared with those of former times, should have humbled us to revise the principle on which we have proceeded.'[5] Anticipating (rightly!) criticism from 'those who have built up a system of administration on which they have set their hearts to call it perfect and infallible', he called for the abandonment of 'the principle of expediency and ... the

4  Edward Irving, *For Missionaries after the Apostolical School: A Series of Orations* (London, 1825).
5  *Ibid.*, p. 129.

rules of prudence'. Missions and faith were being overwhelmed by the prevailing obsession with 'money, money, money', by pursuit of 'the highest names upon a subscription list'.[6] Missions required the rediscovery of 'the nobleness of the Missionary character', with 'its independence of all natural means and indifference to all human patronage, its carelessness of all earthly rewards and contempt of the arithmetic of the visible and temporary things'. Missionaries should depend only on 'the Spirit of God, for sustenance, for patronage, for reward and for a rule of precedence', emulating the simplicity and obedience to the one Lord demonstrated by the original apostles and their disciples.[7]

The Directors were understandably put out and Irving was left to publish his own address, pointedly promising the proceeds to the widow of the Demerara missionary John Smith. Notorious as it was, Irving's address should not be easily dismissed as an early manifestation of the romantic extravagance, theological waywardness and liturgical eccentricity – prophecy and speaking in tongues – which culminated in his exclusion from his pulpit by the trustees in 1832 and death two years later. The desire for independence, direct and uncompromising evangelism, simplicity of lifestyle, complete self-identification with one's audience, freedom from material worries and a total trust in one's God represented an ideal supposedly met by the Apostles and equally attainable now. In Irving's words, 'apostles ... are for *all* times'.[8] This expression of faith was to have an extensive and lasting appeal throughout the century. Just as Irving used the term 'apostolic' and called for a strengthening of faith on primitive Christian lines, missions thus organised soon became known as 'faith' missions.

Those to whom this vision appealed were not simply those who set store by a genuinely powerful faith and maximum economy of means. Many were also united in sharing a pre-millennial eschatology, beliefs often informed by close contact with the Plymouth Brethren established in England in 1830.[9] Although not involved with the Brethren, Irving was instrumental in organising the Albury Conferences. Held annually during Advent at the country house of Henry Drummond from 1826 to 1830, these were the first regular gatherings for the study of prophecy, the millennium and Christ's Second Coming.

The dominant pattern of British Protestant millennial thought in the first half of the century was rooted in enlightenment ideas of progress. In missionary terms, it was associated with the fulfilment of the missionary task in the conversion of the world; this would usher in the millennium of peace, happiness and plenty, at the end of which Christ's Second Coming and the last judgement would take place. The protagonists of a reforming 'Christianity and commerce' strategy were essentially

---

6  *Ibid.*, pp. xiv, xxvi.
7  *Ibid.*, p. 119. The essential biblical text for Irving was Matthew, 10.5–42, together with Mark, 6 and Luke, 9–10.
8  *Ibid.*, pp. xx–xxi.
9  Bebbington, *Evangelicalism in Modern Britain*, chap. 3, esp. pp. 76–84.

aligned with this outlook. Distinct from this 'post-millennialist' belief was that of the 'pre-millennialists', with their pessimistic view of the world moving rapidly towards its end and their expectation of Christ's imminent return to judgement, *after* which the millennium would dawn. Fairly precise calculations of the timing of these events were widely regarded as possible, based on the matching of historical and contemporary happenings with the apocalyptic chronologies set out in the books of Daniel and Revelation. For the missionary the pre-millennialist imperative was to push ahead with evangelism on the widest possible front before the Second Coming occurred.[10]

The systematic formulation of these ideas and their application in the field were slow to occur, held back less by any radical implausibility or theological misgivings than the mounting prestige of the missionary mainstream in the 1830s. They eventually found their expression in the China Inland Mission (CIM) established by J. Hudson Taylor in 1865.

Taylor's venture drew on several sources of inspiration.[11] These included the work of the west-country dentist and surgeon Anthony Norris Groves, who was active as an independent missionary from 1829 to 1852, first in Baghdad and, from 1837, at Chitoor in the Madras Presidency. George Müller, Groves's brother-in-law, demonstrated for Taylor the practicality of working without regular salaried support. Karl Gützlaff recruited Taylor in 1853 to his Chinese Evangelization Society; there Taylor not only met like-minded colleagues but was inducted into the art of living constantly on the brink of bankruptcy.[12] This experience encouraged him to freelance in his own 'faith mission' in Ningpo from 1857 to 1860. After several abortive attempts to forge a connection with existing British societies, he started the CIM. This not only rapidly became the second largest British missionary venture of all but also was widely imitated and prompted adaptations in the practice of the long-established societies.[13]

Characteristic of the faith missions was a determination to operate in isolated and unfamiliar territory, as far as possible beyond any European influence or colonial rule and at a distance from other missionary bodies. China's appeal in the mid-nineteenth century lay in the fact that not only was the European presence still small but it was essentially limited to the coast, Hong Kong and the Treaty Ports, the number of which was increased at first to twelve under the treaty of 1860. For missionaries wishing to prove their faith, inland China presented a major challenge.

The same was true in many parts of Africa, that other arena where faith missions proliferated. David Livingstone's final journeys, from 1866 to his re-emergence late in 1871, when he was run to earth at Ujiji by the journalist H.M. Stanley and to his

10  David Bebbington, 'The Advent Hope in British Evangelicalism since 1800', *Scottish Journal of Religious Studies* 9, 2 (1988), 103–14.

11  Stanley, 'Home Support for Overseas Missions', chap. 7 'The Origins of "Faith" Missions'.

12  For useful introductions to Groves and Müller, *DEB*, Vol. 1, 485–6; Vol. 2, 803–4.

13  The principal study both of Taylor and of the CIM is A.J. Broomhall, *Hudson Taylor and China's Open Century*, 7 vols (Sevenoaks, 1981–89). The CMS was the largest.

death two years later, were important in this connection. Certainly Livingstone saw himself – and historians have tended to accept his view – as consistent in his missionary commitment, in thrall throughout to the traditional missionary pursuit of Christianity and commerce. Nevertheless, his journeys directed attention to the need for advance beyond the territories where the orthodox denominational societies were at work and his career highlighted in particular the needs of the Congo basin and central Africa. Livingstone's discomfort with conventional practice, seen in his impatience of the mission station, his desire to be independent and on the move and his inability to co-operate for long with other European colleagues, may reflect personality and temperament above all else. Yet his correspondence also reveals an awareness of alternative strategies. To a friend in Lanarkshire in 1841 he described how 'Believers everywhere among these people [the Tswana] preach as soon as they feel the value of the gospel, although they have much opposition to contend against and no worldly support save what results from their own industry, they persevere amazingly. The Bechuanas are retailers of news ... They are, too, perpetually on the move from one spot to another. We have people here who have come several hundreds of miles from the interior. This nomadic life is very favourable to the spread of the Gospel, although it is opposed to the spread of civilisation. Ought the Churches at home not [to] take advantage of their news-telling propensities?'[14] Although written in the context of discussion about native agency, the parallels with the practice of the faith missions are inescapable. Equally, Livingstone's last years in central Africa offer numerous similarities, revealing him as well attuned to the practice of the faith missions, even if he did not share their theological romanticism. Simultaneously, Livingstone's dislike of denominationalism provided another carrot to sympathisers with the faith missions. Intrinsic to their reservations about existing missionary societies was the latters' pervasive interdenominationalism. They were reviving the cause originally proclaimed but not sustained by the LMS, the society to which Livingstone himself had originally belonged. If Livingstone, with his fixation on the source of the Nile, is to be regarded as a missionary to the end, it should also perhaps be as one whose activities evolved in ways which were appreciated by radical critics of the traditions from which he came.[15]

Alive to these links, the first of the African faith missions – the Livingstone Inland Mission – was launched in 1878, accompanied by the first of its founders' many books on prophecy.[16] The Livingstone Inland Mission drew on familiar sources. The Guinnesses were friends and firm supporters of Hudson Taylor; their

---

14 Livingstone to Henry Drummond [of Glasgow, not Albury Park], 4 Aug. 1841, printed in David Chamberlin (ed.), *Some Letters from Livingstone 1840–1872* (London, 1940), pp. 26–7.

15 For Livingstone's consistency see, e.g., Ross, *David Livingstone*, pp. 93, 122–3; for alternative emphases, A.D. Roberts, 'David Livingstone', *Oxford Dictionary of National Biography* (forthcoming, Oxford, 2004) and Tim Jeal, *Livingstone* (London, 1973).

16 Mrs H.G. Guinness, *The First Christian Mission on the Congo: The Livingstone Inland Mission* (4th edn, London, 1882) and subsequently *The New World of Central Africa* (London, 1890); Henry Grattan Guinness, *The Approaching End of the Age* (London, 1878).

religious background lay in Dublin Protestantism and the Plymouth Brethren; and their experience brought together independent evangelists and non-denominational missionary training at Harley College in East London, which they had founded in 1872. Rapid expansion at all speed and no cost was the desired end, not least because prophecy accentuated the perennial missionary sense of impatience. With prophetical correctness edging out British patriotism, the Guinnesses argued that four empires preceded the Coming of Christ – Babylonian, Medo-Persian, Greek and Roman. Christians, they insisted, should be aware not only that they lived at the end of the fourth but at the end of its last form, 'the Roman Papacy ... and already that has ceased to exist as a secular government'.[17] Harley House and College, rechristened the East London Institute for Home and Foreign Missions, became the home base for the Livingstone Inland Mission in 1880 until the latter was handed to the American Baptist Missionary Union in 1884. The Congo Balolo Mission, organised by Guinness in 1889 when the Livingstone Inland Mission failed to expand under the American Baptist Missionary Union, was taken under the wing of the Regions Beyond Missionary Union. A northern training branch had opened in 1874 at Hulme Cliff College, Curbar, in Derbyshire and another followed in 1884 in Bromley, Kent. By 1886 the Guinnesses could list 427 missionaries sent out from the Institute, of whom 397 were currently preaching, 88 of them in Africa and many others with the CIM.[18] Their daughters married into the network and their sons became faith mission evangelists.[19]

The requirements for missionary self-support in the Congo necessarily differed from those in China, and the emphasis on local self-sufficiency remained strong. Nevertheless, references in the Guinness writings to the lessons to be learned from the Scottish East African examples of Blantyre and Livingstone, as well as certain South African mission stations, suggest their preparedness to compromise with the traditional institutions associated with settled mission stations.[20] Others, however, appeared more single-minded. F.S. Arnot, a friend of David Livingstone's family, took his lead from Livingstone and the Plymouth Brethren as an independent missionary, establishing himself in 1881 under Lewanika's patronage at Lealui in Zambia.[21] Anxious to distance himself from the ripples of European penetration, he moved on to Garenganze in Katanga and eventually handed over his position in 1889 to Daniel Crawford, another lone Scot with Brethren connections. The spur to his commitment was to reverse the dismal record of modern missions. 'The

17  H. Guinness and F.E. Guinness, *Light for the Last Days. A Study Historic and Prophetic* (London, 1886), chap. 15 'Signs of Our Times', pp. 370–80; see also *The Divine Programme of the World's History* (London, 1888).

18  Mrs H.G. Guinness, *The Wide World and Our Work in it; or, the Story of the East London Institute for Home and Foreign Missions* (London, 1886), appendix.

19  Geraldine, to Hudson Taylor's son, Howard; Lucy, to Karl Kumm, founder of the Sudan United Mission; Whitfield Guinness joined the CIM and Harry the Congo Balolo Mission.

20  Guinness, *The First Christian Mission*, pp. 35–40.

21  Prins, *The Hidden Hippopotamus*, for Lewanika and the missionaries.

cause surely is, that in this, as in other respects we have departed from the divine pattern ... There was no complicated machinery, but there was power. There were no elaborate plans, but they took their directions from the Lord ... Money, which seems the most important thing in this day, is scarcely alluded to in the evangelistic work of early days.'[22]

Other ventures were directed well away from the Congo. With the encouragement of Guinness, George Pearse, who had also been involved at an early stage with the Chinese Evangelization Society and Hudson Taylor, established the North Africa Mission in 1883. Modelling its arrangements on those of the CIM and Livingstone Inland Mission and publishing a monthly record of its work, it spread steadily along the Mediterranean from Morocco to Egypt. Edward Glenny, its Honorary Secretary, later explained part of the thinking behind the venture. 'The older denominational Societies have done excellent work ... but most of them at this time found that their work was brought almost to a standstill on account of their inability to increase their incomes sufficiently; consequently some new departure seemed necessary if the world's evangelization was to be accomplished.'[23]

Rising to this challenge was a further enterprise in the faith mission mould, the Sudan Mission party in 1889–92, led by Graham Wilmot Brooke in association with the CMS.[24] The history of the Sudan Mission is complex and more is said below of its place in the history of the CMS. In conception, however, it was straightforward and of a piece with those mentioned so far. It is well documented and illuminates perhaps more clearly than any the full flowering of the faith missions' inspiration and challenge to tradition.[25]

Brooke was born in 1865, into a military household and a family of mixed Scottish and Irish Protestant persuasion. Educated at Haileybury, he found himself unable to follow his father into the army. Perhaps under the influence of the vigorous evangelical community close to his home in Bromley,[26] he began to develop a missionary interest, especially after travelling alone to Algeria in 1884, where he distributed Gospel translations and was in touch with the newly established North Africa Mission.[27] In 1885–86, inspired like many others by the myth of General Gordon and fascinated with the idea of penetrating the Sudan, he travelled up the

---

22  Frederick S. Arnot, *Garenganze or Seven Years' Pioneer Work in Central Africa* (2nd edn, London, 1889), preface.

23  J. Rutherfurd and Edward H. Glenny, *The Gospel in North Africa* (London, 1900), p. 156.

24  Andrew Porter, 'Evangelical Enthusiasm, Missionary Motivation and West Africa in the Late Nineteenth Century: The Career of G.W. Brooke', *JICH* 6 (1977), 23–46.

25  For the 'Faith missions' and their networks see also Klaus Fiedler, *The Story of Faith Missions* (Oxford, 1994); P.J.Spartalis, *Karl Kumm: Last of the Livingstones, Pioneer Missionary Statesman* (Bonn, 1994); and the forthcoming work of Christof Sauer on Henry Grattan Guinness.

26  In addition to the offshoot of the Guinnesses's East London Institute, this included S.A. Blackwood and Rev. H.E. Brooke (Wilmot Brooke's uncle) both of whom were very active in promoting the Mildmay Conferences. See S.A. Blackwood, *Some Records of the Life of Stevenson Arthur Blackwood* (London, 1896).

27  Rutherfurd and Glenny, *Gospel in North Africa*, p. 219; Brooke Papers, Notebooks F1/2, 3.

Senegal river and was actively involved with the annual Mildmay Conference, which for thirty years had promoted among its causes those of revivalism, a pronounced piety, foreign missions and concern for the Second Coming. Hectic evangelising in London late in 1886 was followed the next summer by a year-long exploratory evangelistic journey to the Congo, again with the Sudan in mind. Unable to surmount its difficulties, Brooke turned to the Niger as the one remaining route inland and left the Congo for Akassa in September 1888. Discussing his plans with CMS missionaries on the spot, he returned to London where he persuaded the CMS to approve his informal association with them, while engaged on his own work as an independent self-supporting missionary. After a further brief visit to the Niger, he married and finally left for Lokoja in February 1890 as joint head of the Sudan Mission party and Honorary Lay Missionary with the CMS. Along with the Sudan Mission's immediate hopes, he eventually died of blackwater fever at Lokoja in March 1892.

Writing from the Congo, Brooke had defined for his father what was in many ways his starting point for the Sudan, uncompromising rejection of the linkage of Christianity and commerce. There is, he said, 'very much confusion ... caused & very much nonsense talked by Evangelicals and Broadchurchmen both confusing the work of saving men from the power of Satan and that of building up political, commercial, & social civilization. I believe these two to be very frequently opposed, & I know they are invariably distinct.'[28] He was convinced that there existed a 'general law' of missionary development. Most societies avoided physical difficulties, seeking out areas already penetrated by 'traders or other immoral self-styled Christians'. In such regions, 'Satan hastens to spread tares, his own servants, teaching the heathen to worship the god of this world under the name of Civilization.' Better, he felt, for the missionary to face physical problems and enter those territories as yet uncontaminated by such influences, where the people were 'still open to first impressions about the worship of God' and displayed no 'mere wish for a knowledge of secular civilization'.[29]

Here lay an important key to Brooke's fascination with the Sudan. All missions to Africa had 'at the outset to decide the great question: shall we follow in the track of traders, or shall we strain every nerve to precede them? ... It will not be open much longer to missions to choose which course they will adopt, for Africa is being opened up.'[30] Brooke and his friends felt the Sudan to be still virgin territory, where the free-ranging evangelist might forestall the corruption certain to follow European trade and partition, a corruption felt more difficult to combat than the influence of Islam.

Brooke's outlook was also one that ultimately found little place for specialists or professionals, such as medical missionaries. The general competence necessary to a self-supporting missionary might allow for some medical skill, but the idea of a

---

28  3 March 1888, Brooke Papers F5/3.
29  Brooke to Rev. A.C.D. Ryder, 14 Sept. 1886, Brooke Papers, F2/1.
30  *Ibid.*

hospital or dispensary, even surgical equipment, involved a settled base and there-fore the expectation that, instead of going to the people, the missionary should wait for them to come to him. As Brooke's colleague Robinson put it, anything that 'belied our professions of simplicity and economy' or diverted people's attention from 'our message' had to go.[31] Ultimately the only worker unmentioned in the Acts of the Apostles but needed in the nineteenth century was the translator.[32] Brooke insisted to the full on the prevailing fashion for simplicity and assimilation to indigenous ways. From the start of his association with the CMS, he was clearly determined to wear native dress and to live on native food; he wished to be completely cut off from all secular powers and temporal assistance should his mission get into difficulties.

It is not surprising to find that Brooke took the CIM as his guide. He referred constantly to Hudson Taylor's 'Rules and Regulations' and found not only Charles Finney's *Lectures on Revivals of Religion* but Taylor's *Days of Blessing in Inland China* 'a revelation ... with regard to Christian life'.[33] Along with his Congo experi-ences these convinced him that missions should be 'in no way whatever directed by subscribers at home', but should follow the CIM's model 'to which God has set His seal by thousands of conversions'.[34] The circles in which he moved and his corre-spondence were dominated by members of the faith mission and pre-millennialist networks. Where he differed from them – and especially from more conventional missionaries also determined to steal a march on the other agencies of British expansion – was in his determination to remove threats to his own venture. Lacking any sense of proportion or caution, he took justification by faith and the authoritar-ianism of the radical challenge to their extremes. This led him into disastrous attempts to reform the CMS's Niger mission which he and his colleagues saw as almost entirely corrupt and a threat from the rear to any Sudan mission.[35]

Brooke was propelled by an apocalyptic pre-millennial vision, one that drove him and others of this persuasion to reject conversion as the first priority of the missionary. A relentless, headlong evangelism was all. 'I see no hope given in the Bible that wickedness in this world will be subdued by civilization or preaching of the gospel – until the Messiah the prince come. And to hasten that time is, I believe

---

31  Brooke, 'Notes on Industrial Work in West African Missions', CMS G3/A3/0 (1890), 222; 'Report on the Sudan Mission School, Lokoja, 1891', CMS G3/A3/0 (1892), 36; *Sudan Mission Leaflet No. 18*; J.A. Robinson to Lang, 21 May 1890, CMS G3/A3/0 (1890), 78; H.H. Dobinson to Lang, 6 Aug. 1891, CMS *ibid.* (1891), 209.

32  Brooke's address, *The Mildmay Conference 1887* (London, 1887), p. 145.

33  Brooke's Journal, 23 April, 17 May 1889, 31 July 1890, Brooke Papers, F4/7; J. Hudson Taylor, *Days of Blessing in Inland China* (London, 1877).

34  Brooke to Leonard K. Shaw, 13 Oct. 1887, Brooke Papers, F5/2. For Shaw, at the centre of active evangelism in Manchester, editor of *The Christian Workers*, financial contributor to the Sudan Mission and distributor of its printed leaflets, see E. Kirlew, *Gilbert R. Kirlew. A Brief Memoir* (London, 1908); L.K. Shaw and T.M. Macdonald to F.E. Wigram (CMS Secretary), 27 April 1892, CMS G/AC4/9/1705; and Brooke Papers, passim.

35  See below, pp. 238–43, 250–2.

the function of foreign missions, "for the gospel must first be preached for a witness, unto all nations and then shall the end come". I therefore should be inclined to frame any missionary plans with a view to giving the simple gospel message to the greatest number possible of ignorant heathen in the shortest possible time.'[36] The alternative for Brooke was awful to contemplate and shows again how his radicalism went hand in hand with a marked conservatism in biblical understanding. Every day spent without 'gospel work', 'Every day that Christ's coming is delayed, means hundreds of souls swept into hell', he jotted down for his talk to a Cambridge audience.[37]

Some hearers at least might be saved, if a simple-minded message were conveyed with single-minded intensity. In advising a fellow African evangelist, Brooke was no less clear as to how this should be done. 'I would humbly urge the importance of making the message bold, urgent and *wholly spiritual* from the very first, of avoiding talking about education or book learning as if that were in any sense "religion", but eagerly pressing on each individual hearer the duty of immediate repentance and submission to Christ and tell them that Christ is shortly coming again. Let them not get the idea that you are recommending a new national religion, but that your message is to individuals and that it is not less binding on the slave because his master rejects it. I am fully alive to the fact that such preaching may spoil your reception at many places and may arouse anger, but I believe it will be honoured of God in bringing men to repentance. Should they enquire about book learning, you must tell them that teaching the people to read God's book in their own tongue is all that we wish to teach, that we have not time for anything else, as all our Members who have spare time must give it up to warning people about Eternity.'[38]

## II

It has now been seen how arguments critical of well-established missionary practice were closely associated with both the cumulative dissatisfaction felt at the outcome of evangelistic efforts and the emergence of pre-millennialist persuasions. In terms of missionary method and theological satisfaction the faith missions were widely felt to offer the best way forward. Directed as they commonly were to areas seen as still cut off from European influences – notably China's interior and those parts of Africa where Islam's presence was either already established or about to become so – they had implications for the connection of missions and empire.

The complexities and the confusion of those relationships in China are not hard to see, for they were to be found even within a single family circle such as that of the Lockharts of Liverpool. Dr William Lockhart, born in 1811, trained in Dublin and at Guy's Hospital in London, was the first British medical missionary, sent by the LMS

---

36  Brooke's address, *The Mildmay Conference 1887* (London, 1887), pp. 141–8.
37  'Notes for Addresses (1886–7)', Brooke Papers, F2/5.
38  Brooke to Rev. J.J. Williams, 13 Nov. 1891, CMS G3/A3/0 (1892), 6.

to open a hospital at Macao in 1839. Shuttling between Batavia, Macao and Chusan in 1840 and at times feeling very cut off,[39] he nevertheless received occasional (in his view far too infrequent) letters from home. One acquaintance, the Reverend William Urwick, in relaying the latest news observed that with the end of 'the war in Syria' attention was shifting to China: 'I have taken some interest in both these departments of military and naval enterprise – as to Syria because the "millenarians" have been … expecting that Mehemet Ali would restore the Jews … and as to China, because it seemed as though some Providential Movement were required to give the gospel access to it.' Urwick evidently had his misgivings over access having been gained by a British war possessing 'somewhat of an ambiguous character'; but this caused him all the more to hope that 'these shakings up of nations prepare the way for the bloodless victories and saving spiritual dominion of the Son of God'.[40] In a similar vein, Lockhart's father retailed how 'the finger of God's Providence is … pointing many eyes to China', especially those of Christians. Considering for how long China had been 'a hopeless spot to work on', 'forbidden ground', they had every reason to be at least as hopeful and enthusiastic as British merchants. After all, 'The warrior, the merchant, the diplomatist are nothing, save as the breakers up of a way for the entrance of the Bible and the Missionary. When they have served this purpose, they are laid by as useless, but the missionary with the Bible in his hand is to be God's special agent to work His gracious designs for long neglected China.'[41] These letters provide pointers to several of the most powerful cross-currents that were to buffet both the Chinese and the agents of British expansion throughout the century. Consideration of them may help towards an understanding of the outcomes of the faith missions' perspectives in confronting the realities of the mission field.

Lockhart's profession stood firmly in a tradition of Western science and civilisation which he and other colleagues, notably in the LMS, were concerned to propagate in tandem with Christianity in the Celestial Empire. At the same time his own views of the relationship between medicine and science were not universally shared. He distanced himself from any direct use of medicine for securing conversions, while insisting that the medical missionary should be clearly identified with the missionary station, 'so that it might be seen and known that the work is done as work for Christ'. That identification should, none the less, not be carried too far. Not only must the hospital be given the utmost attention and constitute his chief work, but, he argued, the medical missionary should be a layman. One could not properly follow two professions: 'if the medical missionary is ordained, either a good surgeon or a good pastor is spoiled'.[42]

---

39 W. Lockhart to S. Lockhart (father) and sister, 19 Jan. 1841, typed copy, SOAS MS 380645/1, p. 142.

40 Urwick to W. Lockhart, 17 Dec. 1840, typed copy, *ibid.*, p. 137.

41 S.B. Lockhart to William Lockhart, 7 Jan. 1841, *ibid.*, p. 138.

42 William Lockhart, *The Medical Missionary in China: A Narrative of Twenty Years Experience* (London, 1861), p. vi. For Lockhart, entries by J. Paquette, *DEB*, Vol. 2, pp. 695–6 and C.F. Grundmann, *BDCM*, p. 407.

From Lockhart's LMS hospitals in Tinghae (1840), Shanghai (1843) and Peking (1861), through the nearly eleven thousand patients treated in his first year's work, to his many later contributions to *Medical Missions at Home and Abroad*, he vigorously sustained the tradition that the builders of the faith missions rejected.[43] LMS missionaries were not alone in this, but were particularly notable.[44] Lockhart's successor at Peking, Dr John Dudgeon, subsequently became Professor of Anatomy at the Interpreters' College; set up under the 1858–60 treaties ending the 'Arrow (or second Opium) War' as a Western language school for mandarins, it rapidly became the vehicle for disseminating a much wider Western knowledge. Continuing a tradition which reached back to Gützlaff and Elijah Bridgman (ABCFM) at Canton in the early 1830s, Dr Joseph Edkins was one of an interdenominational trio publishing the Chinese language 'Peking Magazine', a 'predominantly scientific publication' from 1872 to 1875. Alexander Wylie, of the LMS and later the Bible Society, was distinguished not only for his translations into Chinese of Western mathematical works and for helping found the Shanghai Polytechnic Institute. As a founder member of the North China Branch of the Royal Asiatic Society, he made seminal contributions to Western knowledge of Chinese scholarship. For him 'there was never any contradiction between his secular and religious activities'.[45]

It was also not unknown for the evangelical energy fuelling the CIM's challenge itself to be diverted into more traditional channels. Timothy Richard, converted during the Welsh revival of 1859, influenced by Irving and a firm supporter of the CIM, provides one such instance. As a Baptist missionary in north China and heavily involved in relief work during the disastrous famine of 1876–79, he concluded that Christianity linked to Western civilisation and transferred to China through the educated elite was essential. The BMS, unhappy at this change in direction, seconded him in 1891 to the Society for the Diffusion of Christianity and General Knowledge among the Chinese in Shanghai. Later known as the Christian Literature Society and with Richard as its Secretary, its involvement in educational programmes was widely supported among the missions.[46]

While Lockhart and many after him readily endorsed the close relationship of Christianity and civilisation together with the educational institutions which supported them, they were also closer to the outlook of the faith missions in having serious reservations about aspects of commerce, especially in the form of the

---

43  *Medical Missions at Home and Abroad* was the monthly publication of the Medical Missionary Association, based in London.

44  Walls, *Missionary Movement in Christian History*, chaps 14–15; J.K. Fairbank et al. (eds), *The I.G. in Peking: Letters of Robert Hart Chinese Maritime Customs 1868–1907*, 2 vols (Cambridge, MA, 1975), no. 27.

45  Robert Bickers, 'Alexander Wylie (1815–1887)', *ODNB* (forthcoming, Oxford 2004).

46  Stanley, *History of the BMS*, pp. 180–97, 200–7, 303–7; Lauren Pfister, 'Re-thinking Mission in China: James Hudson Taylor and Timothy Richard', in Andrew Porter (ed.), *The Imperial Horizons of British Protestant Missions, 1880–1914* (Grand Rapids and Richmond, 2003), pp. 183–212.

opium trade. Lockhart condemned as dishonourable and shaming the British official and mercantile approaches to the war of 1839–42 and to the trade that had given rise to it: 'what think you when we entered this a heathen city we found the walls placarded with official papers reprobating the use of opium, threatening the sellers and consumers of the drug with very severe punishment because the opium was a great evil, was poisoning the people and spreading misery and disease and want over the community and we a pretendedly Christian people! An enlightened people! Yes, even an honourable people!!! Hear it – having come hitherto to demand satisfaction for injuries received, [we] are also allowing this hateful traffic to go on, among our own Ships of War and in open day ... in former times, the smugglers had to defend thems[elves] and run the risk of attack and therefore avoided all places where there was an armed Chinese force, but now ... the smugglers are protected by her Majesty the Defender of the Faith's ships, this is the very worst thing that we have done and fills me with disgust and what must the Chinese think of such conduct.'[47] If the imperial British government were not to act against the East India Company in this matter, Christianity and Western values would be a source of mockery: 'if ... the trade be cherished and sustained as before, the heathen may point the finger of scorn at us'.[48]

The trade, as is well known, was 'cherished and sustained'.[49] In the period 1860 to 1900 opium exports into China rose in value from £4.5 million to £9.5 million per annum. Missions and evangelical supporters at home had no illusions as to its damaging effects; they made frequent representations to the East India Company, the imperial government and Members of Parliament and tried to stir up the wider public.[50] Reports on the trade were warmly welcomed. To William Russell at Ningpo, whose memorandum was sent on to the imperial government, there went in return requests for further information together with news of Lord Shaftesbury's attempts to form a committee to force the matter on Parliament and rouse public anger. However, Russell was warned not to be unduly sanguine. 'The parties interested are many and powerful; and commercial morality is frightfully lax. We cannot expect therefore that we shall succeed without a severe struggle. Nor will an evil of such sturdy growth be put down in a day.'[51]

Straith's caution was only too well founded. Not until 1874, after numerous attempts to secure action, was Shaftesbury able to launch the Anglo-Oriental

---

47 W. Lockhart to S. Lockhart (father) and sister, 19 Jan. 1841, typed copy, SOAS MS 380645/1, p. 142.

48 *Ibid.*

49 John Y. Wong, *Deadly Dreams: Opium, Imperialism and the Arrow War (1856–1860) in China* (Cambridge, 1998).

50 For general details, Stock, *History of the CMS*, Vol. 2, pp. 301–6; Findlay and Holdsworth, *History of the WMMS*, Vol. 5, pp. 426–30.

51 H. Straith (CMS Secretary) to Rev. W.A. Russell (Ningpo), 18 Sept. 1855, CMS C.CH/I 1, f. 7; also J. Chapman (CMS Secretary) to W. Welton (Foochow), 18 Sept. 1855, to Henry Reeve (Shanghai), 2 Sept. 1856 and R.H. Cobbold (Ningpo), 3 Sept. 1856, *ibid.*, ff. 35, 43, 51.

Society for the Suppression of the Opium Trade, with strong Quaker support as well as that of prominent figures from the missionary world such as James Legge.[52] Progress towards securing a British withdrawal from the trade remained non-existent and continuing protest only elicited scorn from officials: 'as for Exeter Hall' wrote Sir Robert Hart, head of the Chinese Imperial Maritime Customs, 'donkeys *will* bray to the end of time'.[53] Even missionary opinion was seriously divided as to the wisdom of engaging with government and the political sphere over the question. Robert Cust, ex-India Civil Servant, member of the CMS Parent Committee and prolific writer on missionary themes, by 1890 had concluded that 'it is idle to fight against Nature, free-trade and the liberty of each man to control his own actions in things not forbidden by the laws of civilized nations'.[54] Not only was suppression of the trade impossible; pursuit of suppression put people off associating themselves with missionary endeavours. The extent to which missionary societies were unpopular, Cust believed, was a significant reflection of 'the folly of this small section, always bringing forward their local and peculiar grievances, which have no direct bearing on the Evangelization of the World'. Not only distinguished public figures but 'Even quiet, undemonstrative, but still sincere, Christians feel shy of joining assemblies, which abandon their holy duty of conveying the Gospel to dying souls, to discuss and pass resolutions on the subject of the Cultivation of the Poppy and Manufacture of Opium, the export of Rum and Gin and the Immorality of the British Soldier. Sensible people can see no possible connection between such subjects and the duty imposed upon us all by the parting words of the Risen Saviour. If Missionary Societies desire to constitute themselves Censors and Judges of the Morals of the British people, the Champions of all that think themselves injured and the Denouncers of everything, which they do not understand, they are going beyond their province and trespassing on the duties of secular Societies.'[55]

Cust's remarks were none the less perceptive for being direct and, to some, abrasive. Superficially at least, the opium trade, conjuring up calculations of profits illegitimately won at the expense of innumerable impoverished addicts, was expected to generate the same revulsion as the slave trade had done. That it failed to produce a comparable wave of humanitarian sentiment and active commitment for the missions to ride into inland China is revealing of the nature of both missionary and humanitarian movements. British merchants were generally seen as supplying an extensive market and their withdrawal simply as leading the Chinese to find other sources of supply. The choice of so many Chinese, to consume, trade in and

---

52  F.S. Turner, *British Opium Policy and Its Results in India and China* (London, 1876); Rev. F.S. Turner was the Anglo-Oriental Society's secretary. For Legge, 'the greatest English-speaking sinologist of the nineteenth century', Walls, *The Missionary Movement*, pp. 148, 90, 196; H.E. Legge, *James Legge: Missionary and Scholar* (London, 1905).

53  Hart to James Campbell, 18 Feb. 1883, in Fairbank, *The I.G. in Peking*, no. 403.

54  R.N. Cust, *Notes on Missionary Subjects* (London, 1889), p. 112.

55  *Ibid.*, p. 118.

smuggle opium was also bound up with the inability of China's authorities through ineptitude or crookery to contain it. Continuation of the trade thus revealed the moral weakness and political incompetence of the Chinese at all levels, demonstrating the limits of Chinese civilisation rather than Britain's. Under no circumstances could opium addiction be equated with slaves, opium consumption being self-evidently voluntary, whereas slavery was enforced.

The humanitarians found insufficient enthusiasm for an effective anti-opium crusade and, as Cust's references to trade in spirits and prostitution suggest, remained divided in their concerns. Other groups occupied themselves chiefly with arms or with the extensive coolie trade. The latter was imperfectly regulated in China's case under regulations agreed in 1866 and, as with the Indian traffic, was sufficiently covered by free-trade rhetoric and government oversight to undermine the prospects of any popular campaign aimed at its more objectionable features.[56] Not surprisingly the missions found little enough here with which they could identify themselves in ways likely to bring them extensive support. However, even had the humanitarian lobbies been more effectively united, there was one remaining obstacle to the recreation of a missionary–humanitarian alliance to parallel that of the 1820s to 1840s. Coolies, opium and spirits did not directly threaten missionaries' work in the way that slavery and its institutions had done. Missionaries were murdered, their access to audiences prevented, converts persecuted and mission property not infrequently destroyed by the Chinese especially towards the end of the century.[57] But the direct responsibility of British subjects for such acts, their manipulation and defiance of the law in Britain's own West Indian colonies, had no counterpart in China. While there was little love lost between the missionary community (in any case increasingly international in composition) and other expatriates, British opium traders did not ransack nonconformist chapels.

Where the faith missions tried to sidestep completely all issues of trade and other secular activity, the traditionalists thus preferred even if with limited success to be selective, supporting respectable trades as far as possible at the expense of the others. From CMS headquarters Charles Fenn reassured William Collins, transferred to Peking when the CMS had left Shanghai in 1863, that the Society might 'at some future time take up Shanghae again'. For the time being, however, the 'number of European merchants there makes it an unpromising field for Missionary labour'.[58] Even allowing for the normal excision of the word 'retreat'

---

56  See David Northrup, *Indentured Labour in the Age of Imperialism, 1834–1922* (Cambridge, 1995); Hugh Tinker, *A New System of Slavery: The Export of Indian Labour Overseas, 1830–1920* (London, 1974); Peter Richardson, *Chinese Mine Labour in the Transvaal* (London, 1982); Kay Saunders (ed.), *Indentured Labour in the British Empire, 1840–1920* (London, 1984).

57  Paul Cohen, *China and Christianity: The Missionary Movement and the Growth of Chinese Antiforeignism, 1860–1870* (Cambridge, MA, 1963); 'Christian Missions and Their Impact to 1900', in J.K. Fairbank (ed.), *The Cambridge History of China*, Vol. 10 (Cambridge, 1978), pp. 543–90; Edmund S. Wehrle, *Britain, China and the Antimissionary Riots, 1891–1900* (Minneapolis, 1966).

58  C.C. Fenn (CMS Secretary) to W.H. Collins, 26 Nov. 1866, CMS C.CH/I 1, f. 113.

from the missionary vocabulary, this was mild comment on commercial obstacles. It indicates not only that they were generally such as might be circumvented by moving elsewhere. For most missionary organisers the more extreme responses of the faith missions remained unnecessary, too easily leading one across the frontier from constructive protest into extravagance and impotence.

Returning to the Lockhart exchanges, it is notable that the members of his circle saw the position of China in providential rather than pre-millennial terms. The latter, as seen above, was to become essentially the preserve of Taylor and the CIM tradition, the upheavals in China inviting a general response to the evangelistic image of the country's condition. For Lockhart and those after him missionary approaches were to be defined more in terms of focused responses to particular providential openings, a hospital here, a school or orphanage there, not as a movement akin to the sweep of hunters across a game-filled hillside. However, it was not always easy to distinguish in practice between the two positions. The Taiping Rebellion (1850–64) above all seemed to call for a direct evangelistic response from missionaries of all descriptions.

Encounters with Protestant Christianity in the late 1830s after a time led Hong Xiuquan to develop his own millenarian, anti-Ch'ing vision for China.[59] Using Gützlaff's biblical translations and other devotional literature, Hong gathered much popular support and appeared as the leader of a quasi-Christian movement. Not only the Taipings' openness to Christian ideas but their hostility to idols and opium commended them to Protestant missionaries. They also caused excitement in metropolitan Britain. Uncertainty and a lack of detailed knowledge meant that attitudes of the Taipings and British missionaries towards each other fluctuated.[60] In 1855, Robert Cobbold at Ningpo heard that the 'attention of England has been powerfully turned to China. At one time great expectations were entertained from the rapid successes and Christian principles of Taeping-Wang; and then those expectations were shaken by the mixture of false doctrine in his own publications and more lately by the blasphemies of the Eastern king. Since then the rebels have met with defeat and it almost seems as if the Tartar dynasty would be reestablished in all its pristine power. We are utterly at a loss as to the future'.[61] Only a little later on furlough from Hong Kong, Bishop George Smith published together two forthright addresses, commending the Christian potential of the Taipings and condemning the opium trade.[62]

---

59  Most recently, Jonathan Spence, *God's Chinese Son: The Taiping Heavenly Kingdom of Hong Xiuquan* (New York and London, 1996).

60  Stock, *History of the CMS*, Vol. 2, 296–300, 309–12; S.Y. Teng, *The Taiping Rebellion and the Western Powers* (Oxford, 1971), chap. 9 'Taiping Relations with Western Missionaries', esp. pp. 174–83.

61  J. Chapman (CMS Secretary) to R.H. Cobbold, 18 Sept. 1855, CMS C.CH/I 1, f. 15.

62  George Smith (Bishop of Victoria, Hong Kong), *Our National Relations with China. Being Two Speeches* (London, 1857), 25 March at the Free Trade Hall, Manchester and 5 May at the CMS Anniversary Meeting in Exeter Hall.

Missionaries of several denominations – Anglican, Baptist and Congregationalist – visited key Taiping-held cities, including the capital at Nanjing, in the hope of turning Taiping beliefs into more orthodox channels. Taiping leaders meanwhile encouraged missionaries both for ideological reasons and for as long as they thought themselves capable of winning over the Western powers in their civil war against Peking. By 1860 the pendulum had again swung in Hong Xiuquan's favour and at Salisbury Square 'We have been again led to entertain more hope of the Christianity of the insurgents.'[63] Other missions remained consistently hostile to the Taipings. In the end, evangelicals, in line with British opinion in general, largely turned against them, regarding them 'no longer as imperfect Christians fighting for liberty, but rather as inhuman monsters using religion as a cloak for their evil deeds'. However, there remained a strong feeling for the rest of the century that in missionary terms this episode was a great 'opportunity ... absolutely lost'.[64] Pre-millennialist, faith-mission adherent or not, there thus remained in the minds of Protestant missionaries anticipations of cataclysmic upheaval with profound possibilities for the spread of Christianity in China. China's experience of defeat in the Sino-Japanese War (1895), the Boxer Rebellion (1900) and the revolution of 1911 were carefully scrutinised in the hope that Providence was providing yet another opening. As one who rode the two horses of the CIM and the CMS, the Bishop of Western China, William Cassels, sent a circular letter to his diocese in September 1911. 'With regard to ourselves, I am most anxious that it should be borne in mind that it is most probable that God is going to use this agitation for the extension of His Kingdom and the advancement of the Church. The Taiping rebellion and the Boxer outbreak played their part towards the breaking down of idolatry, the shaking of old foundations and in making the preparation for the setting up of God's Kingdom. This new agitation may carry the work a great deal further.'[65]

William Lockhart was one of the first missionaries into China after the Opium War and throughout his career remained one of a still very small number. Figures are not easily compiled, but there were perhaps seventy to eighty in China during the 1850s and even by 1871 only about a hundred, of whom half were British and of those some fifteen Anglicans. Only after that did the explosion in numbers occur, reaching about 2,800 in the 1890s of whom still about half were British.[66] The numbers of missionaries' dependants would certainly increase these figures substantially. In considering the last of the Lockharts' themes, the relations of missions and British authorities in China, the rapid increase in the size of the missionary community must not be overlooked.

---

63  J. Chapman (CMS Secretary) to F.F. Gough (Ningpo), 3 Oct. 1860, CMS C.CH/I 1, f. 73.

64  Stock, *History of the CMS*, Vol. 2, p. 312.

65  M. Broomhall, *W.W. Cassels First Bishop in Western China* (London, 1926), pp. 277–8. For his career, *CMS Register*, List I, entry 1358.

66  P.D. Coates, *The China Consuls: British Consular Officers, 1843–1943* (Hong Kong, 1988), p. 178; Kenneth S. Latourette, *A History of Christian Missions in China* (London, 1929), pp. 405–10.

There was always a feeling in favour of keeping missionary contacts with official to a minimum. Most pronounced in the CIM, it continued to be present in others. John Burdon, although highly regarded and despite his close connections with the British Legation in Peking, was reminded in 1869 that 'no communications on Missionary subjects should be made direct from [CMS] missionaries to Her Majesty's Government; ... all such communications should pass through the President of the Society or a deputation of the Committee'. The fear in London was that such exchanges might well put at risk the 'kindness and consideration' which it was felt the Society had on the whole received from successive governments.[67] Contact as distinct from more formal communication, however, was altogether another matter in this as in other fields. Confronted with the perennial missionary problem of providing for one's family, Thomas McClatchie (CMS) at Shanghai, already brother-in-law to Sir Harry Parkes, was in touch with Robert Hart to secure a place for his son, as was the Wesleyan George Piercy.[68] Some with missionary connections took official posts: W.H. Medhurst, son of the early LMS missionary, rose to be Consul at Shanghai and receiver of a knighthood. Others eventually left missionary careers for official appointments. Dr Joseph Edkins, after thirty-two years with the LMS, resigned in 1880 to become translator for the Customs Inspectorate-General, as did William Milne for a similar post at the Peking Legation.[69] Such appointments, however, seem to have become less common in later years as the British establishment grew. They were in any case officially viewed with some misgivings, lest irresponsible missionary sympathies affect the supposedly deliberate decisions of government.

Lockhart Sr's idea that the missionary entrée into China would involve a rapid supersession of the roles of merchant and diplomat was of course to prove fanciful. There was a strong feeling in the consular service that until about 1858 a combination of consular caution with an early generation of predominantly scholarly and hardly less cautious missionaries had managed satisfactorily to balance their respective interests. Thereafter, relations deteriorated in all quarters. The influential D.B. Robertson, Consul at Canton, was only one of those who regarded missionaries unsympathetically and worried about mounting religious conflict.[70] Even a society like the CMS worried about the quality of the missionary recruits it was able to find. Youth and enthusiasm, as Barton had noted in India, did not necessarily serve societies well. 'I fear young missionaries are generally rather "bumptious" and do not choose to learn by the experience of their elders, – they still prove the force and

---

67  C.C. Fenn to J.S. Burdon (Peking), 16 Dec. 1869, CMS C.CH/I 1, f. 182; for Burdon, Bishop of Victoria in 1874, *CMS Register*, List I, entry 457.
68  Hart to Campbell, 16 Dec. 1873, 28 Jan. and 24 Feb. 1874, in Fairbank, *The I.G. at Peking*, nos 73, 78, 82. For McClatchie, *CMS Register*, List I, entry 343 and for Piercy, Findlay and Holdsworth, *History of the WMMS*, Vol. 5, pp. 432–4, 439–44, 451, 462.
69  For Milne, *NDNB*; for Edkins, Fairbank, *The I.G. at Peking*, no. 4.
70  Coates, *The China Consuls*, pp. 56–9, 178, 195–7.

truth of Corrie's saying, "It is a happy thing if a young missionary does not do more harm than good the first few years he is out here".[71] 'Our young missionaries go out most of them full of zeal, but they need strength, ballast, method, competence and sureness of view ... for steady hard *work*', Fenn reflected a few years later.[72] In the febrile conditions of fear, suspicion and increasing anti-foreignism, missionary stations in China offered less room than most for misplaced assertiveness and mistaken enthusiasm.

Already by the end of the 1860s, as a consequence especially of purchasing property, the China missions were the subject of severe public criticism. This was seen in correspondence between the home government and Sir Rutherford Alcock, Britain's minister to China, in parliamentary debate and in parts of the press, to an extent that provoked angry protests from the Peking missionaries. Exchanges were enough to confirm the missionary societies' sense, generated in other ways at that time, that the missions were in danger of losing much of the standing carefully built up by mid-century. Passionate defences of the missions were felt necessary.[73] However, it was to China in particular that immature zealots were being attracted – and not only from Britain – especially after 1870. The CIM was held particularly responsible for the erosion of the early nineteenth-century practice whereby the best-qualified and most highly educated volunteers were automatically considered first for India or China.

Tensions undoubtedly grew in the last quarter of the century. There were of course stupid and incompetent officials. C.A. Sinclair at Fuzhou from 1861 to 1886 was reputedly one, on bad terms with everybody.[74] But there was at the same time a growing general irritation at missionary assertiveness and their inflexible attempts to stand on their treaty 'rights'. Two could play at that game and some British consuls as late as 1890 were attempting, even if vainly, to interpret missionary rights outside the treaty ports in a highly restrictive fashion. In Fuzhou at the beginning of the 1890s, consular cases involving missions were averaging one per week and Sir Robert Hart's correspondence more generally recorded increasingly frequent clashes.[75] Positions such as that at Ichang, where W.D. Spence in the early 1880s appreciated 'the delightful countryside and the quiet studious Church of Scotland missionaries who were the only foreign residents besides himself and the Customs staff', were becoming rare.[76]

---

71 John Barton to Henry Venn, 9 March 1861, CMS CI1/037/7. For Daniel Corrie, above, Chapter 2, p. 70.

72 C.C. Fenn to W.H. Collins (Peking), 10 Dec. 1867, CMS C.CH/I 1, f. 141.

73 Fenn to Burdon, 16 Dec. 1869, CMS C.CH/I 1, f. 182 See missionaries' comments in the annual reports of the LMS and the *Chronicle of the London Missionary Society* at the time; also that by Griffith John (LMS), recycled prominently in his biography shortly after the still more fraught events of the Boxer Rebellion: R. Wardlaw Thompson, *Griffith John: The Story of Fifty Years in China* (London, 1906), pp. 251–69.

74 Coates, *The China Consuls*, pp. 211–12.

75 *Ibid.*, p. 214; Fairbank, *The I.G. at Peking*, nos 799, 800, 810, 862, 896.

76 Coates, *The China Consuls*, p. 274.

The complexity of the issues involving missionaries and converts was acute. Not only were disputes fed by anti-foreign and anti-imperialist attitudes found at all levels of Chinese society and notably in the cities where Europeans were concentrated. They were spreading more and more into the countryside and were woven into the structure especially of local kinship, lineage and village conflicts, through the influence and family networks of Chinese Christians both local and from overseas. Not only did missionaries and converts provoke conflicts, wittingly or otherwise; endemic disputes and traditional causes of violence themselves became christianised, as local rivals looked for new sources of influence and identity to strengthen their hands.[77] Missionaries were often at a loss to know where they stood because local quarrels and anti-Christian conflict frequently overlapped. Protestant denominational differences could only too easily be wedded to pre-existing disputes in what was already a deeply divided society. Even experienced missionaries were open to exploitation by opportunists looking to Christianity for political and social advantage rather then specifically religious consolations.

Far from missions ceasing to rely on the British – or Chinese – authorities for their security, the reverse was the case. Consular time given to 'missionary matters' meant less time for commercial issues, precisely the area most consuls considered their prime responsibility. For their part, missionaries did not shrink from playing up and exploiting the official connection; especially in cases where converts' interests were at stake, an ability to call on effective official intervention carried weight in attracting and maintaining church membership. Whatever members of the CIM might wish to believe, most missions were not immune from a need to assert their status. Only a short time after the settlement of 1860, CMS calculations over Hong Kong displayed as much. It was explained to one recently arrived volunteer that 'Your own particular post is in some respects important rather negatively than positively. Hong Kong does not present so many advantages for Missionary effort as some other parts of China, but the effect would be exceedingly bad if in our own seat of Government, nothing were done for the spread of the Gospel, so that if our Mission there is not doing so much good, it is at least preventing some harm.'[78] Competition between French Roman Catholics and Protestants only raised the stakes further, the French apparently being far more ready to take issue and press their claims.

Missionaries' need for defence of their interests and security was thus growing at a time when officials were becoming either less interested or less able to provide it. Some officials were worried by the trend, which they felt was exacerbated by rapidly swelling numbers of young enthusiasts disinclined to accept the wisdom of consular caution. Hart writing late in 1892 observed with foreboding that 'the

---

77  Joseph Tse-Hei Lee, *The Bible and the Gun: Christianity in South China, 1868–1900* (New York, 2002).

78  C.C. Fenn to John Piper, 27 April 1868, C.CH/I 1, f. 145; similarly to C.J. Warren, 14 March 1867, f. 125.

people at various points in interior are again harrying missionaries, but the Yamen [Office of Foreign Affairs] ignores all that it is not specially forced to recognise and foreign ministers, knowing the valuelessness of mere remonstrances and the certainty that no Govt. will nowadays *fight* for a missionary question, are but little inclined to take up the thankless task'.[79] The growth of these attitudes meant that even serious outrages, such as the Ku-tien killings in August 1895, were more likely to go unchecked. 'Diplomacy will inter them decently – and there will be occasion for similar funerals in the future.'[80] Hart was perhaps less than just to the eventual official response on this occasion, but his general prescience was demonstrated only too quickly after the outbreak of the Boxers' rising in 1899. Superficially at least, the disproportionately high number of CIM missionaries and their children killed – 79 out of 188 – demonstrated the impracticality of the radical faith mission approach and the need for continuing reliance by missions on the secular arm. Most missions and British authorities were reinforced in their belief that this was so; Lockhart's optimism was shown to be at least premature. For the CIM, however, the one mission to refuse compensation for their losses, their denial of any need for such reliance outwardly remained intact.[81]

## III

In the nineteenth century Britain emerged as the greatest of all rulers of Muslims and extended its cultural and economic influence among them well beyond the borders of its formal colonies. These developments and those within Islam itself, intertwined with the growth of the missionary movement, aroused evangelical curiosity and optimism. They raised issues concerning missionaries' relations with indigenous governments and the imperial authorities; they highlighted theological issues of significance to supporters of foreign missions. They too, like China, involved missionary societies in political agitation to an unusual extent and had a significant impact on missionary strategy.

It has already been seen how, at the start of the nineteenth century, millennial enthusiasm and eschatological speculation both had an important place in mission-ary thinking. Their impact was uneven, but their pervasiveness and importance in various forms and at different levels in British and American society and their significance in originating and sustaining the LMS, the BMS and Scottish soci-eties, have been clearly established. They prompted evangelical commentators surveying the world scene to draw attention to the significance of Islam. Preoccupations with evangelicalism, Islam and millennial events were not necessar-

79  Hart to Campbell, 30 Oct. 1892, Fairbank, *The I.G. at Peking*, no. 865; for comments in 1893 by F.S.A. Bourne, Consul at Canton, Coates, *The China Consuls*, p. 183.
80  Hart to Campbell, 11 Aug. 1895, Fairbank, *The I.G. at Peking*, no. 982.
81  Broomhall, *Hudson Taylor*, Vol. 7, pp. 456, 621–4 and chaps 10–14; Caroline Child, 'The China Inland Mission and the Boxer Rising of 1900' (unpub. MA dissertation, Reading, 1994).

ily closely combined. Nevertheless, changes in the Muslim world increasingly encouraged eschatological speculation about the 'signs of the times', stimulated study (however inconclusive) of the Bible's prophetic books and spurred on energetic, committed individuals to take up missionary work.

William Carey looked forward to the collapse of Islam following that of Rome.[82] To Melvill Horne, at a time when the 'night is far spent and the day is at hand', the fact that 'the crescent of Mahomet still usurps the places where the cross once triumphed' was one of those considerations enough to stir believers to 'understand the signs of the day and put forth those exertions to which they call us'.[83] By 1810, Anglican figures such as George Faber and Claudius Buchanan were consistently linking prophecy with the waning power of Islam as well as to that of France and Rome and the future of the Jews. William Ellis of the LMS, no Byron *manqué*, nevertheless derived satisfaction from 'the spirit of the times and the aspect of the world' when he saw 'the waning crescent sink, we believe for ever, from the horizon of Greece'.[84]

Initially, much interest centred on Henry Martyn who, between 1806 and 1812 first as an EIC chaplain along with Buchanan and finally as an independent missionary, distinguished himself in translating the Bible into Arabic, Persian and Urdu. To his patron, the Cambridge cleric Charles Simeon, Martyn was a more significant figure even than David Brainerd. To yet another of the early EIC chaplains, Simeon wrote, 'you have heard from dear Martyn, his disputations with the Mahometans and their applications to the father of the Moollahs to write a book on the evidences of the Mahometan religion. The day that such an appeal to reason shall receive the sanction of the Priests, Mahometanism will receive a fatal blow.'[85]

As Simeon's letter suggests, Martyn was one of the first engaged in what soon became the conventional approach to Islam, that of rational disputation with Muslim clerics in the expectation that Muslim defences would collapse and conversion ensue. Learned Muslims – just like educated Hindu Brahmins, it was assumed – would thus ensure that Christianity percolated downwards to their people. For the two men, this approach was bound up with another cause of particular interest to Simeon, that of the conversion of the Jews and their return to the land of Israel.[86] Application on all three fronts – Hindu, Muslim and Jewish –

---

82  De Jong, *As the Waters*, p. 180.

83  Horne, *Letters on Missions*, pp. 20–1.

84  See Buchanan's sermons for 1809–10 frequently reprinted and collected in Claudius Buchanan, *Eight Sermons* (London, 1812); De Jong, *As the Waters*, pp. 163–4, 190–7; William Ellis, *The Command and Encouragement to Communicate the Gospel. A Sermon presented before the London Missionary Society at Craven Chapel on Thursday, May 12, 1831* (London, 1831), pp. 24–5.

85  To Rev. T. Thomason, 17 July 1812, quoted in William Carus (ed.), *The Memoirs of the Life of the Reverend Charles Simeon with a Selection from his Writings and Correspondence*, 2 vols (London, 1847), Vol. 1, p. 353, and Vol. 2, pp. 435–6.

86  Martin, *Evangelicals United*, chap. 9; David Feldman, *Englishmen and Jews: Social Relations and Political Culture, 1840–1914* (New Haven, 1994), pp. 54–65.

would gradually usher in the millennium of peace and Christian harmony after which would follow the Second Coming.

For others, including Buchanan, the grounds for targeting Islam were not only suggested in the 'general contemplation of the prophecies'. They were also supported by rational observation of 'the signs of the times', among which one of the most significant was the expansion of Britain's empire in India.[87] India offered not just a back door into the Near or Middle East; there, under British auspices, Islam and Hinduism could be tackled in the same field. This was something which Martyn's lack of success in the Middle East itself might seem to support. Moreover, in India unlike the Ottoman territories, Islam could far more easily be countered with precisely the same methods by which it was itself promoted – the public reading of religious texts, counterposing Qur'an and Bible and 'the instruction of children'.[88] Thus, alongside the campaign against the East India Company for greater missionary access, there emerged the components of what became the dominant evangelical approach to Islam until the mid-century: a background in post-millennialism, none the less linked to an analysis which tied Biblical prophecy to world events; a preference for an approach via India rather then the Middle East or Ottoman Turkey; and the elevation of 'rational controversy' and school instruction over other methods.

In the 1860s, along with much else in the missionary world, this approach began to change. It did so under the influence of a growing sense that, contrary to expectations, Muslim influence was increasing and a mounting feeling that missionaries had after all neglected Islam to their cost. In Africa at least observers were often correct about the expansion, despite their imperfect knowledge of the continent especially away from the coasts. With the growth of its slave and Malay communities Cape Colony administrators even before 1814 began to support missionaries in part out of a fear of Islam.[89] In Sierra Leone, an earlier sympathy with Islamic influences seems to have begun to give way to critical concern in the 1830s and this crystallised under the impact of explorers' writings published in the 1840s and 1850s.[90] This reflected the fact that for West Africa's inland savannah region, the dominant themes of its history from the early 1800s onwards were those of the Islamic jihads, the development of Islamic states with their Muslim elites and widespread popular conversion to Islam. By mid-century, Islam had also made a significant impact on the northern fringes of Yorubaland, was a noticeable feature

---

87  See especially 'The Star in the East' (preached in Bristol, 26 Feb. 1809), in Buchanan, *Eight Sermons*, pp. 40, 42 and passim.

88  Rev. William Dealtry, *A Sermon preached ... before the Church Missionary Society for Africa and the East being their Thirteenth Anniversary* (2nd edn, London, 1813), pp. 39, 41.

89  Elphick and Giliomee (eds), *Shaping of South African Society*, p. 227; Robert C.-H. Shell, 'Between Christ and Mohammed: Conversion, Slavery and Gender in the Urban Western Cape', in Richard Elphick and Rodney Davenport, *Christianity in South Africa: A Political, Social and Cultural History* (Oxford and Cape Town, 1997), chap. 16.

90  Curtin, *Image of Africa*, pp. 405–6; Fyfe, *Sierra Leone*, passim.

of daily life in Yoruba coastal towns such as Badagry and Lagos and had penetrated a considerable distance down the Niger.[91]

An accurate appreciation of East African conditions was slower in coming and missionaries often failed to understand how little impact Islam had made on rural populations.[92] Nevertheless, from the 1870s CMS missionaries felt some cause for concern and by the 1890s there too Islamic expansion was seriously worrying contemporaries. This was so in Buganda from 1890, despite the establishment of Christian influence in the government after 1884–86 and in Tanganyika from much the same time. There, German policy was felt by 1890 to have given rise to a determination to drive out the Europeans and the colonial government was criticised for employing Arabs and Swahili and for spreading Islamic beliefs through the schools. 'Plantation overseers and railway foremen, as well as subordinate government officials were blamed for proselytism.'[93]

In the 1860s there were figures such as the explorer Richard Burton prepared to anticipate an Islamic conquest of Africa and even in the early 1870s Bosworth Smith wrote of 'Mohammedanism' in Africa as 'spreading itself by giant strides almost year by year'.[94] Hyperbole perhaps, but by the 1880s, there was widespread belief that Islam was making steady headway not only in most parts of that continent but elsewhere too. The editor of the 1888 London missionary conference's proceedings virtually took this 'discouraging fact' for granted.[95] Events in North Africa were regarded as offering particular support for such visions. The Urabist revolt of 1881–82 in Egypt and more especially the rise of Mahdist power in the Sudan, were seen as strong evidence of an Islamic resurgence. Early nationalist critics of the British occupation of Egypt, for example, took a distinctly pan-Islamic line in their periodical *al-Urwa al-Wuthqa* ('The Indissoluble Bond') which was aimed at Muslims everywhere under British rule. Lord Cromer banned the offending publication, playing the while on the susceptibility of British opinion to any suggestion that strong undercurrents of Muslim fanaticism were always ready to erupt. The gradual consolidation of a vociferous nationalist movement only gave added point to these suspicions on the part of a broader British public, while

---

91 H.F.C. Smith, 'A Neglected Theme of West African History: The Islamic Revolutions of the Nineteenth Century', *Journal of the Historical Society of Nigeria* 2 (1961), 169–85; Ayandele, *The Missionary Impact*, pp. 117–18; T.G.O. Gbadamosi, *The Growth of Islam among the Yoruba, 1841–1908* (London, 1978).

92 For contemporary fears of reform movements, Turkish ambitions in Arabia and their Indian implications, R.J. Gavin, 'The Bartle Frere Mission to Zanzibar, 1873', *HJ* 5, 2 (1962), 122–48, esp. 123–9.

93 James D. Holway, 'C.M.S. Contact with Islam in East Africa before 1914', *Journal of Religion in Africa* 4 (1971–72), 200–12; J.A.P. Kieran, 'The Holy Ghost Fathers in East Africa 1863–1914' (unpub. Ph.D. thesis, London, 1966), pp. 358–63, quotation from p. 361.

94 Christine Bolt, *Victorian Attitudes to Race* (London, 1971), pp. 115–16; Reginald Bosworth Smith, *Mohammed and the Mohammedans* (London, 1874), pp. 31–2.

95 Rev. James Johnson (ed.), *Report of the Centenary Conference on the Protestant Missions of the World held in Exeter Hall (June 9th–19th) London, 1888*, 2 vols (London, 1888), p. xviii.

Cromer himself became steadily more concerned at the prospect of a movement shaped by 'pan-Islamic fanaticism'.[96]

Whatever the looseness of contemporary reasoning, the steady development of such general concerns in the second half of the century is understandable. At least some rulers in northern Nigeria interpreted events such as the French invasion of Algeria and the Russo-Turkish War of 1877–78 within a religious framework that demanded solidarity with their co-religionists. Historians have suggested that even a relatively short delay in the partition of Africa among the European powers might well have seen the continent north of the Zambezi absorbed into the Islamic world. Indeed, 'In one sense the partition of Africa was a device to contain or counteract the expansion of militant Islam, which the British as well as the French feared greatly. Partition could be described as a struggle for control of north, west and central Africa between Christian European and Muslim Arab-Africans.'[97] When contemporaries looked to India, some at least discerned a similar phenomenon. Whereas Buddhism and Hinduism were thought to be barely more than static, Islam was seen as expanding its influence in North India and Bengal.[98]

The late nineteenth-century world was thus one in which consciousness of the spread and power of Islam grew markedly. As Sir Charles Eliot, first Commissioner of the East African Protectorate, expressed it, 'In view of the power which Islam has shown of spreading among African races and the damage done on the Upper Nile by the Khalifa and the Dervishes, the existence of this Christian state [Uganda and the East African Protectorate] must be regarded as a great guarantee for the preservation of peace.'[99] However, while practical men such as Eliot thought of holding the balance, evangelicals thought in theological and often more dramatic terms.

Illustrating the vigour of prophetic study, the vicar of Fareham read a paper to a CMS prayer meeting in 1881. 'Many of you, probably, have come to the same conclusion that I have, that the fifth horn in the vision of the ram and the he goat in the eighth chapter of Daniel is a symbol of the Mohammedan power, and that its time for practising and prospering against the Prince of princes is now coming to an end. And many of you, probably, consider that the drying up of the River Euphrates predicted in the sixteenth chapter of Revelation, the effect of which is to be "the kings of the East", or the Eastern kingdoms, finding their way to Christ, is now fulfilling in the exsiccation and absorption of the Mohammedan power as a political and ruling power – that power which certainly has been the most impregnable obstacle to the spread of the Gospel among Eastern kingdoms. Certainly it is

96 Afaf Lutfi al-Sayyid, *Cromer in Egypt* (London, 1966), chap. 5; G.N. Sanderson, 'The Nile Basin and the Eastern Horn, 1870–1908', in Roland Oliver and G.N. Sanderson (eds), *The Cambridge History of Africa: Vol. 6 from 1870 to 1905* (Cambridge, 1985), p. 626, also 620, 628.
97 Ayandele, *The Missionary Impact*, pp. 121–2; Roland Oliver, 'Reviews of Europe and Africa', *JAH* 5 (1964), 134; quotation from Hyam, *Britain's Imperial Century*, p. 216.
98 Bolt, *Victorian Attitudes to Race*, p. 173, with references.
99 In C.S. Goldman (ed.), *The Empire and the Century* (London, 1905), p. 865.

a sign of the times that the Crescent is waning before the Cross, that though Mohammedanism as a religion is not worn out, Mohammedan nations have come under the power or the influence of Christian rulers. Surely, then, the conversion of Mohammedans should be a special subject at missionary conferences. When Daniel knew, from the study of prophecy and the signs of the times, that great religious changes were impending, he set his face unto the Lord God to seek by prayer and supplication the accomplishment of God's promises.'[100]

William Dumergue was not alone in thinking that he and his audience should be following Daniel's example closely. Two decades later, James Stewart, then Duff Missionary Lecturer and neither excitable enthusiast nor mere armchair expositor, in turn defined the problem for his hard-headed listeners at New College, Edinburgh. 'Taking Mohammedanism as a whole, with its strange and wonderful career, the difficulty is how to fit that career, as an event permitted by God, into the progress of the world, or into the evolution of its spiritual history, and how to understand the purpose it was meant to serve.'[101] Here, in other words, was one of the continuing great religious questions of the age.

Like most great questions, it was also an open one. 'No theory seems fully to explain the subject', Stewart continued.[102] Simultaneously, however, writing of the 'Struggle for the Continent' between Christianity, paganism and 'Mohammedanism', he suggested that issues were coming to a climax. 'The struggle between them is not new. It is rather being renewed and this time will probably be final.'[103] Attempts at answers were often unimpressive. In his centenary history of the CMS, Eugene Stock fell back on ambiguity. 'The False Prophet still holds sway over the sacred Lands of the East. Again and again Turkey has seemed to be breaking up. Again and again she has been propped up by the mutual jealousies of the European Powers. Perhaps the reign of Islam over the cities and provinces dear to us for Christ's sake and the Gospel's is to continue till the Lord Himself come.'[104] The significance of Stock's comment, however, lies not in the answer he offered but in the fact that he felt it necessary to raise the question. As Secretary to the CMS, Stock was famously sensitive to the evangelical currents of his day and there seems no reason to reject his feeling that this was an issue of importance to many ordinary and more than a few not-so-ordinary people.

When Stock and Stewart were writing round about 1900, there was already a well-established tradition of practical missionary concern with the Muslim world dating back more than a century.[105] However, few missionaries had followed Martyn,

---

100  Rev. W.S. Dumergue, 'C.M.S. Work among the Mohammedans', *CMI* (Jan. 1882), pp. 18–23.
101  James Stewart, *Dawn in the Dark Continent: Or Africa and Its Missions. The Duff Missionary Lectures for 1902* (Edinburgh and London, 1903), pp. 57–8.
102  *Ibid.*
103  *Ibid.*, p. 40.
104  Stock, *History of the Church Missionary Society*, Vol. 2, p. 155.
105  L.L. Vander Werff, *Christian Missions to Muslims: Anglican and Reformed Approaches in India and the Near East, 1800–1938* (South Pasadena, 1977).

for which there are various explanations. The physical dangers of proselytisation in Muslim countries and the legal penalties for missionaries and still more any converts, were likely to be far greater than elsewhere. Attempts to convert Muslims increasingly seemed unproductive, confirming the long-established Western view of Muslim bigotry and intolerance. In a world of scarce missionary resources it was therefore thought better to deploy them elsewhere.[106] A major problem also seemed to exist in the shape of the ancient Eastern churches which continued their sometimes fitful existence in the Ottoman Turkish Empire, a region which to Henry Venn 'must be regarded as the centre of Mohammedanism'.[107]

Missionary effort in the Ottoman world was felt to hold out little promise when set against the visible evidence of what British and American Protestants saw as decayed and corrupt Christian churches. In India, the practice of religious disputation continued vigorously into the 1850s, and the building of schools and churches in pursuit of influence went on for much longer, but in the Ottoman empire evangelical efforts to confront Islam were often essentially indirect. On one side were those, such as the members of the American Board and, from Britain, chiefly high Anglican churchmen, who continued to support the reform and reinvigoration of the orthodox churches; on the other stood those who had gradually become convinced that the ancient churches were not only corrupt – which encouraged Muslim and Roman Catholic ambition and resurgence – but essentially heretical and their priests superstitious.

In the second camp, especially as the new optimism associated with the establishment in 1841 of the Jerusalem bishopric declined, were many supporters of the CMS. The *Church Missionary Intelligencer* was prone to express despair at the condition of Eastern Christianity. Above all in Jerusalem, it was said, 'Christianity can be contemplated in its last stages of rottenness and humiliation', encouraging the hatred and contempt of Muslims and removing all chance of conversions. For the famous Punjab missionary Robert Clark, it was a debased Christianity which had called Islam into being in the first place and others were firmly convinced that Mariolatry had had much to do with the expansion of Islam into both Arabia and Persia.[108] Lacking much confidence in the possibility of reform in the orthodox churches, many evangelicals therefore had no hesitation in attempting to convert Eastern Christians to a defensible form of their faith. The CMS mission to

---

106 E.g., Rev. James Vaughan, *The Trident, the Crescent and the Cross: A View of the Religious History of India …* (London, 1876), pp. 189–90.

107 Quoted by Stock, *History of the CMS*, Vol. 2, p. 144; Harris, *Nothing but Christ*, pp. 51–8, 73–5, 101–5, 122–32; H.L. Murre-van den Berg, 'Why Protestant Churches? The American Board and the Eastern Churches: Mission among "Nominal" Christians (1820–70)', in Pieter N. Holtrop and Hugh McLeod, *Missions and Missionaries. Studies in Church History Subsidia 13* (Woodbridge, 2000), pp. 98–111.

108 Robert Clark, 'New Protestant Church at Jerusalem', *CMI* 11(March 1875), p. 80; Robert Clark, 'Missions to Mohammedans', *CMI* 2, n.s. (Feb. 1877), 85–96; Robert Bruce, 'Persia in Its Relation to the Kingdom of God', four parts, *CMI* 6–7, n.s. (Nov. 1881– Feb. 1882).

Palestine established in 1851 may have been directed principally at Muslims but it also had eastern Christians in its sights.[109]

The CMS Palestine Mission had a negligible impact and, despite some expressions of pious optimism about fresh opportunities,[110] British effort such as it was in respect of the Ottoman empire seems to have been directed into the Turkish Mission Aid Society (also known as the Western Asia Mission Aid Society), set up to help American efforts in the Levant. In India, the development of Martyn's legacy in the 1840s and 1850s by Dr Carl Pfander and Thomas Valpy French at Agra with the help of sympathetic officials such as William Muir was of considerable intellectual interest, but had only limited impact both locally and in Britain.[111] For large numbers of missionaries and their supporters the sense that evangelical efforts were paltry and ineffectual seemed only to be confirmed by the experience of the Indian Mutiny and rebellion in 1857. Belief in Muslim advance thus blossomed in the 1850s and 1860s along with the parallel feeling that missionary efforts had been both neglectful of Islam and misconceived in practice.

Against this background of Islamic growth and evangelical guilt, mid-century events in the Muslim world precipitated calls for an evangelical response. A writer in the *CM Intelligencer*, noting on the Niger 'the great battle-field, where Islamism, by commercial enterprise and acts of predatory warfare, has been aggressing upon a weak heathenism', suggested that now was the time for action. 'We do not mean that Mohammedanism is impregnable, or that, if it had succeeded in completing its line of defences, that then we should consider its position unassailable and turn away from it in despair ... but it is an advantage to come in before Mohammedanism has completed the absorption of the heathen systems and while the populations, disunited on the subject of religion, are more approachable.'[112] Islam, in other words, could be countered in precisely the same way as corrupt Western influences.

Other aspects of the picture were drawn together, for example, in a missionary appeal made in 1860.[113] J. Müehleisen-Arnold not only defined 'Mohammedans' along with 'Jews' and 'Heathen' as one of the three 'natural divisions' of the mission field but was highly critical of the paucity of Protestant, especially Anglican, efforts to reach them. In these circumstances, 'Can we wonder that ... the late mutiny should not only first break out at Meerut, but that it should breathe a spirit and bear a character, essentially Mohammedan? ... When the God of

---

109 Stock, *History of the CMS*, Vol. 2, chap. 41 'Jerusalem and Constantinople: The Jew, The Turk and The Christian'.

110 E.g., Rev. John Grant, *Religious Aspect of the War with Russia. A sermon ... on the 26th April, 1854* (Dublin, 1854), pp. 17–24.

111 Powell, *Muslims and Missionaries* and her articles listed in the bibliography.

112 Report of the 1857 expedition up the Niger, *CMI* 9, 2 (Feb. 1858), 28–36.

113 Rev. Dr J. Müehleisen-Arnold, *The Society for Propagating the Gospel among the Moslems, in connection with the Church of England; Its First Appeal on behalf of 180 millions of Mohammedans* (London, 1860); *DEB*, Vol. 1, pp. 28–9.

nations saw how ardently England engaged in the Crimean War for the defence of the territorial integrity of Turkey, whilst she made not the faintest effort for the conversion of either Turk or the Sepoy, He inflicted a chastisement upon us which we should do well to consider. The Mohammedans have given us bitter cause last-ingly to remember not only their existence, but also the great work we have to do among them.'[114]

In appealing to the 'essential' nature of Islam, Arnold was reviving older stereo-types that had persisted for centuries. David Livingstone's exposure of the extent of the Swahili-Arab-dominated slave trade tended in the same direction, emphasis-ing Islam's uniform connection with cruelty and fanaticism. At the same time, however, there seem to be new components in the prevailing outlook. Not only were there the calls to action, the sense that Islam could not be left quietly to wither away, the view that great events or at least new opportunities were indicated by distur-bances among Muslims and arguments that Islamic expansion was sufficiently seri-ous to require counter-initiatives by the missionary movement. Just as the American rebellion and the French revolution had done in their time, so the Indian Mutiny also revived to an unparalleled degree the evangelical conviction that national and missionary slackness had resulted in divine reprimand. Bishop Daniel Wilson's last sermon in Calcutta's cathedral, on 'Humiliation in National Troubles', was one of many which reminded churchgoers of the penalties for inac-tion and of the realities of divine judgement as well as providential intervention in human affairs. As Wilson explained, 'He regards nations in their collective capacity. Individuals He chiefly punishes in the next world; but collective bodies, as they will have no future existence, in this.'[115]

Although these emerging views shaped the context in which missions were to address Islam in the later part of the century, action was still slow in coming. 'Islam sees all her frontiers falling in, Rome her centre heaving beneath her', wrote William Arthur, one of the WMMS secretaries: 'humanity, sighing under the feet of both, does not ask, "Will they fall?" but "When?".'[116] Religious revival in 1859 and the attractions of new initiatives in China and Africa, rather than the Islamic heartlands, caught popular attention. The Punjab Missionary conference at Lahore in 1862–63 brought together all the Protestant societies save the SPG, but was not followed up elsewhere and Arnold's society did not take wing. It required a domes-tic British revival in the mid-1870s, together with renewed pre-millennial specula-tion fostered by the Mildmay and Keswick conferences and the Ottoman and Egyptian crises of 1875–82, to forge the serious engagement of the evangelical community with Islam.

---

114 Müerhleisen-Arnold, *Society for Propagating the Gospel*, p. 8.
115 Daniel Wilson, *Humiliation in National Troubles. A Sermon by the Bishop of Calcutta, delivered Friday, July 24th, 1857* (Calcutta, 1857), p. 11; Josiah Bateman, *The Life of the Rt. Rev. Daniel Wilson, D.D.*, 2 vols (London, 1860), Vol. 2, pp. 392–401.
116 John Kent, *Holding the Fort: Studies in Victorian Revivalism* (London, 1978), p. 95.

The international spurs to more effective interest in missions to Muslims lay first in the troubles of the Papacy, which in 1870–71 finally lost its territories outside Rome. Following its suppression in 1864 of CMS and SPG work begun in 1856, the Ottoman empire's troubles also seemed to be escalating, with serious internal disturbances in its Balkan provinces, its loss of Cyprus to Britain and threats to its existence from Russia, bankruptcy and political fragmentation especially in Egypt.

These events were more than sufficient to prompt supporters of missions to reconsider their approaches to Islam. In Anglican circles, signs of this can be seen in papers at the Church Congresses of 1873 and 1874 and a long discussion of recent policy in the *CM Intelligencer* in January 1875. A major conference on missions to Mohammedans was convened at CMS House in Salisbury Square in October 1875 to plan a general forward strategy.[117] Delaying 'new aggressive measures' in Turkey itself until the immediate crisis was over, the conference drew up plans for initiatives in Sierra Leone, Lagos and amongst the Hausa. Noting the recent conference of Indian missionaries in Allahabad in 1873, the gathering asked the Missionary Conferences in Bengal and the North West Provinces to make further plans.[118]

It is difficult to escape the conclusion that millennial awareness influenced this thinking and shaped many people's reactions. Although 'it would be quite out of our province to discuss prophetical questions, however important they may be', wrote the editor of the *CM Intelligencer*, 'we cannot refrain from a passing notice of the wonderful manner in which the whole question of Mohammedanism is now absorbing public attention'. Behind the scenes, several of the regular meetings of the Mission Secretaries Association reviewed Islam's expansion and the best ways of combating it. Still more unusual were the two opportunities its members gave Reverend W.J. Adams of the London Jews Society to speak on prophetic studies and their fulfilment.[119]

The Bishop of Lincoln was moved to give a public lead, feeling it right to demonstrate how contemporary events confirmed views he had long held. A sermon the bishop delivered in September 1876 inevitably suggests the possibility that much of the hostility to Disraeli's policy on the Eastern Question may have been fuelled by a belief that, by defending Ottoman territorial integrity and preventing a Russian occupation of Constantinople, the Prime Minister was confirming British policy on a course which would work against the prophesied

---

117 Stock, *History of the CMS*, Vol. 3, pp. 12–13; 'Recent Manifestations of Mohammedan Intolerance', *CMI* 11 (Jan. 1875), 5–18; 'Minutes of the Conference on Missions to the Mohammedans held ... on the 20th and 21st of October, 1875'.
118 *CMI* 1, n.s. (March 1876), 177–8.
119 'On Missions to Mohammedans', *CMI* 1, n.s. (Jan. 1876), 6–14; London Secretaries Association, minutes Vol. 5: 'The present condition of Israel indicative of an approaching fulfilment of Divine purposes towards them', 8 March 1876 and 'The peculiar claims, advantages and blessedness of Prophetic Studies', 14 Nov. 1877.

collapse of Islam. The conversion of Turks in such circumstances would not only have benefited them, but would bring their personal injection of 'new life into our languid Christianity' and other advantages such as 'an answer to the scepticism of the age and a new proof of the Divine origin of the Gospel'.[120] On other occasions Wordsworth was still more enthusiastic in weaving together worldly events pointing to Islam's demise – 'the acquisition of the island of Cyprus', 'military successes in North-Western India, against a Mohammedan power' – with the apocalyptic symbols contained in the book of Revelation.[121] Gladstone in 1876 and 1880 was perhaps the beneficiary not only of righteous anger at indefensible atrocities but of both pre- and post-millennial enthusiasm.

In the periodical prints, regrets for the insufficiency of past efforts were matched by claims that Muslims as much as Christians were aware they had reached a major turning point. For one prominent convert, 'Either Christianity will win the day, or the people of India will sink into depths of wickedness hitherto unknown. One or other must be the result of the present state of things.' The time had arrived for a unanimous attack and new methods were called for. T.V. French observed how 'everywhere we find Mohammedanism wide awake and on the alert, ... hotly and sorely pressed in a life and death struggle' and argued that progress in north India now depended not on the earlier methods of controversy so much as on aggressive preaching, especially by local Christians.[122] While the missionaries' schools remained prominent, by the end of the decade a broader spectrum of agencies was being pressed forward, now including medical missions and 'women's work among women'. In 1880, for example, the Church of England Zenana Missionary Society was established; by taking advantage of the growing metropolitan demand for women to have a larger role in the work, its organisers were able to extend evangelism into spheres of life normally closed to male missionaries.

Several factors contributed after 1880 to sustain this growth in attention to Islam. Of particular importance was the extension of British control over Islamic areas in Africa. Well ahead of the CMS's re-establishment in 1882 of its operations in Cairo in the wake of Britain's occupation, there was already under way a sustained debate as to the point from which Christian missions might best be launched against Islam. The Society's conference of 1875, referred to above, had

---

120  Christopher Wordsworth, *The Mohammedan Woe and Its Passing Away. A Sermon* (London, 1876), quotation at pp. 27–8.

121  Christopher Wordworth, 'The Decline of Mohammedanism a Signal for a greater spread of the Gospel; which will be to some a Woe', in *Miscellanies Literary and Religious*, 3 vols (London, 1879), Vol. 3, pp. 100–16; also Samuel Garratt, *A Commentary on The Revelation of St. John, considered as The Divine Book of History* (London, 1866; 2nd edn, 1878).

122  Vaughan, *The Trident*, p. 189; Rev. Imad-ud-Din, 'The Results of the Controversy in North India with Mohammedans', *CMI* 11 (Sept. 1875), 276–80; Rev. T.V. French, 'Address on Missionary Effort Among Mohammedans', *CMI* 2, n.s. (Sept. 1877), 577–88; Stock, *History of the CMS*, Vol. 3, p. 120; Alan Guenther, 'Controversy as a "Necessary Evil"? Perspectives on Missions to Muslims in India in the Late Nineteenth Century', *NAMP Position Paper 82* (Cambridge 1998).

already gone some way in this, for example, mapping out a strategy whereby missionaries advanced into the western Sudan from Sierra Leone and up the Niger and endorsing the view that 'Arabic work' should be cultivated rather than Turkish. In his turn Robert Clark urged the case for the Punjab, where he had worked for so long, as a key entry point.[123] Even earlier, the Reverend Henry ('Eloquent') Johnson, a close associate of Bishop Crowther, was sent by the CMS to Palestine during 1874–76, to study Hebrew and Arabic, so equipping himself better for work among the Muslims of the Sierra Leone interior. While there he made the breadth of his own missionary outlook plain. Writing to the CMS Secretary, Edward Hutchinson, he explained that he was 'following the fortunes of the [CMS] East African mission with patriotic interest. I say "patriotic" because I feel that whatever concerns Africa, it matters not in whatever part of the vast Continent, concerns, or should concern me.'[124]

The ripples of the British invasion of Egypt were felt in the missionary world no less than in the corridors of Europe's foreign offices and its millennial significance did not go unremarked. For Major-General Haig of the CMS Parent Committee, 'the days of the Mohammedan Antichrist are numbered. The disintegration of the Turkish Empire proceeds apace'; 'the sudden overthrow of rebellion in Egypt and the occupation of that country by our army' demanded a response and he argued for an initiative at Aden. Haig's writing and lobbying paid off, coinciding as it did with Mahdist successes in the Sudan. The CMS Committee officially adopted Aden as a jumping-off point for the interior in March 1885 and before long the projected importance of Muscat was sufficient to persuade Bishop French, already retired from his work in Lahore, to undertake this new venture. With support from the Free Church of Scotland, the Cambridge Semitic scholar and evangelical Ion Keith-Falconer set himself up at Aden in 1886 and the devotees of Mildmay took up the baton, discussing these issues at length in their 1887 gathering.[125]

Khartoum emerged at this time as a still more powerful focus of evangelical ambitions. As Egyptian control over the Sudan disintegrated, Khartoum was established as the centre of both revolution and the new Mahdist state, exemplar of Islam's late-century reform and expansion. Not only was Muslim excitement at this development mirrored in evangelical fascination with the correspondences between Muslim and Christian views about Christ's Second Advent, the Antichrist and the Mahdi.[126] General Gordon's death in the city early in 1885 gave

---

123 *CMI* 7, n.s. (Nov. 1882), 697; Stock, *History of the CMS*, Vol. 3, p. 119; *CMI* (Feb. 1877), p. 95.

124 Johnson to Hutchinson, 24 June 1875, CMS Archives, C.M./O 38. My gratitude to David Killingray for this reference.

125 Maj.-Gen. F. Haig, 'Aden as Mission Station', *CMI* 7, n.s. (Dec. 1882), 713–22; Herbert Birks, *The Life and Correspondence of Thomas Valpy French, First Bishop of Lahore*, 2 vols (London, 1895), chaps 25–7; R. Sinker, *Memorials of the Hon. Ion Keith-Falconer* (London, 1888), chap. 8 'Aden'; *The Mildmay Conference 1887* (London, 1887).

126 Rev. Worthington Jukes, 'Imam Mahdy and Dajjal, the Muhammedan Antichrist', *CMI* 8, n.s. (Oct 1883), 596–601.

it additional symbolic significance in the confrontation between Christianity and Islam. With his Chinese experience, contempt for convention and his claims to embody Christian principle in action, Gordon was already an influential figure before he returned to the Sudan, both in evangelical circles and especially with the lay young caught up in the revivalist milieu of the period. His death became martyrdom, martyrdom in turn the highest heroism, appealing to the faith missions' emphasis on commitment and sacrifice.

People such as Keith-Falconer saw themselves following Gordon's example; others attempted to follow in his footsteps, which for long meant Cairo. As British forces advanced up the Nile in 1897–98, Douglas Thornton's determination to engage with 'the Mohammedans' led him to review the possible openings; Cairo, he wrote, 'grows upon me more and more, for I believe prophecy indicates the future importance of Egypt in this question'.[127] Shortly after Kitchener's victory at Omdurman (September 1898) marked the military reconquest of the Sudan, Temple Gairdner, for example, travelling secretary of the Student Christian Mission, wrote to his close friend Thornton as the latter departed for Cairo with the CMS. 'You are having the privilege and joy of going to the very land and the very people of one whom we love. May you go in the quietness and peace with which Gordon went (by the same route as you) nearly fifteen years ago to his death. Thanks be to God, loneliness, anxiety, danger, were *less of realities* to him than the still atmosphere where dwell[s] Christ ... Gordon is our friend, our brother.' Gairdner regarded Khartoum as of key importance, but, with missionary activity in the Sudan remaining severely restricted, he joined Thornton in Cairo a year later.[128]

The importance attached to Khartoum and Cairo was enhanced by the fact that influence gained there was influence exerted not only in Africa but throughout the entire Muslim world. Reckoning that 'the Arabic language is read by as many people as Chinese', Thornton regarded Islam as *the* great obstacle; for him Christian victory against Islam in many places hinged on making an impact at its heart. Thornton's mention of Arabic and Chinese provides a useful reminder both of the global terms of reference habitually employed by leading missionaries and society organisers and of how the world was steadily becoming a smaller place. So while he worked away in Cairo, Thornton also read about Emin Pasha in central Africa and 'meditated on Stanford's map of the Nile Valley. Every visitor to the house must have a look at it. Day after day I open it and study its contents. It is the burden of my heart that all these tribes be reached. It was Gordon's wish.'[129]

As seen above, Hausaland – northern Nigeria – offered another important objective. For many missionary recruits in the 1880s and 1890s, the western Sudan

---

127 Sinker, *Memorials*, pp. 100–2; W.H.T. Gairdner, *D.M. Thornton: A Study in Missionary Ideals and Methods* (3rd edn, London 1909), pp. 50–1.
128 C.E. Padwick, *Temple Gairdner of Cairo* (2nd edn, London 1930), pp. 68–9.
129 Gairdner, *Thornton*, pp. 95, 114–5.

rather than India or the Nile valley was 'undoubtedly the opportunity of the hour', as Thornton put it in 1897.[130] It not only combined access to the challenging frontier of Islam's engagement with other African religions but until 1900 was a region seen as still lying beyond both colonial controls and the corrupting effects of Western secular influences. It was thus a perfect arena for those imbued with the enthusiasms of the 'faith' missions and influenced by the pre-millennial concern for rapid and far-reaching evangelisation. In the wake of their onslaught on Bishop Crowther's Niger Mission, Robinson's and Brooke's Sudan Mission Party therefore set to work in the north. Rather than discouraging others, its failure seems to have inspired figures such as Charles H. Robinson, Walter Miller and Bishop Tugwell to press ahead in their turn a few years later.[131]

## IV

The mid-century waning of missionary enthusiasm had a profound effect on the pattern of missionary thought and activity, notwithstanding occasional outbursts of excitement such as accompanied Livingstone's crossing of Africa. The record elsewhere – in India, the West Indies, New Zealand – was heavy with disappointment if not a sense of failure. Historians sensing this atmosphere have been inclined to see a tendency for missions to fall back on a reinvigorated imperial control and intervention as the answer to their problems.[132] However, such a strategy was of limited applicability. Missions, as this chapter has shown, branched out in several new directions. Even in Africa, where the possibilities for territorial empire were most extensive, many missions devised wholly different plans for recovery and advance. These will now be examined. Empire and the interventions of a colonial ruler were one thing, missionary enterprise only too often quite another.

---

130  *Ibid.*, p. 51.

131  Andrew Porter, 'Cambridge, Keswick'; 'Evangelical Enthusiasm'; 'The Hausa Association: Sir George Goldie, the Bishop of Dover and the Niger in the 1890s', *JICH* 7, 2 (1979), 149–79; Frieder Ludwig, 'The Making of a Late Victorian Missionary [J.A.Robinson]', *Neue Zeitschrift für Missionswissenschaft* 47, 4 (1991), 269–90 but esp. 280, 282, 289; and below, Chapter 11, pp. 289, 295.

132  A.J. Temu, *British Protestant Missions* (London, 1972); Nancy Uhlar Murray, 'Nineteenth Century Kenya and the "Imperial Race for Christ"', in B.A. Ogot (ed.), *Kenya in the Nineteenth Century* (Nairobi, 1985), pp. 228–58.

# ~9~
# Missionary traditions, c. 1860–95: adaptations and consequences (1)

Feelings of disaffection, disillusionment or merely disappointment with their record contributed substantially to the mid-century decline in support and enthusiasm for the well-established missionary societies. The radical energy and keen sense of direction, theological as well as geographical, present in the faith missions, represented one positive response to this, examined in the previous chapter. Their romantic vision, incorporating the doctrinal and organisational simplicity of what they supposed to be the world of the first apostles and the early church, had a wide appeal. For most evangelicals, however, the future lay not in wholesale rejection of the recent past and the mounting of new kinds of mission but in the revival and adaptation of existing and more familiar traditions. Despite Anglo-Catholic reservations, Anglican traditions and their partial merger with a broader non-denominational revivalism proved particularly fertile in this respect.

## I

Some of the earliest signs of this process, combining revival and adaptation under the umbrella of a new society, can be found in the Oxford and Cambridge Mission to Central Africa, launched in November 1859 and soon known as the Universities' Mission to Central Africa (UMCA). Its establishment in the context of the residual enthusiasm still felt in Cambridge for David Livingstone's challenge two years before and the mission's first hesitant movements in East Central Africa under Livingstone's direction, have often resulted in its association with the banner of 'Christianity and commerce'. Bishop Wilberforce's peripatetic sermonising on its behalf in 1860, extolling Britain's providential role in opening up Africa's fertility and abundance to Christian commerce, gave further point to the connection. However, this campaign was temporarily significant but ultimately no more than incidental to its development.[1] On this occasion and for some time after, the scientific, anti-slave-trade and legitimate commercial interests were following no more than half-heartedly in a missionary wake. After the death of its first leader, none of these connections was able to prevent the mission's financial collapse, the withdrawal of Trinity College Dublin and Durham universities from the project or the need for not just a temporary withdrawal but an entirely new start from Zanzibar some years later.

---

1 A.R. Ashwell and R.G. Wilberforce, *Life of the Right Reverend Samuel Wilberforce, D.D.*, 3 vols (London, 1880–2), Vol. 2, pp. 421–2, 443–5, 449–50.

Both in conception and in sustaining the UMCA through the early years in Zanzibar, the mission's driving force lay with men of the high church party in the Church of England, such as Selwyn, Samuel Wilberforce and Robert Gray, Bishop of Cape Town. They believed that the future of Anglican overseas missions, perhaps of the Church of England itself, lay in the consecration of 'missionary bishops'. They were more than ever conscious of the ease and rapidity with which nonconformist parties could establish a mission and take the lead in new areas. Nor was the Anglican church simply sluggish by comparison with the voluntary, lay-dominated societies. Some years after its foundation, its second bishop, William Tozer, still felt that Anglican appeal, energy and ecclesiastical principle were in short supply. 'Nothing', he wrote in 1871, 'can be more unsatisfactory than the whole length and breadth of our present mission organization, C.M.S. plainly anti-episcopal, S.P.G. great with factions and dry as dust'.[2] What were required were bishops able to operate on their own and entirely outside the colonial empire. Taking some of their inspiration from the contemporary experience of westward expansion in the United States, they looked to bishops as leaders capable of building up the church from nothing, operating independently of any state and not enthroned as the coping stone in an otherwise complete colonial edifice.[3]

Charles Mackenzie had by 1859 confirmed his high church credentials when as archdeacon of Durban he clashed with Bishop Colenso over the latter's wish to enlarge the role of the laity in the local church organisation. After further serious conflicts with the white members of his Durban congregation over the integration of black and white Christians, he also expressed an interest in plans for a missionary bishopric for Zululand.[4] When these fell through, he offered his services to the SPG and it was for him a short step to acceptance of an invitation to become bishop 'of the mission to the tribes dwelling in the neighbourhood of Lake Nyassa and the River Shiré'. His consecration at Cape Town in 1861 was expensive, not least on account of the £250 passage for participation by the Bishop of St Helena. For campaigners such as Gray, however, obliged to raid his diocesan coffer for the occasion, the precedent was doubtless cheap at the price. Mackenzie thereby became the first purely 'missionary' bishop, attached to no territorial diocese and illustrating the constitutional possibility of complete separation between church and state in the process of missionary expansion.[5] The first link beyond Natal in a chain of

---

2  Tozer to Edward Steere, 21 March 1871, quoted in D.R.J. Neave, 'Aspects of the Universities' Mission to Central Africa, 1858–1900' (unpub. M.Phil. dissertation, York, 1974), p. 6.

3  W.C. Doane, *The Life and Writings of George Washington Doane, D.D., LL.D.*, 4 vols (New York, 1860), Vol. 1, chap. 5, 'English Correspondence – Visit to England' and Vol. 2, pp. 399–425, 'Sermon VIII: The Missionary Bishop'.

4  Harvey Goodwin, *Memoir of Bishop Mackenzie* (Cambridge, 1864), pp. 124–31; Guy, *The Heretic*, pp. 86–9.

5  Charles Gray (ed.), *Life of Robert Gray Bishop of Cape Town and Metropolitan of Africa*, 2 vols (London, 1876), Vol. 1, pp. 465–9.

episcopally led special missions from Cape to Cairo, a vision raised by Gray at Mackenzie's consecration, was in place long before Sir Charles Metcalfe and Cecil Rhodes dreamed of their railway.[6]

In its early days the UMCA received some practical support from members of the SPG, for example through the handling of its finances in a special fund, the provision of publicity and help with office space. However, relations became steadily more acrimonious and were finally broken off in 1881. The narrowly Anglo-Catholic character of the mission was thus strengthened and its base moved out of the universities into the parishes especially of London and the south of England. Simultaneously it expanded significantly on the African mainland and in 1892 was divided into two with the creation of the diocese of Nyasaland (renamed Likoma in 1895). The extension of stations and schools, the growth of an African clergy and indigenous evangelists, provided the necessary bulwarks for institution-alised additions to the UMCA preserve. A new diocese followed for Northern Rhodesia in 1910.

Notwithstanding uncertainty as to how Mackenzie was to develop his mission, the novel hallmarks of the UMCA were evident from the start and were progres-sively accentuated. The pattern of the voluntary society was almost entirely aban-doned. Aided by a small informal committee, Mackenzie was only the first in a line of bishops to play a central part in raising money and selecting volunteers when at home, as well as directing the venture in the field. To be remote, but not entirely cut off, from the other agents of expansion was the ideal. Mackenzie's Natal experience had taught him – as settler colonies had others – the value of work in 'the regions beyond'. 'Nothing can so interfere with missionary operations as the presence of a white population uninfluenced in heart by Christianity.'[7] On the other hand he and his party were happy to take advantage of the hospitality and transport from Simon's Town to the Zambezi provided by sympathetic Royal Navy captains and their vessels on the Cape Station.

The nature of the settlement Mackenzie was to establish was resolved in part by his own admiration for Genadendal and by an unavoidable reliance on liberated slaves. The mission's idea of a Christian village, however, was shaped not by echoes from Sierra Leone but increasingly by the high church ideal of a self-sufficient reli-gious community and the primacy of preaching. This was especially so after renewed expansion on the mainland went ahead under Bishop Steere after 1874.[8] Communities composed predominantly of freed slaves raised all manner of prob-lems involving the exercise of secular authority and relations with local societies unconnected with the mission, something apparently confirmed not only by UMCA experience but still more that of the CMS in their station at Freretown set

---

6  Anderson-Morshead, *History of the UMCA*, pp. 153–4.
7  To H. Goodwin, 27 July 1855, Goodwin, *Memoir*, p. 115.
8  Edward Steere, *The Universities' Mission to Central Africa: A Speech delivered at Oxford* (London, 1875).

up in 1875.[9] They were therefore gradually abandoned by the UMCA in order to preserve the work of evangelisation, celibacy and simplicity of lifestyle and to limit the discipline exercised by the mission to ecclesiastical control of its own church members. 'Missionaries', Steere felt strongly, 'ought to form a Church; what is sometimes formed is rather a Statelet. Forming a Church they have only really power to censure and to expel from communion.' 'Asking for the punishment, by the secular arm, of those who persecute us for our faith seems to me to be a denial of that faith itself.'[10] Another member of the mission later expressed pleasure in that 'Here we are perfectly able to restore the ancient discipline of the Church, to the great and inestimable benefit of the body of the faithful.' In a 'solemn excommunication', 'the power of the Church as a spiritual institution is emphasised and realised'.[11]

The customs of the early church were seen as one defence against involvement with state authority, but they were also valuable in themselves. Chauncy Maples spoke for his colleagues when insisting that 'in all things we must follow primitive custom'. Thus were determined the burial of catechumens, the siting of the altar and baptismal ritual. Any departure from ancient norms required one to 'show reason (and very good reason, too) that our changed circumstances suffice to change the custom'.[12]

No less clear than these concerns with 'apostolic' practice was the departure in other respects from Venn's outlook. With his own early experience of guilds and brotherhoods, Steere took care, not least in his recruitment sermons to undergraduates, to qualify the place of 'civilisation' in a missionary's thinking. 'In some ways civilization is a positive hindrance to the Missionary, from the very comforts which it teaches him to consider indispensable ... Civilization is ... a great and powerful instrument put into our hands for the benefit of those who are now outside its pale, but it is an instrument only and one that is capable of working fearful mischief if we make it substantially our object to raise a civilized nation, rather than a holy Church.'[13] He and his successors were often less concerned with the inculcation of Western belief and civilisation than with making plain the dangers inherent in that civilisation and in the progress of their rivals, Roman Catholicism and Islam.

There was an evident sense of pressure and haste on the part of the clerical members of the mission. This was not necessarily directly millennial in inspiration, but it encouraged in them as in the members of the faith missions an awareness of the need to keep ahead of the corruption inherent in Western expansion.

9  Robert W. Strayer, *The Making of Mission Communities in East Africa* (London and Albany, 1978), pp. 14–20, for the difficulties at Freretown.

10  Steere quoted in R.M. Heanley, *A Memoir of Edward Steere, D.D.,LL.D., Third Missionary Bishop in Central Africa* (London, 1888), pp. 326–7.

11  Chauncy Maples, Journal, 8 July 1885, cited by Ellen Maples, *Chauncy Maples D.D., F.R.G.S. Pioneer Missionary in East Central Africa* (London, 1897), p. 241.

12  *Ibid.*, pp. 142, 237, 241, 262.

13  Address, at a Conference on Missions in Oxford, 1877, *ibid.*, p. 209.

Reservations about the Western impact on Africa were a consistent feature of UMCA writing and comment. Older home supporters, such as Wilberforce, might continue to value the positive rhetoric of 'Christianity and commerce', but this soon ceased to be the language of the UMCA in the field. Mackenzie's criticisms of Natal's settlers, for example, were restated more broadly thirty years later by Maples, at Likoma Island in Lake Nyasa. 'We are getting too much in the world and too civilized here for my tastes. It draws one away from one's real work, all this entertaining of Europeans, the calling of steamers, etc.'[14] A decade further on, Frank Weston worried in particular about the 'debased civilisation' of the European-run plantations and the corrupting impact on African family life of the commercial society of coastal towns; these he thought quite as threatening as the omnipresent expansion of Islam and the practices of 'witchcraft'. Zanzibar, he wrote, 'is more and more immoral – Piccadilly, Sodom and a public bar!'[15] Impatient of anthropological findings while insisting on high standards for Africans as for Europeans, he fretted at the fragility of African Christianity in such a setting.

Dislike of the consequences of modern urban civilisation at home and abroad and a determination to protect Africans from its impact, were important sources of commitment in the mission. For many UMCA recruits this seems to have been derived from their Christian Socialism or their work in urban slum parishes, especially in London. For others, attachment to the rhythms of rural English life or the world of the theological colleges such as Cuddesdon or Westcott House induced a similar aversion. Consciously or unconsciously, missionary work offered British missionaries of all denominations the possibility of escape from an industrial urban society whose failures were by 1880 becoming more and more apparent to contemporaries. Far more strongly than most British African missions, the UMCA welcomed this release. Once in Africa members increasingly rejected the 'civilising mission' which others less perceptive still widely understood and promoted as the Westernisation of African societies. Returning home on furlough in 1901, Weston for example only found his reservations confirmed: 'England seems more worldly and on the surface than ever and there is an absence of real life which makes me very pessimistic.' Back in Tanganyika he deplored more than ever 'the development of plantations' as 'a sore trial to our people and a hindrance to the Gospel'.[16]

Western secular values and malpractice were one source of danger, Islam another. In Central Africa Steere found himself '*fighting against time*. On all sides we are met by signs that the stagnation of Africa is past. The various trading, exploring and missionary expeditions ... have opened the eyes of the natives to their ignorance, backwardness and weakness. Even the very antagonism of the

---

14  Journal, 31 Aug. 1893, cited by Maples, *Chauncy Maples*, p. 350; see also p. 354.
15  H. Maynard Smith, *Frank Bishop of Zanzibar: Life of Frank Weston, D.D., 1871–1924* (London, 1926), pp. 96, 187.
16  Smith, *Frank Bishop of Zanzibar*, pp. 41, 96.

Mohammedans to Christianity has done good in its way, by ... making them enquire into the differences between Christianity and Islam. The whole future of Central Africa is trembling in the balance. The Africans will not remain as they are ... if through lack of men with the apostolic spirit, the English Church is unable to answer their appeal for missionaries, they have no alternative, they must accept Islam.'[17]

The UMCA's preoccupation with Islam, although heightened in the general manner of the late nineteenth century, was none the less essentially pragmatic rather than wildly eschatological. Operating in Zanzibar – exclusively so, from 1864 to 1868 – as for others in north India or ultimately even for men such as Thornton and Gairdner working in Cairo, left missions little alternative. Despite the UMCA's brief association with Livingstone's campaign against Arabs and Portuguese for Christianity and commerce and their ability to benefit from the renewed excitement for the cause in Britain associated with his death and burial in Westminster Abbey in 1873, the mission's approach to Islam was leavened with caution and respect. UMCA members were conscious that this too set them apart from their compatriots. 'A European blunders into the midst of a state of things of which he knows as nearly as possible nothing and having set all law and order, as the natives know them, at defiance, complains that his goods are pilfered and that he can get no redress.' This should hardly come as a surprise, but too often the further consequence was predictable. 'It is a sore temptation to a missionary to see an opportunity, as he thinks, of obtaining a great slice of the country and governing it on Christian principles.'[18]

Such temptations were to be resisted. Islam was only to be understood both in terms of biblical prophecy and as the result of careful study. Maples, looking east towards Mecca as he sailed south through the Red Sea in 1876, reflected on both the contribution to Western learning made by 'the vast intellects of the Arabs' and the biblical writings illuminating 'the great Mohammedan question' and 'the Eastern Antichrist'. His general reading embraced both Ottoman history and prophetical literature.[19] Later he argued that the encounter with Muslims not only necessitated for all missionaries study of the religion itself, 'but what is – as I suppose – a far more difficult thing to accomplish, namely, a thorough investigation into the manner in which that religion has taken hold of his heart and as to the particular points in which lies its subtle attraction for him ... This last knowledge can only be attained by long and patient study of the national character.'[20] Islam was to be

---

17  Heanley, *Memoir of Edward Steere*, p. 220.

18  *Ibid.*, p. 328.

19  Letter, 11 April 1876, Maples, *Chauncy Maples*, pp. 52–3; for his reading, *ibid.*, pp. 269, 292. For Steere on Islam, Heanley, *Memoir of Edward Steere*, chap. 19 'Mohammedanism'.

20  C. Maples, *On the Method of Evangelising Uncultured Races, Monthly Paper No. 9 for the Oxford Mission to Calcutta* (Calcutta, 1882), reprinted in Ellen Maples (ed.), *Journals and Papers of Chauncy Maples D.D., F.R.G.S., Late Bishop of Likoma Lake Nyasa, Africa* (London, 1899), quotation at p. 176.

countered not only by governmental initiatives such as Sir Bartle Frere's diplomatic mission to Zanzibar and the anti-slave-trade treaty of 1873, which helped open the way for renewed Christian evangelism on the mainland. It also required a complex relationship allowing both for mission help with local road building to its school and the Sultan's present of a clock to the new cathedral of Christ Church in Zanzibar, even as missionaries suspected that he hated them all.[21]

Criticisms of Western influences and reflections on Islam led UMCA members at an early stage to a measure of respect and an equal concern to preserve African ways of life and beliefs. Given the deeply ambiguous character of apparently beneficial or at least harmless activity, such as building schools or introducing medical skills, one should first beware easy assumptions of superiority. For Steere, 'nothing can be so false as to suppose that the outward circumstances of a people are a measure either of its barbarism or its civilization ... The chief ornaments of the Apostolic Church would certainly be regarded as uncivilized in the present day and probably we shall ourselves appear so to those who come after us. But the Church of Christ is not affected by distinctions such as these. She has no commission to bring all nations to any other uniformity than that of the faith. She can leave national habits and customs alone, sure that the indwelling Spirit will ... work out in any particular national church that special form of civilization which is best suited to the nation.'[22] Thus Steere thought the despatch of John Swedi, the mission's first ordained African deacon, to the UMCA base at Masasi in 1879, could 'hardly be overrated. The permanent success of our ministry depends in no small degree on its acceptance of all the marked outward features of the native life from which it springs. The heathen cannot suspect Christianity of being a crusade against all they hold dear.'[23]

It was this point where changed circumstances might begin to justify departures from apostolic custom that UMCA members normally preferred to avoid. Maples developed Steere's view in other directions, emphasising the necessity and rightness of adapting the Christian message to different audiences. 'No preconceived idea of how best to preach Christ will be likely to be of use', he argued, notwithstanding the universality of Christian dogma. With respect to modes of evangelism as much as to lifestyle 'the European missionary must become an African to win Africans. He must, so far as is consistent with his Christian principles, assimilate himself to them.'[24]

The missionaries were not so unrealistic as to think that the processes of change could be halted. 'We cannot keep our men out of the commercial movement if we would: the coast towns will always claim many and in claiming their bodies will

21 Heanley, *Memoir of Edward Steere*, p. 262; Maples, *Chauncy Maples*, p. 56.

22 Steere to R.M. Heanley, 4 Feb. 1879, Heanley, *Memoir of Edward Steere*, p. 246.

23 *Ibid.*, p. 245.

24 Maples, *On the Method of Evangelising Uncultured Races*, in Maples (ed.), *Journals and Papers*, pp. 179, 186.

enchain their souls.'[25] Nevertheless, as the European presence expanded it became the goal of the mission to prevent the urban drift and to sustain a 'traditional', essentially rural, African society with its families, tribes and community life, as far as possible. Weston shared Maples's view of the need to Africanise the missionary, by adopting local lifestyles, living simply and ascetically, avoiding any suggestion as a white man of superiority or standing on one's dignity. He told the European missionary, 'If you want to help African women, go and live in their villages and share their life.'[26] Pastoral practice was in turn to be supported by institutional provision. In deepening the structure of the church, converts were generally discouraged from leaving their villages and new archdeaconries were linked to individual tribes.[27] The mission thus should be open to all. Attention to its integration with African life was vital, both to Christianity's expansion and to the building of the church, the most effective obstacle in the way of Islam's advance. The UMCA's attempt at blending Anglo-Catholic Christianity with African ways was one that simultaneously intensified their theologically informed emphasis on community, authority, obedience and discipline.[28]

The UMCA's adaptation to the challenges facing missions in Britain and the circumstances confronting them in Central Africa none the less had distinct limits. Responding like the critics of tradition to the call for apostolic missions, they insisted not only on preaching the apostolic message but also on maintaining the apostolic church, in each case demonstrating the extent to which that apostolic legacy could be reinterpreted. They attached far greater importance to traditional Christian ideas of community than to the individualism so frequently associated with conversion and much contemporary Western thought. Favouring the simplification of missionary operations desired by the faith missions, they were nevertheless not prepared to abandon institutions such as the schools they maintained in Zanzibar. If their responsiveness to local African conditions shows a sympathy or critical understanding alien above all to the faith missions, they could also be as realistic as the most world-weary of missionaries. 'The Makuas and Yaos around us are very far from "stretching out their hands unto God" – in fact, what they *desire* is, to remain in the same ignorance of Him as they were in before we came here' was Maples's wry comment.[29] While willing to acknowledge the complexity of the encounter with Islam, they rejected without reservation the arguments of those in Britain who believed that Islam was either a natural or a desirable religious berth on the Africans' journey to acceptance of Christianity.[30] 'Whatever merits Islam as a

---

25  Smith, *Frank Bishop of Zanzibar*, p. 96.
26  *Ibid.*, p. 137.
27  *Ibid.*, p. 96; Wilson, *History of the UMCA*, p. 189.
28  For later CMS parallels, John Casson, '"To Plant a Garden City in the Slums of Paganism": Handley Hooper and the Future of Africa', *JRA* 28 (1998), pp. 387–410.
29  7 Sept. 1881, in Maples, *Chauncy Maples*, p. 155.
30  Thomas Prasch, 'Which God for Africa: The Islamic-Christian Missionary Debate in Late-Victorian England', *Victorian Studies* 33, 1 (1989–90), 51–73.

religion may have, ... this spurious, so-called Islam, that has penetrated to Nyasaland, has, considered from the point of view of morals, brought about a worse state of things than ... it has in some cases displaced ... While there have always been and still are, many devout Christians ... who ... regard the faith of Islam as a *praeparatio evangeli* for those who, coming out of heathenism, have embraced it and while there are other Christians, we regret to note, who deem that Islam is on the whole the best creed for the regeneration of the African, there are none we feel sure, who, if they really understood the matter, would ... allow that the Mohammedanism affected by certain Yao chiefs and their people, can lead to anything but hopeless degradation and the subversion of all true morality.'[31]

In UMCA attempts to define and reconcile with each other Anglo-Catholic tradition, their experience of a changing Central Africa and Protestant missionary ambitions, they inevitably wrestled with inconsistencies, some of their own making. Maples, although one of the most thoughtful and engaging of the mission's members, offers examples of these difficulties. He joined a mission which attracted above all university-educated men and which contributed as much as any to turn their attention to Africa. Taking his cue from David Livingstone, he too aimed to put missionary work in Africa on a par with that in India. 'It is a mistake', Livingstone had said in Cambridge, 'to suppose that any one, as long as he is pious, will do for this office. Pioneers in everything should be the ablest and best qualified of men.'[32] No longer should the most highly educated automatically be sent out east. So Maples believed 'the work of evangelising the races of savage Africa calls for the best trained intellects and the highest form of mental activity'. Dismissing talk of 'fetishism' or idolatry, he argued that the African possessed deep-rooted religious ideas and 'it is certain that all the secrets of the now prevailing religions of Africa will only be yielded up to a profound and persistent investigation'.[33] It was a view he maintained to the end of his life, insisting in his anniversary sermon to the UMCA in 1895 that the African encounter with Christianity would 'bring out and exhibit new sides of Christian life such as our Western and European natures have not in them to develop'.[34] For the faith missions, of course – but not only them – there was no time for such luxuries; Christian evangelism required minimal preparation and African religions had no potential for the Protestant world. Ironically, however, among the university-trained high churchmen of the UMCA, as with Selwyn in New Zealand insistent on the acquisition of Latin and Greek, there was a tendency to require such high educational attainments in the Western tradition that African messages were only too easily overlooked.

Critical of Western expansion and too much civilisation – but, it would seem, not alert to the possibility or consequences of excessive learning – Maples on one

---

31  Maples, from the *Nyasa News*, 1893, cited by Maples, *Journals and Papers*, p. 248.
32  J. Simmons, *Livingstone and Africa* (London, 1955), p. 79.
33  C. Maples, *The African Church and Its Claims upon the Universities* (Cambridge, 1879), p. 12.
34  Maples (ed.), *Journals and Papers*, pp. 232–3.

occasion had no hesitation in hauling down a Portuguese flag flown by a local chief
in the hope that a British protectorate might be the eventual outcome.[35] Maples, of
course, was not alone. Bishop Smythies too began to hanker after British protection
around Lake Nyasa. For the UMCA as increasingly for other British missions in
the late nineteenth century, some national civilisations were better than others.
Simultaneously, however, both men still rejoiced in the distancing of church and
state which had earlier given Edward Steere satisfaction at the mission's ability to
operate unimpeded across territorial boundaries and continued of great value to
them during the coastal uprising against the Germans in 1888.[36]

Finally, to 'become an African' was for any missionary who recognised the need
– even those accustomed to the ascetic customs of the UMCA – the greatest challenge of all. Bishop Tozer, one of his junior clergy recorded, was inseparable from
his harmonium, even though 'it came up finally in three burdens, the Bishop
himself having taken it to pieces'.[37] In 1892, notwithstanding the legendary walking
abilities of UMCA bishops, the choice of Likoma island as the new diocesan centre
only made sense given access to modern steamers on Lake Nyasa. As for Maples,
Western tradition upheld was sadly in the end his undoing. In September 1895,
only recently returned from his consecration in London at St Paul's Cathedral, his
boat was overturned in a storm on Lake Nyasa. Weighed down by his cassock,
Maples drowned.

## II

The adaptation of the communal religious ideal to missions at home and overseas in
the form of brother- and sisterhoods was not uncommon within the high church
fold. Edward Steere was involved in several such ventures in the 1850s. Looking
back to the religious clubs and associations of the eighteenth century, he saw them
as having immense potential in their concentration of contemplation, self-sacrifice,
resources and leadership. 'In fact all the great institutions which preserved the
Church's life and activity to our own times owe their origins to [that] era and
greatly to the efforts and influence of these Brotherhoods.'[38] Frank Weston, later
Bishop of Zanzibar, was a member of the guild of St Matthew, Stewart Headlam's
Christian Socialist venture formed in 1877. With many Anglo-Catholics and others
who became missionaries overseas, he worked in one of the university college
missions in London's slums which sprang up from the mid-1880s. In Zanzibar he
established a theological college, 'a place of quiet where men might live together
and help one another to learn the secrets of devotion' and, in 1910, achieved the

---

35  Maples, *Chauncy Maples*, pp. 306–8.
36  By G.W. (ed.), E.F. Russell, *The Life of Charles Alan Smythies*, 2nd edn (London, 1899), pp.
    148–58, 161–2.
37  Heanley, *Memoir of Edward Steere*, p. 67.
38  E. Steere, *An Historical Sketch of the English Brotherhoods which existed at the beginning of the eigh-
    teenth century* (London, 1856), p. 32.

establishment of the Community of the Sacred Passion for women, both European and African. 'Might not white women, vowed to chastity, in some way atone for all that black women had suffered from the lust of white men?'[39]

The UMCA with its episcopal leadership and direction did not provide the only pattern. The origin of the brotherhoods in Anglo-Catholic, Tractarian thinking always ensured their respect for episcopal authority, but most operated quite independently under the direction of their own members with the guidance of a religious superior or head of the community. This was the case, for example, in the more familiarly structured setting of north India, where the Cambridge Mission to Delhi and the Oxford Mission to Calcutta began work in, respectively, 1877 and 1881. The Cambridge Mission was intended by its founders, notably B.F. Westcott (Professor of Divinity at Cambridge) and T.V. French (Founder of St John's College, Agra and Bishop of Lahore, 1877–83) to promote higher education and support Christian students.[40] The members of the mission constituted themselves the Brotherhood of the Ascended Christ, leading a communal life in which pastoral work and evangelical preaching were combined with running St Stephen's College. The larger number of unmarried women were drawn together into their own St Stephen's Community, initially with a view to work in the zenanas among Indian women but increasingly engaged in social and medical work of many kinds.[41] The Oxford Mission, regulating themselves as the Brotherhood of the Epiphany, considered there to be a surfeit of 'bazaar' preaching in Calcutta. Amenable to suggestions from the Bishop of Calcutta, it adopted a rural mission in the 1890s, but otherwise, from prime at 6.00 am each day to compline at 9.00 pm, concentrated on its own schools and hostels. Increasingly it worked directly as a mission to the rapidly growing numbers of Calcutta University students. Beginning with three or four clergy, by the late 1890s it had some seven to nine clergy and two laymen at any one time.[42]

In the Indian setting, however, it was unusually difficult to attain the comparative detachment from the state and colonial authority more generally characteristic of the UMCA. From their beginnings both missions had very close connections with the SPG, which since 1814 had played a central role in the appointment and funding of India's Anglican episcopate and these only tightened with time.[43] In 1891, Henry Whitehead, already Principal of the SPG-run Bishop's College in

39  Smith, *Frank Bishop of Zanzibar*, chap. 7, quotations at pp. 35 and 131.
40  T.V. French, *The Proposed Cambridge University Mission in North India: Being the Substance of a Paper read before the Cambridge Mission Aid Society on February 16, 1876* (privately printed, 1876); Birks, *Life and Correspondence of Thomas Valpy French*, Vol. 1, pp. 323–7.
41  *One Hundred Years in Delhi: The Brotherhood of the Ascended Christ 1877–1977* (Delhi, 1977); H.H. Montgomery, *The Life and Letters of George Alfred Lefroy* (London, 1920); Jeffrey Cox, 'Independent English Women in Delhi and Lahore, 1860–1947', in R.W. Davis and R.J. Helmstadter (eds), *Religion and Irreligion in Victorian Society* (London, 1992), pp. 166–84.
42  George Longridge, *A History of the Oxford Mission to Calcutta* (London, 1900).
43  For a useful brief survey of the complexities of this role, Susan Billington Harper, *In the Shadow of the Mahatma: Bishop V.S. Azariah and the Travails of Christianity in British India* (Grand Rapids and Richmond, 2000), chap. 4.

Calcutta, was also appointed superior of the Oxford Mission, while in Delhi the Cambridge Mission took over entirely the SPG's missionary work. Both communities began to furnish bishops for India's dioceses, Lefroy to Lahore and Whitehead to Madras, both in 1899. Following French's appointment to Lahore in 1877, bishops and brotherhoods developed intimate ties. The Oxford Mission's policy while Bishop Johnson was metropolitan (1876–98) was defined by its historian as 'Do nothing without the Bishop'.[44] After a while, the missions' acquisition of city centre sites confirmed their social position and role as frequent visiting places for representatives of the Raj. The Mission House in Cornwallis Street, Calcutta, welcomed among its callers 'soldiers from Fort William, members of the Civil Service, officers in the Army, [and] travellers who are spending the cold weather in India', with no sign of Maples's misgivings about the onrush of 'civilisation'.[45]

No amount of pleading the inaccuracy of their image as missions only for men of standing and 'great intellectual ability' could offset the gradual absorption of the brotherhoods into the larger world of the colonial ruler.[46] Lefroy, for instance, became a member of the Delhi Municipal Council, his responsibilities ranging from the Queen's Jubilee celebrations of 1887 to sanitation. It is not easy to imagine that either of these usefully met what he described as the 'chief inducement' to membership, 'the contact into which it would bring me with some of the leading [Indian] men of the city, to whom our Mission is especially supposed to address itself, but whom we have so far signally failed to reach'.[47] However, there was little sign in either Delhi or Calcutta that the closeness of such contacts was felt in any way to jeopardise the missionary task. The CMS, however, took a different line. In the case of its Indian missionaries, involvement in municipal politics was felt to be undesirable. Officials were unenthusiastic on the grounds that, like political involvement anywhere, it might compromise their position. In India 'belonging to the ruling race' made it doubly difficult for them to be 'regarded simply as a teacher of Divine truth and not as one to whom it may be of temporal advantage to get access'. Each individual case, however, remained subject to review.[48]

Perhaps absorption or its absence did not greatly matter. The paucity of converts was dispiriting to some, for example to Whitehead, impressed as he was by the mass conversions of Indians in the south. Nevertheless, it was frequently downplayed, with the arguments that the careful nurturing of inquirers or potential believers, so necessary but so time-consuming, and the prayers of the missions for India's Christianisation, were the truly vital activities of the brotherhoods. The absence of obvious hostility to their activities disinclined them to question the fact

---

44 Longridge, *Oxford Mission*, p. 194; cf. also pp. 66–80.
45 *Ibid.*, p. 93; for Maples, above, pp. 228–34.
46 *Ibid.*, p. 84.
47 Montgomery, *Life and Letters of Lefroy*, pp. 106–7.
48 W. Gray to Rev. P.M. Zenker and Rev. A.J. Santer, 28 Jan., 12 July 1889, Gray and Stock to Rev. A. Clifford, 16 May 1890, CMS Archives G2I1/L12, ff. 150–1, 260–1, 426.

of their influence. Lefroy thus commented, 'we are here to upset by God's grace their old faiths and customs and to recreate the country in Christ Jesus; and it is only logical to suppose that we should be very much hated and objected to; only logical, but somehow hopelessly the reverse of fact'.[49] The universality of the faith was matched by belief in the utility of Oxbridge teaching transplanted to Bengal and the Punjab. It was felt that the university missions' 'real strength', position and influence with Indians rested not on their social contacts and the production of converts but on their capacity for 'sympathy'. 'It is known now [1899] that every Bengali ... will find a welcome at the Mission House.' The Mission House reflected in microcosm the imperial setting. 'It is because in virtue of our Christian Faith, in virtue of our past heritage, which has made us what we are, we *are* the greater nation, that we are bound by the very sense of our own greatness to be patient, forbearing and sympathetic towards those over whom we rule.'[50]

Whether restatement of providential history or expression of national self-glorification, this assessment was in one sense not as far removed from the UMCA's belief in missionary identification with local peoples as it might at first seem. To both south Asia and Central Africa the Anglo-Catholics brought ideas of 'sympathy' and practical 'consideration', linked to the possibility of insights for the West to be derived from close encounters of the religious kind. These were present in the Cambridge Mission from its foundation as a result of the influential teaching of Professor Westcott.[51] That they lent themselves to expressions of paternalistic self-congratulation should not disguise either their novelty in the missionary world as a whole or their capacity to subvert the language of dominance and imperial control in India. In the world of Hindus and still more of Muslims, the latter as we have seen being readily consigned by some evangelicals to a purely eschatological role in which Islamic beliefs themselves were largely irrelevant, the willingness of Anglo-Catholic missions to treat the beliefs of others with some seriousness was a rarity. It was an assessment at the same time widely separated from the world of the UMCA. The legacy of colonial rule in India at the point of the high church missions' arrival in the 1870s imposed far greater constraints on missionary ambitions than did those prevailing in Central Africa at the same time. The authoritarianism at the heart of the Anglo-Catholic tradition, as well as its members' social connections, were encouraged to assert themselves more readily under the Raj than in circumstances where colonial rule had yet to be established.

## III

The other wing of evangelical Anglicanism, represented by the CMS, regarded these Anglo-Catholic and SPG responses to the conditions of the mid-century and

---

49  G.A. Lefroy to S.S. Allnutt, 13 Aug. 1887, Montgomery, *Life and Letters of Lefroy*, p. 105.
50  Longridge, *History of the Oxford Mission*, pp. 201–2, 206.
51  Cox, 'Independent English women', pp. 166–8.

after as worse than the problems themselves. The CMS retained its suspicion of missionary bishops as hostile to lay influence and prone to monarchical tendencies in all ecclesiastical matters, the latter manifested not least in a desire to control all Anglican missionaries. They were inclined to see religious communities as equally unacceptable, for the propensity to encourage liturgical and ritual experiment if not the outright adoption of Romish aberrations or worse. In the 1870s and 1880s, after the Public Worship Regulation Act of 1874, Anglo-Catholics regarded overseas missions as offering them an opportunity to build a church on lines increasingly under attack at home; their opponents were no less keen to pursue heresy and eccle-siastical corruption wherever it showed itself. On both sides, attitudes to imperial and colonial authority were at first powerfully shaped by domestic denominational rivalry, Anglo-Catholics anxious to escape its reach, low church evangelicals keen to wield it for their own purposes. Nonconformists were as ever uncomfortably placed on the sidelines, unsympathetic to Anglo-Catholicism but keen on religious free-doms and non-interference.

If this route to reform was closed to the CMS, it was also no easier to envisage change in the Society's central strategy, the pursuit of 'Christianity and commerce' linked to the building of native churches on the basis of the 'three selves'. Caught between a lack of donations and volunteers at home and a shortage of converts or financial commitment abroad, Venn and his colleagues needed something either to galvanise the process of church building in the field or to reawaken missionary enthusiasm in the metropole. The appointment and consecration of Samuel Crowther as the first African bishop was designed to achieve the first; their connec-tion with the religious revival associated with the Keswick movement provided the second. Both developments, however, moved the process of missionary adaptation and expansion beyond the control of CMS headquarters.

Crowther's life has attracted much attention.[52] Study in London after the Niger Expedition was the prelude to his ordination in 1843, after which he was sent with others to open the Yoruba mission at Abeokuta. Success there and with J.C. Taylor in Igboland, his translation work and growing familiarity with Lagos and the Niger were followed by his consecration in June 1864 as 'Bishop of the countries of West Africa beyond our [the Queen's] dominions'. In theory this included all those parts of West Africa not already under the jurisdiction of the Bishop of Sierra Leone; in practice it meant chiefly the Niger river basin and parts of Yorubaland.

Crowther's appointment was neither hasty nor ill conceived, but was none the less a gamble. Venn had toyed already with the preferment of Crowther to Sierra Leone, a diocese for which candidates of quality were not easy to find. When he

---

52 The principal studies are Ajayi, *Christian Missions in Nigeria*; Ayandele, *Missionary Impact on Modern Nigeria*; Williams, *Ideal of the Self-Governing Church*; T.E. Yates, *Venn and Victorian Bishops Abroad*; Andrew Porter, articles in *JICH* 5 (1976), 6 (1977) and 7 (1979); John Loiello, 'Samuel Ajayi Crowther, the Church Missionary Society and the Niger Mission 1857–1891' (unpub., Ph.D. thesis, London, 1980).

turned to the Niger, many of the white missionaries, not only CMS, objected, on grounds of their own prior claims, Crowther's insufficient ability and experience, the absence of any church and Venn's somewhat idiosyncratic adoption of a course uncomfortably close for the undiscerning to the precedent recently set by the UMCA. There were also local currents of African opinion critical of Crowther's elevation.[53]

Crowther was acutely aware of the problems but fell in with Venn's plans. In this region the spread of mission stations and schools, the growth of an African professional class in the coastal towns and the penetration of African and European traders up the Niger were being accompanied by anti-slave-trade measures and imperial government action – an aggressively interventionist consular system, warlike engagement with Lagos in 1851 and its annexation in 1861. The missions and churches could not stand back from this process in Yorubaland and the Niger, allowing themselves to be edged aside or even driven out, any more than they could in Sierra Leone or the Gold Coast.[54] Indeed, when in 1865 the imperial Parliament came out against any further forward movement and supported withdrawal from 'the West African Settlements', Crowther's appointment and the place for a native-led, locally financed missionary church made all the more sense. It was hoped in Salisbury Square that Crowther's consecration would boost this development.

For the time being their hopes were well founded. For more than a decade commercial expansion and missionary growth, especially in the Niger delta, went hand in hand. Relations between the CMS and the commercial firms were very close, even within Crowther's own family and, as the bishop cultivated good relations with local rulers, the prospects of locally financed schools and churches brightened. CMS backing for 'native agency' came to mean that church and mission occupied a prominent place in local commercial society.[55] In the late 1860s and early1870s, the Venn vision managed to keep doubters at bay and offered in West Africa evidence that the mid-century crisis of confidence in the traditional strategy had been unjustified. In consequence it provided encouragement to native churches around the world.

Adaptation and reinvigoration of the CMS's tradition thus involved Venn and, he hoped, his successors in taking a lead at the centre in order to stimulate and push forward striking initiatives in church building in the field. Success, Venn expected, would help to re-enthuse supporters of both the missions at home and 'native agency' on the spot, be it in Ceylon, West Africa or south India. It was also hoped that Crowther's activities would help sustain the claims of the CMS to be a church society supportive of episcopacy, in the face of high church criticism. The success Venn desired, however, depended on several conditions. Continuity of policy in

---

53  Williams, *Ideal of the Self-Governing Church*, pp. 28–33.
54  Ajayi, *Christian Missions in Nigeria*, chaps 5–6; for Egba hostility to Europeans, including missions, in the 1860s, pp. 196–204.
55  Ajayi, *Christian Missions in Nigeria*, chap. 7.

Salisbury Square was an obvious sine qua non; it was essential that Venn's policies and outlook should not die with him. Missionaries already in the field, if not enthusiastic, had to be prepared at least to go along with the urging of the central officers. Newly recruited missionaries similarly had to toe the line, suppressing any urge they might have to dismiss the achievements and reasoning of their elders. Finally, Crowther and others in authority had to persuade these different audiences that they were living up to the mission's expectations.

Continuity of policy had to be secured in the face of the great discontinuity of death, Venn in January and Livingstone in April 1873. It was not easily achieved, despite the extremely high regard in which Venn was held. Under his immediate successor, Edward Hutchinson, the situation in the Niger Mission was examined and found wanting. 'Upon a full review of the state of the Niger Mission made by the Committee it appeared evident that this Mission was not in a satisfactory condition and that the Agents both ordained and unordained, with a few noteworthy exceptions, were not maintaining that high tone of Christian life and conversation which could alone give hope of an abundant blessing from on high upon the Mission.'[56] As a result the decision was taken to relieve Bishop Crowther of 'temporalities', that is the secular administrative work and to provide a steamer – the *Henry Venn* – to facilitate his supervision of the mission stations. Two European laymen were appointed to take charge of these aspects of the mission and a Niger Committee was set up at Lagos.[57] The changes were presented to Crowther as a practical aid, as a means to consolidate existing work in the Delta and to pave the way for further expansion upstream and as bringing the Niger into line with CMS administrative arrangements in other missions. 'It must often have struck you that the Niger Mission has held a peculiar position as contrasted with all our other missions. Its entire control and administration has rested with yourself … The growth of the work as well as your own advancing age renders it most necessary that the mission should enjoy the benefit of a permanent system of government that is as far as the temporalities are concerned. It is not of course intended to limit or interfere with your own Episcopal control and direction but as in India that there should be found with you a body who would act as the representatives of the society while you should still remain as the chief pastor and chief missionary too.'[58]

It was not a happy arrangement. For Venn it was of course in the very 'peculiar position' of Crowther's mission that its value had lain and the bishop undoubtedly sensed the determination of some in the CMS to reverse Venn's intention by cutting back African control. The two lay employees, Ashcroft and Kirk, not only exploited their powers to the utmost but diverted the *Henry Venn* to purposes not approved by Crowther, including trading on their own and the mission's account.

56  Hutchinson to James Kirk, 6 Dec. 1878, CMS Archives CA3/L1, f. 329.
57  *Ibid.*; Hutchinson to J.H. Ashcroft, 19 Dec. 1879, *ibid.*, f. 379.
58  Hutchinson to Bishop Crowther, 5 Nov. 1879, *ibid.*, f. 371.

Conflicts were only temporarily defused as the result of another report on the mission, highly critical of many of the African agents and a special conference at Madeira of CMS and Niger Mission members. This time it was suggested that the mission be remodelled on the pattern of mid-China, Palestine, the north Pacific and Ceylon. Among its main features would be a regular Mission Conference and a Finance Committee as the channel of communication with London; the latter would have a clerical secretary who would also represent the Parent Committee on the spot. Immediate practical responsibility for the Upper and Lower Niger was to be divided between the two African archdeacons and it was hoped that all trading by Agents and their families would cease.[59]

There was little consolation for Bishop Crowther in the reassurance offered that 'this arrangement will not in our judgement diminish the interest of the great experiment which is being tried on the Niger. It will still be an African Mission to Africans.'[60] Hutchinson left office under an altogether different cloud, the lay supervisor Ashcroft was dismissed and Venn sympathisers reasserted their over-sight of West African work. However, confidence in the mission was seriously weakened and divisions persisted in CMS House. Throughout the 1880s increasingly stringent criticisms of the mission were made by successive European secretaries, culminating in the grave crisis of 1888–1892. Thomas Phillips, ordained priest by Crowther, resigned from the secretaryship of the mission in summer 1883 after barely nine months, having already caused Eugene Stock considerable problems as to what he should write about the mission in the CMS publications.[61] The central problems were seen as lying in the widespread allegations of the poor quality and corrupt conduct of many African agents; in the ineffectiveness of Crowther's direction and supervision of the mission; and in the division of authority between the Bishop, the Secretary and the Finance Committee. The latter was particularly complex, involving a situation which some suggested could be resolved only by the appointment of a European bishop, capable of commanding the respect and obedience due to an ecclesiastical superior from both black and white Christians.

In correspondence with the Bishop, CMS secretaries focused on the agents and their fitness, identifying the gulf between London and the Niger which they wished to bridge. Lang expressed the Parent Committee's regret at Crowther's refusal to act on complaints against some of the agents, but at the same time acknowledged the principle behind his resistance, that 'you deem it ... inadmissible to disconnect any agent except for some proved offence'. To many at Salisbury Square this was to allow too much tolerance to those unsuited to their posts. 'Our guiding principle is, that the Spiritual work, which alone is the object

59 Report of the Madeira Conference and Deputation Letter to Bishop Crowther, 24 Feb. 1881, *ibid.*, ff. 423–42.
60 F.E. Wigram to Bishop Crowther, 15 June 1881, *ibid.*, f. 449.
61 Stock to Phillips, 3 May 1883, CMS Archives G3/A3/L2, f. 136.

for which the Society exists, can be effectually done only by Spiritual agents and if lack of Spirituality, or incapacity of any kind is apparent in an agent, we sever connection with him. Nor does this severance of connection of itself necessarily involve any stigma on the character of the agent ... We do not feel justified in trying the experiment whether an agent who has avowedly failed to gain influence in one place where he has resided many years, can acquire an influence elsewhere ... It is far better to suffer existing stations to be closed than to leave them manned by inefficient or unworthy agents!'[62]

Effective agents capable of commanding respect on all sides seemed more necessary than ever and not only for the traditional reasons of the CMS's sense of respectability and self-esteem. The responsibility felt to its subscribers and fears that scandalous episodes or rumours might blight mission prospects everywhere, were acute. The early 1880s saw growing Protestant fears about Roman Catholic expansion into the Niger and the possibility that converts might be seduced into transferring their allegiance.[63] Concern for the CMS's reputation seemed well justified by letters of complaint reaching London and when one notorious criminal case involving a CMS agent dragged on for years and was eventually debated at length in the House of Lords.[64] The activities of many newer agents in the Niger Mission, most of them Sierra Leoneans, caused much offence to local people, resulting in vociferous protest from Christians and others especially in the delta. Well-proven African criticism of this African mission was particularly worrying and in the face of evidence that some Nembe converts had been involved in murder the CMS was well aware 'that the eye of the nation will watch the course adopted by the Committee in this matter'.[65]

In the context of correspondence, for example, with the chiefs of Bonny the Society's concern to protect the centrepiece of the Venn policy, while meeting reasonable criticism by tightening control, was clear. 'We are still of opinion', wrote Lang to James Hamilton, Phillips's successor as Secretary, 'that the European influence in the Mission should be as far as possible *outside* the Mission itself. The Secretary's position is so. The special Medical department ... is so. A layman in charge of the Secularities of the Mission would be so ... But a resident European at Bonny in charge of the Established Mission Station there would be distinctly a departure from the whole policy of the Mission, which notwithstanding the many terrible blots which have distressed all the friends of the Mission, has resulted in one of the most remarkable movements in the whole Mission field and yielded results in numbers and in indigenous vigour and enterprise to which we have scarcely a parallel.'[66]

62  Lang to Bishop Crowther, 18 July 1883, *ibid.*, ff. 191–200; see also F.E. Wigram to Archdeacon Johnson, 19 July 1883, *ibid.*, f. 203.
63  F.K. Ekechi, *Missionary Enterprise and Rivalry in Igboland, 1857–1914* (London, 1972), chap. 4.
64  12 April 1883, *House of Lords Hansard Parliamentary Debates*, vol. 278, cols 31–3.
65  G.O.M. Tasie, *Christian Missionary Enterprise in the Niger Delta, 1864–1918* (Leiden, 1978), esp. chap. 3 'The Delta Revolt'; Lang to Hamilton, 13 Nov. 1885, CMS Archives G3/A3/L2, f. 437.
66  Lang to Hamilton, 4 April 1884, *ibid.*, f. 295.

To Bonny's leaders on the same day it was made clear that 'The Committee do not contemplate placing a European Missionary in pastoral charge of any established Mission station on the Niger.'[67] Even Crowther's own request for European assistance on the Upper Niger where vacancies remained unfilled was rejected, except as a temporary measure in the special case of a 'purely Missionary centre, where there is no Christian congregation, but rather a large field for purely evangelistic work among the heathen'.[68]

Crowther failed to appease his critics and acceptable agents remained in short supply. As a result tensions grew to the point that newer – not always younger – European members of the Mission, urged on by Wilmot Brooke and F.N. Eden, a zealot in the cause of episcopal powers and status, decided to force the issues still further into the open.[69] Their action finally split the mission and exposed seriously divided opinions among the Society's leaders as well as its supporters around the country.[70] In 1890 the Niger Mission was completely reorganised and was purged of many of its African agents. Bishop Crowther was forced into retirement and died on New Year's Eve, 1891; no African Anglican diocesan bishop was again appointed until 1951.

## IV

Crowther's departure should not be seen as simply a personal tragedy or the consequence of local political conflicts, although it was both of these things. Nor was its significance confined to the CMS or to Anglicans more generally. Most obviously its wider importance lay in that the Niger experiment of 1864 – indigenous leadership of an indigenous church and its mission – had become in one form or another *the* missionary goal irrespective of denomination. The failure of this first high-profile attempt by a society to address the problems of the 1860s by the direct reassertion and adaptation of its traditional principles raised questions for all who were coming after. It did so first because it was perhaps the most dramatic example of the failure of that strategy and encouraged the wider development and persistence of misgivings about indigenous Christian leadership. However, failure on the Niger was also the consequence of the wave of revivalism associated with the Keswick conferences, which also affected all missions in the last quarter of the nineteenth century. Both developments had bearings on the developing relationship of missionary religion and empire, not least in accentuating the subordination of indigenous peoples to external controls.

---

67  CMS to the Chiefs of Bonny, 4 April 1884, *ibid.*, ff. 287–94, quotation at f. 292.
68  Lang to Bishop Crowther, 11 June 1884, *ibid.*, f. 316.
69  Andrew Porter, 'Evangelical Enthusiasm'; for Eden, Porter, 'The Hausa Association', esp. 152–7. Hamilton, for example, was born in 1831.
70  For example, Canon Samuel Garratt to F.E. Wigram, 23 May 1892, CMS Archives, Home Correspondence Files, 1764.

Evangelicals, finding enthusiasm at a low ebb, have always turned to hopes of religious revival as the main source of new religious life for themselves and their churches. Revivalism therefore has always been a recurrent feature of mission fields overseas as well as the societies' home base. Methodists at work along the West African coast, in Accra, Cape Coast and Lagos in 1876–78 and again in 1885, were excited by the waves of religious fervour sweeping through their congregations and drawing new members into the churches.[71] Wesleyan meetings thrilled to the strains of Moody's and Sankey's hymns in translation and to revival preaching on 'those truths of a Perfect Salvation'.[72] The prevailing spirit was portrayed in the familiar terminology of reassurance at being 'cleansed from all sin … and, through the Spirit's indwelling and guidance … preserved blameless unto the coming of the Lord Jesus'.[73] The emotion, it seemed, was heightened but restrained, the commitment genuine. John Milum, shortly afterwards in 1881 chairman of the Gold Coast district, reacted as William Shrewsbury had done fifty years earlier: 'there is no system so well adapted for evangelising the races among whom we work as the Methodist. Our class system gives us a great hold upon the people and enables us to keep a purer Church than we otherwise could.' If further proof were needed, it was there in the imitation of Wesleyan practice he detected in both the CMS and Basel Mission.[74] Whatever differences of understanding may have existed between cultures, missionaries found in such revivals periodic reconfirmation of the universality of both their message and their audience. Bryan Roe returned from the Lagos revival in 1885 not praising empire but with renewed 'faith in [Africa's] ultimate, social, moral and spiritual regeneration'.[75]

The impact of revivals none the less varied widely. In the metropole by the 1860s, to the elements of spontaneity and cross-fertilisation in such events, there had already been added the contribution of the professional revivalist, men such as Charles Grandison Finney who had developed the techniques of the revivalist preacher to new heights of effectiveness. The malaise of the1860s was more than enough to prompt evangelicals to turn to the possibilities of revival in the following decade. It was within the context of widespread evangelical dissatisfaction with even their own positive achievements that the Mildmay Conferences took root in the 1860s and a fresh wave of American revivalism was received into Britain with the mission of Moody and Sankey in 1874–75. At the same time, the 'Higher Life'

---

71  Rev. George Dyer to WMMS General Secretary, 21 April 1876; Revs Bryan Roe and J.T.F. Halligey, both Lagos, 8 Dec. 1885, WMMS Archives, Files 1876/10, 1885/35, 36.
72  Rev. J. Milum (Lagos) to Rev. W.B. Boyce, 29 Jan. and 18 April 1876, *ibid.*, File 1876/2, 9; W. Penrose (Accra) to WMMS General Secretary, 3 May 1876, *ibid.*, File 1876/14.
73  George Dyer (Cape Coast) to WMMS General Secretary, 21 Sept. 1877 and Rev. J. Jenkin (Cape Coast) to Rev. John Kilner (General Secretary), 2 Sept. 1878, *ibid.*, Files 1877/27, 1878/28. For the Wesleyan tradition on the Coast of preaching 'entire sanctification', W. Terry Coppin, *John Martin: Pioneer Missionary, Hero and Saint* (London, 1910), pp. 34, 64, 123. For this 'holiness' teaching see below, pp. 245–7.
74  Rev. John Milum to Rev. G.T. Perks, 10 April 1877, *ibid.*, File 1877/13.
75  Rev. Bryan Roe (Lagos) to Rev. M.C. Osborn, [Dec. 1885], *ibid.*, File 1885/41.

teaching of Moody's fellow Americans, the Reverend W.E. Boardman, Robert Pearsall Smith and his wife Hannah, provided for those preferring less emotionalism and a theology where at least intelligibility compensated for lack of rigour. Private meetings and conference appearances from spring 1874 to midsummer 1875 convinced many evangelicals and nonconformists that the Pearsall Smiths brought a new and heartening message. So strong was this conviction that in July 1875 the first interdenominational 'Convention for the Promotion of Practical Holiness' was held at Keswick.[76]

'Quakers from America of much theological ignorance' perhaps they were, but many found inspiration in the Pearsall Smiths and Boardman. Their books drew on ideas about personal holiness and sanctification present in both Calvinist and Wesleyan traditions and were widely read.[77] Late Victorian missionary work, especially that of the CMS, came to owe much to the revivalism of which Keswick was the outstanding sign. Charles Harford defined the Keswick message as follows. 'The message of the Convention is addressed ... to those who are the children of God through faith in Christ Jesus and therefore taking the words of the writer of the Epistle to the Hebrews we would say "let us cease to speak of the first principles of Christ and press on unto perfection", or as the margin says, "full growth". Perhaps the words full growth express in the best way the experience that is set forth as the normal position to which Christians should attain. Too many are satisfied with being babes in Christ; they have rejoiced in the knowledge of sins forgiven and new life imparted through Christ, but like the Galatian Christians, having begun in the Spirit they are seeking to be made perfect by the flesh. To such the message of the Keswick Convention is addressed; it sets before them a life of faith and victory, of peace and rest as the rightful heritage of the child of God, into which he may step not by the laborious ascent of some "Scala Sancta", not by long prayers and laborious effort, but by a deliberate and decisive act of faith.'[78]

Although this was written some thirty years after the first convention and reflected some softening of outlines, for example in the preference for the words 'full growth' rather than 'perfection', the essentials of the Smiths' and early Keswick teaching are there. The possibility of a higher life to be enjoyed in this world and attainable by any Christian through a particular act of faith is the central tenet, a revival of older ideas connected with the Wesleyan Methodist concept of

---

76  The following section on Keswick and Cambridge draws on my article 'Cambridge, Keswick and Late Nineteenth Century Attitudes to Africa', *JICH* 5, 1 (1976), pp. 5–34; more recently, for the development of Keswick, D.W. Bebbington, *Holiness in Nineteenth-Century England* (Carlisle, 2000), chap. 4 'The Keswick Tradition'.

77  L.E. Elliott-Binns, *Religion in the Victorian Era* (London, 1936), chap. 12, quotation at p. 223. B.B. Warfield, *Perfectionism*, 2 vols (New York, 1931), pp. 472–3, is no less dismissive of Boardman; for the Smiths, *ibid.*, Vol. 2, chap. 4.

78  C.F. Harford (ed.), *The Keswick Convention. Its Message, Its Method and Its Men* (London, 1907), pp. 5–6.

'Christian Perfection'. Wesley, the Smiths and Keswick speakers all stressed the fact that the ordinary lives of most Christians were highly unsatisfactory. Although through an act of faith one might have become a church member and, being justified by faith, have received 'release and deliverance from the penalty and future punishment of sins past', one still needed liberation from the psychological fact of sin and protection from recurring attacks of past sins. This at Keswick was thought of as 'deliverance from the power of besetting sin, the attainment of victory in the little conflicts of everyday life'.[79]

Consciousness of this state was the first requisite for the advance to the higher life and, so it appeared to many, this was exactly the awareness to which mid-Victorian evangelicals were being led by their sense of disquiet. Such consciousness in any real Christian could only be linked with the immediate desire to be freed from such a situation. It was the contribution of the 'Higher Life' advocates that they could demonstrate a scriptural basis for the belief that Christ offered and promised such freedom here and now. All that was required was the act of faith, complete trust in God on the part of the individual, 'the consecration of the whole being to God [as] a real and definite act, intended to bring the life into closer conformity to the revealed will and Word of God'.[80] The Christian then, by an act of his own will, could make the necessary leap of faith and move to a higher level of existence, achieving not only justification but sanctification by faith. This higher stage produced in the faithful complete happiness and peace of mind, fullness of life and total freedom from any conscious sense of sin, as a result of Christ's dwelling within the individual. Such a change was clearly apparent to one's associates and opened the way to a more intense form of Christian fellowship.

The association with the concepts of conversion and regeneration of the idea of distinct stages, usually separated from each other in time and consciousness, the notion of the individual's responsibility for an act of will and faith which would enable Christ to proceed – these were in many respects novel. They were also acceptable to large numbers of evangelicals, partly because borne out by experience but also because assimilable to a traditional evangelical insistence on the constant necessity for a heightened consciousness of personal sin and trust in the grace of the Redeemer. The doctrine pandered, too, to the feeling that they were a special or peculiar people, in some way set apart from the ordinary run of sinners. Although there was no explicit revival of Calvinistic thinking about the elect, in that grace, sanctification and salvation remained freely available and potentially efficacious for all sinners, it was easy to feel, as some commentators warned, that the select were those who chose to avail themselves of Christ's offering.

Set against a general background of nineteenth-century intellectual developments, the Higher Life teaching offers interesting parallels.[81] It drew heavily on the

---

79  *Ibid.*, p. 78.
80  *Ibid.*, p. 82.
81  Bebbington, *Holiness*, esp. pp. 77–84.

century's romanticism, responded to the appeal of nature, emphasised the need for absolute faith and trust in God and its association of spiritual progress with religious crisis suggests links with patterns of evolutionary thinking. The shift in theological emphasis from the doctrine of the Atonement to that of the Incarnation is matched in the Higher Life concern with practical possibilities of perfection in this world. If one moves from explanations for its easy acceptance and wide appeal to consideration of the potential effects of such teaching, there are historical comparisons still more relevant to the themes of this book. D.B. Davis has discussed the impact of Quaker and Methodist revivalism in the eighteenth century, the route from 'perfectionism' and a novel conception of sin to an attack on the social and religious system supporting the institution of slavery.[82] It is not difficult to see how comparable changes nearly a century later might reinforce the traditional strictness of the missionary societies in matters of religion and ethical standards, paving the way for an assault on existing missionary practice and institutions.

Historically, antinomianism and an excessive authoritarianism have been tendencies inseparable from Perfectionism or Higher Life teaching, and fears of the possible moral and ethical aberrations, rather than dislike of the associated discipline or moral reinvigoration, led prominent evangelicals to be wary of Keswick enthusiasm in the early days. On the eve of the first Convention, for example, Pearsall Smith himself was shipped back to the United States at the insistence of his English friends for committing some unspecified indiscretion. Keswick, however, rapidly proved its respectability and won a place at the heart of English evangelicalism notwithstanding the persistence of theological reservations.[83] Even an eminent nonconformist such as R.W. Dale, who never set foot in Keswick and was highly critical of the Higher Life teaching, welcomed it for the same reason as many whole-hearted supporters. He felt that Keswick teaching 'had rendered a real service to the Christian Church ... by declaring that those whom Christ has redeemed are called to be saints and that holiness even in this life is possible to the believer through the sanctifying power of the Holy Spirit'.[84] It needs little imagination to see that the transfer of such persuasions to the mission field, even in muted form, was unlikely to make for harmonious co-operation.

Of crucial importance to that transfer was the parallel movement from the mid-1870s to found Anglican evangelical training colleges in the major universities, which led to the establishment of Ridley Hall at Cambridge and Wycliffe Hall in Oxford. Although prompted primarily by domestic considerations and the desire to recover evangelical fortunes felt to be under serious threat, the leaders of this movement were closely connected with the missionary societies, especially the

---

82 Davis, *Problem of Slavery in Western Culture*, chap. 10 'Religious Sources of Anti-Slavery Thought: Quakers and the Sectarian Tradition' and pp. 416–21.

83 Bebbington, *Holiness*, pp. 86–8; Charles Price and Ian Randall, *Transforming Keswick* (Carlisle, 2000).

84 A.W.W. Dale, *The Life of R.W. Dale of Birmingham*, 2nd edn, (London, 1899), pp. 329–30, 346–9.

CMS. As a source of missionary volunteers and of activists in societies such as the Inter-Collegiate Christian Unions recruiting undergraduates from other colleges, members of the Halls were second to none. Ridley was of particular significance. Under its first Principal, Handley Moule (1881–99), 514 men passed through the Hall, of whom the astonishing number of 117 became missionaries and a further seventy-six served overseas in such posts as colonial chaplaincies. Although Moule rejected the idea that he actively encouraged men to opt for missionary work, many then and since were convinced that his influence moulded many a missionary's outlook. There is no doubt that his early personal interest in overseas missions was sustained by extensive family links with the CMS. Moreover, throughout his Cambridge days Moule worked very closely with the Reverend John Barton, who in 1877, on returning from India, became vicar of Holy Trinity, the leading evangelical stronghold and a prominent propagandist on behalf of the CMS. Moule, himself 'emphatically a witness for the simple faith',[85] established a tradition of education at Ridley which strongly favoured the exposition of doctrine over more critical studies and encouraged a preference for piety over learning. Without parallel achievements in the development of analytical power or intellectual sympathy, this was a regime likely to produce that dangerous thing, a little learning mingled with heightened self-esteem.

Moule's further contribution to the late century missionary world lay in his encouragement of the link between Keswick and the revivalism in the universities. There was never a clear division between those who went to Keswick and those who kept to Cambridge and Moule found himself steadily drawn to the Keswick message. Especially after his encouragement with Barton of both Moody's immensely successful mission to Cambridge in 1882 and visits by Keswick speakers, the work of the Convention and the University evangelicals was mutually reinforcing. As a consequence of this conjunction, along with work in the university city missions, other vital training grounds for overseas missionaries came to include Cambridge's Jesus Lane Sunday School and, outside university terms, the many seaside beaches such as Scarborough and Llandudno frequented by workers for the Children's Special Service Mission.

Among the potential missionary recruits – not only those from the universities – the experience of a public-school education, a mounting emphasis on good learning, godliness and athleticism and a stress laid on their association with discipline and good character were aspects of a common upbringing from the mid-1870s onwards. These traits were reinforced by dictates derived from more specifically theological influences. It was widely felt in Keswick circles that the utmost attention should be given to 'the formation of the highest type of character in the Christian, before insisting on the normal outcome of Christian activities'. 'Character and not service, was the aim … What we were intended to *be* and not

85  J.B. Harford and F.C. Macdonald, *Handley Carr Glyn Moule, Bishop of Durham. A Biography* (London, 1922), p. 125.

what we were called to *do*, was the prominent thought.'[86] Again R.W. Dale applauded ideas which he saw as rectifying the faults of earlier evangelicals: they 'had been so solicitous for man's salvation as to lose sight of the necessity of his perfection. Too little thought had been given to character and conduct.'[87] With character there was allied community. John Barton emphasised the nature of the Church as 'an *organic living* whole possessing a compact life of its own' and stressed for the benefit of his evangelical listeners the potentially exclusive belief that spiritual life should be regarded less in the manner of the high churchmen as the result of church membership, but rather as 'the *qualifying condition* for it'.[88] Here again was the theological endorsement of the close-knit networks of evangelical life. The apparent intensity of that life, its rapid pace, the abundance of at least superficially close personal relationships, the endless succession of small and more or less intimate meetings – breakfasts, prayer groups, afternoon walks – as well as the tight family ties, strike any reader of their writings. No missionary could but miss this atmosphere and it is clear that for some the most memorable of moments in the mission field were those meetings with their friends and colleagues after long periods spent alone in non-European company.[89] The strong desire to recreate such fellowship, the near-impossibility of doing so, lay behind more than a little European missionary criticism of those who failed to respond as they hoped.

## V

Missionary society administrators viewed the fervour of the years after 1875 with mixed feelings.[90] The general upsurge of interest in missions after years of relative indifference was widely welcomed. At the same time many aspects of the new enthusiasm, as seen above, fitted uncomfortably with the existing structures of missionary activity. Thus the decision of the 'Cambridge Seven' to volunteer for China in 1885 was a source of widespread satisfaction, a highly visible missionary coup confirming beyond doubt the appeal, significance and status of the mission vocation. It incorporated names from Eton, the Royal Artillery and Dragoon Guards, the Trinity College and University Boat Clubs, English test cricket and the Old Reptonian Prayer Union. For Moule it was the outstanding example of 'a movement which has drawn to it man after man of a very noble type and of just the qualities most influential in the young Cambridge world'.[91] Unfortunately for the

---

86  Harford, *Keswick Convention*, p. 77 and chap. 6 'The Message: Its Method of Presentation'.

87  Dale, *Life of R.W. Dale*, p. 349; R.W. Dale, *The Evangelical Revival and Other Sermons* (London, 1880), pp. 33–40. Also Harford, *Keswick Convention*, p. 78.

88  C.E. Barton, *John Barton. A Memoir … with Preface by H.C.G. Moule* (London, 1910), pp. 131–3.

89  For example, M.H.P. Beauchamp, *Days of Blessing in Inland China* (London, 1890).

90  Steven S. Maughan, 'Regions Beyond and the National Church: Domestic Support for the Foreign Missions of the Church of England in the High Imperial Age, 1870–1914' (unpub. Ph.D. thesis, Harvard, 1995).

91  Harford and Macdonald, *Handley Carr Glyn Moule*, p. 120.

older societies, however, the Seven had little hesitation in joining the CIM. The event culminated in four farewell meetings for the CIM party, the last in Exeter Hall at the special request of the YMCA on 4 February 1885 and gave rise to an explosion of publicity for the CIM and its ideals.[92]

The new enthusiasm from which all societies hoped to benefit in some way thus presented them with a serious problem. Unless the long-standing societies adapted their image and appeal they were likely to lose many of the new volunteers either to faith missions such as the CIM, to heterodox organisations such as the Salvation Army or to operators on the fringes of the missionary world such as the Methodist Thomas Champness's Joyful News Evangelists.[93] The CMS found itself inundated with enquiries from volunteers, often too young or otherwise as yet unsuitable but whom it judged wise to encourage; complicated arrangements were discussed to maintain volunteers' links between CMS and other sources of recruits such as the Mildmay Institution.[94] The new spirit of Keswick and revival had to be captured, perhaps tamed, but certainly incorporated into the everyday workings of the mainstream missionary movement. Simultaneously, Keswick itself had to be brought to take more notice of those societies.[95] The CMS's cautious acceptance of this analysis meant that the fate of the Niger Mission was settled in the marketplace for missionary recruits.

We have already seen how the fitness of Crowther's agents, their quality and their 'spirituality' emerged as a central and contentious issue in the development of the Niger Mission experiment. The arrogance, high-handedness and tendency to be hypercritical of the Europeans drawn into the mission are equally plain. It was remarked upon not simply by those Africans who suffered it and their remaining friends at Salisbury Square. To Handley Moule the outstanding characteristics of many of the new missionaries of the 1880s, even before they left home, were their 'uncompromising spirituality and unworldliness'. If for some these were matters of temperament, for most it reflected their wider experience of the evangelical world. It embodied what senior figures within the CMS, like Stock anxious to see the Society move with the times, regarded as a new and desirable manifestation of 'reality' in religion.[96] When approached by men such as Brooke and his friends, the CMS was unwilling to lose them and anxious to turn their idealism and energy to advantage.

The membership of Brooke's and J.A. Robinson's Niger party illustrates the pervasiveness of Cambridge and Keswick influences. Of the seven missionaries, only Brooke and the Reverend P.A. Bennett had not been to university,

92  A.T. Polhill-Turner, *A Story Retold. 'The Cambridge Seven'* (London, 1902), pp. 8–22.

93  Eliza M. Champness, *The Life Story of Thomas Champness* (London, 1907), esp. chaps 17–21.

94  Lang to D.A.L. Hooper, 12 Aug. 1886, CMS Archives, G3/A5/L4, f. 39; Lang to Miss M.W. Harvey, 2 Nov. 1885, CMS Archives, G3/A5/L3, f. 288; *CMS Register*, List II, entry 98.

95  Eugene Stock, chap. 11 'The Missionary Element', in Harford, *The Keswick Convention*.

96  Eugene Stock, *My Recollections* (London, 1909), p. 187.

respectively having made do with Haileybury and the CMS College at Islington. Dr Charles Harford-Battersby, son of the founder of Keswick and member of Moule's college (Trinity), was a prominent member of the Inter-Collegiate Christian Union and at least in his Cambridge days was prone to 'Perfectionist aberrations'. Robinson had been to Christ's College and obtained a first class in the theological tripos; the Reverend F.N. Eden was a product of the aggressively evangelical Pembroke College; and the Reverend Eric Lewis was both a graduate of that most evangelical of all Cambridge colleges, Corpus Christi and a student of Ridley Hall. Henry Dobinson, contemporary with Harford-Battersby at Repton School, had been to Brasenose College, Oxford. It was 'considered quite strange' for him not to have been to Keswick. However, as he recorded, all missionaries, especially the CMS, held Keswick in high regard and it was 'from the ranks of Keswick Convention-goers and other conventions that the Mission ranks are mainly recruited'.[97] There is no doubt that he shared the same outlook as the others at this time.

In approaching the Niger, the European newcomers found little to their satisfaction. Dobinson was the one member of the Niger Expedition who later confessed to burning 'with shame and horror' at the memory of the European criticisms of the mission and its African members 'in those dark days of 1890'; his public apology was appreciated by many Africans but earned him a stern rebuke from Salisbury Square.[98] Yet even Dobinson, very shortly after his arrival at Onitsha in 1890, was telling relations at home how he and his colleagues felt 'the absence of spiritual life out here in the Church. Conversion is practically unknown and has certainly not been required as essential to admission to baptism. A mere knowledge of the Creed, Lord's Prayer and the Ten Commandments has always been reckoned as sufficient ground for baptising any one who offers himself. Can any one be surprised if under such circumstances the Church is impure and rotten through and through?'[99] For those who went out to the Niger at this time it was not the majority of the native Christians along the river but the Muslims of the north – Wilmot Brooke's ultimate evangelistic target – who seemed to mirror their own religious commitment. In the end Brooke, the leader of the expedition to Crowther's Mission, confessed that, although they had come out 'hoping to carry on and expand the work of twenty years ... now after two months we are driven to admit that there is no hope of success until we have first taken down the whole of the past work so that not one stone remains upon another'.[100]

---

97  21 Sept. 1891, H.H. Dobinson, *Letters of Henry Hughes Dobinson Late Archdeacon of the Niger* (London, 1899), p. 117.
98  Quoted by J.B. Webster, *The African Churches among the Yoruba 1888–1922* (Oxford, 1964), pp. 16–17; Ekechi, *Missionary Rivalry*, pp. 68–9.
99  31 March 1890, Dobinson, *Letters*, pp. 49–50.
100  Brooke to General Touch (CMS), 5 June 1890, quoted in Ayandele, *Missionary Impact*, p. 215.

Missionary adjustments to the potentially explosive cocktail of Keswick theology, pre-millennialism and institutional innovation did not generally have such dramatic and destructive impact as occurred on the Niger. However, the CMS was not alone in its difficulties. In West Africa, schism rent one mission after another, for example the Presbyterians at Calabar in 1882 and the Methodists and Baptists at Lagos between 1884 and 1888. Keswick enthusiasms spawned independent missions to Lagos and Freetown in 1886, 1888 and 1889. Many Lagos Christians became the target of criticisms similar to those levied at the Niger agents and were no less resentful; but others displayed evidence of conversion meetings, the personal experience of salvation and a missionary commitment of their own, which the Keswick missioners admired.[101]

Other measures spurred on by these pressures external to the missions included the spread of evangelistic bands similar to the Sudan party. James Horsburgh, already a CMS missionary, lead the New Interior Mission into mid-China in 1891; approved by the CMS as an Honorary Missionary like Brooke, Barclay Fowell Buxton in 1890 led and financed a mission to Japan. All followed one of the most important of these ventures, launched in connection with the Eastern Equatorial Africa Mission.[102] As an honorary missionary attached to the CMS and at his own expense, Douglas Hooper, who had been at Trinity Hall and Ridley, left at the head of this mission party in May 1885. Hooper's enterprise displayed many of the features later to be seen on the Niger. The instructions to the missionaries made much of the guidance of Moule and Barton and the desire of the volunteers to work in 'the regions beyond'. From CMS headquarters the mission was organised with a view to stimulating further university interest, especially after the murder of Bishop Hannington on his way to Buganda in October 1885 and a new rival outburst of enthusiasm for the Far East. A substantial donation of £2000 from Keswick enthusiasts was diverted into support for single women missionaries, for which the number of candidates had grown dramatically with the rise of the conventions. The Secretaries managed as best they could Hooper's recklessness as it steadily came out into the open. He criticised the extravagance of the CMS work, acted on his wish to abandon any but the most essential stores and to live off the country and to his cost ignored the wisest travel precautions. More orthodox members of the party were taken aback by the 'Salvation Army tendencies' of others and by Hooper's wildness. In the end the mission was saved from itself by the impossibility of advancing to Buganda and the presence of the conciliatory European bishops who succeeded Hannington.

On a smaller scale, the nature of the field in north India made a range of other responses more appropriate. The current of the times finally made necessary the

---

101 Webster, *The African Churches*, pp. 43–52.
102 This summary is based on Eastern Equatorial Africa Mission, Letterbooks (1884–88), G3/A5/L3–4 and In-Letters (1885–6), G3/A5, CMS Archives; for Horsburgh and Buxton, *CMS Register*, List I, entries 976, 1152.

closure of the Cathedral Mission College in Calcutta. For fifteen years the CMS had struggled to make it a success, but now 'the almost hopelessness of getting competent men from the Universities for the work of our Colleges' compelled the Society to give it up.[103] It was a regrettable surrender to the prevailing preference for preaching,[104] but was nevertheless a convenient response to the radical complaints against extravagant institutions. Rather than persevere with theological training and English-language higher education, resources were to be redeployed. Mounting concern at the level of vernacular knowledge saw a growing emphasis on the importance for new missionaries to acquire vernacular language skills.[105] Before long this was taken further with requests for the Corresponding Committee to take steps to organise 'some definite Itinerating *system*' with the intention both of reaching more of the rural population and of warding off other locally devised schemes which the Parent Committee found unsatisfactory.[106] The further step dovetailing with the Keswick and faith mission practice was the employment of lay evangelists. Some at least, now to be known as Associated Evangelists, were recruited by the CMS with unusual alacrity in 1890 in response to direct requests from the Society's friends at Keswick. At the same time their presence was for the CMS a useful response to the itinerant activities of the Church Army.[107]

## VI

By stimulating new enthusiasm, rousing volunteers and raising funds, the adaptation and revival of traditions and institutions within the main societies was intended to reassert the continuing possibilities of Christianity's expansion and to quieten the critics of missions. This was to be achieved by demonstrating the unworkability of some new ideas, by allowing them to realise their own limitations and through winning over their supporters by incorporating fashionable priorities as far as possible into standard practice. Thus in this chapter it has been seen how high church Anglicans responded to those needs in East Central Africa and north India, with new missions implanted firmly in their own traditions. The CMS's 'great experiment on the Niger, using Crowther's consecration to forge ahead with

---

103 W. Grey and Hutchinson (CMS Secretaries) to H.P. Parker (Joint Secretary, Calcutta Corresponding Committee), 19 March 1880, CMS Archives CI1/L9, f. 442.

104 In noting this, John Barton also predicted that the latest decision would itself be reversed before long, as indeed it was in 1900 with the foundation of St Paul's College: Barton to W. Grey, 26 April 1888 (copy), CMS Archives, G2I1/L12, f. 14.

105 Grey and Fenn to [? D.T. Barry, Secretary, N. India Mission Corresponding Committee], 13 Dec. 1878 and to H.P. Parker (Secretary, Calcutta Corresponding Committee), 10 April 1879, *ibid.*, L9, ff. 272, 326.

106 *Ibid.* to Parker, 20 Nov. 1883, CMS Archives, G2I1/L10, f. 444.

107 F.E. Wigram to CMS Friends, 1 Aug. 1890 and Instructions to the new evangelists, 7 Oct. 1890, *ibid.*, G2I1/L12, ff. 457, 488; Gray to A.Clifford (Secretary, Calcutta Corresponding Committee), 14 Jan. 1891, *ibid.*, G2I1/L13, f. 18; *Church Missionary Intelligencer* (Feb. 1891).

Venn's established plans, offered another route to an expanding future. The conventional resort to revival as an answer to religious stagnation also found its advocates. This opened the way to what became the Keswick movement, aspects of which appealed in varying degrees to evangelicals around the world and across the denominational spectrum. Finally, it was demonstrated how these new developments could be incorporated into the shifting strategy of a missionary society and applied on the ground.

# Missionary traditions, c. 1860–95: adaptations and consequences (2)

The spreading influence of Keswick's enthusiasm for personal holiness established in many parts of the missionary world a new set of standards by which the reality of the Christianity professed by converts, church members, local catechists and pastors was to be judged. These standards, applied in some cases with an uncompromising rigour and self-destructive single-mindedness as we have seen on the Niger, were frequently married to other newly fashionable tendencies, the most important of which were those associated with the faith missions and changing interpretations of prophecy. These included a powerful non-denominationalism, which cared little for ecclesiastical hallmarks; the hostility to high costs and Western-style institutions, such as schools, colleges, hospitals and orphanages, especially those where theological and secular training were mingled; the emphasis on travelling light and preaching vigorously. Criticisms of past and present practice and demands for new initiatives were an inescapable outcome of this revivalist ideology.

However, it would be mistaken to imagine that the criticisms and challenges of the late century everywhere evoked a willingness to reform or change direction. In a formal manner, for example, Keswick theology and practices appealed less to members of the LMS, BMS and Wesleyans than to Anglicans. Few nonconformists graced the Keswick stage until the 1920s.[1] Claims to novelty were at times little more than old lines backed by new faces. From whichever direction they came, demands for change were often overwhelmed by the din of heels being dug in. Local Christians rejected the consequences of European priorities and demands for change; missionaries were unsympathetic to the requests of their societies; and societies compared their own wisdom or common sense with the perversity of their opponents. Conditions both inside and outside the missions were often such as to curtail creative responses to the promotion of missionary enterprise. Attention must therefore now be turned to a selection of more conservative responses – both towards building up the indigenous churches and by Wesleyans and Presbyterians in India and Africa during partition – that are nevertheless too readily understood as a natural tightening of ties between missions and empire.

---

1 Price and Randall, *Transforming Keswick*, pp. 42–5. My thanks to Dr Brian Stanley for this reference.

## I

One perennial source, both of differences between those in the field and those at home and of conflict between missionaries and local Christians or indigenous audiences, was that of promotion within the indigenous church and Christian community and the transfer of responsibility from European missionary to church members. Although this rarely led to conflicts as complex and dramatic as that surrounding Crowther, it involved a very widespread and persistent assertion of European standards or ideas about the church at the expense of indigenous views. Examples drawn from many parts of the missionary field illustrate how, in less dramatic but no less effective ways, attempts to reinvigorate missionary traditions and to push forward the independence of local churches and the expansion of Christianity could be thwarted.

At their most basic these encounters involved the issue of individuals' pay and status and the interaction of personal ambitions or grievances on both sides. In the larger societies, such as the LMS or the WMMS, European missionaries were far more 'expensive' than native agents: they drew salaries, had travelling expenses, sometimes and with increasingly regularity took leave and as the century wore on incurred pensions as well as allowances for wives and children. For missions such as the CIM and UMCA, many or all of whose missionaries drew no salaries and were unmarried, there was less of a problem. However, it remained the case everywhere that funds always seemed short and the employment of Europeans often meant less opportunity and remuneration for local people unless self-support was made a reality by finance raised on the spot.

For the CMS, its West African missions were uncommonly complicated in this respect. Sierra Leoneans, 'as practically in many respects foreigners in a strange land', had to be provided for differently from either Europeans or local Africans. 'It is obvious that Africans who are natives of the countries where they are living and working, brought up in the country in the midst of their friends, will have acquired simpler habits more in accordance with those of the natives around them and will be enabled to live as regards dress, food, residence etc. far more cheaply than those, whatever their nationality, who have been brought up under very different circumstances at Sierra Leone or elsewhere and have of necessity acquired very different habits of life in all the points specified and who need therefore larger means and better appliances.' The lines were difficult to draw, friction inevitable 'and the natives of the country will be slow to understand or accept the distinction'.[2] Understanding and acceptance were of course the more difficult because conventional ties between salaries, wealth and status were themselves hard to break. Help from family allowances and support for children's education mattered no less to black than to white missionaries.

---

2  R. Lang to J.A. Hamilton, 11 July 1885, CMS Archives, G3/A3/L2, f. 412.

For those feeling financially squeezed – European as well as local inhabitants – and for whom the religious marketplace did not provide sufficient local support, entry into other commercial markets was virtually inevitable. From the early LMS barter trade for coconut oil and arrowroot in the Pacific to CMS agents engaging in the palm oil and other trades of the Niger late in the nineteenth century, the problem remained a live one. In the new climate of the 1880s and 1890s, however, there was also a far stronger tendency to see such involvement not simply as a diversion from evangelism but as evidence of religious and moral inadequacy. Thus were an individual's employment in the mission and chances for advancement both put at risk.

All mission spheres had their own variations on this theme, but most missionaries and agents coped with discomfort and abided by the rules. For them questions of preferment and responsibility were bound up more directly with the future of the mission itself.[3] The Venn strategy was predicated on the assumption that the missionary society's task would eventually end. What came to be referred to as 'the euthanasia of the mission' would occur when the self-financing, self-governing and self-propagating church was secure and missionaries were transferred to a new field.[4] Venn, however, always recognised that persuading European missionaries to relinquish 'their' mission and to move on would be difficult, requiring not only persuasion but a planned process of handing over authority. A major theme in the modern history of overseas missions has been that of the failure, despite persistent attempts by mission administrators, indigenous Christians and individual missionaries to overcome the resistance to what was always seen as premature withdrawal. Historians of the end of empire have long been familiar with a parallel phenomenon in the transfer or surrender of secular power in the process of political and economic decolonisation.

It is not hard to see that individual missionaries had reason to resist the pressures for withdrawal, whatever their origin. Especially for those long in the service of a society, attachment to people and place could be powerful disincentives either to move or to declare oneself redundant. Movement to a new, especially an 'unopened', field, raised all the practical difficulties of starting all over again. Against a common background of self-sacrifice and the privations of much missionary life – hunger, fevers, food shortages, the illness and death of colleagues and their children and the potentially explosive irritations of communal living – it is not surprising that missionaries might wish to hang on to such comforts and routines as they had established. To get on with his work, Bishop Smythies lived off boiled bananas, 'very insipid, tasteless food' but quick to prepare. Eden and Dobinson in the lower Niger found the insect bites bearable, more so than they found their colleague J.A. Robinson, who 'is terribly sensitive and groans and moans all night'.[5] Missionaries with the preferences,

---

3 Williams, *Ideal of the Self-Governing Church*, esp. chaps 3, 4 and 6.
4 For 'euthanasia', *ibid.*, pp. 4–6, 15, 64–5; Shenk, *Henry Venn*, pp. 119–20.
5 Russell (ed.), Life of Charles Alan Smythies, p. 211; 20 March 1890, Dobinson, *Letters of Henry Hughes Dobinson*, p. 41.

energy and perseverance of a Livingstone, James Chalmers or even Wilmot Brooke, enabling them to be either constantly on the move or coping with incessant roughness and isolation, were understandably few. Even transfer home to Britain, with for some at least the likelihood of a new parish or fresh Methodist circuit, presented serious problems of readjustment.

The expression of such preferences, however, was incompatible with the patterns of missionary discourse. Resistance to self-government and independence for new churches from missionary intervention or 'parental' watchfulness had to be justified in terms of benefits and the best interests of the newly converted. The rejection of plans to move forward on the lines laid down by Venn and Anderson could only be allowed to rest on negative arguments, such as the lack of local believers' readiness for responsibility or the risk of damage to the wider evangelical enterprise. Negative images, which had been liable to refinement or dramatisation from the beginning of the modern movement to enhance the importance of the missionary task and to stimulate giving in its support, left their residues. Even when stereotypes might be less prominent than before, experience everywhere indicated that relapse was always a possibility. Such arguments and uncertainties were easily turned, consciously or unconsciously, to support the case for delay in surrendering missionary responsibilities.

Calcutta was but one of the important centres in North India where the arguments between missionaries on the ground and organisers at home can be followed. The site of early Protestant efforts, Calcutta had avoided being directly caught up in the disturbances of 1857 and was able to demonstrate a long and continuous history of missionary endeavour. However, by the mid-1860s it was, Christopher Fenn (north India secretary at Salisbury Square) admitted, not simply a place where there was little sign of success but one where 'there has been much to discourage'.[6] From his correspondents in Calcutta, Fenn received plenty of dismissive comment. The state of the Native Christian community was unsatisfactory, lacking in initiative and prone to lean on European aid. Even those born native Christians were disinclined to take up their heritage, being, it was said, too often stupid, apathetic, impudent and showing a dislike to Europeans.[7] Both London and Calcutta were broadly agreed that the 'weakness of the Native Agency of the Mission is the great blot of our work in North India', while differing over the further steps that might be taken to remedy this situation.[8] These were persistent problems, no different in the 1880s than several decades before.[9]

---

6  Fenn to Timothy Sandys, 4 Nov. 1864, CMS Archives CI1/I2, f. 144. For Sandys, long serving secretary of both the Calcutta Bible Association and the Calcutta Church Missionary Association (1830–64), *CMS Register*, List I, entry 154.

7  Fenn to F.E. Schneider, 13 Sept 1865; to W. Hooper, 30 May 1866; and to T. Sandys, 8 Oct. 1867, CMS Archives, CI1/I2, ff. 263, 370, 481; *CMS Register*, List I, entries 154, 263, 614.

8  Fenn to E.C. Stuart (Secretary, Calcutta Corresponding Committee), 22 July 1867, CMS Archives, CI1/I2, f. 458.

9  Fenn to J. Welland (Secretary, Calcutta Corresponding Committee), *ibid.*, CI1/I3, 1 Dec. 1874; to

However, there was no simple polarisation of views between Indians and Europeans. Like Venn before him, Fenn had no doubt that missionaries were part of the problem and in his correspondence struggled to reconstruct them, a difficult task calling for considerable tact and imagination. He encouraged, impressing on his charges that their experience was not dissimilar to others' and pointing out what he saw as unwarranted modesty or self-criticism in their reports. He warned, both against expecting too much and criticising accordingly and against urging converts 'too much to take employment under Missionary Societies'.[10] He professed ignorance of India and welcomed their letters and suggestions, entering into debate when consulted on tricky issues of episcopacy and native churches.[11] He waxed eloquent against the high church excesses of the Bishop of Colombo and at the same time slipped in the idea that giving Indian Christians more say in their affairs would both create a common anti-ritualist front and allow the 'real strength ... of every Native Christian congregation ... [to] come out to view'.[12]

There were occasions, however, when Fenn felt the need for stronger tactics. As he told Joseph Welland, Secretary to the Calcutta Corresponding Committee, no great improvements were ever introduced by those engaged in the work, but only by outsiders or their pressure. 'Every resolution of every large Missionary Conference is always to the effect that everything in the present mode of action is perfectly right.'[13] Hence the need for the Home Committee at times to overrule the advice of even its ablest and most experienced men. He responded vigorously when he suspected that missionaries were holding back their own support for church building activities in order to give priority to other work that they preferred, but in doing so was careful to take on himself responsibility for a system which nevertheless now needed to be changed. Hence the need, he pointed out to the conservative Robert Clark in the Punjab on one occasion, for the newly introduced Church Councils and Committees. 'Subjection to European Missionaries does not of itself prepare adult Native Christians for independence. Just the reverse ... The only way in which Native Christians can learn to be independent either pecuniarily, or in the way of self-government, is by being practised in it. From this it follows that they must be made independent *before they are fit for it*.'[14] Fenn was also perfectly prepared to egg on the Indian priest P.M. Rudra in his station at Burdwan, to do all he could to counter European resistance to Bengali control over the churches. Explaining how the CMS Committee at home had

B. Davis (Benares), 10 Aug. 1881; and to R. Clark (Secretary, Punjab Corresponding Committee), 18 Aug. 1881, *ibid.*, ff. 368, 371; *CMS Register*, List I, entries 432, 563, 603.

10  Fenn to Hooper, 30 May 1866, CMS Archives, CI1/I2, f. 370.
11  Fenn to Clark, 11 Aug. 1881, *ibid.*, CI1/I3, f. 361.
12  For Bishop R.S. Copleston, the CMS and the 'great Ceylon controversy', Stock, *History of the CMS*, Vol. 3, pp. 203–16; Fenn to James Vaughan, 19 Dec. 1879, CMS Archives, CI1/I3; quotation in Fenn to F.E. Schneider, 13 Sept. 1865, *ibid.*, CI1/I2, f. 263.
13  Fenn to Welland, 25 July 1879, *ibid.*, CI1/I3, f. 337.
14  Fenn to Clark, 18 Aug. 1881, *ibid.*, CI1/I2, f. 371, Fenn's emphasis.

struggled to bring church councils into being at Krishnagar and elsewhere 'in spite of some resistance from Europeans in Bengal itself', he expressed his pleasure at the way in which local Christians were apparently beginning to take advantage of the new openings. 'This throwing off of the foreign yoke by the Bengal Native Christians is exactly what we, the C.M.S. Parent Committee, wish to see brought about.'[15]

## II

It is widely held that Scottish mission traditions in the nineteenth century were uncommonly strong in their twofold attachment, to Duff and to Livingstone. Nevertheless, the emphases associated with both men, on English-language higher education and on Christianity directly linked to commerce, came under increasing scrutiny. Traditional missionary practices established in the 1830s and 1840s remained more or less intact until the 1870s, not least within the Free Church where Duff's influence seems to have increased in the 1860s when, after his retirement from the field, he took over as convenor of the Foreign Missions Committee.[16] However as the influence of the founding fathers in India fell away – Anderson (d. 1855), Wilson (d. 1875) and eventually Duff himself (d. 1878) – and government insistence on 'neutrality' in religious matters persisted, the pressures in the subcontinent to rethink missionary practice grew in both the Church of Scotland and the Free Church. After Livingstone's death and burial in 1874, they were not alone in feeling obliged to meet demands for a mission in East and Central Africa to commemorate his work. However, the revival of 'Christianity and commerce' was no straightforward matter as the process of partition began to unfold. It is necessary to look at both their Indian and their African work in turn.

The disruption of the Scottish churches in the 1840s had left the Established Church with property but deprived of missionaries. The Free Church had taken the manpower but had to rebuild its schools and churches. Both fought to secure as large a share of home support as possible. Consequently Scottish missions continued to feel the dearth of recruits and the scarcity of funds as acutely as any on into the 1860s. In India, against this background, criticism of the missionary record – small returns in numbers of Indian Christians and accusations of extravagance in schools and colleges – were readily forthcoming. The argument that limited resources should be concentrated on more productive, direct evangelism won increasing support. Backing for the Duff tradition was strongest among the European missionaries in the field, while a crude preference for 'evangelism' over 'education' prevailed in home congregations. Even within the churches' Foreign

---

15  Fenn to Piari Mohan Rudra (Burdwan), 29 April 1885, *ibid.*, CI1/I3, f. 380.

16  For example, Sheila M. Brock, 'James Stewart and Lovedale: A Reappraisal of Missionary Attitudes and African Response in the Eastern Cape, South Africa, 1870–1905', (unpub. Ph.D. thesis, Edinburgh, 1974), chaps.1–3.

Missions Committees (FMCs) opinions were often similarly divided. In the FCS, for example, Dr George Smith (Secretary, 1879–1909) and Professor Thomas Lindsay (FMC Convenor, 1885–1900) were respectively protagonists for 'educational' and 'evangelistic' strategies.[17] From the 1870s onwards, although many practical compromises were hammered out locally, the character and preferences of the Scottish enterprise lent ever more towards evangelism and work in the vernacular by both European missionaries and native Indian agents.

The erosion of the 'English school tradition' in India was patchy, a picture related in part to the continuing Indian demand for work in the vernacular, but affected too by the vagaries of missionary income and the endlessly seductive hope that any Christian contact was better than none. Even at the height of their influence and while admiring Duff's achievements, some of his colleagues had found an essential role for vernacular schools.[18] The need for branch schools as feeders to the central Institutions, the employment in them of native Indian teachers, a feeling that country districts should be worked in association with the great cities, all contributed to their continuing vitality. Even if their results were unspectacular, they continued to compete for mission funds with the 'English' schools.

It thus became steadily more common for the argument to be made that the wider the range of activities the greater perhaps might be the chance of a missionary breakthrough. The balance had to be tipped away from higher education toward direct vernacular evangelism. As the convenor of the established church's FMC put it, 'I am not sure that the farther young men advance in literature and science they are led nearer to Christ', because the resulting 'keeness of competition must be a barrier to calm earnest enquiry into Christian truth'.[19] To William Hastie, he wrote, 'Not wishing you to be less of an Educationist, I should rejoice to see you more of an Evangelist than when you went to India; and without question it would be a great blessing, under God, to our old Institution work … if we had at no great distance a more directly Missionary Agency in close connection with Calcutta where the gathering in and the building up of a Christian Church would be the primary and prominent purpose.'[20] That this would make for a more sensible and effective use of scarce resources than the erection of new and distant stations became a familiar refrain.

The failure of native congregations in Bengal to recruit new members prompted suggestions for more vernacular programmes aimed at English-educated Indians.[21] It also led William Milner to conclude that there should generally be

17  For Smith, with his India experience, *BDCM*, pp. 626–7; for Lindsay, *DSCHT*, p. 486.
18  J.Murray Mitchell (Poona) to Alexander Brunton (Convenor FMC, FCS), 31 Dec. 1842, NLS MS/7532(1), f. 195; James Aitken (Poona) to Brunton, 26 Aug. 1840, 30 March 1842, *ibid*., ff. 59, 246.
19  Rev. J.C. Heardman to Wilson (Calcutta), 6 March 1878, NLS MS/7534, f. 98.
20  Heardman to Hastie (Calcutta), 27 Nov. 1879, *ibid*., f. 139. For Hastie's colourful career, *DSCHT*, p. 394.
21  Heardman to Dr Jardine (Calcutta), 3 Jan. 1877, NLS MS/7534, f. 82.

'more evangelistic work alongside of our Education institutions whose direct object would be to give the Gospel to the people *and nothing else*'.[22] In some districts village preaching and itineration kept up over a period seemed to arouse new interest in the missions and to open new opportunities after long periods of insignificant progress. This occurred in Madras, where Adam Andrew and his assistants in the late 1880s found more and more of the lowest castes approaching the mission for assistance. They were responding, Andrew thought, to the preaching of recent years and, as a result of his vernacular ability and interest, a completely new field was taken up by the Free Church's Madras mission.[23]

Debate about the deployment of medical missionaries operated in a similar manner. The placement of medical missionaries had a particular value not least in enabling one denomination to outbid another in areas of competition,[24] but by the 1880s there was wide agreement that to establish them in the larger cities would be superfluous. There Western medicine was both reasonably familiar and accessible. Discussion therefore normally centred on the wisdom of setting up elsewhere either central hospitals or village dispensaries with native agents attended by a travelling doctor; in both cases vernacular competence was thought an essential qualification for the medical missionary.[25]

Mission organisers and doctors themselves, however, felt that more than command of a vernacular language was required if suspicion of medical missions as expensive irrelevancies was to be kept at bay. Debate on a memorial from the Edinburgh Medical Missionary Society finally produced a resolution for the Free Church Assembly's approval, reconciling the role of medic with the mounting pressure for evangelism. 'In order to make the Medical Missionary more efficient in the discharge of his duties it is desirable that the Church should sanction the conferring upon him of some special status, such as that of Evangelist.' It was hoped that this would prevent the specialist from drifting away from the mission.[26] Forty years on from William Lockhart the climate had decidedly changed. From the field itself, Dr Alexander even played down the significance of his own expertise. 'We admit that there is no very pressing humanitarian reason for a medical mission as things are now, but we consider the work to be of distinct value as a means of presenting the pitifulness of the Christian religion, as well as of gathering together large numbers to hear the Gospel.'[27]

---

22  W. Milner to George Smith (Secretary to FMC, FCS), 24 April 1883, NLS MS/7838, f. 79.
23  For Andrew's work with the dalits (outcastes) of Chingleput, 1884–93, see NLS MSS/7845–6.
24  The FCS placed Walker at Conjeveram in 1888 to ward off the Wesleyans, *ibid*., ff. 59–60, in G.M. Rae to Prof. T.M. Lindsay (Convenor, FMC), 26 Feb. 1891.
25  Alex Alexander to Dr George Smith, 27 Feb. 1884, NLS MS/7845, ff. 1–2; Minutes, Special Meeting of the Western India Mission, 6 Dec. 1890, MS/7820, f. 20; Lindsay to Rae, 24 Jan. 1891 and to J.T. Morton, 14 Aug. 1891, MS/7774, ff. 409, 587; Morton to Lindsay, 31 Aug. 1891, MS/7845, ff. 101–2.
26  FMC Minutes, 21 March–9 May 1882, NLS Dep. 298/112, Vol. 7, ff. 128, 132, 145.
27  Alex Alexander to Dr George Smith, 27 Feb. 1884, NLS MS/7845, ff. 1–2.

As in China so in India it was not only the view that traditional methods were unproductive, but also the tendency of missionary effort to press inland away from the major ports and Presidency headquarters, that periodically injected new life into missions' vernacular work. Eventually this led to radical conclusions. Despite personal disagreements with Andrew, James Peattie, secretary to the Free Church Mission Council in Madras, concluded from his work that 'the true solution of the caste-question lies here. Raise the non-castes; give them brain-power enough to take their place in the battle of life with the caste-man; infuse Christian principles into their lives and soon a change will be perceptible in Hindu society. Hindus cannot, in agriculture, do without the Pariahs and hence if the Pariahs were Christianised a great effect would be made on rural Hinduism. Education has not done much yet for the great bulk of the 35 millions of the Madras Presidency.' Vernacular education and evangelising 'among the lower rural classes' was 'the grand lever' for the transformation of Indian society.[28] The work of other missions in Travancore and Tirunelveli (Tinnevelly) taught the same lesson. Duff had represented his College as a mine laid under Hinduism; Peattie's conclusion implied that the charge had been faulty and the mine itself misplaced.

New approaches nevertheless brought serious and persistent problems, one of the most important the resistance among the missionaries themselves to learning the vernaculars. Dr Walker, the Free Church's medical missionary at Conjeveram and Walajabad was noted as still incompetent after five years. The language difficulties encountered in India were certainly very great. However, Walker's failure with Tamil was also attributable, so it was thought, to the fact that senior missionaries in Madras, themselves hardly more qualified, shrank from applying the rules. Although the Foreign Missions Committee at home took a hard line, finally addressing the general problem in 1892 by restricting responsibility and refusing promotion to 'the linguistically challenged', possibilities for evasion apparently still remained.[29] In the Church of Scotland convenors faced the same problem, the Reverend James Williamson pointedly reminding the Calcutta missionaries of the importance now attached to vernacular evangelistic work and the need therefore for staff 'specially devoted' to it.[30] The spirit of Duff, who had never acquired any vernacular, lived on. It was a serious liability in a country where by the 1880s the spread of private schools and the transfer of government schools and colleges into local hands was proceeding rapidly, steadily reducing the significance of the missions' role.

Even as missionary effort seeped into new vernacular channels and Duff's strategy ceased to command its old allegiance, the central institutions continued as

---

28  Peattie to Prof. Thomas Lindsay, 30 March 1893, NLS MS/7846, f. 251.
29  On Walker, see Lindsay to Peattie, 10 Dec. 1892 (Very Private and Confidential), NLS MS/7775, f. 314 and Andrew to Lindsay, 20 June 1893, 7846 f. 310. For the operation of the new rules, e.g., John Stewart to George Smith, 7 June 1893, *ibid.*, f. 305.
30  Williamson to Rev. James Edwards, 21 March 1892, NLS MS/7534, ff. 685-91.

a powerful presence on the scene. Making little concession to new practices and theoretical misgivings, they also lost impetus and co-ordination with the growth of internal conflict and inefficiency. Church of Scotland Convenors frequently expressed despair at the personal bickering in their stations and occasionally sent stern reprimands to Calcutta.[31] The distraction of missionaries in the leading institutions from their central tasks had always been seen as a danger; now the extension of work into the countryside seemed sometimes incompatible with efficient administration and provoked conflicts over the sharing of available funds. In Madras, Andrew eventually abandoned trying to settle financial priorities within the local Mission Council. Instead he complained directly to Edinburgh of a system steadily becoming more anomalous, of 'supervision run mad', of 'a waste of energy ... liable to produce friction amongst the various subordinate agents'.[32]

As in other societies on these issues, so the late 1880s and early 1890s witnessed a crisis in Scottish missions' attempts to recover commitment and adapt traditional approaches to their changing world. Its symptoms were financial, its roots theological. As George Smith explained, 'The growth of the congregational revenue for foreign missions is the test at once of the fidelity of the ministers and office-bearers, the spirituality of the people and the efficiency of the Committee charged with the supervision of this side of the life of the Church.'[33] The problem for the churches lay in the tendency of this basic income to do no more than remain stable or at best rise very slowly. To meet rising expenses or fund any expansion organisers therefore had either to rely on unpredictable sources such as legacies, or put their trust in overseas revenue, especially fees and government grants-in-aid from the very institutions that supporters at home were more and more inclined to reject. Between 1880–81 and 1884–85 congregational giving to the Free Church of Scotland fell from 23 to 18 per cent of total income, while fees and grants remained steady at 26.5 per cent. In 1885–86 congregational giving actually fell in absolute terms and in the next two years total income was down by 14–16 per cent.[34] Major fluctuations of this kind, in enterprises tempted to spend to the limit and disinclined to build up reserves, could only result in debt. This was a fatal course, for while there remained in the church a willingness to meet genuine need, that was not true of debt caused by over-spending. The established church's convenor equally regarded debt as 'the greatest obstacle to our Missionary advance'. 'It causes both the Committee and the missionaries to lose the confidence of Business men.'[35]

---

31  To Hastie, 11 Aug. 1880; to W.A.J. Thomson, sent to Poona partly to ease a difficult situation at Calcutta, 22 Dec. 1880 and 11 May 1881; to Revs. Henry Price, William Harper and C.A. Patterson, 4 Dec. 1890, NLS MS/7534, ff. 173, 184, 197, 502–4.

32  Andrew to Lindsay, 24 Dec. 1891 (Confidential) for quotations and 20 June 1893, NLS MS/7845 f. 174, 7846, f. 310.

33  'Fifty Years of Our Foreign Missions' Revenue', *FCMMR*, May 1885, pp. 162–3.

34  George Smith, 'Ten Years of Our Foreign Missions', *FCSMR*, June 1889, pp. 178–9.

35  Dr J.M. McMurtrie to Rev. D.C. Scott, 23 Feb. 1893, NLS MS/7534, f. 812.

The Free Church's position was better than that of the established church, which in 1887 was forced to consider whether it could any longer sustain 'an effective foreign mission programme'.[36] Nevertheless, in both churches pressures for reduced expenditure and cuts in establishment were constantly transmitted to the field. This search for economy had theological and ecclesiastical consequences, holding back the expansion of institutions deemed expensive and pushing forward 'evangelisation', thought to be cheap. Thus Scottish missions came under pressure to shape their activities in ways that drew on the critical traditions of both Rufus Anderson and those made familiar by the faith missions and supporters of radical revival.

To bring matters to a head, the General Assembly in June 1887 despatched the FMC Convenor at the head of a deputation to review the Indian missions. There can be little doubt that the purpose of the review was to consider the implementation of a principle, not to consider which principle or missionary strategy should be adopted. As Professor of Church History at the Free Church College in Glasgow, Lindsay was highly regarded and self-evidently unlikely to belittle institutions of higher education. However, his views on the 'matter ... occupying the mind of the Church' were well known and he reiterated it only two days after the Assembly's decision. 'My own position ... is defined by one of the statements I made in accepting the convenership – that in India any extension of our operations should be in the line of evangelistic as opposed to the work of our great Colleges. Before I became Convener I had dissented from the proposed extension at Nagpore and since becoming Convener the Committee have refused extension of purely educational work at Poona. I have no desire to interfere with our great Institutions but to my mind the Church has reached the limit it ought to go in that direction.'[37]

Nothing Lindsay saw in India inclined him to change his mind. His tour was kept in the public eye, his 'Notes on Missionary Travel' being regularly printed in the Free Church *Monthly*. These were masterly essays, offering bouquets to all parties while preparing the ground for a Report which, when finally submitted in April 1890, ended the ascendancy of the Duff tradition. To the General Assembly in May Lindsay commended educational missions as 'the only effective means of attacking the caste system', but 'alongside of the educational they must have vigorous, red-hot evangelistic work. That work in India had hitherto been starved.'[38] The Assembly did not demur and after seeking missionaries' views on the Report, the FMC followed suit. After detailed consideration it acknowledged both the past achievement and the need for continued support of the 'Educational Mission Work'. It restated as a generally accepted principle that evangelism and education 'should always be in visible connection with each other'. Nevertheless, 'as the evangelistic work has not been

36  Andrew C. Ross, 'Scottish Missionary Concern 1874–1914. A Golden Era?', *Scottish Historical Review*, LI (1971), pp. 52–72, quotation at p. 63.
37  Lindsay to Andrew, 8 June 1887, NLS MS/7773, f. 41.
38  *FCSM*, July 1890, pp. 204–5.

developed *pari passu* with the other ... [it is] necessary, while in no way sanctioning anything that may ... impair the efficiency of the educational work, specially to foster the evangelistic operations and therefore ... to limit to the present amount the resources spent on the educational institutions and to devote to the evangelistic side whatever increase of contributions may be received and any saving that may be effected in connection with educational work without detriment to its efficiency.'[39]

The traditionalists tried to keep their end up, with Smith welcoming material rebutting 'opponents of Educational Missions' for publication in the *Monthly* and contributing pieces himself designed at least to maintain a balance of interests.[40] In India missionary resistance to the changes, both from Madras and Bombay, was also fierce.[41] To all, Lindsay's message was essentially the same. 'We distinctly cannot afford to go on as we have been doing ... and you must really do something.'[42] It was designed to implement what the FMC on its own had tried for some time, but now hoped to accomplish with the weight of the General Assembly behind it. To William Miller at the Madras Christian College Lindsay even raised the threat of his resignation accompanied by an open explanation to the Assembly, 'that while our educational missionaries profess in public the greatest desire to see evangelical extension, they in private resist in every way attempts to check their ever growing expenditure'.[43]

Miller's position illustrates most graphically the dilemma of the educational missionary. He had arrived in Madras in December 1862, when the mission was at a very low ebb. With justification he could regard himself as the radical reformer. Building up the central school in Madras into a college, fostering the co-operation between churches which led to its adoption as the interdenominational Madras Christian College, acting as its Principal for thirty years, playing important roles both in the University of Madras and in the formulation of government educational policy, point to a career that was in many respects a brilliant success. To find that the pressures for change were leading in quite different directions was hard to accept.[44]

The transition was nevertheless made. Miller's development of Duff's and Anderson's principles was no longer to be a priority. Evangelisation became the key word and in 1892 the Assembly prohibited any further expansion of missionary education. Money was shifted away from Madras towards central India and other non-metropolitan activities; new missionaries were given more time for vernacular study; 'awkward' characters, such as Rae the Madras Secretary, were replaced by

---

39  Minute 91, 16 Dec. 1889, NLS Dep.298/113, Vol. 8 FMC Minutes, p. 285.
40  Smith to Hector, 12 June and 31 Dec. 1890, NLS MS/7774, ff. 208, 380.
41  Lindsay to G.M. Rae, 24 April 1890 (Private and Confidential) and 24 Jan. 1891 and to William Miller, 24 Jan. 1891, NLS MS/7774, ff. 150, 409, 413; to Hector, Sept. 1890 and to Dr D. Mackichan, 18 Sept. 1890, *ibid.*, ff. 280–4.
42  Lindsay to Rae, 24 April 1890 (Private and Confidential), *ibid.*, f. 150.
43  To Miller, 25 April 1891, *ibid.*, ff. 504–9.
44  T. Ambrose Jeyasekeran, 'William Miller and the Meaning of Christian Education in India', *BSIMS*, n.s. 4–5 (1988–9), 42–53.

others more amenable and sympathetic to the church's current ambitions. Administrative changes were introduced to decentralise the missions' local activities, increase the schools' and colleges' reliance on local funds and strengthen the FMC's powers of appointment to local Missionary Councils.[45] A special Village Evangelisation Fund was set up, its moneys to be administered by 'vernacular speaking missionaries in personal superintendence of the work'.[46]

These reflected the domestic pressures and the FMC's determination to swim with the critical current of evangelism, in the expectation of improving their finances and the numbers of volunteers. They were responses shared with both the Church of Scotland and other societies south of the border.[47] The fear, for example, that available funds were being siphoned off towards the CIM and the Salvation Army was everywhere rife and prompted not only the shift towards direct evangelism but fresh attempts to capture the attention of university students.[48] Missionary organisers had begun to draw on influential evangelical speakers such as Arthur Tappan Pierson and, in the atmosphere generated by Keswick and the student conference movement, this had some success.[49] Since its formation in 1870 by the Church of Scotland, the Eastern Himalayan Mission, based at Kalimpong, not far from Darjeeling, had always emphasised vernacular work. It benefited markedly from the growing interest of the University Missionary Association, the Young Men's Guild and the Women's Guild, formed in the 1880s. Even for a mission so recently established, however, emphasis on the vernacular in this case indicated few concessions to local cultures; Presbyterian ecclesiastical organisation and architecture remained resolutely British.[50]

# III

'You must also remember that Africa is our popular mission.'[51] In so saying, the Church of Scotland's FMC Convenor spoke for many mission organisers. Few

---

45 Lindsay to Peattie, 10 Dec. (Very Private and Confidential) and 26 Dec. 1892; to David Reid (Calcutta), 18 July 1894, NLS MS/7775, ff. 314, 351, 996.

46 Lindsay to Peattie, 10 Dec. 1892 (Very Private and Confidential) and to Mackichan, 1 March 1893, *ibid.*, ff. 314, 426.

47 For the parallel Church of Scotland examination of its Indian Missions, see Church of Scotland Minutes of the FMC, 1887–1891, NLS Dep. 298/10, ff. 203–5, 250, 296, 308–11, 426 and following.

48 Lindsay to Peattie, 28 Feb. 1893 and to Mackichan, 1 March 1893, NLS MS/7775, ff. 422–31; McMurtrie to D.C. Scott, 31 Aug. 1893, NLS MS/7534, f. 895.

49 Lindsay to Hector, 1 March 1893, NLS MS/7775, f. 432; McMurtrie to Scott, 4 July 1889, NLS MS/7534, f. 415; Mackichan to Lindsay, 27 April 1894, NLS MS/7821, f. 29. For A.T. Pierson, below at chap. 11, pp. 301–2.

50 Elizabeth G.K. Hewat, *Vision and Achievement, 1796-1956: A History of the Foreign Missions of the Churches united in the Church of Scotland* (Edinburgh and London, 1960), pp. 163–4; C.L. Perry, 'The History of the Expansion of Protestant Christianity among the Nepali Diaspora', (unpub. Ph.D. thesis, Edinburgh, 1994), chap. 2.

51 McMurtrie to Scott, 23 Feb. 1893, NLS MS/7534, f. 812.

denominations did not share with the Scots the feeling that opportunities to open up new areas and to reconsider well-established approaches to evangelisation seemed nowhere more extensive than in Africa. In the decades of the European scramble, however, missionary opportunity was no less mixed with secular restraints, albeit of different kinds, than was the case in India during the same period. The re-awakening of enthusiasm at home and the building of Christian communities abroad generated preoccupations on the part of the missions involved in the pioneering penetration of South, East and Central Africa very different from those at work in British India and sketched out above. Issues of security and state power were frequently uppermost in missionary calculations, a far cry not only from Indian debates over education versus evangelism but even from the blending of Christianity and commerce.

In the 1860s David Livingstone was a prophet without honour in his own country. The Free Church gave short shrift to James Stewart's proposal for a mission to follow up Livingstone's Zambezi expedition. Not until the occasion of his funeral and then in response to external prompting from Sir Bartle Frere, Dr John Kirk and their own local business community, did the Free Church and the established church begin to take such an idea seriously. Coming on this occasion from a man no longer a student but Principal of the Free Church's Institution at Lovedale in the Eastern Cape, Stewart's revived proposal carried greater weight. 'I would humbly suggest', he urged the General Assembly, 'as the truest memorial of Livingstone, the establishment ... of an institution at once industrial and educational, to teach the truths of the Gospel and the arts of civilised life to the natives of the country and which shall be placed in a carefully selected and commanding spot in Central Africa, where ... it might ... become a great centre of commerce, civilisation and Christianity. And this I would call *Livingstonia*.'[52]

The establishment and growth after 1876 of both Livingstonia and the Church of Scotland's parallel but initially chaotic venture at Blantyre, in what was to become Nyasaland and then Malawi, have been exhaustively studied.[53] There were differences in their patterns of development. The Church of Scotland remained centred on Blantyre with contacts to a limited number of villages nearby. The Livingstonia mission was moved from its first site at Cape Maclear to Bandawe and later to Livingstonia at the north-eastern end of Lake Nyasa, emerging as the focal point of some eight principal stations by 1909. Their common characteristic, however, was their position as large residential enclaves, contrasting utterly with the local settlements outside. Observers were struck by the presence of schools, training in everything from brick making to printing, Western-style clothing and

52 John McCracken, *Politics and Christianity in Malawi 1875–1940: The Impact of the Livingstonia Mission in the Northern Province*, 2nd edn (Blantyre, 2000), pp. 57–63; James Wells, *Stewart of Lovedale: The Life of James Stewart* (London, 1909), pp. 125–6.
53 In addition to McCracken, see listed in the bibliography items by Oliver, Hanna, Hugh Macmillan, Andrew Ross.

disciplined worship. It was not surprising that Harry Johnston, Britain's first administrator in Nyasaland and himself an unbeliever who clashed with the Scots there, none the less praised the missions: 'their immediate object is not profit, they can afford to reside at places till they become profitable. They strengthen our hold over the country, they spread the use of the English language, they induct the natives into the best kind of civilization and in fact each mission station is an essay in colonization'.[54]

This was not however the introduction of commerce and Christianity as earlier figures such as Venn, the Sierra Leoneans or even Livingstone himself had understood it. In renewing their grip on tradition, the Scots reshaped the pattern in order to meet the conditions of the Scramble and the fashions of a new age. Crucial parts in this process were played by James Stewart, Robert Laws and David Scott, the latter appointed to re-establish Blantyre after 1881. Whatever the vision that Stewart had harboured in the 1860s of raw materials for export displacing the slave trade, the mission stations from the 1870s were developed essentially as secure, self-supporting and independent settlements. Stewart's outlook was influenced perhaps by Moravian example but certainly by his residence at Lovedale from 1867 on, in many respects the exemplar for the Nyasaland missions.[55]

At Lovedale, descended from the Glasgow Missionary Society's station started in 1821, Stewart took his lead less from Livingstone than from Duff, from Duff's tradition as adapted to the context of a dominant and expansive white settler society. This entailed a prime emphasis not only on education but also on its practical function. The purpose of education for Stewart 'may be answered in one brief word – *Action* ... A man is educated when he is fitted for the position he is intended by the Providence of God to fill ... Any education which is not practical in its character is of no real value to you at your present stage of civilization'. Hence his preoccupation with 'the rudiments of education for all, industrial training for the many and a higher education for the talented few'.[56]

These priorities were transposed to the Livingstonia mission, to which Stewart was temporarily attached in 1876–77. However, they proved no easier to sustain in the Nyasa region than did commercial prospects. Such commerce as was nurtured by the two missions was not under African control but almost entirely in the hands of the African Lakes Company, formed in 1878 to assist the missions' survival. Mission-backed commercial schemes did not flourish; until the development of British administration and the wider economy began to demand labour on a large scale, missionary education provided little more than selected skills of little value to their owners outside the mission stations themselves. The development of cotton, tobacco and coffee ultimately arrived only in the mid-1890s in the wake of white

---

54 Johnston to British South Africa Company, 17 July 1890, cited by Roland Oliver, *Sir Harry Johnston and the Scramble for Africa* (London, 1957), p. 182.

55 Wells, *Stewart of Lovedale*, pp. 74–5, 40.

56 *Ibid.*, pp. 188–9; for his educational credo, also pp. 198–200.

settlers and the establishment of a British protectorate in 1891.[57] For at least two decades Scottish attempts to reinvigorate their missions by developing new African branches were thus seriously constrained. It was above all in their relations with government that their activities underwent significant changes.

The Blantyre mission, starting out as a refuge for liberated or fugitive slaves and the Livingstonia missions, after moving to Bandawe amidst the disputes of the Ngoni and the Tonga peoples, both faced serious problems of disorder and security. There were three kinds of concern: low-level but persistent plundering and theft, affecting not only the missionaries and their supplies but also the African Lakes Company; the constant disruption, spilling over from slave-raiding and local warfare; and the unhelpful or purposely obstructive activities of local Portuguese officials. The latter in particular were seen as hostile to the growing British presence, indifferent or worse to slaving, and, to cap it all, Catholic and heretical. The temptation for the missionaries and their lay helpers to take the law into their own hands, establishing their own judicial system, was inevitably very strong, and, in the case of Blantyre, soon disastrous. There, the punishment by flogging and execution of – in some cases innocent – Africans under missionary auspices naturally caused a great scandal. It revealed, as had Bishop Mackenzie's experience, the vulnerability of missions quite out of their depth in secular administrative matters.[58]

This episode had major consequences. Stewart's long-standing principle, to avoid all missionary involvement in civil jurisdiction, was seen not only as appropriate to ordained ministers but to possess the additional merit of avoiding missionary liability in either British or native courts. At Lovedale, for all his wish to steer clear of politics, Stewart's submission to the magistrate thus illustrated the impossibility for missions everywhere of cutting themselves off from the state, be it indigenous or colonial. They needed its protection, against themselves as much as other offenders. Stewart's principle therefore became established church policy. David Scott, en route for Blantyre, was instructed 'You must always keep in view the fact that you are labouring to found and build up a Christian Church and not laying the foundations of a British Colony or of a small State ... Carefully avoid every temptation to act as judges or rulers in the land.'[59]

The Scots were not previously unaware of this problem and had from the beginning appealed to the British government for consular aid but to little effect. When, in October 1883, a consul for the Nyasa region, Captain C.E. Foot, was appointed, the missions carefully cultivated him and his successors.[60] A consular presence was, of course, not required simply to help prevent another Blantyre scandal. It represented what the missions were coming to want more than anything, the

57  McCracken, *Politics and Christianity*, pp. 114–15, 150, 178–9.
58  For the Blantyre atrocities, *ibid.*, pp. 97–103.
59  A.J. Hanna, *The Beginnings of Nyasaland and North-Eastern Rhodesia 1859–95* (Oxford, 1956), p. 41.
60  McMurtrie to Lord Rosebery (Secretary of State, Foreign Affairs), 14 April 1886, NLS MS/7534, f. 221.

assumption of British rule as the only way of creating a stable world in which they could extend their work. The Anglo-Portuguese Treaty of 1884 concerning the Congo had provoked British missionary and commercial opinion into action and from mid-1886 onwards missionary concern at the advance of Portuguese claims was switched to the east.[61] Both Scottish missions discussed tactics with the UMCA and the African Lakes Company and began to mobilise parliamentary opinion for deputations to the Foreign Office. The Church of Scotland Convenor set about persuading FMC members that detachment and neutrality would no longer suffice: 'we should have the backing of all who have sunk capital or life or labour in our part of Africa. Our object should be the limitation of Portugal, say to the river Ruo and a 3% tariff. The fact is we are "in a hole" in Africa. We have created great and beneficent interests in the interior and Portugal is between us and the sea'.[62] Early in 1887, Scott, home on furlough from Blantyre, was set to work rousing opinion and interest.[63] Here were the bones of a characteristic missionary coalition, which in this case was further extended and kept in being for the next few years.

A high level of missionary agitation in the face of Portuguese pretension and Arab expansion was sustained by two convictions, the one historical, the other political. Despite their own lukewarmness towards Livingstone, Scottish missionary organisers were of the view that imperial government support for his 1858–64 expedition had been such as to create a direct obligation to intervene on behalf of Livingstone's successors and a national interest in central Africa. In addition, as McMurtrie put it, 'I have no hope of anything from the F.O. except through pressure.'[64] To the activists were therefore added ever more churchmen and Scottish Members of Parliament, the Scottish Geographical Society, the Anti-Slavery Society and the indefatiguable campaigner Horace Waller, champion of Livingstone and author for this enterprise of *Title Deeds to Nyasaland* (London, 1887).[65]

The ambiguous position of the missionary party is evident from exchanges relayed to Blantyre of a private meeting of Free Church and Church of Scotland missionary leaders with the Prime Minister and Foreign Secretary, Lord Salisbury, at his London home. These are worth quoting at some length. McMurtrie recorded how 'in regard to our demand that the British Government should use force to

---

61 McMurtrie to Scott, 23 Sept 1886, *ibid.*, f. 263.

62 McMurtrie to Rev. Alexander Hetherwick, 22 Dec. 1886 and to Dr James Rankin, 23 Dec. 1886, *ibid.*, ff. 270, 273.

63 McMurtrie to Hetherwick, 16 Feb. 188[6 sic]7, *ibid.*, f. 295; for the Free Church side of the correspondence, see George Smith's letters in NLS MS/7772–4.

64 To Sir John Neilson Cuthbertson, 29 Feb. 1888 and to Scott, 12 April 1888, *ibid.*, ff. 358, 372.

65 McMurtrie to Scott, 15 Feb., 10 May and to Waller, 14 March 1888, *ibid.*, ff. 363, 372, 376; Tyneside Geographical Society to Dr George Smith, 11 Aug. 1888, NLS MS/7856, f. 35. For Waller's role, Dorothy O. Helly, *Livingstone's Legacy: Horace Waller and Victorian Mythmaking* (Athens, 1987), esp. pp. 281–9, 323–4.

repel the Arabs he [Salisbury] held out no encouragement. (This must *not* go abroad – as it would encourage the Arabs). He said if the British arms met with a repulse it must be avenged and there would be a Gordon and Khartoum business. But, he said (and this is very private) Why not do it yourselves – i.e. employ force in self defence against the Arabs. Lord Balfour said our missionaries felt that their strength lay in the natives seeing that they did not use physical but only moral force. Lord Salisbury replied, with a twinkle in his eye, "Most creditable to the Missionaries and becoming to their sacred calling: but there does not seem to me to be great difference between doing it yourselves and asking us to do it for you!'" McMurtrie continued, '*you*, I know, will not fight, except in the last resort. Certainly the Government would seem committed to look favourably on any measures of force which the trading companies or the missions would be drawn to ... Remember that a growing public opinion may push the Foreign Office further.'[66] Lord Salisbury was widely distrusted. The Free Church Missions Committee Secretary, remembering 'how he [Salisbury] deluded the country in the second Afghan War' and finding him 'obsequious to Germany', was convinced that 'if Germany comes in our way we go to the wall under this Government'. Keeping up the public pressure he therefore agreed was essential.[67]

At intervals other possibilities for securing the region were contemplated, such as a charter for the African Lakes Company. After Hetherwick's furlough early in 1889, spent like Scott's the previous year in rousing public feeling, Harry Johnston's raising of the British flag on the river Ruo and declaring a British protectorate over the Shiré Highlands in the summer was widely welcomed. So too was Salisbury's firm stand against the Portuguese in 1890. However, pleased as the missions were to think that they 'had changed the policy of the Government two years ago, or less',[68] a settlement with the Portuguese in the treaty finally ratified in 1891 was not the end of the affair.

The missions not only wanted British administration; they also wanted it on their own terms. Although they insisted on the need for African agreement to any arrangements, they disagreed both amongst themselves and with British policymakers on the form an administration should take.[69] At first they had welcomed the formation of the British South Africa Company and the prospects both of its northward expansion and its absorption of the African Lakes Company. To the north, William Mackinnon and his chartered venture, the Imperial British East Africa Company, were also looked to for assistance.[70] Their meeting with Cecil Rhodes early in 1891 at the Westminster Palace Hotel, his customary London

---

66  McMurtrie to Scott, 10 May 1888, NLS MS/7534, ff. 376–8.
67  For the Free Church correspondence, see NLS MS/7773, especially George Smith to Robert Laws, 9 May and 4 July 1888, at ff. 325, 347.
68  McMurtrie to Rev. Archibald Scott (Edinburgh), 2 March 1891, *ibid.*, f. 551.
69  McCracken, *Politics and Christianity*, pp. 198–216.
70  George Smith to Robert Laws, 3 July 1889 and to Dr Henry, 24 Oct. 1889, NLS MS/7773, f. 721, MS/7774, f. 31; 'Our Foreign Missions', *Free Church of Scotland Monthly Record* (Oct 1889).

watering hole, and the news that he was financially supporting Johnston and the Central Africa Protectorate, also generated enthusiasm. 'We had a very satisfactory interview with Mr. Rhodes ... He has very different ideas from Consul Johnston as to the Arabs ... When he is done with the Portuguese, he says he will shoot every Arab who refuses to leave the country.'[71]

Johnston himself was indeed another matter altogether, far less worried by missionary criticisms than members of the Foreign Missions Committees supposed. Even in 1891 his activity provoked George Smith to 'trust that "the State" in the shape of Consuls may not prove as bad for our Church in Nyasa-land as Portugal and the Arabs'.[72] For much of 1892–93 the Scottish missions found themselves fighting another campaign, this time against the violence of Johnston's methods and his alienation of many former allies. This involved taking issue with taxation policy and with his support for white settler interests. Official endorsement of resident whites whose conduct was 'a great hindrance to the success, not only of missionary enterprise but of civilizing agencies of every kind', had to be curbed. On this further step, again the churches felt themselves divided, with Blantyre in particular deeply uncomfortable with the choice facing them. Public campaigning would 'give a handle to the adversaries of Government. On the other hand we cannot let our mission be destroyed.'[73] Further meetings with Lord Salisbury, Lord Rosebery and Foreign Office officials inevitably followed, with much trading of charge and counter-charge. Within the missions, confidence in the British South Africa Company, Rhodes's policies and Johnston's dependence on them was rapidly declining. Consequently, 'We want no colonials here. The attitude of the Cape towards the nigger is unendurable. From what I hear of Mashonaland, I have no faith in the B.S.A., simply a huge monopoly. They have no right here as Administrators. It was Home British that opened this door and it must be Home British that must administer it.'[74] Johnston resented the criticism, gave as good as he got and damned the Church of Scotland Mission as 'disloyal to the Administration'. As for his suggestion that missionaries did not care for the spread of religion, the reaction in Edinburgh was predictable. 'The man who could write that has permitted his judgment to be wholly warped.'[75]

The history of the subsequent breach between Rhodes and Johnston and the role of the imperial government which took over the Nyasaland protectorate itself in 1895, is beyond the scope of this book and readily available elsewhere. It has been the purpose here to show the problems into which missions could be rapidly drawn in the confused circumstances of Africa's partition. Principles of

---

71 McMurtrie to Rev. Archibald Scott (Edinburgh), 2 March 1891, NLS MS/7534, f. 551.
72 George Smith to Robert Laws, 26 Feb. 1891, NLS MS/7774, f. 447.
73 McMurtrie to Lord Balfour of Burleigh, 16 May, 19 July 1892, *ibid.*, ff. 717, 731; also correspondence at ff. 692–7, 712, 715–7, 736, 741–70, 772–805, 895.
74 Rev. W.A. Scott to Dr Scott, 7 June 1892, enclosed in McMurtrie to Rosebery, 29 Aug. 1892, *ibid.*, ff. 741–70; McMurtrie to Scott, 31 Aug. 1893, f. 895.
75 McMurtrie to Lord Balfour of Burleigh, 31 Aug. 1893, *ibid.*, ff. 897–901.

evangelistic strategy and ecclesiastical organisation, theoretical views on the extent of missionary engagement in secular or civil affairs, the nature of their relations with governments at all levels, were easily swept into the melting pot. Threats from hostile or rival parties – Swahili Arab slavers, Roman Catholic Portuguese, monopolistic chartered companies – changed priorities and brought the search for familiar authority and the security of the missions to the fore. Beyond the main mission stations, the expansion of Christian influence was largely left to the haphazard outcome of initiatives by individual African Christians; within them, there developed highly autocratic church structures and social arrangements. Dependence on imperial officials replaced dependence on the tolerance of local leaders, with the unavoidable consequence being missions' close involvement in the building of empire. Even as the promise of new security was held out to them, missionary enterprise simultaneously faced the creation of unexpected difficulties by the new colonial order. The careful revival and adaptation of missionary traditions was a starting point rapidly left behind in the competition between missions and their rivals to define both the pattern of Christianity's expansion and the character of empire.

## IV

Although some missions managed to maintain their traditional approach to evangelisation far longer than others without serious disruption, questions of reform could not be sidestepped for ever. The Wesleyan Methodists were uncommonly tenacious and unquestioning of their district and circuit organisation and ministerial control in European hands. In some ways this was justified by the flexibility which it offered in extending the territorial reach of the mission. In Madras, for example, once the possibilities on the ground were appreciated by local missionaries, the extension of evangelism to the villages in the early 1880s was accomplished with little of the agony experienced by the Free Church of Scotland.[76] Both in Madras and in other areas such as Hyderabad it was a shift in emphasis all the more easily incorporated as a result of the relatively late and limited involvement of the Methodists in higher education.

That involvement, not only in boarding schools and colleges but in industrial missions, in orphanages and in extensive ministering to European congregations, was nevertheless more than enough to attract critical attention. In the 1860s significant increases in WMMS home support were still insufficient to sustain existing work. A tour of inspection by the chairman of the Madras District in 1867 revealed a depressing scene, 'struggling Missionaries and Mission buildings falling into decay' and 'a Mission starved both in men and money'. Ten years later Dr Ebenezer Jenkins, an enthusiast for schools who had worked in Madras from 1846 to 1861, returned a report on the district elaborating on the lamentable failure to

---

76 Findlay and Holdsworth, *History of the WMMS*, Vol. 5, pp. 240–4, 320.

develop a native Indian ministry.[77] The same sense of limited progress if not stagnation unrelieved by any domestic enthusiasm was again recognised in the mid-1880s but hardly eased by increased grants followed by immediate retrenchment. In the Bengal District, the new chairman in 1876 was no less critical of the Society's poor record over some fifteen years. 'Believe me', Baugh wrote, 'one or two Missionaries doing mixed work, frequently exchanged and never mastering a knowledge of the language or of the manners of the people, is really no more than playing at mission work, very little more than mere waste of time and money. If very much more is not done *speedily* we ought, in all honour, to abandon our attempts.'[78]

These characteristics both exacerbated and reflected the WMMS's financial difficulties. The Society's income, having risen far more than that of its rivals in the 1850s and 1860s, subsequently fell no less dramatically by 1894 to a level which matched that of thirty years before. Despite a rising domestic church membership, giving per head fell by a third.[79] Failure to grapple with wider strategic thinking as other societies had begun to do long before meant that the crisis when it was finally faced in 1889–90 was the more severe. As it had done in the case of the Scottish missions, India again provided a catalyst.

By 1886 the government of India was deeply unpopular in the ranks of Britain's Nonconformists for its operation of the Contagious Diseases Acts. Based on a recognition of the size of the Indian Army and the inevitability of prostitution, these acts were designed to regulate it in ways that would help to reconcile a measure of protection for Indian women with the health and entertainment of British and Indian soldiers. Subject to an unremitting barrage of criticism from the fanatical Quaker activist Alfred Dyer, Josephine Butler and other leading figures of the 'Purity' campaign, the government of India's position was not helped by its half-hearted attempts to reform the system with a new Cantonment Act in 1889.[80] As the row dragged on, missionaries in India were drawn into the protests and those both at home and abroad who were felt to have been insufficiently vocal critics of the system also found themselves in the firing line. Fuel was added to the flames by the fact that 'the Dyer party', being no less violently opposed to the 'education' strategy in missionary work, was as a result doubly critical of figures such as Dr Miller of Madras, thought to be indifferent to the 'state regulation of vice'.[81]

---

77  *Ibid.*, pp. 200, 225–7, 233.

78  *Ibid.*, p. 352.

79  *Ibid.*, Vol. 1, pp. 193–4.

80  Kenneth Ballhatchet, *Race, Sex and Class under the Raj: Imperial Attitudes and Policies and their Critics, 1793–1905* (London, 1980), chap. 2; Ronald Hyam, *Empire and Sexuality: the British Experience* (Manchester, 1990), pp. 64–71, 121–7.

81  Criticisms of the India missionaries over this question temporarily climaxed at the 1892/3 all-India Decennial Missionary Conference. See Peattie to Smith, 19 Jan. 1893; to Lindsay, 30 March 1893, NLS MS/7846, ff. 175, 251; and further letters at MS/7775, ff. 422–5, 494, 618–24, 677.

Scarcely less prominent on both campaign fronts was the outstanding Methodist preacher and editor of the *Methodist Times*, the Reverend Hugh Price Hughes. For Hughes, committed to overseas missions, the issues in debate offered basic reasons for the decline in Methodist enthusiasm for that cause. They starkly revealed the limitations of the civilisation being imparted to Indians alongside missionary Christianity and indicated the need for a far-reaching review of missionary activity. Hughes, already at odds with the FMC, therefore lent his support to charges coming from other directions. With his own misgivings about the prominence of formal Western education in the missionary enterprise, Hughes warmed to the Reverend J. Gelson Gregson's onslaught on Indian missions. Gregson, experienced missionary and temperance worker, had recently returned from India. Speaking at the Mildmay Second Advent Conference in March 1886, he attacked the dominance of 'printing presses, exotic Christian villages and corrupting Christian compounds' for their perpetuation of denominationalism instead of promoting evangelism.[82] Missionary arrangements in India he repeatedly portrayed as an inadequate educational system rather than a means to conversion. Hughes was attracted by the hyperbole of Gregson's outraged sensibility, which represented schools as 'unscriptural Christian hothouses' producing 'missionary parasites, subsidized with missionary money'. 'In the Divine missionary report in the book of Acts, we have no record of theological seminaries or educational colleges.' Native Christians should not be offered land or salaried employment, but left as witnesses to the fact that God would provide for the body as well as the soul. Gregson then went on to sketch out a system of itinerant preaching, of Christian territorial occupation as a prelude to Christ's Second Advent.[83] Other sources drawn on by Hughes included the prominent Baptist Member of Parliament W.S. Caine and Thomas Champness.

The spring of 1889 saw the appearance in the *Methodist Times*, with disquietingly vigorous editorial endorsement, four articles by the Reverend Dr Henry Lunn, who had been briefly a medical missionary in south India and was now assisting Hughes at the Wesleyans' West London Mission. Such detailed and open criticism, together with the two men's defence of a new missionary policy, opened up within the Wesleyan community what became known as 'the Missionary Controversy'. This was undeniably a bitter and damaging dispute, holding up to the WMMS the model of the faith missions and finding the Society seriously wanting.[84] The Wesleyan Conference of 1889, the public protests of the specially

---

82  'The Coming of the Lord as an incentive to Missionary Zeal', *Report of the Mildmay Second Advent Conference, 2–4 March 1886* (London, 1886), pp. 174–8. Gregson was a Baptist missionary in India 1858–66 and 1872–79; until 1886 he was engaged in temperance work with the Indian Army and was pastor at Mussoorie.

83  J. Gelson Gregson, *Apostolic Missions for the Present Day* (London, 1887), pp. 4–6, 13.

84  Findlay and Holdsworth, *History of the WMMS*, Vol. 1, pp. 133–60; D.P. Hughes, *The Life of Hugh Price Hughes* (London, 1904), chap. 13; MCA, File PLP 57–6, Hugh Price Hughes correspondence, July 1890.

convened meeting of Wesleyan missionaries at Bangalore and the Missionary Committee of Enquiry together guaranteed maximum exposure for the whole affair. The Society's linen, clean as well as unclean, was not only washed but aired and ironed in public; the criticisms, defence, enquiry report and evidence received were all printed together for posterity.[85]

It hardly mattered, save to the individuals concerned, that eventually the missionaries were exonerated from the charges of extravagance and unacceptable worldliness and those aspects of Hughes's and Lunn's detailed case rejected by the Enquiry. The unsatisfactory state of Wesleyan missions was hard to gainsay and the Conference's early resolutions on the affair, favouring 'a large extension of evangelistic work', appeared to concede the issue on missionary methods.[86] In insisting on a distinction between 'the well-meant but mistaken policy of the saintly Dr. Duff and the old-fashioned policy of the apostle Paul and our Methodist forefathers', Hughes was arguing for three principles. 'We believe (1) that educational agencies should be quite subordinate to the direct work of preaching the gospel; (2) that educational agents should be, as far as possible, laymen; and (3) that the advantages of education should be given mainly to our own native converts and especially to those of them who may become catechists or ministers.'[87] The question of missionaries' standard of living was for Hughes of lesser significance, introduced in a period of financial hardship for the Society as a way of finding the means to support wider evangelism, not as an intrinsically vital issue. The WMMS was being pointed by its critics in the direction of the CIM and the Salvation Army, pushed along the road that, as Lunn noted and was seen above, the CMS and the Oxford Mission to Calcutta had already begun to travel.[88]

The WMMS centenary historians agreed with others at the time in rejecting as inappropriate the 'asceticism' of the CIM, an attitude with some basis in experience but reinforced, if nothing more, by the persistent Methodist leaning towards enhanced status and establishment contact. There was in this tendency a line of descent, from William Shaw at the Cape in the 1830s to the Methodists' isolated stand among nonconformists in their support for the Boer War (1899–1902), which gives substance to the general complaints raised by Hughes and his allies over India.[89] The 'Missionary Controversy' had the further consequence of seriously damaging the Society's missions. A further fall in total income at home was translated into severe limits imposed on missionary expenditure in Madras, while in Hyderabad restrictions were reckoned to have set back Wesleyan activity by two decades. As Findlay and Holdsworth accepted, before the controversy, 'the visible and measureable results of Indian Missions ... appeared to spell failure and to call

85  *The Missionary Controversy. Discussion, Evidence and Report* (WMMS, London, 1890).
86  Findlay and Holdsworth, *History of the WMMS*, I, p. 145.
87  *The Missionary Controversy*, pp. 83–4.
88  *Ibid.*, pp. 14, 86, 196.
89  Above Chapter 4, pp. 112–15; Stephen Koss, 'Wesleyanism and Empire', *HJ*, 18, 1 (1975), 105–18.

for some new policy'.[90] However, the manner of its conduct was such as to post-pone indefinitely the Society's adaptation. Far less successfully than other societies was the WMMS able to adapt, reapply or rethink its traditional approaches. Not only did Shrewsbury's confidence in Methodist perfection die hard.[91] When the centenary history was written between 1914 and 1924, the task of soothing hurt feelings and the attempt to rescue the Society's Indian past was evidently still in progress.

V

The experience of the Scottish missions north of the Zambezi was in varying degrees widely shared. Most churches and societies, funds permitting, felt obliged to extend their operations in Africa as it attracted renewed popular attention after 1870. In these circumstances, revival and adaptation were promoted less by rethinking established missionary practice than by applying it in new geographical settings. Contemporaneous and in many respects analogous with events unfolding on the Zambezi and the Shiré were those further north in Buganda. There the CMS mission, established at the centre of the kingdom's political life, was caught up in the increasingly complex and violent rivalries of Protestant, Catholics, Muslims and traditionalists.[92] Captivated by accounts of extensive conversions and martyrdom, public attention in Britain hardly slackened after Bishop James Hannington's murder on his way into Buganda in 1885. Following the routing of their rivals by the local Protestant interest, aided by Captain Frederick Lugard and the forces of the chartered Imperial British East Africa Company, extensive missionary agitation was of critical importance in extracting from the Liberal government a decision to retain Buganda and establish the East African Protectorate in 1895.[93]

Evangelicals not only wanted to revive the home base of the missionary move-ment but required settings in which to pursue their goal with minimum disruption. Widespread African resistance and mounting European intervention convinced many of them that Africa could not provide adequate stability. Inevitably, therefore, missions looked for a solution first in the expansion of British influence and territo-rial control and then by making demands on British administrators. For this reason missionary representatives were to be found not only knocking repeatedly at official doors in London's Whitehall but also pacing the corridors and committee rooms at international conferences. Dr Robert Laws from Livingstonia, Frederick Moir of

---

90  Findlay and Holdsworth, *History of the WMMS*, Vol. 1, p. 155, Vol. 5, pp. 234, 324–5.
91  Above, Chapter 4, p. 138.
92  *A.M. Mackay, Pioneer Missionary of the Church Missionary Society to Uganda. By His Sister* (London, 1890; repr. 1970).
93  Tudor Griffiths, 'Bishop Alfred Tucker and the establishment of a British Protectorate in Uganda 1890–94', *JRA* 31 (2001), 92–114; [D.] Anthony Low, 'British Public Opinion and the Uganda Question: October–December 1892', *Uganda Journal* 18, 2 (1954), 81–100.

the African Lakes Company and William Ewing from Glasgow's Presbyterian business community represented the Free Church at the West Africa Conference in Berlin in 1884–85. Claiming the successful recognition of Scottish missionary interests under Article 6 of the Berlin Act, the Free Church *Monthly* concluded that 'This is what the Berlin Conference has secured for the Church of Christ and very specially for our own section of it ... Thus David Livingstone is avenged.'[94] At the Brussels Conference of 1890 on the ending of the slave trade, missionary pressure groups seem to have been similarly engaged. The Scottish churches were there in force, the Free Church developing contacts with the Moravians and the Berlin Evangelical Missionary Society among others and the BMS working closely with the Anti-Slavery Society.[95]

The Congo River and its headwaters not only impinged on the Scottish sphere and attracted the faith missions such as the Livingstone Inland Mission; they also offered openings attractive to others no less orthodox than the Presbyterians. Starting in 1877, the BMS, aided by successive benefactions from the Yorkshireman Robert Arthington and the armed force of Leopold II's forces under H.M. Stanley, slowly developed a chain of stations on traditional lines, in the ultimately misplaced expectation that Leopold's International Association and the Congo Free State would provide an acceptable framework for missionary enterprise.[96] As BMS hopes and optimistic respect for Leopold's ambitions indicate, growing reliance on the intervention of European empire-builders was an outstanding feature of the period from the early 1880s well into the next decade. Unable to muster the resources and finding difficulty in squaring the use of force with their profession and their consciences, many missionaries – as Lord Salisbury pointedly remarked – preferred secular agencies under the direction of Providence to open the way for them. They were faced, however, with British imperial authorities generally reluctant to take direct control. Convinced at the same time that 'tribalism' could not sustain itself in the face of broader processes disrupting African societies, anxious themselves both to move ahead and to shorten any period of disruption, missionaries in Africa as elsewhere therefore saw their role as that of mediators of change.

This was very marked in southern Africa. As the region's mineral revolution took off, John Mackenzie, in 1877 chairman of the LMS Bechuanaland District Committee, reflected on how 'We find ourselves present where the meeting of races is taking place and it is in our power to assist the weak, to guide the ignorant, to rouse the slumbering and the slothful on the one hand and on the other and as far as

---

94 'The New Deal in Central Africa', *FCMMR,* Jan. 1885, 3; 'The New Africa', *ibid.,* (June 1885), 173–5.

95 Suzanne Miers, *Britain and the Ending of the Slave Trade* (London, 1975), pp. 229–38; Slade, *English-Speaking Missions in the Congo,* pp. 86–95; Dr George Smith to President, International Slavery Conference, Brussels, 21 Jan. 1890 and to Robert Laws, 11 Feb. 13 March, 5 Nov. 1890, NLS MS/7774, ff. 81, 105, 108, 338, 365.

96 Stanley, *Baptist Missionary Society,* pp. 117–39.

we can, to restrain from evil and from wrong the enterprising and somewhat reckless European.'[97] Mackenzie continued to develop the LMS tradition established by his forerunners, pressing for imperial intervention to protect local peoples against the rapacity of settler development and, by the 1880s, significant industrialisation with its greatly enlarged demands for labour. Elsewhere in South Africa, missionaries such as J.S. Moffat (son of Robert) and Bishop Knight-Bruce supported the British South Africa Company in its early phases for similar ends. As the company's reputation became tarnished, others such as the Wesleyans in Bechuanaland also followed Mackenzie and W.C. Willoughby, turning in 1894–95 to the imperial government for assistance in safeguarding missionary spheres of interest against company or settler intrusion.

A similar trajectory can be seen among missions in West Africa. Missionary interests had been prominent in earlier confrontations such as those over Lagos in 1851 and 1861. In 1892, however, their part in bringing about the military expedition against the Ijebu has given rise to its being labelled 'the Missionary war'. As one American evangelist commented at the time, 'War is often a means of opening a door for the gospel to enter a country. A sword of steel often goes before a sword of the spirit. The landing of troops here now may be part of the divine plan for answering our prayers and opening Ijebu and other interior countries to the gospel.'[98] In a similar vein, at the time of the Ashanti conflict in 1895, the Superintendent of the Wesleyan Methodists' Gold Coast missions welcomed the 'most righteous' invasion, declaring that he would 'like to see Britain in possession of the whole of Africa'. 'Although not necessarily avowed Christian men in every instance, yet the officers of the two services serving under Her Majesty's flag represent Justice and Humanity ... I should consider myself worse than despicable if I failed to declare my firm conviction that the British Army and Navy are today used by God for the accomplishment of His purposes.'[99]

## VI

Even in the late nineteenth-century context of expanding territorial empire, however, it would be seriously mistaken to see in such examples of the endorsement of imperial power indications of a deep-rooted or persistent missionary commitment to empire and direct British rule. Nor do they indicate an abandonment of the long-held preference for avoiding politics, let alone the development of a new wish for theocratic states of their own. Large areas of Africa were among the most volatile, disturbed and insecure parts of the globe; serious problems of security and order were not uncommon elsewhere, in China and the Pacific for example. These

---

97  A.J. Dachs, 'Missionary Imperialism in Bechuanaland 1813–1896' (unpub. Ph.D. thesis, Cambridge, 1968), p. 122.

98  C.C. Newton, 12 April 1892, in Ayandele, *Missionary Impact*, pp. 54–69, quotations at pp. 55, 67.

99  Denis Kemp, *Nine Years at the Gold Coast* (London, 1898), pp. 194, 232–4, 256.

conditions were felt to threaten not only missionary enterprise but European ambitions more generally, especially for trade and settlement. Missionaries not surprisingly shared the widespread conviction that external, formal intervention by the European or Western powers was on balance necessary and probably beneficial for the majority of those concerned.

Empire, however, was valued by most missionaries on grounds of expediency, according to its contribution to the attainment of missionary goals. Some empires – normally but not necessarily one's own – were better than others; imperial structures were more useful in certain times and places than in others, just as some forms of commerce were acceptable while others were not. Imperial expansion might appear promising in its early phases, but cease to be so once it had settled down. Officials, initially uncertain of their ground, might welcome missionary advice and local knowledge to start with, but abandon it as their confidence grew. In India, missionaries were late arrivals and government not readily trusted; in parts of colonial Africa, missionaries, frequently among the first Europeans on the scene, soon lost such advantages as that conferred and found the pattern of empire taking on unacceptably restrictive forms. Even in the late nineteenth century, as secular empire-builders closed in on every side and missions became once again ever more fit and proper subjects for government regulation, the original missionary sense of self-sufficiency constantly resurfaced. The widespread preference for evangelisation over education itself carried theological and ecclesiastical implications and involved a self-conscious distancing from the state with its political and administrative entanglements or diversions.

The ambiguities of these relationships are not easily recaptured.[100] Nevertheless, significant elements can be seen in the following letter sent home to Scotland from Hugli in 1893. 'It goes against the grain of an orthodox Imperialist like me to do anything in the way of complaining to Parliament about the Indian Government. I think our rulers here are often much injured and hampered by that sort of thing. This feeling on my part does not spring from personal bias. For from European officials in India I have never received anything better than bare civility and very often worse ... However, I'm a missionary first and an Imperialist afterwards and I did not come out here to watch my work being stopped by "judicial calmness".'[101] In the late nineteenth-century world of expanding colonialism and administrative restraints on missions, to be a 'missionary first' had for a time seemed to necessitate a greater dependence on imperial protection. By 1900 it increasingly meant once more the distancing of evangelicals from empire. The processes that contributed to this further readjustment are the subject of the next chapter.

---

100 But see James G. Greenlee and Charles M. Johnston, *Good Citizens: British Missionaries and Imperial States, 1870–1918* (Montreal, 1999).
101 William McCulloch to Dr George Smith, 29 Nov. 1893, NLS MS/7839, f. 108.

# Beyond the centenaries:
# missions versus empire, 1890–1914

Centenary celebrations in the 1890s for the Baptists, the LMS and the CMS, bicentenaries for the SPCK and the SPG, naturally focused on how far the missions had come and on their prospects for future success. The *Centenary Report* of the LMS in 1895, anticipating the extravagant claims of some modern historians, went so far as to suggest that little in the presence of Britain overseas had not been shaped by missionary effort. The 'only way to get a just estimate of the missionary history of the past century is to read with it the story of material progress and of territorial expansion, the story also of political and religious development in Britain … The extension of trade, the facility of colonisation, the enlargement of territory, the scientific knowledge of the world and its peoples, the suppression of international wrongs, the possibility of free and useful intercourse between the different races, have been largely helped by the earnest labours of the band of unassuming missionaries.'[1]

Nevertheless, even at the time, the celebratory nature of the occasions was far from unqualified. For example, the LMS Directors found the state of their funds and income so serious that they halted the Forward Movement of the previous year. They resolved to accept no more offers of service and to send no volunteers overseas, even those currently in training, until things markedly improved. Their Centenary Fund was devoted to paying off the Society's accumulated debt.[2] On behalf of the CMS, Eugene Stock in his *History* frankly expressed the organisers' disappointment at the response to its own centenary initiatives, notwithstanding the substantial increase in total income that occurred in 1896-97 and was more than sustained through to 1914.[3] In a few places attention was given to the obstacles that had been encountered along the way. The LMS looked back ruefully to the failure of its scheme for the separation of the West Indian churches and the ever more discouraging prospects for its work in South Africa. Little attention was paid, however, to the issues that distanced missions from empire, or to the fluctuations in missions' views of that relationship, such as have provided much of the material for this book. Nor was much written about the changes of direction in that relationship then under way. These issues are the particular concern of this chapter.

---

1 *Centenary Report of the London Missionary Society* (London, 1895), p. 2.

2 *Ibid.*, pp. 11, 15–17.

3 Stock, *History of the CMS*, Vol. 3, pp. 715–20; for SPG and CMS income totals, Maughan, 'Regions Beyond and the National Church', table 1.2, p. 71.

## I

The development of racial thought has long been acknowledged as intimately bound up with the growth of Britain's modern empire. The explanation of significant differences – in physical characteristics, social customs, religions, technologies and political systems – between societies in terms of racial superiority was not only held to account for the growth of empires but provided a justification for their continued existence and explained the necessary patterns of rule applied to them. However, although the Western characterisation of races provided a new intellectual and social cement for the agents of Britain's expanding empire, for the missions its very exclusivity created serious problems. The growth of nineteenth-century racial perspectives, so at odds with Christianity's egalitarianism, both distanced missions from empire and undermined the missionary enterprise; at the same time, through the hostility it provoked, it weakened empire itself.

At the beginning of the nineteenth century, when missionaries themselves were objects of restraint and ridicule among the empire's white ruling elites, they nevertheless shared with most of their critics a belief in the fundamental unity of humanity. It was generally held that there existed a single, divinely created, human race, whose members shared a common, rational human nature. Drawing out the ethnological implications of Livingstone's work, William Monk concluded that 'Having seen that the Africans are really "bone of our bone" and "flesh of our flesh", the way is hence cleared for the argument that we are bound, as brothers, to act for their temporal and spiritual good'.[4] These essential conditions underpinned the expectations of administrators and humanitarians as well as evangelicals that liberty, prosperity, civilisation and Christianity would advance together. Under British auspices above all, individual and social progress would edge out savagery, inhumanity and degradation.

In most quarters, this universalist outlook was gradually undermined during the nineteenth century.[5] It was eroded by the unexpected slowness in the transformation of the extra-European world and the consequential widening of the technological gulf and the disparity in wealth between the British and indigenous peoples. Interpreted as evidence of resistance to British ways despite the benefits of long periods of British contact or rule, events such as the Indian Mutiny, West Indian decline, the Jamaican rebellion and China's Boxer Rising, led people to question the rationality or basic capacity of non-Europeans. Increasingly the idea took hold that racial hallmarks and degrees of cultural sophistication were inseparably linked. Intellectual and scientific developments in phrenology, anthropology

---

4  Rev. William Monk (ed.), *Dr. Livingstone's Cambridge Lectures* (Cambridge, 1858), p. 85.
5  The universalist outlook was undermined probably more slowly in Britain than elsewhere: Peter Mandler, '"Race" and "Nation" in Mid-Victorian Thought', in S. Collini, R. Whatmore and B. Young (eds), *History, Religion and Culture: British Intellectual History 1750–1950* (Cambridge, 2000), pp. 224–44.

and evolutionary thought also seemed to impart a physical or biological reality to the concept of 'race'. As belief in the reality and permanence of racial categories spread after 1860, so the concept of 'race' was gradually incorporated into justifications for the growth and maintenance of empire. It was also woven into the structure of imperial and colonial institutions, as a crystallising sense of racial hierarchy eclipsed the possibility of blacks wielding authority over whites and kindled a new sense of responsibility in 'the white man's burden'.

Imperial officials gave articulate voice to these shifts in outlook. Sir William Hunter, retired from the Indian Civil Service and 'speaking as an Englishman' to the Royal Society of Arts, declared his 'conviction that English Missionary enterprise is the highest modern expression of the world-wide national life of our race. I regard it as the spiritual complement of England's instinct for colonial and Imperial rule. And I believe that any falling off in England's Missionary efforts will be a sure sign of swiftly coming decay.'[6] From experience of East and Central Africa, Sir Harry Johnston reflected on the potential contribution of races other than the white to the region's development. 'I think the admixture of yellow that the negro requires should come from India and that Eastern Africa and British Central Africa should become the America of the Hindu. The mixture of the two races would give the Indian the physical development which he lacks and he in his turn would transmit to his half negro offspring the industry, ambition and aspiration towards a civilized life which the negro so markedly lacks.'[7]

Within the missionary world, however, these changes were less apparent. This is not to suggest that missions and their supporters were immune to currents of thought running wide and deep in the British societies at home and abroad of which they were members. There was always a risk that generally ethnocentric views of the world consciously or unconsciously imbibed by missionary volunteers at home might be transmuted overseas into a more explicit sense of racial hierarchy. For this reason, Bishop Knight-Bruce thought that all appointments in South Africa should last for no more than four or five years, 'so that the inevitable tendency to fall into the ways of the country would be stopped in the individual ... Especially should this be the case with the Clergy.'[8] However, institutional routines were as likely to be the source of problems as they were to provide safe-

---

6 'Sir William W. Hunter on the Religions of India', reprinted in *The Mission Field* (April 1888), pp. 130–40.

7 H.H. Johnston, *Report [on] ... British Central Africa*, 1894, p. 31, quoted by H. Alan C. Cairns, *Prelude to Imperialism: British Reactions to Central African Society, 1840–1890* (London, 1965), p. 207. This did not prevent him from commenting elsewhere that 'Some of the best, hardest-working and most satisfactory sensible missionaries I have ever known have been West Indians – in colour as dark as the Africans they go to teach, but in excellence of mind, heart and brain capacity, fully equal to their European colleagues', Johnston, *British Central Africa* (London, 1897), p. 203. I am most grateful for this reference to David Killingray.

8 G.W.H. Knight-Bruce, 'The Mashonaland Mission of Bishop Knight-Bruce', ed. C.E. Fripp, *Gold and the Gospel in Mashonaland 1888* (London, 1949), p. 121.

guards against them. All the more notable therefore are features of the missionary movement that went some way to neutralise the influence of the explicitly exclusive racist attitudes so often to be found elsewhere.

A striking feature of missionary commentary was its inattention to if not confusion over categorisation. Generalisations about missionaries' standpoint on questions of race derived from their language are often therefore very difficult and unreliable. Terms such as 'race', 'blood', 'tribe', 'nation', 'parent stock' and 'mankind' jostled with each other in ways which suggested widespread uncertainty if not ignorance as to the bases of social and political development and organisation and a sense of the multiple purposes – inclusive as well as exclusive – that might be served by racial terminology. Introducing the report of the 1888 international missionary conference held in London, the editor drew attention to its demonstration of 'the great extent to which the work in heathen lands is in the hands of the races derived from the great Saxon stock'. Writing off the record of 'the Latin races' as ruined by Roman Catholicism, he concluded, 'It is to the race which is sending the blessings of Christianity to the heathen to which God is giving success as the colonisers and conquerors of the world.'[9] On this occasion the term 'race' served a suitably integrative purpose. Racial terminology was appropriate to a community and to a gathering of this kind that transcended the narrower horizons of either a purely British empire or an individual European nation. 'Race' stood proxy for a community defined in cultural terms, in this case by its Protestant Christianity. The conference was thus also representative of a community from which other 'races' were not to be excluded, open as all equally were to the availability of grace and redemption.

In the late nineteenth century as earlier, missionary outlooks continued to rest on the conviction of universality. This persuasion depended not on biological or other scientific reasoning but on two fundamental biblical principles: the availability to all members of the human race of grace and redemption from sin and the atonement for the sins of the whole world represented in Christ's death and resurrection. Henry Rowley, a member of the UMCA and Mackenzie's Zambezi expedition, later wrote of the debate about the peopling of Africa. Although 'this science is still within the region of conjecture … whatever revelations it may yet make, we may be very sure that they will be found in perfect harmony with the declaration of Holy Scripture, that "God made man in his own image" and that "He hath made of one blood all nations of men for to dwell on all the face of the earth"'.[10] Rowley and other colleagues were thus able to argue that such differences and diversity as were present among local African groupings on the arrival of Europeans were no less than those of Europe and Asia and could be easily accounted for by diffusion, isolation, political disorganisation, slavery and consequent degeneration. These were processes no less operative among Africans than among 'our own countrymen …

---

9  Rev. James Johnston, *Report of the Centenary Conference of the Protestant Missions of the World*, 2 vols (London, 1888), pp. xv–xvii.
10  Henry Rowley, *Africa Unveiled* (London, 1876), pp. 30–1.

left to themselves for any length of time in the wilds of Australia or America'.[11] Biological race and its cultural consequences had little place either here or more widely among missionaries.

In the 1890s, Bishop Knight-Bruce similarly condemned as utterly misleading any attempt to speak of 'native character'. 'Natives are about as different in their characters as Europeans would be', brought up under similar conditions.[12] He also moved freely between 'race' and 'nation', distinguishing between groups principally by the nature of their government. He found 'the difference between a Christian [Khama's Ngwato] and a Heathen [Lobengula's Ndebele] nation ... very striking – the brutality of one rule compared with the righteousness of the other. Khama is so eminently a gentleman – in appearance, manners, thought: in speaking to him one entirely forgets that he is brown and not white. Lobengula is so eminently not – the people seem to have many of the bad qualities of the lowest class of Whitechapel rough.'[13] The 'Bantu' (despite the term's linguistic connotations) and Bechuana Knight-Bruce referred to only as races, the Sotho and Ndebele as both races and nations.[14]

The CMS medical missionary Septimus Pruen argued along the same lines. Behavioural and character traits observable in Africans, like the 'sins' to which they were prone, were in no wise innate or inborn but a matter of circumstance and upbringing, just as they were with Europeans. The attainment of the high expectations that Christianity required of adherents depended on individual faith and divine grace. 'Without God's Holy Spirit, the African would certainly be unequal to the task, but so would the cultivated Englishman.'[15]

At the turn of the nineteenth century, missionaries were to be found grappling with the problems of racism and race conflict in two principal ways. They were, first of all, concerned to combat at least their harshest expressions in the encounter between indigenous peoples and other agents of British expansion. This struggle, of course, in form at least was nothing new and it had lost none of its edge since the early days of the missionary movement in the West Indies or Cape Colony. Pruen, for example, was appalled at the treatment of Africans, Christian or not, on the Zanzibari coast. 'The natives out here seem to be treated as if they were an inferior race of animals', by Europeans, who also regarded it as 'a crushing accusation against the members of the Universities' Mission, that "they actually treat those niggers as if they were brothers"'.[16] Knight-Bruce in Mashonaland was left angry and amazed 'at the unspeakable want of knowledge, injustice, rapid self-contradic-

---

11  *Ibid.*, pp. 32, 37.
12  G.W.H. Knight-Bruce, *Memories of Mashonaland* (London, 1895), p. 153.
13  *Ibid.*, Journals, from *Gold and the Gospel*, p. 84.
14  *Ibid.*, pp. 64, 75–6, 94–5, 104, 124.
15  S.T. Pruen, *The Arab and the African: Experiences in Eastern Equatorial Africa during a residence of three years* (London, 1891), pp. 270–2, 287, 299.
16  Pruen (Lindi) to Lang, 30 June 1886, CMS Archives G3/A5, f. 220.

tions, [and] ungrounded assertions ... contrary to fact' that characterised the behaviour even of 'the higher class of Colonist' towards Africans. As Robert Cust, the CMS stalwart and defender of Bishop Crowther, put it, 'The Albocracy of the age is terribly heartless.'[17]

James Stewart, albeit a man of very determined views on how Africans might realistically advance themselves within the restrictions established by white colonial society, was nevertheless widely regarded as a champion of African rights against the 'barbarous colour-madness of many of his fellow-countrymen'.[18] He was faced in 1897 with the formation of the Presbyterian Church of South Africa, which prompted serious debate over the future of the mission congregations at Lovedale and nearby. Their members, overwhelmingly African, voted not to join a united church and were strongly supported by Stewart and his colleagues. The African decision was easy to understand. 'They argue from political analogy. They have not benefited by the transfer from the Queen to the Colony and would gladly return to live at peace under the aegis of the Crown. They fear a similar sequel' if incorporated into a united church dominated by colonists.[19] As for the missionaries, their opposition to union was a consequence of 'the very absence of race prejudice on the part of the Kaffrarian Presbytery and their sympathy with the native people, their knowledge of the race prejudice existing among many of the European colonists in South Africa and their anxiety to preserve the rights and privileges of the native Christians in the face of such tendencies known to exist'.[20] This was a point well made, not least for its expression by J.D. Don, the missionary vexatiously prosecuted in connection with a notorious case at Burghersdorp in 1885 in which a white colonist murdered an African.[21]

The possibility or existence of dissension along racial and ethnic lines *within* the missions or local churches was both common and far more difficult to counter. Where missionaries themselves displayed such attitudes, resignation or dismissal sometimes rooted them out. J.H. Ashcroft, for example, appointed lay agent in 1878 to deal with the Niger Mission's accounts and to manage the steamer *Henry Venn*, was dismissed in 1882 as a result of his overbearing demeanour toward the Africans.[22] Others, such as Thomas Phillips, Ashcroft's successor and the first European to be ordained by an African bishop, also resigned unexpectedly soon, the consequence perhaps of having similarly adopted such critical stereotyping.[23] None

---

17  Knight-Bruce, Journals, from *Gold and the Gospel*, p. 84; Cust, *Notes on Missionary Subjects*, p. xiii.

18  Wells, *Stewart of Lovedale*, pp. 283–4.

19  Rev. J.D. Don to Young, 15 Feb. 1897, quoted in Brock, 'James Stewart and Lovedale, p. 53.

20  Don's analysis, quoted in *ibid.*, p. 53; Don to Prof. T.M. Lindsay (FCS mission secretary), Jan. 1899, NLS MS/7798, f. 230.

21  For the Don–Pelser case, correspondence Aug. 1885–April 1886, NLS MS/7797; Shepherd, *Lovedale*, pp. 224–6 and Brock, 'James Stewart', pp. 254–60.

22  *CMS Register*, List I, entry 576; Rev. Robert Lang (CMS Clerical Secretary and noted cricketer) to Rev. T. Phillips (Private and Confidential), 19 Jan. 1883, CMS Archives G3/A3/L2, f. 112.

23  *CMS Register*, List I, entry 953.

the less, a widespread awareness of racial or ethnic characteristics contributed to a general discourse of paternalistic benevolence, cloaked in references to 'the African character and habits' or the 'idiosyncrasies of the African mind'.[24] Other comparative comments might employ a common terminology, but, used in different periods, could also take on a quite distinct and disparaging content. Touring in his diocese in 1824, Bishop Heber had noted that most Indians he encountered 'in stature and apparent strength ... were certainly much inferior to the generality of our ship's company' and some 'with very graceful figures, [were] distinguished by a mildness of countenance almost approaching to effeminacy'.[25] Such terminology employed sixty or seventy years later, as Harry Johnston demonstrated, could convey an altogether harsher stereotyping.[26]

Missionaries had increasingly to respond to charges of discrimination and were frequently faced with the need to avert schism or to minimise the impact on the church of local anti-British, anti-colonial or nationalist movements. Such incidents too frequently entailed the loss of able and influential mission members from the local Christian community. According to the Secretary of the SPG, with a degree of understatement disguising its widespread occurrence, 'without question there are indications that we are not exactly beloved, nor does education improve matters'.[27]

This facet of missionary enterprise has received a great deal of attention and scholars have focused on two closely related issues. Taking their lead from Henry Venn, they have asked why progress towards the establishment of indigenous native churches was not only limited but also seemed c.1900 to be in danger of slowing still further. They have also considered the responses of local Christians both to this situation and to the failure to develop indigenous ministries on a scale sufficient to hasten the 'euthanasia' of the missions. The answers given to these questions reveal widespread agreement. Even among one-time supporters of Venn's principles there developed a sense of caution and misgivings as to the capacity – financial, administrative, ethical, spiritual – of indigenous Christians in many places to sustain churches from their own resources. These reservations were only reinforced by the emergence of young, impatient and far more narrowly ethnocentric or racially conscious missionaries in the 1880s and 1890s. Inclined to be hypercritical, often enthused by a new and uncompromising spirituality, they found much wrong with present circumstances and little to praise in the past. The need to prolong European missionary supervision they therefore regarded as essential. Although the impact of these different influences was seen at its most extreme in

---

24  Lang to Phillips, 25 Nov. 1882, 11 May 1883, *ibid.*, ff. 89, 154.
25  Reginald Heber, 6 Oct. 1824, *Narrative of a Journey through the Upper Provinces of India from Calcutta to Bombay, 1824–1825*, 2 vols (London, 1844), Vol. 1, pp. 21, 25.
26  Johnston, *Report* (note 7 above); Mrinalini Sinha, *Colonial Masculinity: The 'Manly Englishman' and the 'Effeminate Bengali' in the Late Nineteenth Century* (Manchester, 1995).
27  Bishop H.H. Montgomery, 'The Attitude of the White Man Towards the Darker Races', *The East and the West*, Jan. 1903, p. 54.

West Africa and the impact of the Niger mission crisis was felt far and wide, similar developments were quite independently part of the experience of many missions and indigenous Christians.

Crowther's successor in 1893, Bishop J.S. Hill, was not only a European. He also brought to his diocese of Western Equatorial Africa the qualifications not only of a CMS missionary in Lagos but, in a wry reflection on the concern for appropriate qualifications, most recently ten years as a prison chaplain in New Zealand! The opportunity provided by his unexpected death the next year was not taken. African opinion was overridden and, although the African archdeacon James Johnson became assistant bishop for the Niger Delta Pastorate, Herbert Tugwell's consecration settled the issue of ultimate authority until 1920. In all three of these West African cases the overriding concern was preservation of the CMS's own control over the development of the local church.[28]

In the UMCA, Dr John Hine (Bishop of Nyasaland, 1896–1908) felt there should be 'no more native priests for ten years ... of that I am pretty certain. And an increasing number of permanent deacons. We are pushing the native too fast and it demoralizes him ... we push the simple native too much and he soon gets out of control and is anything but a blessing.' His successor, Frank Weston, agreed. 'I myself feel most strongly that there is a danger that we are going too fast about the native ministry ... because the English workers are not sufficient to keep an eye on the Africans when ordained.'[29]

The pattern of events in India matched that elsewhere. Despite the ample numbers of Indian priests and suggestions from the 1850s onwards that the time had come for the elevation of an Indian to a diocesan bishopric, an assistant bishop, V.S. Azariah, was not consecrated until 1912. Azariah became a full diocesan bishop legally as well as practically only in 1930 and no more than two further Indian assistant bishops were appointed before 1947.[30]

This general development of institutional divisions between British missionaries and indigenous church members may suggest a process of church growth and ecclesiastical evolution shaped above all by perceptions of race. It can also be called on to support the view that the functioning of institutions in the colonial setting itself greatly enhanced the sense that a racial calculus dominated the encounter.[31] It is a development also easily linked to the further argument, that the missionary movement was so shot through with the presuppositions of racial superiority that its integration with other processes of empire building and its role as a colossal buttress of empire are unquestionable.

---

28  Williams, *Ideal of the Self-Governing Church*, pp. 182–97, 230–43.
29  Hine to Duncan Travers (UMCA Secretary), Ash Wednesday 1902, cited by Jermone T. Moriyama, 'The Evolution of an African Ministry in the Work of the Universities' Mission to Central Africa in Tanzania, 1864–1909' (unpub. Ph.D. thesis, London, 1984), p. 254; Weston, *Central Africa*, July, 1908, pp. 181–2, and May 1909, p. 115.
30  Harper, *In the Shadow of the Mahatma*, chap. 4 and pp. 153–63.
31  See Chapter 10 above, section 1.

All these arguments, notwithstanding their logical attraction and contemporary appeal, are none the less oversimplified and one-sided. Evidence of quite other lines of thinking is provided, for instance, by supporters of missions convinced that racial distinctions were unsustainable. Even a crude division between Caucasian, Mongolian and Ethiopian was undermined by the scientific observation of human variety. The 'mixtures between these races are so extensive and numerous', wrote the geographer S.R. Pattison in his volume for the Religious Tract Society, that the 'actual condition of things in regard to race is unstable as a whole', demonstrating 'everywhere a capacity for change more or less from one form into another'. That 'the unity of man extends to his religious faculties as well as to his physical and intellectual conditions' is demonstrated by the universal responsiveness of differ-ent cultures to the evangelical message.[32]

Not only did racial and ethnocentric convictions vary in degree from individual to individual but such convictions were always one element among others in deter-mining the course of missionary thinking and activity.[33] Thus Bishop Hill, thrown into the thicket of controversy, found himself charged by both whites and blacks with 'unduly siding with the natives' and 'with race prejudices and intolerant arro-gancy'.[34] J.D. Don, engaged in the Free Church of Scotland debate about mission-ary priorities in the development and expansion of the church, asked 'Shall we continue to raise such native ministers [i.e. "ordained … like their European brethren"], or confine ourselves to the type now called evangelists?' He was acutely aware that either course could be construed as racist, especially 'in a mission like ours' where 'the number cannot be largely or rapidly increased'. To concentrate on producing indigenous evangelists would appear to block African advancement and leadership; to offer the higher education necessary to that smaller number possess-ing the ability and able to exercise authority in administering the sacraments and superintending the church was equally open to accusations of discrimination. Given the practical problems facing ordained missionaries at the Cape, who had to deal with local officials, property rights, poaching by other missions and the super-intendence of schools, Don favoured current practice. His aim was 'to procure a good supply of men possessing the lower qualification', from among whom 'men might be chosen from time to time who approved themselves worthy of receiving a higher education and of being raised to the higher position'. However, there was no escaping the difficulty of pursuing this middle way to general satisfaction.[35]

In India an episcopal appointment and the advance of V.S. Azariah in particular raised a horde of considerations, weighing very differently with various involved parties. The desire for a colour-blind rather than a racially divided church

---

32  S.R. Pattison, *Gospel Ethnology*, new cheaper edition (London, c.1890), pp. 13–14, 21, 35.

33  See above, pp. 247, 283–9.

34  Williams, *Ideal of the Self*-Governing Church, pp. 193–4.

35  J.D. Don to Prof. T.M. Lindsay (FCS missions secretary), 17 May 1892, NLS MS/7798, f. 32; cf. Don to Lindsay, 24 Jan. 1898, *ibid.*, f. 194, showing his changing views.

produced great concern for candidates' abilities and background. The perceived 'failure' of church council schemes in Tinnevelly was little less worrying for India's Christians than the Crowther crisis. The practical consequences of Azariah's own inexperience – he was ordained deacon only in June 1909 – and his low caste status as a Nadar mingled with concerns over nationalist responses to ecclesiastical or episcopal authority and legal or constitutional questions.[36] These debates are not reducible simply to examples of race conflict or contests over imperial hegemony, although these were elements in the situation. No more plausibly can it be argued that controversies thrived because, as a result of insufficient political will and resolution, liberal intentions were merely suffocated by racist predisposition.

Critical contemporaries among missionaries and converts, feeling themselves excluded, patronised or threatened under whatever arrangements existed for promoting church life and growth, were none the less inclined to play the racial card, regardless of its precise relevance. Bishop Weston, sensitive to his mission's overwhelming dependence on the efforts of African Christians but justifiably worried about the fragility of African Christianity in the conditions of the plantations and coastal towns, strove to reconcile the need for trust in his clergy with the dangers of 'a premature grant of home rule' to local churches.[37] He also attempted to work out the UMCA's ideals of celibacy and 'the religious life' by building up close-knit religious communities for both men and women. Given his profound concern with ecclesiastical order and clerical authority, the need for discipline, self-sacrifice and obedience counted for much with Weston and his colleagues. They took pleasure in the fact that, in dealing with moral or marital lapses, it was not only possible but positively beneficial to impose traditional ecclesiastical rulings.[38] Despite Weston's anxiety that 'we should not lose confidence in the African ministry',[39] his combination of paternalism and ethnocentricity was not a success. Not only was the development of an African ministry curtailed but there developed 'a quiet but persistent rebellion against Weston amongst the African clergy', with an inevitable sequence of suspensions and dismissals.[40] The divisions opened up undoubtedly bore a racial character, but to characterise this entirely negatively as 'race conflict' would fall little short of caricature.

The capacity of missionaries to alienate not only church members but often those less formally attached to Christian communities and the consequences of that alienation, is well known.[41] In Africa above all the growth of independent local churches born of separation from the mission-controlled bodies was particularly pronounced. Crowther's experience was followed by the breakaway of the Niger

36  Harper, *In the Shadow of the Mahatma*, pp. 153–63.
37  Smith, *Frank Bishop of Zanzibar*, p. 88.
38  Ellen Maples, *Chauncy Maples*, p. 241.
39  Smith, *Frank Bishop of Zanzibar*, pp. 87–8.
40  Moriyama, 'Evolution of an African Ministry', p. 286.
41  For an introduction, Hastings, *The Church in Africa*, esp. chaps 7 and 9.

Delta Pastorate, dedicated under James ('Holy') Johnson to African leadership and Anglican practice; this was disrupted in its turn when in 1901 the Bethel African Church broke away from the Pastorate. The Baptist and Methodist missionary-led churches of Sierra Leone and the Gold Coast experienced similar divisions. In contrast to these so-called 'Ethiopian' churches were other 'Zionist' movements, built around charismatic individuals or Christian 'prophets'. They incorporated much from traditional African religions, had a greater mass appeal and were regarded by Europeans as often dangerously radical, especially in South and Central Africa where they were most numerous.

These separatist movements were clear signs of the manner in which Christian evangelism contributed to the distancing of indigenous peoples from colonial institutions and culture, either by providing models that could be independently developed or by contributing ideas and ritual to otherwise indigenous religious movements. Their role in developing the cultural distinctiveness and political independence of Africans has been considerable. Nevertheless, it is a role that should not be exaggerated. Most Christians, in Asia still more than Africa, continued to belong to the mission congregations and churches directly descended from them, but they too often distanced themselves from colonial and missionary connections. They were able to do so because, while missions imparted education and belief, they could not control their diffusion, eventual impact and adaptation. Nor could missions, whatever their misgivings, free themselves from the consequences of their small numbers and necessary reliance on indigenous Christians as agents and evangelists.

## II

At the turn of the nineteenth century, Islam remained a major evangelical preoccupation, a provocative stimulus to missionary dynamism as well as global awareness especially among the younger generation of missionaries recruited in the 1890s. Not just for missionaries but for many other people the 'Moslem Menace' was coming to match that of the 'Yellow Peril'. Thus Lord Salisbury linked both in less inflammatory language but none the less with a frank warning to missions to tread very carefully in such areas of the world.[42] Such official caution and apparent lack of sympathy outraged many missionaries; it only seemed to confirm the imperial government's indifference to what the missions saw as a great opportunity. Thus in correspondence with the American evangelist and world student leader John R. Mott, for example, the LMS missionary J.N. Farquhar wrote of 'a great awakening' among Muslims in India 'leading to a) greater political activity b) far greater educational enthusiasm c) a revival of Mohammedanism'. 'All this', he felt, 'opens the way for Xn. influence.' Thinking on a world scale, Farquhar saw 'two problems ...

---

42  Speech at SPG Anniversary Meeting, reported in *The Times*, 20 June 1900, p. 10b; Greenlee and Johnston, *Good Citizens*, chap. 4, esp. pp. 113–14.

beyond all others, the Oriental problem and the Mohammedan problem'; in conjunction with the missionary movement, he looked to organisations such as the Young Men's Christian Association and the World Student Christian Federation[43] to meet 'the very crisis of the evolution of Asia' and the contemporary impact on Islamic societies of 'the explosive forces of Western thought'. Farquhar's was a global view and, together with its sense of urgency, one shared by many others, such as the up-and-coming J.H. Oldham.[44]

In response to such analyses, major conferences to examine Islam and the work of the missions were convened at Cairo in 1906 and at Lucknow in 1911.[45] At the Pan-Anglican Congress in 1908 and still more at the World Missionary Conference of 1910 in Edinburgh, the problem of Islam was also given much careful attention. This scrutiny reflected not only specifically evangelical preoccupations with Providence and eschatology but a general characteristic of the period, in that almost wherever observers looked, whether or not they were sympathetic to missions, they found large segments of the extra-European and colonial world in turmoil and encountered widespread pressures for social and political change. Delegates to the Lucknow Conference saw the unrest and divisions in the Islamic world as 'startling evidence of the finger of God in history', opportunities to be seized at once.[46] Critics mocked the 'irrational arrogance and aggressiveness' which they detected in the missions on these issues and, as on many previous occasions, blamed them for being at least partly responsible for ethnic and nationalist discontents. Experienced administrators such as Sir Evelyn Baring dismissed the widely held evangelical notion of a Muslim domino effect triggered off by events in the Middle East; in Sir Alfred Lyall's words, 'The Mahdi's fortunes do not interest India'.[47] Nevertheless there was widespread agreement that movements as diverse as the Boxer Rebellion and republican revolution in China, nationalist movements in India and Egypt, indigenous rights protection movements in West Africa, independent churches and local revolt in South Africa and Japan's defeat of Russia in the war of 1905 were evidence of unprecedented upheavals. In the eyes of the missions they required a distinct evangelical response.

---

43  See below, pp. 301–5.
44  Farquhar to Mott, 15 April 1909, Mott Papers 45/29/521; Oldham to Mott, 16 Aug. 1913, Mott Papers 45/64/1175. Farquhar was then National Student Secretary of the YMCA of India and Ceylon.
45  *Methods of Mission Work among Moslems. Being those Papers read at the First Missionary Conference on behalf of the Muslim World held at Cairo April 4th–9th 1906* (London and New York, 1906); for Lucknow, note 46 below.
46  E.M. Wherry, S.M. Zwemer and C.G. Mylrea (eds), *Islam and Missions. Being Papers read at the Second Missionary Conference on behalf of the Mohammedan World at Lucknow, January 23–28, 1911* (London, 1911), p. 22; for an overview, Susan Bayly, 'The Evolution of Colonial Cultures: Nineteenth-Century Asia', in Andrew Porter (ed.), *OHBE Vol. 3: The Nineteenth Century* (Oxford, 1999), pp. 447–69.
47  Arthur Glyn Leonard, *Islam. Her Moral and Spiritual Value. A Rational and Psychological Study* (London, 1909), p. 136; Cromer, Earl of, *Modern Egypt*, 2 vols (London, 1908), Vol. 1, pp. 551–2.

In their debates about Islam the principal missionary conferences in the years before the First World War revealed general agreement on two fundamental issues: the extent of discontent in the Muslim world and the priority to be given to Africa. 'There never was such unrest, politically, socially and spiritually, in Moslem lands as there is today and ... this very unrest is accompanied by a new sense of solidarity and an attempt to unify the disintegrating forces of Islam.' The latter was particularly evident in Africa. Participants at the Lucknow gathering endorsed Edinburgh's conclusion, that the 'absorption of native races into Islam is proceeding rapidly and continuously in practically all parts of the continent ... Either Christianity or Islam will prevail throughout Africa.'[48]

These discussions not surprisingly re-echoed long-standing evangelical perceptions – notably the interpretation of Muslim unrest as evidence of the break-up of hostile historic structures; conflicting views on the extent to which these changes were signs either of Islam's resurgence or of Christianity's opportunity; and the worries about expansion. For reasons which drew strongly on traditional criticisms of Islam – its lack of moral sense, its impact on women, its bigotry, formalism and materialism and its association with slavery – it was also recognised as Christianity's main opponent to a degree probably greater than ever before.

Continued scrutiny of the signs of the times as well as the spirit of the conferences frequently reinforced fresh eschatological reflections. During the Edinburgh Conference, Handley Moule, by then Bishop of Durham after three decades of tending Cambridge's evangelical enthusiasts, appealed to 'the thought of *the Lord's Return*' as a necessary check on all other differences of opinion. Temple Gairdner in his review of Edinburgh also noted the opening speakers' consciousness of an imminent Second Coming. In a less eirenic vein, he identified the present world crisis as one with other key historical moments such as that immediately before Christ's first coming. No St John the Divine was required 'to see The Beast rising from the world-tide and presenting once more the immemorial alternative, "Naturism or Deeper into God". The spectacle of the East, with half a worldful of men, suddenly drawn into the full current of world-thought is one scene in the vision of the modern Apocalypse. The spectacle of the West rapidly surrendering to a radically atheist philosophy of Nature is the other.'[49] The sense of crisis, urgency and pessimism evident in many of these comments made in the years after 1900 points to the persistence of a pronounced pre-millennial outlook of the kind which had become popular between 1870 and 1890. However, such continuities as existed in the shifting relationship between evangelicalism, Islam and millennial expectations were also counterbalanced by equally noticeable changes.

Although General Gordon cast a long shadow, the imperial government ensured that his legacy in the Sudan was ultimately an institutional one in the

---

48  Wherry, Zwemer and Mylrea (eds), *Islam and Missions*, pp. 25, 17.
49  H.C.G. Moule to John R. Mott, 22 June 1910, Mott Papers 45/60/1117; W.H.T. Gairdner, *'Edinburgh 1910'. An Account and Interpretation of the World Missionary Conference* (London, 1910), p. 152.

shape of Gordon College and the cathedral begun in Khartoum between 1900 and 1904. Christian teaching and preaching remained tightly constrained under British rule and pre-millennialist missionary practice in the manner of the CIM or Wilmot Brooke was quite impossible. Cromer, loftily looking back at his Egyptian career, allowed that 'The missionary, the philanthropist, the social reformer and others of the same sort, should have a fair field. Their intentions are excellent, although at times their judgment may be defective. They will, if under some control, probably do much good on a small scale.' However, they could not be trusted to operate unrestrained.[50] Centralised institutions made possible official watchfulness and intervention.

Similar misgivings, akin also to those that had periodically disturbed officials in India, were felt also by men in authority on the Niger. In the 1890s, George Goldie was keen that the Royal Niger Company should benefit from missionary business and was anxious for missionary support to increase backing for his chartered monopoly. However, he also found it necessary to curb their ventures into the Niger territories lest they provoke hostility. A.H. Hallen, for instance, who had spoken at the British Association in 1892 on 'Opening Relations with the Hausa Race of Western Soudan', was refused entry. Goldie thought him 'a firebrand', dangerous in a territory 'where even the best tempered and least selfish men become splenetic'![51] Generally speaking, the CMS leaders welcomed Goldie's assistance and approved his commercial practices, including restraint of the liquor trade.[52] However, as his influence finally collapsed in 1898 and the imperial government took over northern Nigeria in 1900, the CMS seized its chance, despatching a missionary expedition under Bishop Tugwell to Kano in December 1899. 'The end is drawing near. The kings of Hausa cities are renouncing their religious allegiance to the Sultan of Sokoto. The people prophesy the advent of the whiteman with the Christian religion ... The sacred writings of the Hausas predict the second coming of Christ as the victorious leader of a great army. Next year [1900] is marked out as the time.'[53] Not surprisingly this optimistic convergence of indigenous and Christian prophecies came to little in practice. The visit to Kano was an embarrassing failure, while increasingly the Fulani emirs and Lugard's administrative successors combined to make effective missionary work all but impossible. Not until 1924 was the CMS permitted to establish itself in the foreigners' quarters in Kano.[54]

---

50 Cromer, *Modern Egypt*, Vol. 2, p. 234.
51 *Report of the British Association for the Advancement of Science*, Vol. 62 (Edinburgh, 1892), p. 817; also *Proceedings of the Royal Geographical Society*, 14 (Oct. 1892), 715; Goldie to C.H. Robinson, 30 Aug. and 6 Sept. 1893, Robinson–Hallen correspondence, Galton MSS 77.
52 E.A. Ayandele, 'The Relations between the Church Missionary Society and the Royal Niger Company, 1886–1900', *JHSN*, 4 (1968), 399–418.
53 *Niger and Yoruba Notes* (CMS, Jan. 1900), cited by Ayandele, *The Missionary Impact*, pp. 127–8.
54 Ayandele, *The Missionary Impact*, chap. 4 'The Crescent and the Cross in Northern Nigeria, 1900–1914'.

There consequently emerged in the writing and conference reports of this decade a bitter and sustained criticism of the practice of British colonial rule in Muslim areas. Eugene Stock's pointed observation, that 'the Government has seemed so unduly careful of Mohammedan feeling and so little disposed to take a reasonable stand as a Christian nation', echoed complaints made both after the Indian Mutiny and during the Eastern Crisis of 1875–78 and was later felt to apply in many territories besides the Sudan.[55] Still more irksome than the official restraint of missionary enterprise was its consequence in promoting Muslim expansion. In a work jointly published by the British missionary societies, Gairdner expressed a widely held view when he wrote that 'the *pax Britannica* makes a ring-fence, within which Islam finds exceptionally favourable opportunities of spreading Eastward still'.[56]

There were also influences apart from government prohibitions that undermined the persistence among missionaries to Muslims of an aggressively evangelistic pre-millennial strategy. Despite a tendency to view Islam as a united whole, the second half of the century seems to have witnessed the growth among missionaries of divided opinions over approaches to Muslims. In part, this reflected differences between conditions in North India and those elsewhere, especially in Africa. There is little evidence to suggest that a combination of pre-millennial enthusiasms and the peripatetics' dislike of bricks and mortar ever played much part in the thinking of those now going to India. Although, for example, G.A. Lefroy of the Cambridge Mission to Delhi described his 'first literary enterprise' as 'a small book on prophecy strictly for Mahommedan consumption', his interest in the subject was apparently limited. The official enquiries and self-examination of several societies in the 1850s and 1860s and the far-reaching 'missionary controversy' of the 1880s and 1890s, drew attention to the serious need for preaching and economy; but they rarely led to the closure of those educational institutions which had already been developed in India. So too the sense that earlier methods of engaging with Islam had been unproductive placed a premium on the training for direct evangelism of a body of local Christian preachers, thereby directly reaffirming the importance of the schooling provided in such institutions as the Church Missionary College at Lahore.[57]

British scholars at home and in India also moved gradually towards alternative understandings of Islam, by starting with the assumption that revelation and religious development were a continuing historical process and working towards some sort of accommodation rather than persisting in confrontation.[58] This approach

---

55  Eugene Stock, *History of the Church Missionary Society. Supplementary Volume the Fourth* (London, 1916), p. 108.

56  Stock, *History of the CMS*, Vol. 4, p. 115; W.H.T. Gairdner, *The Reproach of Islam* (London, 1909), p. 25; also Karl Kumm of the SUM, speaking at Edinburgh, Gairdner, *'Edinburgh 1910'*, p. 73.

57  Montgomery, *Life and Letters of Lefroy*, pp. 75, 94; Vaughan, *The Trident*, pp. 190–1.

58  Clinton Bennett, Victorian *Images of Islam* (London, 1992); Alan Guenther, 'Changing Perceptions of Islam: Thomas Patrick Hughes as Missionary and Scholar', *NAMP Symposium Paper* (Boston, 1998).

also gained ground at a popular level, especially as acquaintance with African conditions grew from the mid-1870s and writers developed the case for Islam's positive contribution to Africa's advance from its position at the bottom of a racial and cultural hierarchy.[59] In the late 1880s the merits of Islam in sub-Saharan Africa became a subject of acute public debate after Canon Isaac Taylor proclaimed its value to Africans as a half-way house en route to Christianity at the Church Congress meeting in 1887.[60]

That debate was essentially inconclusive, providing some with a stick with which to beat missionaries and prompting others to think more carefully about the nature and conduct of Christian–Muslim relations. The extensive tolerance for Islam, which it revealed, was also reinforced from other directions. Archbishop Benson in 1892 argued before the SPG's Annual Meeting for an approach to Islam that rested on respect and recognition of its equal capacity with Christianity to form excellent characters. Knowledge gained from his own travels in North Africa and a sense of the comparisons to be drawn with Roman Catholicism to Islam's credit, led him to press for tolerance and mutual regard. 'We must not approach them as if they knew they were themselves deficient, and that it was only pride and obstinacy that prevented them from listening to us.' Without understanding and an appreciation that the same processes were at work in the formation of sincere Muslims as with Christians, 'we shall have no chance in dealing with a religion like Mahomedanism'.[61] These views gained Benson much criticism. Lefroy in Delhi, for example, regretted that the Archbishop had ignored the dark side of Islam. However, they made sense to many even within the missionary world. Members of the UMCA who saw themselves in the front line against Islam's expansion not infrequently compared Muslims favourably to many of the Europeans whom they saw as undermining their work. Bishop Weston, for instance, 'feared Islam not a little, but he feared Commercialism more'.[62]

Curbed by government restraints, confronted with the case for practicality, even some of those immersed in the ardent milieu of pre-millennial enthusiasm found their ideas developing in a detached and scholarly manner under the pervasive influence of historical modes of theological criticism and comparative inquiry. This subverted any simple-minded identification of Islam with Antichrist, even while on all sides there continued the conviction that Islam was destined to be

---

59 See for example, Smith, *Mohammed and the Mohammedans*; Edward Blyden, *Christianity, Islam and the Negro Race*, 2nd edn (London, 1888); W. Winwood Reade, *The Martyrdom of Man* (London, 1875; 15th edn, 1896) ; T.W. Arnold, *The Preaching of Islam: A History of the Propagation of the Muslim Faith* (London, 1896).

60 Thomas Prasch, 'Which God for Africa: The Islamic–Christian Missionary Debate in Late-Victorian England', *Victorian Studies* 33, 1 (1989–90), 51–73.

61 A.C. Benson, *The Life of Edward White Benson*, 2 vols (London, 1899, repr. 1900), Vol. 2, pp. 412–23, 456–61, quotation at p. 460.

62 Montgomery, *Life and Letters of Lefroy*, pp. 90–2; Smith, *Frank Bishop of Zanzibar*, pp. 242, 97 and chap. 5.

replaced by Christianity. This was probably true of Keith-Falconer, who has already been mentioned. In the early 1900s, in the case of Gairdner, Thornton and many of their contemporaries the former intensity of their pre-millennial persuasions was becoming less pronounced. 'Cabin'd, cribb'd, confin'd' in Cairo while, as they initially thought, biding their time for the Sudan,[63] they gradually took up for themselves the long-standing tasks of translation, publication, schooling, journalism and the promotion of literature societies. 'Remember', Thornton wrote, 'that ... what you write here in Arabic will soon reach India, as quickly as it can reach England. It will find an entrance into other Moslem lands.' Several years later, he was still referring to that 'great language of Arabic, which binds together the continents of Asia and Africa'.[64] Curbed by Cromer in the Sudan, they responded to opportunity in Cairo by moving away from the Consul-General in Egypt itself. They adopted the strategy of 'foreigners like Lanfranc and Anselm and Aidan in England', siding 'where it is right and lawful to do so, with national aspirations, that we cultivate friendship, remove misunderstandings and are resorted to as counsellors'. This was to step in and 'help the nation', by preventing the emergence of 'an educated class of agnostics on the one hand and a recrudescence of Islam in its most fanatical form on the other'.[65] The development of Gairdner's work in Cairo, where he eventually died in 1928, provides an important example of how a new generation of missionaries and their teachers were drawn steadily towards both a sympathetically critical study of Muslim religious texts and their appeal and away from any deferential or even reluctant alignment with British rule.

It was in such ways that an overwhelmingly gradualist, essentially optimistic, post-millennial strategy again reasserted itself in missions to Muslims. Missionary rhetoric still preserved traces of pessimism and pre-millennial expectations, but missionary practice was again turning away from a romantic radical rejection of the past to the renewed development of older traditions. In the course of the century, the focus of missionary interest had shifted periodically between India, the Near or Middle East and sub-Saharan Africa. The consequential growth of a deeper understanding, wider contacts and a more accommodating attitude towards Islam had an important impact. In one sense growing familiarity with Islam had created the problem for James Stewart referred to above, 'how to fit that career ... into the progress of the world'. At the same time Stewart's question, 'how to understand the [Providential] purpose it was meant to serve', was by 1914 once again unlikely to be answered with references to Antichrist or the interpretative framework of pre-millennialism that had once looked so promising. The further area of missionary convergence lay in the contribution made by the experience of

63 Padwick, *Temple Gairdner*, pp. 80–2, 87.
64 To Gairdner, Cairo, n.d. [1899], Gairdner, *D.M. Thornton*, p. 62; Thornton, memo (1906), *ibid.*, p. 171.
65 Thornton to H.C.G. Moule, 2 Feb. 1906, quoted in Gairdner, *Douglas Thornton*, pp. 192–3 and 232; Padwick, *Temple Gairdner*, chap. 9 'Apologetics, 1903–07'.

missionaries to Muslims, especially in Africa, to the renewed distancing of missions from the new colonial state.

### III

Earlier chapters have indicated how at different levels the international networks of the missionary movement were built up in the early and mid-nineteenth century. British missions were woven into the global web along with continental Protestants and missionary colleagues from all parts of the English-speaking world, especially the United States, by recruitment, intermarriage, personal friendships, revival movements and scholarly exchanges. Despite the conventional picture of the late nineteenth century as an age of intensified national rivalries, before the First World War there was no diminution but rather an increase in these countervailing tendencies.

The activity of colonising powers during the Scramble, for instance, often pushed missionaries together. Events in East and Central Africa coinciding with the 1890 Brussels Conference generated contacts, seen above, between the Free Church of Scotland mission, the German province of the Moravians and the Berlin Evangelical Missionary Society.[66] As the century passed, missionary experience itself spurred on the growth of international co-operation through the widespread adoption of agreements over missions' spheres of activity. These 'comity' arrangements – among British societies as well as between British and foreign – were designed to prevent overlapping and therefore uneconomic evangelism. Combining as they did an acceptance of the interchangeability of denominations as territory was exchanged or yielded up by different societies, they were not only a solution to potential disputes but could at times be sources of conflict, national as well as denominational. Relations between the LMS and the Norwegian Missionary Society in Madagascar show both sides of the picture. After the reopening of Madagascar to missions in 1861, the LMS returned, only to be met by Bishop Schreuder's challenge on behalf of the Norwegian Missionary Society, newly arrived in 1866.[67] Relations were subsequently much more amicable. In 1892, one of the LMS secretaries, the Reverend George Cousins, joined the Norwegian Missionary Society in Stavanger to celebrate their fiftieth anniversary. In the 1890s confidential committee and other administrative papers were exchanged and later in 1912–13 the English societies took the lead in the protests by the Protestant community at French official restrictions. United in adversity and demanding 'an end ... to Arbitrary Government', the local Protestant missionaries – Quakers, LMS, Norwegian Missionary Society, SPG, Lutheran, involving

---

66  George Smith to Robert Laws, 5 and 27 Nov. 1890, NLS MS/7774, ff. 338, 365. Above, p. 279.

67  Joseph Mullens (LMS Secretary) to Christian Dons (NMS General Secretary), 16 Dec. 1871, NMS Archives, Box 56A, microfilm 1, pp. 28–9; *Norwegian Mission to Madagascar* (LMS Printed for Directors only: London, 1872), *ibid.*, General Secretariat Box 4/6. For the general history, Finn Fuglestad and Jarle Simensen (eds), *Norwegian Missions in African History: Vol. 2: Madagascar* (Oslo, 1986), chap. 3.

Americans, British, French and Norwegian – followed their home societies in holding their own international conference to agree the principles of a co-operative working of the entire island.[68]

At quite another level, time-honoured customs offered missionaries practical help, encouragement, flattery and evidence not only of mutual regard but intellectual and social esteem. R.N. Cust offered American visitors temporary membership of the Athenaeum or the Travellers Club during their stay and secured the election of Dr Means to the Royal Geographical Society.[69] The Welsh Baptist Timothy Richard received honorary degrees in 1895 and 1901 from Emory and Brown universities and the BMS Secretary E.B. Underhill from Rochester. The CIM extended its recruitment to the United States in 1888 and Henry Grattan Guinness not only collected a doctorate from Brown in 1889 but inspired the establishment of missionary training institutes in Boston and Minneapolis. Missionary travel with its opportunities for friendship and enlightenment greatly increased. Rufus Anderson travelling to Bombay in 1854 recorded in his diary pleasurable conversations with three other missionary passengers.[70] Fifty years on, A.J. Brown sailed home from Bombay at the end of his Asian tour of inspection. He was able to organise a questionnaire and a conference for twenty-two other missionaries on board, including members of the SPG, LMS, CMS, Basel, Gossner, Zenana Bible and Medical and the Moravian missions.[71]

One feature of this process and a notable indicator of the growth of the missionary enterprise was the increasing frequency of missionary conferences. International gatherings began with the London and New York meetings convened in 1854. Thereafter Liverpool (1860), London (1878, 1888), New York (1900) and Edinburgh (1910) punctuated the period and the sense of self-generated expansion is palpable. With a certain chronological laxity the 1888 assembly took the title of 'Centenary' conference; New York in 1900 was the first 'ecumenical' international missionary conference. Edinburgh was not only the first 'World' missionary conference but reflected its organisers' determination not to let things slip in its rosy after-glow, by the establishment of a 'Continuation Committee' which in 1921 was further reorganised as the International Missionary Council.[72] Local missionary conferences became both much more feasible and as frequent as funds

---

68  *LMS Chronicle* (Sept. 1892), pp. 201–2; Report of the three English missions, 28 Feb. 1912, NMS Archives General Secretariat Box 18/13; 'International Conference on Missionary Work in Madagascar, LMS House, 15 June 1912', *ibid*, Box 185/13; 'Private and Confidential. Report of a Conference of Missionaries and Delegates of Missions held in Tananarive, Madagascar, October 1913', *ibid.*, Box 185/12, pp. i–iv, 1–88.

69  Cust to Means, 17 Dec. 1879, ABC 14/5/188.

70  Rufus Anderson, Oct. 1854, Journal vol. 2, ABC/30/12.

71  Brown, entry 4 March 1902 and pp. 158–73, Journal, Special Collections Record Group 2, Yale Divinity School. Arthur Judson Brown was administrative secretary to the Presbyterian Board of Foreign Missions in New York, 1895–1929.

72  For Edinburgh and its aftermath, Keith Clements, *Faith on the Frontier: A Life of J.H. Oldham* (Edinburgh and Geneva, 1999), chaps 5–8.

allowed. Beginning at Allahabad in 1872 there developed a regular decennial pattern of all-India missionary gatherings, interspersed with the local and provincial meetings of individual denominations.[73] In Europe and America it would seem that even the burgeoning international exhibitions were turned to missionary account. The Great Exhibition in Hyde Park in 1851, the Crystal Palace, the Paris exhibition of 1855 and, in 1893, the 'Parliament of Religions' in association with the World Fair at Chicago and the Foreign Missions Conference of North America all offer evidence of a presence so far little studied.[74]

Aspects of these missionary and other related conferences, such as the Keswick conventions, have occasionally found their historians and gatherings, notably that at Edinburgh in 1910, have a place in the history of the ecumenical movement among the churches.[75] However their impact has generally attracted little attention. It has therefore been shown above how the implications of regular meetings such as Mildmay and Keswick spilled over with considerable effect from the domestic history of British religion into that of missionary activity overseas. They drove wedges between missions and empire as did the conferences on the state of the Muslim world, by questioning the relevance and value of Western institutions or practices for the missions' primary goals of evangelism, conversion and church building. In this international world of evangelical revivalism and conference activity, the emergent student movement was yet another influential development that produced a similar impact.

The Student Volunteer Movement (SVM), as it was called in North America and the British Student Volunteer Missionary Union shared a common root in the Young Men's Christian Association (YMCA), originally founded by George Williams and his fellow office workers in 1844. Actively concerned at first with home missions and part of a much wider movement – not confined to Britain – intended to safeguard the immortal souls of easily corruptible young men adrift in the modern city, the YMCA was also marked from the start according to its historian by 'missionary aggressiveness as much as intensity of devotion'. Captivated by the LMS idols, Robert Moffat and John Williams, members quickly developed a serious interest in overseas missions. With revival 'never far from the heart of the YMCA's concerns', they took to heart equally the urgent message of contemporary American revivalists such as Asa Mahan and Charles Finney. [76]

---

73  Calcutta (1882–83), Bombay (1892–93), Madras (1902); they were held at the turn of the year to escape the summer heat.

74  See Clyde Binfield, *George Williams and the Y.M.C.A.: A Study in Victorian Social Attitudes* (London, 1973), pp. 171–7, 368. Paul Greenhalgh, *Ephemeral Vistas: The Expositions Universelles, Great Exhibitions and World's Fairs, 1851–1939* (Manchester, 1988), ignores this aspect.

75  J.C. Pollock, *The Keswick Story* (London, 1964); Bebbington, *Evangelicalism in Modern Britain*, chap. 5 'Holiness unto the Lord: Keswick and its Context in the Later Nineteenth Century'; Ruth Rouse and Stephen Charles Neill (eds), *A History of the Ecumenical Movement 1517–1948* (London, 1954), pp. 355–62, 405–7.

76  Binfield, *George Williams*, pp. 100, 104–5, 116, 129, 198–9.

The rapid broadening of the YMCA's base in associations throughout Europe and the emigrant worlds of both North America and the British colonies took place in the 1850s and 1860s. It began to develop an international perspective on missionary activity and established its own North American missionary department in 1879. From an early date revivalist preachers such as Dwight Moody and A.T. Pierson had close YMCA links and in the 1880s the Association's missionary programme was much stronger in the United States than in Britain.[77] Under the influence of his own conversion and pre-millennial enthusiasms, Pierson, for example, began to develop the overseas missions theme, quickly developing a nationwide reputation. He was soon among those regularly addressing the summer bible schools and conferences at Northfield in Massachusetts begun by Moody for lay evangelical workers about1880. The initiative of Luther Wishard, travelling college secretary for the YMCA, prompted Moody and through him Pierson to hold a conference at Mount Hermon near Northfield in July 1886, the first of its kind for college students. Those who attended were members of the inter-collegiate YMCA, came from prestigious institutions such as Princeton and Yale as well as small colleges and included figures such as R.P. Wilder and J.R. Mott who were very soon to be prominent in the SVM.

After hectic canvassing of universities and colleges across the eastern states, the SVM itself was launched two years later, in 1888, at the annual Northfield conference. Hudson Taylor from the CIM was one of the principal speakers. Additional impetus was derived from the revival of activity by the Evangelical Alliance and through the influence of Pierson's own publications, notably *The Crisis of Missions* (London, 1886) and articles on both 'The Problem of Missions' and 'Our Lord's Second Coming'.[78] Indeed, Pierson was a ubiquitous presence at this time. He attended the Niagara Conferences, rather appropriately the home of millennial enthusiasts and site of the CIM's launch in North America;[79] with the assistance of figures such as F.B. Meyer, one of the few British Baptists noted for his Keswick connections, he took up the editorship of the *Mission Review*, establishing its international influence. He was prominent among the large contingent of American delegates at the 1888 London Centenary Conference. In this emotive setting at Northfield, one hundred students volunteered themselves for missionary work and the SVM was under way. Its commencement was followed up with another tour of the colleges and its first major convention in 1891.

---

77  Essential to an understanding of Anglo–American thought and networks is Dana Lee Robert, *Occupy until I Come* (Grand Rapids, 2003), based on 'Arthur Tappan Pierson and Forward Movements of Late Nineteenth Century Evangelicalism' (Ph.D. dissertation, Yale, 1984); 'Arthur Tappan Pierson 1837–1911', in Gerald H. Anderson, Robert T. Coote, Norman A. Horner and James M. Phillips (eds), *Mission Legacies* (Maryknoll, 1994), pp. 28–36.

78  Robert, 'Arthur Tappan Pierson' (dissertation), pp. 206–23, which also notes his *Evangelical Work in Principle and Practice* (New York, 1887, London, 1888).

79  H.W. Frost (CIM, Toronto) to R.P. Wilder, 29 Sept. 1898, Wilder Papers 38/2/19.

Many students on the British side of the Atlantic were already prepared to respond when Robert Wilder launched his campaign in the British universities in 1891.[80] Key figures such as J.E.K. Studd (brother of one of the 'Cambridge Seven' who had joined the CIM) and Henry Drummond (biology lecturer and Scottish evangelist), thanks to Moody, had already visited America and were instrumental in getting British student evangelistic campaigns into their stride. Moody's own campaigns in Britain in 1873–74 and 1884–85 had also contributed much to prepare the ground. Through Moody's connections and with the help of Eugene Stock, the work of the SVM was brought into close touch with the Keswick circle. Wilder's appearance at Keswick in 1891 generated much enthusiastic support, an intense evangelistic tour and the inauguration of the Student Volunteer Missionary Union (SMVU) of Great Britain and Ireland at a conference in Edinburgh early in April 1892.[81]

The student movement thus brought together into a new synthesis an older evangelical strand represented by the Young Men's and Young Women's Christian Associations and the later nineteenth century's revivalist enthusiasm from Mildmay and Keswick, the latter with their apocalyptic and 'practical holiness' concerns. Like the SVM, the SVMU was not itself a missionary society; it publicised the need for evangelistic work, encouraged individuals to commit themselves to it and assisted them in finding suitable positions. In the United States it functioned essentially as an overseas missionary arm of the Young Men's and Young Women's Christian Associations and in Britain principally as an additional recruiting agency for the larger mission societies. It was overwhelmingly lay in membership and was exceedingly youthful: at the SVMU's first international students' conference held at Liverpool in January 1896, 715 of the 927 participants were college or university students.[82] It is therefore not surprising to find, along with Stock and Georgina Gollock of the CMS, Ralph Wardlaw Thompson (LMS Secretary), George Smith (Free Church of Scotland) and Hudson Taylor (CIM) nurturing the student movement from the outset. Inside the universities figures such as John Barton similarly sought to multiply and tighten the connections.[83]

The SVMU not only promised to tap more effectively than ever before what had always been seen as a potentially vital reserve of missionary commitment but was felt to have made good its promises, not least by Stock, who counted 506 missionaries sent

---

80  Extracts from the Journal of R.P. Wilder: The Origin of the Student Volunteer Missionary Union of Great Britain and Ireland [1891–92], Wilder Papers 38/13/139.

81  Tissington Tatlow, *The Story of the Student Christian Movement of Great Britain and Ireland* (London, 1933), chap. 1.

82  Tatlow, *Story of the SCM*, pp. 71–2; Stock, *History of the CMS*, Vol. 3, pp. 654–5; cf. C. Howard Hopkins, *John R. Mott, 1865–1955: A Biography* (Grand Rapids, 1979), p. 230.

83  Gollock, recruited as an administrator from the YWCA, was a moving spirit in CMS women's work; see Stock, *History of the CMS*, Vol. 3, p. 660; F.E. Wigram (CMS), Wardlaw Thompson and Stock to Wilder, respectively 24 Nov. 1892, 28 June 1895 and 19 July 1895, Wilder Papers 38/2/15 and 17; Rev. John Barton to CMS Secretaries, Letters 1892–3 in CMS Archives, Home Correspondence G/AC4.

out on its account between 1892 and 1898.[84] No wonder Stock was at his most flat-
tering in persuading Mott to speak at the CMS anniversary in 1898. 'It is a very rare
thing for us to put up any friend not one of us. I mean Ch. of E[ngland]. I only know of
three cases in the ninety nine years completed today ... But we look upon you as the
leading representative of the most real and vigorous missionary movement of the day
and we are putting you on the programme second, next after the Bishop of London.'[85]
The movement was also energetic and optimistic, to a fault in the view of some older
missionaries and derived much besides its dynamism from the Americans who came
regularly in significant numbers to the Keswick conventions and the SVMU gatherings systematically linked to them. The SVMU's adoption at Liverpool in 1896 of the
American SVM's 'watchword', 'The Evangelization of the World in this
Generation', was contested by a minority notably from Germany for its naivety and
superficiality. However, those critics following Gustav Warneck were concerned to
place missions in the pattern of world history, giving to them a precision absent from
most eschatological and providential speculation. In its own way the SVMU shared
this systematic concern.[86] The decision at Liverpool thus formalised sentiments that
had been gathering strength for as much as two decades and conveyed the new flavour
most effectively.[87]

The new slogan reflected the urgency of the missionary cause. SVMU organisers not only set about mobilising student opinion outside the universities, among
Sunday School teachers, in the theological colleges and in the YMCA and YWCA
branches. They joined their American and continental counterparts in founding
the World Student Christian Federation in 1894 to provide a global umbrella for all
national bodies such as the SVM or SVMU. The SVMU's asceticism was several
degrees lower than that of the early faith missions. Nevertheless, theologically and
strategically the emphasis on evangelism reflected the haste and underlying influence of the pre-millennial conviction that if evangelistic efforts were stepped up
then the Second Coming would be advanced. The watchword also pointed to the
movement's pronounced ecumenism and non-denominational character, both
features important when it came to extending the international nature of the movement, even if more of a problem when engaging the episcopal interests of the SPG
and UMCA. In line with YMCA traditions it gave great emphasis to the role of the
laity as missionary evangelists in their ordinary lives, at home as well as abroad.
This was more than appropriate in a world where the formalities of a clerical career
had become more and more esteemed among missionaries.

---

84  Stock, *History of the CMS*, Vol. 3, pp. 689–90.
85  Stock to Mott, 12 April 1898, Mott Papers 45/86/1532.
86  Clements, *Faith on the Frontier*, pp. 61–2; for Warneck, Anderson et al. (eds), *Mission Legacies*,
    pp. 373–82.
87  Hopkins, *Mott*, pp. 231–2; Tatlow, *Story of the SCM*, chap. 5, pp. 109–10; Hutchison, *Errand to the
    World*, pp. 129–44; Richard Pierard, 'Significant Currents in German Protestant Missiology',
    *NAMP/CWC Position Paper 102* (Cambridge, 1998), pp. 4, 16–20; Clements, *Faith on the Frontier*,
    pp. 65–6.

The significance of the Student Volunteer Movement for British – not to mention worldwide – missionary enterprise was enormous. More than anything else in the 1890s it was the chief source of fresh ideas and enthusiasm for the traditional overseas societies. It generated recruits, funds and inspiration sufficient to survive even the great hiatus and missionary reconstruction imposed by the war of 1914–18. It represented the latest of the many successive injections of revivalism into Protestant missions since the early eighteenth century and its leaders either took advantage of existing institutions or created new organisations to channel its energy and commitment towards constructive missionary ends. It focused its efforts above all on those parts of the world – India and still more countries in the Far East – where there were large and rapidly growing numbers of Western-educated students to be won over and mobilised.

Amongst the institutions or organisations it utilised, however, empire counted for little. It would have been surprising indeed if the foreign constituents of bodies such as the SVMU, the YM/WCA, the WSCF and hundreds of student, missionary and bible study associations around the world had wished it otherwise. One of the few missionary leaders who seriously attempted to tie mission to empire was H.H. Montgomery, Bishop of Tasmania and in July 1901 newly appointed secretary of the SPG. Professing a keen sense of racial and cultural hierarchy, he planned to overcome the divisions within the Anglican church at home and abroad by promoting unity around the cause of Christian missions. However, the Pan-Anglican Congress of 1908 which he masterminded fell flat and the youthful shock troops of the Junior Clergy Missionary Association on whom he relied failed to attract many followers. Montgomery's vision collapsed amidst fresh outbreaks of sectarianism, a persistent Anglican preoccupation with domestic matters and failure to agree on the meaning of an 'imperial' Christianity.[88]

Wholly different was the outcome of the SCM's own activity: the World Missionary Conference held in June 1910 in Edinburgh was essentially its creation. The idea was broached in SVMU circles in terms of the need for an essentially practical conference devoted to careful analysis of missionary problems and the co-ordination of common solutions worldwide. Scottish interest provided the venue, but it was Mott and his colleagues who managed to control the planning and organisation from 1908 onwards. J.H. Oldham above all played a critical role, not only as secretary and administrator but also in securing the presence at the conference of all the major Anglican interests, including the SPG and representatives of the Anglo-Catholic tradition.[89]

---

88  Steven Maughan, 'Imperial Christianity?', in Andrew Porter (ed.), *The Imperial Horizons of British Protestant Missions, 1880–1914* (Grand Rapids and Richmond, 2003), a briefer version of which appears in Daniel O'Connor et al. (eds), *Three Centuries of Mission* (London, 2000), pp. 358–70.

89  Stock, *History of the CMS*, Vol. 4, pp. 26, 557–63; Hopkins, *Mott*, chap. 7; Clements, *Faith on the Frontier*, chap. 5; Timothy Yates, *Christian Mission in the Twentieth Century* (Cambridge, 1994: repr. 1999), pp. 7–33.

This is not the place to explore the details of evangelical manoeuvres and the complex compromises associated with Edinburgh. Such work as exists suggests that these deserve a book of their own.[90] Edinburgh's relevance here lies in its expression of the new international forces driving the global enterprise, their distance from and willingness to criticise Britain's imperial policy and colonial practice and their emphasis on the potential both of new audiences for the Christian message and of a systematically organised missionary movement with a reach not attained hitherto. Two of the preparatory Commissions' Reports presented for debate at Edinburgh illuminate these themes. Commission VII on the relations of missions and governments concentrated not, as might have been expected, on the positive possibilities of alliances between them but on the unsatisfactory performance of European governments prone to place obstacles in the way of evangelism and to provide inadequate basic support. Recent experiences in China and the Congo Free State were amongst those that had struck deep.[91] Commission VIII, focusing on 'co-operation and the promotion of unity', in effect provided the missionary movement's general response to the failings of government and other agencies. It considered the many ways in which missions' effectiveness could be fostered and their duplication or division minimised, both at home and in their efforts abroad. The report offered a vigorous commentary on the potential of missionary agency and the capacity of missions to fend for themselves as a real presence on the international scene.[92] It might be said that the wheel had turned almost full circle and the days of Melvill Horne or the 1840s had come again. For Wesleyans in particular, the inspiration and practical experience of involvement at Edinburgh in 1910 transferred to their own 'Centenary Movement' helped the centenary itself in 1913 to a resounding success in terms of both new funds and fresh initiatives.[93] The confident, self-sufficiency of the missions was once more being reasserted and governments along with empire were being pushed to one side.

## IV

Between 1820 and 1850 the shifting, ambiguous character of missions' relations with the humanitarian movement was abundantly demonstrated. Not only did missionaries themselves play the humanitarian card, emphasising how support for

---

90  For example, Brian Stanley, 'Church, State and the Hierarchy of "Civilization": The Making of the "Missions and Governments" Report at the World Missionary Conference, Edinburgh 1910', in Andrew Porter (ed.), *The Imperial Horizons of British Protestant Missions, 1880–1914* (Grand Rapids and Richmond, 2003), pp. 58–84.

91  *World Missionary Conference, 1910. Report of Commission VII* (Edinburgh, London and New York, 1910); see also below, pp. 309–11.

92  *World Missionary Conference, 1910. Report of Commission VIII: Co–Operation and the Promotion of Unity* (Edinburgh, London and New York, 1910).

93  James Lewis, *William Goudie* (London, 1923), pp. 136, 140, 155, 162. Goudie, General Secretary to the Centenary Movement 1909–14, was also a member of Edinburgh's Commission II 'The Church in the Mission Field'.

them would further humanitarian ends. Secular humanitarians were also persuaded that missionaries at work were some of their best allies and temporarily carried the missionary movement forward to an exhilarating position of independence and public esteem. That achieved, however, missions for the time being found little further place for the humanitarians in their planning. Conscious as they were of their primary aim of conversion, fearful of its being overshadowed by the diversion of sentimental social reform, missions turned again to their own lasts. The ending of that close co-operation, generated by the issues of emancipation and aboriginal protection, contributes substantially to any explanation of the depressed condition of both movements in the mid nineteenth century. Failing to hang together, they hung separately.[94] Their history is instructive for the historian as to the danger of assuming that missionaries were necessarily also humanitarians. However, as the nineteenth century moved on, changing evangelical circumstances led once more to the combination of the two outlooks and sometimes to practical co-operation. This was possible because missionaries' understanding of both the nature of evangelism and humanitarianism changed.

Alignment with the anti-slavery movement in a bid for imperial action to free the slaves arose, as was seen above, less from missionary commitment to the cause itself than from the wish to create an environment in which missionary activity went unhindered and Christian principle could be lived out in practice. This approach – promoting the missions' prime goal by the application of humanitarian means – was to be repeated time and again through the century. It lay, for example, behind missionary initiatives in India, perhaps most notably in their combined efforts, following the 1855 Calcutta Missionary Conference, on behalf of the Bengal indigo cultivators in 1859–62. These led to the perverse trial and imprisonment of James Long in Calcutta on the charge that he had libelled the indigo planters. Long, G.G. Cuthbert (both CMS) and their colleagues from various denominations were keenly aware of the parallels between events in Bengal and earlier conditions in West Africa, the Cape Colony and the British West Indies. As Long wrote to the Secretary in London, 'Indigo Planting interferes with our own works as much as the Slave Trade does with Mission work on the coast of Africa.' 'The Missionary Conference considered that they were as much bound to enter on this question as Missionary bodies were on the subject of the Slave Trade of West Indie [*sic*] Slavery.'[95] Their criticisms of the indigo planting system were substantially borne out by the government of Bengal's Indigo Commission and, when the planters pursued their vendetta against Long for his publications, the CMS stood behind him. Henry Venn's comparisons were telling: the Society's Parent (main) Committee 'class his case with many other excellent men who have been subject to similar treatment while a moral conflict has been in progress for the relief of the

---

94  See Chapters 4 and 6 above.
95  Long to CMS Parent Committee, 9 and 23 April 1860, cited by Oddie, *Missionaries, Rebellion and Proto-Nationalism*, pp. 111–12.

oppressed as in the case of Missionary Dr Philip at the Cape and the Missionary Smith in the West Indies'.[96]

The indigo question was simply one of the most notorious examples in India where the entanglement of poverty, debt, insecurity of land tenure or property rights, forced labour, persecution of Christian converts or inquirers and a corrupt judicial system drove missionaries to press government for reforms. Long also drew West Indian parallels when missionaries in the 1850s confronted the wider abuses of zamindari power in Bengal. This marked the start of a prolonged campaign that eventually contributed to the reforms embodied in the Bengal Tenancy Act of 1885.[97] Similar pressure was later applied to government for reform of the land tenure system in Madras by Free Church of Scotland and Wesleyan missionaries working with the 'pariahs'. In the 1880s and 1890s Adam Andrew (FCS) and William Goudie (WMMS) backed by the local missionary conference took the issues to the provincial and then the home governments.[98]

This cluster of issues generated levels of agreement among missionaries missing on many other questions. When it came to 'vice', prostitution, child marriage, opium and temperance, opinions among missionaries as elsewhere were very divided as to the extent of apparent outrages and how best to tackle them. Missionaries were often uncertain how far they would be justified in diverting scarce resources and attention to matters which the fact of serious disagreement itself showed they generally regarded as less significant obstacles to evangelism and teaching. It is therefore not surprising to find labour issues in particular recurring among missions' prime concerns, not only in India but elsewhere. The pattern of missionary engagement was none the less haphazard and sporadic, no more capable of generating sustained public support in Britain than were the lobbying activities of the Anti-Slavery Society and the Aborigines Protection Society. It tended to point in two directions, either pushing the imperial government towards the establishment of general legal frameworks and institutional controls on abuses or persuading it to use such powers and resources as it possessed to take effective action in individual cases.

In the western Pacific, the expansion of white settlement and plantations both in the islands and in northern Australia also brought the expansion of labour recruitment and migration. The increase of unregulated economic exploitation produced anarchic conditions, frequently with degrees of violence amounting to low-level warfare. Missionaries found themselves caught up in it, sometimes as unwitting victims, often as participants in self-defence and retribution. Such were, for example, John Paton and the New Hebrides Mission forced out of Tanna in 1862, whose presence at the retributory shelling of Tanna villages by the Royal

---

96  Venn to Rev. E.C. Stuart, 10 Sept. 1861, cited in *ibid.*, p. 134.
97  G.A. Oddie, *Social Protest in India: British Protestant Missionaries and Social Reforms 1850–1900* (Delhi, 1979), pp. 110–28, at p. 116.
98  *Ibid.*, pp. 128–46; Lewis, *William Goudie*, pp. 35–6, 39–40, 51, 57–9.

Navy became a byword for 'missionary imperialism'; and Bishop Patteson of the Melanesian Mission murdered at Nukapu in the Solomon Islands in 1871.[99] Mission societies therefore supported a succession of imperial interventions designed to bring a measure of stability: the Pacific Islanders' Protection Act (1872 and 1875), the annexation of Fiji (1873–74), the establishment of a British High Commissioner for the Western Pacific and protectorates over the Gilbert and Ellis Islands and the Solomons in 1892–93.[100]

In West Africa, missionaries after 1874 periodically agitated for action against domestic slavery and other forms of involuntary servitude on the Gold Coast. Further south, Wesleyan and LMS missionaries returned at regular intervals in the 1880s and 1890s to the need for protection of indigenous peoples rights to land and labour in Bechuanaland against the power of footloose settlers and the British South Africa Company. Rather different was the recruitment in 1904–6 for the Transvaal gold mines of Chinese labour to assist a postwar economic recovery. In Britain the National Free Church Council joined hands with labour protesters and nonconformist ministers including leaders such as Dr John Clifford took to their pulpits, in active opposition alongside other campaigners.[101] However the absence of an evangelistic dimension to this South African question meant that the missions did not choose to get involved.

Of far greater significance than the past several decades of humanitarian skirmishes, however, was the last missionary engagement before 1914 on the labour front in the Congo Free State. Hitherto, British missions had concentrated attention either on areas where, in the absence of other European governments, the imperial government might be expected to act in their defence, or on places where British authority was already established and might be exercised without undue difficulty. The Congo Free State, however, was not only the creation of an international agreement between the great powers but was also under another sovereign authority, King Leopold II of the Belgians. Leopold's aggressive diplomacy and bland assurances notwithstanding, during the 1890s plentiful evidence was accumulating that the Free State's administration operated in ways wholly contrary to the terms agreed at Berlin and Brussels. Officials discriminated against missions other than those of Belgian Catholic orders, restricted trade not under their own control and used murder and mutilation to enforce local production of the tropical commodities – especially rubber – on which the state's revenues depended.[102]

99 James Paton (ed.), *John G. Paton, Missionary to the New Hebrides: An Autobiography*, 2 vols (London, 1889–90), Vol. 1, chaps 5–10, Vol. 2 chap. 4; Garrett, *To Live Among the Stars*, pp. 175–7, 182–8; Sir John Gutch, *Martyr of the Islands: The Life and Death of John Coleridge Patteson* (London, 1971).

100 W. David McIntyre, *The Imperial Frontier in the Tropics, 1865–75* (London, 1967); Deryck Scarr, *Fragments of Empire: A History of the Western Pacific High Commission, 1877–1914* (Canberra, 1967).

101 Kevin Grant, '"A Civilised Savagery": British Humanitarian Politics and European Imperialism in Africa, 1884–1926' (unpub. Ph.D. thesis, Berkeley, 1997), pp. 139–41.

102 Slade, *English-Speaking Missions in the Congo*; David Lagergren, *Mission and State in the Congo ... 1885–1903* (Uppsala, 1970).

Being dependent on Leopold's permission and challenged by Roman Catholic competitors, the principal societies in the Congo basin, the British BMS and Congo Balolo Mission, were reluctant to jeopardise their position. In addition to its own intrinsic importance, the Congo offered them yet another line of assault on Islam.[103] Mission administrators at home such as Alfred Baynes, the BMS Secretary and missionaries on the spot, such as George Grenfell and W.H. Bentley, were at first unwilling to credit and subsequently were reluctant to reveal, the exploitation and atrocities about which they knew. They relied on their own contacts, quiet diplomacy and moral pressure to bring reforms, in the circumstances a fruitless strategy that not only revealed missionary weakness but demonstrated how the 'avoidance of politics' was itself a highly political act.[104] Only after reports from the American Baptists working in the Congo and agitation by the Aborigines Protection Society, was the situation fully brought to light. E.D. Morel, with a valuable background in West African trade and shipping, uncovered damning evidence of the rapacity of Free State agents and the atrocities committed against the Congolese. Rebuffed by the British Foreign Office but determined to bring the regime to account, Morel wrote *Red Rubber* (1904) and, urged on by the British consul, Sir Roger Casement, singlemindedly mounted a public campaign.

Essential to the success of the agitation, despite Morel's reluctance to recognise and later acknowledge it, was the alliance he formed with Dr Harry Guinness and John and Alice Harris of the Congo Balolo Mission. Their extensive speaking tours, appalling photographic evidence and ability to activate the religious networks, churches and mission supporters to provide funds and publicity, far outstripped anything Morel's Congo Reform Association was able to achieve on its own.[105] Baptist and Quaker opinion in particular was mobilised on a scale that paralleled Wilberforce's and Sturge's achievements sixty and more years before.

However, despite the appeal of a single issue and a clearly defined goal – Congo exploitation and the end of Leopold's rule – this was not to be resolved in a narrowly British context. International considerations – fears that its own colonial record might be questioned or the European balance of power be upset – caused the British government to hesitate. The successful outcome in which Leopold was compelled to abandon control to the Belgian parliament in 1908 required not only the continued mobilisation of missionary supporters to the end but emphasis on the international obligations involved. As Morel explained in his private account of the campaign, humanitarian obligations, derived from 'British honour' and 'British imperial responsibilities in Africa' associated with Britain's original support for Leopold's enterprise, were important. But so were two other principles, 'human pity the world over' and 'international commercial rights ... inseparable from

---

103  Slade, *English-Speaking Missions in the Congo*, pp. 135–6.
104  Stanley, *History of the BMS*, pp. 122–39.
105  Grant, '"A Civilised Savagery"', chap. 3.

native economic and personal liberties'.[106] He should have added 'missionary liberties', for the Congo question involved the missions in the internationalisation of both colonial issues and the humanitarian movement, features not only of the decade but increasingly of the new century.[107]

The missionary sense of humanitarian obligation also shifted in other directions, perhaps most evidently in the development of medical missions. Something of a bridge was crossed in 1841 with the formation of the Edinburgh Medical Missionary Society. However, it was not until after the formation of the London Medical Missionary Association in 1878 that the missionary societies generally took seriously the appointment of properly qualified doctors as an important aid to the propagation of Christianity. Apart from uneasiness at the costs of salaries and equipment, there were other purely pragmatic reasons for delay. Until the impact of the professional association, the General Medical Council set up in 1858, began to make itself felt, the competence of many doctors and the efficacy of treatment were often limited. Some cures were worse than none at all.[108]

While it might be hoped that missionaries, their families and their efficacy as evangelists might benefit from the availability of medical care, the extension of missionary medicine to indigenous populations remained for many a quite separate matter. As an experiment the CMS sent Dr Edward Forster to Mombasa for a year or so in 1874. His view of the situation was at best cool. 'Mombasa is a veritable Sodom: people frequently come for medicines to increase their virility or sexual desires; to have impotency, the effects of their own lusts, removed; you will observe how common are diseases connected with sexual lusts; these constitute a large share of our work; the affected are of every class, no more feeling of shame apparently being felt by the higher Arab than by the poorest slave.'[109] From the association of illness with sin Forster thus went on to imply that signs of remorse and repentance ought to be necessary preconditions for any treatment. Without them many treatments could hardly be justified. Greater experience weighed against this view, drawing H.K. Binns at nearby Taita (Taveta) towards the most commonly persuasive of justifications for medical missions, that they were the only or at least the most effective means of conversion. Binns explained how he had 'thought very much of the nature of the work

---

106 Morel's history was finally published by Wm Roger Louis and Jean Stengers, *E.D. Morel's History of the Congo Reform Movement* (Oxford, 1967), quotation at pp. 63, 68.

107 See, for instance, Donal Lowry, '"The Boers were the beginning of the end"? The Wider Impact of the South African War', in Donal Lowry (ed.), *The South African War Reappraised* (Manchester, 2000), pp. 203–46; Clements, *Faith on the Frontier*, chap. 7 'World Missions and World War 1914–18'.

108 C. Peter Williams, 'Healing and Evangelism: The Place of Medicine in Later Victorian Protestant Missionary Thinking' and Andrew F. Walls, '"The Heavy Artillery of the Missionary Army": The Domestic Importance of the Nineteenth-Century Medical Missionary', in W.J. Shiels (ed.), *Studies in Church History* 19 (Oxford, 1982), pp. 271–85, 287–97.

109 'Quarterly Report of Medical Work done in Mombasa and Neighbourhood, September 1875', cited by J.V. Thomas, 'The Role of the Medical Missionary in British East Africa 1874–1904' (unpub. D.Phil. thesis, Oxford, 1982), p. 53; for Forster, *CMS Register*, List I, entry 791.

there and have come to the conclusion that a Medical Mission is the one to win the hearts of the people; sickness is very prevalent especially among the young, ophthalmia being the most common. If we could only start a hospital, with a doctor and his wife ... they would soon win their way to the hearts of the people and could thus be able ... to lead them to the Great Physician.'[110]

Not only could medical assistance open the most unpromising areas but it could hardly be detached from evangelism. It has been well argued that increasingly the broader British domestic climate of social reform and theological change placed additional premiums on the work of the medical missionary.[111] The obligations of benevolence towards bodies and souls in this world were appealed to more frequently as belief in eternal punishment declined. Increasingly the expression of humanitarian sympathies in the form of healing and support for the medical missionary came to be seen not only as a useful adjunct to the task of evangelism but as integral to Christianity itself. The BMS, for example, seems to have stuck by the principle that the medical role was subordinate to the evangelistic until the 1880s. However, in despatching James and Agnes Watson to Chingzhou in northern China in 1885, the Society seems for the first time to have abandoned this insistence. By the mid-1890s, an appreciation of medical missions and a willingness to support them adequately was well established in the Society and, following the CMS's tardy step of 1894, a Baptist Medical Missionary Auxiliary was formed in 1901.[112]

The Report of the London Centenary Conference in 1888, while sensitive to conflicting views on the place of medical missionaries, roundly asserted that 'The doctrine of Christ is no mere system of metaphysics on the one hand, nor is it a system of asceticism on the other. It is religion which cares for the body as well as for the soul.'[113] As illustration of this precept, the LMS increased its European medical missionaries from six in 1880 to twenty-two in a total strength of 258 in 1895 and forty-five out of 277 in 1905, not counting the great increase in numbers of native medical staff.[114] From Blantyre Dr McVicar in his *Report* for 1900 indicated the way of the future under the heading 'The Hospital as a Missionary Agency'. 'There are many people who look upon the medical work in a Mission as being simply an advertisement for the Mission ... This prostitution of medical science seems to me to be deplorable. I believe that in a country like this, where the people are themselves so helpless, medical work is per se not merely the best possible demonstration of Christianity, but it is Christianity, applied Christianity.'[115]

110  May 1883, cited by Thomas, 'Role', p. 84; for Binns, *CMS Register*, List I, entry 805.
111  Williams, 'Healing and Evangelism', pp. 278–80.
112  Stanley, *History of the BMS*, pp. 235–6, 238–9.
113  'Special Missionary Subjects. Medical Missions', in Johnson, *Report of the Centenary Conference*, Vol. 1, pp. 378–96, quotation at p. 380.
114  Norman Goodall, *A History of the London Missionary Society 1895–1945* (Oxford, 1954), p. 508. For details of Scottish medical work, T.G. Gehani, 'A Critical Review of the work of Scottish Presbyterian Missions in India, 1878–1914' (unpub. Ph.D. thesis, Strathclyde, 1966), pp. 289–315.
115  Thomas, 'Role', pp. 229–30.

The phrase 'applied Christianity' has particular implications for the connection between missions and humanitarianism. As seen above, missionaries' humanitarian commitment since the early nineteenth century had normally been interpreted with reference to those activities of missionaries, with or without assistance from others, that were designed to remove obstacles to both evangelism and the Christian life of indigenous peoples. Missionary humanitarianism was in other words primarily functional, an aid to the propagation of the faith, rather than a natural, spontaneous expression, a working out in practice, of the fundamentals of an individual missionary's own belief. By the end of the nineteenth century the emphasis was changing and rapidly growing levels of medical activity by the missions were the chief expression of that change.[116] At Edinburgh in 1910 their importance was so widely emphasised that the Report of Commission I valued them and their 'practical demonstration of the spirit of Christianity' on a par with educational missions.[117]

The expansion of medical training and medical volunteers, the proliferation of leprosaria, dispensaries and hospitals, have a place in the domestic context of mounting church concern with social policy and reform in Britain itself.[118] However, they were not the only indicators of a new missionary order. The Report to the Edinburgh Conference of the Commission on Co-operation and the Promotion of Unity included a short section on 'Works of Philanthropy and Beneficence'. 'Co-operation in [such] works', its author argued, 'is another very natural exhibition of the Christian spirit on the part of missionaries. It is found specially in times of famine, war, or other public calamity ... In times of famine, flood, earthquake and fire, Christian men do not discuss whether they should co-operate, but simply do so as a matter of course.'[119] The *Report* offered as an example the famine of 1907 in North Kiangsu, but this was only the latest of the public environmental catastrophes to which missions had felt compelled to turn. Beginning with the devastating succession of floods, droughts, typhoons and locust plagues that hit China between 1876 and 1880, events especially in China drew missions into relief work.[120] Timothy Richard's work marked a watershed in this respect. The comparative detachment displayed by a missionary such as Griffith

---

116 J.S. Dennis, *Centennial Survey of Foreign Missions* (Edinburgh, 1902); H.P. Beach and B. St John, *World Statistics of Christian Missions* (New York, 1916).

117 *World Missionary Conference, 1910: Report of Commission I, Carrying the Gospel to all the Non-Christian World* (Edinburgh, London and New York, 1910), pp. 313–14, also 183, 188, 198–9, 310–11, for their special importance in Muslim areas.

118 E.R. Norman, *Church and Society in England 1770–1970 – A Historical Study* (Oxford, 1976), chap. 8 'Christian Social Ideals, 1900–1920'.

119 *World Missionary Conference, 1910. Report of Commission VIII*, pp. 79–80.

120 Broomhall, *Hudson Taylor*, Vol. 6, chap. 5; P.R. Bohr, *Famine in China and the Missionary: Timothy Richard as Relief Administrator and Advocate of National Reform, 1876–1884* (Cambridge, MA, 1972); Timothy Richard, *Forty-Five Years in China: Reminiscences by Timothy Richard* (London, 1916).

John (LMS) during the calamities of the 1860s and 1870s was gradually eroded in the face of endemic natural disasters in later years.[121] In 1885, Richard's speech to the BMS Annual Meeting was one of those picked out by observers as evidence that 'the emphasis in Christian Missions had changed'. 'Formerly the stress had been laid on saving the heathen from the sufferings of hell in the next world, now foreign Missions existed also to save the heathen from the hell of suffering in this world.'[122]

In South Africa, for Andrew Smith of the Free Church mission, it was important to support the movement for Africans' right to freehold lands and individual title. Under present conditions, he wrote from Kingwilliamstown, 'they are either cooped up in Locations, with pieces of arable ground on the run-rig principle and some commonage – very bare. They are much like the crofters in Lewis and the Outer [?] Hebrides and like them condemned to stagnation and poverty, with no motive to improve their position and no possibility of doing so. Otherwise they hold a tract under tribal tenure and are equally helpless as individuals and cannot build decent dwellings on commonage, with no security of tenure. Things as they are seem drifting on to the creation of another Ireland; but the free-hold movement is making some progress. As tenure of land lies at the base of the whole social structure, a change in that would create a revolution.'[123]

Broadening conceptions of missionary work and evangelism in the late nineteenth century went well beyond a simple desire to impress local peoples with the technological prowess of a Christian society. The relief and medical provision associated with the 'social experiments' and 'attempts at social service' of William Goudie and his Madras colleagues from 1882–1906 was an example close to home of the general truth observed in the Wesleyans' centenary history, that 'the humanitarian character of Christian service receives today an ever-increasing emphasis'.[124]

## V

This review of thinking and activity in what is often regarded as 'the high imperial age' suggests that missions' relationship with empire and its agents had lost nothing of its ambiguity. The rhetoric of empire building and the multiplication of imperial and colonial interests included a powerful sense of 'national mission' but still demonstrated only a limited capacity for shaping or assimilating the theory and practice of Christian missions. The stronger the sense of racial distinctions the less successful the missions were in promoting the growth of the Christian churches. In

---

121 R. Wardlaw Thompson, *Griffith John: The Story of Fifty Years in China*, rev. popular edn (London, 1908), pp. 233–41, 327.

122 Richard, *Forty-Five Years*, p. 189.

123 Andrew Smith to George Smith, July 1893, NLS MS/7798, f. 65; cf. Don to Smith, 15 April 1895, *ibid.*, f. 101.

124 Lewis, *William Goudie*, pp. 58, 61, 91 and passim; Findlay and Holdsworth, *History of the WMMS*, Vol. 5, pp. 171–2.

the Muslim world, changes in missionary approaches to evangelism and the extension of colonial controls only increased the conflict of views between missions and
Western rulers. The internationalisation of the missionary movement and its
dynamics tended increasingly to separate national ambitions for empire and the
global pursuit or fulfilment of evangelical goals. Those goals were in any case shifting. To a greater understanding of other religions was attached both a heightened
concern with Christianity as a 'practical' religion and a redefined missionary sense
of service. An important part of the missionary movement's attempts to sustain its
appeal and generate renewed support thus involved its re-appropriation of the
secular humanitarian goals so significant to its progress in the first half of the nineteenth century.

# Conclusion: the 'anti–imperialism' of Protestant missions?

'One of the difficulties of the student of missions is that the work is now being done on so extensive a scale, and under such diverse conditions, that it becomes increasingly necessary to restrict the area of observation and to specialize study in one field and even to the work of one society, if he would really become fully acquainted with the subject.' Worthy of note more than a century ago, the problem has only grown since the two secretaries of the LMS wrote at the time of Queen Victoria's Silver Jubilee.[1] It is perhaps a reflection of the unwieldy scope of modern missionary enterprise that much of the discussion of missionaries has persisted in following the well-worn paths defined in a recent Oxford University sermon. 'The two charges brought against the missionary are that he was an advocate of imperialism and the destroyer of indigenous culture and values.'[2] Missions and missionaries, even when they conformed to these stereotypes so entrenched in Western historiography, were without doubt the supporters and embodiment of much else. This book has therefore attempted to escape these methodological and intellectual restraints, by embracing a wide range of Protestant missions and examining afresh on a broad front their relationships with empire.

## I

In reflecting on themes developed in earlier chapters and notwithstanding the disclaimer in the Introduction, recent scholarship on the impact of Protestant missions overseas requires some attention for its role in defining the boundaries of this book. Whatever the ambiguities of the relationship between missions and empire and the many pressures distancing missions and their goals from empire and notwithstanding missionaries' own lack of a steadfast imperial commitment, the possibility remains that missionaries might still be effective imperialists. Missionaries might not advocate empire, but were often associated with institutions or beliefs identified by local peoples with imperialism. Powerful cases have been made by scholars such as T.O. Beidelman and the Comaroffs to the effect that despite their best intentions missions might be effective empire builders.

---

1 R. Wardlaw Thompson and Arthur N. Johnson, *British Foreign Missions 1837–1897* (London, 1899), p. 218.
2 Krishnan Srinivasan, *Mission and Message. The Ramsden Sermon 17 November 2002* (Oxford, 2003), p. 2.

In addressing this issue, it is helpful to remember both the relative weakness of the missions and that, notwithstanding their critics, they were also widely seen by local people to have contributed positively to the societies they set out to evangelise. Historians, both of empire and of the missionary encounter or impact in different parts of the world, have come to recognise in recent years not only the dependence of missions (like all agents of empire) on indigenous co-operation but the adaptability of local cultures to missionary messages. Missionary personnel and mission Christianity have not only encountered indifference and hostility: both with and without conversions, they have also been turned constantly to local advantage. There has been no intention here to survey in any detail the appropriation by indigenous societies of aspects of Christianity. However, a number of general points about the local impact of missionaries must be made, bearing as they do on the interplay of missions and empire.[3]

Although not all contemporaries agreed, nevertheless, as we have seen, one of the most important features of missionaries' work lay in their contribution of education through schools and colleges. Christianity, especially in its Protestant forms, was a religion dependent on literacy which alone made it possible for converts or others to read and study the Bible; literacy, in its turn, was dependent upon instruction and Protestant evangelists therefore readily turned to teaching. It is now, of course, commonplace to see in the process of schooling a mode of discipline and social control and tempting to see in both indigenous societies and colonial settings a very special need for ruling elites to exploit education for that end.

In considering the role of mission schools as empire-building agents, however, it is particularly important to remember that those who ran them were quite unable to prevent non-Europeans from exploiting mission education for other than religious ends. Historians have long recognised that the interest of African rulers in having missionaries reside at their capitals was, at least at first, hardly ever a religious one. On the Niger, 'Neither the Egba nor the Efik chiefs had the least interest in the white man's creed per se; none of them wished the spiritual side of missionary enterprise any success.'[4] Ayandele's conclusion can be applied equally to Wesleyans on the Gold Coast in the 1840s, the CMS or UMCA in East Africa forty years later and to those many Hindu protestors who, fearing subornation of their children and the subversion of their faith, over the years led the periodic withdrawals of pupils from mission schools. The missions' attraction lay in the education they provided, which was seen as helping people to acquire the white man's many advantages, as opening the way to the wide range of activities associated with literate societies. In Africa, India and elsewhere, schools, like the printing press and books, were welcomed as means to that end.

The cultural impact of schools was thus fundamentally determined by what colonial peoples wanted to take from them, with the result that there was no

---

3 The following argument borrows from my article '"Cultural Imperialism" and Protestant Missionary Enterprise, 1780–1914', *JICH* 25 (1997), pp. 367–91, at pp. 382–8.
4 Ayandele, *The Missionary Impact*, p. 9.

predominant 'missionary' or 'colonial' education. It was also restricted by the fact that throughout the colonial period the direct social and geographical reach of missionary education was very limited. Even as late as 1948, after twenty-five years of extensive government additions to missionary efforts, no more than four per cent of the Gold Coast's population had received an education to Standard VII, the highest level of elementary schooling.[5] That missionaries everywhere fretted at the lack of support they felt their work received, is another potent reminder not only of their thwarted ambitions but also of their restricted individual scope. It is therefore essential that today's assessments of the 'imperial' role of missions should take account both of the limits to their ability to control the influence of their message and to the diverse routes by which it was diffused among the populations with whom they engaged.

Equally significant to this discussion is the fact that missionary work and education, despite their manifest limits, often had a vital liberating impact and was welcomed for that reason. There is no doubt that the spread of literacy and knowledge of other languages both widened horizons at many different social levels and greatly enhanced the ability of ordinary people to question or subvert traditional attitudes as well as imperial and colonial assumptions. Examples of such developments can be found in very different places. In India, missionary assistance and example provided low caste groups with the means to defend their interests, improve their status and even survive physically in the face of famine, epidemic and persecution.[6] In both India and Africa, Christian teaching frequently provided a spur to the revival and reform of indigenous religions.[7] Missionary education and work with the vernaculars provided the means whereby many communities were enabled to disinter their own history, offsetting with a new pride the progressive development of their own society against that of the British. Indeed, some historically minded anthropologists have reached the conclusion that time was of the essence. 'The religious encounter was less a matter of the clash of world views, considered as timeless sets of moral and theological alternatives, than it was a contest between rival narratives or schemes for how individuals and communities should project themselves over time.'[8] Although the sense of time and historical

---

5  *Gold Coast Census Report* (1948).

6  See, e.g., Oddie, *Social Protest in India; Hindu and Christian in South-East India* (London, 1991); Dick Kooiman, 'The Gospel of Coffee: Mission, Education and Employment in Travancore (19th Century)', in Kooiman, Otto van den Muijzenberg and Peter van der Veer (eds), *Conversion, Competition and Conflict: Essays on the Role of Religion in Asia* (Amsterdam, 1984), pp. 185–214; 'Mass Movement, Famine and Epidemic. A Study in Interrelationship', *ICHR* 22, 2 (1988), 109–25; Bugge, 'Mission and Tamil Society', chap. 6.

7  Powell, *Muslims and Missionaries*; Kenneth W. Jones, *Socio-Religious Movements in British India* (Cambridge, 1989).

8  Paul Jenkins (ed.), *The Recovery of the West African Past: African Pastors and African History in the Nineteenth Century: C.C. Reindorf and Samuel Johnson* (Basel, 1998); J.D.Y. Peel, 'For Who Hath Despised the Day of Small Things? Missionary Narratives and Historical Anthropology', *CSSH* 37, 3 (1995), 581–607, quotation at 600.

development introduced by missionaries differed from the traditional understanding of the Yoruba, John Peel has shown how the outcome was one in which the Yoruba emerged as more effective creators of their present as well as their past.[9] Practice and interpretation nevertheless differed considerably between regions. Missionary time for the Tswana, according to the Comaroffs, was a source of restraint, 'the religious calendar of the church ... embracing the everyday lives of its participants in a continuous regime of instruction, veneration and surveillance'. By contrast, Bishop Steere in Zanzibar insisted that the clock presented to Christ Church by the Sultan of Zanzibar 'should keep Eastern time' and 'great was the satisfaction of the natives at the decision'.[10]

That missionary contributions to individuals and their communities were often greatly valued in these and many other ways is clearly illustrated by recent work on the history of women. Increasingly sensitive to the complexity of missionaries' impact and their interaction with indigenous societies, these studies are uncovering much to which earlier nationalist or decidedly secular writers remained oblivious. Some have little time for unqualified feminist assumptions about the imposition of Western 'patriarchialism' through church practice. Elizabeth Isichei, for example, has argued that 'it seems to be much more generally true in Africa that women experience Christianity as empowering. It gave them a place to stand, from which they could bypass or challenge male-dominated sacred worlds.'[11] No wonder it has been noted that at least in Africa the great majority of early baptisms were of women.[12] Indeed it can be argued that the work of European female missionaries seriously undermined metropolitan norms and thus inhibited any 'cultural imperialism' that might have been involved in the process of translation to new settings. It has already been noted that Europe's dissenting and evangelical movements had a long record of opening up opportunity for women and this was still more so overseas. The circumstances of missionary life led to debate about the role of women and inevitable departures from many of the rigidities of socially or functionally separate spheres. The extent of female responsibility, the demonstration of practical co-operation with men, both extended missionaries' own experience and offered a range of unfamiliar examples – in one historian's words, 'introduced new conceptions of gender' – to indigenous women.[13] There are, for instance, many cases of mission stations providing refuges for women anxious to avoid the marriages

---

9  Peel, *Religious Encounter and the Making of the Yoruba*.

10  Comaroff, *Of Revelation and Revolution*, Vol. 1, p. 234; Anderson-Morshead, *History of the UMCA*, p. 88.

11  Elizabeth Isichei, 'Does Christianity Empower Women? The Case of the Anaguta of Central Nigeria', in Fiona Bowie, Deborah Kirkwood and Shirley Ardener (eds), *Women and Missions: Past and Present. Anthropological and Historical Perceptions* (Providence and Oxford, 1993), p. 209.

12  Adrian Hastings, in *ibid.*, p. 112.

13  Kwok Pui-Lan, 'The Image of the "White Lady": Gender and Race in Christian Mission', in Anne Carr and Elizabeth Schussler Fiorenza (eds), *The Special Nature of Women?* (London and Philadelphia, 1991), p. 25.

demanded by tribal convention and for freed or escaped slaves. For both metropolitan and local societies, especially in India, the late nineteenth-century growth in
numbers of female medical missionaries and teachers also marked in many ways a
radical departure.[14]

Even the occurrence of explicit conversions to Christianity is now recognised
by historians to represent far more than a simple surrender to white power or an
accommodation to the enlargement of scale and outlook introduced by colonial
contacts. Recent writings show that Christian beliefs were evidently attractive
because they addressed important aspects of everyday life inadequately dealt with
by traditional religions, offering answers, for example, to the experience of evil in
the shape of poverty and disease and facing up to the fact of death in new ways.[15]
Religious uncertainty was not the prerogative solely of Western societies; the
homogeneity of pre-Christian traditions cannot be taken for granted and even the
presence of a mission was certain to provoke questions.[16] Alternative answers
were the more persuasive when, as was so often and increasingly the case, they
were conveyed by indigenous Christians rather than white missionaries. The work
of these local evangelists also meant that the fundamental egalitarianism of the
Christian message was felt in colonial Africa or India just as it had been a century
before when West Indian plantation owners did their utmost to limit missionary
teaching. At times, the attractions of conversion were many, offering prospects of
emancipation even if this entailed exchanging one set of beliefs and practices for
another. Not only was it Christianity rather than any more resolutely rational or
secular beliefs that relieved Africans from the fears and uncertainty associated
with witchcraft. Christianity as appropriated by Africans also appears in many
places to have kept at bay the secularisation of their society, providing them with
a defence of their conviction as to 'the essentially unified and "spiritual" nature of
human existence'.[17] The very variety of individual decisions and Christian communities suggests that the existence of converts offers little guide to the reality or
extent of the hegemonic influence or cultural domination so often attributed to
missions.

---

14  Margaret Donaldson, 'Missionaries and the Liberation of Women: A Case Study from South Africa',
    *Journal of Theology for Southern Africa* 53 (1985), 4–12; 'The Invisible Factor: Nineteenth Century
    Feminist Evangelical Concern for Human Rights', *Journal for the Study of Religion* 2, 2 (1989), 3–15;
    Rosemary Fitzgerald, 'A "peculiar and exceptional measure": The Call for Women Medical
    Missionaries for India in the Later Nineteenth Century', in Robert A. Bickers and Rosemary Seton
    (eds), *Missionary Encounters: Sources and Issues* (London, 1996), pp. 174–96.
15  Robin Horton, 'Conversion', *Africa* 41, 2 (1971), 85–108; 'On the Rationality of Conversion',
    2 parts, *Africa* 45, 3–4 (1975), 219–35, 373–99; Gray, *Black Christians and White Missionaries*,
    part 2.
16  Cf. Greg Dening, *Islands and Beaches: Discourse on a Silent Land: Marquesas 1774–1880* (Honolulu,
    1980; repr. Chicago, 1988), p. 201.
17  Kwame Bediako, *Christianity in Africa: The Renewal of a Non-Western Religion* (Edinburgh, 1995);
    and the review by Richard Gray, *Bulletin of the School of Oriental and African Studies* 60 (1997),
    202–3.

The continued presence and success of missionaries almost anywhere depended on their value and usefulness, the willingness of local leaders and their people to co-operate with them and the possibility of Christianity being construed in a manner answering to local circumstances. Missionaries soon learnt that they were not automatically welcome; African or Asian co-operation based on fear was of little value and permanent acceptance was to be won only by negotiation and compromise. However much missionaries might regret it, local peoples inevitably combined their own curiosity with an awareness that among whites Christian belief and forms of worship were subjects of debate and matters of choice. Frequently challenged by other expatriates even if not engaged in their own disputes with rival denominations, missionaries could not afford to be too dogmatic or inflexible in the face of indigenous questions or challenges to their ideas and authority. The penalty for inflexibility was commonly rejection.

Despite the notionally 'imperial' pretensions of their doctrines, Christian missions were thus likely to make cultural concessions. Their limited material resources, small numbers and relative closeness to local peoples always left them conscious of their own weakness. Many of them were quicker than other Europeans to sense the criticism and ambitions of those among whom they worked. That powerful element in the thinking of most missions that looked to the euthanasia of their enterprise persisted not only because it embodied European concerns about scarce resources but because it also coincided with indigenous aspirations to a better future.

When therefore missionaries themselves appeared to stand in the way of local interests or, say, the process of church development, then local resentment, resistance and declarations of independency were the inevitable consequences. However, as the history of the CMS and other societies indicates, mission strategies from Henry Venn onwards were ahead of secular authorities in anticipating the need for withdrawal, however tardy their initiatives may seem with today's hindsight. The reluctance of many missionaries on the ground to relinquish control is not to be readily written off as evidence of determination to retain a state of colonial subordination. Far from signifying the success with which imperial norms were being inculcated or imposed, it was also a significant indication of the extent to which British norms had *failed* to take root. In the same way, missionary policy-makers' desire for retrenchment and their plans to move on were evidence less of feelings of triumph or success than of a pervasive (if sometimes mistrustful) recognition that only local people themselves, acting on their own initiative, could continue the task effectively.

Scholars who see empire-building in the consequences of missions too easily ignore that missionary insight and neglect the considerable power which local societies possessed to deflect or selectively absorb Western influences. There is now a substantial historiography that explores the subtle interplay of influences in missionary encounters with non-European peoples. In their investigations of such issues as the relation of missions to the landscape, the development of missionary rituals and techniques of conversion and the social or political standing of converts, scholars have demonstrated both the flexibility and the limited power of missions and the progressive reshaping of many missionaries themselves.[18] In many settings, it would seem appropriate to argue that the imperialism associated with missionary efforts and the changes they oversaw were not those of the expanding metropole but of local classes and ethnic communities who were able to turn missionary offerings to their own advantage.

One most striking example of this process can be seen in the southern African Ngwato kingdom, the subject of a major study by Paul Landau.[19] It is one all the more telling for involving another of the Tswana polities that provided the basis for the Comaroffs' entirely opposite conclusions. Landau finds quite untenable their view that Tswana Christians merely identified with or were engulfed by a faith defined and interpreted by missionaries as they consolidated Britain's colonial power. The establishment of Khama's political position in the second half of the nineteenth century, together with the consolidation and expansion of the Ngwato kingdom, clearly hinged on their successful appropriation and control of Christianity. The Ngwato church, in a process of local social transformation which involved the development of new and powerful roles for women, for individual missionaries and even for the LMS itself, was made to serve the purpose of the Ngwato monarchy in its control of the kingdom.

If these lessons of the past were taken fully into account in the discussion of religion and empire, there might be a wider recognition that the history of British Protestant missions in fact seems to present us with a paradox. In the sphere of missionary enterprise, indigenous choices and capacity for resistance or adaptation shaped a process of cultural exchange which often bore little relation to broader imbalances of material power between colonisers and colonised. Highly effective as missions frequently were in promoting cultural change, whether they worked inside or outside Britain's empire, they were amongst the weakest agents of 'cultural imperialism'.[20] In so far as they were beginning before 1914 to provoke, equip and even sympathise with the first stirrings of indigenous political nationalisms – in Egypt or India – they were nurturing seeds of empire's twentieth-century

---

18  For African examples, 'Concluding Summary' by T.O. Ranger, in K.H. Petersen (ed.), *Religion, Development and African Identity* (Uppsala, 1987), pp. 145–62; Prins, *The Hidden Hippopotamus*; Terence Ranger, 'Taking Hold of the Land: Holy Places and Pilgrimage in Twentieth Century Zimbabwe', *Past and Present* 117 (1987), 158–94; Justin Willis, 'The Nature of a Mission Community: the Universities' Mission to Central Africa in Bonde', *Past and Present* 140 (1993), 127–54; David Maxwell with Ingrid Lawrie (ed.), *Christianity and the African Imagination: Essays in Honour of Adrian Hastings* (Leiden, 2002).

19  Paul S. Landau, *The Realm of the Word. Language, Gender and Christianity in a Southern African Kingdom* (London, 1995).

20  See Lamin Sanneh, *Translating the Message: The Missionary Impact on Culture* (New York, 1993). Here Sanneh develops his concept of 'translatability', arguing that missionaries' adoption of vernacular languages commenced a far-reaching process of renewal, revival and reform consistent with enhanced indigenous control and self-understanding. He argues that this step 'was tantamount to adopting indigenous cultural criteria for the message, a piece of radical indigenisation far greater than the standard portrayal of mission as Western cultural imperialism', p. 3.

demise. The undercurrents of such support from Western missionaries in India and Africa were seriously worrying to some organisers of the World Conference at Edinburgh in 1910.[21]

## II

In revising our understanding as to the roles of missions in the replacement and adaptation of indigenous cultures and religions, recent scholars have thus been led not merely to redefine but significantly to enhance the parts played by indigenous Christians and their supporters. In these circumstances, the co-existence of attempts to sustain traditionally far-reaching claims for 'missionary imperialism' with others that insist on the increasing importance of local agency has become increasingly problematical. The logic of this redefinition has made still more necessary a serious reconsideration of both the position of missions as advocates and agents of empire and the dynamics of their own autonomous expansion overseas. The more historians have appreciated the powers of appropriation and talent for adaptation possessed by local societies, the more important has become an understanding of the varied and variable offerings brought by the missions in their metropolitan baggage.

The foregoing chapters have argued that an important aspect of that reconsideration must be to re-examine the place of empire in the thought, planning and development of Protestant missions. That place has been determined in both negative and positive ways. By and large most missionaries did not want to be imperial propagandists and colonial rulers, any more than they intended to be consistent or uncritical supporters of capitalist enterprise. The shifting character of their relations with imperial authorities and other agencies of metropolitan expansion; their ambiguous dealings with indigenous rulers or interest groups; and their weakness as empire-builders or propagandists, were all substantially influenced by that fact. Both those who organised mission societies and those who volunteered for missionary service wanted to share their own religious enthusiasm, to convert non-Christians, to build up new churches and to promote the kingdom of God on earth. These goals, their roots in biblical revelation and religious revival, the timing of missionary initiatives in their pursuit, the means by which they were to be promoted and their curtailment in unfavourable circumstances have therefore been at the heart of this book.

The growing scale of Britain's worldwide presence of course made it impossible for missionaries to escape all involvement either with empire or with other facets of Britain's expansion abroad. However, that involvement was both patchy and discontinuous while also highly competitive, decidedly negative as well as optimistically engaged.[22] Attitudes ranged from total indifference or harsh criticism of

---

21 Stanley, 'Church, State and the Hierarchy of "Civilization"', in Porter (ed.), *Imperial Horizons*, pp. 69–73.

22 See above, pp. 140–2, 267–74; also Steven Maughan, 'Imperial Christianity?', in Porter (ed.), *Imperial Horizons of British Protestant Missions*, pp. 32–57.

empire, through discomfort and toleration, to enthusiastic support. The great majority of missionaries displayed a fitful interest in empire, giving it their temporary and often grudging attention chiefly when it hindered evangelisation or might bring its authority to bear in a necessary defence of missions' past achievements or basic freedom to carry on their work.[23]

The argument developed here has paid particular attention to the many influences that strained relations between missions and empire and often pushed them apart. At their most extreme, these were perhaps to be seen in the activities of the 'faith missions', inspired by a radical theology and anxious to distance themselves as far as possible from Western influences. Occasionally missions found themselves at the other pole. Despite their best intentions they were nevertheless overtaken by empire, especially in regions of white settlement and nowhere perhaps more so than in southern Africa, with its growing and assertive white communities anxious to subordinate the black and coloured populations to the expanding demands of a settler capitalist economy. Van der Kemp had early on experienced this at the hands not only of Dutch colonists but also of the South African Missionary Society.[24] Yet even there in the late nineteenth century sharply contrasting positions were to be found and denominational differences as well as sectarian histories could still be critically important when it came to formulating criticisms of both Westernisation and intensified colonial controls.[25] Missionary bishops supported by the SPG, such as Henry Callaway (1872–73) and Bransby Key (1883–1901) at St John's, Kaffraria and William Carter, Bishop of Zululand (1891–1903), were convinced of the lasting value of much in African culture and customary life. However, Anglicans were divided amongst themselves on these issues. Episcopal readiness to compromise with those divisions within the church, together with the weight of political power ranged against them, made the bishops ineffective defenders of Africans' interests, notwithstanding their opposition to measures such as the Glen Grey Act (1894), Swaziland's transfer to the Transvaal, Zululand's incorporation into Natal and locally devised legislation on African land-holding. The SPG's and WMMS's commitment to multiracial congregations and the continued link between mission and church also restricted African advancement. For the time being, only in the LMS with its Congregationalist principles was the earlier tradition of political action and vociferous protest kept alive and openings for Africans protected.[26]

Missionaries in South Africa, to an extent less common elsewhere before 1914, were in particular danger of being linked closely to, even imprisoned by, wider

23  Brian Stanley, 'Nineteenth-Century Liberation Theology: Nonconformist Missionaries and Imperialism', *Baptist Quarterly: Journal of the Baptist Historical Society* 33, 1 (1987), 5–18.
24  See above, p. 77; Janet Hodgson, 'Mission and Empire: A Case Study of Convergent Ideologies in Nineteenth-Century Southern Africa', *Journal of Theology for Southern Africa* 38 (1982), 34–48.
25  Cf. Peter Hinchliff, 'The English Speaking Churches and South Africa in the Nineteenth Century', *Journal of Theology for Southern Africa*, 9 (1974), 28–38.
26  Margaret Blunden, 'The Anglican Church and the Politics of Southern Africa, 1888–1909' (unpub. D.Phil. thesis., Oxford, 1980), chaps 1–2, 4 and pp. 197–8, 233.

processes of empire-building. In the 1890s, for instance, Wesleyan Methodist missionaries were amongst the staunchest supporters of the Cape Colony's territorial expansion. In this they not only echoed Shaw and his colleagues sixty years before but sustained a broader Wesleyan tradition of support for empire which eventually ranged them on the side of the imperial government in the South African War of 1899–1902. For other nonconformist churches in South Africa, however, it was more explicitly their missionary orientation, the institutional separation of mission society from the church, that generated support for the war – a British victory being seen to 'serve the interests of missionary endeavours and end the power of the Dutch Reformed churches'.[27] At the turn of the nineteenth century in South Africa the situation was one in which local regional developments were rapidly closing off openings once available to British missions. Nevertheless, even in these circumstances, the persistence of British Protestant missions with the education, medical training and ordination of Africans broadcast an egalitarian and essentially anti-colonial message that made them objects of profound suspicion to white settlers of every kind.[28]

In other settings the entanglement of missions with empire could be at once less constraining and more far-reaching in its impact. In Kenya on the eve of the First World War, changing colonial conditions and striking disputes arising from a local missionary conference caused worldwide reverberations that threatened to polarise approaches to the evangelical task. The conference, held at Kikuyu in 1913, was the latest of several between the Church of Scotland mission, the CMS and other Protestants, designed to tackle growing problems associated with the existence of missionary society spheres and the increasing movement of converts and mission workers out of their own denomination's 'area'. Presided over by Dr W.G. Peel and J.J. Willis, bishops respectively of Mombasa and Uganda and intended also to foster their common cause against the rival forces of Roman Catholicism and Islam, the conference drew up proposals under Anglican leadership for an ecclesiastical federation and the possibility of common baptismal procedures and inter-communion.[29]

This apparent blurring or even abandonment of denominational divisions occurred at an unusually critical moment. It came hard on the heels of the

---

27  Above, pp. 136–9, 147–9; Stephen Koss, 'Wesleyanism and Empire', 105–18; Greg Cuthbertson, 'Preaching Imperialism: Wesleyan Methodism and the War', in David Omissi and Andrew Thompson (eds), *The Impact of the South African War* (Basingstoke, 2002), pp. 157–72; 'Pricking the "nonconformist conscience": Religion against the South African War', in Donal Lowry (ed.), *The South African War Reappraised* (Manchester, 2000), p. 180. See also Greenlee and Johnston, *Good Citizens*, chap. 3.

28  For contemporary perceptions of the unsatisfactory state of South African Missions and the intractable nature of the field see, for example, *World Missionary Conference 1910: Report of Commission I Carrying the Gospel to all the Non-Christian World* (Edinburgh, London and New York, 1910), pp. 227–30, 244; Richard Elphick, 'Evangelical Missions and Racial "Equalization" in South Africa, 1890–1914', *NAMP Symposium Paper* (Boston, 1998).

29  For accounts of Kikuyu, Oliver, *Missionary Factor in East Africa*, pp. 222–30; Stock, *History of the CMS*, Vol. 4, pp. 409–24.

Edinburgh Conference of 1910, when it had seemed to many that the cause of interdenominational Christianity, so fitted for the mission field by its preoccupation with the 'essentials' of the faith, had made a great leap forward. It also followed the series of regional gatherings that culminated in the National Conference of missionaries and churchmen at Calcutta in December 1912. Organised by J.R. Mott and his allies, the final Report on Co-operation and Unity, with its sugges-tions for inter-communion, was presented by the newly appointed metropolitan bishop and high churchman, G.A. Lefroy.[30] These developments, seen against the contemporary European background of modernist theological criticism, only exac-erbated the mounting fears of many Anglo-Catholics for the coherence of the Church of England and its doctrines. Anglo-Catholics, already suspicious of the wisdom and consequences of the high church representation at Edinburgh, only found their worries steadily confirmed.[31] While some high church bishops, not only Lefroy, sooner or later took these developments in their stride, to Bishop Weston at Zanzibar Indian events and more especially Kikuyu seemed shocking. He denounced the Kikuyu scheme, accused his fellow bishops of promoting heresy and schism, appealed to the Archbishop of Canterbury and immediately rushed his views into print.[32]

The detailed outcome of Weston's protests need not concern us here.[33] The bishop gained some of his points and as a result added to his leadership of the UMCA for the next decade the role of influential exponent for the Anglo-Catholic position in the Anglican church as well as advocate of alternative plans for missions' co-operation and unity. Storm in a colonial teapot this might seem, but to the British missions and churchmen involved its significance at the time stretched far wider. For Weston himself, whose mission operated across German as well as British colonial territory, it was no merely national church that was involved but the nature and authority of the Christian Church worldwide. Others saw an equal need to take the episode seriously. It was not only felt to merit examination by the Central Consultative Body of the Lambeth Conference. Bishop Willis later pointed out that the issues it raised 'affected every part of the great world-wide Anglican Communion ... the great Nonconformist bodies ... [and] the Church of Scotland ... From India, from Australia, from America, from all parts of the world letters

---

30  Stock, *History of the CMS*, Vol. 4, chap. 16 'India: The Anglican Church and Union Movements', esp. pp. 185–90.

31  Stuart Mews, 'Kikuyu and Edinburgh: The Interaction of Attitudes to Two Conferences', in G.J. Cuming and Derek Baker (eds), *Councils and Assemblies. Studies in Church History* 7 (Cambridge, 1971), 345–59.

32  For Bishop Whitehead of Madras, Stock, *History of the CMS*, Vol. 4, pp. 413–14; and for Palmer of Bombay, Gerald Studdert-Kennedy, 'Theology and Authority, Constitution and Improvisation: The Colonial Church in India', in J.M. Brown and R.E. Frykenberg (eds), *Christians, Cultural Interactions and India's Religious Traditions* (Grand Rapids and London, 2002), pp. 169–70; Frank Weston, *Ecclesia Anglicana: For What Does She Stand?* (Zanzibar, 1913).

33  G.K.A. Bell, *Randall Davidson Archbishop of Canterbury*, 3rd edn (London, 1952), chap. 42 'Kikuyu'.

either approving or condemning the action poured in.'[34] There was thus far more to the uproar over the Kikuyu conference than the transfer to a colonial setting of sectional disputes already well rehearsed in Britain itself. Christian unity and the side-stepping of denominational differences were not imperial but global questions. On the eve of the First World War, no less than in the midst of the late eighteenth century's wars, missionaries were still conscious that they operated in a world that was neither national nor imperial, but global, in scope.

## III

The process that so unsettled Bishop Weston was accepted by others as part of a benign development of Christian traditions. The Christianity that was transplanted, the Christianity that developed in settings overseas, had always tended to diverge from British metropolitan norms, both through a natural evolution and frequently at the insistence of missionaries themselves.[35] It could scarcely have been otherwise. Whatever the setting in which the transmission of missionary messages took place, it is difficult to see that any uniform pattern could have been imposed on the outlook and thought-patterns of non-European societies, colonising their languages and confining them within a colonial discourse of Western manufacture.

To start with, the backgrounds and skills of the agents of linguistic change were enormously varied. Even a brief roll-call of missionary agents involved in these activities – such as William Carey and his Indian pundits; George Pope, a Prince Edward Islander with affinities for Tamil and Balliol College; Hannah Kilham, of artisan family and seceder from first Anglicanism, then Wesleyan Methodism; J. Friedrich Schön, graduate of Basel; T.J. Bowen, the one-time American soldier from Georgia; the Ulster Presbyterian Hope Waddell, assisted in Old Calabar by helpers from Jamaica; and Samuel Crowther, freed Yoruba slave with his many Sierra Leonean assistants – is suggestive of the breadth of theology, education, class, nationality and ability involved. Such differences help explain the disputes over adequate vocabulary and correct meanings that everywhere attended the appearance of grammars, dictionaries and translations.

It is equally significant that even missionaries acquainted with local languages often had to rely heavily on interpreters, again of varying competence.[36] Also like other Europeans, missionaries were no less prone to take a utilitarian approach to language, acquiring such portions as suited their role and neglecting the rest.[37]

---

34  Stock, *History of the CMS*, Vol. 4, p. 424.
35  Brian Stanley, 'The Reshaping of Christian Tradition: Western Denominational Identity in a Non-Western Context', in R.N. Swanson (ed.), *Unity and Diversity in the Church. Studies in Church History 32* (Oxford, 1992), 399–426.
36  For the problems of interpreters, Robert Moffat, *Missionary Labours and Scenes in Southern Africa* (London, 1842), pp. 291–5.
37  Bernard S. Cohn, 'The Command of Language and the Language of Command', in Ranajit Guha (ed.), *Subaltern Studies* 4 (Delhi, 1985), 276–329.

Such selectivity probably heightened the contrasting potential in any case revealed in different languages for coping with the exposition of Christianity. No less than their Jesuit predecessors in China, Catholic missionaries, for example, in the Pacific Islands invented new words for matrimony and the mass, created novel word associations and sought out old myths for new purposes. Scottish missionaries in the Niger Delta struggled with the local Efik language which lacked the means to express concepts such as 'resurrection', 'temptation', 'individual responsibility' and human 'sinfulness'. They responded in what was essentially a two-way process: they redefined Efik words to overcome the constraints of indigenous language and explain the Gospel's meaning in local terms and they selected certain Christian symbols rather than others for emphasis as more congruent with categories of Efik belief.[38] Recent study of the London Missionary Society's work with the Tswana refers to Robert Moffat's bible as a 'hybrid creation', true to the language of no one party.[39] In both cases, therefore, what one might call 'cultural concessions' were being made on all sides throughout the process. The fusion of language and ideas produced a complexity of influences which is at odds with an insistence on a Western 'cultural imperialism'. Missions were frequently unable to set the terms of their discussions with local people and in such circumstances the employment or transmission of a 'colonial discourse' is hard to imagine.[40]

The growing missionary responsiveness to non-Christian and world religions after 1900 worked in the same direction. A degree of flexibility and openness had long been a particular feature of the LMS.[41] Rarely was it more emphatically spelt out than in the Society's General Instructions of 1873. 'Do not ANGLICISE YOUR CONVERTS. Remember that the people are foreigners. Let them continue as such. Let their foreign individuality be maintained. Build upon it, so far as it is sound and good; and Christianize, but do not needlessly change it. Do not seek to make the people Englishmen. Seek to develop and mould a pure, refined and Christian character, native to the soil.'[42] Exhortations from missionary headquarters as to the need for sensitivity towards indigenous cultures could easily be forgotten in the heat of the evangelical moment and were always likely to be selectively followed. Nevertheless, the gradual broadening of missionary training, especially in the two decades before 1914 and the accumulation of missionary high scholarship, both developments reaching well beyond the LMS, inevitably deepened that

---

38  Dening, *Islands and Beaches*, pp. 193–4, 204; W. Harrison Daniel, 'Patterns in Mission Preaching: The Representation of the Christian Message and Efik Response in the Scottish Calabar Mission, Nigeria, 1846–1900' (unpub. Ph.D. thesis, Edinburgh, 1993).

39  Comaroff, *Of Revelation and Revolution*, Vol. 1, pp. 217–18. The Comaroffs do not seem to appreciate the extent to which acknowledgement of the Tswana contribution or the limits to that of the missionaries weakens any general insistence on missionary hegemony.

40  Porter, '"Cultural Imperialism"', pp. 378–9.

41  Jonathan Bonk, *The Theory and Practice of Missionary Identification, 1860–1920* (New York, 1989).

42  *General Regulations for the Guidance of the English Missionaries of the Society* (London, 1873), Part II General Instructions for Missionaries, Article 12k.

concern.[43] Enhanced cultural awareness was slowly extended to the intelligent scrutiny of indigenous faith and beliefs. 'After all', wrote George Allan, 'the perfection of cricket is not of the essence of Christianity.'[44]

This was especially true of Asian religions. In India, the 1890s witnessed a further significant movement of Hindu religious revivalism and reform, representing, some would argue, a form of religious or cultural 'nationalism' paralleling or overlapping the 'political nationalism' of the infant Indian National Congress formed in 1885. It was led by figures such as Sri Ramakrishna and Swami Vivekananda and further encouraged by the Hindu Tract and Theosophical Societies. In part this movement was born out of a vigorous and hostile reaction against Western influences and it provoked in return no less vigorous ripostes, such as John Jones's *India's Problem*.[45] However, it also produced another very different series of exchanges, on both sides far more questioning and exploratory of each other's faiths.[46] Among British missionaries, the outstanding but not the only figure in this developing tradition was J.N. Farquhar, a Scottish educational missionary on the staff of the Indian YMCA from 1902 to 23. Farquhar's writings embodied an acknowledgement that non-Christian religions contained at least a measure of revelation. This development reflected in part changes of focus in British theology, away from a preoccupation with Christ's death and atonement towards a concern with his incarnation, which at the same time helped to encourage the opening up of comparative religious studies. Thus it was that Farquhar could write increasingly of Christianity as 'the crown of Hinduism', the title given to his most influential work. This 'fulfilment theology' as it was called presented an interpretation of Christ's historic role and Christianity itself as the completion or fulfilment of the world's major religions, the final outcome of a process already set in motion by Hindu teachers and reformers.[47] For others, such as the SPG missionary C.F. Andrews, the Bible itself was 'a truly Eastern book … written by Easterners; it contains the universal truths' and bore careful study alongside other books of the East.[48] Eastern customs such as those embodied in the caste system were viewed in a new or sometimes softer light.

---

43  Andrew F. Walls, *The Missionary Movement in Christian History: Studies in the Transmission of the Faith* (New York and Edinburgh, 1996), chaps 15–16.

44  G.A. Allan, *Civilization and Foreign Missions* (London, 1900), p. 44.

45  John P. Jones, *India's Problem: Krishna or Christ* (New York and London, 1903), e.g. at pp. 112–13. Jones was a missionary with the ABCFM.

46  For a recent discussion, Chandra Mallampalli, 'British Missions and Indian Nationalism, 1880–1908: Imitation and Autonomy in Calcutta and Madras', in Andrew Porter (ed.), *The Imperial Horizons of British Protestant Missions, 1880–1914* (Grand Rapids and Woodbridge, 2003), chap. 8.

47  J.N. Farquhar, *The Crown of Hinduism* (Oxford, 1913); for a study of these themes, Eric J. Sharpe, *Not to Destroy but to Fulfil: The Contribution of J.N. Farquhar to Protestant Missionary Thought in India before 1914* (Uppsala, 1965).

48  Eric J. Sharpe, 'C.F. Andrews 1871–1940', in Gerald Anderson et al. (eds), *Mission Legacies* (New York, 1994), quotation at p. 318. On Andrews see the works by O'Connor and Tinker listed in the bibliography.

Similar processes of re-evaluation can be detected in writings on both Islam and Buddhism at this time. However, it is not the intention here to explore the alternative understandings of Christianity's competitors that theologies and missionaries were developing at the start of the twentieth century. They not only have their place elsewhere.[49] They were also slow to have an impact and they have been presented as a newly liberal value system no less keen 'than its predecessors to fashion the non-European world in a particular Western image'.[50] However, in terms of the themes that have been developed above, in so far as these views represented a retreat from claims to a Christian monopoly of truth and insight, they not only weakened the potential intellectual and cultural connections between missions and empire but also offered support for indigenous cultures everywhere. They were in tune with the movement discussed earlier from active proselytisation to a missionary ethic of practical witness through service and the relief of suffering.[51] At a time when pessimism about non-Western abilities and a general acceptance of racial hierarchy both flourished, such missionary views provided an important counterpoise.

Although missions could not avoid empire, they were determined to put it in its place. The extent of their determination, the universal sweep of their theology, the global extent of their contacts and their consciousness, deserve more acknowledgement than they have generally received. Missions also operated in a world where many different pressures – political, theological, economic and intellectual – combined, as we have seen, to distance them from empire no less than to draw them together. These pressures too deserve serious recognition. Aggressive crusading was far from representing the only evangelical approach to the missionary task. The variety and nuance of missionary standpoints, their detachment from empire and the measure of anti-imperialism, all associated with Britain's Christian missionary enterprise, have an important place in the history both of empire and of missions. It is to be hoped that this book will contribute towards a clearer understanding of that complex relationship.

---

49 For example, Kenneth Cracknell, *Justice, Courtesy and Love: Missionaries and Theologians Encountering the World Religions, 1846–1914* (London, 1995).

50 Stanley, *Bible and the Flag*, pp. 164–5; Mallampalli, 'British Missions and Indian Nationalism', pp. 179–82.

51 See above, pp. 307–14.

# Select bibliography

The bibliography is divided into the following sections:

Archives and manuscript collections
Primary printed sources
Secondary books and articles
Periodicals
Works of reference
Unpublished dissertations

## Archives and manuscript collections

**Birmingham University Library**
Church Missionary Society
G.W. Brooke

**Bodleian Library (Rhodes House), Oxford**
Dr John Philip Papers [notes and transcripts in W.M. Macmillan Papers]
Society for the Propagation of the Gospel
Universities' Mission to Central Africa

**Cambridge University Library**
British and Foreign Bible Society
London Secretaries Association
Thornton Family Papers

**Houghton Library, Harvard University**
American Board of Commissioners for Foreign Missions

**John Rylands University Library of Manchester**
Methodist Church Archives

**National Library of Scotland**
Church of Scotland
Free Church of Scotland
United Presbyterian Church

**Ridley Hall, Cambridge**
H.C.G. Moule Papers

**School of Oriental and African Studies, London University**
Council for World Mission [London Missionary Society]
Lockhart Papers
Wesleyan Methodist Missionary Society

**Trinity College, Cambridge**
E.W. Benson

**Yale Divinity School**
A. Judson Brown
D..L. Moody
John R. Mott
Horace Waller
R.P. Wilder
Miscellaneous Personal Papers
Missions Pamphlet Collection
Sermons and Addresses
Student Volunteer Movement for Foreign Missions

## Primary printed sources

[ABCFM] *Letters of the American Missionaries, 1835–1838*, ed. D.J. Kotze (Van Riebeeck Society: Cape Town, 1950)

[Aborigines Committee] *Report from the Select Committee on Aborigines (British Settlements) PP*(1836) VII (538)

[Aborigines Committee] *Report from the Select Committee on Aborigines (British Settlements)*, *PP*(1837) VII (425)

Allan, G.A. *Civilization and Foreign Missions* (London, 1900)

Anderson, Rufus. *History of the Sandwich Islands Mission* (Boston, 1870)

Anderson-Morshead, A.E.M. *The History of the Universities' Mission to Central Africa 1859–1909* (London, 1909*)*

Arnold, T.W. *The Preaching of Islam: A History of the Propagation of the Muslim Faith* (London, 1896)

Arnot, Frederick S. *Garenganze or Seven Years' Pioneer Work in Central Africa* (2nd edn, London, 1889)

[Asbury, Francis] Elmer T. Clark (ed.). *The Journal and Letters of Francis Asbury*, 3 vols (London and Nashville, 1958)

Ashwell, A.R. and Wilberforce, R.G. *Life of the Right Reverend Samuel Wilberforce, D.D.*, 3 vols (London, 1880–82)

*Atlas des Missions Catholiques. Par le R.P.O. Werner* [trans. from the German, orig. published Freiburg, 1884] (Bureau des Missions Catholiques, Lyons, 1886)

[Baptist Missionary Society] *The Centenary Volume of the Baptist Missionary Society, 1792–1892* (London, 1892)

Barton, C.E. *John Barton. A Memoir ... with Preface by H.C.G. Moule* (London, 1910)

Bateman, Josiah. *The Life of the Rt. Rev. Daniel Wilson, D.D.*, 2 vols (London, 1860)

Beauchamp, M.H.P. *Days of Blessing in Inland China* (London, 1890)

Benson, A.C. *The Life of Edward White Benson*, 2 vols (London, 1899, repr. 1900)

Birks, Herbert. *The Life and Correspondence of Thomas Valpy French, First Bishop of Lahore*, 2 vols (London, 1895)

Blackwood, S.A. *Some Records of the Life of Stevenson Arthur Blackwood* (London, 1896)

Blyden, E.W. *Christianity, Islam and the Negro Race*, 2nd edn (London, 1888)

Bogue, David. 'Objections against a mission to the heathen, stated and considered', *Sermons preached in London at the Formation of the Missionary Society* (London, 1795)

Boyce, William. B. *Notes on South African Affairs, from 1834 to 1838* (Graham's Town, 1838)

Bray, Thomas. *A Memorial representing the present State of Religion on the Continent of North America* (London, 1700)

Bridgman, Elijah C. *Glimpses of Canton: The Diary of Elijah C. Bridgman 1834–1838*, with a Foreword by Martha Lund-Smalley (New Haven, 1998)

Buchanan, Claudius. *Memoir of the Expediency of an Ecclesiastical Establishment for British India* (London, 1805)

Buchanan, Claudius. 'A Sermon preached at the Parish Church of St. Andrew by the Wardrobe … June 12, 1810', *Proceedings of the Church Missionary Society for Africa and the East* 3 (London, 1810–12), 9–50

Buchanan, Claudius. *Eight Sermons* (new edn, London, 1812)

Buchanan, Claudius. *Colonial Ecclesiastical Establishment: Being a Brief View of the State of the Colonies of Great Britain, and of her Asiatic Empire, in respect to Religious Instruction: Prefaced by some considerations on the National Duty of affording it. To which is added, A Sketch of an Ecclesiastical Establishment for British India. Humbly Submitted to the Consideration of the Imperial Parliament* (London, 1813)

Buxton, Charles ed. *Memoirs of Sir Thomas Fowell Buxton, Bart.*, new edn (London, 1882)

Buxton, Thomas Fowell. *The African Slave Trade* (London, 1839)

Buxton, Thomas Fowell. *The Remedy* (London, 1839)

Buxton, Thomas Fowell. *The African Slave Trade and Its Remedy* (London, 1840)

Byron, George A. *An Examination of Charges against the American Missionaries at the Sandwich Islands, as alleged in the Voyage of the Ship Blonde, and in the Quarterly Review* (Cambridge, 1828)

Carey, William. *An Enquiry into the Obligations of Christians, to use Means for the Conversion of the Heathens* (Leicester, 1792)

Casalis, Eugene. *My Life in Basutoland: A Story of Missionary Enterprise in South Africa* (London, 1889)

Chalmers, Thomas. *The Utility of Missions ascertained by Experience: A Sermon preached before the Society in Scotland for Propagating Christian Knowledge … June 2, 1814*, 2nd edn (Edinburgh, 1816)

[Champion, George] *The Journal of an American Missionary in the Cape Colony 1835 by George Champion*, ed. Alan R. Booth (Cape Town, 1968)

Champness, Eliza M. *The Life Story of Thomas Champness* (London, 1907)

[Church Missionary Society] *Summary View of the Designs and Proceedings of the Society for Missions to Africa and the East* (London, 1812)

Coates, D., Beecham, John, and Ellis, William. *Christianity the Means of Civilization* (London, 1837)

Coillard, François. *On the Threshold of Central Africa* (London, 1902)

Coke, Thomas. *Address to the Pious and Benevolent, proposing an annual subscription for the support of the missionaries in the Highlands and islands of Scotland, the Isles of Jersey, Guernsey and Newfoundland, the West Indies, and the Provinces of Nova Scotia and Quebec* (London, 1786)

Coke, Thomas. *The Recent Occurrences of Europe Considered in relation to such prophecies as are either fulfilling or unfulfilled. First published in 1807, in an appendix to his Commentary on the Bible* (London, 1809)

Colenso, J.W. *The Pentateuch and Book of Joshua critically examined*, 4 vols (London, 1862–63)

Coppin, W. Terry. *John Martin: Pioneer Missionary, Hero and Saint* (London, 1910)

Cromer, Earl of. *Modern Egypt*, 2 vols (London, 1908)

Cust, R.N. *Notes on Missionary Subjects* (London, 1889)

Dale, A.W.W. *The Life of R.W. Dale of Birmingham*, 2nd edn (London, 1899)

Dale, R.W. *The Evangelical Revival and Other Sermons* (London, 1880)

[Davies, John] *The History of the Tahitian Mission 1799–1830 written by John Davies Missionary to the South Sea Islands*, ed. C.W. Newbury (Hakluyt Society 2nd series, 116, Cambridge, 1961)

Dealtry, William. *A Sermon preached … before the Church Missionary Society for Africa and the East being their Thirteenth Anniversary* (2nd edn, London, 1813)

Dennis, J.S. *Centennial Survey of Foreign Missions* (Edinburgh, 1902)

Doane, W.C. ed. *The Life and Writings of George Washington Doane, D.D., LL.D.*, 4 vols (New York, 1860)

Dobinson, H.H. *Letters of Henry Hughes Dobinson Late Archdeacon of the Niger* (London, 1899)

Duff, Alexander. *The Church of Scotland's India Missions* (Edinburgh, 1835)

[Edwards, Jonathan] *The Works of Jonathan Edwards Vol. 5: Apocalyptic Writings*, ed. Stephen J. Stein (New Haven and London, 1977)

Edwards, Jonathan. *Account of the Life of the Late Reverend Mr. David Brainerd* (1749) [For the latest scholarly edition, *The Works of Jonathan Edwards Vol. 7*, ed. Norman Petit (New Haven and London, 1985)]

Ellis, John Eimeo. *Life of William Ellis Missionary to the South Seas and to Madagascar* (London, 1873)

Ellis, William. *Narrative of a Tour through Hawaii* (London, 1826)

Ellis, William. *Polynesian Researches, during a residence of nearly six years in the South Sea Islands*, 2 vols (London, 1829)

Ellis, William. *The Command and Encouragement to Communicate the Gospel. A Sermon presented before the London Missionary Society at Craven Chapel on Thursday, May 12, 1831* (London, 1831)

Ellis, William. *Vindication of the South Sea Missions from the Misrepresentations of Otto Von Kotzebue, Captain in the Russian Navy, with an Appendix* (London, 1831)

Ellis, William. *Memoir of Mary M. Ellis* (London, 1835)

Ellis, William. *Three Visits to Madagascar* (London, 1858)

Ellis, William. *The American Mission in the Sandwich Islands: A Vindication and an Appeal in relation to the proceedings of the Reformed Catholic Mission at Honolulu* (London, 1866).

*Essays and Reviews* (London, 1860)

Farquhar, J.N. *The Crown of Hinduism* (Oxford, 1913)

French, T.V. *The Proposed Cambridge University Mission in North India: Being the Substance of a Paper read before the Cambridge Mission Aid Society on February 16, 1876* (privately printed, 1876)

Gairdner, W.H.T. *D.M. Thornton: A Study in Missionary Ideals and Methods* (3rd edn, London 1909)

Gairdner, W.H.T. *The Reproach of Islam* (London, 1909)

Gairdner, W.H.T. *'Edinburgh 1910'. An Account and Interpretation of the World Missionary Conference* (London, 1910)

Garratt, Samuel. *A Commentary on The Revelation of St. John, considered as The Divine Book of History* (London, 1866; 2nd edn, 1878)

Goldman, C.S. (ed.). *The Empire and the Century* (London, 1905)

Goodwin, Harvey. *Memoir of Bishop Mackenzie* (Cambridge, 1864)

Grant, Anthony. *The Past and Prospective Extension of the Gospel by Missions to the Heathen. The Bampton Lectures for 1843*, 2nd edn (London, 1845)

Grant, Charles. *A Proposal for establishing a Protestant Mission in Bengal and Behar* (unpublished London, 1787)

Grant, Charles. *Observations on the State of Society among the Asiatic Subjects of Great Britain, particularly with respect to morals; and the means of improving it ... written chiefly in the year 1792, PP* (1812–13), Vol. 10: republished in *PP* (1831–32), Vol. 8 (734)

Grant, John. *Religious Aspect of the War with Russia. A sermon ... on the 26th April, 1854* (Dublin, 1854)

Gray, Charles (ed.). *Life of Robert Gray Bishop of Cape Town and Metropolitan of Africa*, 2 vols (London, 1876)

Gregson, J. Gelson. *Apostolic Missions for the Present Day* (London, 1887)

Guinness, Henry Grattan. *The Approaching End of the Age* (London, 1878)

Guinness, Mrs H.G. *The First Christian Mission on the Congo: The Livingstone Inland Mission* (4th edn, London, 1882)

Guinness, Mrs H.G. *The Wide World and Our Work in it; or, the Story of the East London Institute for Home and Foreign Missions* (London, 1886)

Guinness, Mrs H.G. *The New World of Central Africa* (London, 1890)

Guinness, H., and Guinness, F.E. Light *for the Last Days. A Study Historic and Prophetic* (London, 1886),

Guinness, H., and Guinness, F.E. *The Divine Programme of the World's History* (London, 1888).

Hanna, W. *Memoirs of the Life and Writings of Thomas Chalmers*, 4 vols (Edinburgh, 1849–52)

Harford, C.F. ed. *The Keswick Convention. Its Message, Its Method and Its Men* (London, 1907)

Harford, J.B., and Macdonald, F.C. *Handley Carr Glyn Moule, Bishop of Durham. A Biography* (London, 1922)

[Hart, Robert] *The I.G. in Peking: Letters of Robert Hart Chinese Maritime Customs 1868–1907* eds J.K. Fairbank et al., 2 vols (Cambridge, MA, 1975)

H[aweis]., T[homas]. 'The Very Probable Success of a proper Mission to the South Sea Islands', *Evangelical Magazine* (July 1795), 261–70

Haweis, Thomas. *A View of the Present State of Evangelical Religion throughout the World; with a view to promote missionary exertions* (London, 1812)

Heanley, R.M. *A Memoir of Edward Steere, D.D., LL.D., Third Missionary Bishop in Central Africa* (London, 1888)

[Heber, Reginald] *Narrative of a Journey through the Upper Provinces of India, from Calcutta to Bombay, 1824–1825 (With Notes upon Ceylon) An Account of a Journey to Madras and the Southern Provinces, 1826, and Letters written in India*, ed. Amelia Heber, 2 vols (London, 1844)

Hill, George. *Lectures in Divinity*, 3 vols (Edinburgh, 1821)

[Hodgson, T.L.] *The Journal of the Rev. T.L. Hodgson Missionary to the Seleka-Rolong and the Griquas, 1821–31*, ed. R.L. Cope (Johannesburg, 1977)

Horne, Melvill. *Letters on Missions; addressed to the Protestant Ministers of the British Churches* (Bristol, 1794)

Hughes, D.P. *The Life of Hugh Price Hughes* (London, 1904)

Irving, Edward. *For Missionaries after the Apostolical School: A Series of Orations* (London, 1825)

James, J.A. *Missionary Prospects: A sermon the substance of which was delivered ... at the opening of Hoxton College as a missionary academy* (Birmingham, 1826)

Johnston, Harry H. *British Central Africa* (London, 1897)

Johnston, James (ed.). *Report of the Centenary Conference on the Protestant Missions of the World held in Exeter Hall (June 9th–19th) London, 1888*, 2 vols (London, 1888)

Jones, John P. *India's Problem: Krishna or Christ* (New York and London, 1903)

Kemp, Denis. *Nine Years at the Gold Coast* (London, 1898)

Kirlew, E. *Gilbert R. Kirlew. A Brief Memoir* (London, 1908)

*The Kitchingman Papers: Missionary Letters and Journals, 1817 to 1848*, eds Basil le Cordeur and Christopher Saunders (Johannesburg, 1976)

Knight, William. *Memoir of the Rev. H. Venn* (London, 1880; 2nd rev. edn 1882)

Knight-Bruce, G.W.H. 'The Mashonaland Mission of Bishop Knight-Bruce', ed. C.E. Fripp, *Gold and the Gospel in Mashonaland 1888* (London, 1949)

Knight-Bruce, G.W.H. *Memories of Mashonaland* (London, 1895)

Knight-Bruce, G.W.H. Journals, from *Gold and the Gospel in Mashonaland 1888*, ed. C.E. Fripp (London, 1949)

Latrobe, C.I. *Journal of a Visit to South Africa in 1815, and 1816* (London, 1818)

Legge, H.E. *James Legge: Missionary and Scholar* (London, 1905)

Leonard, Arthur Glyn. *Islam. Her Moral and Spiritual Value. A Rational and Psychological Study* (London, 1909)

Lewis, James. *William Goudie* (London, 1923)

*Some Letters from Livingstone 1840–1872*, ed. David Chamberlin (London, 1940)

*David Livingstone Letters and Documents 1841–1872*, ed. Timothy Holmes (Livingstone, Lusaka, Bloomington and London, 1990)

*David Livingstone Family Letters 1841–1856*, ed. I. Schapera, 2 vols (London, 1959)

*Livingstone's Missionary Correspondence 1841–1856*, ed. I. Schapera (London, 1961)

*Livingstone's Private Journals 1851–1853*, ed. I. Schapera (London, 1960)

*David Livingstone's African Journal, 1853–1856*, ed. I. Schapera, 2 vols (London, 1963)

Livingstone, David. *Missionary Travels and Researches in South Africa* (London, 1857)

*Dr. Livingstone's Cambridge Lectures*, ed. William Monk (Cambridge, 1858)

*The Zambezi Expedition of David Livingstone, 1858–1863*, ed. J.P.R. Wallis, 2 vols (London, 1956)

*The Zambezi Doctors: David Livingstone's Letters to John Kirk 1858–1872*, ed. Reginald Foskett (Edinburgh, 1964)

*David Livingstone's Shire Journal, 1861–1864*, ed. Gary W. Clendennen (Aberdeen, 1992)

*The Last Journals of David Livingstone, in Central Africa, from 1865 to His Death*, ed. Horace Waller, 2 vols (London, 1874 and 1956)

Livingstone, David, and Livingstone, Charles. *A Narrative of an Expedition to the Zambesi and its Tributaries, and of the Discovery of the Lakes Shirwa and Nyassa, 1858–1864* (London, 1865)

Lockhart, William. *The Medical Missionary in China: A Narrative of Twenty Years Experience* (London, 1861)

[London Missionary Society] *General Regulations for the Guidance of the English Missionaries of the Society* (London, 1873)

Longridge, George. *A History of the Oxford Mission to Calcutta* (London, 1900)

*Zachary Macaulay and the Development of the Sierra Leone Company, 1793–4. Part I: Journal, June–October 1793*, ed. Suzanne Schwarz (2nd edn, Leipzig, 2000)

*A.M. Mackay, Pioneer Missionary of the Church Missionary Society to Uganda. By His Sister* (London, 1890; repr. 1970)

Mackintosh, C.W. *Coillard of the Zambezi* (London, 1907)

Manross, W.W. *The Fulham Papers in the Lambeth Palace Library: American Colonial Section Calendar and Indexes* (Oxford, 1965)

Manross, William W. *S.P.G. Papers in the Lambeth Palace Library. Calendar and Indexes* (Oxford, 1974)

Maples, C. *The African Church and Its Claims upon the Universities* (Cambridge, 1879)

Maples, C. *On the Method of Evangelising Uncultured Races, Monthly Paper No. 9 for the Oxford Mission to Calcutta* (Calcutta, 1882)

*Journals and Papers of Chauncy Maples D.D., F.R.G.S., Late Bishop of Likoma Lake Nyasa, Africa*, ed. Ellen Maples (London, 1899)

Maples, Ellen. *Chauncy Maples D.D., F.R.G.S. Pioneer Missionary in East Central Africa* (London, 1897)

*The Letters and Journals of Samuel Marsden, 1765–1838*, ed. J.R. Elder (Dunedin, 1932)

Marshman, J.C. *Hints relative to Native Schools, together with the outline of an institution for their extension and management* (Calcutta, 1816)

Marshman, J.C. *The Life and Times of Carey, Marshman, and Ward*, 2 vols (London, 1859)

Martyn, Henry. *Sermons* (Calcutta, 1822)

[Martyn, Henry] *Journals and Letters of the Reverend Henry Martyn*, ed. S. Wilberforce, 2 vols (London, 1837)

[Methodist Missionary Society] *A Statement of the Receipts and Disbursements of the Methodist Missions, in the year 1803 and 1804* (London, 1804)

[Methodist Missionary Society] *The Missionary Controversy. Discussion, Evidence and Report* (WMMS, London, 1890)

*Methods of Mission Work among Moslems. Being those Papers read at the First Missionary Conference on behalf of the Muslim World held at Cairo April 4th–9th 1906* (London and New York, 1906)

*Report of the Mildmay Second Advent Conference, 2–4 March 1886* (London, 1886)

*The Mildmay Conference 1887* (London, 1887)

Moffat, Robert. *Missionary Labours and Scenes in Southern Africa* (London, 1842)

Montgomery, H.H. *The Life and Letters of George Alfred Lefroy* (London, 1920)

*E.D. Morel's History of the Congo Reform Movement*, eds Wm Roger Louis and Jean Stengers (Oxford, 1967)

Muhleisen-Arnold, J. *The Society for Propagating the Gospel among the Moslems, in connection with the Church of England; Its First Appeal on behalf of 180 millions of Mohammedans* (London, 1860)

Mullens, Joseph. *Results of Missionary Labour in India* (London, 1852)

Mullens, Joseph. *Missions in South India Visited and Described* (London, 1854)

Mullens, Joseph. *A Brief Review of Ten Years Missionary Labour in India 1852–61* (London, 1863)

Müller, F. Max. *On Missions. A Lecture delivered in Westminster Abbey on December 3, 1873. With an introductory Sermon by Arthur Penrhyn Stanley Dean of Westminster* (London, 1873)

[New England Company] *Some Correspondence between the Governors and Treasurers of the New England Company in London and the Commissioners of the United Colonies in America, The Missionaries of the Company and Others between the Years 1657 and 1712* (London, 1896)

Orme, William. *A Defence of the Missions in the South Seas and Sandwich Islands against the mis-representations contained in a late number of the Quarterly Review in a letter to the editor of the Journal* (London, 1827)

Padwick, C.E. *Temple Gairdner of Cairo* (2nd edn, London 1930)

Paton, James (ed.). *John G. Paton Missionary to the New Hebrides: An Autobiography*, 2 vols (London, 1889–90)

Pattison, S.R. *Gospel Ethnology*, new cheaper edition (London, c.1890)

Perry, W.S. (ed.) *Historical Collections relating to the American Colonial Church*, 5 vols (New York, 1870–78)

Philip, John. *Necessity of Divine Influence. A Sermon preached before the Missionary Society … May 12, 1813* (London, 1813)

Philip, John. *Researches in South Africa Illustrating the Civil, Moral, and Religious Condition of Native Tribes*, 2 vols (London, 1828)

Pierson, A.T. *Evangelical Work in Principle and Practice* (New York, 1887, London, 1888)

Polhill-Turner, A.T. *A Story Retold. 'The Cambridge Seven'* (London, 1902)

Pratt, J.H. (ed.) *Eclectic Notes: or, Notes of of Discussions on Religious Topics at the Meeting of the Eclectic Society, London, during the years 1798–1814*, 2nd edn (London, 1865)

Pratt, J. and J.H. (eds) *Memoir of the Reverend Josiah Pratt* (London, 1849)

*The Protestant and Missionary Map of the World* (London, 1846)

Pruen, S.T. *The Arab and the African: Experiences in Eastern Equatorial Africa during a residence of three years* (London, 1891)

Reade, W. Winwood. *The Martyrdom of Man* (London, 1875)

Richard, Timothy. *Forty-Five Years in China: Reminscences by Timothy Richard* (London, 1916)

Rowley, Henry. *Africa Unveiled* (London, 1876)

Rutherfurd, J. and Glenny, Edward H. *The Gospel in North Africa* (London, 1900)

Schön, J.F., and Crowther, S.A. *Journals of the Rev. James Frederick Schön and Mr Samuel Crowther* (London, 1842)

Scott, John. *Letters and Papers of the Late Rev. Thomas Scott* (London, 1824)

Selwyn, G.A. *Are Cathedral Institutions Useless? A Practical Answer to this Question addressed to W.E. Gladstone, Esq. M.P.* (London, 1838)

Selwyn, G.A. *How shall we sing the Lord's Song in a Strange Land? A Sermon preached in the Cathedral Church of St. Peter, Exeter … previous to his departure from England* (1842)

Selwyn, G.A. *Thanksgiving Sermon: Preached … on His Arrival in His Diocese* (Paihia, 1842)

Selwyn, G.A. *A Charge delivered to the Clergy of the Diocese of New Zealand at the Diocesan Synod … September 23, 1847* (repr. London, 1849)

*The Journal of Henry Sewell, 1851–7*, ed. W.D. McIntyre, 2 vols (Christchurch, 1980)

Shaw, William. *A Defence of the Wesleyan Missionaries in South Africa: Comprising Copies of a Correspondence with the Rev. Dr John Philip DD* (London, 1839)

Shrewsbury, J.V.B. *Memorials of the Rev. William J. Shrewsbury* (London, 1867, 2nd edn 1868)

[Sierra Leone] *Report from the Committee on the Petition of the Court of Directors of the Sierra Leone Company, PP* (1801–2) 2 (339)

*The Memoirs of the Life of the Reverend Charles Simeon with a Selection from his Writings and Correspondence*, ed. William Carus, 2 vols (London, 1847)

Sinker, R. *Memorials of the Hon. Ion Keith-Falconer* (London, 1888)

Smith, George. *A Narrative of an Exploratory Visit to each of the Consular Cities of China and to the Islands of Hong Kong and Chusan, on behalf of the Church Missionary Society …* (London, 1847)

Smith, George [Bishop of Victoria, Hong Kong]. *Our National Relations with China. Being Two Speeches* (London, 1857)

Smith, George. *The Life of John Wilson, D.D. F.R.S.* (London, 1878)

Smith, H. Maynard. *Frank Bishop of Zanzibar: Life of Frank Weston, D.D., 1871–1924* (London, 1926)

Smith, Reginald Bosworth. *Mohammed and the Mohammedans* (London, 1874)

Smith, Sydney. 'Methodism', *Edinburgh Review*, 11 (1808), 341–62

Southey, Charles Cuthbert (ed.). *The Life and Correspondence of the late Robert Southey*, 6 vols (London, 1849–50)

Spangenberg, A.G. *A Candid Declaration of the Church known by the name of Unitas Fratrum, relative to their labour among the heathen* (London, 1768)

Stewart, Charles Samuel. *Journal of a Residence in the Sandwich Islands, during the years 1823, 1824, and 1825 ... With an Introduction and occasional notes by William Ellis* (London, 1828)

Steere, Edward. *An Historical Sketch of the English Brotherhoods which existed at the beginning of the eighteenth century* (London, 1856)

Steere, Edward. *The Universities' Mission to Central Africa: A Speech delivered at Oxford* (London, 1875)

Stewart, James. *Dawn in the Dark Continent: Or Africa and Its Missions. The Duff Missionary Lectures for 1902* (Edinburgh and London, 1903)

Stock, E. 'The Missionary Element', in Charles E. Harford, *Keswick Convention*, chap. 9

Stock, E. *My Recollections* (London, 1909)

Taylor, J. Hudson. *Days of Blessing in Inland China* (London, 1877).

Thompson, R. Wardlaw. *Griffith John: The Story of Fifty Years in China* (London, 1906; rev. popular edn, London, 1908)

Thompson, R. Wardlaw, and Johnson, Arthur N. *British Foreign Missions 1837–1897* (London, 1899)

Tucker, H.W. *Memoir of the Life and Episcopate of George Augustus Selwyn, D.D.*, 2 vols (London, 1879)

Turner, F.S. *British Opium Policy and Its Results in India and China* (London, 1876)

*Journal of Voyages and Travels by the Rev. Daniel Tyerman and George Bennett*, ed. James Montgomery, 2 vols (London, 1831)

Underhill, E.B. *The West Indies: Their Social and Religious Condition* (London, 1862)

Vaughan, James. *The Trident, the Crescent, and the Cross: A View of the Religious History of India ...* (London, 1876)

Venn, Henry. *Retrospect and Prospect of the Operations of the Church Missionary Society 1865* (London, 1865)

Venn, Henry. *The Native Pastorate and Organization of Native Churches* (London, n.d.)

von Kotzebue, O.E. *A New Voyage round the World in the years 1823, 24, 25 and 26*, 2 vols (London, 1830)

W., G., and Russell, E.F. (eds) *The Life of Charles Alan Smythies*, 2nd edn (London, 1899)

Waddell, H.M. *Twenty-nine Years in the West Indies and Central Africa, 1829–58* (London, 1963 edn)

*Anecdotes of the Life of Richard Watson, Bishop of Llandaff; Written by Himself at Different Intervals, and Revised in 1814* (London, 1817)

Wells, James. *Stewart of Lovedale: The Life of James Stewart* (London, 1909)

Weston, Frank. *Ecclesia Anglicana: For What Does She Stand?* (Zanzibar, 1913)

Wherry, E.M., Zwemer, S.M., and Mylrea, C.G. (eds) *Islam and Missions. Being Papers read at the Second Missionary Conference on behalf of the Mohammedan World at Lucknow, January 23–28, 1911* (London, 1911)

Wilberforce, R.I., and Wilberforce, S. *The Life of William Wilberforce*, 5 vols (London, 1838)

Wilberforce, Samuel. *Speeches on Missions*, ed. Henry Rowley (London, 1874)

Williams, John. *A Narrative of Missionary Enterprises in the South Sea Islands* (London, 1837)

Willison, John. *The Balm of Gilead, for healing a Diseased Land; ... And a Scripture Prophecy of the Increase of Christ's Kingdom, and the Destruction of Antichrist* (Dundee, 1742; Glasgow, 1765, etc.)

Wilson, Daniel. *Humiliation in National Troubles. A Sermon by the Bishop of Calcutta, delivered Friday, July 24th, 1857* (Calcutta, 1857)

Wordsworth, Christopher. *The Mohammedan Woe and Its Passing Away. A Sermon* (London, 1876)

Wordsworth, Christopher. 'The Decline of Mohammedanism a Signal for a greater spread of the Gospel; which will be to some a Woe', in *Miscellanies Literary and Religious*, 3 vols (London, 1879), Vol. 3, 100–16

*World Missionary Conference 1910: Reports of Commissions*, 9 vols (Edinburgh, London and New York, 1910)

Wyld, J. *An Atlas of Maps of different parts of the World designed to show the Stations of the Protestant Missionaries* (London, 1839)

## Secondary books and articles

Adams, Peter. *Fatal Necessity: British Intervention in New Zealand, 1830–1847* (Auckland and Oxford, 1977)

Ajayi, J.F. Ade. 'Henry Venn and the Policy of Development', *Journal of the Historical Society of Nigeria* 1 (1959), 331–42

Ajayi, J.F. Ade. *Christian Missions in Nigeria 1841–1891: The Making of a New Elite* (London, 1965)

Anstey, Roger. *The Atlantic Slave Trade and British Abolition, 1760–1810* (London, 1975)

Armitage, David. *The Ideological Origins of the British Empire* (Cambridge, 2000)

Austen, Ralph A., and Smith, Woodruff D. 'Images of Africa and British Slave Trade Abolition: The Transition to an Imperialist Ideology', *African Historical Studies* 2 (1969), 63–89

Axtell, James. *The Invasion Within: The Contest of Cultures in Colonial North America* (New York and Oxford, 1985)

Ayandele, E.A. *The Missionary Impact on Modern Nigeria 1842–1914* (London, 1966)

Ayandele, E.A. 'The relations between the Church Missionary Society and the Royal Niger Company, 1886–1900', *JHSN* 4 (1968), 399–418

Ballhatchet, Kenneth. *Race, Sex and Class under the Raj: Imperial Attitudes and Politics and Their Critics, 1793–1905* (London, 1980)

Bayly, C.A. *Imperial Meridian: The British Empire and the World, 1780–1830* (London, 1989)

Bayly, Susan B. *Saints Goddesses and Kings: Muslims and Christians in South Indian Society* (Cambridge, 1989)

Bayly, Susan. 'The Evolution of Colonial Cultures: Nineteenth-Century Asia', in Andrew Porter (ed.), *OHBE Vol. 3: The Nineteenth Century* (Oxford, 1999), pp. 447–69

Bebbington, David W. *Evangelicalism in Modern Britain* (London, 1988)

Bebbington, David W. 'The Advent Hope in British Evangelicalism since 1800', *Scottish Journal of Religious Studies* 9, 2 (1988)

Bebbington, David W. *Holiness in Nineteenth-Century England* (Carlisle, 2000)

Beck, Roger B. 'Cape Colonial Officials and Christian Missionaries in the Early Nineteenth Century', in Holger Bernt Hansen and Michael Twaddle (eds), *Christian Missionaries and the State in the Third World* (Oxford and Athens, GA, 2001), 76–86.

Bediako, Kwame. *Christianity in Africa: The Renewal of a Non-Western Religion* (Edinburgh, 1995)

Beidelman, Thomas O. 'Social Theory and the Study of Christian Missions in Africa', *Africa* 44 (1974), 235–49

Beidelman, Thomas O. 'Contradictions between the Sacred and the Secular Life: The Church Missionary Society in Ukaguru, Tanzania, East Africa, 1876–1914', *CSSH* 23 (1981), 73–95

Beidelman, Thomas O. *Colonial Evangelism: A Socio-Historical Study of an East African Mission at the Grassroots* (Bloomington, 1982)

Belich, James. *Making Peoples: A History of the New Zealanders From Polynesian Settlement to the End of the Nineteenth Century* (Auckland and London, 1996)

Bell, G.K.A. *Randall Davidson Archbishop of Canterbury*, 3rd edn (London, 1952)

Bennett, Clinton. *Victorian Images of Islam* (London, 1992)

Bennett, J. Harry. *Bondsmen and Bishops: Slavery and Apprenticeship on the Codrington Plantation of Barbados, 1710–1838* (Berkeley, 1958)

Bickers, Robert. 'Alexander Wylie (1815–1887)', *ODNB* (forthcoming, Oxford, 2004).

Binfield, Clyde. *George Williams and the Y.M.C.A.: A Study in Victorian Social Attitudes* (London, 1973)

Binney, Judith. 'Whatever Happened to Poor Mr Yate? An Exercise in Voyeurism', *New Zealand Journal of History* 9, 2 (1975), 111–25

Birtwhistle, N.A. 'Methodist Missions', in R. Davies, G. Rupp, and A.R. George (eds), *A History of the Methodist Church of Great Britain*, Vol. 3 (London, 1983), 1–116

Blackburn, Robin. *The Overthrow of Colonial Slavery, 1776–1848* (London and New York, 1988)

Bloch, Ruth H. *Visionary Republic: Millennial Themes in American Thought, 1756–1800* (Cambridge, 1985)

Bohr, P.R. *Famine in China and the Missionary: Timothy Richard as Relief Administrator and Advocate of National Reform, 1876–1884* (Cambridge, MA, 1972)

Bolt, Christine. *Victorian Attitudes to Race* (London, 1971)

Bonk, Jonathan. *The Theory and Practice of Missionary Identification, 1860–1920* (New York, 1989)

Bonomi, Patricia U. *Under the Cope of Heaven: Religion, Society and Politics in Colonial America* (Oxford and New York, 1986)

Bowie, Fiona, Kirkwood, Deborah, and Ardener, Shirley (eds). *Women and Missions: Past and Present. Anthropological and Historical Perceptions* (Providence and Oxford, 1993)

Bredekamp, Henry, and Ross, Robert (eds). *Missions and Christianity in South African History* (Johannesburg, 1995)

Breen, Louise A. 'Praying with the Enemy: Daniel Gookin, King Philip's War and the Dangers of Intercultural Mediatorship', in Martin Daunton and Rick Halpern (eds), *Empire and Others: British Encounters with Indigenous Peoples, 1600–1850* (London, 1999), 101–22

Breward, Ian. *A History of the Churches in Australia* (Oxford, 2001)

Bridenbaugh, Carl. *Mitre and Sceptre: Transatlantic Faiths, Ideas, Personalities and Politics, 1689–1775* (New York, 1962)

Brock, Peggy. *Outback Ghettos: Aborigines, Institutionalization and Survival* (Cambridge, 1993)

Brock, Peggy. 'Mission Encounters in the Colonial World: British Columbia and South-West Australia', *Journal of Religious History* 24, 2 (2000), 159–79

Broomhall, A.J. *Hudson Taylor and China's Open Century*, 7 vols (Sevenoaks, 1981–89)

Broomhall, M. *W.W. Cassels First Bishop in Western China* (London, 1926)

Brown, P.R.L. *The Rise of Western Christendom*, 2nd edn (Oxford, 1997)

Bundy, David. 'The Development of Models of Missions in Methodism during the Early American Republic with Attention to the Antecedents of the Holiness Movement', *NAMP Position Paper 48* (Cambridge, 1997)

Butler, Jon. *Awash in a Sea of Faith: Christianizing the American People* (Cambridge, MA, and London, 1990)

Cairns, H. Alan C. *Prelude to Imperialism: British Reactions to Central African Society, 1840–1890* (London, 1965)

Carey, Hilary M. '"The debt of justice": Aborigines, Missions and the Humanitarians 1830–1845', *NAMP Symposium Paper* (Boston, 1998)

Carson, P.S.E. 'An Imperial Dilemma: The Propagation of Christianity in Early Colonial India', *JICH* 18, 2 (1990), 169–90

Casson, John. '"To Plant a Garden City in the Slums of Paganism": Handley Hooper and the Future of Africa', *JRA* 28 (1998), 387–410

Cell, John. 'The Imperial Conscience', in Peter Marsh (ed.), *The Conscience of the Victorian State* (Syracuse, 1979), 173–213

Chadwick, Owen. *Mackenzie's Grave* (London, 1959)

Chadwick, Owen. *The Victorian Church*, Vol. 1 (3rd edn, London, 1971), and Vol. 2 (2nd edn, London, 1972)

Chambers, D. 'The Church of Scotland's Nineteenth Century Foreign Missions Scheme: Evangelical or Moderate Revival?', *Journal of Religious History* 9, 2 (1976), 115–38

Chen, Jerome. *China and the West: Society and Culture 1815–1937* (London, 1979)

Christensen, Torben, and Hutchison, W.R. (eds) *Missionary Ideologies in the Imperialist Era 1880–1920* (Copenhagen, 1982)

Clements, Keith. *Faith on the Frontier: A Life of J.H. Oldham* (Edinburgh and Geneva, 1999)

Cnattingius, H. *Bishops and Societies: A Study of Anglican Colonial and Missionary Expansion, 1698–1850* (London, 1952)

Coates, P.D. *The China Consuls: British Consular Officers, 1843–1943* (Hong Kong, 1988)

Cohen, Paul. *China and Christianity: The Missionary Movement and the Growth of Chinese Antiforeignism, 1860–1870* (Cambridge, MA, 1963)

Cohen, Paul. 'Christian Missions and Their Impact to 1900', in J.K. Fairbank (ed.), *The Cambridge History of China*, Vol. 10 (Cambridge, 1978)

Cohn, Bernard S. 'The Command of Language and the Language of Command', in Ranajit Guha (ed.), *Subaltern Studies* 4 (Delhi, 1985), 276–329

Comaroff, Jean and John. *Of Revelation and Revolution*, 2 vols (Chicago, 1991 and 1997)

Comaroff, Jean and John. *Of Revelation and Revolution*, Vol. 1, 'Book Feature', *SAHJ* 31 (1994), 273–309

Coupland, Reginald. *Wilberforce* (Oxford, 1923)

Cox, Jeffrey. 'Independent English Women in Delhi and Lahore, 1860–1947', in R.W. Davis and R.J. Helmstadter (eds), *Religion and Irreligion in Victorian Society* (London, 1992), 166–84

Cox, Jeffrey. 'George Alfred Lefroy: Anglicans, Untouchables, and Imperial Institutions', in Susan Pedersen and Peter Mandler (eds), *After the Victorians: Essays in Honour of John Clive* (London, 1994), 55–76

Cox, Jeffrey. 'Religion and Imperial Power in Nineteenth-Century Britain', in R.W. Davis and R.J. Helmstadter (eds), *Freedom and Religion in the Nineteenth Century* (Palo Alto, 1997), 339–72, 424–8

Cox, Jeffrey. *Imperial Faultlines: Christianity and Colonial Power in India, 1818–1940* (Stanford, 2002)

Cracknell, Kenneth. *Justice, Courtesy, and Love: Missionaries and Theologians Encountering the World Religions, 1846–1914* (London, 1995)

Curtin, Philip D. *The Image of Africa: British Ideas and Action, 1780–1850* (London, 1965)

Cuthbertson, Greg. 'Preaching Imperialism: Wesleyan Methodism and the War', in David Omissi and Andrew Thompson (eds), *The Impact of the South African War* (Basingstoke, 2002), 157–72

Cuthbertson, Greg. 'Pricking the "nonconformist conscience": Religion against the South African War', in Donal Lowry (ed.), *The South African War Reappraised* (Manchester, 2000), 169–87

Da Costa, Emilia Viotti. *Crowns of Glory, Tears of Blood: The Demerara Slave Rebellion of 1823* (New York and Oxford, 1994)

Darch, John H. 'The Church Missionary Society and the Governors of Lagos, 1862–72', *JEccH* 52, 2 (2001), 313–33

Davidson, Allan K. *Evangelicals & Attitudes to India, 1786–1813: Missionary Publicity and Claudius Buchanan* (Sutton Courtenay, 1990)

Davies, Ronald E. 'Jonathan Edwards and His Influence on the Development of the Missionary Movement from Britain', *NAMP Position Paper 6* (Cambridge, 1996)

Davis, David Brion. *The Problem of Slavery in Western Culture* (Harmondsworth, 1966 Penguin edition, 1970)

Davis, David Brion. *Slavery and Human Progress* (New York, 1984)

Daw, E.D. *Church and State in the Empire: The Evolution of Imperial Policy 1846–1856* (Canberra, 1977)

De Jong, J.A. *As the Waters Cover the Sea. Millennial Expectations in the Rise of Anglo-American Missions 1640–1810* (Kampen, 1970)

De Kock, Leon. *Civilizing Barbarians: Missionary Narrative and African Textual Response in Nineteenth-Century South Africa* (Johannesburg, 1996)

De Silva, K.M. *Social Policy and Missionary Organizations in Ceylon, 1840–1855* (London, 1965)

Dening, Greg. *Islands and Beaches: Discourse on a Silent Land: Marquesas 1774–1880* (Honolulu, 1980; repr. Chicago, 1988)

Doll, Peter M. *Revolution, Reaction, and National Identity. Imperial Anglicanism in British North America, 1745–1795* (Madison and London, 2000)

Donaldson, Margaret. 'Missionaries and the Liberation of Women: A Case Study from South Africa', *Journal of Theology for Southern Africa* 53 (1985), 4–12

Donaldson, Margaret. 'The Invisible Factor: Nineteenth Century Feminist Evangelical Concern for Human Rights', *Journal for the Study of Religion* 2, 2 (1989), 3–15

Douglas, Bronwen. 'Encounters with the Enemy? Academic Readings of Missionary Narratives on Melanesians', *CSSH* 43, 1 (2001), 37–64

Drayton, Richard. *Nature's Government: Science, Imperial Britain, and the 'Improvement' of the World* (New Haven and London, 2000)

Du Plessis, J. *A History of Christian Missions in South Africa* (London, 1911)

Ekechi, F.K. *Missionary Enterprise and Rivalry in Igboland, 1857–1914* (London, 1972)

Ekechi, F.K. 'Studies on Missions in Africa', in Toyin Falola (ed.), *African Historiography. Essays in Honour of Jacob Ade Ajayi* (Harlow, 1993), 145–65

Elbourne, Elizabeth. 'The Foundation of the Church Missionary Society: The Anglican Missionary Impulse', in John Walsh, Colin Haydon and Stephen Taylor (eds), *The Church of England c.1689–c.1833* (Cambridge, 1993), 247–64

Elbourne, Elizabeth. 'Freedom at Issue: Vagrancy Legislation and the Meaning of Freedom in Britain and the Cape Colony, 1799 to 1842', *Slavery and Abolition* 15, 2 (1994), 114–50

Elbourne, Elizabeth. *Blood Ground: Colonialism, Missions, and the Contest for Christianity in the Cape Colony and Britain, 1799–1853* (Montreal and London, 2002)

Elliott-Binns, L.E. *Religion in the Victorian Era* (London, 1936)

Elphick, Richard. 'Africans and the Christian Campaign in South Africa', in H. Lamar and L.M. Thompson (eds), *The Frontier in History: North America and Southern Africa Compared* (New Haven, 1981), 270–307

Elphick, Richard. 'Evangelical Missions and Racial "Equalization" in South Africa, 1890–1914', *NAMP Symposium Paper* (Boston, 1998)

Elphick, Richard, and Giliomee, Hermann (eds). *The Shaping of South African Society 1652–c.1840* (Cape Town and Middletown, CT, 1989)

Elphick, Richard, and Davenport, Rodney (comp. and eds). *Christianity in South Africa: A Political, Social and Cultural History* (Oxford and Cape Town, 1997)

Embree, A.T. *Charles Grant and British Rule in India* (London, 1963)

Embree, A.T. 'Christianity and the State in Victorian India: Confrontation and Collaboration', in R.W. Davis and R.J. Helmstadter (eds), *Religion and Irreligion in Victorian Society: Essays in honour of R.K. Webb* (London, 1992), 151–65

Enklaar, Ido H. *Life and Work of Dr. J.Th. Van Der Kemp, 1747–1811: Missionary Pioneer and Protagonist of Racial Equality in South Africa* (Cape Town and Rotterdam, 1988)

Etherington, Norman. 'An American Errand into the South African Wilderness', *Church History* 39 (1970), 62–71

Etherington, Norman. 'Gender Issues in South-East African Missions, 1835–85', in Henry Bredekamp and Robert Ross (eds), *Missions and Christianity in South African History* (Johannesburg, 1995), 135–52

Etherington, Norman. 'Missions and Empire', in Robin W. Winks (ed.), *OHBE Vol. 5 Historiography* (Oxford, 1999), 303–14

Feldman, David. *Englishmen and Jews: Social Relations and Political Culture, 1840–1914* (New Haven, 1994)

Fiedler, Klaus. *The Story of Faith Missions* (Oxford, 1994)

Findlay, G.G., and Holdsworth, W.W. *The History of the Wesleyan Methodist Missionary Society*, 5 vols (London, 1921)

Fingard, Judith. *The Anglican Design in Loyalist Nova Scotia, 1783–1816* (London, 1972)

Fisch, Jorg. 'A Pamphlet War on Christian Missions in India, 1807–1809', *Journal of Asian History* 19 (1985), 22–70

Fisher, Humphrey. 'Conversion Reconsidered: Some Historical Aspects of Religious Conversion in Black Africa', *Africa* 43, 1 (1973), 27–40

Fitzgerald, Rosemary. 'A "peculiar and exceptional measure": The Call for Women Medical Missionaries for India in the Later Nineteenth Century', in Robert A. Bickers and Rosemary Seton (eds), *Missionary Encounters: Sources and Issues* (London, 1996), 174–96

Fletcher, R.A. *The Conversion of Europe: From Paganism to Christianity, 371–1386 AD* (London, 1997)

Forrester, Duncan. *Caste and Christianity: Attitudes and Policies on Caste of Anglo-Saxon Protestant Missionaries in India* (London, 1980)

France, W.F. *The Oversea Episcopate: Centenary History of the Colonial Bishoprics Fund, 1841–1941* (London, 1941)

Francis-Dehqani, Guli. 'CMS Women Missionaries in Persia: Perceptions of Muslim Women and Islam, 1884–1934', in Kevin Ward and Brian Stanley (eds), *The Church Mission Society and World Christianity, 1799–1999* (Grand Rapids and Richmond, 2000), 91–119

Fyfe, Christopher. *A History of Sierra Leone* (Oxford, 1962)

Gaitskell, Deborah. 'Rethinking Gender Roles: The Field Experience of Women Missionaires in South Africa', in Andrew Porter (ed.), *The Imperial Horizons of British Protestant Missions, 1880–1914* (Grand Rapids and Richmond, 2003), 131–57

Gallagher, J. 'Fowell Buxton and the New African Policy, 1838–42', *Cambridge Historical Journal* 10 (1950), 36–58

Garrett, John. *To Live Among the Stars: Christian Origins in Oceania* (Geneva and Suva, 1982)

Gascoigne, John. *Science in the Service of Empire: Joseph Banks, the British State, and the Uses of Science in the Age of Revolution* (Cambridge, 1988)

Gavin, R.J. 'The Bartle Frere Mission to Zanzibar, 1873', *HJ* 5, 2 (1962), 122–48

Gbadamosi, T.G.O. *The Growth of Islam among the Yoruba, 1841–1908* (London, 1978)

Gernet, Jacques. *China and the Christian Impact* (Paris, 1982; English trans, Cambridge, 1985)

Gidney, W.T. *The History of the London Society for Promoting Christianity among the Jews from 1809 to 1908* (London, 1908)

Gill, Sean. *Women and the Church of England from the Eighteenth Century to the Present* (London, 1994)

Goodall, Norman. *A History of the London Missionary Society 1895–1945* (Oxford, 1954)

Gow, Bonar A. *Madagascar and the Protestant Impact: The Work of the British Missions, 1818–95* (London, 1979)

Grant, Kevin. 'Christian Critics of Empire: Missionaries, Lantern Lectures, and the Congo Reform Campaign in Britain', *JICH* 29, 2 (2001), 27–58

Gray, Richard. 'Christianity', in A.D. Roberts (ed.), *The Cambridge History of Africa Vol. 7 1905–1940* (Cambridge, 1986)

Gray, Richard. *Black Christians, White Missionaries* (New Haven and London, 1990)

Green, W.A. 'The Creolization of Caribbean History', *JICH* 14, 3 (1986), 149–69

Greenhalgh, Paul. *Ephemeral Vistas: The Expositions Universelles, Great Exhibitions and World's Fairs, 1851–1939* (Manchester, 1988)

Greenlee, James G., and Johnston, Charles M. *Good Citizens: British Missionaries and Imperial States, 1870–1918* (Montreal, 1999)

Griffiths, Tudor. 'Bishop Alfred Tucker and the Establishment of a British Protectorate in Uganda 1890–94', *JRA* 31 (2001), 92–114

Grimshaw, Patricia. *Paths of Duty: American Missionary Wives in Nineteenth-Century Hawaii* (Honolulu, 1989)

Groves, Charles P. *The Planting of Christianity in Africa*, 4 vols (London, 1948–58)

Grunder, Horst. 'Christian Missionary Activities in Africa in the Age of Imperialism and the Berlin Conference of 1884–1885', in Stig Forster, Wolfgang J. Mommsen, and Ronald Robinson (eds), *Bismarck, Europe, and Africa: The Berlin Africa Conference 1884–1885 and the Onset of Partition* (Oxford and London, 1988), 85–103

Guenther, Alan. 'Controversy as a "Necessary Evil"? Perspectives on Missions to Muslims in India in the Late Nineteenth Century', *NAMP Position Paper 82* (Cambridge 1998)

Guenther, Alan. 'Changing Perceptions of Islam: Thomas Patrick Hughes as Missionary and Scholar', *NAMP Symposium Paper* (Boston, 1998)

Guenther, Alan. 'The Image of the Prophet as Found in Missionary Writings of the Late Nineteenth Century', *The Muslim World* 90, 1–2 (2000), 43–70

Gunson, Niel. *Messengers of Grace: Evangelical Missionaries in the South Seas 1797–1860* (Melbourne, 1978)

Gutch, John. *Martyr of the Islands: The Life and Death of John Coleridge Patteson* (London, 1971)

Guy, Jeff. *The Heretic: A Study of the Life of John William Colenso 1814–1883* (Johannesburg and Pietermaritzburg, 1983).

Hall, Catherine. 'White Visions, Black Lives: The Free Villages of Jamaica', *History Workshop* 36 (1993), 100–32

Hall, Catherine. *Civilising Subjects: Metropole and Colony in the English Imagination, 1830–1867* (Cambridge, 2002)

Handy, Robert T. *A History of the Churches in the United States and Canada* (Oxford, 1976)

Hanna, A.J. *The Beginnings of Nyasaland and North-Eastern Rhodesia, 1859–95* (Oxford, 1956)

Hansen, Holger Bernt. 'European Ideas, Colonial Attitudes and African Realities: The Introduction of a Church Constitution in Uganda, 1898–1909', *IJAHS* 13, 2 (1980), 240–80

Hansen, Holger Bernt. *Mission, Church and State in a Colonial Setting: Uganda 1890–1925* (London, 1984)

Hansen, Holger Bernt, and Twaddle, Michael (eds). *Christian Missionaries and the State in the Third World* (Oxford and Athens, GA, 2001)

Harlow, Vincent T. *The Founding of the Second British Empire, 1763–1793*, 2 vols (London, 1952, 1964)

Harper, Susan Billington. *In the Shadow of the Mahatma: Bishop V.S. Azariah and the Travails of Christianity in British India* (Grand Rapids and Richmond, 2000)

Harris, Paul W. *Nothing but Christ: Rufus Anderson and the Ideology of Protestant Foreign Missions* (Oxford and New York, 1999)

Harrison, Brian. *Waiting for China: The Anglo-Chinese College at Malacca, 1818–1843, and Early Nineteenth-Century Missions* (Hong Kong, 1979)

Harrison, J.F.C. *The Second Coming: Popular Millenarianism 1780–1850* (London, 1979)

Hastings, Adrian. *A History of African Christianity, 1950–1975* (Cambridge, 1979)

Hastings, Adrian. *The Church in Africa 1450–1950* (Oxford, 1994)

Helly, Dorothy O. *Livingstone's Legacy: Horace Waller and Victorian Mythmaking* (Athens, OH, 1987)

Hempton, David. 'Evangelicalism and Eschatology', *JEccH* 31, 1 (1980), 179–94

Hempton, David. *Religion and Political Culture in Britain and Ireland* (Cambridge, 1996)

Hempton, David. *Religion of the People: Methodism and Popular Religion, c.1750–1900* (London, 1996)

Hennel, Michael. *John Venn and the Clapham Sect* (London, 1958)

Hertzler, James R. 'English Baptists Interpret Continental Mennonites in the Early Nineteenth Century', *Mennonite Quarterly Review* 54, 1 (1980), 42–52

Heuman, Gad. *'The Killing Time': The Morant Bay Rebellion in Jamaica* (London, 1994)

Hewat, Elizabeth G.K. *Vision and Achievement, 1796–1956: A History of the Foreign Missions of the Churches united in the Church of Scotland* (Edinburgh and London, 1960)

Hewitt, Gordon. *The Problems of Success: A History of the Church Missionary Society 1910–1942*, 2 vols (London, 1977)

Hilliard, David. *God's Gentlemen: A History of the Melanesian Mission* (St Lucia, 1978)

Hilton, Boyd. *The Age of Atonement: The Influence of Evangelicalism on Social and Economic Thought, 1785–1865* (Oxford, 1988)

Hinsley, F.H. (ed.) *Material Progress and World-Wide Problems, 1870–1898: New Cambridge Modern History* 11 (Cambridge, 1976 edition )

Hinchliff, Peter. 'The English Speaking Churches and South Africa in the Nineteenth Century', *Journal of Theology for Southern Africa* 9 (1974), 28–38

Hodacs, Hanna. *Converging World Views: The European Expansion and Early-Nineteenth-Century Anglo-Swedish Contacts* (Uppsala, 2003)

Hodgson, Janet. 'Mission and Empire: A Case Study of Convergent Ideologies in Nineteenth-Century Southern Africa', *Journal of Theology for Southern Africa* 38 (1982), 34–48

Hodgson, Janet. 'A Battle for Sacred Power: Christian Beginnings among the Xhosa', in Richard Elphick and Rodney Davenport (eds), *Christianity in South Africa: A Political, Social and Cultural History* (Oxford and Cape Town, 1997), 68–88

Hole, Charles. *The Early History of the Church Missionary Society for Africa and the East to the end of A.D. 1814* (London, 1896)

Holt, Thomas C. *The Problem of Freedom: Race, Labor, and Politics in Jamaica and Britain, 1832–1938* (Baltimore, 1992)

Holtrop, Pieter N., and McLeod, Hugh (eds). *Missions and Missionaries. Studies in Church History Subsidia 13* (Woodbridge, 2000)

Holway, James D. 'C.M.S. Contact with Islam in East Africa before 1914', *Journal of Religion in Africa* 4 (1971–72), 200–12

Hopkins, C. Howard. *John R. Mott, 1865–1955: A Biography* (Grand Rapids, 1979)

Horton, Robin. 'Conversion', *Africa* 41, 2 (1971), 85–108

Horton, Robin. 'On the Rationality of Conversion', 2 parts, *Africa* 45, 3–4 (1975), 219–35, 373–99

Howe, Stephen. *Ireland and Empire: Colonial Legacies in Irish History and Culture* (Oxford, 2000)

Hutchison, William R. *Errand to the World: American Protestant Thought and Foreign Missions* (Chicago, 1987)

Hyam, Ronald. *Empire and Sexuality: The British Experience* (Manchester, 1990)

Hyam, Ronald. *Britain's Imperial Century, 1815–1914: A Study of Empire and Expansion*, 3rd edn (Basingstoke and New York, 2002)

Ingham, Kenneth. *Reformers in India, 1793–1833: An Account of the Work of Christian Missionaries on Behalf of Social Reform* (Cambridge, 1956)

Ingleby, J.C. *Missionaries, Education and India: Issues in Protestant Missionary Education in the Long Nineteenth Century* (Delhi, 2000)

Isichei, Elizabeth. *A History of Christianity in Africa* (Grand Rapids, 1995).

Isichei, Elizabeth. 'Does Christianity Empower Women? The Case of the Anaguta of Central Nigeria', in Fiona Bowie, Deborah Kirkwood and Shirley Ardener (eds), *Women and Missions: Past and Present. Anthropological and Historical Perceptions* (Providence and Oxford, 1993), 209–28

Jakobsson, Stiv. *Am I Not a Man and a Brother? British Missions and the Abolition of the Slave Trade and Slavery in West Africa and the West Indies, 1786–1838* (Uppsala, 1972)

Jeal, Tim. *Livingstone* (London, 1973)

Jenkins, Paul (ed.) *The Recovery of the West African Past: African Pastors and African History in the Nineteenth Century: C.C. Reindorf and Samuel Johnson* (Basel, 1998)

Jenkins, Paul. 'The Church Missionary Society and the Basel Mission: An Early Experiment in Inter-European Cooperation', in Kevin Ward and Brian Stanley (eds), *The Church Mission Society and World Christianity 1799–1999* (Grand Rapids and Richmond, 2000), 43–65

Jeyasekeran, T. Ambrose. 'William Miller and the Meaning of Christian Education in India', *BSIMS*, n.s. 4–5 (1988–89), 42–53

Joll, James. *Europe Since 1870* (Harmondsworth, 1976 edn)

Jones, K.W. *Socio-Religious Reform Movements in British India* (Cambridge, 1989)

Kass A.M. and E.H. *Perfecting the World: The Life and Times of Dr Thomas Hodgkin, 1798–1866* (Boston and New York, 1988)

Keegan, Timothy. *Colonial South Africa and the Origins of the Racial Order* (London, 1996)

Kellaway, William. *The New England Company, 1649–1776: Missionary Society to the American Indians* (London, 1961)

Kent, John. *Holding the Fort: Studies in Victorian Revivalism* (London, 1978)

Killingray, David. 'The Black Atlantic Missionary Movement and Africa, 1780–1920s', *Journal of Religion in Africa* 33, 1 (2003), 3–31

Kitzan, Laurence. 'The London Missionary Society and the Problem of Authority in India, 1798–1833', *Church History* 40 (1971), 457–73

Klingberg, Frank J. *Anglican Humanitarianism in Colonial New York* (Philadelphia, 1940)

Knox, R.A. *Enthusiasm: A Chapter in the History of Religion with Special Reference to the XVII and XVIII Centuries* (Oxford, 1950; repr. 1959)

Kooiman, Dick. 'The Gospel of Coffee: Mission, Education and Employment in Travancore (19th Century)', in Kooiman, Otto van den Muijzenberg and Peter van der Veer (eds), *Conversion, Competition and Conflict: Essays on the Role of Religion in Asia* (Amsterdam, 1984), 185–214

Kooiman, Dick. 'Mass Movement, Famine and Epidemic. A Study in Interrelationship', *ICHR* 22, 2 (1988), 109–25

Koskinen, Aarne A. *Missionary Influence as a Political Factor in the Pacific Islands* (Helsinki, 1953)

Koss, Stephen. 'Wesleyanism and Empire', *HJ* 18, 1 (1975), 105–18

Kwok Pui-Lan. 'The Image of the "White Lady": Gender and Race in Christian Mission', in Anne Carr and Elizabeth Schussler Fiorenza (eds), *The Special Nature of Women?* (London and Philadelphia, 1991)

Lagergren, David. *Mission and State in the Congo … 1885–1903* (Uppsala, 1970)

Laird, M.A. *Missionaries and Education in Bengal, 1793–1837* (Oxford, 1972)

Landau, Paul S. *The Realm of the Word. Language, Gender, and Christianity in a Southern African Kingdom* (London, 1995)

Landes, David. *The Wealth and Poverty of Nations* (New York and London, 1998)

Langmore, Diane. *Missionary Lives: Papua, 1874–1914* (Honolulu, 1989)

Laracy, H. 'Selwyn in Pacific Perspective', in Warren E. Limbrick (ed.), *Bishop Selwyn in New Zealand 1841–68* (Palmerston North, 1983), 121–35

Latourette, Kenneth S. *A History of Christian Missions in China* (London, 1929)

Latourette, Kenneth S. *A History of the Expansion of Christianity*, 7 vols (London, 1937–45)

Latourette, Kenneth S. *Christianity in a Revolutionary Age*, 5 vols (New York, 1957–61)

Lee, Joseph Tse-Hei. *The Bible and the Gun: Christianity in South China, 1868–1900* (New York, 2002)

Lewis, James. *William Goudie* (London, 1923)

Lloyd, T.O. *The British Empire, 1558–1995* (Oxford, 1996)

Lovett, Richard. *The History of the London Missionary Society 1795–1895*, 2 vols (London, 1895)

Low, D.A. 'British Public Opinion and the Uganda Question, October–December 1892', *Uganda Journal* 18, 2 (1954), 81–100

Low, D.A. *Lion Rampant. Essays in the History of British Imperialism* (London, 1974), chap. 4 'Empire and Christianity'

Lowe, Kate. 'The Beliefs, Aspirations and Methods of the First Missionaries in British Hong Kong, 1841–5', in Pieter N. Holtrop and Hugh McLeod (eds), *Missions and Missionaries. Studies in Church History Subsidia 13* (Woodbridge, 2000), 50–64.

Lowry, Donal. '"The Boers were the beginning of the end"? The Wider Impact of the South African War', in Donal Lowry (ed.), *The South African War Reappraised* (Manchester, 2000)

Ludwig, Frieder. 'The Making of a Late Victorian Missionary [J.A. Robinson]', *Neue Zeitschrift für Missionswissenschaft* 47, 4 (1991), 269–90

Lynn, Martin. 'Commerce, Christianity and the Origins of the "Creoles" of Fernando Po', *Journal of African History* 25 (1984), 257–78

McCracken, John. *Politics and Christianity in Malawi 1875–1940: The Impact of the Livingstonia Mission in the Northern Province*, 2nd edn (Blantyre, 2000)

McIntyre, W. David. *The Imperial Frontier in the Tropics, 1865–75* (London, 1967)

McLeod, Hugh. *Religion and the People of Western Europe, 1789–1970* (Oxford, 1981)

Macmillan, W.M. *The Cape Colour Question: A Historical Survey* (London, 1927)

Macmillan, W.M. *Bantu, Boer and Briton: The Making of the South African Native Problem*, 2nd edn (Oxford, 1963)

Madden, A.F. *Select Documents on the Constitutional History of the British Empire and Commonwealth, Vol. 1 'The Empire of the Bretaignes', 1175–1688* (Westport, New York, and London, 1985)

Mallampalli, Chandra. 'British Missions and Indian Nationalism, 1880–1908: Imitation and Autonomy in Calcutta and Madras', in Andrew Porter (ed.), *The Imperial Horizons of British Protestant Missions, 1880–1914* (Grand Rapids and Richmond, 2003), 158–82

Mandler, Peter. '"Race" and "Nation" in Mid-Victorian Thought', in S. Collini, R. Whatmore and B. Young (eds), *History, Religion and Culture: British Intellectual History 1750–1950* (Cambridge, 2000), pp. 224–44

Marshall, P.J. (ed.), *The Oxford History of the British Empire Vol. 2 The Eighteenth Century* (Oxford, 1998)

Marshall, P.J. 'Britain without America – A Second Empire?', in (ed.), *OHBE Vol. 2 The Eighteenth Century* (Oxford, 1998), 576–95

Marshall, P.J. 'Presidential Address: Britain and the World in the Eighteenth Century', 4 parts, *Transactions of the Royal Historical Society* 6th Series, 8–11 (1998–2001)

Marshall, P.J. and Williams, Glyndwr. *The Great Map of Mankind: British Perceptions of the World in the Age of Enlightenment* (London, 1982)

Martin, Roger H. *Evangelicals United: Ecumenical Stirrings in Pre-Victorian Britain, 1795–1830* (Metuchen, NJ, and London, 1983)

Mason, J.C.S. *The Moravian Church and the Missionary Awakening in England 1760–1800* (Woodbridge, 2001)

Maughan, Steven. 'Imperial Christianity? Bishop Montgomery and the Foreign Missions of the Church of England, 1895–1915', in Andrew Porter (ed.), *The Imperial Horizons of British Protestant Missions, 1880–1914* (Grand Rapids and Richmond, 2003), 32–57

Maxwell, David (ed.) with Lawrie, Ingrid. *Christianity and the African Imagination: Essays in Honour of Adrian Hastings* (Leiden, 2002)

Maxwell, Ian Douglas. 'Civilization of Christianity? The Scottish Debate on Mission Methods, 1750–1835', in Brian Stanley (ed.), *Christian Missions and the Enlightenment* (Grand Rapids and Richmond, 2001), 123–40

Meek, Donald E. 'Scottish Highlanders, North American Indians and the SSPCK: Some Cultural Perspectives', *Records of the Scottish Church History Society* 23, 3 (1989), 378–96

Menezes, M.N. *British Policy towards the Amerindians in British Guiana 1803–1873* (Oxford, 1977)

Merrell, James H. '"The Customes of Our Countrey": Indians and Colonists in Early America', in Bernard Bailyn and Philip D. Morgan (eds), *Strangers Within the Realm: Cultural Margins of the First British Empire* (Chapel Hill, 1991), 117–56

Mews, Stuart. 'Kikuyu and Edinburgh: The Interaction of Attitudes to Two Conferences', in G.J. Cuming and Derek Baker (eds), *Councils and Assemblies. Studies in Church History* 7 (Cambridge, 1971), 345–59

Meyer, Lysle E. 'T.J. Bowen and Central Africa: A Nineteenth-Century Missionary Delusion', *IJAHS* 15, 2 (1982), 247–60

Miers, Suzanne. *Britain and the Ending of the Slave Trade* (London, 1975)

Mitra, S.K. 'The Vellore Mutiny of 1806 and the Question of Christian Missions to India', *ICHR* 7 (1973), 75–82

Moore, R.J. *Sir Charles Wood's Indian Policy 1853–66* (Manchester, 1966)

Munro, Doug, and Thornley, Andrew. 'Pacific Islander Pastors and Missionaries: Some Historiographical and Analytical Issues', *Pacific Studies* 23, 3/4 (2000), 1–31

Murray, D.J. *The West Indies and the Development of Colonial Government 1801–34* (Oxford, 1965)

Murray, Iain H. *Jonathan Edwards: A New Biography* (Edinburgh, 1987, repr. 1996)

Murray, Jocelyn. *Proclaim the Good News: A Short History of the Church Missionary Society* (London, 1985)

Murray, Jocelyn. 'The Role of Women in the Church Missionary Society, 1799–1917', in Kevin Ward and Brian Stanley (eds), *The Church Mission Society and World Christianity, 1799–1992* (Grand Rapids and Richmond, 2000), 66–90

Murray, Nancy Uhlar. 'Nineteenth Century Kenya and the "Imperial Race for Christ"', in B.A. Ogot (ed.), *Kenya in the Nineteenth Century* (Nairobi, 1985), 228–58

Murre-van den Berg, H.L. 'Why Protestant Churches? The American Board and the Eastern Churches: Mission among "Nominal" Christians (1820–70)', in Pieter N. Holtrop and Hugh McLeod (eds), *Missions and Missionaries. Studies in Church History Subsidia 13* (Woodbridge, 2000), 98–111

Neill, Stephen. *A History of Christian Missions* (2nd edn, Harmondsworth, 1986)

Neill, Stephen. *A History of Christianity in India, 1707–1858* (Cambridge, 1985)

Noll, Mark A., Bebbington, David W., and Rawlyk, George A. *Evangelicalism: Comparative Studies of Popular Protestantism in North America, the British Isles, and Beyond, 1700–1990* (New York and Oxford, 1994)

Norman, E.R. *Church and Society in England 1770–1970: A Historical Study* (Oxford, 1976)

Northrup, David. *Indentured Labour in the Age of Imperialism, 1834–1922* (Cambridge, 1995)

O'Brien, Susan. 'A Transatlantic Community of Saints: The Great Awakening and the First Evangelical Network, 1735–1755', *American Historical Review* 91, 4 (1986), 811–32

O'Brien, Susan. 'Eighteenth-Century Publishing Networks in the First Years of Transatlantic Evangelicalism', in Mark A. Noll, David W. Bebbington and George A. Rawlyk (eds), *Evangelicalism: Comparative Studies of Popular Protestantism in North America, the British Isles, and Beyond, 1700–1990* (New York and Oxford, 1994), 38–57

O'Connor, Daniel. *Gospel, Raj and Swaraj: The Missionary Years of C.F. Andrews 1904–14* (Frankfurt-am-Main, 1990)

O'Connor, Daniel, and others (eds). *Three Centuries of Mission: The United Society for the Propagation of the Gospel 1701–2000* (London and New York, 2000)

Oddie, Geoffrey A. 'India and Missionary Motives, c.1850–1900', *JEccH* 25, 1 (1974), 61–74

Oddie, Geoffrey A. *Social Protest in India: British Protestant Missionaries and Social Reforms 1850–1900* (Delhi, 1979)

Oddie, Geoffrey A. *Hindu and Christian in South-East India* (London, 1991)

Oddie, Geoffrey A. *Missionaries, Rebellion and Proto-Nationalism: James Long of Bengal 1814–87* (Richmond, 1999)

Oldfield, J.R. *Popular Politics and British Anti-Slavery: The Mobilisation of Public Opinion against the Slave Trade, 1787–1807* (London, 1998)

Oliver, Roland. *The Missionary Factor in East Africa* (1952; 2nd edn, London, 1965)

Oliver, Roland. *Sir Harry Johnston and the Scramble for Africa* (London, 1957)

Oliver, W.H. *Prophets and Millennialists: The Uses of Biblical Prophecy in England from the 1790s to the 1840s* (Auckland, 1978)

Olson, Alison. 'The Eighteenth Century Empire: The London Dissenters' Lobbies and the American Colonies', *Journal of American Studies* 26, 1 (1992), 41–58

*One Hundred Years in Delhi: The Brotherhood of the Ascended Christ 1877–1977* (Delhi, 1977)

Pascoe, C.F. *Two Hundred Years of the S.P.G.: An Historical Account of the Society for the Propagation of the Gospel in Foreign Parts, 1701–1900*, 2 vols (London, 1901)

Peel, J.D.Y. 'For Who Hath Despised the Day of Small Things? Missionary Narratives and Historical Anthropology', *CSSH* 37, 3 (1995), 581–607

Peel, J.D.Y. *Religious Encounter and the Making of the Yoruba* (Bloomington, 2000)

Peterson, John. *Province of Freedom: A History of Sierra Leone, 1787–1870* (London, 1969)

Pfister, Lauren. 'Re-thinking Mission in China: James Hudson Taylor and Timothy Richard', in Andrew Porter (ed.), *The Imperial Horizons of British Protestant Missions, 1880–1914* (Grand Rapids and Richmond, 2003), pp. 183–212

Pierard, Richard. 'Significant Currents in German Protestant Missiology', *NAMP/CWC Position Paper 102* (Cambridge, 1998)

Piggin, F.S. *Making Evangelical Missionaries, 1780–1856: The Social Background, Motives and Training of British Missionaries to India* (Appleford, 1981)

Pinnington, John E. 'Common Principles in the Early Years of the Church Missionary Society: The Problem of the "German" Missionaries', *Journal of Theological Studies* 20, 2 (1969), 527–32

Pollock, J.C. *The Keswick Story* (London, 1964)

Porter, Andrew. 'Cambridge, Keswick and Late Nineteenth-Century Attitudes to Africa', *JICH* 6, 1 (1976), 5–34

Porter, Andrew. 'Evangelical Enthusiasm, Missionary Motivation and West Africa in the Late Nineteenth Century: The Career of G.W. Brooke', *JICH* 6 (1977), 23–46

Porter, Andrew. 'Late Nineteenth-Century Anglican Missionary Expansion: A Consideration of Some Non-Anglican Sources of Inspiration', in D. Baker (ed.), *Religious Motivation. Biographical and Sociological Problems for the Church Historian* (Oxford, 1978), 349–65

Porter, Andrew. 'The Hausa Association: Sir George Goldie, the Bishop of Dover, and the Niger in the 1890s', *JICH* 7, 2 (1979), 149–79

Porter, Andrew. '"Commerce and Christianity": The Rise and Fall of a Nineteenth Century Missionary Slogan', *HJ* 28, 3 (1985), 597–621

Porter, Andrew. 'Religion and Empire: British Expansion in the Long Nineteenth Century, 1780–1914'. *JIHC* 20, 3 (1992), 15–31

Porter, Andrew. '"Cultural Imperialism" and Protestant Missionary Enterprise, 1780–1914', *JICH* 25 (1997), 367–91

Porter, Andrew. 'Trusteeship, Anti-Slavery, and Humanitarianism', in Andrew Porter (ed.), *OHBE Vol 3 The Nineteenth Century* (Oxford, 1999), 198–221

Porter, Andrew. 'Religion, Missionary Enthusiasm, and Empire', in Andrew Porter (ed.), *OHBE Vol 3 The Nineteenth Century* (Oxford, 1999), 222–46

Porter, Andrew. 'Language, "Native Agency" and Missionary Control: Rufus Anderson's Journey to India, 1854–5', in Pieter N. Holtrop and Hugh McLeod (eds), *Missions and Missionaries. Studies in Church History Subsidia 13* (Woodbridge, 2000), 81–97

Porter, Andrew (ed.). *The Imperial Horizons of British Protestant Missions, 1880–1914* (Grand Rapids, and Cambridge, 2003)

Porter, Bernard. *The Lion's Share* (3rd edn, London, 1996)

Potts, E.D. *British Baptist Missionaries in India, 1793–1837: The History of Serampore and Its Missions* (Cambridge, 1967)

Powell, Avril A. *Muslims and Missionaries in Pre-Mutiny India* (London, 1993)

Powell, Avril A. 'Processes of Conversion to Christianity in Nineteenth Century North-Western India', in Geoffrey Oddie (ed.), *Religious Conversion Movements in South Asia* (London, 1997)

Powell, Avril A. 'Reciprocities and Divergences Concerning Religious Traditions in Two Families of Scholars in North India', in Jamal Malik (ed.), *Perspectives of Mutual Encounters in South Asian History 1760–1860* (Leiden, 2000), 188–222

Prasch, Thomas. 'Which God for Africa: The Islamic-Christian Missionary Debate in Late-Victorian England', *Victorian Studies* 33, 1 (1989–90), 51–73

Price, Charles, and Randall, Ian. *Transforming Keswick* (Carlisle, 2000)

Prins, Gwyn. *The Hidden Hippotamus. Reappraisal in African History: the Early Colonial Experience in Western Zambia* (Cambridge, 1980)

Raison-Jourde, Françoise. *Bible et Pouvoir à Madagascar au XIXe siècle* (Paris, 1991)

Ranger, Terence. 'White Presence and Power in Africa', *JAH* 20 (1979), 463–9

Ranger, Terence. 'Concluding Summary', in K.H. Petersen (ed.), *Religion, Development and African Identity* (Uppsala, 1987), pp. 145–62

Ranger, Terence. 'Taking Hold of the Land: Holy Places and Pilgrimage in Twentieth Century Zimbabwe', *Past and Present* 117 (1987), 158–94

Richardson, Peter. *Chinese Mine Labour in the Transvaal* (London, 1982)

Robert, Dana. *Occupy until I Come: A.T. Pierson and the Evangelization of the World* (Grand Rapids, 2003)

Roberts, A.D. 'David Livingstone', *The Oxford Dictionary of National Biography* (forthcoming, Oxford, 2004)

Rooy, Sidney H. *The Theology of Missions in the Puritan Tradition: A Study of Representative Puritans: Richard Sibbes, Richard Baxter, John Eliot, Cotton Mather, and Jonathan Edwards* (Delft, 1965)

Ross, Andrew C. 'Scottish Missionary Concern 1874–1914. A Golden Era?', *Scottish Historical Review*, 51 (1971), 52–72

Ross, Andrew C. *John Philip (1775–1851): Missions, Race and Politics in South Africa* (Aberdeen, 1986)

Ross, Andrew C. 'John Philip: Towards a Reassessment', in Hugh Macmillan and Shula Marks (eds), *Africa and Empire: W.M. Macmillan, Historian and Social Critic* (London, 1989), 125–39, 299–305

Ross, Andrew C. *Blantyre Mission and the Making of Modern Malawi* (Blantyre, 1996)

Ross, Andrew C. *David Livingstone: Mission and Empire* (London, 2002)

Ross, Robert. 'James Cropper, John Philip and the Researches in South Africa', in Hugh Macmillan and Shula Marks (eds), *Africa and Empire: W.M. Macmillan, Historian and Social Critic* (London, 1989), 140–52, 302–5

Rouse, Ruth, and Neill, Stephen Charles (eds). *A History of the Ecumenical Movement 1517–1948* (London, 1954)

Rowell, Geoffrey. *Hell and the Victorians: A Study of the Nineteenth-Century Theological Controversies Concerning Eternal Punishment and the Future Life* (Oxford, 1974)

Rutherford, Noel. *Shirley Baker and the King of Tonga* (Melbourne, 1971)

Sachs, William L. *The Transformation of Anglicanism: From State Church to Global Communion* (Cambridge, 1993)

Samson, Jane. *Imperial Benevolence: Making British Authority in the Pacific Islands* (Honolulu, 1998)

Sandeen, E.R. *The Roots of Fundamentalism: British and American Millenarianism, 1800–1930* (Chicago, 1970)

Sanders, Peter. *Moshoeshoe Chief of the Sotho* (London, 1975)

Sanderson, G.N. 'The Nile Basin and the Eastern Horn, 1870–1908', in Roland Oliver and G.N. Sanderson (eds), *The Cambridge History of Africa: Vol. 6 from 1870 to 1905* (Cambridge, 1985), 592–679

Sanneh, Lamin. *Translating the Message: The Missionary Impact on Culture* (New York, 1993)

Saunders, Kay (ed.). *Indentured Labour in the British Empire, 1840–1920* (London, 1984)

Savage, David W. 'Evangelical Education Policy in Britain and India, 1857–1860', *JICH* 22 (1994), 432–61

al-Sayyid, Afaf Lutfi. *Cromer in Egypt* (London, 1966)

Scarr, Deryck. *Fragments of Empire: A History of the Western Pacific High Commission, 1877–1914* (Canberra, 1967)

Semmel, Bernard. *The Governor Eyre Controversy* (London, 1962)

Semple, Rhonda. *Missionary Women: Gender, Professionalism and the Victorian Idea of Christian Mission* (Woodbridge, 2003)

Semple, Rhonda. '"The Conversion and Highest Welfare of Each Pupil": The Work of the China Inland Mission at Chefoo', *JICH* 31, 1 (2003), 29–50

Sharpe, Eric J. *Not to Destroy but to Fulfil: The Contribution of J.N. Farquhar to Protestant Missionary Thought in India before 1914* (Uppsala, 1965)

Sharpe, Eric J. 'C.F. Andrews 1871–1940', in Gerald Anderson et al. (eds), *Mission Legacies* (New York, 1994)

Shell, Robert C.-H. 'Between Christ and Mohammed: Conversion, Slavery, and Gender in the Western Cape', in Richard Elphick and Rodney Davenport (eds), *Christianity in South Africa: A Political, Social and Cultural History* (Oxford and Cape Town, 1997), 268–77, 446–7

Shenk, Wilbert R. 'Rufus Anderson and Henry Venn: A Special Relationship?', *IBMR* 5 (1981), 168–72

Shenk, Wilbert R. *Henry Venn – Missionary Statesman* (Maryknoll, NY, 1983)

Shenk, Wilbert R. 'The Role of Theory in Anglo-American Mission Thought and Practice', *Mission Studies* 11, 2 (1994), 155–72

Shepherd, R.H.W. *Lovedale South Africa: The Story of a Century 1841–1941* (Lovedale, 1941)

Shineberg, Dorothy. *They Came for Sandalwood* (Cambridge, 1967)

Short, K.R.M. 'Jamaican Christian Missions and the Great Slave Rebellion of 1831–2', *JEccH* 27, 1 (1976), 57–72

Simensen, Jarle (ed.). *Norwegian Missions in African History: Vol. 1: South Africa 1845–1906;* Finn Fuglestad and Jarle Siemensen (eds), *Vol. 2: Madagascar* (Oslo, 1986)

Simmons, J. *Livingstone and Africa* (London, 1955)

Simpson, Donald. *Dark Companions: The African Contribution to the European Exploration of East Africa* (London, 1975)

Sinha, Mrinalini. *Colonial Masculinity: The 'Manly Englishman' and the 'Effeminate Bengali' in the Late Nineteenth Century* (Manchester, 1995)

Slade, Ruth. *English-Speaking Missions in the Congo Independent State, 1878–1908* (Académie Royale des Sciences Coloniales, Tome 16, Brussels, 1959)

Smith, A. Christopher. 'William Carey 1761–1834. Protestant Pioneer of the Modern Mission Era', in Gerald H. Anderson et al. (eds), *Mission Legacies. Biographical Studies of Leaders of the Modern Missionary Movement* (Maryland, NY, 1994), 245–54

Smith, Edwin W. *The Life and Times of Daniel Lindley (1801–80)* (London, 1949)

Smith, George. *The Life of William Carey, D.D., Shoemaker and Missionary* (London, 1885)

Smith, H.F.C. 'A Neglected Theme of West African History: The Islamic Revolutions of the Nineteenth Century', *Journal of the Historical Society of Nigeria* 2 (1961), 169–85

Spartalis, P.J. *Karl Kumm: Last of the Livingstones, Pioneer Missionary Statesman* (Bonn, 1994)

Spence, Jonathan. *God's Chinese Son: The Taiping Heavenly Kingdom of Hong Xiuquan* (New York and London, 1996)

Srinivasan, Krishnan. *Mission and Message. The Ramsden Sermon 17 November 2002* (Oxford, 2003)

Stafford, Robert A. *Scientist of Empire: Sir Roderick Murchison, Scientific Exploration and Victorian Imperialism* (Cambridge, 1989)

Stanley, Brian. '"Commerce and Christianity": Providence Theory, the Missionary Movement, and the Imperialism of Free Trade, 1842–1860', *HJ* 26 (1983), 71–94

Stanley, Brian. 'Nineteenth-Century Liberation Theology: Nonconformist Missionaries and Imperialism', *Baptist Quarterly: The Journal of the Baptist Historical Society* 33, 1 (1987), 5–18

Stanley, Brian. *The Bible and the Flag: Protestant Missions and British Imperialism in the Nineteenth and Twentieth Centuries* (Leicester, 1990)

Stanley, Brian. *The History of the Baptist Missionary Society 1792–1992* (Edinburgh, 1992)

Stanley, Brian. 'The Reshaping of Christian Tradition: Western Denominational Identity in a Non-Western Context', in R.N. Swanson (ed.), *Unity and Diversity in the Church. Studies in Church History 32* (Oxford, 1992), 399–426

Stanley, Brian (ed.). *Christian Missions and the Enlightenment* (Richmond, Grand Rapids and Cambridge, 2001)

Stanley, Brian. 'Christianity and Civilization in English Evangelical Mission Thought, 1792–1857', in Stanley (ed.), *Christian Missions and the Enlightenment* (Grand Rapids and Richmond, 2001), pp. 169–97

Stanley, Brian. 'Church, State, and the Hierarchy of "Civilization": The Making of the "Missions and Governments" Report at the World Missionary Conference, Edinburgh 1910', in Andrew Porter (ed.), *The Imperial Horizons of British Protestant Missions, 1880–1914* (Grand Rapids and Richmond, 2003), 58–84

Stein, Burton. *Thomas Munro: The Origins of the Colonial State and His Vision of Empire* (Delhi, 1989)

Stock, Eugene. *The History of the Church Missionary Society: Its Environment, Its Men and Its Work*, 4 vols (London, 1899, 1916)

Stone, Norman. *Europe Transformed 1878–1919* (London, 1983)

Strayer, Robert. *The Making of Mission Communities in East Africa: Anglicans and Africans in Colonial Kenya, 1875–1935* (London and Albany, 1978)

Stuart, Doug. 'The Making of a Missionary Disaster: The Makololo and the London Missionary Society', *NAMP Position Paper 29* (Cambridge, 1997)

Studdert-Kennedy, Gerald. 'Theology and Authority, Constitution and Improvisation: The Colonial Church in India', in J.M. Brown and R.E. Frykenberg (eds), *Christians, Cultural Interactions, and India's Religious Traditions* (Grand Rapids and London, 2002), pp. 154–82

Sundkler, Bengt. *Christianity in Africa* (Cambridge, 2001)

Tasie, G.O.M. *Christian Missionary Enterprise in the Niger Delta, 1864–1918* (Leiden, 1978)

Tatlow, Tissington. *The Story of the Student Christian Movement of Great Britain and Ireland* (London, 1933)

Taylor, S.J. 'Whigs, Bishops and America: The Politics of Church Reform in Mid-Eighteenth Century England', *HJ* 36, 2 (1993), 331–56

Temperley, Howard. *British Anti-Slavery 1833–1870* (London, 1972)

Temperley, Howard. *White Dreams, Black Africa: The Antislavery Expedition to the Niger* (New Haven and London, 1991)

Temu, A.J. *British Protestant Missions* (London, 1972)

Teng, S.Y. *The Taiping Rebellion and the Western Powers* (Oxford, 1971)

Thomas, Nicholas. 'Colonial Conversions: Difference, Hierarchy, and History in Early Twentieth-Century Evangelical Propaganda', *CSSH* 34, 2 (1992), 366–89

Thomas, Nicholas. *Colonialism's Culture: Anthropology, Travel and Government* (Cambridge and Oxford, 1994)

Thompson, H.P. *Into All Lands: The History of the Society for the Propagation of the Gospel in Foreign Parts 1701–1950* (London, 1951)

Thorne, Susan. *Congregational Missions and the Making of an Imperial Culture in Nineteenth-Century England* (Stanford, 1999)

Tinker, Hugh. *A New System of Slavery: The Export of Indian Labour Overseas, 1840–1920* (London, 1974)

Tinker, Hugh. *The Ordeal of Love: C.F. Andrews and India* (Delhi, 1979)

Turner, Mary. *Slaves and Missionaries. The Disintegration of Jamaican Slave Society 1787–1834* (Urbana and London, 1982)

Turner, Michael J. 'The Limits of Abolition: Government, Saints and the "African Question", c.1780–1820', *English Historical Review* 112 (1997), 319–57

Tyrrell, Alex. 'The "Moral Radical Party" and the Anglo-Jamaican Campaign for the Abolition of the Negro Apprenticeship System', *English Historical Review* 99 (1984), 481–502

Tyrrell, Alex. *Joseph Sturge and the Moral Radical Party in Early Victorian Britain* (London, 1987)

Unruh, John D. *The Plains Across: Emigrants, Wagon Trains and the American West* (London, 1992 edn; first pub. 1979)

Van den Berg, J. *Constrained by Jesus' Love: An Inquiry into the Motives of the Missionary Awakening in Great Britain in the Period between 1698 and 1815* (Kampen, 1965)

Vander Werff, L.L. *Christian Missions to Muslims: Anglican and Reformed Approaches in India and the Near East, 1800–1938* (South Pasadena, 1977)

Vickers, John A. *Thomas Coke Apostle of Methodism* (London, 1969)

Vickers, John A. 'The Genesis of Methodist Missions', *NAMP Position Paper 10* (Cambridge, 1996)

Viswanathan, Gauri. *Masks of Conquest: Literary Study and British Rule in India* (New York, 1989; repr. Delhi, 1998)

Walls, Andrew F. '"The Heavy Artillery of the Missionary Army": The Domestic Importance of the Nineteenth-Century Medical Missionary', W.J. Shiels (ed.), *Studies in Church History* 19 (Oxford, 1982), 287–97

Walls, Andrew F. *The Missionary Movement in Christian History: Studies in the Transmission of the Faith* (New York and Edinburgh, 1996)

Walls, Andrew F. 'The Eighteenth-Century Protestant Missionary Awakening in its European Context', in Brian Stanley (ed.), *Christian Missions and the Enlightenment* (Grand Rapids and Richmond, 2001), 22–44

Ward, Kevin, and Stanley, Brian (eds). *The Church Mission Society and World Christianity, 1799–1999* (Grand Rapids and Richmond, 2000)

Ward, W.R. *The Protestant Evangelical Awakening* (Cambridge, 1992)

Warfield, B.B. *Perfectionism*, 2 vols (New York, 1931)

Warren, M.A.C. *Crowded Canvas: Some Experiences of a Life-Time* (London, 1974)

Washbrook, D.A. 'India 1818–1860: The Two Faces of Colonialism', in Andrew Porter (ed.), *OHBE Vol. 3 The Nineteenth Century* (Oxford, 1999), 395–421

Watts, M.R. *The Dissenters*, 2 vols (Oxford, 1978, 1995)

Webster, J.B. 'The Bible and the Plough', *Journal of the Historical Society of Nigeria* 4 (1963), 418–34

Webster, J.B. *The African Churches among the Yoruba 1888–1922* (Oxford, 1964)

Wehrle, Edmund S. *Britain, China and the Antimissionary Riots, 1891–1900* (Minneapolis, 1966)

White, Gavin. '"Highly Preposterous": Origins of Scottish Missions', *Records of the Scottish Church History Society* 19, 2 (1976), 111–24

White, Landeg. *Magomero: Portrait of an African Village* (Cambridge, 1989 edn)

Williams, C. Peter. '"Not Quite Gentlemen": An Examination of "Middling Class" Protestant Missionaries from Britain, c.1850–1900', *JEccH* 31, 3 (1980), 301–15

Williams, C. Peter. 'Healing and Evangelism: The Place of Medicine in Later Victorian Protestant Missionary Thinking', in W.J. Shiels (ed.), *Studies in Church History* 19 (Oxford, 1982), 271–85

Williams, C. Peter. *The Ideal of the Self-Governing Church: A Study in Victorian Missionary Strategy* (Leiden, 1990)

Williams, C. Peter. '"The Missing Link"; The Recruitment of Women Missionaries in some English Evangelical Missionary Societies in the Nineteenth Century', in Fiona Bowie, Deborah Kirkwood, and Shirley Ardener (eds), *Women and Missions: Past and Present. Anthropological and Historical Perceptions* (Providence and Oxford, 1993), 43–69

Williams, Donovan. 'Social and Economic Aspects of Christian Mission Stations in Caffraria 1816–1854', 2 parts, *Historia* 31, 2 (1985) 33–48, and 32, 1 (1986), 25–56

Willis, Justin. 'The Nature of a Mission Community: The Universities' Mission to Central Africa in Bonde', *Past and Present* 140 (1993), 127–54

Wilson, Kathleen. *The Island Race: Englishness, Empire and Gender in the Eighteenth Century* (London and New York, 2003)

Wolffe, John. *God and Greater Britain: Religion and National Life in Britain and Ireland 1843–1945* (London and New York, 1994)

Wong, John Y. *Deadly Dreams: Opium, Imperialism, and the Arrow War (1856–1860) in China* (Cambridge, 1998)

Wood, Donald. 'A Slave Missionary and the Worldly Powers: John Wray in Guiana', in Holger Bernt Hansen and Michael Twaddle (eds), *Christian Missionaries and the State in the Third World* (Oxford and Athens, GA, 2001), 30–8

Wood, Ian. *The Missionary Life: Saints and the Evangelisation of Europe 400–1050* (Harlow, 2001)

Yates, T.E. *Venn and Victorian Bishops Abroad: The Missionary Policies of Henry Venn and Their Repercussions upon the Anglican Episcopate of the Colonial Period, 1841–1872* (Uppsala and London, 1978)

Yates, T.E. *Christian Mission in the Twentieth Century* (Cambridge, 1994: repr. 1999)

# Periodicals

*Central Africa*
*Church Missionary Intelligencer*
*Church Missionary Juvenile Instructor*
*Church Missionary Review*
*Cobbett's Parliamentary Debates*
*The East and the West*
*Eclectic Review*
*Edinburgh Review*
*Evangelical Magazine*
*Free Church of Scotland Missionary Review*
*Free Church [of Scotland] Monthly Missionary Review*
*Juvenile Missionary Herald*
*Report of the [London] Missionary Society*
*Medical Missions at Home and Abroad*
*Methodist Annual Reports*
*Mission Field*

*Missionary Herald*
*Parliamentary Debates*
*Parliamentary Register*
*Proceedings of the Royal Geographical Society*
*Report of the British Association for the Advancement of Science*
*Sudan Mission Leaflet*

## Works of reference

Anderson, Gerald H., Coote, Robert T., Horner, Norman A. and Phillips, James M. (eds), *Mission Legacies. Biographical Studies of Leaders of the Modern Missionary Movement* (Maryknoll, NY, 1994)

Anderson, Gerald H. *Biographical Dictionary of Christian Missions* (Grand Rapids, 1998; 1999)

*Australian Dictionary of Biography*, 13 vols and index (Carlton, New York and London, 1966–93)

Beach, H.P. and John, B.St. *World Statistics of Christian Missions* (New York, 1916)

Cameron, N.M. de S. (ed.) *Dictionary of Scottish Church History and Theology* (Edinburgh, 1993)

*Dictionary of Canadian Biography*, 14 vols (Toronto, 1969, 1974–98)

*Dictionary of New Zealand Biography*, 5 vols (Wellington, 1990–2000)

*Dictionary of South African Biography*, 5 vols *(Cape Town, 1968–87)*

Lewis, Donald M. (ed.) *The Blackwell Dictionary of Evangelical Biography 1730–1860* (Oxford, 1995)

*Oxford Dictionary of National Biography* (forthcoming, Oxford, 2004)

*Register of Missionaries and Native Clergy, From 1804 to 1904* (Church Missionary Society, privately printed, London 1895)

Sibree, J. (ed.) *London Missionary Society: A Register of Missionaries, Deputations, etc., from 1796 to 1923*, 4th edn (London, 1923)

Walls, Andrew F. 'Missions', in N.M. de S. Cameron (ed.), *Dictionary of Scottish Church History and Theology* (Edinburgh, 1993), 567–94

## Unpublished dissertations

Ballhatchet, Helen. 'Between Idolatry and Infidelity: The Christian Missionary in Japan, 1874–1912' (Ph.D. thesis, London, 1985)

Blunden, Margaret. 'The Anglican Church and the Politics of Southern Africa, 1888–1909' (D.Phil. thesis, Oxford, 1980)

Brock, Sheila M. 'James Stewart and Lovedale: A Reappraisal of Missionary Attitudes and African Response in the Eastern Cape, South Africa, 1870–1905' (Ph.D. thesis, Edinburgh, 1974)

Bugge, Henriette. 'Mission and Tamil Society: Sixty Years of Interaction, 1840–1900' (Ph.D. thesis, Copenhagen, 1991)

Carson, Penelope S.E. 'Soldiers of Christ: Evangelicals and India, 1784–1833' (Ph.D. thesis, London, 1988)

Child, Caroline. 'The China Inland Mission and the Boxer Rising of 1900' (MA dissertation, Reading, 1994)

Close, Robin E. 'Literacy, Identity and Protest: The Khoi of South Africa and the Objibwa of Upper Canada, c. 1820–1850' (Ph.D. thesis, Cambridge, 2003)

Dachs, A.J. 'Missionary Imperialism in Bechuanaland 1813–1896' (Ph.D. thesis, Cambridge, 1968)

Daniel, W. Harrison. 'Patterns in Mission Preaching: The Representation of the Christian Message and Efik Response in the Scottish Calabar Mission, Nigeria, 1846–1900' (Ph.D. thesis, Edinburgh, 1993)

Gehani, T.G. 'A Critical Review of the work of Scottish Presbyterian Missions in India, 1878–1914' (Ph.D, thesis, Strathclyde, 1966)

Grant, Kevin. '"A Civilised Savagery": British Humanitarian Politics and European Imperialism in Africa, 1884–1926' (Ph.D. thesis, Berkeley, 1997)

Haggis, Jane. 'Professional Ladies and Working Wives: Female Missionaries in the London Missionary Society and its South Travancore District, South India in the Nineteenth Century' (Ph.D. thesis, Manchester, 1991)

Hickford, Mark. 'Making "territorial rights of the natives": Britain and New Zealand, 1830–1847' (D.Phil. thesis, Oxford, 1999)

Hitchen, John Mason. 'Formation of the Nineteenth-Century Missionary Worldview: The Case of James Chalmers' (Ph.D. thesis, Aberdeen, 1984)

Kieran, J.A.P. 'The Holy Ghost Fathers in East Africa 1863–1914' (Ph.D. thesis, London, 1966)

Laidlaw, Zoe. 'Networks, Patronage and Information in Colonial Government: Britain, New South Wales and the Cape Colony, 1826–43' (D.Phil. thesis, Oxford, 2001)

Lee, Joseph Tse-Hei. 'Conversion or Protection? Collective Violence and Christian Movements in Late Nineteenth-Century Chaozhu, South China' (Ph.D. thesis, London, 2000)

Loiello, John. 'Samuel Ajayi Crowther, the Church Missionary Society, and the Niger Mission 1857–1891' (Ph.D. thesis, London, 1980)

Lumley, James. 'Progress or Decline? The Funding of the LMS Missions in Cape Colony, 1848–1872' (MA dissertation, King's College London, 1998)

Lynn, Martin. 'John Beecroft and West Africa, 1829–54' (Ph.D. thesis, London, 1978)

McKelvie, G.D. 'The Development of Official Anglican Interest in World Mission, 1783–1809: with Special Reference to Bishop Beilby Porteus', 2 vols (Ph.D. thesis, Aberdeen, 1984)

Macmillan, H.W. 'The Origins and Development of the African Lakes Company, 1878–1908 (Ph.D. thesis, Edinburgh, 1970)

Maughan, Steven S. 'Regions Beyond and the National Church: Domestic Support for the Foreign Missions of the Church of England in the High Imperial Age, 1870–1914' (Ph.D. thesis, Harvard, 1995)

Moriyama, Jerome T. 'The Evolution of an African Ministry in the Work of the Universities' Mission to Central Africa in Tanzania 1864–1909' (Ph.D. thesis, London, 1984)

Neave, D.R.J. 'Aspects of the Universities' Mission to Central Africa, 1858–1900' (M.Phil. thesis, York, 1974)

Perry, Alan F. 'The American Board of Commissioners for Foreign Missions and the London Missionary Society in the Nineteenth Century: A Study of Ideas' (Ph.D. thesis, Washington, 1974)

Perry, C.L. 'The History of the Expansion of Protestant Christianity among the Nepali Diaspora' (Ph.D. thesis, Edinburgh, 1994)

Ray, Louise. 'The Impact of the London Missionary Society as an Agent of Cultural Imperialism in Madagascar, 1818–1836' (MA dissertation, King's College London, 1999)

Robert, Dana Lee. 'Arthur Tappan Pierson and Forward Movements of Late Nineteenth Century Evangelicalism' (Ph.D. thesis, Yale, 1984)

Roxborogh, W.J. 'Thomas Chalmers and the Mission of the Church with Special Reference to the Rise of the Missionary Movement in Scotland' (Ph.D. thesis, Aberdeen, 1978)

Semple, Rhonda. '"Ladies of Much Ability and Intelligence": Gendered Relations in British Protestant Missions, 1865–1910' (Ph.D., London, 2000)

Stanley, Brian. 'Home Support for British Overseas Missions in Early Victorian England, c.1838–1873' (Ph.D. thesis, Cambridge, 1979)

Thomas, J.V. 'The Role of the Medical Missionary in British East Africa 1874–1904' (D.Phil. thesis, Oxford, 1982)

# Index

Note: abbreviations following individual names indicate principal religious/missionary affiliation.